Learning Intelligence: Innovative and Digital Transformative Learning Strategies

AF896388

Kumaran Rajaram

Learning Intelligence: Innovative and Digital Transformative Learning Strategies

Cultural and Social Engineering Perspectives

Springer

Kumaran Rajaram
Division of Leadership, Management and Organization, Nanyang Business School
Nanyang Technological University
Singapore, Singapore

https://doi.org/10.1007/978-981-19-9201-8

This Springer imprint is published by the registered company Springer Nature Singapore Pte Ltd.
The registered company address is: 152 Beach Road, #21-01/04 Gateway East, Singapore 189721, Singapore
(www.springernature.com/mycopy)

Preface

> *"The one true goal of education is to leave a person asking questions"*
> *—Author unknown*

It has been sixteen years since I started the insightful journey that commenced back then in 2006 during my stint as the Director of Academic Affairs and Head, Strategy and Business Development managing local and international students. To develop a strong rooted learning culture and culture of learning in the institution, I needed to create and execute strategies that leverage from the notion 'learning intelligence' that focuses on the institution's concrete goals, comprehending the learning needs and practices, and quantify the learning outcomes. I was intrigued to solve the complex challenges for learners in pursuit of their studies at the university setting from a socio-culturally dislocated environment, having to understand their unique learning styles, behaviours, cognitive process, rooted values and beliefs and culture of learning. Beyond my role as a senior leader in the institution that enables me to make key decisions for transformation and change, I took on a concurrent role as a researcher in area of learning intelligence, science, culture and internationalization of higher education. The inspiration to dive deeper on the strategic, tactical and operational issues was motivated from the varying complex questions that emerged through the real-life challenges that I had to deal with and have experienced.

Deputy Academic Director (Liaison), Nanyang Technopreneurship Centre

My aspiration is to put my contemporary cutting-edge learning and teaching scholarship research insights and reflections together to benefit the larger academic community in a book titled: *"Learning Intelligence: Innovative and Transformative Learning Strategies: Cultural and Social Engineering Perspectives"*. This compelling journey began back then in 2012 when I am invited to join as a faculty with Nanyang Business School, Nanyang Technological University, Singapore. As appointed as the course chair-director, I am responsible to oversee 8–10 senior instructors and over 450 students, including exchange students from various countries globally. I am also appointed as the deputy academic director (liaison) with Nanyang

Technoprenuership Centre, where I lead and manage students in the entrepreneurship specialization. I was intrigued by the rapid changes to explore and experiment ways to transform the learning culture and re-design the curriculum to enhance the contents knowledge and competencies to be acquired through addressing the complex learning challenges that emerge and were embedded in the pursuit of students' university education. The reflection on my personal values and beliefs on teaching and learning drives the mission that unfolds in three key dimensions: (a) inculcate positive and nurturing learning environment; (b) stimulate learner's interest for learning; and (c) ingrain a mindset of life-long learning. I continually made attempts through diverse and creative ways to understand students' learning preferences, empathizing with their learning challenges, learning culture and culture of learning as well as the programme's primary focus and intended learning outcomes. This allows me to customize the instructional techniques to meet students' expectations so that effective acquisition of knowledge will be achieved. I believe effective teaching happens when there is a good balance of interactivity, dialogue and exchange of perspectives between the teacher and students. Hence, by endeavouring to appreciate the varying students' aspirations, I can facilitate a conducive learning environment that inspires and encircles everyone's aspirations in the class. We should be creative to utilize varying instructional approaches, via both the traditional approaches and technological interventions that stimulate optimal learning in the students. Collaborative and cooperative learning enables one to grow intellectually, develop internally and enhance their individual personality. It is imperative to develop a culture of innovation and creativity, developing an entrepreneurial and problem-solving mindset. This encourages students to not only optimize their inner talent and potential but also nurture them to be enterprising, enabling them to be critical thinkers embracing diverse perspectives. In a concurrent appointment, I serve as a cradle research fellow in the area of organizational and learning science, learning culture and culture of learning, learning analytics, competencies development and internationalization of higher education. The inspiration to dive deeper on these learning, human capital and training development, competency and skills augmentations and teaching areas was derived from the varying questions that emerge through the real-life encounters and challenges that I had to deal with and have experienced from the strategic, tactical levels (during my prior stints as chief executive officer (CEO), Global Leadership, Management and Learning Intelligence Consultancy, Asia Pacific; Head, Technical specialization, Electrical and Mechanical Engineering, Training Institute; Director of Academic Affairs and Head, Strategy and Business Development; Founder, Executive Director & Principal Consultant, Research Lab for Learning Culture and Innovations) and operational level (as a professor presently who deals directly with the students). Back then, the immediate goal was to examine and resolve the challenges creatively by addressing the influencing and contributing factors. Now, I have since embarked tackling these vital and pressing research questions and having them experimented, validated and analysed by putting together in this book. Hence, this serves as the fundamental motivation to perform cutting-edge research.

In today's rapidly evolving and changing learning environment, educators in higher education need to be mindful, agile and thoughtful in designing the course curriculum to achieve quality, depth and rigor of training and its deliverables in any context of specialization. Today's higher education at university requires to nurture students to become competent and globally employable business leaders and managers, having them realize and internalize their role as change catalysts in building a productive and sustainable world, where enterprises of all sorts can be leveraged on humanistic as well as economic interventions. University education expects to train, equip and develop students' competencies to nurture them to be globally sought-after business leaders. Hence, some of the vital questions that we need to reflect upon are: What is the crucial role of learning in the 21st century? Why education systems need to be re-designed to meet the challenges of a highly uncertain future?

As Rajaram, K. (2021) advocates: *"Learning happens when the learners question the norms; search for information to address the varying perspectives; explore the unknown without being spoon-fed with model answers; self-think critically on how to resolve issues at hand; experience discomfort in the progress and are put in an ambiguous situation, while working towards resolving an assigned task. This allows one to think, reflect and strive towards the process of finding the answers to the unanswered queries and unresolved issues. During the learning phase, the process of learning is the focus if learning in terms of depth and quality is to occur".*

The broad study on learning intelligence investigated from varying dimensional contexts is an imperative and topical contemporary issue in responding to today's rapid changing higher education climate. Educating students equipped with quality, job-ready 'know-hows' and skills and competencies require higher education institutions and universities to be agile, function with a growth mindset and be on top of the game. The primary emphasis in ensuring high quality and effective delivery of the course programmes should be re-iterated to maintain a consistently high standard and rigor. This requires evidence-based inputs to understand the influence of learning design based on the learning culture, learning characteristics derived from the culture of learning, social and geographical issues that are deeply rooted and complex. The context from socio-cultural dimensional aspects in the higher educational learning eco-system, its learning design, pedagogical and assessment aspects have been relatively under-researched. Much of the academic success for students is dependent on the educational and socio-cultural congruence between themselves and the institution they study in. This study makes a vital contribution in comprehending the learning strategies, its related socio-cultural aspects as well as the notion that surrounds learning intelligence and how it should be applied.

This book serves as an important and timely intervention where the innovative, evidence-based and contemporary learning strategies are presented with deep discussions, academic literature and supported with research findings. The learning and teaching strategies presented are adopted in "real-time" learning environments targeted towards outcome-based and competency-based learning goals. The book will address the complex challenges and limitations in contemporary learning and teaching in higher education supported with evidence, hence providing possible approaches to address them. The book addresses an interesting scope of topics largely clustered into four categories, namely (a) cultural and social engineering of learning; (b) innovation and transformation in learning; (c) digital transformation and data analytics in learning; and (d) assessment and feedback for learning that are all contemporary, relevant and essential. The topics under each of these themes are categorized based on the scope of its primary contents; however inline to the title of the book, in each of the topic, there will an inclusion of varying concepts related to socio-cultural aspects such as collaboration, cooperation, interdependency, group processing, dynamics and conformity based on the context and contents of that topic. For the first theme of social-cultural engineering, there are two topics that are addressed, specifically focusing on cultural intelligence and cognitive empathy. Next, three topics are covered under the theme, innovation and transformation in learning, namely exploiting disruptive innovation, blended learning and authentic learning—digital transformation and innovations. Each of these topics within its cluster includes a section discussing on how learning needs to be socially adapted and culturally aligned with sensitivity. Under the final theme of assessment and feedback, the topic assessment, assessment rubrics and feedback, intertwined with socio-cultural issues, are addressed.

This will be of interest for the academic community to examine how these learning strategies could be adopted by leveraging on the latest digitalization, together with cultural and social aspects to engage learners through collaboration and independent learning. This will be of large interest for the academic community to explore and examine how these learning transformative strategies, 'know-hows' interventions and innovations could be adopted or to be served as exemplary practices to be potentially customized and used in context especially in varying socio-cultural complexities. There is a high focus and inclination on outcome-based and authentic learning, assessment and feedback, fixated on how to better facilitate the classes leveraging on technology-enabled learning that engages and facilitates much higher level of collaborative, team-based and cooperative learning in the process of education. The book addresses an interesting scope of topics that are both contemporary and essential to almost all academics and senior leaders, policy makers of higher education institutions, affiliated stakeholders as well as practitioners who has a high responsibility to develop an eco-system to nurture, develop, train and equip learners at both the undergraduate and post-graduate levels at the university with the relevant contents' knowledge, skills and competencies.

I aim to value-add through the scholarly work in this book as an avenue of contribution to higher education institutions and university leaders, researchers, educators, learning science practitioners and other stakeholders globally in this field to help them attain their institutional and individualized goals.

Singapore, Singapore Kumaran Rajaram, Ph.D. (Distinction)

Praise for *Learning Intelligence: Innovative and Digital Transformative Learning Strategies*

"Dr. Rajaram's book makes a vital contribution to the field of learning science and teaching scholarship in higher education to be adopted by working professionals in the future workplace context. The book delivers a total of 10 chapters that are rich in evidence and provide practice-oriented frameworks for those involved in advancing transformative and innovative learning strategies in socio-cultural contexts. The amazing set of insights and practical – and policy-related recommendations serve as positive transformational changes in higher education, focusing on specifics of the much under-researched notion of learning intelligence. As institutions must deal with evolving and complex challenges brought about by, for example, digitalization, strategic re-positioning and health crisis, socio-cultural complexities, the forward-looking and visionary strategic, tactical and operations proposals integrated into the book provide safeguard for sustainable development in transformative and innovative teaching and learning context of higher education."

—Dr. Churchill, Daniel, *Associate Professor, Academic Unit of Teacher Education and Learning Leadership, Faculty of Education, The University of Hong Kong*

"I recommend the book to anyone interested to know where the education landscape is heading next. Modern education requests that we become not only experts in our specific academic domains but also masters of technologies that help improve the effectiveness, efficiency and engagement of teaching. As the world is becoming increasingly flat and with a growing sentiment on ESG, we must embed more cultural intelligence and cognitive empathy in our school environment and curriculum. In the end, innovation is the key to succeeding in every field, including delivering quality teaching at universities. If we want to educate future leaders who will transform industries and societies, we, as teachers, must equip ourselves with a continuously learning mentality and technology know-how. If you share the same vision, I recommend reading this illuminating book."

—Professor Xin Simba Chang, *Associate Dean (Research), Nanyang Business School, Nanyang Technological University, Singapore*

"This timely work overviews important educational discourses about the complex and changing learning environment. It also presents innovative and tested strategies about nurturing students to be business leaders. What is particularly striking is the focus on balance between teaching practical competencies while at the same time developing mindfulness and empathy. The result is an innovative book offering holistic guidance beyond a priori knowledge."

—Mark Brooke (Ed.D.), *Senior Lecturer, Centre for English Language Communication, National University of Singapore*

"Today's world has challenged us at many levels. We live in highly volatile and unpredictable times. We have seen and will continue to witness disruptions arising from new innovations and technological advancements, as well as unprecedented events both within and outside of human control. The higher education sector will not be immune to these disruptions and must be resilient and versatile to cater to a world in which change is the only constant. Dr. Kumaran Rajaram's "Learning Intelligence: Innovative and Transformative Learning Strategies, Cultural and Social Engineering Perspectives" aptly captures the challenges and opportunities in the higher-education sector. While the book touches on a wide range of topics, its detailed and in-depth reflections on how the higher-education sector can harness immersive technologies and AI are exceptionally relevant to the modern educator. There is much for educators to learn from the pedagogically sound, coherent and evidenced-based approach adopted by the book written is simple and accessible language suitable to readers of any background and experience."

—Dr. Althaf Marsoof, *Assistant Professor, Division of Business Law, Nanyang Business School, Nanyang Technological University, Singapore*

"Higher education, learning and pedagogy is expected to not only reflect but, also, predict and even shape societal, cultural and technological changes. University education, and business education in particular, needs to continuously and creatively adapt to new needs, tools, priorities. "Learning Intelligence: Innovative and Transformative Learning Strategies" by Dr. Kumaran Rajaram exactly discusses these topics and prepares everyone involved in higher education to rethink, assess and re-design the whole spectrum of the educational process. The added value that this book brings lies on that, on top of explaining what needs to be done, Dr. Rajaram convincingly details why it is needed and, critically, how this can be done. Combining scientific evidence with practical approaches (based on Dr. Rajaram's extensive experience of teaching a demanding multicultural audience) but, as well, a futuristic approach, the book offers invaluable theoretical and applied knowledge. Yet, Dr. Rajaram brings in something more, namely a vision on how the learning environment in the next ten to twenty years should be. Dr. Rajaram envisions higher education as a learning process through which students, over and above acquiring skills and knowledge, realise their role as carriers of change. In a world that faces increasingly more complex and universal challenges requiring global and local solutions, I think most of us would agree that ensuring that students have the knowledge, confidence and courage to act is the most important skill we want to inculcate. Dr. Rajaram's book shows us the way to do it."

—George Christopoulos, Ph.D., *University of Cambridge (Neuroscience), Associate Professor, Assistant Dean (Research), Nanyang Business School, Nanyang Technological University, Singapore*

"In March 2018, OECD published a position paper in which it proposed an initial framework designed to help countries address two key questions: (1) What knowledge, skills, attitudes, and values will today's students need to thrive and shape their world, and (2) How can instructional systems develop these knowledge, skills, attitudes, and values effectively? These two questions are well addressed by Dr. Kumaran Rajaram in his ground-breaking new book, Learning Intelligence: Innovative and Transformative Learning Strategies. A major theme in the book is the focus on the future of learning, bridging the human and technological aspects of learning, which educators will find captivating. As an educator as well as an intelligence scholar and practitioner, I was captivated by the 3 Is in the book: (1) innovative approach, (2) informed by research, (3) inspirational insights that would challenge us to rethink and reimagine learning intelligence."

—Associate Professor Tan Joo Seng, *Division of Strategy, International Business and Entrepreneurship, Nanyang Business School, Nanyang Technological University, Singapore*

"Dr. Kumaran Rajaram's book on learning intelligence from cultural and social engineering perspectives for higher education is indeed a must read for all future-ready educators. It provides a comprehensive and in-depth analyses of practice-oriented strategies that are evidence-based. The learner-centered approach to motivate learning with "just-in-time" social psychological interventions for cognitive empathy and to maximize the learner's potential is refreshing. Employing disruptive innovation and transformative frameworks for learning innovation, he provides the authentic backdrop helping educators to prepare learners to be resilient and engage with the VUCA world where black swan events are becoming not uncommon. His book guides us through familiar grounds of blended learning strategies with a twist for higher impact and efficacy. Further, it nudges educators to venture into unchartered waters in higher learning that includes immersive technologies and AI for education. The educator is challenged to be a learner as well through embedding analytics in instruction using design learning to continually improve one's teaching in instilling 21st century skills and beyond. This book helps educators to be well-equipped and competent with the key skills for future learning. Most importantly, it encourages scholarship of teaching and learning to reflect and rethink teaching philosophies and guiding principles for a more collaborative and cohesive learning environment for the future of education."

—S. H. Annabel Chen, *Professor of Psychology, School of Social Sciences | Clinical Neuropsychologist | Director, Centre for Research and Development in Learning (CRADLE) | Director (NTU), Centre for Lifelong Learning and Individualised Cognition (CLIC) a collaboration with Cambridge University (a NRF-CREATE programme) | LKCMedicine and National Institute of Education (joint appointments) | Nanyang Technological University, Singapore*

"University education has moved beyond training for the workforce to educating people for the uncertain future. This move requires a new form of pedagogy that is rooted in the science of learning. This book essentially is the translation of the science of learning into the practice of education. The chapters here provide evidence-based frameworks and guidance towards being engaged in teaching. Specifically, the guidance is rooted in current practice which may be applicable for developing "future-ready" citizens. Readers will quickly notice that the author is strongly advocating the development of intra- and inter-personal competencies as the mechanism through which technical competencies may be developed. How may we, as educators, be assured that has taken place? This book advocates learning analytics as the basis for the assurance of learning. In sum, this book should be of interest to educators whose values share the author's evidence-based approach to education."

—Associate Professor Damien Joseph, *Associate Dean (Undergraduate Academics), Nanyang Business School, Nanyang Technological University, Singapore*

"Dr. Rajaram's book brings to the foreground the social and cultural dimension of teaching and learning, an important but often neglected area. Educators can find insightful observations and useful research findings that they can adopt for their practice. Dr. Rajaram also discussed challenges in the uncertain world today and explore pragmatic strategies in education that will better place us with the emergence of potentially disruptive education technologies such as Mixed Reality and Artificial Intelligence. This book will be a great companion for both educators and policy makers."

—Dr. Ho Shen Yong, *Principal Lecturer, Executive Director, Institute of Pedagogical Innovation, Nanyang Technological University, Singapore*

Contents

Part I Introduction

1 Future of Learning: Teaching and Learning Strategies 3
Kumaran Rajaram
1.1 What's New: The Future Learning 4
1.2 Trends and Drivers 4
1.2.1 Globalization 6
1.2.2 Demographic: Diversity of Learners 7
1.2.3 Labour Market and Employer Demands 8
1.2.4 Emerging Technologies 9
1.3 Learning Intelligence 10
1.3.1 Strategic Level Planning and Interventions 12
1.3.2 Tactical Level Planning and Interventions 12
1.3.3 Operational Level Planning and Interventions 12
1.4 Key Evolving Challenges and Concerns of Future Learning 18
1.5 The 21st Century Classroom: How to Learn and Teach? 19
1.5.1 Evolving Teaching Methodologies 20
1.5.2 Blended Learning 21
1.5.3 Online Learning 22
1.5.4 Mobile Learning 22
1.5.5 Simulations, Gamification and Video Games 23
1.6 Learning Strategies for the Future 24
1.7 Educators of the Future 25
1.7.1 Cross-Cultural Competence 25
1.7.2 Empathy: Leadership Skills Development 25
1.7.3 Teacher-Thinking 26
1.7.4 Growth Mindset: Lifelong Learning 26
1.7.5 Collaborative and Networked Learning 27
1.8 Future Curriculum Learning Design and Assessment 27
1.8.1 Collaboration 28
1.8.2 Co-creation with Learners 29

1.8.3 Connectedness ... 29
1.8.4 Technological Disruptions and Interventions ... 30
1.8.5 Assessments ... 31
1.9 Learning Mobility—The New Expectation of Learning "Anywhere and Anytime" ... 32
1.10 Individualized and Personalized Learning: Customization for Learners ... 35
1.11 Sociocultural Interventions for Future ... 36
1.12 Recommendations ... 38
1.13 Concluding Thoughts: Implications for Future Learning ... 46
References ... 48

Part II Cultural and Social Engineering of Learning

2 Cultural Intelligence in Teaching and Learning ... 57
Kumaran Rajaram
2.1 Introduction ... 58
2.2 Cultural Intelligence and Its Impact on Higher Education (HE) ... 59
2.3 Globalization of Higher Education ... 67
2.4 Cultural Intelligence: Analysis from an Education Perspective—Effects on Teaching and Learning in Higher Education ... 71
2.4.1 Strategic-Tactical and Operational Levels ... 72
2.4.2 Increasing Cultural Diversity Within Student Populations ... 73
2.5 Sociocultural Localized Context and Transnational Education ... 74
2.6 Cross-Cultural Teaching ... 75
2.7 Pedagogical Learning Design: Learning Strategies and Instructional Techniques for Cross-Cultural Context ... 76
2.7.1 Virtual Learning ... 78
2.7.2 Flipped Classroom ... 78
2.7.3 Cooperative Learning ... 79
2.7.4 Blended Learning ... 79
2.7.5 Experiential Learning ... 80
2.8 Enhancing Learning Efficacy Through Pedagogical Learning Design ... 80
2.9 Challenges in Cross-Cultural Teaching ... 81
2.9.1 Communication ... 82
2.9.2 Assessment ... 82
2.9.3 Class Participation ... 83
2.9.4 Differences in Learning Orientation ... 84
2.9.5 Facilitating Cross-Cultural Group Work ... 84
2.9.6 Use of Technology ... 85

2.9.7 Student-Teacher Relationships 85
2.10 Multicultural Teaching Efficacy 86
2.11 Measurement of Multicultural Teaching Efficacy: Frameworks and Scales 90
2.12 Student Engagement: Cross-Cultural Learning Contexts 92
2.12.1 Differences in Learning Styles 94
2.12.2 Fear of Judgement from Peers 95
2.12.3 Increasing Use of IT in Classrooms 95
2.12.4 Lack of Confidence 96
2.13 Teachers' Training: Proficiency in Adapting in a Cross-Cultural Context 96
2.14 Teachers' Outlook Towards Culturally Diverse Students 98
2.15 Correct Mix of Teaching Strategies for High Efficacy of Learning in Cross-Cultural Settings 99
2.16 Concluding Thoughts 100
References 106

3 Social-Psychological Intervention: Development of Cognitive Empathy 119
Kumaran Rajaram
3.1 Introduction 120
3.2 Leadership Competencies 121
3.3 Empathy 124
3.3.1 Cognitive Empathy 125
3.3.2 Teaching Empathy 126
3.4 Design Thinking 128
3.5 Social-Psychological Interventions 129
3.6 Hypotheses 131
3.7 Methods 132
3.7.1 Settings 132
3.7.2 Data Sources 133
3.7.3 Procedures 134
3.7.4 Measures and Reliability 135
3.8 Results 137
3.8.1 Assignment Completion by Conditions 137
3.8.2 Use of Management and Design Thinking Terms by Conditions 138
3.8.3 Assignment Solution by Conditions 138
3.8.4 Presence of Empathy by Condition 140
3.9 Discussion 140
3.10 Conclusion 141
References 142

Part III Innovation and Transformation in Learning

4 Exploiting Disruptive Innovation in Learning and Teaching 149
Samson Tan
4.1 Introduction 150
4.2 Impact of Globalization on Higher Education 152
4.2.1 Higher Education in a VUCA World 154
4.2.2 The 21st Century Learners in Higher Education 156
4.3 The Influence of Technology on Higher Education 157
4.3.1 The Impact of the Fourth Industrial Revolution on Education 159
4.3.2 COVID-19 Pandemic Impact on Education 161
4.4 A New Framework for Innovation in Teaching and Learning 163
4.4.1 Clayton Christensen and Disruptive Innovation 163
4.4.2 Transformative Strategic Framework for Innovation in Teaching and Learning 165
4.5 A Revised Framework for Innovation in Teaching and Learning 165
4.6 Implementation of Innovation Through Diffusion of Innovation 168
4.6.1 The Gartner Hype Cycle 168
4.6.2 The Diffusion of Innovation Model 169
4.6.3 The Synergy Gartner Hype Cycle and the Diffusion of Innovation Model 170
4.7 Conclusion 171
References 171

5 Blended Learning 177
Kumaran Rajaram
5.1 Introduction 178
5.2 Blended Learning 179
5.2.1 Benefits of Blended Learning 181
5.2.2 Types of Blended Learning 183
5.2.3 Approach Adopted: How Blended Learning Is Conducted? 183
5.2.4 Impact 184
5.2.5 Level 184
5.3 Technology Enhanced Learning (TEL) 192
5.3.1 Impact of Technology Enhanced Learning (TEL) 193
5.3.2 The Link of TEL to Blended Learning 194
5.4 Blended Learning Design 195
5.4.1 Online Learning 196
5.4.2 Voice-over Lectures 197
5.4.3 Animations 197
5.4.4 Quizzes 197
5.4.5 Online Reflection Journal 198

5.4.6 Face-to-Face Learning ... 198
5.4.7 Face-to-Face Seminars with Technological Interventions ... 199
5.5 Assessment of Blended Learning ... 200
5.5.1 Online Learning Assessment ... 200
5.5.2 Face-to-Face Learning Assessment ... 202
5.6 Social-Cultural Aspects of Blended Learning ... 203
5.6.1 Online Learning ... 203
5.6.2 Face-to-Face Learning ... 204
5.7 Application to Teaching and Learning ... 206
5.7.1 Global Perspectives ... 206
5.7.2 Financial Costs of Blended Learning ... 208
5.7.3 Future of Blended Learning Pedagogy ... 209
5.7.4 Perspectives of Students and Instructors ... 209
5.8 Concluding Thoughts and Future Directions ... 210
References ... 212

6 Authentic Learning Digital Transformation and Innovations ... 217
Kumaran Rajaram
6.1 Introduction ... 218
6.2 Digital Transformation in Learning and Learning Innovations ... 219
6.3 Learning Interventions ... 223
6.4 Learning Transformation ... 223
6.4.1 Social Engineering ... 226
6.4.2 Learning Culture and Culture of Learning ... 227
6.5 Pedagogy ... 229
6.5.1 E-Learning ... 229
6.5.2 Blended Learning ... 229
6.5.3 Flipped Classroom ... 230
6.5.4 Virtual Reality and the Future of Pedagogy ... 230
6.6 Class Participation ... 230
6.6.1 Facilitation of Class Participation ... 232
6.6.2 Meta-Analysis: Aspects of Class Participation and Its Impact on Learning Outcomes and Processes ... 233
6.6.3 Learning Intervention: K^mAlive Learning Application—Class Participation Functionality ... 233
6.7 Critical Thinking ... 239
6.7.1 Meta-Analysis: Instructional Approaches to Enhance Critical Thinking, Its Impact on Learning and Application to Employability ... 240
6.7.2 Facilitation of Critical Thinking ... 241
6.7.3 Learning Intervention: K^mAlive Learning Application—Critical Reflection Functionality ... 247

6.8 Peer Evaluation ... 248
6.8.1 Meta-Analysis: Types of Peer Evaluation ... 250
6.8.2 Facilitation of Peer Evaluation ... 254
6.8.3 Learning Intervention: K^mAlive Learning Application—Peer Review Functionality ... 255
6.9 Group Discussions and Group Review ... 256
6.9.1 Meta-Analysis: Approaches to Group Discussion and Its Impact to Learning ... 258
6.9.2 Facilitation of Group Discussion and Group Review ... 258
6.9.3 Learning Intervention: K^mAlive Learning Application—Group Discussion and Group Review Functionality ... 266
6.10 Leadership, Human and Soft (Employability) Skills and Competencies ... 269
6.10.1 Meta-Analysis: Leadership, Human and Soft (Employability) Skills Development, Impact on Learning and Application to Future Work ... 271
6.10.2 Training of Leadership, Human and Soft (Employability) Skills ... 277
6.10.3 Learning Intervention: K^mAlive Learning Application—Leadership, Human and Soft (Employability) Skills Functionality ... 278
6.11 Application to Teaching and Learning Practice ... 284
6.12 Recommended Learning Interventions with Sociocultural Engineering Strategies ... 286
6.12.1 Class Participation ... 286
6.12.2 Critical Thinking ... 287
6.12.3 Peer Evaluation ... 288
6.12.4 Group Discussions and Group Review ... 288
6.12.5 Leadership and Soft Skills Competencies ... 289
6.13 Practical Implications and Recommendations ... 289
6.14 Concluding Thoughts ... 291
References ... 292

Part IV Digital Transformation and Data Analytics in Learning

7 Harnessing Immersive Technologies for Innovation in Teaching and Learnings ... 305
Samson Tan
7.1 Introduction ... 306
7.2 Literature Review Immersive Learning ... 307
7.2.1 Jensen and Konradsen (2018) ... 308
7.2.2 Merchant et al. (2014) ... 309
7.2.3 Wu et al. (2020) ... 310

7.2.4 Radianti et al. (2020) ... 310
7.3 Meta-Analysis of Immersive Learning ... 311
7.3.1 Immersive Technology ... 312
7.3.2 Learning Outcome Evaluation ... 313
7.3.3 Application in Domain Knowledge ... 313
7.3.4 Defining the Types of Knowledge or Learning Content ... 314
7.3.5 Contextualising Immersive Technologies for Innovation in Teaching and Learning ... 314
7.4 Reframing Immersive Technology for Innovation in Teaching and Learning ... 317
7.4.1 Immersion ... 318
7.4.2 Presence ... 319
7.4.3 Interactivity ... 321
7.4.4 Agency ... 322
7.4.5 Sociocultural Dynamics ... 323
7.5 Immersive Learning Design Model ... 324
7.5.1 Tacgin's Instructional Design Model for Immersive Virtual Reality Learning Environments ... 325
7.5.2 Dalgarno and Lee's (2010) Affordance Model for 3D Virtual Learning Environments ... 325
7.5.3 Makransky and Petersen's (2021) Cognitive Affective Model of Immersive Learning (CAMIL) ... 326
7.5.4 Revised Instructional Model for Immersive Learning ... 327
7.6 Conclusion ... 329
References ... 329

8 Harnessing Artificial Intelligence for Innovation in Education ... 335
Samson Tan
8.1 Introduction ... 336
8.2 What Is Artificial Intelligence (AI)? ... 337
8.3 Will AI Take Over from Humans? ... 339
8.3.1 Human Intelligence (HI) and Artificial Intelligence (AI) ... 340
8.3.2 Impact of AI on Society ... 341
8.4 A Framework for Artificial Intelligence in Education ... 342
8.5 Applying Artificial Intelligence in Education (AIEd) ... 344
8.6 Trends and Developments of Personalized Adaptive Learning Systems (PALS) ... 346
8.6.1 Distribution of Learning Content ... 346
8.6.2 Distribution of System Support/Hardware ... 346
8.6.3 Distribution of Learning Outcomes ... 348
8.6.4 Distribution of Parameters of Personalized Adaptive Learning ... 349

8.7 Designing an AI-Powered New Personalized Adaptive Learning ... 350
8.8 Teacher-Facing AIEd ... 351
8.8.1 Automated Grading or Marking ... 352
8.8.2 Feedback ... 353
8.9 System-Facing AIEd Applications ... 353
8.9.1 Profiling and Prediction ... 353
8.9.2 Admission Decisions and Course Scheduling ... 354
8.9.3 Drop-Out and Retention ... 355
8.9.4 Student Models and Academic Achievement ... 355
8.10 Future of Artificial Intelligence in Education (AIEd) ... 356
8.10.1 AIEd Augment Our Physical Landscape ... 356
8.10.2 AIEd Connect to the Internet of Things ... 357
8.11 Conclusion ... 358
References ... 359

Part V Assessment and Feedback for Learning

9 Assessment, Assessment Rubrics and Feedback ... 367
Kumaran Rajaram
9.1 Introduction ... 368
9.2 Assessment ... 369
9.2.1 Importance of Assessments ... 371
9.2.2 Categories of Assessments ... 372
9.2.3 Assessments for Developing Varying Learning Outcomes ... 373
9.3 Feedback ... 374
9.3.1 Importance of Feedback ... 377
9.3.2 Guidelines to Provide Effective Feedback ... 378
9.4 Types of Feedback ... 383
9.4.1 Formative Feedback ... 383
9.4.2 Summative Feedback ... 385
9.4.3 Formal Feedback ... 386
9.4.4 Informal Feedback ... 386
9.5 Assessment Rubrics ... 387
9.5.1 Use of Assessment Rubrics ... 390
9.5.2 Types of Assessment Rubrics ... 392
9.6 Social-Cultural Aspects of Assessment ... 394
9.7 Background of Study ... 397
9.8 Method ... 399
9.8.1 Participants ... 399
9.8.2 Procedure ... 399
9.9 Analysis ... 400
9.10 Findings ... 400
9.11 Discussion ... 405

9.12 Strategies for the Effective Adoption of Assessments and Feedback ... 408
9.12.1 Effective Design and Structural Process of Assessments ... 410
9.12.2 Well-Devised Plan and Effective Execution of Strategies ... 410
9.12.3 Engineering the Sociocultural Eco-System: Strategies to Handle Diverse Student Population ... 411
9.12.4 Utilizing Digitalization and Technological Interventions to Enhance Feedback ... 413
9.13 Concluding Thoughts ... 416
Appendix A: Interview Questions for Instructors and Course Designers ... 417
Appendix B: Interview Questions for Students ... 418
References ... 418

Part VI Conclusion

10 Concluding Thoughts ... 429
Kumaran Rajaram
10.1 Cultural Intelligence in Teaching and Learning ... 430
10.2 Blended Learning Strategy ... 432
10.3 Future of Learning: Teaching and Learning Strategies ... 433
10.4 Innovation and Transformation in Learning ... 437
10.5 Social-Psychological Intervention ... 439
10.6 Digital Transformation: Data-Driven Learning ... 440
10.7 Assessment and Feedback for Learning: Now and the Future ... 442
10.8 Artificial Intelligence and Immersive Learning for the Future ... 443
10.9 Cultural and Social Perspectives ... 446
References ... 447

Index ... 451

List of Figures

Fig. 1.1 Conceptual framework for learning intelligence 11
Fig. 1.2 Transformational model for future of learning in Higher Education 41
Fig. 2.1 Components of cultural intelligence and its application to teaching and learning 64
Fig. 2.2 Visual diagram that presents the impact of cultural intelligence (CQ) 65
Fig. 3.1 Principles of management LAMS sequence 132
Fig. 3.2 Design thinking LAMS sequence 132
Fig. 3.3 Use of terms by conditions 139
Fig. 3.4 Focus of advice by conditions 139
Fig. 4.1 Revised transformative strategic framework for learning innovation 167
Fig. 5.1 Conceptual framework for blended learning (Extracted from Rajaram, 2021) 180
Fig. 5.2 Conceptual framework: ways blended learning can be categorized 183
Fig. 5.3 Blended learning design conceptual framework 196
Fig. 5.4 Elements of blended learning 207
Fig. 6.1 Learning transformation framework (Adapted from @Reserach Lab for Learning Innovation and Culture of Learning, Rajaram [2020]) 226
Fig. 6.2 Instructor's panel view: Instructor-centred class participation functionality 237
Fig. 6.3 Instructor's panel view: Student-centred class participation functionality 238
Fig. 6.4 Instructor's panel view: critical reflection functionality 247
Fig. 6.5 Instructor's panel view: Peer review functionality 256
Fig. 6.6 Instructor's panel view: Group Review functionality 266
Fig. 6.7 Instructor's panel view: Group Discussion functionality 267
Fig. 6.8 Instructor's panel view for the pre-evaluation functionality 279

Fig. 6.9 Instructor's panel view for the in-class evaluation functionality 280
Fig. 6.10 Instructor's panel view for post evaluation functionality 281
Fig. 6.11 Instructor's panel view: Peer evaluation functionality 282
Fig. 6.12 Instructor's panel view of role-based evaluation: leader evaluation 283
Fig. 6.13 The instructor's panel view of role-based evaluation 283
Fig. 6.14 Instructor's panel view of role-based evaluation: devil's advocate evaluation 284
Fig. 6.15 Instructor's panel view of within group evaluation 285
Fig. 6.16 Framework of learning interventions and socio-cultural considerations 287
Fig. 7.1 Proposed instructional design model 328
Fig. 9.1 Social-cultural aspects of assessments and feedback 398
Fig. 9.2 Recommended strategies for effective adoption of assessments and feedback 409
Fig. 9.3 Conceptual framework—scaffolded guiding principles on feedback process cycle 414

List of Tables

Table 1.1 Scope and impact on learning from multiple intelligences (MI) 15
Table 1.2 Key components for a digital infrastructure that supports learning mobility 34
Table 2.1 Dimensions and sub-dimensions of cultural intelligence (CQ) 60
Table 2.2 Definitions of cultural intelligence and its competency traits 62
Table 2.3 An instructional guide on practice-oriented strategies for cross-cultural teaching and facilitation 87
Table 2.4 Frameworks for measuring multicultural teaching efficacy 91
Table 2.5 Teaching techniques and the impact it has on the students' learning 101
Table 3.1 LAMS sequence resource descriptions by conditions 134
Table 3.2 Means comparison of demographic measures between conditions 137
Table 3.3 Mean comparison of used terms between conditions 138
Table 5.1 Meta-analysis: different models of blended learning, its applied contexts and impacts on learning 185
Table 5.2 Three distinct design approaches in terms of the impact of blended learning 190
Table 5.3 Levels of blended learning approaches 192
Table 6.1 Digital learning interventions and tools 224
Table 6.2 Aspects of class participation and its impact on learning processes and outcomes 234
Table 6.3 Instructional approaches to enhance critical thinking, its impact on learning and application to employability 242
Table 6.4 Categorization of peer evaluation, its impact on learning and application to future work 251
Table 6.5 Categorization of group discussion, its impact on learning and its application to future work 259

Table 6.6 Categorization of Group Review, its impact on learning and its application to future work 262
Table 6.7 Presents the leadership skills development, its impact on learning and application to future work 272
Table 6.8 Presents the human, soft (employability) skills development, its impact on learning and application to future work 275
Table 9.1 Three-tier conceptual framework for categorization of assessment methods 375
Table 9.2 Conceptual framework: guiding principles—conditions for high efficacy and effective feedback 380
Table 9.3 Categorization on the types of feedback 384
Table 9.4 Students' perspectives—key emerging themes 401
Table 9.5 Themes and responses of students' perceived reasons for e-assessment rubrics to be adopted 402
Table 9.6 Themes and responses for benefits of using e-assessment rubrics for instructors 404
Table 9.7 Themes and responses for benefits of using e-assessment rubrics for students 406
Table 9.8 Emerging key indicators for effectiveness of e-Assessment Rubrics: Perspectives from students and instructors and course designers 407
Table 10.1 Institutional implementation strategies for blended learning 434

Part I
Introduction

Chapter 1
Future of Learning: Teaching and Learning Strategies

Kumaran Rajaram

Abstract This chapter is an introductory chapter titled "Future of Learning: Teaching and Learning Strategies". In this chapter of the book, the primary purpose of the proposed learning strategies advocated in this book will be discussed, the significance and timeliness of the topics covered inline to the current educational climate and future classroom teaching. An overview and discussion on the current teaching and learning "gaps", crisis and challenges facing the higher education will be highlighted to provide readers the context and urgency on the need to shift the learning culture through rethinking, challenging the status quo and norms through re-design and transformation. The need to be more mindful on social engineering and cultural intelligence in teaching will be emphasized for educators to be aware, updated and re-calibrated to fit well in the rapidly evolving culturally diverse learning environment. The valuable contributions are presented through rigorous discussion on innovative learning strategies, digital transformations, social engineering and cultural intelligence in teaching and learning context. The motivation of this attempt is to equip learners with the social and humanizing elements while appreciating the latest and advanced technological learning design and support systems. Each chapter's scope and its research gaps will be discussed succinctly yet comprehensively to get the readers understand the value that this book offers. Possible remedies to the identified research gaps are discussed. The will commence by presenting the background, context of teaching and learning in higher education at present, the urgency and need to rethink, transform and be resilient to adapt to evolving changes through relevant learning strategies, digital transformation, social and cultural engineering strategies that are innovative driven. Each chapter presents the research gaps and recommends the appropriate evidence-based approach adopted to deal with the issues accordingly. The methodologies and research design adopted are described. The concluding paragraphs enable the reader to understand the importance of the proposed chapters and its strong connectivity among them.

K. Rajaram (✉)
Division of Leadership, Management and Organization, Nanyang Business School, Nanyang Technological University, Singapore, Singapore
e-mail: rkumaran@ntu.edu.sg

K. Rajaram, *Learning Intelligence: Innovative and Digital Transformative Learning Strategies*, https://doi.org/10.1007/978-981-19-9201-8_1

1.1 What's New: The Future Learning

The role and expectations of higher education are continuously and constantly evolving and changing, where higher education institutes are influenced by a multitude of external forces that also vary as years unfold. As such, many have started to ponder and marvel how the future of learning process and its nuances will evolve in the near and distant future. The trends that we witness and experience in today's higher education landscape are momentously influenced by rapid evolving technological developments, globalization, varying employer demands and so on. Higher education institutions must be committed to be agile, proactively look out for and respond promptly to new developments in the sector to remain competitive. This enables institutions to re-align and re-design the pedagogies to be adopted in classrooms in accordance with the students' needs. Moreover, it also provides teachers with the required training to upgrade their skills to ensure that they are fully equipped to manage the complexities in a twenty-first century classroom. As a contingency strategy, institutions should be aware of the potential setbacks that they would potentially encounter, that allows them to plan and prepare to deal with it effectively.

Pedagogy and curriculum learning design are vital aspects in the eco-system of providing high quality where it serves as a pivoting role in propelling forward the future of higher education. The way in which teachers teach and students learn has certainly changed over the years and is expected to continue changing in the future. The future cannot be predicted with 100% certainty. Just like how the COVID-19 pandemic forced global experimentation with remote teaching, an abrupt major event or development of new technology could take us by surprise and seriously disrupt the flow of higher education institutes.

The effects of COVID-19 pandemic could be well acknowledged with more than one billion students' education pursuit has been disrupted. Nonetheless, in the flip side, we must acknowledge that it has certainly given us a hard push, to rethink while working around the limitations that enabled us an opportunity to rethink and innovate learning, teaching strategies and re-image, reinvent education. It has also re-emphasized the urgency to review and accelerate the transformation from traditional classroom of teaching and learning that was still lingering and deeply entrenched in many educational institutions. That said, educators generally seek out to explore and experiment innovative strategies to move away from a teacher-centric towards student-centric/student-oriented learning environment where it is inclined towards higher level of engagement, collaborative dialogues, inter-intra and peer feedback.

1.2 Trends and Drivers

RMIT (n.d.) reported in reference to Professor Tricia McLaughlin, there are four key aspects in which education is set to transform in the near future. Firstly, there will be a substantive increase in collaborative learning pedagogies in general where more students become co-creators of their own learning. Secondly, technology will be an enabler to have classrooms to be facilitated anytime and anywhere. Thirdly, teachers will start to have more individualized and personalized learning plans for students that enable them to learn at a pace that best suits their abilities, imperatively accommodate to their speed of acquiring knowledge and to engage with contents that is most beneficial to them. Lastly, the purpose of assessments will move beyond attaining good grades results. These changes are already observable in classrooms today and are likely to be even more prominent as we progress and propel forward.

In a similar vein, Redecker et al. (2011) advocated that personalization, collaboration and informalization (informal learning) will be at the core of future learning. The standard of future learning will be characterized by lifelong learning and moulded by the pervasiveness of information and communication technologies. Several vital trends and drivers influencing the future of learning were presented in the Conceptual Map of the Future of Learning by Redecker et al. (2011). The framework comprises of four key thrusts, namely drivers, labour market trends and demands, education and training and ICT trends. The thrust on drivers influences the labour market trends and demands in general. These elements include demography, globalization, immigration, technology and labour market. The education and training section focuses on new skills and new ways of learning, focusing explicitly on personalization, collaboration and informalization. Personalization on the front of new skills development focuses on personal skills such as initiative, resilience, responsibility, risk-taking and creativity, whereas on the front of new ways of learning, personalization focused on being learner-centred approach such as to be tailor-made and targeted, active and constructive, and motivating and engaging. Collaboration on the front of new skills development addresses social skills such as teamwork, networking, empathy, compassion and co-constructing, whereas on the front of new ways of learning, it focuses on social learning such as peer-learning and sharing and collaborating in communities. Informalization on the front of new skills development addresses the development of learning skills such as managing, organizing, meta-cognitive skills and failing forward, whereas on the new ways of learning front, it focuses on life wide learning such as anywhere, anytime approach, blending virtual and real, and combining source/providers. The last pillar that influences the entire education and training eco-system is the ICT trends. Some examples include augmented reality, data mining, learning analytics, electronic tutors, 3D virtual worlds, social networks, games, mobiles, e-books, OER, portfolios and learning management system (LMS).

Drawing from their research and other relevant literature, in the next section, we list and elaborate the key trends and drivers that would potentially have a significant influence on the future direction of teaching and learning in higher education.

1.2.1 Globalization

Globalization impacts all aspects of operations from an international, national, industrial and societal contexts, including the evolution of higher education. In fact, globalization is primarily a driving force for many of the evolving trends. The classroom learning (Carnoy & Rhoten, 2002), learning climate, learning eco-system, infrastructure and processes, teaching strategies adopted and culture of learning (Rajaram, 2021) are subtly but would ultimately be in continuous process of transformation by the varying forces of globalization. The spillover effects could also be seen in varying aspects of the knowledge production process that includes the overall delivery of school educational systems, national policies and local cultural, social practices. A potential decrease in public funding and the rapid adoption of information technology to expand the quantity of education at a low cost are other implications that need to be managed. The ripple effects of globalization make higher education institutions and universities to work much harder to compete, stay relevant, contemporary and survive in terms of sustainability in a global market.

The implications and impacts of globalization manifest in the higher education market in a multitude of ways. A few such examples include the intensification of competition for international students, the increase in transnational programmes and the prevalence of for-profit providers (De Wit, 2011). Imperatively, with the higher education markets becoming global and commodified, competition has since become more intense. As such, students around the globe are coming out from their home country to pursue their higher education or university education and enhance their value and standing in terms of their academic and professional development, preparing them for new global workforce. Naturally, with an increase in international students, the composition of students in the higher education institutions is much more diverse than ever. This element of diversity is viewed as the drivers for the growth and future of higher education. Further to this, the effect of globalization is experienced in the rapid growing demand of adopting of technological advancements on how higher education institutions deliver programmes today.

Globalization has certainly enabled for an increased international cooperation that allows universities to form alliances to compete in the global mass higher education market (Chan, 2004) and hence position themselves more strategically in terms of sustainability and providing much higher value proposition to the targeted market. When done right, this allows cooperating institutions to value add inline to the needs of the targeted segment and thus attract more students in view of competitiveness. Globalization has played a pivotal role in increasing the significance of English language abilities resulting in many non-native speakers pursuing degrees in English-speaking countries such as the United States or the United Kingdom.

1.2.2 Demographic: Diversity of Learners

Diversity in terms of nationality and ethnicity are a few of the major changes in demographics that have been observed in student populations over the years progressively. The projections of the Bureau of the Census in the United States report that there will be a population of 393.9 million immigrants by the year 2050 with an average annual growth rate of 0.77% per year. It is proposed that 55% of the net growth is likely to be ascribed to immigrants and their descendants. Further to this, the number of international students in general has been positively increasing over the years (Duffin, 2020a, 2020b). This was well illustrated in the statistics on the number of international students in the United States from 2003/04 to 2019/20, which is presented by Statista via https://www.statista.com/statistics/237681/international-students-in-the-us/. The increase in cultural diversity can be largely attributed to the continuous increasing number of immigrants and their children along with international students. This trend can also be largely mirrored, resonated and experienced in other developed countries as well.

Diversity can also present itself in other varying forms such as gender, sexual orientation, age, socio-economic class and disability. When we examined from a dimension of diversity, all students from varying cultural diversity can be viewed as having their own individual strengths and weaknesses because of the varying environments embedded with unique values and beliefs with which they grew up in or simply due to a matter of personality differences that are largely influenced by the cultural norms and practices and climate. As such, it is imperative that higher education institutes must pay closer attention to ensuring that their programmes consider the learning culture, norms that tie closely to their efficacy of learning, mental well-being and welfare by acknowledging the needs of these culturally different students. This has a ripple effect on the increased trend for more individualized learning. For instance, self-paced learning prevents fast learners from feeling restricted and bored, and slow learners from feeling left behind.

The benefit of this evolving shift in demographics is for the students having the opportunity to interact and work with peers who come from varying cultural backgrounds. The ability to work in such a dynamic environment with social and cultural differences is a crucial skill for students to have today as it equips them to be job ready to work in diverse cultural teams and beyond. Soft skills such as teamwork, embracing differences yet working cordially with respect and communicating with sensitivity and mindfulness, are becoming increasingly vital traits employers desire in fresh graduates, equally as the emphasis given to the technical/hard skills. This shift in employer expectations and demands is certainly a contributing factor that helps to influence and shape the future of higher education.

1.2.3 Labour Market and Employer Demands

The work climate, culture and environment are rapidly evolving embedded with more complexities from social, cultural and operational perspectives. With digitalization as part of the driving force forward, jobs are now re-designed and require new, different skillset, knowledge and abilities to fill them. Skills' "gaps", mismatch and potential workforce fragility provide stronger impetus to re-access having a transformed curriculum. The efforts taken by varying stakeholders in wanting to close the "skills gaps" of the learning in school and the "know-hows and skills" for work have called for a revolution of upskilling and reskilling with over one billion workers by 2030 needing to reskill. Beyond the advocation and promotional efforts of lifelong learning in preparing the society for job disruptions, there must be equal emphasis on continuous review, revamp, improvisation and updating of the education models to avoid a disconnect with the realities of the future.

Employers depend largely on employees to enhance their organization's competitiveness (Pang et al., 2018) and growth in terms of sustainability, tied to employees' capabilities and outputs that could potentially affect overall organizational performance. If a company makes poor recruitment decisions, they will incur a loss from both monetary and non-monetary aspects. Hence, it is crucial for them to hire the right people with the essential "know-hows", skill and competencies. This pressing need from employers explains why higher education institutes have been increasingly pressured to develop graduates with relevant, contemporary employability skills and prepare students adequately for the continuously evolving workforce (Suleman, 2017).

It is most certain and becomes apparent that jobs of the future will require new and higher levels of skillsets. Redecker et al. (2011) state that the main drivers that impact relevancy and currency of skills include the progressive de-valuing of shelf-life of knowledge, increased level of information availability, and the persisting pressures of generalization and specialization of the workforce (Redecker et al., 2011). Europe is an example where economies are moving towards an increased demand in knowledge and skill intensive jobs related to technical and managerial work. This major shift in employer demands is not just visible in Europe but across the globe as well. The World Economic Forum emphasized the shift in skill demands and composition, which was presented in the Future of Jobs Report, World Economic Forum that could be retrieved from https://reports.weforum.org/future-of-jobs-2016/shareable-infographics/. Institutions must have the relevant contemporary knowledge and the capacity to train and equip students with these skills.

World Economic Forum in January 2020 highlighted in a report that proposes skills that could be clustered in eight categories for contemporary modern education: Innovation and creativity, problem-based and collaborative learning; technology; interpersonal; global citizenship; personalized and self-paced learning; accessible and inclusive learning; and lifelong and student-driven learning. The expectation of future generation workers is to be equipped with skills that even smart and highly technologically advanced machines cannot replicate or at least perform as competently as humans. This entails emotional, social and care support roles, embracing cultural intelligence and work that requires frequent human interactions and collaborations. The new job roles and its scopes are to be much less specific, defined and more fluid. Hence, being agile, willingness to adapt and align speedily, having an entrepreneurial and growth mindset by being creative and innovative are core competencies that need to be cultivated, advocated and ingrained throughout one's education on top of the basic subject contents knowledge to be acquired. Besides this, a mindset of grit, crisis readiness and fortitude embedded with a basic awareness of global emerging trends is to be ingrained through social learning which could be done via societal and community service learning. Such skills would come handy to deal with unprecedented circumstances, manage future work crisis and avoid social panic situations, for example COVID-19 pandemic. Moreover, futures literacy is a skill that enables people to comprehend and vision, and imagine the future in a beneficial way, inspiring and encouraging innovative solutions for future issues. Information and media literacy empowers individuals to independently discern facts from fake news and disinformation campaigns. Contemporary and future education models should emphasize and put weightage on ethos such as upholding integrity behaviour, personal ethics and values to nurture responsible global citizens who not only comprehend but can also affirmatively and actively contribute to crucial issues such as social disparity, biases and discriminative aspects and sustainability.

Aside the focus on relevant and modern skills development, the future labour market is influenced by the emergence of new technological advancements and disruptions. Not only do employees have to upskill and reskill by learning to work with technological innovations, but digitalization can also make jobs redundant, resulting in unemployment. James (2019) advocated three types of skills universities need to introduce into the curriculum to prepare students for future employment, namely practical technological skills, data skills and social skills. We are already seeing the use of technology in varying functional roles within higher education classrooms that has shown a significant increase over the years. Technological disruptions do not only affect what we need to learn now but imperatively how we would be learning in the future and beyond.

1.2.4 Emerging Technologies

Generally, technology investments made by schools worldwide has increased more than a 100-fold in the last two decades (Lim et al., 2013). Most of these investments were made on the assumption that technology-mediated learning environments provide opportunities for students to search for and analyse information, solve problems, communicate and collaborate. The overall direction is that institutions are expected to have students to be equipped with competencies that enable them to compete in the twenty-first century and beyond marketplace.

Moreover, over 60% of higher education institutions have either reorganized or have plans to reorganize their information technology units within two years (Elzarka, 2012). The demand for innovative and instruction-focused technologies has progressively continued to rise, and the use of other technologies such as e-portfolios, learning management systems and wireless classrooms has been growing as well.

Generally, emerging technologies in education can be viewed as volatile in having them embedded within the learning processes and curriculum designs. However, it is still vital for institutions to discover and explore new ways of adopting and implementing them in classrooms. This enables education institutions to remain up to date and at the same time develop key competencies in students for them to be upskilled and reskilled to stay relevant for the future workforce. Technology has a large influence on how course contents are taught and delivered and the type of learning design pedagogies adopted.

1.3 Learning Intelligence

Learning intelligence refers to an institution or organization's learning and development, innovations, transformations and capabilities. To put it in context, it can be explicitly defined as the institution or organization's capability to define, describe learning goals, comprehend the rapidly evolving learning needs, requirements and practices, and quantify via interpreting learning outcomes. The next primary question is for us to relate and understand the role of intelligence in learning. The definitions of learning and intelligence are different and could be viewed as separate aspects that can be discussed independently. However, interestingly, the distinction between these two concepts becomes vague when it comes to the actual learning process. Evidence reports that the relationship between learning and intelligence shows minimal difference in measures of individual's intelligence, such as an intelligence quotient (IQ) test and measures of their ability to learn. This establishes a strong correlation and identity between the notions of intelligence and learning.

All of these insights from a holistic context advocate that the efficacy of learning can be enhanced by focusing on learning practices or their intellectual development. As such, educators have more autonomy to diversify students' learning through social-culturally and intellectually meaningful as well as rewarding approaches such as virtual and augmented reality, artificial intelligence, personalized/self-paced learning or gamification. Figure 1.1 presents the conceptual framework for learning intelligence.

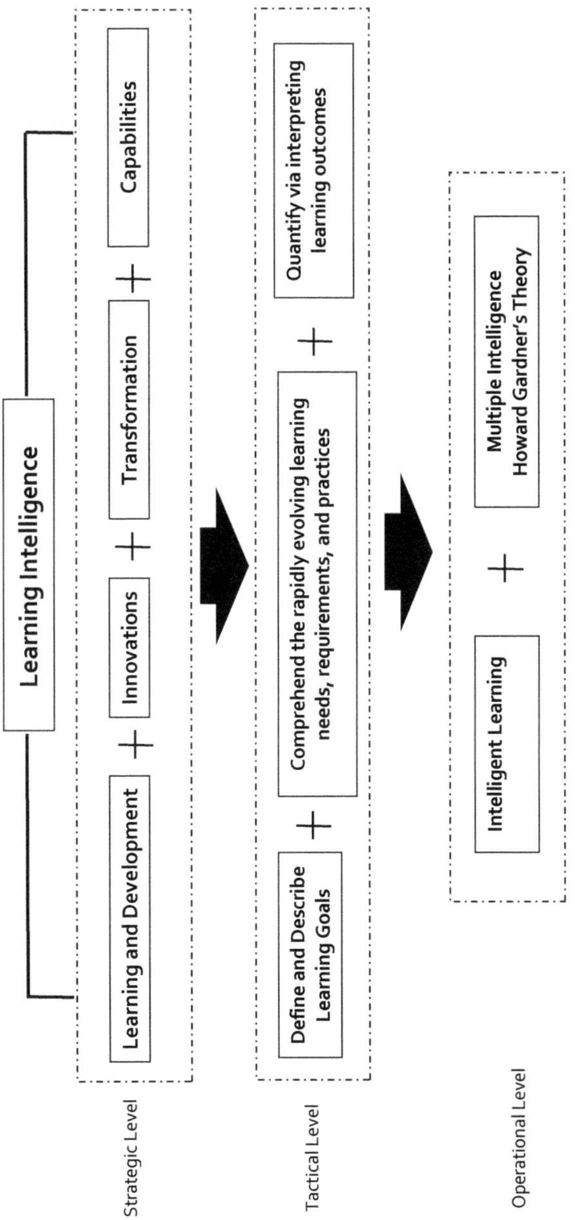

Fig. 1.1 Conceptual framework for learning intelligence

1.3.1 Strategic Level Planning and Interventions

Under the strategic level, four key thrusts are involved in formulating and applying the learning intelligence notion, namely (a) learning and development; (b) innovations; (c) transformation; and (d) capabilities. There must be an eco-system built to ensure the processes of learning and development are well established. For example, investing in a validated system that tracks and monitors strategic key performance indicators for (a) the organization or institution; (b) its division and/or department learning level goals; and (c) its employees' individual professional growth. Next, the institution or organization must draw out strategic learning plans that need to be cascaded down to be achieved by the varying respective divisions/departments. These strategic goals include having to well understand the skills, applied knowledge and competencies required and devising a strategic road map. Next is building the strategic eco-system supported by policies that advocate creativity to flourish, more importantly to shape an innovative culture to be ingrained with the institution/organization. On a similar vein, the plan for transformation goals must be implemented through policy advocate and processes as enablers. Further to that, the relevant resources and manpower as an investment to develop the relevant capabilities must be drawn out and allocated.

1.3.2 Tactical Level Planning and Interventions

Under the tactical level, three key thrusts are involved in cascading the strategic level directions in applying the learning intelligence notion, namely (a) define and describe learning goals; (b) comprehend the rapidly evolving learning needs, requirements and practices; and (c) quantify via interpreting learning outcomes. At the division/department level, the learning goals are to be defined from the context of the institution's strategic plan and direction. The learning goals should be explicitly described to comprehend the emphasis and focus. To have this done, the evolving learning needs, requirements and practices must be carefully examined, understood and interpreted. This enables the division/department to then decide on the identification of areas of learning to be focused on and making it available for access. The learning outcomes can be quantified to explicitly monitor and measure the impact.

1.3.3 Operational Level Planning and Interventions

1.3.3.1 Intelligent Learning

At this juncture, having a clear and deep understanding of the term "intelligent learning" enables us to distinguish it with the term learning intelligence. Intelligent learning refers to the occurrence or phase when learning and development departments, educators and learners collaborate and work together to have the essentials sorted out and get the things right. When the learning process is optimized, and the learning outcomes are achievable, then learners are engaged in intelligent learning. Besides that, by giving due consideration to the environmental aspects, we are able to increase the efficacy of the intended learning outcomes and goals. An intelligent learning environment refers to the educational strategy or approach where learners are immersed in a deep learning, problem-solving and critical thinking climate, space or situation. An example to illustrate this would be maritime students or sailors who use a ship simulator to be exposed to real-situational circumstances for their learning and training purposes.

1.3.3.2 Howard Gardner's Theory of Multiple Intelligences

In Howard Gardner's theory of multiple intelligences (1983, 1993), that is a primarily learner-based philosophy, the traditional views of intelligence were challenged and the existence of nine discrete "intelligences" in human beings, combinable in various ways to form an intellectual repertoire of different intelligences, was argued and advocated.

Gardner provided a basis upon which to identify, value and develop learners' abilities. These intelligences were clustered into nine intelligences progressively, namely:

- **Logical-Mathematical**: It is characterized as the ability to perform logical reasoning, utilize the numbers effectively (Armstrong, 2009) and think logically (Richards & Rodgers, 2014). Other abilities include problem-solving, exploring patterns, calculating and outlining.
- **Verbal-Linguistic**: It refers to using language in an innovative and unique way (Richards & Rodgers, 2014). It relates to rhythms, sounds of words, that include human voice as well as environmental and instrumental sounds. It uses syntax, semantics, phonology and pragmatic dimensions of language or its practical use, for example, rhetoric, explanation, mnemonics and metalanguage.
- **Visual-Spatial**: It refers to the abilities to design, invent, imagine and create. It involves the bodily-kinesthetic aspects, namely learning through physical movement, mimicking and touching. It can be defined as the "…capacity to visualize to graphically represent visual or spatial ideas, and to orient oneself appropriately in a spatial matrix" (Armstrong, 2009, p. 7).
- **Interpersonal**: It relates and understands others' feelings. Gardner (2011) defines this intelligence as "the ability to notice and make distinctions among other individuals and specifically, among their moods, temperaments, motivations and intentions" (p. 253).
- **Intrapersonal**: The primary aspect of this intelligence is focused on one's inner self where it makes one understands one's own emotions, motivations and moods. Gardner (2006) defined this intelligence as the ability "to form an accurate,

veridical model of oneself and to be able to use that model to operate effectively in life" (pp. 49–50).

- **Naturalist**: This intelligence was added to the list in 1995. Gardner describes this as a half intelligence intertwined with spiritualist intelligence. It comprises of individuals who are sensitive to patterns and make connections to elements in nature while enjoying and respecting other species and the environment. The sensitivity is tied to other natural phenomena such as mountains and cloud formations (Armstrong, 2009).
- **Musical-Rhythmic**: It refers to the capacity to comprehend and express elements of music that includes rhythmic and melodic patterns through formal analytic means or figural or intuitive means.
- **Bodily-Kinesthetic**: It refers to the ability to use mental capabilities to organize body movements, showing the related cooperation between mental and physical activities. These includes physical tasks such as acting out or dancing (Green & Tanner, 2005).
- **Existential**: This was added to the list as the ninth intelligence in 1999 and is referred to as the intelligence of big questions. It refers to the ability to raise and contemplate big questions (Gardner, 2006).

In an interview with Mindshift Connections in April 1997, Gardner stated that multiple intelligence (MI) is most useful for two educational ends: (a) Enables learners to realize desired outcomes through planned education programmes and (b) allows learners to comprehend vital theories and concepts in the disciplines (Gardner, 1997).

The fundamental thrust of Gardner's theory notion underlies the questions, "*Why are we teaching people what we are teaching in the way we are teaching, and why do we value our current system of educating human beings as the best, and as the most wholesome, accurate way of assessing the intelligence of a human being?*".

The design methodology adopted to deliver knowledge may not be well aligned to the capabilities of learners. Thus, this drives unproductive outcomes and failures on the quality aspects of the learning process. Learners must be self-aware of their strengths and weaknesses to enhance their self-learning journey and overcome their challenges by being adaptive to diverse tasks. The strategy adopted must embed the notion of understanding learners' cognitive process and the socio-constructivist process.

In trying to figure out how best to experiment using the intelligence in classrooms, several strategies were adopted, and these can be summarized as follows: (a) Adopting Gardner's theory as a legitimate planning guide to offer students a variety of learning activities; (b) categorizing the types of intelligence into its particular activities; (c) incorporating specific intelligences to the relevant topics to cover all aspects of intelligences holistically; and (d) ensuring all topics are covered with relevant intelligences incorporated. Gardner's theory aims to address the needs of the students, where activities are designed to relate to students' strengths and weaknesses. It enables them to work on their profiles which were less well developed while building on their areas of strength.

The emphasis must be in the range of activities offered as a planned, integral part of the curriculum, rather than randomly selected for sake of variety. Gardner himself is critical of a simplistic approach where the activities to be included must be carefully thought through that nurture different intelligences instead of an ad hoc approach for the sake of variety or diverse coverage. Based on the foundational inspirations from Hopper and Hurry (2000)'s insights, an enhanced, detailed and transformed guiding interventions have been newly formulated. Table 1.1 presents the enhanced version on the scope and impact of learning from multiple intelligences.

Tensions between process versus contents

The different values in society could be well experienced as tensions that emerge from the perceptions of the need to place emphasis on how people learn (process of learning) versus what people learn (the content of learning). Small (1977) advocates the notion of the distinction between education and school, where he claimed that by

Table 1.1 Scope and impact on learning from multiple intelligences (MI)

Increased awareness on the way learning happens and about its learning process	1. Emphasis is on students' exploration and self-learning process. 2. Exposure of learners to varying differentiated learning approaches and them of being responsible for their own learning and attaining its outcomes. 3. More focused efforts and much greater emphasis on exploring strategies in which students learn best. 4. Enable reasonable flexibility and adequate autonomy provided for the curriculum to be tailor-made to fit the learning needs of students. 5. Identify the embedded learning challenges and have them explicitly addressed to enhance the efficacy of the intended learning outcomes.
Increased emphasis on individual learning processes and personalized learning	1. The focus is on personalized learning where the emphasis is on individuals devising their learning processes where they are made accountable for their own learning. 2. The belief that all individuals are unique, and they do not have the same kinds of minds is adopted; the efficacy of education for individuals works most effectively when these differences and strengths are taken into due consideration instead of being ignored. 3. The approach of learners keeping their records of learning progress and achievements as part of a planned process helps in the development of the learner's autonomy (Greenhalgh, 1994). 4. The fourfold Kolb's (1984) influential framework advocates an array of learning styles to fit individual learning styles. When learners utilize their preferred learning styles, they widened their opportunities for success in learning (Greenhalgh, 1994). 5. "Learning happens when the learners start questioning the norms; searching for information to address the varying perspectives; explore the unknown without being spoon-fed with model answers; self-think critically on how to resolve issues at hand; experience discomfort in the progress and are put in an ambiguous situation, while working towards resolving an assigned task. This allows one to think, reflect and strive towards the process of finding the answers to the queries and unanswered issues. The process of the learning phase is the focus if learning in terms of depth and quality is to occur" (Rajaram, 2021, p. vii).

(continued)

Table 1.1 (continued)

Enhanced stimulation of the active, team-based and collaborative learning process	1. Students' motivation increases dramatically when they acknowledge, resonate and relate through relevant diverse activities in lessons, where it would not be an end in itself but a means of learning. 2. Once the students can grasp and comprehend the aspects which they had previously not known, they would be committed in projecting themselves in a positive light to their peers. 3. Less time taken to deal with the behavioural disruptions that could potentially cause classroom anxiety which is reduced to enable a more conducive climate of learning. 4. Facilitates the process of creating awareness to recognize their ability to learn and the sense of learning, which is a core element in enhancing self-esteem, especially for those who regard themselves as failures or at least their perceived notion as such. 5. The shift of accountability involved in the learning process enables an affirmative effect between student–teacher relationships.

going to school, one may not necessarily be educated, and conversely, getting back to school does not necessarily give one an education. This was reiterated drawing on the work of Illich who mentioned that the actual participation constitutes socially valuable learning where the participation involves learners in every phase of the learning process with full autonomy of what to be learned and how it is to be learned.

The tensions between process and content are at times irreconcilable; hence, this may potentially lead to the collapse of the system. Generally, students can take control and monitor their own learning progress. However, they tend to be demotivated and block off their own learning processes by not mobilizing their learning skills when they perceive little relevance of what is being taught. The key emphasis in learning should be not merely facilitating the "right" or "wrong" contents; rather, it is about mobilizing intellectual inquisitiveness, enabling to make balanced judgements, nurturing reasoning skills and resourcefulness while equipping individuals to make sense of the world in which they live in.

On the flip side, multiple intelligences (MI) theory has come under scrutiny where it was criticized for being fundamentally flawed (Best, 1996; White, 1998). The MI theory has been manipulated, distorted and diluted to fit a wide range of pedagogical, educational and curricular strategies some of which have gained much criticism, including Gardner himself. Using the analogy of a beacon, by providing a light from the beacon, and not in the beacon itself, the value of MI approach can be acknowledged. The focus of the critics was on the actual machinations of the beacon rather than the broader implications of the light shining from it. Hence, we could reiterate that the MI notion does shed an alternative light on aspects of the contemporary and current debates in education. Despite the non-novelty of the theory, it is certainly timely and refreshing to reiterate the key thrusts that it sheds light on for both the learners and the teachers. Basically, on the aspect of how it enables learners to access, manage and develop their own learning processes.

The Impact: On Cross-Cultural Aspects and Context

The increased attention in the use of multiple intelligences is primarily because of the discrepancy that often exists between school tasks and the learners' "spectrum of intelligences" (Gardner, 1983). Culture distinctively influences the development of learners' intelligences by defining what is valued for every individual who potentially differs from cultural, social and other diversity elements. The primary question to reflect on the efficacy of how students are identified and developed is, are they well noticed based on their intelligences, strengths and sociocultural backgrounds?

Three core requirements need to be addressed for a certain type of intelligence to be developed: (1) The opportunity must be given or facilitated for learning; (2) the learning culture must place emphasis and value on the specific intelligences development; and (3) the learner must put in efforts and place importance on developing that intelligence.

Educators can elevate students through engaging them actively with the application of multiple intelligences. This intervention assists nurture-specific intelligences that students may lack which are vital for their future success by developing culturally responsive methods to engage students who have challenges in learning. Culturally responsive and personalized learning experiences enable students to reach their fullest potential at their own pace, while providing them with positive reinforcement (Teele, 1990).

It is not necessary to address all of the intelligences in everything educators teach (Gardner, 1983, 1993, 1994). Different projects can provide students the alternative to explore a topic using their strongest intelligence. Some students might develop a model, write or illustrate content, for example. The topic must be taught to students in a manner that is relevant, appropriate and applicable to them in the near future.

A culturally responsive assessment is required to promote equitable educational experiences via multiple intelligences. David Lazear (1994) identified key principles in providing instruction for culturally responsive assessment that adopts multiple intelligences notion as follows:

- Assessment should drive the learning design, the adoption of pedagogical approach and its curriculum design.
- Assessment should be at the core of the education process, focusing on authenticity.
- Assessment practices should resemble assessment in the "real world".
- Assessment design and execution must involve educators and students to be active partners who have worked together in demonstrating learning.
- Assessment requires time and efforts, and hence, educators must be given adequate time to create and administer instruments.
- Assessment practices should be designed for students' benefit.
- Assessment should be individualized and developmentally appropriate.

All in all, educators must continuously rethink and review on the current instructional and assessment practices, examining it from a multi-sociocultural lens to be agile and adaptable to the rapid evolving changes. Educators should adopt a reverse engineering approach where the planning, facilitation and assessment must be based on the learner's individual needs while taking due consideration of the sociocultural settings. As a clear relationship exists between multiple intelligences and culture (Reiff, 1993, 1996), educational experiences must reflect the understanding of each learner's culture.

1.4 Key Evolving Challenges and Concerns of Future Learning

Higher education institutes are under continuous call by varying stakeholders to remain relevant and contemporary in the twenty-first century and beyond for the future. Hence, it is imperative that they commit towards the journey of radical transformation to teaching and learning space that have been brought about by digital technologies and the Internet in the last decade (Burkle et al., 2018). Adopting a growth mindset and agility in their outlook enables them to address the rapidly evolving changes and disruptions. On the contrary, major and sudden breakthroughs in teaching and learning aspects, while potentially beneficial, can also be highly detrimental should institutions are unprepared to deal and manage it. Further to these challenges brought about by technological disruptions and advancements, institutions should also examine the varying challenges relating to the topics such as sustainability, multi-disciplinary training, easy and affordable access to education and learning in diversity, distinctive embedded nuances within different learning cultures and culture of learning which are pressing topics today and likely in the future as well.

One of the pressing concerns is the implications and the ripple effects of fiscal challenges faced by the higher education institutions and universities. There are varying aspects of factors that contribute to the financial predicaments of institutions. Some of these includes the lack of adequate or sufficiently sustainable government support and progressive increase in operational and functional costs. This has put institutions to search and look out for other streams of cash inflow. This could potentially include providing online (asynchronous) and virtual (synchronous) programmes that can be accessed anywhere in the world. These programmes could be collaborated with corporations to provide upskilling and reskilling professional certifications. However, on the flip side, pursuing such non-traditional funding sources can bring on challenges and complications of its own as predicaments. For example, corporate sponsorships and contract clauses could significantly interfere with an institute's research through pre-invention license agreements, publication delays, pre-publication access to research results, censorship and so on.

Another recent and more contemporary-inclined concern is that of online programmes, where illegal downloads and uploads can severely impact an institute's revenue stream and reputation. In the similar vein, other potential challenges particularly for online learning includes (1) will there be a negative effect or implication in a perceived reduced quality of education due to the absence of physical presence and a lesser direct face-to-face human engagement; (2) increased faculty training costs, perhaps in getting more experienced yet competent facilitators adept who are technologically inclined; (3) faculty resistance; (4) employer bias and perception against online degrees in terms of its rigour and quality; (5) increased cost of technological advancements and infrastructure; (6) programme start-up costs and challenges; (7) potential reduction on student and professor interactions; (8) irrelevance and outdatedness of previous location advantage; and (9) potential infringement on existing programmes (Palvia et al., 2018; Rajaram, 2021). The potential future challenges may be plentiful, however, as the pace of change within higher education continues to speed up. PwC (2020) identified that increased risks will largely fall into one of four clusters, namely: (1) Brand preservation; (2) information security; (3) regulatory; and (4) operational. Overall, it is crucial for higher education institutions to acknowledge honestly the potential challenges that they may face and be resourceful, humble to learn from others while making the necessary arrangements to tackle them appropriately.

1.5 The 21st Century Classroom: How to Learn and Teach?

21st Century Classroom can be defined as a classroom that embeds the elements and the learning culture and climate of futuristic learning. Futuristic learning entails a major shift focusing on student-centric learning where inter-group, intra-group collaboration, peer review, higher-order skills training beyond knowledge acquisition, leveraging on digitalization in learning and crisis, unprecedented situational handling leadership and social literacy skills. The advancement of educational technology has certainly assisted in transforming classrooms across the globe. In a twenty-first century classroom today, teachers can easily access information and resources that their predecessors would find inconceivable. For example, teachers can access information on the Internet at anytime, anywhere at any location; they can gain access to infinite information and numerous data sets, visuals/images and videos of events across the world. The high potential and capabilities of technology are expected to get even better as time progresses. It is imperative for institutes to be mindful and ensure that technology is not merely used as simply a way to deliver information, which may be the reason but should never be the only purpose. Through the limitations offered by such educational technology integration, institutions may possibly overlook many impactful and positive contributions that technology can make in twenty-first century classrooms. Hence, teachers should leverage the use of technology as deemed fit to the situational and circumstance context to engage students with real-world problem-solving, conceptual development and critical thinking (Irving, 2006).

The goal of future education is to facilitate and create a seamless pathway for students to gain the twenty-first century and beyond employability skills and competencies (Donovan et al., 2014) that makes students job ready and address the demands of today's workforce. Many educational reforms are not able to sustain or fail largely due to varying definitions that describe the reform, and perhaps the term "twenty-first century skills' are interchangeably used without a clear and well-defined description. Some focus on the use of technology for communication and collaboration while others are inclined on digital literacy. Despite this lack of consistency, there have been numerous efforts to define and describe twenty-first century skills and learning. In general, these skills are those that go beyond the classroom context. Advances in technology make it essential for students to have functional and critical thinking skills such as information, media and ICT literacy. Moreover, in a globally competitive information age, it is also vital for students to develop skills such as agility, resilient, flexibility, adaptability, leadership and other employability skills. Thus, with the introduction of skills and competencies required for the twenty-first century and beyond, it is no surprise that modes and approaches of learning have changed over the past years (Davidson & Goldberg, 2009). With emerging technologies, modes of teaching have also changed. In the next section, we shall discuss and examine the newer teaching techniques, methodologies and learning strategies that have been influenced by digitalization and technological advancements.

1.5.1 Evolving Teaching Methodologies

Industry experts years ago had predicted that massive open online courses (MOOCs) would potentially cause face-to-face higher education institutes to become obsolete (Govindarajan and Srivastava (2020). In contrary, this is clearly not the case today, where higher education institutes have responded adequately well and have changed significantly compared to a decade ago. More specifically, there have been numerous changes to the ways in which higher education is facilitated and the course instruction being delivered, more so adjusting rapidly through learning from COVID-19 pandemic.

These changes have certainly been the effects of digitalization, technological advancements along with the easy access and usability of Internet. Many higher education institutes have started to focus on the application of technology and the Internet of Things (IoT), a global network that links devices, objects and things to the Internet infrastructure interact with the internal and external environments (Aldowah et al., 2017). The Internet, in particular, has a significant presence in higher education institutions, where the capability of technologies to disrupt teaching, learning and assessment is well understood. Overall, the Internet and technological developments have greatly impacted higher education. Now let us examine more specifically on how teaching methodologies and strategies have evolved for the future.

1.5.2 Blended Learning

Blended learning entails the combination of face-to-face (physical or virtual and synchronous) and online (asynchronous) learning, with an emphasis on technology-based/ technology-enabled learning (Rajaram, 2021). Blended learning enhances cost effectiveness and increase access and flexibility (Sharma et al., 2019). For example, if the number of students' size is very large, say in few hundreds, then it could be economical to have them all go through the asynchronous online learning where the time spent explicitly for face to face will be more productive. The students could be engaged through discussions that incline towards higher order of applied learning. Further to that, it can also help improve pedagogical practices and student learning outcomes. In terms of pedagogical learning design, blended learning enables increased interactions between students and teachers, while facilitating skills and learning agility, and capacity development. With an array of varying benefits, it is no surprise that blended learning programmes are becoming even more popular and in demand today. A report by Allen et al. (2007) found that 36% of schools in the United States offer at least one blended programme with the majority of them being associate degree programmes. The penetration rate of blended programmes by the type of school was examined in different types of schools advocated by Allen et al. (2007). Overall, this number is expected to be much higher today, especially with the emergence of newer technologies, rapid evolution of digital transformation interventions and the current pandemic COVID-19 situation.

In their studies in 2007, it was reported as follows: (a) The penetration rate for the certificate programme peaked for the doctoral/research and associates type of school clusters, followed by masters and baccalaureate type of school clusters, with the specialized type of school cluster scoring the least impact; (b) for the associate program, the peak of penetration was from the doctoral/research and associates type of school clusters, followed by the masters and baccalaureate type of school clusters, with again the specialized type of school cluster scoring the least impact; (c) for the bachelors program, the peak of penetration is attained at the masters and doctoral/research type of school clusters, followed by the baccalaureate and specialized segments, with the associates type of school cluster having the minimal effect; (d) the penetration rate for the master's programme peaked for doctoral/research and masters type of school clusters, followed by baccalaureate and specialized type of school clusters, with the specialized type of school cluster being rated with the minimal impact This research analysis enabled potential improvised design to occur, having the relevant elements carefully embedded in the design of blended learning.

Alexander et al. (2019) state that blended learning is seen to have increased steadily as a favoured course delivery model alongside with varying other fully online options. Personalized or adaptive courseware and web conferencing tools are some of the digital solutions that are used in blended learning to achieve the intended learning outcomes. Blended learning is preferred by students primarily due to reasons such as flexibility, ease of access and the integration of advanced multimedia. To support and assist in the growth of blended learning pedagogy, higher education institutions must support and expose faculty in the learning design experiences that optimize the use of digital platforms that comprise collaboration and student-centred learning design.

1.5.3 Online Learning

Online learning has shown significant growth and demand over the last decade, as the Internet and the recent COVID-19 pandemic have literally forced schools, including higher education institutions, to accept and work in a remote virtual learning space to continue its essential operations of facilitating lectures, seminars, tutorials and students' consultations. It is noteworthy to point out that online learning was prominent even before the COVID-19 pandemic due to the rapid evolution of digitalization, more global learning collaborations and the emphasis towards the concept of self-directed and personalized that enables students to learn at their own pace. In fact, online learning has shown clear and significant growth in adoption in the last decade. Forecasts have predicted that the online education market will be worth $350 billion by 2025 (Koskal, 2020). The progressive steady growth of online learning is clear in the United States, where the number of students enrolled in distance learning courses has been steadily increasing over the years, as presented by Duffin (2020a, 2020b), U.S. student distance learning enrolment 2012–2018, that could be retrieved from https://www.statista.com/statistics/944245/student-distance-learning-enrollment-usa/

For higher education institutions, online learning can free resources from courses that can be commoditized and enabling these resources to be directed to research-based teaching, personalized problem-solving and mentorship. Students would have more space to manage their time since they are not required to spend all their time in campus, and instead use their time effectively in campuses for extra curriculum activities, optional electives, group work discussions, consultations with faculty, more peer-to-peer or intra-inter group interactions and career guidance, all of which apparently cannot be done from home (Govindarajan & Srivastava, 2020).

Online education is becoming an essential strategy, especially experiencing how it has made a huge impact on learning during COVID-19 pandemic for higher education institutions and universities, perhaps to all segments of education. Hence, it is undoubtedly clear that given the rapid growth of online learning, higher education institutions must figure out ways to provide quality online programmes, explicitly to investigate the efficacy of online learning.

1.5.4 Mobile Learning

Mobile learning or m-learning is viewed as separate aspect from other forms of technology-supported learning due to the differences in the way it mediates and facilitates learning experiences. Its ability to enable learners to learn at any time or place makes mobile learning an unique form of learning. The five distinct affordances that mobile learning offers include (1) portability; (2) affordable and ubiquitous access; (3) "just-in-time" learning opportunities; (4) connection and convergence; and (5) individualized and personalized experiences (Melhuish & Falloon, 2010).

The concept of mobile learning has been there for more than a decade; however, today, its focus is no longer solely on applications, but rather very much inclined towards the connectivity and convenience it brings to the learning experiences. As mobile devices become more affordable and accessible to students across the globe, the possibility of m-learning becomes limitless. In fact, the ownership of mobile devices has been steadily increasing. Research conducted by the Pew Research Center in 2018 reported that 59% of adults globally own a smartphone, whereas research from the EDUCAUSE Center for Analysis and Research reported that 95% of undergraduate students own smartphones (Alexander et al., 2019).

Most students generally support the adoption of m-learning and have a positive outlook towards it. Four in five students claimed that they have used a mobile device for coursework (Magda & Aslanian, 2018). Students used mobile devices for a wide range of learning activities, including accessing of course readings, communicating with professors and peers, accessing the learning management system, conducting research and writing up course work reports.

1.5.5 Simulations, Gamification and Video Games

Simulation, as a learning activity, is a growing trend in many diverse fields (Damewood, 2016). Simulation is a system that represents or stands in for another system, and its purpose is to enable process, procedure or skills practice in a controlled environment. For example, in the nursing field, substituting portion of the clinical hours with simulation learning hours is becoming a common and growing trend. Simulation allows students to apply information learnt and sets aside time for reflection that helps transfer information into knowledge. In the same vein, video games can also be used as an avenue or a strategy to facilitate simulation.

Educators seemed to be dismissive of video games (Shaffer et al., 2005). In a contrary, corporations, the government and the military have already recognized and made use of their significant educational power. They argue that games and learning are activities that are most powerful when they are personally meaningful, experiential, social and epistemological concurrently. Video games enable learners to participate in a new imaginary world and think, talk and act in unique and creative ways. For instance, the game "Real Lives 2010" is a simulation game that allows players to live a life in any country of the world with events occurring throughout their life based on real-world statistics. This game could be used to relate to students the varying forms of struggles that are ubiquitous around the world. The benefits and usefulness of video games are well acknowledged by K-12 teachers, with almost

60% of them adopt digital games at least once weekly in teaching and 18% utilizing them daily (Novotney, 2015).

Video games enable the development of effective social practices (Shaffer et al., 2005). Video games present players with a simulated world that, if well-constructed, can go beyond teaching facts and skills and embody certain aspects of social practices. There are strong implications on how video games can potentially impact higher education of the future.

1.6 Learning Strategies for the Future

As teaching and learning methodologies evolve, so will students. Students play a vital role in the higher education process, and so institutions must acknowledge on how students themselves may influence the entire learning experience. Matthias (n.d) from PA Consulting (n.d), as reported in Times Higher Education, stated that students presently have clearer goals and higher expectations on the type of relationship they require to develop with higher education institutions to achieve their educational goals, aspirations, and ambitions. The present and future students would not only have varied but certainly have much higher expectations in their educational journey. Moreover, they would also adopt different behaviours and attitudes when it comes to learning strategies.

Hence, it is imperative for educators to be agile and respond to these changing needs. Primarily, these students would come with much better exposed in terms of digitalization tools and platforms in their high schools and extended learning resources that enable them to appreciate a wider breadth of knowledge, especially from a multi-disciplinary context and with a more diverse collaborative learning methodologies and service-learning techniques. Hence, the learning strategies need to be designed with the rapidly changing needs and demands in mind so that higher education institutions can produce "job-ready" and industry-inclined graduates. Some contemporary strategies include enhanced level of team-based, active and collaborative learning; advanced practical hands-on exposure with increased frequency, for example, more internships planted within the programme curriculum; work and study programme embedded to see more connectivity of their classroom learning and its application to workplace context; multi-disciplinary curriculum where there are courses that need to be taken with other subject disciplines. This process enhances students' learning exposure and enriches their learning capacity through intermingling with other student profiles that enable them to appreciate subjects that are beyond their core specialization. Hence, the mantra is to adopt the strategy of being agile and responsive by performing continuous reviews to closely align to the needs of employers and other stakeholders so that the "gap" of skills and knowledge required for these students to be equipped is continuously addressed and closed.

1.7 Educators of the Future

Educators must rethink on what and how their roles have evolved to meet the needs of the future of education. The roles of higher education teachers must also be re-examined, in the similar vein on how the higher education curriculum is to be continuously reviewed and adjusted to reflect the twenty-first century ideas about knowledge and learning. As pointed out by Bolstad et al. (2012), teachers' roles need to be reconsidered if the common consensus towards the primary role of education is not just to transmit knowledge but also to cultivate people's ability to engage with and generate knowledge (Bolstad et al., 2012). Therefore, it is crucial that educators receive adequate training that will allow them to develop the necessary skills and competencies required for future classrooms. Some of the core skills that we believe are essential in the twenty-first century classroom and beyond are presented below with supporting discussions:

1.7.1 Cross-Cultural Competence

With many higher education institutes adopting an international approach or striving towards internationalization, teachers at present and of the future are expected to deal with students from diverse backgrounds. In a study conducted by Ballantyne et al. (1999) in Australia, it was discovered that the phrase "cross-cultural teaching and learning" emerged as the primary element to describe, contextualize and describe exemplary teaching in universities. This study is further supported by Salmona et al. (2015) who reported that the development of enhanced cultural competence was one of the key factors identified as crucial for future teachers. Both of these studies are indicators of how cross-cultural skills are extremely essential, relevant, contemporary and importantly necessary in today's higher education contexts. In today's multicultural, diverse climate and environment, educators are to be equipped so that they could train the students to acquire the relevant skills and knowledge to deal with the conflicts positively, see them as opportunities to strengthen professional relationships and shift the mindset to embrace diversity and working in complex culturally intertwined contexts.

1.7.2 Empathy: Leadership Skills Development

Empathy is a concept that came about in the early 1990s by Theodor Lipps and Edward Titchener (Davis, 1996; Rajaram, 2021). Empathy can be defined and described fundamentally as the psychological process of a person reflecting the feeling of another person or the ability to empathize. According to Bouton (2016), teaching and training of empathy is a vital skill for pre-service teachers (Bouton,

2016) and educators in higher education to be equipped with, developed and trained. This is especially true in the current context where there are often trends of mismatched aspects of diversity between teachers and students. Besides playing an important role in dealing with cultural sensitivity and diversity issues in the school system, empathy can also assist teachers in expanding social skills, emotional intelligence, moral development and so on. Further to that, empathy allows teachers to better analyse, relate and understand students' behaviour at depth. This allows them to undertake a more student-centred approach which is a shift that has been progressively happening for quite some time in the higher education domain. Rajaram (2021) has advocated and validated through an evidence-based approach that takes an effective psychological intervention known to elicit cognitive growth in a variety of contents and translates it into a university setting to develop students' cognitive empathy as part of the leadership skills in a university business course. In the similar vein, the conceptual strategy could be adopted for educators as well to enhance their cognitive empathy as part of the professional skills development. The primary basis is to have social-psychological interventions provoke individuals to address potential cognitive blocks that may inhibit positive learning behaviours. This research was significant and highly effective for three primary reasons, namely: "(1) it attempted to prime participants for the development of a non-content-based skill, in this study it was cognitive empathy, with a generalizable activity sequence; (2) it compared the effects of this priming activity against participants receiving more domain-specific content; (3) it introduced methods of analyzing participant work for holistic solutions and for indicators of graduate attributes instead of merely addressing content knowledge and domain-specific skills" (Rajaram, 2021, p. 121).

1.7.3 Teacher-Thinking

The development of cognitive competency of the concept "Teacher-Thinking" is embedded with several processes such as perception, reflection, problem-solving, inquiring and the manipulation of ideas (Huang, 2015). Teacher-thinking is one of the key skills for educators to develop and work on as it enables one to synthesize and perceive significant functions in their teaching work. It serves primarily as a foundational and fundamental element for an educator's decision-making. Hence, as classrooms become more complex with additional technological tools that are being added into the mix, teacher-thinking skills become even more crucial for educators to be able to keep up with the fast-paced classroom.

1.7.4 Growth Mindset: Lifelong Learning

Twenty-first century education entails educators to adopt a growth mindset that makes it necessary for them to see themselves and act as lifelong learners. It also requires them to have the ability to adjust, align and adapt to changing educational circumstances, evolving expectations and needs of students. For example, a teacher may be placed out of their comfort zone when teaching with new technological tools or embracing digitalization in teaching. However, if that teacher views this as a learning opportunity with a growth and positive mindset, then it enables him/her to overcome such discomfort and grow the required knowledge and skills. Without the fundamental trait/qualities of a lifelong learner, educators may potentially reduce the efficacy of their own teaching abilities and stagnate the growth of their students.

Researchers at the NZCER project Teachers' Work argued that the learning environments are a result of an interplay between individual teachers' knowledge, skills and dispositions, and the context within which they were working. Therefore, while a highly educated workforce is imperative for twenty-first century education, in the same vein, it is equally crucial that higher education institutes facilitate and support teachers' ongoing professional learning needs.

1.7.5 Collaborative and Networked Learning

For a long time, professional networks served as an avenue/platform where educators have shared knowledge, best practices which well served as professional development. Future-oriented learning will involve more cross-disciplinary collaboration, embedded with new strategies of mentoring and learning relationships among educators and educational leaders (Bolstad et al., 2012; Rajaram, 2021). Berry (1993) mentioned faculty are expected to connect and build industry networks by bringing them into the university community to value-add to the current resources and enhance recognition. Teachers wanted to network basically to improve their own practices and thought processes as well as to overcome the possibility of being isolated or avoid loneliness. Establishing a learning community allows educators to gain a richer, more diverse perspectives and be more open to appreciate the varying aspects and differences in pedagogical practices.

1.8 Future Curriculum Learning Design and Assessment

Curriculum could be viewed as the core intellectual centre of schooling and its main message system (Williamson, 2013). Curriculum links both academic, vocational knowledge and skills with personal identity as well as the culture of society. Moreover, it also determines the contents to be studied and the methods for studying it. As a whole, curriculum can describe the values and aims used to justify a particular program, all the educational processes and learning that go on within it.

Twenty years ago, Kress (2000) advocated that generally, most curricula in Western schools remained the same when compared to schools of the nineteenth century where the goal was to produce homogeneously conceived citizens who could contribute to the labour force and satisfy the needs of the nineteenth century nation. On a similar vein, Williamson (2013) characterized curricula of the past as "factory schooling" where students are prepared for life in largely routine low-skills industrial jobs. The curriculum of the future in the 1980s was expected to focus on creating a more educated, flexible and highly skilled workforce as factory schooling lost relevance. Today, we are facing a myriad of new, complex and unique needs, concerns that must be addressed by higher education to ensure its longevity in the long run. These new circumstances require more thought through, novel, improvised responses equating to new goals and curricula which are more appropriate and suitable to attain these goals.

Adopting a twenty-first century curriculum must facilitate the bandwidth to blend knowledge, thinking, innovation skills, media, information and communication technology (ICT) literacy, and real-life experiences in the context of core academic subjects (Alismail & McGuire, 2015). Students need to develop twenty-first century skills such as critical thinking, problem-solving and ability to collaborate by working in teams so that they are adequately ready to pursue their future careers and endeavours. Higher education institutions have addressed the changing nature of the world by employing new, innovative pedagogical techniques that are relevant in today's rapidly changing situational contexts. However, these new pedagogical strategies are often designed to encompass several teaching and learning themes including collaboration, co-creation with learners, connectedness and technological disruptions. The next section will present discussions on the future curriculum design through having it evaluated by these themes and addressing the future of assessments.

1.8.1 Collaboration

Collaboration in learning delivers quality learning outcomes in terms of comprehension of contents instead of merely a means to develop or assess knowledge (Child & Shaw, 2016; Rajaram, 2020, 2021). It is described as a technique that facilitates learning mechanisms such as induction, deduction and associative learning. It involves groups of learners working together to solve a problem, complete a task or create a product (Laal et al., 2012). In a collaborative learning environment, students are challenged both socially and emotionally and are actively engaged.

There is a growing emphasis on project and enquiry-based learning as research has proven that collaboration has positive impact on student's learning and knowledge retention. It increases the social competencies of students and allows them to learn and incorporate knowledge from multiple sources. There has been an increasing need for students to apply what they have learnt in social settings. Organizations today require innovation to happen through combining the potential and expertise of their employees through collaboration. Furthermore, the recent advancements in technology have created new opportunities for how collaboration occurs.

Hence, it is of no surprise that collaboration has now become a twenty-first century trend. There is an essential need in society for people to be able to work together on varying issues, and thus, there is an apparent shift from individual efforts to group work and from independence to community. The importance of collaboration is viewed through the use of group work as a means to assess student learning.

1.8.2 Co-creation with Learners

According to the OECD (2018), future-ready students need to exercise agency in their own education as well as throughout their life. Agency implies a sense of responsibility to participate and to influence people for the better. For educators to enable agency, they must recognize learners' individuality and acknowledge the relationships that influence their learning. The concept of co-creation or co-agency encompasses the future of curriculum design. Co-agency, as described by the OECD, refers to the interactive and mutually supportive relationships that help learners achieve their goals.

Co-creation allows students to contribute towards their own learning. By actively participating in class, students will not be limited to only learning from their teacher's perspective; rather, co-creation allows teachers to widen their views and the opinions through students who likely would give them novel ideas which are not thought of before. Interactive exchanges between teacher and learner are another aspect that surrounds the future of curriculum design. Teachers should intentionally plan to allocate more time to interact with students within the classrooms in their classrooms.

1.8.3 Connectedness

To better prepare students for the workforce, higher education institutes should ensure that students are equipped with adequate practical knowledge and a good understanding of their individual chosen career paths. Perhaps, this could be possibly done by encouraging connectedness in varying ways between higher education institutes and corporate organizations, allowing students to experience the real work setting and make early connections with industry professionals. Work experience and being equipped with the skills, ability to transit quickly to business operational requirements, have become more imperative in the twenty-first century and beyond because industries are increasingly looking out for graduates with the relevant, necessary competencies and skills to succeed in the respective given roles. The term "connectedness" in this context refers to how curriculum will be designed to enable students to learn in real workforce type of environments, or even close to a simulated setting outside the classroom.

There has been a growing number of higher education institutes incorporating some type of work placement within their programmes or adding an internship scheme at the end of a programme (Helyer & Lee, 2014). The goal is to allow students to learn through hands-on experience, acquire the "know-hows" in the real corporate settings and leverage, and use what they have. The transferable and generic skills are even more crucial than ever in today's rapid changing world, especially with so much of uncertainties and evolution in the future job requirements. Hence, it is vital for graduates to be agile, respond with a growth mindset to be adaptable and resilient to thrive. Internship, work experiences gained via work-study programmes and part-time work, for example, allow students to gain some of these actual work skills which enhance their adaptability and transition to workforce more speedily by understanding the realities of work upon graduation. It also gives students some level of connectedness with the working world. Moreover, it allows them to expand their professional network by making professional connections and build relationships with employees and working adults who can guide, mentor and provide them with relevant, expert advice and recent, contemporary insights.

1.8.4 Technological Disruptions and Interventions

Technological disruptions and interventions are emerging theme that envelops the radical changes in pedagogy. New technological innovations have assisted higher education institutes to deploy new teaching methodologies, for example flipped classroom, blended learning, higher emphasis on cooperative and collaborative learning and so on. Enhancements in technological tools, platforms and the integration of digitalization have enabled for the betterment of fully online programmes as well as the development of effective virtual learning environments with high level of student engagement and quality learning process efficacy. Mobile learning, data analytics through technological interventions, mixed reality, artificial intelligence (AI), blockchain and virtual assistants are a few key developments in technology and digitalization (Alexander et al., 2019). Besides having technology and digitalization assist in teaching and learning arena, it also helps higher education institutes to accelerate and advance the capabilities and capacities for data analytics. Analytical technologies are increasingly and more widely adopted generally; for instance, data mining techniques are progressively gaining significance in the education sector. Higher education institutes can creatively use these techniques to influence and perhaps incorporate interventions to enhance the learning processes and outcomes. For example, data mining techniques can facilitate policy makers in higher education to be equipped with data-based models that support their goals to enhance the efficiency, efficacy and quality of teaching and learning. Hence, these techniques can create systemic change by helping institutions seek solutions for specific issues. Overall, relevant technological interventions and systems can provide support in the higher education decision-making processes (Aldowah et al., 2019). Ketamo et al. (2019) experimented using artificial intelligence and other technologies to build a real-time understanding of skills, competencies, knowledge and abilities that workplaces seek. Primarily, the goal of this project was to overcome the specific contextualized challenges and frustrations of ensuring that curriculum design is up-to-date inline of preparing graduates for the rapidly evolving the work setting. This serves as highly useful and beneficial for institutes to align students' learning and the attributes developed to be useful upon graduation and to enter the workforce. This reiterates on how technology and digitalization can potentially assist institutes to modify curricula in totality or altogether. Both of these studies presented show how technological disruptions become one of a key consideration it comes to curriculum design, where potential benefits can be attained. Pedagogical strategies such as online or blended learning are largely influenced and impacted by this intervention.

1.8.5 Assessments

Aside the curricula, the assessment design of the future also does come into as a reflective question when discussing and planning the future of higher education. For example, the COVID-19 pandemic reiterated or re-emphasized the relevance and imperativeness of virtual (synchronous) or fully online/e-(asynchronous) assessments. Times Higher Education (2020) reported that in the next five years, universities must embrace technology to transform the way assessment is facilitated to enhance its efficacy in terms of quality, speed and accuracy. Five distinct ways were identified by which technology will potentially affect assessments, namely to be more authentic, accessible, automated, continuous and secure. Moreover, further to technological interventions, there are other related drivers that influence assessments for the future. The mega trends for assessment include, namely (1) increases in computational power and statistical methods; (2) dynamics of population change; and (3) the rhetoric and politics of accountability. Changes in assessment are largely a resultant of increased class sizes, modified curricula and the need to support students better. At the same time, assessment options are constrained by regulations and external quality assurance demands. These are largely driven by concerns over standards, reliability and plagiarism. Hence, it is key for institutes to address these concerns and provide due considerations given the rapid evolving and changing environment.

One of the highest emerging themes in the academic literature on educational assessment is the increase in emphasis on exploring, understanding and exploiting the influences of specific assessment approaches on student learning process and outcomes. Another theme directs to the extent to which assessments meet the key goals, objectives and intended learning outcomes of a course. Both of these themes advocate and emphasize how the holistic goals of assessments have shifted from merely just focusing on grades to focusing learning in a more student-centred approach. Assessments no longer serve just as a way to assess student learning, but now are transforming to become tools that can assist in student development. Therefore, the concepts of assessment for learning and authentic assessments are expected to grow in prominence in the future. Ultimately, the conceptualizations of both pedagogies embedded with the relevant and appropriate assessments would significantly influence and impact the factors affecting higher education.

1.9 Learning Mobility—The New Expectation of Learning "Anywhere and Anytime"

The development and wide adoption of the Internet as well as mobile devices have allowed for higher education institutes to add on a new or improvised mode of delivery for their programmes. For instance, online learning allows students to access their course resources and materials from anywhere in the world with an Internet connection and a mobile device or laptop, while asynchronous learning allows students to learn at their own pace. The combination of these two modes of learning creates a situation or a convenient possibility where learning can occur anywhere and anytime. We refer to this concept as learning mobility where it encompasses choices such as e-learning, m-learning and distance learning.

Learning mobility is essential now and in the future due to evolving changes in demographics and landscape of higher education. For instance, there has been an increasing number of adult learners enrolling into higher education institutes. This is reported by statistics from the United States (US) Department of Education, Maryville University (n.d.), explicitly pointing to the number of adults of 20 or older going back to school since 1970 with projected numbers for 2019 and 2024 that could be retrieved from https://online.maryville.edu/blog/going-back-to-school-statistics/

Adult learners have specific needs that they seek support from higher education institutes such flexibility, more tailored-made learning design to align in their learning endeavours due to heavy commitments outside of school such as family, personal and/or work. Learners who are working and pursuing their studies concurrently are generally inclined towards higher "anytime and anywhere" tendencies due to the need for them to create a balance between their work, school personal and family life (Du et al., 2019). The study reported that a higher level of self-directed learning has a greater potential of better performance, although there could be potential adverse impact on learning performance. This is pointed out and reiterated by Rajaram (2021) where he advocates that to increase the efficacy in self-directed learning, it would be crucial to embed well-designed and essential interventions to (1) assess the learners' knowledge gained through online quizzes; (2) provide immediate formative feedback; and (3) facilitate an avenue to engage and address their queries possibly with some level of human intervention. Apparently, the increased frequency of transitions between learning locations can potentially result in much poorer information retention as compared to when the learning occurs in a more consistent and sustainable environment. Aside from demographics, external influences play a vital role in the adoption of learning mobility options. Unforeseen circumstances such as the SARS outbreak or the recent COVID-19 pandemic highlight the need for institutes to be prepared for situational circumstances where students may not be able to physically attend classes on campus. In the case of the COVID-19 pandemic, travel bans and social distancing measures prevented face-to-face learning activities. Hence, the learning mobility options, its supporting resources and the platforms it operates are vital aspects for higher education institutes to consider.

While it comes across that self-directed learning, i.e., “anytime and anywhere learning” is useful and highly beneficial, we should acknowledge the limitations, concerns that it comes with. Online or distance learning introduces and intensifies certain barriers in social interaction, technology, student support, pedagogy and accessibility (Morris, 2010).

Firstly, fully online or distance learners can feel alone and isolated due to a lack of interaction and communication between their peers and teachers, resulting in a lack of social interactiveness and engagement. Secondly, a technological barrier and limitation occurs when students feel discomfort in adopting technological tools or platforms which add on to embedded elements such as technically inclined challenges, Internet and technology-inclined costs and accessibility, and technical “know-hows” and skills. Thirdly, the lack of student support or limitations that are tied to them, namely (1) lack of social-cultural eco-systems and processes built in to meditate the complex learning challenges due to diversity; (2) inadequate time for students to be able to gain in-depth comprehension of contents due to the lack of interactivity component embedded in the system; and (3) lack of academic experience where teachers are not able to empathize, resonate to the students’ needs with an agile and responsive mindset. Fourthly, effective implementation of pedagogical barriers and limitations may occur as not all classroom instructors may be equipped with the relevant skills or “know-hows” or deemed effective when operating online. Senior aged faculty members may potentially struggle in keeping up and facilitating interactive and individualized lessons online due to the inability to catch up speedily with the current technological advancements. Finally, the presence of a digital divide suggests that some students may not have decent broadband connections to access the online resources and course materials. Further to this, physically disabled students may face limitations and barriers if there are insufficient supportive or assistive technologies. This specific barrier relates and intertwines to the sociocultural aspects of institutes and beyond.

With such limitations and barriers in mind, it is imperative for higher education institutes to comprehend how they can overcome by addressing and eventually resolving such issues. Therefore, it is vital for them to come up with a guiding framework that supports learning mobility which could be applied to their operations. To facilitate learning mobility, a few primary components are essential to be considered which will assist in building an effective digital infrastructure. These components include universal broadband connectivity, a plan for facilitating digital citizenship, investment in professional learning to allow for necessary pedagogical transformations, engagement of parents and community partners, and the establishment of appropriate assessment and data systems (Thigpen, 2014). The aforementioned components are elaborated in Table 1.2.

Table 1.2 Key components for a digital infrastructure that supports learning mobility

Component	Description
Broadband connectivity	To function in twenty-first century classrooms, both students and educators need to have fast and reliable connections to the Internet. This is so that they can effectively use a range of digital tools, including online communication tools such as Zoom, Microsoft Teams and Google Hangouts. A decent broadband connection also allows learners to work with their teachers and peers using online collaborative tools. Moreover, it allows them to take advantage of secure cloud capabilities such as data storage. It is recommended that school campuses have a minimum of 100 Mbps (megabits per second) for every 1,000 students and staff to meet the demands of online learning
Digital citizenship	The concept of digital citizenship refers to the knowledge required to participate effectively and responsibly in a digital world and includes digital literacy and online safety and ethics. The way in which students interact with digital tools as well as their engagement with digital content influences the extent to which they benefit from digital learning. Digital literacy is particularly important because youth are increasingly getting their news through online media platforms such as YouTube, Twitter and Facebook. Thus, it is important that schools teach learners to effectively discern the credibility and accuracy of information they see online
Professional learning	Educators play a crucial role in a comprehensive digital infrastructure. They require their own systems of support and training to fully take advantage of the potential of digital learning. Therefore, there is a need for educators to move to a professional learning model. Rather than simply understanding how to use a technological tool, they also need to understand how the tools can be used to transform their classroom
Engagement of stakeholders	Communities surrounding students can support and shape individualized learning pathways. Connecting learning opportunities across youth-serving institutions will improve overall engagement and interest in school. Communities can involve themselves in helping achieve student learning goals through apprenticeships, community-based exhibitions and supporting the alignment of afterschool programming with in-school curricula
Assessment and data systems	Creating personalized and student-centred digital learning opportunities heavily relies on access to real-time data on student performance which can be used to evaluate instructional practice. Through assessment and data systems, schools will be able to continually adjust and improve learning pathways for each individual student. A comprehensive digital infrastructure should provide educators with relevant and timely data which can help them in designing pedagogy to be used in classrooms

1.10 Individualized and Personalized Learning: Customization for Learners

One major trend in higher education is the increasingly individualized and personalized approach to learning. Personalized learning involves differentiation and individualization to connect to a specific learner's interests and experiences (Bartle, 2015). It enables teachers to curate to the needs and abilities of each individual student. The goal of personalized learning is to ensure that the educational system responds directly to the students' diverse needs rather than implementing a "one-size-fits-all" model that may not be as efficient. Educational reforms in higher education are already making personalized learning a reality (McLoughlin, 2013), for example pedagogical models that support the principles of personalized learning including connectivist learning, online collaborative learning and pedagogy 2.0.

Other pedagogical techniques include personalized learning include flipped classrooms, e-learning, MOOCs and mobile learning Li and Wong (2020). Personalized learning benefits students as it utilizes their differences as a leveraging factor to customize when it comes to instruction and assessments. It can assist teachers recognize individual strengths and demands of students and is unlike the "one-size-fits-all" model that has been found to lead to undesirable outcomes such as higher drop-out rates. Li and Wong (2020) have presented the data for 2001–2009 versus 2010–2018 on specific objectives of personalized learning in their study. Elements that were rated in range between 10 and 34% for both category of years 2001–2009 and 2010–2018 include (a) increase learning effectiveness; (b) provide personalized learning path; (c) increase learning satisfaction; (d) enhance learning motivation; (e) enhance learners' engagement; and (f) enrich learning experience. However, elements that were rated below 10% for both category of years 2001–2009 and 2010–2018 include (a) cater for learners' interest; (b) increase teaching effectiveness; (c) promote lifelong learning; (d) achieve learning objective; (e) enhance collaborative learning; (f) address individual learning style; (g) predict learners' performance; (h) provide personalized learning support; (i) promote learners' self-regulation; (j) identify learners at-risk; and (k) others.

FitzGerald, Jones, Kucirkova and Scanlon (2018) reported that the potential benefits of personalized learning can be classified into three distinct levels, namely (1) learner, teacher and institution. At the student level, the benefit could be focused on personalization that can potentially increase motivation and learner empowerment and improve attitudes to learning. At the teacher level, personalized learning can support teachers via learner feedback, some of that can be automated so that teachers can focus on more higher quality commentary. At the institutional level, personalization has been found to be able to help tackle underachievement in education and raise standards in compulsory education.

On the flip side, we also need to acknowledge the challenges of personalized learning which are discussed by Bartle (2015) who listed four potential obstacles. Firstly, students tend to not know where their knowledge is lacking. To take ownership and co-author their personalized learning, it is vital that students have an adequate comprehension of the required progressive steps of their learning. Secondly, students may take a superficial or rather surface level approach when it comes to online learning, so it is crucial that it is designed to facilitate the process of deep learning and secondary interventions that encourages this. Thirdly, teachers should be willing and have the ability to shift their pedagogy to a student-centred approach, especially since the skills and inclination of values that a teacher advocates have been found to affect student achievement. Lastly, accreditation requirements may pose a challenge or limiting factor as it potentially restricts the flexibility of courses.

Bingham et al. (2016) add on to the potential challenges in the implementation of personalized learning. These researchers reported that inaccurate data, challenges in developing student autonomy and problems with managing students' use of technology will potentially led teachers retreating back to more traditional and low-tech practices. From a holistic perspective, they claimed that understanding and anticipating challenges prior to future implementation are imperative so that institutes can better plan resource allocation. Further to this, it enables institutes to identify precursors of favourable or unfavourable student learning outcomes.

1.11 Sociocultural Interventions for Future

Higher education institutes are facing major shifts and changing trends in their demographics. Aside from an increase in the profile of adult learners, there have also been progressive general growth in the enrolment of female students (UNESCO Institute for Statistics, 2020), students with disabilities (Koshy, 2019), low-income students (Fry & Cilluffo, 2019), international students (Zong & Batalova, 2018) and many other sociocultural categorizations. These different groups of students contribute to the growing diversity of higher education campuses. While we could acknowledge that diversity does bring about benefits, institutes must also thoroughly and carefully consider on how it can impact the overall learning experience of every student in varying ways. Furthermore, these groups are the ones who are often marginalized and face inequities in their daily lives. Hence, it is crucial that institutes consider these inequities, provide adequate accommodations and establish relevant policies to ensure that all students have equal learning opportunities.

The trend towards diversity could be primarily because higher education has become a necessity for students around the world to attain livable wages and to build successful long-term careers. An estimated 85% of current jobs and about 90% of the fastest-growing, best-paying jobs require employees to have some form of post-secondary education (Adams Becker et al., 2017). Despite that, it is reported that the United States is on the road to producing 11 million fewer certificates and degrees than the national economy will require by 2025. Certain inequities around the globe can be attributed to the cause of this student underachievement. For instance, half of all people from high-income families earn a bachelor's degree by age 25, but this number goes down to just one in ten for those in low-income families. In the case of students with disabilities, the evidence points towards lower rates of college adjustment experienced compared to their peers with disabilities (Kim & Kutscher, 2020). Students with disabilities are also reported to be marginalized and face alienation, stigma and discrimination. These factors and other contributing aspects contribute to the undermining of their confidence and academic success. As a whole, these studies highlight how the varying factors beyond the student's or institute's control can significantly impact learning experiences.

Aside impacting students, sociocultural factors can also impact teachers and influence academic change and development in higher education. A study by Englund et al. (2018), examining the working environments of teachers on an online pharmacy programme, verifies this claim along with other findings. Their study shows that communication and dialogue are crucial components of cultural construction. Different teaching departments may have their own established, customized culture, and hence, there can be tensions and restrictions when they are expected to work with one another. The finding is especially imperative in the current context where there is an increased focus on interdisciplinary knowledge, thus requiring faculty from various departments to work with each other and together. This is also crucial as more foreign educators enter local institutes, bringing certain aspects and nuances of their cultural values and norms into their departments. Therefore, higher education institutes must ensure that not only they monitor sociocultural influences amidst students but also among teachers as well.

It is expected that the future of higher education will become more technology-centric, given that online education is a long-term strategy for many tertiary institutes. We can foresee certain issues of the future that arise from sociocultural factors. For instance, digital tools and platforms that offer beyond basic features today that majority of students from higher-income families can access may not be as financially viable for easy access to students from lower-income families. We could expect this trend will continue to unfold as technological tools and gadgets consistently continue to upgrade. Perhaps, some students may be able to afford the speediest Internet services while others may not be as fortunate. This can result in severe disparities in the quality of learning between these two groups of learners. Thigpen (2014) reports that 30% of households in the United States do not have high-speed broadband while many lack decent speeds for students to adequately and properly utilize modern digital learning tools at home. Nonetheless, the relevant and effective use of technology has great potential to improve student outcomes for under-served students. It is crucial for higher education institutes to ensure an equitable access to technology is advocated and facilitated to ensure the efficacy of the reach is optimized. While the student profile population of higher education institutes is becoming increasingly diverse, policymakers and faculty need to be acknowledged and be aware of the potential obstacles they need to likely overcome in the future. Hence, it is imperative for higher education institutes to place more targeted emphasis on the sociocultural elements that potentially influence the experiences of teachers and students.

1.12 Recommendations

Despite the unpredictability of the future of learning with a full hundred percent certainty largely caused by the consistent evolving changes, speed of innovations and from time to time intervened by unpredictable events, specific trends and drivers could potentially point to the direction of the future of learning. Hence based on the analysis, I have proposed recommendations based on these observed trends, by clustering them into three levels of higher education institutes, namely at the micro (teacher level), meso (school and programme level) and macro (university/institutional level).

At the micro-level, teachers are strongly advocated to upgrade their ICT skills as the demand and need for flexible online offerings have continued to increase over the years (Roddy et al., 2017) and are expected to further increase down the road in the near future. As online learning continues to expand, it is becoming increasingly clear that there is a need for competent online instructors. Although some aspects of face-to-face teaching competencies can be potentially transferred to online contexts, this may not be adequate in dealing with the varying unique aspects of online teaching. There is a rising need for teachers to effectively communicate, manage technology, and deliver and assess contents. Teachers should closely monitor students' progress and follow up on issues to ensure that they minimize student disengagement. Further to that, without sufficient technological skills, teachers may be unable to overcome technology-related challenges during online lessons which could impact students' overall learning experience. Ideally, institutions should provide teachers with relevant training so that they can upgrade their knowledge and skills. However, teachers should also remain proactive and look towards lifelong learning due to the constant emergence of new evolving technologies.

At the programme level, higher education institutes are expected to shift towards more resilient teaching, in accordance with a whitepaper written for Coursera (2020). They state that in the subsequent phases of the COVID-19 pandemic, higher education institutes should be ready to shift to a fully online format at any given phase. However, even in the phase beyond the post-crisis, there remains a need for agile teaching models since an unexpected crisis could occur anytime. Therefore, they suggest that institutes should expose, train and benefit students through flexible teaching models that are resilient against uncertainties but at the same time able to meet the changing and rising expectations of students in terms of value and quality. Resilient teaching largely points towards the fact that each course is explicitly design around a set of well-defined and scoped learning goals, with supporting learning activities that help students advance towards those goals and guide them through a scaffolded process. They illustrated the case of Duke University who uses the term "flexible teaching" to describe their student-centred, engaging, adaptive and inclusive approach. The authors suggest that blended learning is a core aspect of resilient teaching as it provides students more and varying options. In all, it is suggested that programmes are designed to be student-centred, interactive and inclusive so that schools will be able to effectively deal with the new era of education.

At the institutional level, it is vital for higher education management and policymakers to ensure that policies are adapted to the current times. According to KPMG International (2020), many higher education institutions around the world are at or approaching crossroads when it comes to strategy and operating models. Wiley Education Services (n.d.) suggests three key initiatives that administrators can focus on so that their institute may be better able to deal with the new developments in the higher education environment that continues to evolve due to advancements in technology, increased competition, variations in student demographics, and changing student and employer demands. These recommendations include increasing access to new students, overcoming faculty technology concerns, refining and supporting the students' journey. Moreover, recommendations at the policy level include creating a safe and equitable learning environment and climate for all students. For instance, institutions can review their financial aid policies to assist and retain lower-income students. They can also ensure stricter anti-discrimination policies to ensure minority students' safety. There should also be fair accommodations for students with disabilities. It is imperative that the emphasis of policies should not only focus on the institution itself but also be more student-focused as this will also benefit the institution from a more holistic level.

To assist the various stakeholders, namely the senior management, researchers and educators on the transformation for future learning, I have conceptualized a guiding framework that is presented in Fig. 1.2 that serves as a scaffolded analysis and flow of process. The framework is categorized into three clusters, namely external interventions (external environment), internal interventions (internal environment) and outcomes (impact on stakeholders). Higher education institutions are affected by, and affect, their environment. The external interventions serve as inputs for the institutions to align and create continuously relevant strategies (internal interventions): (1) internationalization and globalization: As institutions open their recruitment to international students, the courses offered need to be mindful of the cultural aspects in designing their pedagogical design and so on. It also relates to the rapid evolution and demands on educational services to be offered beyond domestic market that involves inter-institutional cross-country collaborations; (2) digitalization, technology evolution, advancement and trends: The evolving changes in technological disruptions and infrastructure needs to be dealt with by higher education institutions. For example, the contemporary upgraded technologies require a "rethink" on how the existing information technology infrastructure could be re-aligned to meet the changing rapid demands to be relevant; (3) social and cultural transformation: With the rapid acceleration of globalization and the urgent need to collaborate globally requires higher education institutions to be agile and responsive by being mindful of the culturally, socially embedded strategies adopted and executed; (4) demographic changes and shifts: The profile, type of students interested to attend undergraduate and postgraduate programmes are changing distinctively, for example, more adult learners such as mid-career professionals or talent pool who are identified to be senior leaders are coming back to pursue both their undergraduate and postgraduate qualifications; (5) changing immigration profile: Students internationally are showing more interest in pursuing their studies overseas to enhance their exposure and experience, where some are deciding to reside in those countries after their studies. Aside this, there are more opportunities or call for foreign talents who are being invited as expatriates to take up job positions, as such their children will now potentially be attending the higher institutions in that country. (6) Education policies locally and globally: There will be continuous changes and new policy initiatives on education in every country that impacts domestic issues pertaining to educational strategies adopted while the changes that are made in other countries do have ripple effects due to the inter-connectivity of the movement of the students across countries. (7) Changing needs of the job roles: As the world evolves and the needs, demands and expectations of the people, consumers and varying stakeholders' changes, hence this requires the functional job roles and responsibilities to transform. Hence, the higher education institutions need to speedily respond to these "gaps" by having them addressed appropriately through reviewing and re-aligning on how they could train and equip the students with the new skills and competencies.

The outputs are the strategies to be executed to meet the demands and expectations of varying stakeholders. This comes under the purview of internal environment that comprises of internal interventions as illustrated below. Figure 1.2 presents a validated framework on the transformational model for future learning in higher education that encompasses three primary thrusts, namely external environment, internal environment and potential outcomes that shape as deliverables. In the below section, the core elements that comprise within the internal environment of higher education institutions and serve as vital influencing factors to shape the deliverables are illustrated as follows:

(1) Continual Learning: Re-value the lifespan of educational qualifications—learning for and through life. Many years ago, we may have adopted the mindset of preparing for almost 20 years for our very first job, perhaps the only job for life. Can we afford to remain with that traditional mindset with the rapid evolution of changes that have been happening around us? Perhaps we have to accept the reality of aligning and changing roles, responsibilities and even jobs. The key reflection is the relevancy and update-ness of the skills and knowledge as years unfold ahead, after your graduation from a higher education institution. As the efficacy of the already equipped "know-hows" decreases rapidly as years pass, then the need to acquire new skills and knowledge must be ramped up to stay relevant and contemporary. So, there is an urgent need of mindset shift, where one must acknowledge that learning never ends and no one time qualification is adequate. The perception of learning for and through life must not mean that there is a body of knowledge and competencies that once acquired will prepare us for the rest of our life. Instead, learning for life must be the process of continual learning for the rest of an individual's life, throughout in a progressive manner. No amount of intense and prepared education frontloading can prepare one completely for life. The only possible strategy to propel ahead is through continual learning through varying means that enable one to remain contemporary, relevant and current for the entity of

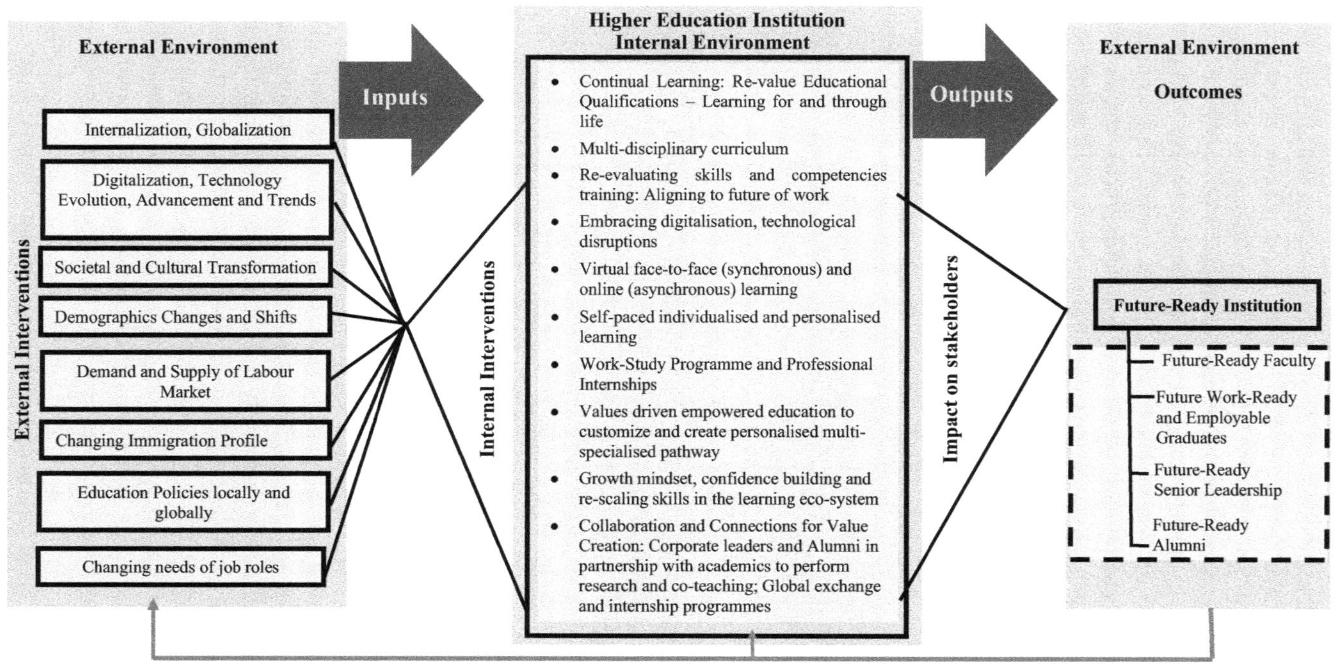

Fig. 1.2 Transformational model for future of learning in Higher Education

one's life. Hence, the value proposition of the academic qualifications needs to be re-evaluated from the varying different stakeholders' perspectives and today's complex, dynamic and evolving environment and climate. Vital questions such: (a) Are the students ready for the future job roles in terms of applied knowledge and "know-hows"? (b) Are these students' skills-set required for the future jobs adequate? (c) How can we create an eco-system where there is a progressive structure of academic qualification renewable with professional experience add-on over an individual's life-time stint? This requires a major revamp of the entire higher educational structural process and its related eco-system governing it to be reviewed and transformed. (f) How can the learning loops fastened in process to shorten the time to market for skills and knowledge, commencing from frontier research, leading industrial technologies and breakthrough market practices to academia and back to the market. Obviously, this strategy drives the competitiveness as a people and system. Hence, the outreach, collaboration and partnership strategy need to be sharpen specifically in the arena of internships, academia and industrial collaborations as well as alumni engagement.

(2) Multi-disciplinary curriculum: There is an urgent need to cross-fertilize students for them to be exposed and acquire knowledge in subjects beyond their core specialization. This enables them to intermingle with students of other specializations where such collaborations are valuable in terms of exchanging and learning from varying collective perspectives. (a) Are the modules flexible combined and recombined across multi-disciplinary contexts, provide empowerment to design their own curriculum, build their own degree courses that enable students to pivot and flex across rapidly changing, evolving sectors and to create new value propositions for the evolving market? (b) What are new skills or knowledge "know-hows" that need to be introduced to enhance the efficacy in transiting to the workplace? For instance, the skills to learn, learn speedily, unlearn and relearn, collaborate across multiple disciplines, cultures and perspectives to create something unique become more imperative than the focus on grade at a particular point in life and ever before.

(3) Re-evaluating skills and competencies training—Aligning to future work: The relevant skills and competencies required for the rapidly changing job roles must be identified and the training must be incorporated through appropriate learning design and pedagogical approaches at the programme level. This allows students to be progressively trained on these skills while they are in the university which enables them to proficient when they step into the workforce.

(4) Embracing digitalization, technological disruptions: School leadership needs to reiterate the urgency and importance on the shift and change of mindset towards embracing the technological disruptions in support with innovative pedagogical learning designs to deal with the rapid changing needs.

(5) Virtual face-to-face (synchronous) and online (asynchronous) learning: The capacity in terms of information technology infrastructure, competent trained faculty and the sustainable resources needs to be ready and available so that fully virtual seminars / lectures as well as fully online asynchronous learning

could be supported and delivered with high efficacy in terms of quality and impact.

(6) Self-paced individualized and personalized learning: The pressing need in developing and facilitating more individualized tailor-made learning becomes essential as the diversity of students (i.e., faster learners versus slower learners; students from varying social and cultural backgrounds; students with different strengths and weakness in a particular area of study).

(7) Work-study programme and professional internships: The eco-system needs to be developed where students are able to work while pursuing their studies becomes vital today to ensure they are able to relate and apply their acquired classroom knowledge, concurrently enabling them to be progressively upscaled on the "know-hows" and required skills. This includes work-study programme where students are able to go for an adequate period away on a job placing taking say a 6-month block off during the pursuit of their study or alternatively make special arrangements to work on say for example, 1–2 days full-time with an organization and the remaining days taking up 50% of the normal study load. Such flexible arrangements allow students to acquire their classrooms learning, having them applied on job immediately and bring back questions or clarifications to be discussed in class. Such scaffolded learning structure certainly allows students to go through a process which is highly productive as they could experience the authentic value of in-class learning while having them applied during their professional attachment job roles at workplace.

(8) Values driven empowered education to customize and create personalized multi-specialized pathway: Every institution needs to create their own values that are to be advocated and highly emphasized to be ingrained during students' stint in pursuit of their studies. This plays a vital role in having to be empowered in their own learning. Aside this, the course learning structure should be designed to assist shape students' personalized multi-specialized pathway, where they are empowered to identify courses within a structured yet flexible and multi-pronged pathway, enabling them to expand their knowledge base beyond their core area of specialization. In a world of contesting ideas, principles, ideology, beliefs and values, the confidence in charting one's own destiny based on pragmatic, focused and disciplined search for what works best for our people in context, instead be slaves of ideology. There is a need to define one's way of life based on one's own set of values. Teachers are to be equipped with the "know-hows" and confidence to chart own customized learning solutions to modern rapid challenges bestowed to shape up "job-ready" graduates based on a pragmatic, focused and disciplined search for what works best for the students on context, rather than be slaves of ideology; and defining, shaping the customized set of values to stand out and succeed.

Two key values that are vital to be ingrained in the eco-system, includes (1) the sense of beyond self-fulfilment and self-growth, to be nurtured on service leadership where the values overarch to the contributions and service to the society, world and the country one belongs to; (2) the responsibility to define success beyond oneself to overcome challenges with tenacity and in unity through leading with conviction and excelling with confidence.

(9) Growth mindset, confidence building and re-scaling skills in the learning eco-system: It is vital to have multiple interventions that enable students to be ingrained with the growth mindset where the eco-system has adequate controls put in place to enable continuous re-scaling and up-scaling of relevant skills. The capacity for us to be confident and respond with a growth mindset commences from comprehending our strengths, weakness and interests. This rudimentary aspect is vital to be ingrained as values from our foundational years of school, especially reiterated in the pursuit of one's university education. The intervention on re-scaling skills enables students to better comprehend and appreciate the evolving needs, changes diversity and complexity that they are expected to navigate and face in the future. The key thrust is to have the humility to learn from others, around the globe, but never relegate to merely imitating other's ideas without thoroughly relating and applying the context. The strategic ethos is to build the eco-system that enables students to other's successes as well as failures, but ultimately they must have the courage and confidence to develop their own solutions to their own challenges—in any context of their future workplace.

(10) Collaboration and Connections for Value Creation: Corporate leaders and alumni in partnership with academics to perform research and co-teaching; global exchange and internship programmes: The industrial partnership and collaboration to inject timely contemporary discussions and insights into the learning process are essential. These interventions are targeted to produce a future-ready institution that comprises of (a) future-ready faculty: Are those who are equipped with deep rooted ethos and values that enable propelling of the learning to greater heights through empowered grounded beliefs and leadership; (b) future work-ready and employable graduates: The ultimate goal of every institution to ensure students is ready for employment with equipped with the relevant "know-hows" and skills; (c) future-ready senior leadership: To lead and navigate the rapid evolving changes, the leadership of the institution needs to have the compelling vision and competence to navigate through unprecedented challenges, make tough decisions and agile to change course as required to meet the rapid changing needs; (d) future-ready alumni: The service leadership with intertwined bonded relationship with the institution and the mindset to work collaboratively by value-adding as to be the new norm for the graduates who become alumni of the institution. Finally, there is a feedback loop that serves as a channel to provide necessary inputs back to the external and internal aspects of the interventions.

Universities and higher education institutions are not merely transmitters of knowledge and skills, where many online asynchronous learning contents, platforms and providers can fulfil that fundamentally. Instead, we must be agile and responsive to leverage on technological interventions to transfer baseline foundational knowledge and skills through self-directed and paced, adaptive learning while harnessing on the accumulated and real-time data converted to meaningful information to focus our teaching efforts. By doing so, it enables teachers to increase their bandwidth by re-directing their efforts, time and energy to nurture and develop higher-order skills to connect, collaborate and create. Further to this, it is vital for leaders of university and higher education institutes (HEIs), educators and students to be catalyst of interconnectedness where each of them is to serve as bridges or connectors to collaborate and create value. In a fast paced, rapidly evolving more diverse and divided world, yet more intertwined and interconnected, all stakeholders, especially universities and HEIs leadership, have to build and maintain a strong network of connections and partnerships to stay relevant and current, keep the bonding, togetherness strong, intact and remain open. Hence, it's imperative to deepen the connections in three dimensions, namely with the world, with industry and with the local and global community. As the world evolves multi-dimensionally and perhaps more than before threatens to fragment along geopolitical, ideological, cultural and technological lines, university and HEIs and its leaders at all levels that includes educators can distinguish themselves as an unwavering platform for people to connect, collaborate and create to transcend those lines. Thus, there is an urgent need to rejuvenate and re-ignite the strategic push with necessary interventions to have students nurtured by understanding and interacting with the world—one way for universities and HEIs to connect and reconnect even more assertively and in a large scale with the world through their exchange and professional attachments or internship programmes, even as COVID-19 pandemic wears on. The key point is to send students overseas to learn and welcome foreign students to add diversity to the universities and HEIs campuses while enabling these students to enhance their understanding of the world. The strategic positioning of HEIs and universities is to continuously explore creative ways to build and create a unique brand that resembles for being trusted and accepted as a principled partner that others can rely, put their trust on as well as wanting to partner and work with. The value proposition is not merely the ability to just appreciate and celebrate diversity but to also bridge divergence and create new convergence. Secondly, HEIs and universities need to further tighten its connections and affiliations with academia and industry. Perhaps, the concept of how internships could be introduced beyond a fixated credit bearing should be explored and applied in context across the various schools of specializations. For instance, the internships could be acknowledged as a service where it could be tied to their progressive work experience. Flexibility must be enabled for students to lengthen their pursuit of studies, for instance if they would like to take a 6-month full-time interning position where they could apply what they have learned in a classroom context or alternatively, they could do a part-time internship through a work-study programme where they commit 1–2 days interning and the rest of the days at school. Such arrangements enable students to intern with industry without being constrained by time and subject of study. Students in future should be able to complete their programmes at their own time, if they have the desire and opportunity to intersperse their internship and studies. Another radical yet future directed strategy is to adopt the applied learning eco-systematic model that brings the university into the workplace and allows students to learn by working with real-life tools to solve real-life industry challenges and needs. For this initiative to be rolled out well, faculty plays a critical role as they become the connecting link between industry and universities. Universities must create more opportunities for faculty to keep pace with the latest industry innovations and create free-flowing exchanges of ideas and personnel between industry and universities. Further to this, universities need to review and rebalance their pre-employment training or PET and focus on continuing education and training (CET) as well as their staff composition and manpower resources to sustain and execute the needful. Finally, universities must aspire to move towards the eco-system of being "in the community, with the community and for the community", so that they are able to better engage the world's talent to put the hands, hearts and heads together create a dynamic, unwavering and exciting future of tomorrow.

This transformation model for future of learning in higher education serves as a guide to comprehend the intertwined elements that serve as a control mechanism that affects, shapes and impacts the potential outcomes.

1.13 Concluding Thoughts: Implications for Future Learning

At all three levels, namely strategic (institutional), tactical (program) and operational (micro) levels, recommendations provided cover several distinct yet interlinking key themes that bring about their own implications—student centricity, flexible learning and technology integration. These themes are identified to be some of the most vital aspects to be duly considered when higher education institutes come up with proposed remedies or solutions for future learning.

Based on the discussions and recommendations proposed, it is clear that institutes should adopt a more student-centred and personalized approach in teaching, administrative aspects and policy development. It is ideal and recommended for future learning to place more focus and emphasis on the development of students. Student-centred learning fosters communication and collaborative skills (Aguti et al., 2014), while student-centred approaches are largely effective, for example, when multicultural issues are examined as they are able to benefit from the varying perspectives that made available to them (Wright, 2011). This is very relevant in today's increasingly diverse classrooms where students are expected to work with individuals from dissimilar backgrounds. Through such collaborative interactions, students are exposed to much wider perspectives where they learn how to respect, acknowledge and deal with differences in views due to varying norms, beliefs and cultural backgrounds in a tactful yet fruitful manner. Student centricity can further benefit under-served students through policy changes revolving around funding and more. On the contrary, there are also negative implications of student centricity and in particular, student-centred learning. An issue raised in a study by Abbasi and Hadadi (2014) of English language learners in Iran revolves around the practicality of student-centred teaching. Interestingly, students interviewed were unfamiliar with the concept and felt that they would be much more comfortable learning the way they used to. Those students who have experienced such student-centred teaching approaches were reluctant in taking responsibility for their own learning due to the embedded sociocultural norms of them being much lesser tolerant of uncertainty situational contexts. They complained that the instructor was not doing much in the classroom as their accepted perceived notion is for teachers to provide the essential information and they to be at the receiving end. The authors justified this by emphasizing that this could be due to their previous learning experiences where they have been largely performing the role of a passive listener where instructors were the only ones taking control. Therefore, instructors need to be aware of the potential setbacks and hence be mindful on how they could progressively assist and guide students to shift their mindsets while letting them experience the benefits of such student-centred approaches. In the similar vein, such situation could potentially occur in higher education classrooms where students come from varying diverse social and cultural backgrounds. Hence, it is imperative that instructors are mindful and create space, an echo-system, a learning environment and climate where all students are encouraged to participate that makes them feel secured and motivated to do so.

The next theme encompasses discussions and recommendations revolving around flexible learning. Unpredictable global events, for example. COVID-19 pandemic raises concerns regarding the adoption of correct and appropriate learning design pedagogy. As such recommendations to adopt models such as flipped, blended learning models are advocated. The benefit of launching blended learning programmes is that it enables institutions to reach a global audience in a relatively short time while able to bring about large returns on investment. On the learning aspect, it enhances level of active learning process (Bonk & Graham, 2005), student engagement and higher-order cognitive learning (Rajaram, 2021). Flexibility is vital given the changing student demographics such as the increase in adult learners who need to balance work, school and their own personal lives. Implementing blended learning models can be more complex than it seems (Garrison & Vaughan, 2007), where it potentially involves large start-up costs. Blended learning or even fully online programmes can face significant competition with institutions or corporations offering MOOCs delivering similar content at a lower rate.

Finally, technological integration is another prevalent theme that was discussed and reflected upon. We see technology being adopted and digital disruptions intervening via online learning and technology-enhanced learning. The use of technology enhances the level of students' engagement (Schindler et al., 2017), facilitate feedback (Lilllejord et al., 2018), potentially transform the learning process to achieve higher-order learning outcomes, enhance the level of students' engagement and improve knowledge and skill acquisition. Moreover, technology can help institutes collate big data that assist in developing more student-centred and personalized learning paths for students. Such collated data can assist institutes to identify specific gaps in learning and hence allow teachers to create targeted solutions (Nazarenko & Khronusova, 2017). At the policy level, the use of real-time data enables making effective decisions. On the flip side, such implementation of technology has its drawbacks as well. For example, students may get distracted by such interventions, wasting valuable, precious and limited time available in classrooms. Another issue could also be the unequal availability of technologies for all, especially those from low socio-economic status. A key concern is also that technology could only potentially benefit those with access and alienate those without (Kemp et al., 2014). There have also been disagreements as to whether online learning can fully replace face-to-face learning fully or is it to be seen as a complementary to further value-add effectively. These diverging and biased perspectives may impact the rate at which some recommendations are adopted.

The future of learning entails numerous opportunities but certainly subject to volatility and filled with unprecedented interventions as there are varying influential factors that the higher education environment is exposed to with continuous, constant evolution. Higher education institutes are expected to take charge and act on the key trends pointing towards the direction of future learning. Institutes cannot simply go with the flow and reactively respond to changes in the environment; rather, they need to be proactive by anticipating and preparing well ahead to effectively and promptly deal with the rapid changes.

References

Abbasi, H., & Hadadi, A. (2014). The possible negative outcomes of putting learners in spotlight. *Procedia—Social and Behavioral Sciences, 98*, 3–8. https://doi.org/10.1016/j.sbspro.2014.03.381

Adams Becker, S., Cummins, M., Davis, A., Freeman, A., Hall Giesinger, C., & Ananthanarayanan, V. (2017). *NMC Horizon report: 2017 Higher education edition*. The New Media Consortium. https://library.educause.edu/-/media/files/library/2017/2/2017horizonreporthe.pdf

Aguti, B., Walters, R. J., & Wills, G. B. (2014). Effective use of e-learning technologies to promote Student Centered Learning Paradigms within Higher Education Institutions. *International Journal for E-Learning Security, 4*(2), 391–398. https://doi.org/10.20533/ijels.2046.4568.2014.0051

Armstrong, T. (2009). *Multiple intelligences in the classroom* (3rd ed.). The Association for Supervision and Curriculum Development.

Aldowah, H., Ul Rehman, S., Ghazal, S., & Naufal Umar, I. (2017). Internet of things in higher education: A study on future learning. *Journal of Physics: Conference Series, 892*, 012017. https://doi.org/10.1088/1742-6596/892/1/012017

Aldowah, H., Al-Samarraie, H., & Fauzy, W. M. (2019). Educational data mining and learning analytics for 21st century higher education: A review and synthesis. *Telematics and Informatics, 37*, 13–49. https://doi.org/10.1016/j.tele.2019.01.007

Alexander, B., Ashford-Rowe, K., Barajas-Murphy, N., Dobbin, G., Knott, J., McCormack, M., & Weber, N. (2019). *EDUCAUSE Horizon report 2019 higher education edition*. https://library.educause.edu/resources/2019/4/2019-horizon-report

Alismail, H. A., & McGuire, P. (2015). 21st century standards and curriculum: Current research and practice. *Journal of Education and Practice, 6*(6), 150–154. https://files.eric.ed.gov/fulltext/EJ1083656.pdf

Allen, I. E., Seaman, J., & Garrett, R. (2007). *Blending in: The extent and promise of blended education in the United States*. Sloan-C.

Ballantyne, R., Bain, J. D., & Packer, J. (1999). Researching university teaching in Australia: Themes and issues in academics' reflections. *Studies in Higher Education, 24*(2), 237–257. https://doi.org/10.1080/03075079912331379918

Bartle, E. (2015). *Personalised learning: An overview.* https://itali.uq.edu.au/files/1279/Discussion-paper-Personalised_learning_an_overview.pdf
Best, R. (1996). *Gardner's MI theory: Critical considerations and an alternative conception.* Proceedings: Conference on Learning and the Arts, 1996, October 17–19, Stavanger, Norway.
Berry, L. L. (1993). Our roles as educators: Present and future. *Journal of Marketing Education, 15*(3), 3–8. https://doi.org/10.1177/027347539301500302
Bingham, A. J., Pane, J. F., Steiner, E. D., & Hamilton, L. S. (2016). Ahead of the curve: Implementation challenges in personalized learning school models. *Educational Policy, 32*(3), 454–489. https://doi.org/10.1177/0895904816637688
Bolstad, R., Gilbert, J., McDowall, S., Bull, A., Boyd, S., & Hipkins, R. (2012). *Supporting future-oriented learning and teaching: A New Zealand perspective.* Ministry of Education, New Zealand. https://www.educationcounts.govt.nz/publications/schooling/supporting-future-oriented-learning-and-teaching-a-new-zealand-perspective
Bonk, C. J., & Graham, C. R. (2005). *The handbook of blended learning: Global perspectives, local designs.* Pfeiffer.
Bouton, B. (2016). Empathy research and teacher preparation: Benefits and obstacles. *SRATE Journal, 25*(2), 16–25. https://eric.ed.gov/?id=EJ1113829
Burkle, M., Tait, A., Nørgård, R. T., Guri-Rosenblit, S., & Canals, L. (2018). The universities of the future: Educational and organizational challenges. https://www.springeropen.com/collections/futureuni
Carnoy, & Rhoten. (2002). What does globalization mean for educational change? A comparative approach. *Comparative Education Review, 46*(1), 1–9. https://doi.org/10.2307/3542019
Chan, W. W. Y. (2004). International cooperation in higher education: Theory and practice. *Journal of Studies in International Education, 8*(1), 32–55. https://doi.org/10.1177/1028315303254429
Child, S., & Shaw, S. (2016). Collaboration in the 21st century: Implications for assessment. https://www.cambridgeassessment.org.uk/Images/374626-collaboration-in-the-21st-century-implications-for-assessment.pdf
Coursera. (2020). *Building the future of higher education: Best practices for resilient teaching.* https://www.coursera.org/campus/resilient-teaching-best-practices/?utm_campaign=campus&utm_content=resilient-teaching-wp-the-digital-hub&utm_medium=digital-hub&utm_source=the
Damewood, A. M. (2016). Current trends in higher education technology: Simulation. *TechTrends, 60*(3), 268–271. https://doi.org/10.1007/s11528-016-0048-1
Davidson, C. N., & Goldberg, D. T. (2009). *The future of learning institutions in a digital age.* https://doi.org/10.7551/mitpress/8517.001.0001
Davis, M. (1996). *Empathy: A social psychological approach.* Boulder, CO: Westview Press.
De Wit, H. (2011). Globalization and Internationalisation of Higher Education. *Revista De Universidad y Sociedad Del Conocimiento (RUSC), 8*(2), 241–248. https://doi.org/10.7238/rusc.v8i2.1247
Donovan, L., Green, T. D., & Mason, C. (2014). Examining the 21st century classroom: Developing an innovation configuration map. *Journal of Educational Computing Research, 50*(2), 161–178. https://doi.org/10.2190/ec.50.2.a
Du, X., Yang, J., Shelton, B., & Hung, J.-L. (2019). Is learning anytime, anywhere a good strategy for success? Identifying successful spatial-temporal patterns of on-the-job and full-time students. *Information Discovery and Delivery, 47*(4), 173–181. https://doi.org/10.1108/idd-09-2019-0060
Duffin, E. (2020). US. Student distance learning enrollment 2012–2018. http://www.statista.com/statistics/944245/student-distance-learning-enrollment-usa/
Elzarka, S. (2012). Technology use in higher education instruction. *CGU Theses and Dissertations,* 1–131. https://doi.org/10.5642/cguetd/39
Englund, C., Olofsson, A. D., & Price, L. (2018). The influence of sociocultural and structural contexts in academic change and development in higher education. *Higher Education, 76*(6), 1051–1069. https://doi.org/10.1007/s10734-018-0254-1

FitzGerald, E., Jones, A., Kucirkova, N., & Scanlon, E. (2018). A literature synthesis of personalised technology-enhanced learning: what works and why. *Research in Learning Technology*, *26*(0), 1–16. https://doi.org/10.25304/rlt.v26.2095

Fry, R., & Cilluffo, A. (2019, May 22). A rising share of undergraduates are from poor families, especially at less selective colleges. https://www.pewresearch.org/social-trends/2019/05/22/a-rising-share-of-undergraduates-are-from-poor-families-especially-at-less-selective-colleges/#:~:text=The%20growth%20in%20the%20share,1996%20to%2027%25%20in%202016

Gardner, H. (1983). *Frames of mind: The theory of multiple intelligences.* Basic Books.

Gardner, H. (1993). *Multiple intelligences: The theory in practice.* Basic Books.

Gardner, H. (1994). Intelligences in theory and practice: A response to Elliot W. Eisner, Robert J. Sternberg, and Henry M. Levin. *Teachers College Record,* 95(4), 567–582.

Gardner, H. (1997). *An Interview with Howard Gardner.* Mindshift Connection: Multiple Intelligences. Zephyr Press.

Gardner, H. (2006). *The development and education of the mind: The selected works of Howard Gardner*. Routledge.

Gardner, H. (2011). *Frames of mind: The theory of multiple intelligences* (3rd ed.). Basic Books.

Garrison & Vaughan (2007). *Blended learning in higher education: Framework, principles, and guidelines*, John Wiley & Sons, Inc.

Greenhalgh, P. (1994). *Emotional Growth and Learning.* Routledge.

Green, C., & Tanner, R. (2005). Multiple intelligences and online teacher education. *ELT Journal, 59*(4), 312–321. https://doi.org/10.1093/elt/cci060

Govindarajan, V., & Srivastava, A. (2020). What the shift to virtual learning could mean for the future of higher ed. https://hbr.org/2020/03/what-the-shift-to-virtual-learning-could-mean-for-the-future-of-higher-ed

Helyer, R., & Lee, D. (2014). The role of work experience in the future employability of higher education graduates. *Higher Education Quarterly, 68*(3), 348–372. https://doi.org/10.1111/hequ.12055

Hopper, B., & Hurry, P. (2000). Learning the MI way: The effects on students' learning of using the theory of multiple intelligences. *Pastoral Care in Education, 18*(4), 26–32. https://doi.org/10.1111/1468-0122.00176

Huang, J.-L. (2015). Cultivating teacher thinking: Ideas and practice. *Educational Research for Policy and Practice, 14*(3), 247–257. https://doi.org/10.1007/s10671-015-9184-1

Institute for Prospective Technological Studies, Redecker, C., Leis, M., Leendertse, M., Punie, Y., Gijsbers, G., Hoogveld, B. (2011). *The Future of Learning: Preparing for Change.* Publications Office of the European Union. https://doi.org/10.2791/64117

Irving, K. E. (2006). The impact of technology on the 21st century classroom. In J. Rhoton & P. Shane (Eds.), *Teaching science in the 21st century: Teaching science in the twenty-first century* (pp. 3–19). NSTA Press.

James, F. (2019, November 6). *What do employers want from tomorrow's university graduates?* https://www.qs.com/what-employers-want-tomorrows-university-graduates/#:%7E:text=Soft%20skills%20such%20as%20creativity,core%20skill%20set%20in%202020

Kemp, A. T., Preston, J., Page, C. S., Harper, R., Dillard, B. R., Flynn, J., & Yamaguchi, M. (2014). Technology and teaching: A conversation among faculty regarding the pros and cons of technology. *The Qualitative Report*, *19*, 1–23. https://files.eric.ed.gov/fulltext/EJ1043545.pdf

Ketamo, H., Moisio, A., Passi-Rauste, A., & Alamäki, A. (2019). Mapping the future curriculum: Adopting artificial intelligence and analytics in forecasting competence needs. *Proceedings of the 10th European Conference on Intangibles and Intellectual Capital ECIIC 2019*, 144–153. https://www.theseus.fi/handle/10024/172083

Kim, M. M., & Kutscher, E. L. (2020). College students with disabilities: Factors influencing growth in academic ability and confidence. *Research in Higher Education*, 1–23. https://doi.org/10.1007/s11162-020-09595-8

Koksal, I. (2020, May 2). The rise of online learning. https://www.forbes.com/sites/ilkerkoksal/2020/05/02/the-rise-of-online-learning/?sh=4af38b9872f3

Kolb (1984). *Experiential Learning Experience as the source of learning and development*, Prentice-Hall.
Koshy, P. (2019). *Ncsehe briefing note: Equity student participation in Australian higher education 2013–2018*. https://www.ncsehe.edu.au/publications/briefing-note-equity-student-participation-in-australian-higher-education-2013-2018/
KPMG International. (2020). *The future of higher education in a disruptive world*. https://assets.kpmg/content/dam/kpmg/xx/pdf/2020/10/future-of-higher-education.pdf
Kress, G. (2000). A curriculum for the future. *Cambridge Journal of Education, 30*(1), 133–145. https://doi.org/10.1080/03057640050005825
Lazear, D. (1994). *Multiple intelligence approaches to assessment: Solving the assessment conundrum*. Zephyr Press.
Laal, M., Laal, M., & Kermanshahi, Z. K. (2012). 21st Century learning; Learning in collaboration. *Procedia—Social and Behavioral Sciences, 47*, 1696–1701. https://doi.org/10.1016/j.sbspro.2012.06.885
Li, K. C., & Wong, B. T.-M. (2020). Features and trends of personalised learning: a review of journal publications from 2001 to 2018. *Interactive Learning Environments*, 1–14. https://doi.org/10.1080/10494820.2020.1811735
Lillejord, S., Børte, K., Nesje, K., & Ruud, E. (2018). *Learning and teaching with technology in higher education—A systematic review*. https://www.forskningsradet.no/siteassets/publikasjoner/1254035532334.pdf
Lim, C. P., Zhao, Y., Tondeur, J., Chai, C. S., & Tsai, C. C. (2013). Bridging the gap: Technology trends and use of technology in schools. *Educational Technology & Society, 16*(2), 59–68. https://www.ds.unipi.gr/et&s/journals/16_2/6.pdf
Magda, A. J., & Aslanian, C. B. (2018). *Online college students 2018: Comprehensive data on demands and preferences*. The Learning House, Inc. https://www.learninghouse.com/wp-content/uploads/2018/06/OCS-2018-Report-FINAL.pdf
Maryville University. (n.d.). Adult students in higher education statistics. https://online.maryville.edu/blog/going-back-to-school-statistics/
McLoughlin, C. (2013). *The pedagogy of personalised learning: exemplars, MOOCS and related learning theories*. https://acuresearchbank.acu.edu.au/download/adcf45887d75ffd4148c0246e51b78d27f76d2e06f9dc22def3724abf4ed97d4/69985/MCLOUGHLIN_2012_The_pedagogy_of_personalised_learning_exemplars.pdf
Melhuish, K., & Falloon, G. (2010). Looking to the future: M-learning with the iPad. *Computers in New Zealand Schools*, 1–16. https://hdl.handle.net/10289/5050
Morris, T. A. (2010). Anytime/anywhere online learning: Does it remove barriers for adult learners? In T. Kidd (Ed.), *Online education and adult learning: New frontiers for teaching practices* (1st ed., pp. 115–123). Information Science Reference.
Nazarenko, M. A., & Khronusova, T. V. (2017). Big data in modern higher education. Benefits and criticism. *2017 International Conference 'Quality Management, Transport and Information Security, Information Technologies' (IT&QM&IS)*, 676–679. https://doi.org/10.1109/itmqis.2017.8085914
Novotney, A. (2015). *Gaming to learn*. https://www.apa.org/monitor/2015/04/gaming
OECD. (2018). *The future of education and skills: Education 2030*. https://www.oecd.org/education/2030/E2030%20Position%20Paper%20(05.04.2018).pdf
PA Consulting. (n.d.). Student 4.0: How universities can become student centric institutions. https://www.timeshighereducation.com/hub/p/student-40-how-universities-can-become-student-centric-institutions
Palvia, S., Aeron, P., Gupta, P., Mahapatra, D., Parida, R., Rosner, R., & Sindhi, S. (2018). Online education: Worldwide status, challenges, trends, and implications. *Journal of Global Information Technology Management, 21*(4), 233–241. https://doi.org/10.1080/1097198x.2018.1542262
Pang, E., Wong, M., Leung, C. H., & Coombes, J. (2018). Competencies for fresh graduates' success at work: Perspectives of employers. *Industry and Higher Education, 33*(1), 55–65. https://doi.org/10.1177/0950422218792333

PwC. (2020). *Perspectives in higher education.* https://www.pwc.com/us/en/industries/health-industries/library/higher-education-perspectives.html

Rajaram, K. (2020). *Educating Mainland Chinese Learners in Business Education: Pedagogical and Cultural Perspectives* – Singapore Experiences. Springer.

Rajaram, K. (2021). *Evidence-Based Teaching for the 21st Century Classroom and Beyond – Innovative-Driven Learning Strategies.* Springer.

Redecker, C. , Leis, M., Leendertse, M., Punie, Y., Gijsbers, G., Krischner, P., Stoyanovand, S., & Hoogveld, B. (2011). The future of learning: Preparing for the change, JRC Scientific and Technical Report.

Reiff, J. (1993, February). Learning styles and culture: Promises and problems. *Paper presented at the annual meeting of the National Association for Multicultural Education.*

Reiff, J. (1996, April). Bridging home and school through multiple intelligences. *Paper presented at the annual meeting of the Association for Childhood Education*, International, Minneapolis, MN.

Richards, J. C., & Rodgers, T. S. (2014). *Approaches and methods in language teaching* (3rd ed.). Cambridge University Press.

RMIT University. (n.d.). The future of learning and teaching: Big changes ahead for education. https://www.rmit.edu.au/study-with-us/education/discover-education/the-future-of-learning-and-teaching-big-changes-ahead-for-education

Roddy, C., Amiet, D. L., Chung, J., Holt, C., Shaw, L., McKenzie, S., & Mundy, M. E. (2017). Applying best practice online learning, teaching, and support to intensive online environments: An integrative review. *Frontiers in Education, 2*, 1–10. https://doi.org/10.3389/feduc.2017.00059

Salmona, M., Partlo, M., Kaczynski, D., & Leonard, S. (2015). Developing culturally competent teachers: An international student teaching field experience. *Australian Journal of Teacher Education, 40*(40), 35–53. https://doi.org/10.14221/ajte.2015v40n4.3

Schindler, L. A., Burkholder, G. J., Morad, O. A., & Marsh, C. (2017). Computer-based technology and student engagement: A critical review of the literature. *International Journal of Educational Technology in Higher Education, 14*(1), 1–28. https://doi.org/10.1186/s41239-017-0063-0

Shaffer, D. W., Squire, K. R., Halverson, R., & Gee, J. P. (2005). Video games and the future of learning. *Phi Delta Kappan, 87*(2), 105–111. https://doi.org/10.1177/003172170508700205

Sharma, B., Nand, R., Naseem, M., & Reddy, E. V. (2019). Effectiveness of online presence in a blended higher learning environment in the Pacific. *Studies in Higher Education, 45*(8), 1547–1565. https://doi.org/10.1080/03075079.2019.1602756

Statista, & Duffin, E. (2020a, May 5). U.S. student distance learning enrollment 2012–2018. https://www.statista.com/statistics/944245/student-distance-learning-enrollment-usa/

Statista, & Duffin, E. (2020b, November 23). International students in the U.S. 2003–2020. https://www.statista.com/statistics/237681/international-students-in-the-us/

Small, C. (1977). *Music-Society-Education.* John Calder (Publishing) Ltd.

Suleman, F. (2017). The employability skills of higher education graduates: Insights into conceptual frameworks and methodological options. *Higher Education, 76*(2), 263–278. https://doi.org/10.1007/s10734-017-0207-0

Teele, S. (1990). *Teaching and assessment strategies appropriate for the multiple intelligences* (rev. 1992). University of California.

Thigpen, K. (2014). *Creating anytime, anywhere learning for all students: Key elements of a comprehensive digital infrastructure.* https://all4ed.org/reports-factsheets/creating-anytime-anywhere-learning-for-all-students-key-elements-of-a-comprehensive-digital-infrastructure/

Times Higher Education. (n.d.). How has the coronavirus accelerated the future of assessment? Retrieved from https://www.timeshighereducation.com/hub/jisc/p/how-has-coronavirus-accelerated-future-assessment

UNESCO Institute for Statistics. (2020). School enrollment, tertiary, female (%gross). Retrieved from https://data.worldbank.org/indicator/SE.TER.ENRR.FE

Wiley Education Services. (n.d.). Dealing with change: How universities can evolve for the future while maintaining mission. https://edservices.wiley.com/three-key-considerations-for-future-of-higher-education/

Williamson, B. (2013). *The future of the curriculum*. Amsterdam University Press.

White, J. (1998). *Do Howard Gardner's multiple intelligences add up?* Institute of Education, University of London.

Wright, G. (2011). Student-Centered Learning in Higher Education. *International Journal of Teaching and Learning in Higher*, *23*(3), 92–97.

Zong, J., & Batalova, J. (2018, May 9). *International students in the United States in 2017*. https://www.migrationpolicy.org/article/international-students-united-states-2017

Part II
Cultural and Social Engineering of Learning

Chapter 2
Cultural Intelligence in Teaching and Learning

Kumaran Rajaram

Abstract This chapter focuses on the aspects of cultural intelligence within the context of teaching and learning. As the world is becoming increasingly flat (Ang et al., 2007; Darling-Hammond, 2010), the classroom is viewed as a mirror that often reflects this phenomenon at a microcosmic level. As teachers continue to work with an increasingly culturally and linguistically diverse student population, their roles and responsibility have become more complex in addressing not only the academic and institutional demands of their work but also the interpersonal and intrapersonal demands of meeting the needs of all learners. We need to acknowledge that by purely emphasizing on the academic knowledge in developing our student's learning, we will miss out the rich resources linked to diverse presence in the higher education institutions and universities. The ability to communicate and practice cultural intelligence is based on the idea that every individual through interaction mediated by language can resolve situations that we could not resolve ourselves through academic or practical intelligence. It is crucial to transform the concepts of learning to promote forms that encourage interaction and behavioural actions. To make the changes, it requires processes and mechanisms where everyone in the community can participate in students' learning and in that of others. The learning process must be transformed in a way that allows the wider community to participate and contribute. The chapter commences with an overview on the urgency and importance of "social-cultural consciousness" for teachers to effectively manage and negotiate their interactions with students mediated by sociocultural backgrounds. Next, it presents the theoretical aspects and discussion of cultural intelligence, cultural competence and cultural engineering & re-engineering. Thereafter, the role of cultural intelligence in teaching and the role of culture for students' learning are discussed. Finally, the chapter wraps up with strategies and recommendations in practice that has worked effectively well in dealing with multicultural students' profile.

K. Rajaram (✉)
Division of Leadership, Management and Organization, Nanyang Business School, Nanyang Technological University, Singapore, Singapore
e-mail: rkumaran@ntu.edu.sg

K. Rajaram, *Learning Intelligence: Innovative and Digital Transformative Learning Strategies*, https://doi.org/10.1007/978-981-19-9201-8_2

2.1 Introduction

As the world becomes more interconnected to effectively function that is tied closely to its economic growth, enhancing its sociocultural infrastructure due to the cross-cultural functions and operations, awareness and competency of cultural 'know-hows' becomes increasingly vital. Globalization, while enabling vast benefits and opportunities, for example, culturally diverse interactions, also brings with it the increased 'probability of cultural misunderstandings, tensions and conflicts' (Ang et al., 2011, p. 582). The primary questions that emerge: (a) Why is culture not uniformly consistent?; (b) Why are some able to be easily adjusted and adaptable to new cultures while others seem to struggle?

The prominence and the rapid evolution of globalization with a steady increase in the multicultural workplaces has led cultural intelligence (CQ) to be a trending topic in recent times (Earley et al., 2006; Livermore, 2011). CQ is an essential element in today's rapid evolving global economy that impacts cross-cultural adjustment, corporate strategy and much more (Earley et al., 2006), especially for the future where diversity at various levels becomes part of the operating norm. The wave of globalization has also impacted the Higher education. There has been an increasing trend in international student mobility that serves as the source where higher education institutions and universities around the globe become much more accessible. The availability of varying fully online platforms, for example, MOOCs means that one could pursue their education via asynchronous and synchronous online modes, where they do not necessarily have to leave their country of living to experience culturally diverse classrooms. Hence, understanding and having CQ skills and competencies developed increasingly imperative in the education sector to be able to strategically cope with the fast-changing climate.

Cultural intelligence—otherwise known as CQ—is defined as a multidimensional capacity that enables the effective functioning within culturally new and varied contexts that comprises cognitive/metacognitive, motivation and behavioural elements (Ng & Earley, 2006). Some of the earliest proponents of CQ defined it as one's ability to act effectively in culturally diverse situations (Earley & Ang, 2003). Earley and Ang (2003) distinguishes CQ from social intelligence and emotional intelligence (EQ) stating that CQ "is not simply a minor adaptation" of either. While CQ is complementary to other intelligences like EQ (Mosakowski & Earley, 2004; Thomas et al., 2008; Van Dyne et al., 2012), a person with high EQ within his or her own domain may not necessarily be able to adapt and identify the social nuances of other cultures. However, not all scholarly definitions of CQ are identical. Thomas et al. (2008) suggest that the variations of each definition result in differences in its implied outcomes or applications. We could relate this to the context of how the scholarly work focuses its underlying constructs that make up CQ, or more commonly known as 'dimensions'. CQ is often described as multidimensional that comprises cognitive and behavioural characteristics although these labels defined may vary in context from article to article (Ang & Van Dyne, 2008; Bücker et al., 2015; Earley & Ang, 2003; Thomas, 2006; Van Dyne et al., 2012). For the purpose of illustrating the constructs that make up CQ, Van Dyne et al.'s (2012) dimensions were chosen as a reference since it builds upon previously established and well-discussed research. In total, CQ comprises 11 sub-dimensions that were derived from Earley and Ang's (2003) earlier conceptualization of the four factors construct of CQ. Earley and Ang (2003) proposed three interconnected ways in which intelligence can be viewed: Cognitive (including metacognitive), motivational and behavioural, which was the derivation based on the multiple intelligences' framework (Sternberg & Detterman, 1986). Metacognition subsequently was presented as an element on its own, resulting in the four factors construct of CQ (Ang et al., 2007). Table 2.1 presents the illustrations on the dimensions and sub-dimensions of cultural intelligence (CQ) based on the aforementioned scholarly work.

Although the four-factor construct serves as a guiding framework by and large, there have been some criticisms as well as alternative suggestions for improvements. For example, most notably by Thomas et al. (2008) who identifies CQ as a system of facets that interact with one another. The facets include cultural knowledge, cultural metacognition and cultural skills. Both constructs by Earley and Ang (2003) and Thomas et al. (2008) have their similarities where they both identify CQ as multi-faceted and distinct from social intelligence and emotional intelligence. However, Thomas et al. (2008) criticized Earley and Ang's (2003) concept for being an aggregate construct as it lacks clarity in the relationships between the factors and the overall construct (Ott & Michailova, 2016). Another difference identified by Ott and Michailova (2016) reported another variation unlike Earley and Ang (2003). Thomas et al. (2008) referred to the motivational facet as not a requirement for CQ. Nevertheless, most scholarly work has chosen to build upon Earley and Ang's four factors construct.

To have a holistic perspective of the scholarly definitions of CQ, we analysed the key themes and commonalities to identify the more prevalent components. Table 2.2. presents the established and contemporary scholarly definitions of CQ. We have included a column to sieve out the competency traits required for CQ that emerged from the scholarly definitions. These competencies are required for one to be able to be equipped with the varying dimensional aspects of cultural intelligence.

The varying scholarly definitions addresses the scope of cultural intelligence. Further analysis enabled us to identify the components that encompasses cultural intelligence which is illustrated in Fig. 2.1. These components are what one must undertake in order to achieve an affirmative outcome of cultural intelligence.

2.2 Cultural Intelligence and Its Impact on Higher Education (HE)

Internationalization of higher education is defined as the process by which higher education institutions compete for students globally and the processes by which they attempt to prepare students for a globalized world, which is often positively linked to

Table 2.1 Dimensions and sub-dimensions of cultural intelligence (CQ)

Dimensions of cultural intelligence	Definitions of the Dimensions of Cultural Intelligence (Ang & Van Dyne, 2008, pp. 4–6)	Sub-dimensions of cultural intelligence	Definitions of the sub -dimensions of cultural intelligence (Van Dyne et al., 2012, pp. 298–305)
Metacognitive	"an individual's level of conscious cultural awareness during cross-cultural interactions"	1. Planning	"strategizing before a culturally diverse encounter"
		2. Awareness	"knowing about cultural thinking and knowledge of self and others in real time"
		3. Checking	"reviewing assumptions and adjusting mental maps when actual experiences differ from expectations"
Cognitive	"knowledge of norms, practices, and conventions in different cultures that has been acquired from educational and personal experiences"	1. Culture-General Knowledge	"knowledge of the universal elements that constitute a cultural environment"
		2. Context-Specific Knowledge	"declarative knowledge about manifestations of cultural universals in a specific domain and procedural knowledge of how to be effective in that domain"
Motivational	"the capability to direct attention and energy toward learning about and functioning in situations characterized by cultural differences"	1. Intrinsic Interest	"valuing culturally diverse experience in and of itself because it is inherently satisfying"
		2. Extrinsic Interest	"valuing the tangible, personal benefits that can be derived from culturally diverse experiences"
		3. Self-efficacy to Adjust	"having task-specific confidence in culturally diverse situations"
Behavioural	"the capability to exhibit appropriate verbal and nonverbal actions when interacting with people from different cultures"	1. Verbal Behaviour	"flexibility in vocalization"
		2. Non-verbal Behaviour	"flexibility in communication that is conveyed via gestures, facial expressions, and body language, rather than through words"

(continued)

Table 2.1 (continued)

Dimensions of cultural intelligence	Definitions of the Dimensions of Cultural Intelligence (Ang & Van Dyne, 2008, pp. 4–6)	Sub-dimensions of cultural intelligence	Definitions of the sub -dimensions of cultural intelligence (Van Dyne et al., 2012, pp. 298–305)
		3. Speech Acts	"flexibility in manner of communicating specific types of messages such that requests, invitations, apologies, gratitude, disagreement, and saying 'no' are expressed appropriately based on local standards"

factors that influence global university rankings, such as research funding (Robson & Wihlborg, 2019). Interestingly, international students are viewed as a source of cash flow revenue for higher education institutions (Choudaha, 2017). As educational institutions become more globalized, the prevalence of cross-cultural interactions in day-to-day operations increases exponentially, making higher education institution grounds ideal for developing cultural intelligence competencies in their students.

The embedment of cultural intelligence within higher education institutions is especially vital now and for the future as the prominence and embracing of internationalization are growing steadily. Global corporations are in search for talents who are culturally competent (Ramsey & Lorenz, 2016) and able to effectively function in international teams (Crossman & Clarke, 2009), adaptable, culturally mindful and sensitive. Higher education institutions should place much higher emphasis on cross-cultural education in order to prepare students for the increasingly complex and multicultural society (MacNab, 2011). This does not only benefit graduates who will potentially be nurtured to be culturally competent, but also the higher education institutions themselves since graduate employability is often a considerable factor in determining the reputation, quality of as well as the institutional global ranking.

A study by Eisenberg et al. (2013) found that educational interventions influenced the cultural intelligence levels of students. Hence, higher education institutions must be mindful of how the cultural intelligence aspects are being integrated into its strategy and operations. For example, study abroad programmes are one of the primary approaches that many higher education institutions adopt to enhance their students' cultural intelligence (Holtbrügge & Engelhard, 2016) and dexterity through providing avenues for them to be exposed to cultural diversity. Next, we shall examine in detail on how cultural intelligence will influence the higher education institutions from a holistic perspective.

Cultural intelligence (CQ) has a significant impact at the strategic, tactical and operational levels for higher education institutions. At the strategic level, cultural

Table 2.2 Definitions of cultural intelligence and its competency traits

Source	Definition of cultural intelligence	Competency traits required in cultural intelligence
Earley and Ang (2003)	"…capability to adapt effectively to new cultural contexts…"	Adaptative
Thomas and Inkson (2003)	"…involves understanding the fundamentals of intercultural interaction, developing a mindful approach to intercultural interactions, and finally building adaptive skills and a repertoire of behaviours so that one is effective in different intercultural situations"	Understanding; Mindful; Adaptative
Mosakowski and Earley (2004)	"is the ability to make sense of unfamiliar contexts and then blend in"	Logical and sensitive
Earley and Peterson (2004)	"reflects a person's capability to gather, interpret, and act upon these radically different cues to function effectively across cultural settings or in a multicultural situation"	Interpretive and aligned
Pedersen (2004)	"…the ability to engage in a set of behaviors that uses skills (i.e., language or interpersonal skills) and qualities (e.g., tolerance for ambiguity, flexibility) that are tuned appropriately to the culture-based values and attitudes of the people with whom one interacts"	Adaptative
Thomas (2006)	"…the ability to interact effectively with people who are culturally different"	Articulative; sensitive
Ang et al. (2007)	"…capability to function and manage effectively in culturally diverse settings…"	Adaptative; flexible
Thomas et al. (2008)	"…a system of interacting knowledge and skills, linked by cultural metacognition, that allows people to adapt to, select, and shape the cultural aspects of their environment"	Adaptative; cognitive agility
Crowne (2008)	"The ability to interact effectively in multiple cultures…"	Mindful communication and interaction

(continued)

Table 2.2 (continued)

Source	Definition of cultural intelligence	Competency traits required in cultural intelligence
Ang and Van Dyne (2008)	"…an individual's capability to function effectively in situations characterized by cultural diversity"	Adaptative; Sensitivity; Emotional and Social Intelligence
Livermore (2009)	"…the capability to function effectively across national, ethnic, and organizational cultures."	Adaptative; mindful
Van Dyne et al. (2010)	"…the ability to function effectively in a diverse context where assumptions, values, and traditions of one's upbringing are not uniformly shared with those with whom one needs to act"	Behavioural and cognitive agility
Van Dyne et al. (2012)	"…an individual's capability to detect, assimilate, reason, and act on cultural cues appropriately in situations characterized by cultural diversity"	Cognitive and behavioural agility; Adaptative; flexible; mindful
Fang et al. (2018)	"…the capability by which expatriates, managers, and others involved in cross-cultural interactions function effectively in a globalized world…"	Mindful communication and interaction
Roy et al. (2018)	"…an individual's ability and skills to manage themselves and interact with others across cultures"	Adaptative; Mindful communication and interaction
Hu et al. (2020)	"…an individual's competence in effectively engaging with a culturally diversified environment…"	Agility, Engaging with an open mindset
Richter et al. (2020)	"…an individual's capability to adapt effectively to, and function effectively in, new cultural contexts"	Adaptative

intelligence plays a vital role due to its strong connective link with transformational leadership (Keung & Rockinson-Szapkiw, 2013; Velarde et al., 2020) and organizational commitment (Anvari et al., 2014). It was found that leaders who are transformative in their actions could potentially better manage multicultural environments (Keung & Rockinson-Szapkiw, 2013), implying that institutions should look to hire leaders with high cultural intelligences due to their efficiency and effectiveness to adapt compared to those with lower cultural intelligences. The leaders' subsequent top-down dissemination of knowledge could also affect how cultural intelligence

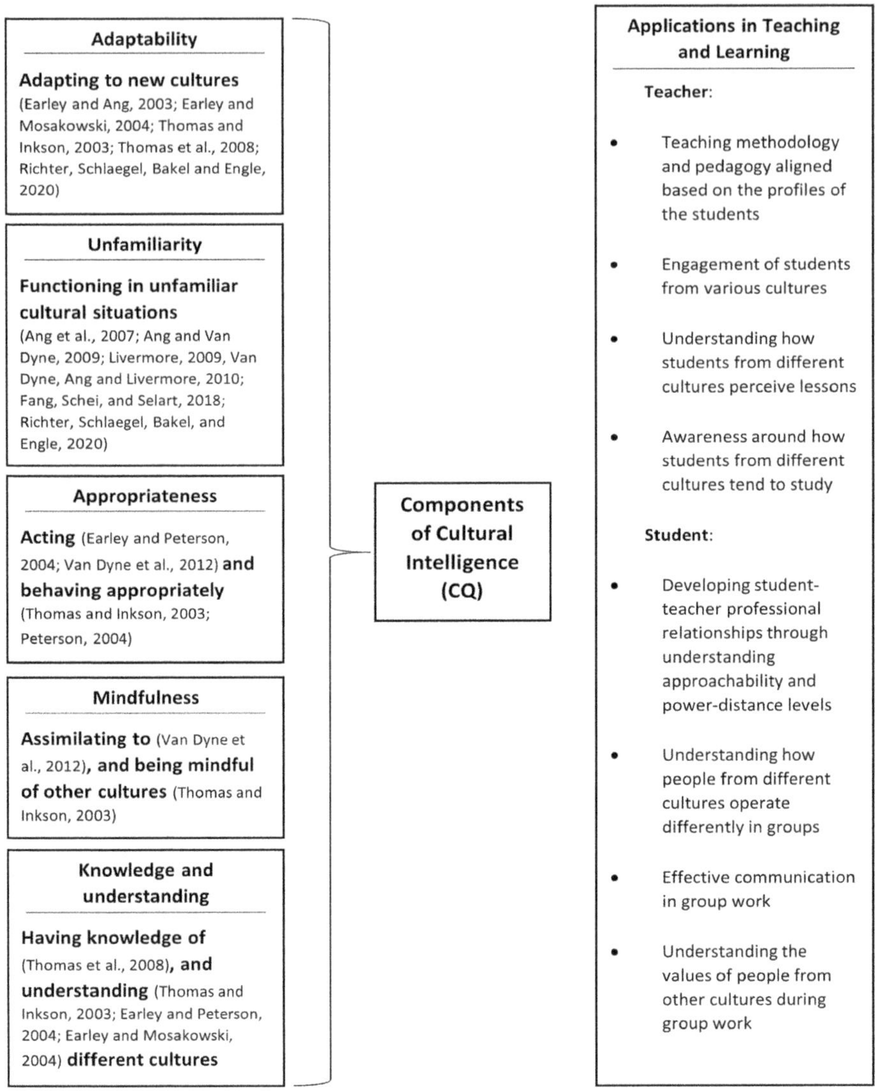

Fig. 2.1 Components of cultural intelligence and its application to teaching and learning

development is integrated into staff training and subsequently on student curriculum. This could be deduced by acknowledging that those with a better understanding on the factors influencing CQ development are better able to train individuals to be effective in culturally diverse situations (Rosenblatt et al., 2013). The influence of CQ affects other aspects of Higher Education Institutes, such as design and development of site plans, where mixing international and domestic students in hostels can facilitate cross-cultural interactions (Holtbrügge & Engelhard, 2016).

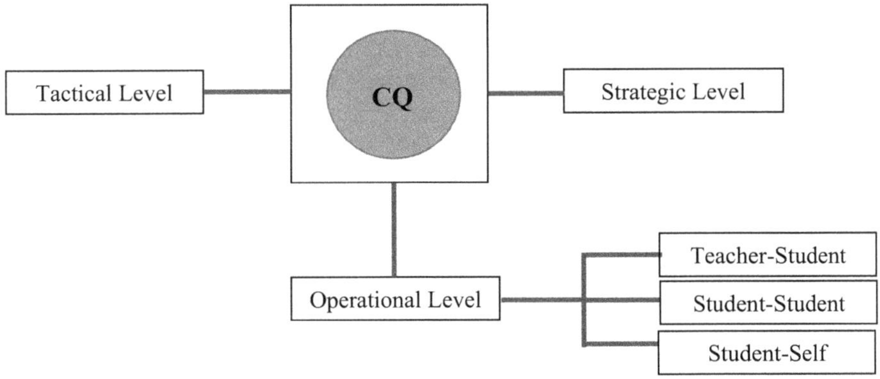

Fig. 2.2 Visual diagram that presents the impact of cultural intelligence (CQ)

At the tactical level, CQ competency levels may vary from institutions to institutions across different countries based on the exposure of varying cultures, embedded values, norms and practices. This could be well validated by, for example, it was found in a research study that Australian accounting academics had a lower average CQ compared to other professional groups (Tharapos, 2015). Another study conducted by Beneroso and Alosaimi (2020) with final-year engineering undergraduates in the United Kingdom (UK) found that international students had greater cognitive CQ while domestic students had greater motivational CQ. Examining CQ at a more granular level, it enables schools to devise and/or align management approaches that caters to its own unique and targeted group of stakeholders.

At the operational-level, CQ can impact teaching and learning in higher education on three levels of interactions and exchanges across: (a) teacher-student; (b) student-student; and (c) student-self contexts, which is presented in a visual form in Fig. 2.2.

In the "teacher-student context", CQ affects the pedagogical methods employed by the teacher which is subsequently experienced and absorbed by the students. In a more globalized context, teaching effectively and engaging students becomes more complex, complicated as teachers are required to adjust in order to accommodate the diversity present in classrooms. Thus, teachers are expected not only to teach with cultural intelligence but also must develop culturally intelligent students. Goh (2012) reiterates the importance of integrating CQ into the curriculum by providing several suggestions on how to do so. A good understanding of CQ by teachers allows them to address and provide guidance to their students and subsequently instil skills that will allow them to engage in this globalized world (Molina, 2013).

The "student-student" context focuses on students' interactions collaborating and engaging with students from other cultures. Multicultural teams are often viewed to have high potential for innovation and creativity (Bouncken et al., 2016), although there can be issues in communication that arise from differences in cognition and behaviour (Spencer-Rodgers & McGovern, 2002). This explains the influence of cultural diversity on interpersonal trust and team performance (Ang & Van Dyne,

2008; Moon, 2013). However, these issues have been found and reported to be negated by CQ. For example, in multicultural teams, CQ was found to reduce the negative effect of cultural diversity on interpersonal trust (Ang & Van Dyne, 2008). Interestingly, culturally diverse teams with higher levels of CQ are also likely to show greater rates of performance improvement (Moon, 2013).

The "student-self" context examines the impact of CQ on an individual basis. In the context comprising international students, CQ acts as a moderating factor and lessens the impact of culture shock and reverse culture shock (Presbitero, 2016), where it enables foreign students to be more comfortable and adjust better to culturally diverse situations. Furthermore, evidence shows that there is a positive correlation between CQ and academic success, specifically in the context of studies comprising of international students (Iskhakova, 2018; Khan et al., 2020).

Livermore (2011) reported that the number one predictor of success in the current borderless world is cultural intelligence. Research conducted in 30+ countries over many years revealed that those equipped with high cultural intelligence are more competent in handling challenges in life and work, especially with the global nature and contemporary aspects of today's societal context (Livermore, 2011). CQ emerges an essential competency in addressing the complex challenges with the rapid, evolving globalization and cross-cultural international trade. On a similar capacity, CQ epitomizes a promising future and progress in the area of cross-cultural teaching, learning and training. To adequately equip leaders and students' nuances of contemporary and multi-sociocultural future, cross-cultural training and competency building are essential (Bandura, 2002; Brislin et al., 2008; Hofstede, 2003; Ng et al., 2009; Oddou, 2005; Schmidt-Wilk, 2010). Scholars (Black & Gregersen, 1999; Gordon, 2008; Schmidt-Wilk, 2010) advocate the need to advance the capacity for multicultural competency aspects to be able to operate in culturally unique and complex environments. The United States and UK, as two of the top host countries in the world, have long benefited from attracting large numbers of international students (Upton & Butters, 2019).

Teachers' CQ's competency enables them to empower students intellectually and through sociocultural intelligence leveraging on cultural referents to educate and impart knowledge, skills and values. Students come with different social values, norms and diverse cultural backgrounds equipped with their own cognitively trained minds to seek valuable knowledge through information exchanges within the learning contest and environment. The presence of diverse international students within the work groups enables augment learning gains applied to different international contexts during ad hoc interactions in class and in the process of engaging with each other while doing up group assignments. Research evidence states that impalpable exchanges and interactions may foster deeper insights and appreciation of working in international contexts attaining a more broadened approach in dealing with workplace challenges, that prepares and equips students in coping with increasingly multicultural and interdependent work environments. Leask (2009, p. 207) denotes this as the "hidden curriculum", an active interplay of informal and incidental learning journey both in and out of the classroom that shapes the experiences of the students. Despite the overlook of this hidden curriculum, its role should not be underestimated due to its vital role of building stronger cultural awareness and knowledge of on what comprises as effective practice in aiming for international infusion (Leask & Bridge, 2013).

Theoretical Evidence-Based Discussions

2.3 Globalization of Higher Education

Globalization suggests unrestricted flow of goods and services across international borders in an unified world economy. This process is driven by market and environmental forces where the focus is on markets as opposed to respective countries to promote economic development and social well-being. The resultant of rapid and evolving globalization attracts multinational and transnational companies to expand in markets not bound by national or geographical borders. The globalization progress has largely benefited from the rise of a knowledge economy and technological advances. The universities creating knowledge is valued for their intellectual capital where it emerges as a vital element of invention and a driving force of economic growth in the globalized knowledge economy.

The mobility of international students for the purposes of education has been a norm, however, the international mobility of universities and programmes on a larger, more universal scale is a more recent development (Gürü, 2011). Universities have expanded their global operations into the international arena, supported by technological and communication advances, together with unmet demand for university education elsewhere in the world (Gribble & Ziguras, 2003; McBurnie & Ziguras, 2001). The goal is to access some of the world's more sophisticated education models and provision of education by foreign institutions becomes an avenue to rapidly develop local education systems (McBurnie & Ziguras, 2007). This results in rapid development and accumulation of human knowledge in these countries and subsequently impacting its economic development (McBurnie & Ziguras, 2007). International education is viewed as critical components for sharing knowledge, building intellectual capital and remaining competitive in a globalizing world' (Bhandari & Blumenthal, 2013, p. 2). Although there are obvious benefits by operating in global markets for education purposes, Lemaitre (2002) reported that education seemed to be absent from most of the scholarship surrounding globalization.

The strategy to sustain and elevate the globalization of higher education is to understand, view the progressive and rapid rising strengths of overseas universities as opportunities and not a threat. The exchange of ideas and people put forth by academic competition is only benefitable for the developing nations as knowledge building is the common good for the public where many other nations and individuals can use. The advancement of one country need not affect another country negatively, indeed in a contrary, it helps all to collectively rise with the collaborative efforts in the innovation and economic growth forefront to emerge in a win-win proposition of ever-greater magnitude for all concerned.

The term ‘globalization’ has slightly different contextual meanings for different people (Kellner, 1998; Nayyar, 2007). Globalization is largely referred to as a process of integration into the world economy (Nayyar, 2007). It could also be used in a normative sense to determine a strategy of development based on a swift integration with the world. Largely, globalization can be defined as a process associated with increasing economic openness, growing economic interdependence and deepening economic integration in the world economy. It is vital to differentiate the term ‘globalization’ from ‘internationalization’ as the two terms are often used interchangeably and somewhat loosely even though they do not mean exactly the same (Yang, 2003). This could be well validated by the distinction made by Cantwell and Maldonado-Maldonado (2009) where they state “..globalization is something that happens to universities and internationalization is how universities respond.” (p. 290). In recent times, due to the rapid evolution of inter-connectivity issues, many universities globally are now focusing on internationalization as one of their key strategic priorities (Robson & Wihlborg, 2019) in terms of their strategic positioning that enhances their reputation, global presence and diversity embracement.

Globalization has increasingly become a vital topic that arises in debates involving the future of higher education (Yang, 2003). Globalization influences how universities function and create more efficient, effective and accountable institutions (Salmi, 2009; Waghid, 2002). A more informed understanding of globalization and global trends can enrich higher education curriculum (Salmi, 2009; Waghid, 2002). Globalization provides the capacity to empower and outreach to a large number of people globally by providing them the opportunity for higher educational qualifications (Lieven & Martin, 2006). Besides this, the positive global relationships among the faculty may assist in advancing research, science and innovation. Moreover, the cross-institutional and disciplinary collaborations among the various universities globally enhance each other’s capabilities and reputational growth. For example, hosting and participating in international conferences elevates the global reputation of universities (Williams & Van Dyke, 2007). The sharing of resources globally can play a great role to address national and global problems and to address future economic needs (Teichler, 2003). In today’s rapid evolution of learning climate and technological disruption, globalization positively drives the agenda of digitalization as rightfully pointed by the researchers (Fee, 2009; Killen, 2010; Yang, 2003) pointed out that it creates an environment conducive to electronic learning. This spills over to other aspects, say a push for innovative higher education programmes, such as recognition of prior learning can be spread across the globe to benefit more students (Lieven & Martin, 2006; Teichler, 2003). Ultimately, we could be convinced that with these optimistic implications professionalization in higher education and the realization for sound support systems and structures are likely to intensify (Teichler, 2003; Williams & Van Dyke, 2007).

The effects of globalization could be seen with the rapid expansion of the global higher education market due to the discourse of global competition and we could deduce that this phenomenon to a large extent is motivated economically. We could see that globalization has been major influence in changing the landscape of higher education (De Wit, 2011; Nayyar, 2007). These changes manifest in many ways that are rightfully pointed out by De Wit (2011), such as the intensification of competition for international students and academics, the increase in transnational education programmes, the emergence of international for-profit providers in higher education and the changing position of countries like India and China in the world economy and in the higher education sector. At the forefront, we could clearly acknowledge that an increase in international students yield more funds to universities (Yang, 2003). This can be seen as a positive impact where world-class standards and quality assurance systems could potentially be replicated throughout the world (Lieven & Martin, 2006, Salmi, 2009; Teichler, 2003). Further to this, it facilitates universities to be ranked globally which affects the international reputation of the institution (Williams & Van Dyke, 2007). Through these changes, universities are in a much better position to take on an affirmative role to educate and nurture global citizens who would be able to value-add and create a better world for all.

Globalization has also allowed for increased international cooperation which allows universities to forge alliances to be able to compete in the global and mass higher educational market (Chan, 2004). This is well reported by research scholars (Lieven & Martin, 2006; Salmi, 2009; Teichler, 2003). Further to that, the practice of universities ranking has a major influence on the international reputation of the institution (Williams & Van Dyke, 2007). For example, universities in Singapore adopt the strategy of internationalization through collaborative arrangements with other prestigious universities from varying parts of the globe. More specifically, Yale University and the National University of Singapore (NUS) established a liberal arts college in Singapore, named Yale-NUS College that comes under the purview of the Singapore government. While graduates receive NUS degrees, Yale plays a major role in developing the curriculum and hiring faculty. Both parties are beneficiaries in their own rights gaining from this internationalized initiative. This certainly creates more opportunities for students to gain internationally recognized qualifications (Lieven & Martin, 2006; Teichler, 2003). This collaborative partnership assists Singapore in meeting its aspirations to be a regional and eventually a global education hub. At the same time, it draws globally talented students to Yale's programmes and helps attract more foreign students to Yale's Connecticut campus and vice-versa.

While we have examined and discussed the various numerous positive effects of globalization, let us now examine the dark side of it. Higher education institutions are also concerned over the potential negative impacts of the globalization and internationalization of higher education.

From a strategic level, globalization has resulted in a general decline in public funding that goes towards higher education despite the increasing trend of students' enrolment. The burden of funding higher education has shifted largely onto the shoulders of individuals. Due to this resulting effect, the quality of academic teaching has suffered across a range of countries, resulting in diminishing students contact hours, especially with senior and experienced staff, who often appear sporadically and whose lecturing standards decline in quality due to constant repetition, lack of updated course materials and resources. Such negative effects have affected higher education at an enormous scale, especially in the humanities and social sciences (Yang, 2003).

Recent research on internationalization of higher education in Asia-Pacific countries shows that there is strong concern about the potential negative impact of globalization that leads to the homogenization of national identities and cultures (Yang, 2003). For example, Nguyen (2007) reports varying concerns of the impact of globalization in higher education. Countries like China and Vietnam could potentially be flooded with foreign and private education providers that offer a variety of popular subjects and attractive course packages that are inclined towards attracting the bulk, which may be strategized from a more profit-driven context. This poses a ripple effect to the local state universities, perhaps having to compete with these providers leaving them with non-profitable subjects, such as arts and humanities. Obviously, this may not be applicable to all clusters of universities where the lower tier ones are more susceptible as they may be focusing on the similar target profile group of students who are more inclined to completing their degrees at a faster pace and at a much more economical means. The commercialization of higher education and the profit motive in certain cases supersede the need for quality provision and erodes the traditional values, intellectual character and critical thinking of university life (Lieven & Martin, 2006; Yang, 2003). The need to operate profit-making enterprises distracts academic staff from their legitimate academic functions (Yang, 2003). Additionally, although globalization promotes multiculturalism, however with the increasing number of students studying overseas, there are valid concerns about the social and political ripple effect consequences when students return in large numbers back to their home countries. One such example would be language. English has become the common language for foreign providers to deliver academic programmes, especially if they are to be well-recognized and accredited by global stakeholders. Consequently, on the contrary, it may lead to weakening of national values and identities, unless there is a highly well-structured emphasis and processes put in place to give equal importance to their own mother tongue languages. This effect could be seen in countries where students are migrated to a foreign country where the emphasis on their own mother tongue language is very much reduced, hence the probability of them not to appreciate the embedded nuances within the language is very high. Aside this, the much-reduced usage of the language also creates the pathway for it to be eventually diminished. Furthermore, the presence of many foreign providers could also potentially further increase the social division in these countries, if proper social processes are not consistently well advocated and embedded within the eco-system put in place. Affluent students and those from the middle class may potentially choose to enrol in private, foreign institutions, leaving public institutions, which are already poorly funded and unable to afford to offer the best academic environment, to cater the larger majority of students, especially the students from financially worst-off situations. The resultant effect of this would potentially brand these countries of having low-quality standards of higher education. Globalization has widened the digital divide between richer and poorer countries. The richer countries have abundant resources that enable them to support the digital transformation and building of the infrastructure, whereas the poorer countries are left far behind due to their inability to proceed due to their financial constraints. Further to this, there is a poor understanding of the higher education systems of the developing world (Horsthemke & Enslin, 2008; Lieven & Martin, 2006; Yang, 2003). This puts countries in this cluster in a great disadvantage, resulting in a large gap in terms of advancement or progress. In the similar vein, global imperialism or colonialism is created when the "strongest" universities (mostly from the UK and United States) are strengthened and "weaker" universities are weakened because they do not have the resources to globalize (Horsthemke & Enslin, 2008; Yang, 2003). This leads to the widening of "gaps" in the quality standards and the effectiveness in how higher education is offered in these developed versus developing countries. This clearly indicates that the most advantaged people in developing nations are empowered, while the poor remains disadvantaged, thus the "elitist" nature of higher education is perpetuated (Horsthemke & Enslin, 2008; Lieven & Martin, 2006; Yang, 2003).

Besides this, while national qualifications frameworks exist in many countries, the absence of regional and global qualifications frameworks stifle student mobility (Eisenhart, 2008; Lieven & Martin, 2006). Such uncertainly caused by globalization and ambivalence is likely to lead to increased managerialism in higher education and could be resisted by academics and administrators (Teichler, 2003). Finally, the effect could be well felt and experienced through the dominant cultural values and systems that are spread throughout the world and may threaten the survival of local cultures and customs (Yang, 2003). The safeguarding of these traditional cultural values and norms may be in conflict due to the embracing of the sought-after dominant ones that emerge due to globalization.

2.4 Cultural Intelligence: Analysis from an Education Perspective—Effects on Teaching and Learning in Higher Education

Globalization has an embryonic and strong effect on education that is well translated into educational policies that influences teaching practices and teacher education (Wang et al., 2011). Apple (2011) advocates that globalization emerges near the top of the list as a crucial topic within the critical education literature, as the emphasis is on how the social and ideological dynamics are fundamentally restructuring what education does and those who benefit from it. The literature evidence indicates that cultural competence has not intersected with much depth with the literature on teaching and learning contexts. Goh (2012) reiterated that despite the seminal and groundbreaking theories about cultural competence—cultural intelligence (CQ; Earley & Ang, 2003)—the notion has not yet had much presences in education and teacher education. Although there are some discussions overarching CQ on pedagogies adopted, for example, the experiential education approaches (Tchaicha & Davis, 2005). A few others have highlighted the strength of such approaches in enhancing self-awareness (Lee, 1966) and in teaching management-related topics, such as negotiation, within a cultural framework (Weiss, 2003). The fundamental question of why cultural intelligence is to be taught to students and the compelling reason for them to acquire this knowledge and skills need to be reflected upon, thoroughly justified. The primary driver force is globalization where one must be trained, equipped to deal with people from varying culture as businesses rapidly expand overseas and the competency to develop, equip them with character and citizenship education (Goh, 2012).

Internationalization has also impacted teaching and learning within higher education institutes. Universities across the world are increasingly under intense pressure to equip more people with proficiencies that can be used efficiently in the knowledge economy (Naidoo & Jamieson, 2005).

2.4.1 Strategic-Tactical and Operational Levels

At the strategic-tactical level, globalization's effect could be experienced through the ripple effects and impact by triggering organizational change (Vaira, 2004). Consequences related to globalization and the knowledge economy have brought forth developments that apply pressures on universities to commodify teaching and learning and to "sell" it in the international educational marketplace (Naidoo & Jamieson, 2005). Therefore, academic success for institutions now shifts from being evaluated according to academic principles to being measured according to strict financial criteria such as the number of students enrolled and the amount of financial surplus created. This commodification has a significant impact on students' learning process and their commitment to the quality of learning they are exposed to.

For example, as argued by Naidoo and Jamieson (2005), technological advances associated with globalization that have given rise to virtual higher education are particularly vulnerable to the tendency for commodification. One of the primary reasons that could be tied to this would be that virtual education provides much easier and faster ways of gaining academic qualifications, sometimes compressing the duration of the course in higher education. This is tied to varying reasons of motive that enhances the business aspect of the institution rather than the academic rigour and standards to be upheld. Firstly, it could be attributed to the ease and convenience of distributing learning resources and materials electronically upon its production. Secondly, since learners can be easily located anywhere within an Internet connection, there is a high potential for saving physical space. Furthermore, required tutoring of lessons for the courses enrolled to be read and course assessments can be delivered much more thriftily through economies of scale. This makes virtual education highly attractive to both the higher education provider and the students who enrolled, the target group. Universities are also generally getting less access to public funds or require the meeting of much more stringent measures from the government. This could also explain of why they are attracted to such forms of learning and teaching and why any opportunities to produce teaching more economically are seized upon.

Globalization can also very well explain why many higher education institutes in non-native English-speaking countries are offering English-taught courses. China's increasing participation in the global economy and world affairs has sped up the development of education of English majors in China (Chang, 2006). Similarly, in Spain, multilingual internationalization is especially noticeable in bilingual universities such as the University of the Basque Country in Spain, where English-medium instruction is becoming more popular (Doiz et al., 2013) as well as Japan where there is increased pressure to provide entirely English-taught degree programmes (Huang, 2014).

2.4.2 *Increasing Cultural Diversity Within Student Populations*

Globalization and internationalization have resulted in higher education institutes being challenged with increasing cultural diversity. The surge of international students is an attribute of new globalized times (Doherty & Singh, 2005), due to varying reasons such as students wanting to have an overseas study exposure, expatriate parents being invited to work overseas and so on. The comprehension of different cultures is of paramount importance to be able to provide quality education across varying cultural contexts and situations. Higher education institutes could certainly do much more in educating and equipping their students for a globally connected and culturally diverse world (Asmar, 2005).

Although drawing criticisms by scholars in its categorization over the years, Hofstede's cultural dimensions (1981) primarily advocate those different countries are characterized by varying cultural dimensions. One such key challenge is dealing with the diverse learning styles which could be somewhat associated and correlated with varying viewpoints, norms, values, beliefs and other aspects within cultures. Interestingly culture has a significant effect in deciding a person's preference for abstract conceptualization compared to concrete experience (Joy & Kolb, 2009). This study also reported that individuals tend to have more abstract learning styles in countries that are high in in-group collectivism, institutional collectivism, uncertainty avoidance, future orientation and gender egalitarianism whereas individuals adopt more reflective learning styles in countries that are considered high in in-group collectivism, uncertainty avoidance and assertiveness. Hence, it is imperative for higher education institutes to be mindful of the cultural and social backgrounds of their students.

Hybridized universities are the output effects due to globalization. Studies have shown that most former colonies have inherited university models from their previous colonizers. However, Asian countries have not only adopted Western models of higher education, but they also have adapted models to suit local needs, sociocultural aspects and rapidly evolving market conditions. Hawkins (2013) pointed out modern universities in many Asian settings have been adapted that resulted in a mixture of indigenous elements overlaid with Western forms. These Asian customs were firmly established in the local context prior to Western intervention, hence would continue to prevail in vital aspects of social, cultural and educational happenings in the Asian region (Lee et al., 2017).

In the context of communication, Prescott and Hellstén (2005) emphasized the nuances of contextualized speech by identifying inferential characteristics that are otherwise considered hidden, inaccessible for inspection and scrutiny. These cultural readings of speech draw attention specifically on the importance of features that are crucial for executing socioculturally effective teaching and learning strategies for communication within international education.

2.5 Sociocultural Localized Context and Transnational Education

Besides the increased international students' mobility, transnational education has been a value proposition undertaken by higher education institutions to further advance their strategic positioning. As more institutions and programmes have collaborated in partnerships across borders, this strategic intervention becomes more prevalent. The term 'transnational education' is defined as a situation where the students pursuing an educational programme are located not in the country where the awarding institution is based (McBurnie & Ziguras, 2007). The formation of an international branch campus can affect a diverse range of stakeholders in both home and host countries. These stakeholders potentially would have varying inclination, where some are against the opening of the international branch campuses due to multiple reasons while others have some apprehension over the ways these campuses operate in another sociocultural setting. Questions as such arise: (a) Whether the quality and rigour of the programme could be maintained?; (b) how does the learning culture affect the learning design of the programme? Culture has an impact in effective management of transnational education. This could be validated as a study by Eldridge and Cranston (2009) discovered that between Australian and Thai universities, the cultural differences between these two institutions affects both the academic and operational management of their transnational higher education programmes.

Satisfying stakeholders is one of the core challenges of transnational education. For example, observations made on transnational education in Malaysia found that clashing stakeholder objectives, lack of clarity and good understanding on transnational education and discrepancies between policy versus implementation have brought about issues in the diverse areas of strategic management, administrative and logistics eco-system, operational controls that in due course affects the smooth execution of transnational education. While conflicts between institutional partners can affect collaborative partnerships, tensions among stakeholders within the same institution can also negatively affect that potentially lessen the benefits of partnership (Hill et al., 2014). The recognition of academic qualification, i.e. a joint degree, when the schools are in two different countries in transnational higher education can more challenging than a conventional degree as they do not belong to any single national higher education system rather a combination of both (Hou et al., 2017). But in a contrary, if these partnerships are of equally well-recognized and well-reputed institutions, then usually the recognition is viewed as the best from each side, for example, East and West.

Hence, it is important that higher education institutions have certain well-established processes and structures, plus competent leaders who will aid in their success when tackling foreign markets. Institutions that are flexible, quick to learn and have the competencies required to pilot organizational change are usually the institutions that have the greatest chances of success overseas (Wilkins, 2017). Higher education institutions need to continuously endeavour to fit in with their host cultures while concurrently to work towards in achieving academic freedom, improve local, social, political and legal conditions. One strategy that institutions have adopted to overcome precariousness and cultural distance between home and host countries is to work with partners based in the host country. Working with a local partner who have a much better understanding of the local environment would potentially help minimize the risks of setting up a campus abroad. Legitimacy could also be attained much faster when institutions avoid any actions that may be deemed culturally unacceptable.

We could predict that the potential outcome of culturally competent behaviour is a higher level of engaged and effective inter-sociocultural interaction. The next question is then to understand the specific behavioural indicators in action are. To address this question, literature points us to the research work performed on adaption to foreign culture (e.g. Richard & Brislin, 1981; Cushner & Brislin, 1996; Ruben & Kealey, 1979 and the expatriate adjustment, example Aycan, 1997). Leveraging from these research studies and what they have analysed, two primary characteristics of an effective intercultural interaction emerges, namely (a) individual personalized adaptation projecting positive experiences and well-being, experiencing comfort when engaging an individual from another culture, where there is no heightened level of anxiety in comparison to be dealing with an individual in their own cultural context; (b) good interpersonal relationships with culturally different others as relationships integrally dyadic in nature (Thomas et al., 2008).

2.6 Cross-Cultural Teaching

Cultural issues have become more prominent that require urgent attention in higher education (Palfreyman & McBride, 2007). With ever more diverse student populations, higher education institutions have been increasingly pressurized to internationalize their teaching, research and service-related activities (De Beuckelaer et al., 2012). In a study by Ballantyne et al. (1999) in Australia, the phrase "cross-cultural teaching and learning" was identified as one of several keywords or phrases that is used to contextualize and describe exemplary teaching by university academics. This is an example of the importance that cross-cultural teaching has gained that makes it inevitable and so essential in today's globalized higher education contexts and circumstances. Teachers need to empathize and comprehend that an imbalance in teaching and learning is created when the teacher teaches from one cultural point of view whereas the students' primary learning experiences come from another cultural dimension (Chávez & Longerbeam, 2016).

Literature does distinguish the key differences between Western and non-Western aspects of teaching and learning. The cultural differences encountered by staff at higher education institutes can be well-explained by Hofstede's model of cultural dimensions: (a) individualism–collectivism; (b) uncertainty avoidance; (c) power distance; (d) masculinity–femininity; (e) long-term or short-term orientation; and (f) indulgence or self-restraint (Bovill et al., 2014). Culture influences how students prefer their teachers to act and deliver the lessons. For example, in a study by Watkins (2000), British students depicted a good teacher as someone who can grab the students' interest, explain concepts clearly, use effective instructional techniques and facilitate a scope of learning activities, whereas the mainland Chinese students preferred the teacher to have deep knowledge, be able to answer questions and act as a good moral model (Rajaram, 2021).

Hence, the learning design and instructional techniques to be adopted for cross-cultural teaching should be carefully examined. Academic discussions advocate that there are multiple ways to approach cross-cultural teaching. Biggs (2001) distinguished three foci in cross-cultural teaching, namely a teacher can focus on student differences (are focused more the abilities and capacity of the student, the sociocultural backgrounds and so on); on instructional or teaching techniques (the different types of pedagogical approaches in terms of instructor-centred versus student-centred); and on students' learning processes (the interventions that enable students to enhance their learning abilities and competencies). The increase in diversity in the student profile has created both challenges and opportunities for universities to deliver an internationalized curriculum (Ryan, 2012). The following section will discuss the pedagogical practices and how they are perceived in different cultures. Further to that we would analyse the challenges instructors face when teaching and engaging students across cultures.

2.7 Pedagogical Learning Design: Learning Strategies and Instructional Techniques for Cross-Cultural Context

Pedagogical learning design is a key element that needs to be duly considered when the efficacy of cross-cultural learning and teaching is involved. Globalization has shaped homogeneous learning designs and pedagogic practices largely due to the influence of Western educational approaches in non-Western countries and societies

(Deng, 2011; Nguyen et al., 2009; Rajaram, 2021). However, Western pedagogical techniques may not necessarily fit into Eastern contexts, hence potentially cause cultural conflicts and mismatches. But a careful re-alignment with specific changes within the learning design enables the attainment of a much higher efficacy on the learning quality aspects and avoid mismatches due to cultural nuances. From the students' preference perspective, in fact, international students show a keen desire for curriculum internationalization. A study conducted by Cheng et al. (2016) found that Chinese students studying in Scottish and Australian universities wanted more international perspectives in the course contents.

Therefore, in the case of higher educational institutions with multicultural classrooms, culturally appropriate pedagogy becomes in-demand to cater to students from culturally diverse backgrounds (Zhao, 2007). This enables culturally sensitive learning environment to optimize the transnational students' learning outcomes (Wang & Moore, 2007). Moreover, the differences in teaching and learning preferences could be attributed to the varying cultures embedded with the different values and beliefs that impact behaviours.

The studies done on learning styles tend to centre around the dissimilarity between Asian, especially from Confucian Heritage Cultures (CHC), and Western samples (Eaves, 2011). Some scholars claim that higher cognitive abilities are able to be assessed via competitive assessments where Asian learners who are perceived to be compliant and favouring repetitive learning or memorization appear to outperform Western counterparts (Baumgart & Halse, 1999; Watkins & Biggs, 1996). This view is contradicting and in contrast to Western learning environments that prioritize metacognition, meaningful earning and outcomes that seek higher levels of cognitive functioning through a deep learning attitude over surface ones. We should not come to a conclusion with a few such research studies with limited or standalone samples, instead, take a more holistic view on how the learning process is carried out by identifying specific variables and its context.

The learning design and the type of pedagogical strategy that comprises instructional techniques should be mindfully selected to cater to the different styles of learning that vary across different cultures. In Charlesworth (2008)'s study, for example, she found that Indonesian students scored the lowest on the activist scale and highest on the reflector scale, whereas Chinese students scored the highest on the theorist scale and about the same on the activist scale as the Indonesians. On the pragmatist scale, the French sample shows a significantly higher score that sets them apart from their peers. Despite the general variations in learning styles, it is crucial to not generalize as learning styles can be influenced by other aspects such as subject discipline, perceived workload intensity and individual differences (Eaves, 2011). The following section will illustrate the pedagogic practices and their application in varying cultural contexts.

2.7.1 Virtual Learning

Virtual learning refers to online teaching that is exclusively done via synchronous and asynchronous modes. A vital aspect that needs to be managed in global virtual teams is the difference in the perceptions of time or time visions of members, that can affect team dynamics and success (Saunders et al., 2004). Every culture takes a different view on the aspect of time. For instance, American, Anglo-Saxon, Germanic and Scandinavian cultures tend to have a linear view of time and look at it as a limited commodity, while Japanese cultures view time as a gradual transition from one activity to another. Institutes that offer massive online open courses (MOOCs) or have online modules must take into account not only the discrepancies between foreign participants in their respective time zone, but also how to handle conflicting time visions.

In virtual learning, the type of information technology (IT) infrastructure adopted, operational platforms (e.g. Internet, learning management systems), and user-friendly resources are a few key elements to be duly considered. For example, in a study conducted with Maori (indigenous people of New Zealand), it was discovered that although they adopted and welcomed Western technology, majority do not have easy access to Internet access. Hence, in such situations and circumstances, it is key for Higher Education Institutes to provide appropriate support.

2.7.2 Flipped Classroom

In a flipped classroom, students are expected to be involved in prior learning, for example, watch instructional videos, read articles, attempt quizzes and do up the assigned pre-class tasks. Flipped learning is when direct instruction moves from class-oriented learning space to individual learning space and the class-oriented space is then transformed into an interactive learning space (Bergmann & Sams, 2014; Rajaram, 2019, 2021).

The active nature of flipped learning, especially during the in-class physical lessons or synchronous learning during virtual class has varying level of efficacy when measured across cultural contexts. Asian students, in particular those for Confucian Heritage Learners, are generally seen as timid and reluctant to ask questions or speak up (Ho, 2020). This is largely pointed to the fact that they are ingrained in the values of collectivism, refrain from speaking up and asserting their own personality, that can be perceived as breaking group norms and being defiant. On the similar vein, students from the west who are more individualistic, largely from low power distance and uncertainly avoidance culture tends to be more outspoken, asserting their differing views and projecting their own individualized personality.

2.7.3 Cooperative Learning

Cooperative learning involves students working on learning activities in small groups and acknowledged for their contributions and participations based on their group's performance. When we plan to execute this learning design, we must be mindful of how it will be for varying cultural profile of students. As Ghahraman and Tamimy (2017) rightfully pointed out that cultural nuances affect the efficacy of cooperative learning, where the needful must be appropriately adjusted to be culturally responsive.

A clear illustration could be primarily a mismatch that happens when applying Western cooperative learning methodology to Asia contexts without any changes or adjustments to be applied to the Asian contexts. In such cases, factors that require perhaps different emphasis on leadership and group composition need to be focused on. In a similar vein, mainland Chinese learners tend to work well in groups largely because of the collectivist mentality where they tend mostly to suppress their personal interests, avoid confrontation and criticize their peers (Nguyen et al., 2006; Rajaram, 2010; Rajaram & Bordia, 2011). In contrary, evidence points out to show that the efficacy of group dynamics for the same group of students does shift if they are exposed to a learning culture (either locally or overseas) that emphasis or rewards on individualist behavioural interventions over a prolonged phase (Rajaram, 2013, 2021; Rajaram & Bordia, 2013; Rajaram & Collins, 2013).

2.7.4 Blended Learning

Blended learning is defined by scholars (Maarop & Embi, 2016; Rajaram, 2021) as a teaching and learning approach comprises of a combination of traditional face-to-face learning and distributed learning, with an emphasis on online instructional approaches. In the unprecedented and rapid changing learning climate, Rajaram (2021) advocated a new definition of how blended learning has to be visualized and executed. He advocated that blended learning must also be performed from a fully virtual mode, where the face-to-face in-class learning will be equated to synchronous mode of learning (i.e. virtual face-to-face real-time) and asynchronous online learning serves to address the portion away from the classroom. The adoption of active blended learning help to establish student-centric learning that empowers learners, shifting from traditional teaching models (Lomer & Anthony-Okeke, 2019), where it is viewed as a preferred approach, considering face-to-face communication and collaborative work are seen as essential in Asia (Latchem & Jung, 2009) and beyond internationally.

Hence, the primary question is how a physical or virtual face-to-face session could be evaluated as effective or high in terms of quality efficacy when examined form cultural dimensional aspects? This requires the necessary cultural nuances and aspects to be incorporated within the learning design so that its effectiveness and engagement of the students could be enhanced. For example, when the profile of students is inclined towards more of the collective-oriented nature that comprises introverts, then enabling students to blog or leveraging on platforms for them to write to express their thoughts by means of class participation results in a much higher rate of engagement. These students are provided a secured platform where their active intellectual participation can be well-acknowledged and recognized. By not addressing these minor yet vital aspects may potentially undermine the 'silent' stereotype causing them to be disengaged that causes negative repercussions in their learning process.

2.7.5 Experiential Learning

Experiential learning involves learning from experience or learning by doing. Experiential learning primarily immerses learners in an encounter and promotes reflection on the experience to acquire new skills, behaviours or ways of thinking.

These experiential learning techniques are appropriate in closing the "gap" between classroom and real-world practice (Valentine & Speece, 2002), in the West. When this pedagogical learning design was extended to undergraduate courses in Asia, the students appreciated the experience and receptivity was generally affirmative. This suggests that experiential learning methods do work in non-Western cultures as well. Nonetheless, in the Asian context, the specific aspects of the learning design need to be modified somewhat taking the sociocultural aspects into due consideration to have it function effectively, while ensuring the modifications or adaptations should not be too radical that moves away from the core emphasis of the pedagogical value proposition. In most experiential learning methods, small group work is already an aspect and as such becomes very compatible with Asian sociocultural norms. In Western higher education institutions, these modifications can be well extended to appeal to international students from Asian countries and beyond.

2.8 Enhancing Learning Efficacy Through Pedagogical Learning Design

The pedagogical learning and teaching practices adopted do assist teachers in higher education to develop cultural intelligence (CQ) competencies and skills in students. Goh (2012) provides suggestions of classroom activities that build on the four capabilities of CQ (Van Dyne et al., 2010), namely drive (motivational CQ), knowledge (cognitive CQ), strategy (metacognitive CQ) and action (behavioural CQ). For example, to instil the aspects of motivational CQ, the learning activity would enable students to experience and resonate the direct benefits of being multiculturally and globally literate, while an activity that utilizes CQ strategy uses case studies to promote higher order and sophisticated thinking.

A study by Ramsey and Lorenz (2016) pointed out that CQ is a skill that could be learned and acquired in a classroom context. Students who were surveyed reading a cross-cultural management (CCM) course in a master's in business administration (MBA) programme were found to have their level of CQ increased after the course. The CQ was positively correlated to students' level of satisfaction of the course. Higher education institutions should offer a wide ranging of cultural training to prepare students for a globalized career path. Universities need to acknowledge the challenges faced in designing CCM courses. For example, the programmes tend to rely too much on delivering knowledge or the cognitive aspect of CQ rather than training on relevant skills associated with the metacognitive aspects of CQ. There is a high tendency to prescribe the national cultural values and behaviours of individuals of that culture that it is operating on. There tends to be a lack of focus and specificity in the type of training each individual needs or requires. Hence, universities should aim to cover all four aspects of CQ to fully leverage optimize the potential of CCM courses.

Virtual developments should also be duly considered. A study conducted by Erez et al. (2013) discovered the possibility to enhance CQ through active participation in a virtual multicultural team project where it was reported that global training programmes can improve participant's CQ. Hence, this could be one of the strategies higher education institutes that offer massive online open courses (MOOC) enable CQ development without necessarily having their students travel abroad. Aside this, culture-in-context learning can also be facilitated virtually by using serious games (Schumacher & Festing, 2020). The process of higher-order cognitive thinking and exchanges of perspective through such simulated gamification allows CQ skills to be developed.

2.9 Challenges in Cross-Cultural Teaching

Varying challenges may potentially arise when teachers engage in cross-cultural teaching. The comprehension of these potential setbacks is vital so that it enables teachers to be better aware hence much prepared to navigate and deal with evolving challenges. In the following section, we will be examining cross-cultural aspects that focuses on international students in higher education institutes.

2.9.1 Communication

Whenever educators discuss issues pertaining to teaching international students, they tend to generally be inclined or some more emphasis on language competency than on any other issues (Robertson et al., 2000). For example, in Western-based universities, where English language is used as the language of instruction, teachers struggle communicating to international students who are not native English speakers (Carroll & Ryan, 2005). Transnational students may be unfamiliar with the local language used. Although generally, majority of students go through and had to pass standardized English exams such as IELTS (International English Language Testing System), the qualifying basic test certainly differs quite distinctively from the standard of English used for reading a course at the university level.

Even if students from diverse cultural backgrounds have an adequate competency level in the English language, the style and slang in which they communicate will often vary. The different ways they speak and write in their own culture and language get largely transferred directly when they use the English language. This puts the pressure on educators to empathize, resonate, listen more, comprehend the difficulties foreign students may potentially face when it comes to verbal and written communication. Further to that, aside from grammar and vocabulary, other aspects of communication such as intonation, body language and presentation styles may also be possibly overlooked (Cortazzi & Jin, 2002).

2.9.2 Assessment

The approach in assessing students' learning is another issue that requires deep reflection and pondering when it is examined from a cross-cultural context. To enhance the efficacy in evaluating students, we need to comprehend the differences in attitudes and outlook taken towards learning between students from varying sociocultures. For example, the preference for written exams versus coursework; high level of strictness versus moderate level of strictness (i.e. some level of leniency applied). For example, Austrians generally adopt a more lenient approach towards plagiarism or cheating whereas German students have a much stronger preference for written exams and have a preference towards a mix of different types of assessments (Apfelthaler et al., 2007). Evidence also points out that students who share similar learning styles tend to have similar assessment preferences across cultures. For example, a study in a United Kingdom (UK) university found that domestic and foreign students have more preference for coursework and were less inclined towards examinations (Bartram & Bailey, 2010).

2.9.3 Class Participation

Research scholar Rajaram (2021) defines class participation as follows:

> Class participation as a learning pedagogy enables students to speak up, express themselves, ask questions in class, by facilitating through an open and easy platform that lessens communication barrier. This mode of instruction allows students to learn to express their opinions and to exchange perspectives with others. Moreover, class participation serves as an interactive and reflective platform to engage both the instructors and peers to discuss the topics covered at a much greater depth. (p. 84)

The aspect of class participation for international students' participation in Anglo-Western universities has been discussed widely in the literature (Straker, 2016). The level of commitment to learning, the intensity of participation in class discussions and the level of enthusiasm to partake in intellectual conversations normally vary among students. Hence, this creates the challenge for teachers to inspire, motivate and engage students while at the same time not cast aside lesser experienced or introverted students who are wary about speaking up (Ituarte & Davis, 2007; Rajaram, 2021). It is theorized that greater consciousness of social boundaries is reflected in Eastern cultures that may be the root cause of this reservation. While most students from Western cultures share similar alphabets, clothing style and religious beliefs, Asian students from various countries such as India, China and Thailand often have less to relate to, and so the transition from a collectivist culture to a more individualistic one may be much more challenging for them. Thus, international students do not only have to overcome language barriers but also the dissimilarities in the cultural ways locals interact with one another. Besides this, another potential reason for the lack of class participation of international students, particularly Asian students in Western higher education institutes, could be primarily due to language anxiety. The relationship between language competency and class participation was significant for both language anxiety and fear of negative evaluation (Lee, 2007). Other cultural differences such as gender and age could also possibly impact the level of class participation. For example, students may feel exasperated by students who put in lesser efforts in their academic studies compared to their intense involvement social activities. Students who are younger in age compared to slightly older aged students may also feel intimidated to participate in front of more matured students for fear of revealing their lack of experience or simply have a different outlook or perspective due to their exposure. This could be explained as some countries require individuals slightly longer years to complete their high school education or have certain national service requirements to be fulfilled, for example, in Singapore, males have to complete their national service after their high school before their university education.

2.9.4 Differences in Learning Orientation

There are varying distinctive differences in the design and process of learning when examined across varying nationalities. We could term it as the learning culture and culture of learning. Learning culture "should not be understood as the context or environment within which learning takes place, rather the progressive outcome through the learning and social practices that are being embedded in the learning design" (Rajaram, 2021, p. 251), whereas culture of learning can be defined as the advocated, accepted behavioural norms and values of learners in a certain setting that could be clustered as national culture, institutional sub-culture, or even more specific groups that sub-cultures could potentially exist. Many of these aspects are interrelated to differences in power and status. The differences in learning styles and preferences can be attributed to the cultural dimensions that can be ascribed to different countries. For example, students from collectivist countries were more positively inclined to working in groups that are somewhat homogenous. These dissimilarities vary from country to country. In Singapore, for example, a combination of low uncertainty avoidance, high power distance and medium masculinity make students very competitive and risk-taking. They, therefore, are very proactive in their own growth on education and enjoy partaking in discussions with their teacher. They are alright with working hard and going beyond the required scope of classes. Hence, if teachers are more inclined towards being timid and adopt a differential behaviour with students, they may feel challenged and disparaged. Whereas in Thailand, the learning culture can be categorized to be low in terms of individualism, where students dislike to stand out among others. Therefore, a teacher must well comprehend these cultural implications and nuances by having them incorporated in the learning design and in adopting the correct mix of instructional techniques and nuances to better cater to transnational students.

2.9.5 Facilitating Cross-Cultural Group Work

Teachers play a significant role in structuring interaction between students from diverse backgrounds (Arkoudis et al., 2012). There must be a thought through scaffolded design and process in facilitating this diverse group of students. General challenges about cross-cultural group work are often misconstrued as stemming from merely only students' cultural diversity. These issues primarily arise due to the complexity of cross-cultural group work itself, from students' lack of skills in working in such situational context, but largely from the inappropriate ways in which group work is organized and assessed. For example, a good number of teachers use group work as a way to handle and deal with large numbers of students rather than an intended strategy to enhance their learning process and achieve better learning outcomes. Some common mistakes include devising tasks that are better off when done individually, setting the numbers in a group not to be too large not anticipating inevitable conflicts and unprepared to deal with those conflicts.

An example to illustrate the conflict occurrences will be domestic students blaming international students in the same group for pulling their grades down due to their quality of work, or unequal contributions, the varying norms and values that emerges when working as a team together, different outlook or approach taken in terms of expressing ideas and perceived notions or where the importance and emphasis are placed. On the flip side, international students may feel upset that their ideas or contributions are ignored or if they are forced to work with local students who lack motivation and diligence. These dissatisfactions are intertwined to language competence and disagreements arising from cross-cultural misunderstandings. They can be interpreted as incompetence, arrogance and correlated with negative connotations.

2.9.6 Use of Technology

The degree of usage, adoption and sophistication of technology in higher education institutes has been progressively increasing. The competency in using the advanced computer systems, applications and technological interventions by students provided by higher education institutes is vital in determining its accessibility and adoption. For newcomers, there will be a lack of familiarity with the hardware and technical terms associated with the technological platforms and computers. Likewise in other new situations, there will be a phase of initiation to go through, that follows a potentially a steep learning curve. Aside from regional diversity aspects, teachers should consider socioeconomic and age diversity aspects among their students as well, and how these interventions affect their capacity to engage with technology in their pursuit of their studies.

In a study, Huang et al. (2019) discovered that the cultural values and beliefs of the Chinese and Spanish university teachers influenced their decision to use technology. The study also highlighted that the take-up rate of the technology by the teachers is largely determined by how important it is to the students, and how they perceived interest and inclination to that. This echoes the student-centred pedagogical inclination that is adopted in both China and Spain.

2.9.7 Student-Teacher Relationships

There has been a considerable amount of research work done on the relationship between educators and international students. The key point that we would like to establish is that the cultural element in a teaching and learning setting plays a vital role to be duly considered. This consideration of culture applies across (a) efficacy in terms of student engagement for learning and social well-being; (b) perceived notion of values, qualities of a good teacher and role model where students are inspired of;

and (c) the approach to develop trust and professional bonding. We could illustrate this with some specific occurrences. For example, supervising international students may require more time, efforts and skills than supervising local students, where in a study by Brown and Atkins (1988), they pointed out this very point by comparing it to a sample of local British students. On a similar vein, in terms of preference towards teacher-student relationships, evidence indicates that British-oriented learners prefer their teachers to be patient and sympathetic for students who has difficulty following the lesson whereas the mainland Chinese students will consider their relationship with a good teacher to be one that is friendly, approachable and warm beyond the classroom. We could acknowledge that such add-on demands and workload, more than often cause problems for both these international students and their supervisors. The key issue emerges from the perceived level of adjustment either of them are expected to make due to a certain degree of cultural influence. We could simply make sense of this by relating to cultural values that emphasise to be more individualistic and masculine on their sociocultural values in having their views asserted versus more collective and feminine on their sociocultural values in having them expressed. This implies and potentially would cause a mismatch of expectations inline to their academic roles and responsibilities (Macrae, 2002).

To address the key challenges on cross-cultural teaching, the following recommendations are proposed, that is presented in Table 2.3—An instructional guide on practice-oriented strategies for cross-cultural teaching and facilitation. These are collated and successfully validated via positive outcomes through years of observations, engagements and vast experience teaching, facilitating in varying cross-cultural settings.

2.10 Multicultural Teaching Efficacy

To train students and equip them with CQ, teachers themselves must be well equipped and to teach with cultural intelligence. That means that how culturally intelligent our students become is a function of a teachers' own level of cultural intelligence. It is important to clarify this idea here. In my years of teacher preparation, I have never encountered a teacher whose personal goal is to teach in a culturally unintelligent manner. Similarly, it seems obviously shallow and disappointing to not expect our students to be multiculturally educated and globally engaged as end products of a primary and secondary education. No one enters the teaching profession to teach like a racist or to intentionally express bigotry. Neither do we take pride in students who develop myopic or narrow views of the world. But because the culturally diverse demographics of classrooms today create frequent value conflicts, it is not difficult to conduct oneself in a manner that unintentionally offends or, at worst, discriminates students from cultural backgrounds different than our own. Bonk et al. (2005) make it clear that shifting country and classroom demographics around the world requires all teachers to be prepared to teach diverse learners.

Table 2.3 An instructional guide on practice-oriented strategies for cross-cultural teaching and facilitation

Strategies for cross-cultural teaching	
Challenges	Validated practice-oriented recommendations
Communication	• Teachers are to reflect and comprehend the explicit differences from the cognitive and behavioural aspects that arises when engaging the culturally diverse groups of students • Teachers are to be aware of how both verbal and non-verbal forms of communication may differ from culture to culture. This could possibly lead to or affect teachers' and students' comprehension of each other's communication and work. Despite passing standardized languages tests that are stipulated for, educators should not jump to the conclusion that international students are instantly capable of communicating or verbally articulating at a university standard, especially if the course is very technical and comprised of complicated terminologies • Teachers are to understand the communication styles adopted for learning by students in that culture and how teaching techniques that have been effective. This enables teachers to understand learners' preferences, perceived learning effectiveness, their beliefs, conjectures and cultural norms ingrained as behavioural, habitual acts • Teachers are to be mindful in making conclusions about cultural variations to students who represent that culture. Teachers should be sensitive to the cultural profile of students. They need to acknowledge that these students are not that culture as not every individual conforms to all cultural nuances and trends. Teachers need to be aware that the cultural generalizations themselves differ in how they are viewed, experienced and realized according to the circumstance and context applied. Hence, a strategy would be to cluster students to have a broad sense of the larger divide that enables teachers to develop a more customized way of teaching, acknowledging the variations • Students are to be strongly encouraged to participate in language and communication-related self-improvement workshops offered by the university. In the spirit of enhancing and advocating for diversity, students could also be provided varying avenues or appropriate options to upskill themselves progressively on such cross-cultural language courses • Engage students and teachers on their expectations and perceived quality level, rigour, effectiveness of teaching: For example, what are their expectations on teachers and students' roles, tutorials, seminars, lectures, quality work, written reports • Observe the behaviours and communication styles, i.e. how they talk and listen to each other and to their teachers. Identify the explicit sociocultural aspects, for example: Questioning style, the approach taken on agreeing versus disagreeing, how key perspectives are articulated as well as the process of its discourse, the intonation, level of specificity, how the teamwork is played out, the level of being authentic the level of respect shown, attitudes, approach to authority, critical review and evaluation, the level of authenticity, innovativeness and creativity and the level, role of memorization • Adopt an open mindset, practice synergy and collaboration: The core intervention is to comprehend the learning culture and culture of learning in context. Primarily, observe, comprehend the style, approach adopted in both teachers' and students' thought-process, communication methods, styles, their perceived notions and preferences. Engage and assist them to emphasize, resonate, understand and imperatively appreciate each other's cultures. Reflect and ponder on how the current learning and teaching approaches could be tweaked or improvised to have these cultural nuances, expectations incorporated • Propose to the schools to allow the use of e or manual dictionaries during timed exams to reduce the stress on international students should they come across a word they do not understand as it is not a test on their language rather subject contents • Propose and seek necessary permission to record lectures and seminars/tutorials so that international students are able to revisit and listen to contents covered that they may not have understood during the live session

(continued)

Table 2.3 (continued)

Strategies for cross-cultural teaching	
Challenges	Validated practice-oriented recommendations
Assessment	• Incorporate quality and well-guided verbal and written English language courses as the connecting bridge before these international students qualify to read their mainstream courses • Teachers and learning course designers should undergo appropriate training to comprehend the epistemological foundations of Western-based education that covers the social-cultural values, beliefs and norms of international students. On the students' side, they are to be made aware and educated on the context, nature, creation & value of the sociocultural knowledge, rather than merely asked to follow rules of behaviour without the rationale being understood. Primarily a structured and scaffolded eco-system is to be put in place to render assistance and guidance to students as deemed appropriate • Teachers should engage students' feedback, understand their concerns and explain the rationale on the type of assessment adopted • Institutions should highlight the type of assessment each of the courses in the programme that has been put in place during the course phase selection, so that students are aware and much better prepared beforehand. This may cause students to focus more on getting good grades over pursuing a course that they are interested in. However, this could be potentially mitigated if teachers can inspire and spark interests in them if they are initially uninterested
Class Participation	• An appropriate learning system or process has been modelled to have the experience of students validated, taken the language usage and proficiency into due consideration and the teachers to be equipped with the competency to facilitate authentic exchanges among learners ensuring that they feel secured, comfortable in contributing and sharing their thoughts • Teachers should continuously try to review and explore contemporary techniques that have high efficacy in terms of engagement, learning effectiveness across varying cultural contexts which enables students to actively participate and contribute in class (i.e. via both oral and written modes) • Teachers should not equate reluctance to speak up as incapability. Students may simply feel anxious or shy, for example, "lose face" or being judged by others. Hence, teachers should encourage students to step out of their comfort zone by enabling a "safe" learning environment to reduce this anxiety
Facilitating Cross-cultural Group Work	• Teachers are to devise clear instructions on the grouping criteria where there is a good spread of international and local students, rather than having them placed singly in groups alone or in only a few groups. Empower the students to form their own groups but with strict and clear requirements on the diversity aspects to be addressed. They could confirm their final decisions with the teachers to serve as a validation of the process and meeting the requirements. By this, there is a good balance of providing them autonomy but to work within stipulated rules to be adhered by • The group size should be in the range of four to six, should not be too big that reduces the efficacy of group work. However, when the diversity of the group is very high, then it is advisable to keep the group size smaller • Teachers are to encourage self-reflection and curiosity among students from different cultures. This should help to facilitate an open dialogue where international students can discuss, exchange their thoughts and share their own cultural values, norms to explore how to best work together navigating the differences • Teachers are to be mindful, aware and sensitive to potential conflicts and acknowledge the areas that are not necessarily easy to collaborate and work together. Hence, teachers should engage these students and explore how to assist by providing the required interventions • Pedagogical strategies such as service and experiential learning are advocated to enhance the authenticity of group work that facilitates students to be exposed to practical, social, cultural and educational aspects where it allows engagement with others who have not interacted with others different from themselves. Such natural occurrences, exchanges, self-conflict resolutions enhance cross-cultural 'know-hows', build-up relationships and to work around the challenges that embeds within the context

(continued)

Table 2.3 (continued)

Strategies for cross-cultural teaching	
Challenges	Validated practice-oriented recommendations
Differences in Learning Orientation	• Teachers should acknowledge and be sensitive that different cultures learn differently and to have an open-mind, practice flexibility on the adjustments, adaptive responses with agility that they could possibly make in the classrooms to facilitate and accommodate the learning styles • Teachers should avoid clustering cultures as "Western" or "non-Western" as there are significant cultural variations in countries within those categories • Teachers, especially in partnership with the diverse profile of students, should be encouraged to make thorough and continuous review on topics such as teachers as experts versus the role of partnership in learning focusing on student-centred teaching, collaborative group work versus individual work, application-based learning versus memorization or rote-inclined learning, open communication (individualistic culture) versus group or acceptable views basis (collective culture), the emphasis and inclination towards oral/verbal versus written course work • Institutions should mindfully create their culture of learning and learning culture, carefully identifying the influencing factors that emerges from both internal and external environments of higher education institutions. The type of emphasis in learning and pedagogical approaches may not necessarily be by the faculty but potentially influenced by the varying interactions with the learners, learning environment, climate, external learning community, expert advocates and so on. Hence, it is imperative to have a broader perspective by looking beyond the narrow view of individual views or approaches adopted
Use of Technology	• Learners are to be exposed to the identified learning technologies at the early phase itself and have them use it • A peer support approach should be adopted. The more experienced or senior students who have used these learning technologies could possibly guide the new or less experienced ones. This enables the transfer of 'know-hows' to be facilitated more effectively as these senior students know the challenges, hence able to empathize and resonate while training, equipping them the essentials • Teachers should be aware of the rapid changing landscape of higher education. As the urgency and need increase for varying reasons to incorporate online asynchronous and synchronous learning, it becomes more crucial to ensure students are well prepared and equipped with the skills to be engaged, learn more effectively • Teachers have to be aware of students who may not have the means to effectively study online
Student–Teacher Relationships	• Different cultures have different expectations on how the professional relationship between the students and teachers transpires. The expectations, for example, in terms of the direct involvement versus empowered or more autonomy-inclined approach, the power distance (low versus high) that exists or at least perceived by the two stakeholders, the roles, responsibilities and how these should be carried out in execution and so on. Hence, it is essential to ensure teachers make it clear on their role and involvement in the student's learning journey from the beginning to minimize the possibility of any misunderstandings that may occur

Teaching efficacy is the level of a teacher's conviction and belief on his or her capacity to influence students' performance. Teaching efficacy is a type of self-efficacy and a cognitive process where individuals construct beliefs about their capacity to perform at a given level of attainment (Tschannen-Moran et al., 1998). However, in a multicultural context, varying other factors have to be duly considered in determining the level of efficacy of a teacher's performance. Hence, multicultural efficacy can be defined as the teaching performance in a cross-cultural context and the level of teacher's confidence in such teaching contexts. This competency of multicultural efficacy is vital in facilitating cross-cultural classrooms embedded with varying social-cultural nuances (Kang et al., 2019).

Teaching efficacy has a strong positive correlation to students' achievements (Ashton & Webb, 1986; Dembo & Gibson, 1985; Silverman, 2008) and to lesson designs in regard to students' abilities, cultures and interests (Dilworth, 2004; McCown et al., 1996). Multicultural efficacy generally goes beyond multicultural attitudes largely because being equipped with them does not necessarily mean that a teacher can apply effectively them in a classroom context (Guyton & Wesche, 2005). Studies show that higher levels of self-efficacy help to mediate levels of stress and burnout in teachers (Schwarzer & Hallum, 2008). This emerges as a highly relevant factor, correlated directly to the 'diversity-related burnout' aspect among teachers in dealing with culturally diverse learners (Tatar & Horenczyk, 2003). The importance weighed on multicultural teaching efficacy could be intertwined to the fact that teachers play a vital role to teach cultural intelligence to develop culturally intelligent students (Goh, 2012). Hence, by simply modifying curriculum designs and applying new pedagogical methods may not be adequate to prepare students for a global workforce. Hence, teachers have to be sufficiently capable of managing global cross-cultural classrooms.

There is a disconnect between the multicultural self-efficacy, attitudes of teachers and their understanding of multiculturalism (Strickland, 2018). Evidence shows that there was an inconsistency between high multicultural self-efficacy and positive multicultural attitudes, with teachers' responses related to their conceptualization of multiculturalism. This implies the existence of colour-blind racist attitudes which involves seeing people as the same and ignoring racial identity (Bonilla-Silva, 2006).

In the similar vein of having scales in measuring teaching efficacy, scales measuring a teacher's sense of multicultural efficacy can be used to compare with educational outcomes (Silverman, 2008). Table 2.4 presents a brief description on frameworks and the items used to measure multicultural teaching efficacy.

2.11 Measurement of Multicultural Teaching Efficacy: Frameworks and Scales

The multicultural efficacy scale (MES), based on Bennett (1990), was further built upon by Guyton and Wesche (2005). It comprises of four dimensions of a conceptual

Table 2.4 Frameworks for measuring multicultural teaching efficacy

Frameworks	Source	Description
Multicultural Efficacy Scale (MES)	Guyton and Wesche (2005)	35 items categorized into 3 subscales: Experience, attitude and efficacy. There is an additional item which classifies the participants in accordance with what they view as the core purpose of multicultural teaching
The Teachers' Sense of Multicultural Efficacy Scale (TSMES)	Silverman (2008)	15 items that can be arranged into 2 factors: Individual-based items and society-based items
Teacher Efficacy Scale for Classroom Diversity (TESCD)	Kitsantas (2012)	10 items that address the different situations that a teacher may encounter in the classroom (e.g. language differences, ethnic distinctions and so on)

model of multicultural teacher framework and other conceptions of multiculturalism for a content framework. The motivation on the development of this scale is to measure the complexity of the progress of multicultural education. 665 undergraduates and graduate teacher education students from several geographic regions across the United States contributed in validating the MES. 160 items were placed into one of five subscales (Guyton & Wesche, 2005). After multiple rounds of testing and prototyping, the data was reduced to 35 items and three subscales which are experience, attitude and efficacy. Experience is a derivation of information, enabling surveyors to compare results but not affecting the scoring of multicultural efficacy. Attitude is tied to situations connected to race relations and preferences of classroom diversity. Efficacy is crucial to the convictions of teachers in their effectiveness of addressing multicultural issues.

The teacher's sense of multicultural efficacy scale (TSMES) provides a way to assess teacher efficacy explicitly for educating diverse students and for education on diversity issues, and offer potential explanations on educational inequity (Silverman, 2008). Beliefs of self-efficacy are derived from behavioural relations, individual characteristics and the environment according to the claims by Silverman (2008). 152 pre-service teachers from a range of undergraduate programmes at a university in the United States were used to validate this framework. The development of the scale's item was based on the concept that teachers require to have relevant skills to teach cross-cultural students. Items of the TSMES were reduced to 15 items from 110 items and 15 general demographic questions. These items are categorized as individual-based items and societal-based items. When it comes to individual-based multicultural education, teachers feel more efficacious as compared to society-based multicultural education. This evidence implies that beyond the classroom contexts, teachers do not realize their capability to affect any of the identified specific factors.

The teacher efficacy scale for classroom diversity (TESCD) was developed by Kitsantas (2012). The items utilized to measure efficacy is prevalent in highly diverse classrooms to assess the confidence in the ability to find a solution over utilizing culturally appropriate teaching techniques. The sample size used for this study comprises of 417 participants, of whom those included were diverse with pre-service teachers from major ethnic groups in the United States, such as Caucasian, African American, Hispanic and Asian. Scenarios were built based on the academic literature on cultural diversity and students' diversity. These scenarios were adopted as they encouraged teachers to think beyond their extent of self-efficacy in various cultural situations. The scenario items were eventually reduced to four from 14 where each item required teachers to experience a situation compromising cultural diversity. The participants were asked to indicate how confident they would be in effectively handling the respective situational circumstances based on a scale ranging from 0 to 100.

We have examined three varying multicultural efficacy scales, the items used and the type of measurement it focuses on. Multicultural teaching is a complex concept that is affected by a multitude of elements, hence qualitative measures such as interviews and evaluations can certainly help support results from the use of these frameworks. We could resonate this fundamentally to the fact that self-efficacy may not necessarily be the exact representation of the cross-cultural teaching competency of teachers. Further to that, the frameworks were largely developed and tested in Western countries with largely homogeneous, apart from the TESCD sample sizes of participants are mainly from European descent. Hence, its applicability to other cultural contexts is not distinctly investigated in the studies. To validate this point, we could point an example, say the study by Gorski et al. (2012) found that White and other race participants displayed higher levels of efficacy compared to African American participants. Thus, it is vital to consider the varying intervening elements together the evolution of teaching since the conceptions of these frameworks and how these aspects affect or influence the multicultural teaching efficacy. For example, the prominence of online learning and distance learning may potentially influence a teacher's sense of multicultural efficacy.

2.12 Student Engagement: Cross-Cultural Learning Contexts

There has been much debate among scholars about the precise nature of student engagement, explicitly due to the lack of distinction between the state of engagement, it's antecedents and consequences (Kahu, 2013). Despite this, most could agree that the underlying construct of student engagement is based on the premise that it is related to students' effective usage of their time and energy (Pike et al., 2011). In classrooms, student engagement can be linked to the extent to which students participate in purposeful learning activities (Leask & Carroll, 2011). Conceptually, student engagement can be categorized as is multidimensional (Bowden et al., 2019; Fredricks et al., 2004; Kahu, 2013). Student engagement comprises of four distinct yet interrelated dimensions, namely affective, social, behavioural and cognitive engagement (Bowden et al., 2019). These four dimensions are intertwined and are collective at work to motivate a student's striving, persistence and retention.

Evidence states that student engagement is positively correlated to learning outcomes (Foster & Rahinel, 2008; Pike et al., 2011). Those involved in post-secondary education would generally agree that enhancing student engagement impact student's success and subsequently, society (Foster & Rahniel, 2008). This is supported by a research study that explains the role that tertiary experiences play in shaping students' general well-being that has an impact on the collective societal well-being (Bowden et al., 2019). Students' success is influenced by a multitude of factors as it is not so straightforward and easy to determine the type of institutional strategies to improve engagement that would have an impact on the academic and industry performance as a whole (Foster & Rahniel, 2008). As majority of the engagement measures are devised at the broad institutional level, this potentially contributes to the "gap", explicitly the lack of clarity in the role of the teacher. Teachers have a large influence to improve their success in both the classroom and industry. This could be done by creating opportunities to participate and collaborate with peers, providing time to discuss concepts and answer questions and creating challenging assignments that require students to analyse information and make judgements. We must acknowledge that the benefits of cultural diversity will not come into fruition without any intervention. Higher education institutes place too much emphasis on expecting that the benefits would naturally manifest with much lesser emphasis on strategic and informed intervention to enhance inclusion and engagement (Leask & Carroll, 2011).

Engagement with international students increases the cross-cultural learning among the students as well as the institute's community (Arthur, 2017). Opportunities to develop students' intellectual and social engagement increase the sense of belonging to the host institution. Building an inclusive environment for all students is imperative. Forging friendships between domestic and international students should be advocated and encouraged as it reduces the feel of loneliness and homesickness among the international students. The environments in higher education institutions play a crucial role in shaping student attitudes and behaviours towards their diverse profile of peers. Studies show that engagement is a learned behaviour, hence by having it facilitated among diverse students, institutions can create the conditions to promote developmental change.

It is vital to comprehend how engagement of international students varies from one cultural group to another. In a comparative study between American students and international students, it was found that compared to White and Black international students, Asian international students were less engaged in active and collaborative learning and diversity-related activities (Zhao et al., 2005). The satisfaction level on the quality of their campus environment is also lower than the other two groups. Hence, teachers should not generalize all international students, rather they should take due consideration on the varying cultures they come from. The study also reported that the international students' density had positive effects on diversity-related experiences as well as improved aspects of students' engagement, for example, perceptions of the campus environment. This could be related to the likelihood of international students sourcing friends of similar backgrounds and facilitating a strong foundation to build a social support system. As studies support the notion of engagement being a learned behaviour, this makes it possible for institutions to facilitate developmental change. Hall et al. (2010) mentioned that those who had past experiences interacting with people from outside their culture before entering university were more predisposed in engaging international students. Higher education institutes should continue to work on building the cross-cultural competencies of their staff and students. The efforts or approaches should also be continued beyond classrooms, perhaps in a social setting, for example, service learning, fieldwork projects and even networking or informal events. Effective cross-cultural engagements occur in both the informal and formal curriculums (Leask & Carroll, 2011). The formal curriculum revolves around the planned and sequenced programme of teaching and learning organized around defined contents and assessed in varying ways. On the flip side, the informal curriculum refers to the various extra-curricular activities that take place within campus. Besides engagement on cultural variation in class, engagement in campus life plays a key role in the retention and success of international students (Glass et al., 2017). Contrast to the concept of student engagement is student disengagement. Disengagement occurs when students choose to reject learning opportunities or prefer not to be involved mindfully in the learning process. Dean and Jolly (2012) reported that learning activities can cause cognitive dissonance in students. Their study reported that the contributing cause could be due to the differences in learning environment norms, racial norms, economic class norms and other intertwined factors. Some coping mechanisms may help them manage anxiety and allow them to engage in activities but this may not always be the case.

Next, we shall discuss the challenges faced by teachers and students in a cross-cultural context and environment that may potentially result in disengagement of students.

2.12.1 Differences in Learning Styles

Students from various cultures have different learning styles (Ladd & Ruby Jr., 1999; Wong, 2004). In a cross-cultural setting, teachers have to address students who have differing preferences towards learning. Addressing and aligning to culturally driven learning styles of students is essential to encourage students' interest that enables personal interactions between the students and teachers to occur (Bhattacharyya & Shariff, 2014).

Different learning styles are viewed as a challenge because it impacts how a learning activity is experienced (Kolb, 1984). For example, teachers who are committed to experiential learning design approaches may make assumptions that such activities would result in positive involvement on all students. However, this is not the case as activities such as simulations were not helpful for those who adopts the "abstract conceptualizer" learning style, whereas it is helpful for those who are inclined to the "concrete experiencer" learning style.

Another reason is that some learning styles are simply more influential on the dimensions of engagement. Halif et al. (2020) reported that only the visual learning style was able to influence all dimensions of student engagement. These results show that visual learners had higher classroom engagement as opposed to both auditory and kinesthetic learners. From a cross-cultural perspective, some learning cultures emphasize an array of values, norms and behavioural aspects that are inclined more towards visual learning style than the others.

2.12.2 Fear of Judgement from Peers

Learning activities set by teachers may trigger a negative or a fear-based memory (Dean & Jolly, 2012). This may result in a student becoming reluctant to get involved in both classroom and out-of-classroom activities. This could be largely due to the fear of judgement being made by their teachers or peers.

Next, language difficulties can also be recognized as one of the primary contributing aspects of fear. International students were so sensitive to their language inadequacies that engaging and involved participation in class is mostly challenging (Robertson et al., 2000). Qualitative study by Lee and Rice (2007) who found that international students in the United States often felt uncomfortable about participating in group work or interacting with peers due to concerns and doubts about English language proficiency.

This hypersensitivity of their language inadequacy can stem from the fear of 'losing face' that is a common phenomenon especially in Chinese Heritage Culture (CHC) cultures. Students may feel worried and have perceived perspectives or inclinations of being judged by others. Some international students may not often talk, or stop talking, with tutors and other students to avoid grammatical mistakes and largely being avoided from feeling embarrassed (Su, 2012).

2.12.3 Increasing Use of IT in Classrooms

In today's digitized age, capturing students' engagement online is a key concern. Inactivity and passivity online are viewed as symptoms of disengagement and predictors of negative outcomes, such as dissatisfaction and dropout (Morgan-Thomas & Dudau, 2019). Technology may threaten to distract rather than engage students. In a study conducted by Zhao et al. (2005), it was reported that international students seemed to be more comfortable and perceived to be confident in using computer technology for preparing class assignments and in communicating with their teachers and peers. In a flip side while this may help them feel more at ease, it potentially contributes to social isolation as it could be considered as a substitute for face-to-face interactions. International students may use technology instead of talking directly to peers or instructors to avoid embarrassing exchanges created by language barriers and unfamiliarity with cultural idioms.

2.12.4 Lack of Confidence

To effectively engage international students, acknowledging the varying constraints, teachers must have the confidence in their ability to do so. A study by Caruana (2010) found that academic staff were (a) uncertain and (b) lacked confidence in dealing with issues related to the internationalization of the curriculum as well as (c) struggled to have the institutional policies into practice. This may well have validated their persistent use of largely ineffective strategies while dealing and working with culturally diverse groups of learners with evidence pointing to the lack of impact. Therefore, it is imperative for institutions to allocate relevant resources, train their staff so that they are better prepared to deal with the increasingly diverse classrooms.

2.13 Teachers' Training: Proficiency in Adapting in a Cross-Cultural Context

With increasing diversity in classrooms, teachers are expected to work effectively with students from varying cultural backgrounds (Gopal, 2011; Keengwe, 2010; Rajaram, 2013, 2021). Teachers' cross-cultural trainings can assist them to manage, handle and engage students from varying cultures.

Cross-cultural training is vital as it enables participants in making preemptive determinations of what types of behaviours to emulate. It also enhances one's awareness and empathy (Heng, 2016). The correct mix of determinations will enable them to act appropriately without any trial-and-error approaches. Hence, a participant will be reassured the potential occurrences of inappropriate actions, avoiding associated negative consequences to be experienced by someone who is untrained. Such positive experiences subsequently lead to positive outcomes such as higher levels of job satisfaction (Black & Mendenhall, 1990).

Relevant training increases the efficacy in ingraining the competency of cultural intelligence (CQ). Cultural intelligence (CQ) is a vital managerial competency as we could acknowledge that an individual with high CQ is able to comprehend human behaviour much better, hence is therefore in a better stead to lead, manage people in a manner that could potentially enhance business success. Higher cultural intelligence enables effective communication within the work environment, good cultural judgement and informed decision-making. A person with high CQ is better in adjusting and adapting in culturally diverse situations, that turn enhances their effectiveness at workplace. When this is applied to the higher education context, it implies that teachers with higher cultural intelligence are able to lead and manage highly diverse classrooms.

Petrović (2011) advocates that learning design of teachers' training should incorporate and promote primary factors, such as openness to intercultural interaction, intercultural learning, readiness to recognize and utilize multiculturalism, cultural diversity as a learning resource, mutual respect and mindfulness. This enhancement of CQ training for teachers can be vary impactful in their dealings with the diverse profile of students that could only influence them positively. Improving cross-cultural competencies is a nonlinear procedure that involves stimulating an individual's cognitive elements, affective elements and behavioural components (Mendenhall et al., 2013). Gopal (2011) developed a framework that focuses on three core elements of Deardorff's (2009) process model, namely attitudes, knowledge and comprehension and skills. For each core element, there are sub-aspects that encompass within that, namely (a) attitudes (valuing other cultures; motivation; openness to other cultures, ethnocentricity); (b) knowledge and comprehension (cultural self-awareness, gender roles, language); and (c) skills (self-reflection, reflexivity, communication skills). When these core elements act together, they produce two desired outcomes: (a) a shift in one's frame of reference, in which adaptability and flexibility play a central role; and (b) a shift in effective behaviour in intercultural situations and communication. Therefore, the ideal strategy is to be facilitate training to resolve around targeting each one of these core elements and address the aspects that lie within that.

For example, training can be facilitated through experiential learning design. Experiential learning is an approach that elicits a deeper understanding of self, culture and literacy practices where it adopts an explorative method to use this knowledge for educational change. It enables teachers to relate and resonate to their students' daily experiences as second language learners from varying cultural contexts. Hence, a thorough comprehension is developed through engaging with realities outside their own cultures and to continue understanding through comparing assumptions and beliefs (Dantas, 2007). In this case, experiential learning can identify the first two core elements in gaining intercultural competence.

Another approach would be training through cross-cultural simulations (Cruz & Patterson, 2005). A simulation is an instructional technique that attempts to recreate certain aspects of reality for the purpose of gaining information, clarifying values, understanding other cultures, or developing a skill. By using kinesthetic and affective modes of learning, participants learn by doing, feeling, analysing and reflecting. The sequence and implementation of the experience are usually stipulated, although participants act and react as their individual personalities and backgrounds prescribed. Thus, cross-cultural simulations are an effective way to incorporate the skills element along with the other two elements. Teachers should be encouraged or put through this assimilation eco-system to train and equip them to improve their cross-cultural competencies.

2.14 Teachers' Outlook Towards Culturally Diverse Students

It is of key importance that teachers fundamentally recognize, comprehend and appreciate their own worldviews in order to successfully engaging the diverse profile of students. This is vital as only then they are able to better understand and relate to their students' outlook and their perceived sociocultural worldviews. Evidence points explicitly to the fact that teachers themselves do face and have to deal with their own racism and biases to be able to effectively and efficiently communicate with their students (McAllister & Irvine, 2000). Although these biases do vary from instructor to instructor, the broad and holistic studies discussed in this section will enable us to make some concluding generalizations.

International students bring a range of cultures to the classroom context where it motivates teachers in working around such diversity as emerged by a study on teachers at an Australian University (Sawir, 2013). Though novel values and beliefs are expected to be advocated, teachers may have underlying prejudices and perceived stereotype perceptions that may not always be true of students from other cultures. For example, mainland Chinese students, for instance, are often perceived to be passive and overly reliant, not able to articulate their thoughts clearly. This claim could be validated by a few studies by scholars (Heng, 2016; Jenkins, 2000) who are faculty members from a US Higher Education Institution who reported that Chinese students were not able to read or orally summarize papers which they attributed this to their poor English language and lack of motivation. In essence, faculty members associated students' feeble command of the English language and motivation towards their cultural background. These faculty perceive those Chinese learners are not keen in assimilating or enhancing their English language through socialization. We could agree with (Gorski, 2011) that this is a deficit approach adopted by teachers where their approach towards these students is based on their perceptions and stereotype notions inclined towards the students' weaknesses rather than their strengths.

In contrary, a study conducted university in London showed that while challenges are amplified by language and cultural differences as it points towards the fact that managing international students could be challenging but if it is examined from a more optimistic view, these experiences do bring about diverse valuable and enriching perspectives (Kingston & Forland, 2007). Evidence showed that although international students disliked group discussions and presentations initially, they eventually adjusted and adapted, while beginning to enjoy the variety of assessment approaches. The differences in standards that exist between faculty and international students point to the increasingly diverse student population that requires constant monitoring and adaption to fit the current times. Evidence from research does stress the inadequacy of guidance for teachers who are required to manage diverse spectrum of international students.

"Colour blindness" is an alternate view some teachers strongly uphold as a belief while teaching diverse classrooms. Here "Colour blindness" is referred to when one view everyone as the same without any biased view on their skin colour or their cultural background. In contrary, those with colour-blind racism or discrimination disregard the multitude of struggles and challenges faced by individuals of different cultures and otherizes them (Bonilla-Silva, 2006). For example, studies revealed by McCoy et al. (2015) that faculty members interact with students from a "colorblind perspective". By adopting race-neutral and colour blind language, faculty labelled their students as academically inferior, less prepared and less interested in pursuing their studies.

A teacher's performance in cross-cultural settings may be potentially disrupted by these rudimentary problems. Hence, training should be regularly conducted to assist teachers to unlearn the innate biases and discriminatory actions which they may hold and act upon, while to relearn and equip themselves with the essentials. Evasion of stereotypes and discrimination is possible, but the beholder must first be aware of the possibility for bias, be mindful and cautious of it, and have adequate cognitive capacity to act upon it. Cross-cultural training is useful and helpful, as it promotes empathy where it enables for individuals to view things from various perspectives (Dovidio & Gaertner, 2010).

Smith-Maddox and Solórzano (2002) developed a theoretical framework on ingrained ideologies by creating a space in a social foundations course for teacher candidates to unlearn their stereotypical knowledge of race while analysing and theorizing what it means to teach a diverse student population. With this methodological approach, the student teachers can have an immersion experience in culturally diverse communities to comprehend, relate and explore the societal and systemic challenges people from other cultures face. This approach facilitates a learning experience that creates the conditions for teachers to examine the moral and ethical dilemmas of teaching and learning while challenging their own intrinsic assumptions and engage in conversations about social and cultural differences.

Behavioural modification is another way of changing an individual's actions via their behavioural CQ abilities. Behaviours that are sanctioned in a particular culture are identified and transferred as the "know-hows" to a learner. Simulations and role-plays are conducted, and reinforcement and punishment are used to guide behavioural change. Those who wish to increase cultural intelligence learn to break out from their old habits to acquire a new repertoire of behaviours considered and accepted in the identified culture (Earley & Peterson, 2004).

Application to Teaching and Learning Practice

2.15 Correct Mix of Teaching Strategies for High Efficacy of Learning in Cross-Cultural Settings

Teaching in a classroom with different cultural clusters of students requires mindful facilitation with a good sensitivity of being aware of the distinctive cultural nuances that exists within the group of students. The teacher must understand these differences adequately well so that two primary aspects could be fundamentally addressed, namely: (a) the learning design, on how the contents could be effectively facilitated through the correct mix of pedagogies; (b) the sociocultural cognitive and behavioural norms and patterns. The learning design should comprise elements that enables the students to resonate and be inclined to work towards with a tolerance level of discomfort and unfamiliarity but not totally away from their sociocultural values and beliefs. This plays a vital role in ensuring students can operate within a space which enables them to grow yet be re-assuring them that it is doable where they feel secured, not in a disengaged manner. However, once they are conditioned and adapted to these new changes then instructors can progressively equip these students to be accustomed to the specific nuances embedded within that.

We have identified and collated a list of teaching techniques and provided collated validated recommendations provided by the studies. Table 2.5. presents the teaching techniques and the impact it has on the students' learning.

2.16 Concluding Thoughts

More than so in the past decade, cultural intelligence or CQ has been a trending topic not just among research scholars but also widely an issue to be pondered upon in varying organizations, public and private. Globalization has enabled these organizations to function via cross borders, where this has caused the movement of people to be rapidly increasing at an unprecedented scale. The ability and skills required to interact and work with people from all over the world have become a skill and competency that is vital especially in a more diverse environment. Higher education has never been more accessible. We are no longer-geographically bound, nor do we have to be the elite few who get access to further our education. An example to validate this could be pointed to the enrolment in tertiary education which has grown in the United States from 47.37% of the total population of secondary school graduates in 1970 to just over 84% in 2014 (Roser & Ortiz-Ospina, 2013). This sharp increase shows the reach to not only local students in a country but more so for anyone globally. Globalization has enabled individuals from all ages, socioeconomic class and geographical cultures access to what was once a seemingly rare commodity.

This chapter provides insights on the importance of culture and its interconnectedness to teaching and learning practices in higher education context. With evermore diverse classrooms, the vital skill of cultural intelligence (CQ) has emerged to be on the spotlight. Evidence clearly points that CQ, while complementary to other varying intelligences (Mosakowski & Earley, 2004; Thomas et al., 2008; Van Dyne et al., 2012), it stands on its own as an unique intelligence. We find contrary perspectives that although there are discrepancies with regard to the exact dimensions of CQ, literature generally agrees that it is a multidimensional concept (Ott & Michailova, 2016). We identified the core components of CQ as defined by scholarly work, namely adaptability, unfamiliarity, appropriateness, mindfulness, and knowledge and understanding, and how these individual elements could be applied to the context of teaching and learning practices. We emphasized and elaborated on how

Table 2.5 Teaching techniques and the impact it has on the students' learning

Mode of delivery/pedagogy	Sample description	Description of the mode of delivery/pedagogy	Impact
Asynchronous electronic discussion boards Rollag (2010)	Used by instructors at Babson College in the United States that facilitates online case discussions in their MBA programme	Asynchronous communication allows people that may not share the same space and time to actively participate in the production of shared knowledge	The quality and effectiveness of discussions were often equal or better online than in-person. This is a result of students having more time to devise and edit their responses. Further to that, since discussions are over a longer period, students were able to make more than one contribution and the class had more time to collectively analyse the subject at depth
Self-Practice (Role-Play) Learning to negotiate reality Antal and Friedman (2008)	A 22-h course that ran over three and a half days for eight semesters at the Leipzig Graduate School of Management, with the goal of leading students through a conscious process of analysis and experimentation	Learning to negotiate reality involves becoming conscious of and unlearning deep-rooted cognitive processes and behavioural responses that hinder constructive cross-cultural interactions The objective of the course was to bring students to the point where they are able to make the informed choice of learning to negotiate reality and are able to deepen learning by self-practising	The course allowed students to realize that the focus is not about 'foreigners' or 'culture' but their own innate reasoning and behaviour towards cross-cultural interactions Rather than being overwhelmed or unable to understand cultural norms and values, the course teaches them that they can make conscious choices about how to interpret and respond to situations that are frustrating or confusing

(continued)

Table 2.5 (continued)

Mode of delivery/pedagogy	Sample description	Description of the mode of delivery/pedagogy	Impact
"Think, Write, Share" Woods et al. (2006)	Study 1: Two focus groups—The first group consisted of six international students, each from different countries and aged between 21 and 30, who were studying postgraduate programmes. The second focus group consisted of five experienced business teachers of ages 26 to 44 who had worked teaching international undergraduate and postgraduate students Study 2: Surveys were administered to 52 experienced teachers who volunteered from two universities. The teachers had an average age of 39.7 years	The "think-write-share" strategy is to assist students who require more time to frame their responses in the discussion language. This technique provides students to write their answers to a given question within a specified time limit. Thereafter, students share their answers in class, usually starting with students who have weaker English language skills	International students have more time to develop their ideas in English which helps if they have language competence issues
"Question Clarity" Woods et al. (2006)	Study 1: Two focus groups—The first group consisted of six international students, each from different countries and aged between 21 to 30, who were studying postgraduate programmes. The second focus group consisted of five experienced business teachers of ages 26 to 44 who had worked teaching international undergraduate and postgraduate students Study 2: Surveys were administered to 52 experienced teachers who volunteered from two universities. The teachers had an average age of 39.7 years	This strategy involves visibly writing or displaying the discussion question as a method for clarification	The visual prompt aids as an anchor point so students can remain focused on the subject of discussion. This method of using visual aids has been proven to be helpful in cross-cultural interactions

(continued)

Table 2.5 (continued)

Mode of delivery/pedagogy	Sample description	Description of the mode of delivery/pedagogy	Impact
"Peer Explanation" Woods et al. (2006)	Study 1: Two focus groups—The first group consisted of six international students, each from different countries and aged between 21 and 30, who were studying postgraduate programmes. The second focus group consisted of five experienced business teachers of ages 26 to 44 who had worked teaching international undergraduate and postgraduate students Study 2: Surveys were administered to 52 experienced teachers who volunteered from two universities. The teachers had an average age of 39.7 years	This strategy involves assigning students who have understood the concept being taught to small groups so that they can help explain	This is a mutually beneficial strategy as it helps clarify concepts while those who help can gain benefits from peer-mentoring. Students could help other students who are struggling to catch up due to their lack of language competency or skills
"Student Examples" Woods et al. (2006)	Study 1: Two focus groups—The first group consisted of six international students, each from different countries and aged between 21 and 30, who were studying postgraduate programmes. The second focus group consisted of five experienced business teachers of ages 26 to 44 who had worked teaching international undergraduate and postgraduate students Study 2: Surveys were administered to 52 experienced teachers who volunteered from two universities. The teachers had an average age of 39.7 years	This strategy asks international students to think of examples based on their background and experience that relates to the concept that is being taught	This not only validates the experience of the international student but also enhances the experience of domestic students. It also helps students make the link between tacit knowing and explicit knowledge

(continued)

Table 2.5 (continued)

Mode of delivery/pedagogy	Sample description	Description of the mode of delivery/pedagogy	Impact
"Break Up and Report Back" Woods et al. (2006)	Study 1: Two focus groups—The first group consisted of six international students, each from different countries and aged between 21 and 30, who were studying postgraduate programmes. The second focus group consisted of five experienced business teachers of ages 26 to 44 who had worked teaching international undergraduate and postgraduate students Study 2: Surveys were administered to 52 experienced teachers who volunteered from two universities. The teachers had an average age of 39.7 years	This strategy involves the teacher dividing the class into smaller culturally mixed groups Each group would be given a time limit to complete a given task and the teacher should inform the students that one person from each group should be appointed to present their responses to the entire class	This strategy provides a less threatening small group environment where the student with weaker language skills can first test out their understanding as well as their responses to the questions asked before speaking to the larger group
Icebreakers Crose (2011)	NA	Icebreakers allow for informal interactions to take place and allow students to get to know each other. This involves utilizing a large portion of the first-class session for students to know each other and allow for informal interactions to occur	Using icebreakers can allow students to learn what each of their peers like to be referred to as well as provide an opportunity for them to learn to correctly pronounce unfamiliar names. This helps in forming bonds outside of the classrooms which is beneficial to both international and domestic students

being equipped with CQ skills is not just imperative for students who will be going out to the global workforce but also for teachers and higher education institution leaders to have.

Globalization is one of the contributing causes for CQ skills to be rated highly. The effects of globalization on higher education have caused universities and higher education institutes to focus on internationalization as a key strategic priority (Robson & Wihlborg, 2019). Example of positive effects includes the rapid development of the higher education global market (De Wit, 2011; Nayyar, 2007) and international cooperation between institutes (Chan, 2004), whereas for negative effects, it includes lower public funding and homogenization of national identities and cultures (Yang, 2003). Hence, we see several effects and trends emerging on teaching and learning in higher education institutes, both the strategic and operational levels. This includes the commodification of higher education, the prominence of transnational programmes and more. Globalization has made higher education institutes aware of the increasing cultural diversity where having a good comprehension of different cultures of its staff and faculty is foremost important (Bovill, Jordan & Watters, 2015). This influences on how these institutions approach the aspects of teaching and learning at strategic, tactical and operational fronts with the primary emphasis on how to deal with cultural diversity.

We also dived into the interconnectedness between culture and the adoption as well as preferences of instructional pedagogy and techniques. Hofstede's cultural dimensions model could be referenced to as one of the frameworks for cross-cultural teaching to explain the cultural differences experienced by teachers and students (Bovill et al., 2014). We discussed how certain pedagogical strategies are more prevalent or preferred in specific cultural contexts, though it is vital to note that this does not necessarily equate to learning effectiveness. The correct mix of techniques to be identified can be based on the outcome of different learning styles associated with varying cultures (Charlesworth, 2008). We also explored how it is possible for CQ to be taught and the skills learned, acquired in the classroom context (Ramsey & Lorenz, 2016). The challenges and limitations faced by teachers teaching in cross-cultural contexts and climate were examined. Multicultural teaching efficacy was discussed as it has a positive correlation to student accomplishments (Ashton & Webb, 1986; Dembo & Gibson, 1985; Silverman, 2008). Three frameworks revolving around the measurement of multicultural teaching efficacy were examined. Student engagement, which is positively linked to learning outcomes (Foster & Rahinel, 2008; Pike et al., 2011), was also discoursed. We discovered that dissimilar cultures are engaged differently and challenges in engagement could be potentially due to some of the aspects such as difference in learning styles, fear of judgement from peers, increasing use of technology and lack of confidence. With an increasing diversity in numbers with challenges of engaging students as one of the core issues requires teachers to be trained effectively to be equipped with skills to work in multicultural settings (Gopal, 2011; Keengwe, 2010). Such trainings provided in cross cultural contexts enhances cultural competencies such as CQ (Du Plessis, 2011), and facilitate in attaining positive outcomes such as job satisfaction (Black & Mendenhall, 1990).

References

Ang, S., & Van Dyne, L. (2008). *Handbook of cultural intelligence: Theory measurement and application* (1st ed.). Routledge.
Ang, S., Van Dyne, L., Koh, C., Ng, K. Y., Templer, K. J., Tay, C., & Chandrasekar, N. A. (2007). Cultural intelligence: Its measurement and effects on cultural judgment and decision making, cultural adaptation and task performance. *Management and Organization Review, 3*(3), 335–371. https://doi.org/10.1111/j.1740-8784.2007.00082.x
Ang, et al. (2011). *Cultural Intelligence, from Part VI - Kinds of Intelligence, Chapter 29,* edited by Robert J. Sternberg and Scott Barry Kaufman. New Cambridge University Press.
Antal, A. B., & Friedman, V. J. (2008). Learning to negotiate reality: A strategy for teaching intercultural competencies. *Journal of Management Education, 32*(3), 363–386. https://doi.org/10.1177/1052562907308794
Anvari, R., Irum, S., Ashfaq, M., & Atiyaye, D. M. (2014). The impact of leader's cultural intelligence on organizational commitment. *Asian Social Science, 10*(17), 45–51. https://doi.org/10.5539/ass.v10n17p45
Apfelthaler, G., Hansen, K., Keuchel, S., Mueller, C., Neubauer, M., Ong, S. H., & Tapachai, N. (2007). Cross-cultural differences in learning and education: Stereotypes, myths and realities. In D. Palfreyman & D. L. McBride (Eds.), *Learning and teaching across cultures in higher education.* Palgrave Macmillan. https://doi.org/10.1057/9780230590427
Apple, M. W. (2011). Global crises, social justice, and teacher education. *Journal of Teacher Education, 62*(2), 222–234.
Arkoudis, S., Watty, K., Baik, C., Yu, X., Borland, H., Chang, S., Lang, I., Lang, J., & Pearce, A. (2012). Finding common ground: Enhancing interaction between domestic and international students in higher education. *Teaching in Higher Education, 18*(3), 222–235. https://doi.org/10.1080/13562517.2012.719156
Arthur, N. (2017). Supporting international students through strengthening their social resources. *Studies in Higher Education, 42*(5), 887–894. https://doi.org/10.1080/03075079.2017.1293876
Ashton, P. T., & Webb, R. B. (1986). *Making a difference: Teachers' sense of efficacy and student achievement.* Longman.
Asmar, C. (2005). Internationalising students: Reassessing diasporic and local student difference. *Studies in Higher Education, 30*(3), 291–309. https://doi.org/10.1080/03075070500095713
Atkins, M., & Brown, G. (1988). *Effective teaching in higher education.* Taylor & Francis.
Aycan, Z. (1997). Expatriate adjustment as a multifaceted phenomenon: Individual and organization level predictors. *The International Journal Human Resource Management, 8*, 434–456.
Ballantyne, R., Bain, J. D., & Packer, J. (1999). Researching university teaching in Australia: Themes and issues in academics' reflections. *Studies in Higher Education, 24*(2), 237–257. https://doi.org/10.1080/03075079912331379918
Bandura, A. (2002). Social cognitive theory in cultural context. *Applied Psychology: An International Review, 51*, 269–290.
Barker, J. (2002). The purpose of study, attitudes to study and staff-student relationships. In D. McNamara & R. Harris (Eds.), *Overseas students in higher education.* Routledge. https://doi.org/10.4324/9780203040065
Bartram, B., & Bailey, C. (2010). Assessment preferences: A comparison of UK/international students at an English university. *Research in Post-Compulsory Education, 15*(2), 177–187. https://doi.org/10.1080/13596741003790716
Baumgart, N., & Halse, C. (1999). Approaches to learning across cultures: The role of assessment. *Assessment in Education: Principles, Policy & Practice, 6*(3), 321–339. https://doi.org/10.1080/09695949992775
Bednar, D. A., & Brandenburg, M. (1984). Relationships between communicator style and perceived teaching effectiveness in management classes. *Academy of Management Proceedings, 1*, 111–115. https://doi.org/10.5465/ambpp.1984.4978285

Beneroso, D., & Alosaimi, N. (2020). Cultural intelligence of chemical engineering students: A demographics study. *Education for Chemical Engineers, 32*, 32–39. https://doi.org/10.1016/j.ece.2020.05.003
Bennett, C. N. (1990). Preservice multicutural techer education: Predictors of student readiness. *Teaching and Teacher Education, 6*, 243–254.
Bergman, P., McLaughlin, M., Bass, M., Pauly, E., & Zellman, G. (1977). *Federal programs supporting educational change: Vol. VII. Factors affecting implementation and continuation* (ERIC Document Reproduction Service No. 140 432). RAND.
Bergmann, J., & Sams, A. (2014). *Flipped learning: Gateway to student engagement*. International Society for Technology in Education.
Bhandari, R. & Blumenthal, P. (2013). International Students and Global Mobility in Higher Education: National Trends and New Directions. Palgrave Macmillan.
Bhattacharyya, E., & Shariff, A. B. M. S. (2014). Learning style and its impact in higher education and human capital needs. *Procedia—Social and Behavioral Sciences, 123*, 485–494. https://doi.org/10.1016/j.sbspro.2014.01.1448
Biggs, J. B. (2001). Teaching across cultures. In F. Salili, C. Y. Chiu, & Y. Y. Hong (Eds.), *Student motivation* (Plenum series on human exceptionality). Springer. https://doi.org/10.1007/978-1-4615-1273-8_14
Black, J., & an Gregerson, H. (1999). The right way to manager expatriates. *Harvard Business Review, 77*, 52–63.
Black, J. S., & Mendenhall, M. (1990). Cross-cultural training effectiveness: A review and a theoretical framework for future research. *The Academy of Management Review, 15*(1), 113–136. https://doi.org/10.2307/258109
Bodenhausen, G. V., Macrae, C. N., & Garst, J. (1998). Stereotypes in thought and deed: Social-cognitive origins of intergroup discrimination. In C. Sedikides, J. Schopler, & C. A. Insko (Eds.), *Intergroup cognition and intergroup behavior* (pp. 311–335). Lawrence Erlbaum Associates Publishers.
Bonilla-Silva, E. (2006). *Racism without racists: Color-blind racism and the persistence of racial inequality in the United States* (2nd ed.). Rowman & Littlefield.
Bonk, C. J., Graham, C. R., Cross, J., & Moore, M. G. (2005). *The handbook of blended learning: Global perspectives, local designs* (1st ed.). Pfeiffer.
Bouncken, R., Brem, A., & Kraus, S. (2016). Multi-cultural teams as sources for creativity and innovation: The role of cultural diversity on team performance. *International Journal of Innovation Management, 20*(1), 1650012. https://doi.org/10.1142/s1363919616500122
Bovill, C., Jordan, L., & Watters, N. (2014). Transnational approaches to teaching and learning in higher education: Challenges and possible guiding principles. *Teaching in Higher Education, 20*(1), 12–23. https://doi.org/10.1080/13562517.2014.945162
Bovill, C., Jordan, L., & Watters, N. (2015). Transnational approaches to teaching and learning in higher education: Challenges and possible guiding principles. *Teaching in Higher Education, 20*, 12–23.
Bowden, J. L.-H., Tickle, L., & Naumann, K. (2019). The four pillars of tertiary student engagement and success: A holistic measurement approach. *Studies in Higher Education*, 1–18. https://doi.org/10.1080/03075079.2019.1672647
Brislin, R., MacNab, B., & Nayani, F. (2008). Cross-cultural training: Applications and research. In P. Smith, F. Peterson, & D. Thomas (Eds.), *Handbook of crosscultural management research.* (pp. 397–410). Sage.
Brookfield, S. D., & Preskill, S. (2005). *Discussion as a way of teaching: Tools and techniques for democratic classrooms* (2nd ed.). Jossey-Bass.
Brown, G., & Atkins, M. (1988). *Effective teaching in higher education*. Routledge.
Bücker, J., Furrer, O., & Lin, Y. (2015). Measuring cultural intelligence (CQ). *International Journal of Cross-Cultural Management, 15*(3), 259–284. https://doi.org/10.1177/1470595815606741

Cantwell, B., & Maldonado-Maldonado, A. (2009). Four stories: Confronting contemporary ideas about globalisation and internationalisation in higher education. *Globalisation, Societies and Education, 7*(3), 289–306. https://doi.org/10.1080/14767720903166103
Carroll, J., & Ryan, J. (2005). *Teaching international students: Improving learning for all.* Routledge.
Caruana, V. (2010). The relevance of the internationalized curriculum to graduate capability: The role of new lecturers' attitudes in shaping the 'student voice'. In E. Jones (Ed.), *Internationalization and the student voice: Higher education perspectives.* Routledge.
Chan, W. W. Y. (2004). International cooperation in higher education: Theory and practice. *Journal of Studies in International Education, 8*(1), 32–55. https://doi.org/10.1177/1028315303254429
Chang, J. (2006). Globalization and English in Chinese higher education. *World Englishes, 25*(3–4), 513–525. https://doi.org/10.1111/j.1467-971x.2006.00484.x
Charlesworth, Z. M. (2008). Learning styles across cultures: Suggestions for educators. *Education + Training, 50*(2), 115–127. https://doi.org/10.1108/00400910810862100
Chávez, A. F., & Longerbeam, S. D. (2016). *Teaching across cultural strengths: A guide to balancing integrated and individuated cultural frameworks in college teaching.* Stylus Publishing.
Cheng, M., Adekola, O. A., Shah, M., & Valyrakis, M. (2016). Exploring Chinese students' experience of curriculum internationalization: A comparative study of Scotland and Australia. *Studies in Higher Education, 43*(4), 754–768. https://doi.org/10.1080/03075079.2016.1198894
Choudaha, R. (2017). Are international students "cash cows"? *International Higher Education, 90*, 5–6. https://doi.org/10.6017/ihe.2017.90.9993
Cook, L. (1991). Cooperative learning: A successful college teaching strategy. *Innovative Higher Education, 16*(1), 27–38. https://doi.org/10.1007/bf00911556
Cortazzi, M., & Jin, L. (2002). Communication for learning across cultures. In D. McNamara & R. Harris (Eds.), *Overseas students in higher education.* Routledge. https://doi.org/10.4324/9780203040065
Crose, B. (2011). Internationalization of the higher education classroom: Strategies to facilitate intercultural learning and academic success. *International Journal of Teaching and Learning in Higher Education, 23*(3), 388–395. https://eric.ed.gov/?id=EJ946165
Crossman, J. E., & Clarke, M. (2009). International experience and graduate employability: Stakeholder perceptions on the connection. *Higher Education, 59*(5), 599–613. https://doi.org/10.1007/s10734-009-9268-z
Crowne, K. A. (2008). What leads to cultural intelligence? *Business Horizons, 51*(5), 391–399. https://doi.org/10.1016/j.bushor.2008.03.010
Crowne, K. A. (2019). Investigating antecedents of transformational leadership in students. *Journal of International Education in Business, 12*(1), 80–94. https://doi.org/10.1108/jieb-07-2018-0029
Cruz, B. C., & Patterson, J. (2005). Cross-cultural simulations in teacher education: Developing empathy and understanding. *Multicultural Perspectives, 7*(2), 40–47. https://doi.org/10.1207/s15327892mcp0702_7
Cushner, K., & Brislin, R. (1996). *Intercultural interactions: A practical guide* (2nd ed.). Sage.
Dantas, M. L. (2007). Building teacher competency to work with diverse learners in the context of international education. *Teacher Education Quarterly, 34*(1), 75–94. https://www.jstor.org/stable/23478853?seq=1
Darling-Hammond, L. (2010). Teacher education and the american future. *Journal of Teacher Education, 61*, 35–47.
De Beuckelaer, A., Lievens, F., & Bücker, J. (2012). The role of faculty members' cross-cultural competencies in their perceived teaching quality: Evidence from culturally-diverse classes in four European countries. *The Journal of Higher Education, 83*(2), 217–248. https://doi.org/10.1080/00221546.2012.11777240
De Wit, H. (2011). Globalization and internationalisation of higher education. *RUSC Universities and Knowledge Society Journal, 8*(2), 77. https://doi.org/10.7238/rusc.v8i2.1247
De Wit, H. (2017). Global: Internationalization of higher education: Nine misconceptions. In G. Mihut, P. G. Altbach, & H. De Wit (Eds.), *Understanding higher education internationalization:*

Global perspectives on higher education. SensePublishers. https://doi.org/10.1007/978-94-6351-161-2_2

Dean, K. L., & Jolly, J. P. (2012). Student identity, disengagement, and learning. *Academy of Management Learning & Education, 11*(2), 228–243. https://doi.org/10.5465/amle.2009.0081

Deardorff, D. K. (2009). *The SAGE Handbook of Intercultural Competence*. SAGE.

Dembo, M. H., & Gibson, S. (1985). Teachers' sense of efficacy: An important factor in school improvement. *The Elementary School Journal, 86*(2), 173–184. https://doi.org/10.1086/461441

Deng, Z. (2011). Confucianism, modernization and Chinese pedagogy: An introduction. *Journal of Curriculum Studies, 43*(5), 561–568. https://doi.org/10.1080/00220272.2011.617837

Dilworth, P. P. (2004). Multicultural citizenship education: Case studies from social studies classrooms. *Theory & Research in Social Education, 32*(2), 153–186. https://doi.org/10.1080/00933104.2004.10473251

Doherty, C., & Singh, P. (2005). How the west is done: Simulating western pedagogy in a curriculum for Asian International Students. In P. Ninnes & M. Hellstén (Eds.), *Internationalizing higher education: CERC studies in comparative education* (Vol. 16). Springer. https://doi.org/10.1007/1-4020-3784-8_4

Doiz, A., Lasagabaster, D., & Sierra, J. (2013). Globalisation, internationalisation, multilingualism and linguistic strains in higher education. *Studies in Higher Education, 38*(9), 1407–1421. https://doi.org/10.1080/03075079.2011.642349

Dovidio, J. F., & Gaertner, S. L. (2010). *Intergroup bias: Handbook of social psychology*, 1084–1121. https://doi.org/10.1002/9780470561119.socpsy002029

Du Plessis, Y. (2011). Cultural intelligence as managerial competence. *Alternation, 18*(1), 28–46. http://hdl.handle.net/2263/18778

Earley, C. P., & Ang, S. (2003). *Cultural intelligence: Individual interactions across cultures* (Stanford Business Books [Paperback]) (1st ed.). Stanford Business Books.

Earley, C. P., Ang, S., & Tan, J. (2006). *CQ: Developing cultural intelligence at work* (1st ed.). Stanford Business Books.

Earley, P. C., & Peterson, R. S. (2004). The elusive cultural Chameleon: Cultural intelligence as a new approach to intercultural training for the global manager. *Academy of Management Learning & Education, 3*(1), 100–115. https://doi.org/10.5465/amle.2004.12436826

Eaves, M. (2011). The relevance of learning styles for international pedagogy in higher education. *Teachers and Teaching, 17*(6), 677–691. https://doi.org/10.1080/13540602.2011.625143

Eisenberg, J., Lee, H.-J., Brück, F., Brenner, B., Claes, M.-T., Mironski, J., & Bell, R. (2013). Can business schools make students culturally competent? Effects of cross-cultural management courses on cultural intelligence. *Academy of Management Learning & Education, 12*(4), 603–621. https://doi.org/10.5465/amle.2012.0022

Eisenhart, M. (2008). Globalization and science education in a community-based after-school program. *Cultural Studies of Science Education, 3*(1), 73–95.

Eldridge, K., & Cranston, N. (2009). Managing transnational education: Does national culture really matter? *Journal of Higher Education Policy and Management, 31*(1), 67–79. https://doi.org/10.1080/13600800802559286

Erez, M., Lisak, A., Harush, R., Glikson, E., Nouri, R., & Shokef, E. (2013). Going global: Developing management students' cultural intelligence and global identity in culturally diverse virtual teams. *Academy of Management Learning & Education, 12*(3), 330–355. https://doi.org/10.5465/amle.2012.0200

Fang, F., Schei, V., & Selart, M. (2018). Hype or hope? A new look at the research on cultural intelligence. *International Journal of Intercultural Relations, 66*, 148–171. https://doi.org/10.1016/j.ijintrel.2018.04.002

Fee, K. (2009). *Delivering E-Learning A Complete Strategy for Design, Application and Assessment*. Kogan Page.

Foster, M. K., & Rahinel, R. (2008). Student engagement and competency development. *Academy of Management Proceedings, 1*, 1–5. https://doi.org/10.5465/ambpp.2008.33664597

Fredricks, J. A., Blumenfeld, P. C., & Paris, A. H. (2004). School engagement: Potential of the concept, state of the evidence. *Review of Educational Research, 74*(1), 59–109. https://doi.org/10.3102/00346543074001059

Ghahraman, V., & Tamimy, M. (2017). The role of culture in cooperative learning. *International Journal of Language Studies, 11*(2), 89–120. https://www.researchgate.net/publication/320395633_The_role_of_culture_in_cooperative_learning

Glass, C. R., Gesing, P., Hales, A., & Cong, C. (2017). Faculty as bridges to co-curricular engagement and community for first-generation international students. *Studies in Higher Education, 42*(5), 895–910. https://doi.org/10.1080/03075079.2017.1293877

Goh, M. (2012). Teaching with cultural intelligence: Developing multiculturally educated and globally engaged citizens. *Asia Pacific Journal of Education, 32*(4), 395–415. https://doi.org/10.1080/02188791.2012.738679

Gopal, A. (2011). Internationalization of higher education: Preparing faculty to teach cross-culturally. *International Journal of Teaching and Learning in Higher Education, 23*(3), 373–381. https://eric.ed.gov/?id=EJ946163.

Gopinathan, S., & Lee, M. H. (2011). Challenging and co-opting globalisation: Singapore's strategies in higher education. *Journal of Higher Education Policy and Management, 33*(3), 287–299. https://doi.org/10.1080/1360080x.2011.565001

Gordon, M. (2008). *Assess Notes Nursing Assessment & Diagnostic Reasoning*. Davis Company Press.

Gorski, P. C. (2011). Unlearning deficit ideology and the scornful gaze: Thoughts on authenticating the class discourse in education. *Counterpoints, 402*, 152–173. https://www.jstor.org/stable/42981081

Gorski, P. C., Davis, S. N., & Reiter, A. (2012). Self-efficacy and multicultural teacher education in the United States: The factors that influence who feels qualified to be a multicultural teacher educator. *Multicultural Perspectives, 14*(4), 220–228. https://doi.org/10.1080/15210960.2012.725332

Gribble, K., & Ziguras, J. (2003). Learning to Teach Offshore: Pre-Departure training for lecturers in transnational programs. *Higher Education Research and Development, 22*(2), 205–216.

Gudykunst, W. B. (2005). *Theorizing about intercultural communication*. Sage.

Gürü, K. (2011). Higher Education and International Student Mobility in the Global Knowledge Economy. State University of New York Press.

Guyton, E. M., & Wesche, M. V. (2005). The multicultural efficacy scale: Development, item selection, and reliability. *Multicultural Perspectives, 7*(4), 21–29. https://doi.org/10.1207/s15327892mcp0704_4

Halif, M. M., Hassan, N., Sumardi, N. A., Shekh Omar, A., Ali, S., Abdul Aziz, R., Abdul Majid, A., & Salleh, N. F. (2020). Moderating effects of student motivation on the relationship between learning styles and student engagement. *Asian Journal of University Education, 16*(2), 93. https://doi.org/10.24191/ajue.v16i2.10301

Hall, W. D., Cabrera, A. F., & Milem, J. F. (2010). A tale of two groups: Differences between minority students and non-minority students in their predispositions to and engagement with diverse peers at a predominantly White Institution. *Research in Higher Education, 52*(4), 420–439. https://doi.org/10.1007/s11162-010-9201-4

Hartini, H., Yaakub, S., Abdul-Talib, A. N., & Saud, M. B. (2017). The effects of cultural intelligence on international students' engagement. *International Journal of Business, Economics and Law, 12*(2), 18–25. https://www.ijbel.com/wp-content/uploads/2017/05/BUS-89.pdf

Hativa, N., Barak, R., & Simhi, E. (2001). Exemplary university teachers. *The Journal of Higher Education, 72*(6), 699–729. https://doi.org/10.1080/00221546.2001.11777122

Hawkins, J. N. (2013). East-west? Tradition and the development of hybrid higher education in Asia. *The Dynamics of Higher Education Development in East Asia*, 51–67. https://doi.org/10.1057/9781137347374_4

Henderson, M., Selwyn, N., & Aston, R. (2015). What works and why? Student perceptions of 'useful' digital technology in university teaching and learning. *Studies in Higher Education, 42*(8), 1567–1579. https://doi.org/10.1080/03075079.2015.1007946

Heng, T. T. (2016). Different is not deficient: Contradicting stereotypes of Chinese international students in US higher education. *Studies in Higher Education, 43*(1), 22–36. https://doi.org/10.1080/03075079.2016.1152466

Hill, C., Cheong, K.-C., Leong, Y.-C., & Fernandez-Chung, R. (2014). TNE—Trans-national education or tensions between national and external? A case study of Malaysia. *Studies in Higher Education, 39*(6), 952–966. https://doi.org/10.1080/03075079.2012.754862

Ho, S. (2020). Culture and learning: Confucian heritage learners, social-oriented achievement, and innovative pedagogies. *Diversity and Inclusion in Global Higher Education*, 117–159. https://doi.org/10.1007/978-981-15-1628-3_5

Hofstede, G. (1981). Culture and organizations. *International Studies of Management and Organization, 10*(4), 15–41.

Hofstede, G. (2003). The universal and the specific in 21st century management. In D. Tjosvold & K. Leung (Eds.), *Cross-cultural management* (pp. 29–42). Ashgate.

Holbrook, R. L. (2014). Moving images: Effective teaching with film and television in management. *Academy of Management Learning & Education, 13*(4), 680–683. https://doi.org/10.5465/amle.2014.0309

Holtbrügge, D., & Engelhard, F. (2016). Study abroad programs: Individual motivations, cultural intelligence, and the mediating role of cultural boundary spanning. *Academy of Management Learning & Education, 15*(3), 435–455. https://doi.org/10.5465/amle.2015.0128

Horsthemke, K. & Enslin, P. (2008). African philosophy of education: The price of unchallengeability. *Studies on the Philosophy of Education.*

Hou, A.Y.-C., Morse, R., & Wang, W. (2017). Recognition of academic qualifications in transnational higher education and challenges for recognizing a joint degree in Europe and Asia. *Studies in Higher Education, 42*(7), 1211–1228. https://doi.org/10.1080/03075079.2015.1085010

Hu, S., Liu, H., Zhang, S., & Wang, G. (2020). Proactive personality and cross-cultural adjustment: Roles of social media usage and cultural intelligence. *International Journal of Intercultural Relations, 74*, 42–57. https://doi.org/10.1016/j.ijintrel.2019.10.002

Huang, F. (2014). Challenges for higher education and research: A perspective from Japan. *Studies in Higher Education, 39*(8), 1428–1438. https://doi.org/10.1080/03075079.2014.949535

Huang, F., Teo, T., Sánchez-Prieto, J. C., García-Peñalvo, F. J., & Olmos-Miguelåñez, S. (2019). Cultural values and technology adoption: A model comparison with university teachers from China and Spain. *Computers & Education, 133*, 69–81. https://doi.org/10.1016/j.compedu.2019.01.012

Iskhakova, M. (2018). Does cross-cultural competence matter when going global: Cultural intelligence and its impact on performance of international students in Australia. *Journal of Intercultural Communication Research, 47*(2), 121–140. https://doi.org/10.1080/17475759.2018.1437463

Ituarte, S., & Davis, G. (2007). Perception of 'self' and 'other': Social boundaries that influence teaching and learning in increasingly diverse us classrooms. In D. Palfreyman & D. L. McBride (Eds.), *Learning and teaching across cultures in higher education.* Palgrave Macmillan. https://doi.org/10.1057/9780230590427

Jenkins, J. (2000). *The phonology of English as an international language.* Oxford University Press.

Joy, S., & Kolb, D. A. (2009). Are there cultural differences in learning style? *International Journal of Intercultural Relations, 33*(1), 69–85. https://doi.org/10.1016/j.ijintrel.2008.11.002

Kahu, E. R. (2013). Framing student engagement in higher education. *Studies in Higher Education, 38*(5), 758–773. https://doi.org/10.1080/03075079.2011.598505

Kang, H.-S. T., Kim, E.-J., & Park, S. (2019). Multicultural teaching efficacy and cultural intelligence of teachers. *International Journal of Educational Management, 33*(2), 265–275. https://doi.org/10.1108/ijem-11-2017-0318

Keengwe, J. (2010). Fostering cross cultural competence in preservice teachers through multicultural education experiences. *Early Childhood Education Journal, 38*(3), 197–204. https://doi.org/10.1007/s10643-010-0401-5

Kellner, D. (1998). Globalization and the postmodern turn. In R. Axtmann (Ed.), *Globalization and Europe: Theoretical and empirical investigations*. Pinters.

Keung, E. K., & Rockinson-Szapkiw, A. J. (2013). The relationship between transformational leadership and cultural intelligence. *Journal of Educational Administration, 51*(6), 836–854. https://doi.org/10.1108/jea-04-2012-0049

Khan, K. Z., Wang, X., Malik, S., & Ganiyu, S. A. (2020). Measuring the effects of emotional intelligence, cultural intelligence and cultural adjustment on the academic performance of international students. *Open Journal of Social Sciences, 8*(9), 16–38. https://doi.org/10.4236/jss.2020.89002

Khosa, D. K., & Volet, S. E. (2013). Promoting effective collaborative case-based learning at university: A metacognitive intervention. *Studies in Higher Education, 38*(6), 870–889. https://doi.org/10.1080/03075079.2011.604409

Killen, R. (2010). *Teaching strategies for quality teaching and learning*. Juta.

Kingston, E., & Forland, H. (2007). Bridging the gap in expectations between international students and academic staff. *Journal of Studies in International Education, 12*(2), 204–221. https://doi.org/10.1177/1028315307307654

Kitsantas, A. (2012). Teacher Efficacy Scale for Classroom Diversity (TESCD): A validation study—Profesorado. *Revista de Curriculum y Formación Del Profesorado, 16*(1), 35–44. http://www.ugr.es/~recfpro/rev161ART3en.pdf

Kolb, D. (1984). *Experiential learning: Experience as the source of learning and development*. Prentice Hall.

Kreber, C. (2009). Different perspectives on internationalization in higher education. *New Directions for Teaching and Learning, 118*, 1–14. https://doi.org/10.1002/tl.348

Ladd, P. D., & Ruby, R., Jr. (1999). Learning style and adjustment issues of international students. *Journal of Education for Business, 74*(6), 363–367. https://doi.org/10.1080/08832329909601712

Latchem, C., & Jung, I. (2009). *Distance and blended learning in Asia* (Open and flexible learning series) (1st ed.). Routledge.

Leask, B. (2009). Using formal and informal curricula to improve interactions between home and international students. *Journal of Students in International Education, 13*, 205–221.

Leask and Bridge (2013). *Comparing internationalization of the cirriculum in action across disciplines: Theoretical and practical perspectives, compare, 43*(1), pp. 79–101.

Leask, B., & Carroll, J. (2011). Moving beyond 'wishing and hoping': Internationalization and student experiences of inclusion and engagement. *Higher Education Research & Development, 30*(5), 647–659. https://doi.org/10.1080/07294360.2011.598454

Lee, E. L. (2007). Linguistic and cultural factors in East Asian students' oral participation in U.S. university classrooms. *International Education, 36*(3), 29–47.

Lee, J. A. (1966). Cultural analysis in overseas operations. *Harvard Business Review*, 106–114.

Lee, J. J., & Rice, C. (2007). Welcome to America? International student perceptions of discrimination. *Higher Education, 53*(3), 381–409. https://doi.org/10.1007/s10734-005-4508-3

Lee, M., Wan, C. D., & Sirat, M. (2017). Hybrid universities in Malaysia. *Studies in Higher Education, 42*(10), 1870–1886. https://doi.org/10.1080/03075079.2017.1376871

Lemaitre, M. J. (2022). *Quality as politics, Quality in Higher Education*. Taylor & Francis.

Lengnick-Hall, C. A., & Sanders, M. M. (1997). Designing effective learning systems for management education: Student roles, requisite variety, and practicing what we teach. *Academy of Management Journal, 40*(6), 1334–1368. https://doi.org/10.5465/257036

Lewis, L. H., & Williams, C. J. (1994). Experiential learning: Past and present. *New Directions for Adult and Continuing Education, 62*, 5–16. https://doi.org/10.1002/ace.36719946203

Lieven, M., & Martin, G. (2006). Higher education in a global market: The case of british overseas provision in Israel. *Higher Education, 52*, 41–68.

Livermore, D. (2009). *Leading with cultural intelligence: The new secret to success*. AMACOM.

Livermore, D. (2011). *The cultural intelligence difference: Master the one skill you can't do without in today's global economy* (1st ed.). AMACOM.

Loke, H. Y., Chia, Y.-T., & Gopinathan, S. (2017). Hybridity, the developmental state and globalisation: The case of Singapore's universities. *Studies in Higher Education, 42*(10), 1887–1898. https://doi.org/10.1080/03075079.2017.1376874

Lomer, S., & Anthony-Okeke, L. (2019). Ethically engaging international students: Student generated material in an active blended learning model. *Teaching in Higher Education, 24*(5), 613–632. https://doi.org/10.1080/13562517.2019.1617264

Maarop, A. H., & Embi, M. A. (2016). Implementation of blended learning in higher learning institutions: A review of literature. *International Education Studies, 9*(3), 41.

MacNab, B. R. (2011). An experiential approach to cultural intelligence education. *Journal of Management Education, 36*(1), 66–94. https://doi.org/10.1177/1052562911412587

Macrae, M. (2002). The induction of international students to academic life in the United Kingdom. In D. McNamara & R. Harris (Eds.), *Overseas students in higher education*. Routledge. https://doi.org/10.4324/9780203040065

Manikutty, S., Anuradha, N. S., & Hansen, K. (2007). Does culture influence learning styles in higher education? *International Journal of Learning and Change, 2*(1), 70. https://doi.org/10.1504/ijlc.2007.014896

Marginson, S., & van der Wende, M. (2007). To rank or to be ranked: The impact of global rankings in higher education. *Journal of Studies in International Education, 11*(3–4), 306–329. https://doi.org/10.1177/1028315307303544

May, M., & Bartlett, A. (1995). "They've got a problem with English": Perceptions of the difficulties of international post graduate students. In P. Thomas (Ed.), *Teaching for development: An international review of Australian and non-formal education for Asia and the Pacific*. National Centre for Development Studies, Australian National University.

McAllister, G., & Irvine, J. J. (2000). Cross cultural competency and multicultural teacher education. *Review of Educational Research, 70*(1), 3–24. https://doi.org/10.3102/00346543070001003

McBurnie, G., & Ziguras, C. (2001). The regulation of transnational higher education in Southeast Asia: Case studies of Hong Kong, Malaysia and Australia. *Higher Education, 42*(1), 85–105.

McBurnie, G., & Ziguras, C. (2007). *Transnational education: Issues and trends in offshore higher education*. Routledge.

McCown, R., Driscoll, M., & Roop, P. G. (1996). *Educational psychology: A learning-centered approach to classroom practice* (2nd ed.). Allyn & Bacon Publishers.

McCoy, D. L., Winkle-Wagner, R., & Luedke, C. L. (2015). Colorblind mentoring? Exploring white faculty mentoring of students of color. *Journal of Diversity in Higher Education, 8*(4), 225–242. https://doi.org/10.1037/a0038676

Mendenhall, M. E., Arnardottir, A. A., Oddou, G. R., & Burke, L. A. (2013). Developing cross-cultural competencies in management education via cognitive-behavior therapy. *Academy of Management Learning & Education, 12*(3), 436–451. https://doi.org/10.5465/amle.2012.0237

Meyer, M., Bushney, M. J., & Ukpere, W. I. (2011). The impact of globalisation on higher education: Achieving a balance between local and global needs and realities. *African Journal of Business Management, 5*(15), 6569–6578. https://doi.org/10.5897/AJBM11.205

Molina, S. (2013). Romanticizing culture: The role of teachers' cultural intelligence in working with diversity. *CATESOL Journal, 21*, 220–244. https://www.researchgate.net/publication/311856359_romanticizing_culture_the_role_of_teachers'_cultural_intelligence_in_working_with_diversity

Moon, T. (2013). The effects of cultural intelligence on performance in multicultural teams. *Journal of Applied Social Psychology, 43*(12), 2414–2425. https://doi.org/10.1111/jasp.12189

Morey, A. I. (2000). Changing higher education curricula for a global and multicultural world. *Higher Education in Europe, 25*(1), 25–39. https://doi.org/10.1080/03797720050002170

Morgan-Thomas, A., & Dudau, A. (2019). Of possums, hogs, and horses: Capturing the duality of student engagement in e learning. *Academy of Management Learning & Education, 18*(4), 564–580. https://doi.org/10.5465/amle.2018.0029

Mosakowski, E., & Earley, P. C. (2004, October). Cultural intelligence. *Harvard Business Review*. https://hbr.org/2004/10/cultural-intelligence
Naidoo, R., & Jamieson, I. (2005). Knowledge in the marketplace: The global commodification of teaching and learning in higher education. In P. Ninnes & M. Hellstén (Eds.), *Internationalizing higher education: CERC studies in comparative education* (Vol. 16). Springer. https://doi.org/10.1007/1-4020-3784-8_3
Nayyar, D. (2007). Globalisation: What does it mean for higher education? *Economic and Political Weekly, 42*(50), 30–35. https://www.jstor.org/stable/40277048
Ng, C. L. (2007). Teaching business studies to far east students in the UK. In D. Palfreyman & D. L. McBride (Eds.), *Learning and teaching across cultures in higher education*. Palgrave Macmillan. https://doi.org/10.1057/9780230590427
Ng, K. Y., & Earley, P. C. (2006). Culture and intelligence: Old constructs. *New Frontiers. Group and Organization Management, 31*(4), 4–19.
Ng, K., Van Dyne, L., & Ang, S. (2009). From experience to experiential learning: CQ as a learning capability for global leadership development. *Academy of Management Learning & Education, 8*, 511–526.
Nguyen, H. (2007). Impacts of globalization on higher education in China and Vietnam: Policy and practice. *Conference: 4th Education in a Changing Environment Conference* (pp. 68–77). https://www.researchgate.net/publication/216792907_Impacts_of_globalization_on_higher_education_in_China_and_Vietnam_Policy_and_practice
Nguyen, P. M., Elliott, J. G., Terlouw, C., & Pilot, A. (2009). Neocolonialism in education: Cooperative learning in an Asian context. *Comparative Education, 45*(1), 109–130. https://doi.org/10.1080/03050060802661428
Nguyen, P. M., Terlouw, C., & Pilot, A. (2006). Culturally appropriate pedagogy: The case of group learning in a Confucian heritage culture context. *Intercultural Education, 17*(1), 1–19. https://doi.org/10.1080/14675980500502172
Oddou, G. (2005). A cross-culture exercise: Expat in the marketplace. *Journal of Management Education, 29*, 758–768.
Ott, D. L., & Michailova, S. (2016). Cultural intelligence: A review and new research avenues. *International Journal of Management Reviews, 20*(1), 99–119. https://doi.org/10.1111/ijmr.12118
Palfreyman, D., & McBride, D. (2007). *Learning and teaching across cultures in higher education* (2007th ed.). Palgrave Macmillan.
Pedersen, P. (2004). *110 experiences for multicultural learning*. American Psychological Association.
Petrović, D. S. (2011). How do teachers perceive their cultural intelligence? *Procedia—Social and Behavioral Sciences, 11*, 276–280. https://doi.org/10.1016/j.sbspro.2011.01.076
Pike, G. R., Smart, J. C., & Ethington, C. A. (2011). The mediating effects of student engagement on the relationships between academic disciplines and learning outcomes: An extension of Holland's theory. *Research in Higher Education, 53*(5), 550–575. https://doi.org/10.1007/s11162-011-9239-y
Poultney, V., & Fordham, J. (2018). Researching reciprocal leadership. *Management in Education, 32*(1), 32–39. https://doi.org/10.1177/0892020617748151
Presbitero, A. (2016). Culture shock and reverse culture shock: The moderating role of cultural intelligence in international students' adaptation. *International Journal of Intercultural Relations, 53*, 28–38. https://doi.org/10.1016/j.ijintrel.2016.05.004
Prescott, A., & Hellstén, M. (2005). Hanging together even with non-native speakers: The international student transition experience. In P. Ninnes & M. Hellstén (Eds.), *Internationalizing higher education: CERC studies in comparative education* (Vol. 16). Springer. https://doi.org/10.1007/1-4020-3784-8_5
Prowse, J., & Goddard, J. T. (2010). Teaching across cultures: Canada and Qatar. *Canadian Journal of Higher Education, 40*(1), 31–52. https://eric.ed.gov/?id=EJ904269

Rajaram, K. (2010). Culture Clash: teaching western-based business education to mainland Chinese students in Singapore, Doctoral Dissertation, University of South Australia, Adelaide.
Rajaram, K. (2013). Followers of Confucianism or a new generation? Learning culture of mainland Chinese in pursuit of western based business education away from mainland China. *International Journal of Teaching & Learning in Higher Education, 25*(3), 369–377.
Rajaram, K. (2019). Flipped classrooms: Scaffolding support system with real-time learning interventions. *Asian Journal of the Scholarship of Teaching and Learning, 9*(1), 30–58.
Rajaram, K. (2021). *Evidence-based teaching for the 21st century classroom and beyond—innovative-driven learning strategies*. Springer.
Rajaram, K., & Bordia, S. (2011). Culture clash: Teaching western-based management education to mainland Chinese students in Singapore. *Journal of International Education in Business, 4*(1), 63–83.
Rajaram, K., & Bordia, S. (2013). East versus west: Effectiveness of knowledge acquisition and impact of cultural dislocation issues for mainland Chinese students across ten commonly used instructional techniques. *International Journal for the Scholarship of Teaching and Learning, 7*(1), 1–21 (ISSN 1931-4744).
Rajaram, K., & Collins, J. (2013). Qualitative identification of learning effectiveness measures among mainland Chinese students in culturally dislocated study environments. *Journal of International Education in Business, 6*(2), 179–199.
Ramsey, J. R., & Lorenz, M. P. (2016). Exploring the impact of cross-cultural management education on cultural intelligence, student satisfaction, and commitment. *Academy of Management Learning & Education, 15*(1), 79–99. https://doi.org/10.5465/amle.2014.0124
Richard, W., & Brislin, R. W. (1981). *Cross-cultural Encounters, Face-to-face Interaction*, Pergamon Press.
Richter, N. F., Schlaegel, C., Bakel, M. V., & Engle, R. L. (2020). The expanded model of cultural intelligence and its explanatory power in the context of expatriation intention. *European Journal of International Management, 14*(2), 381. https://doi.org/10.1504/ejim.2020.105545
Robertson, M., Line, M., Jones, S., & Thomas, S. (2000). International students, learning environments and perceptions: A case study using the Delphi technique. *Higher Education Research & Development, 19*(1), 89–102. https://doi.org/10.1080/07294360050020499
Robson, S., & Wihlborg, M. (2019). Internationalization of higher education: Impacts, challenges and future possibilities. *European Educational Research Journal, 18*(2), 127–134. https://doi.org/10.1177/1474904119834779
Rollag, K. (2010). Teaching business cases online through discussion boards: Strategies and best practices. *Journal of Management Education, 34*(4), 499–526. https://doi.org/10.1177/1052562910368940
Rosenblatt, V., Worthley, R., & MacNab, B. (2013). From contact to development in experiential cultural intelligence education: The mediating influence of expectancy disconfirmation. *Academy of Management Learning & Education, 12*(3), 356–379. https://doi.org/10.5465/amle.2012.0199
Roser, M. & Ortiz-Ospina, E. (2013). *Primary and Secondary Education*. Retrieved from https://ourworldindata.org/primary-and-secondary-education
Roy, A., Newman, A., Ellenberger, T., & Pyman, A. (2018). Outcomes of international student mobility programs: A systematic review and agenda for future research. *Studies in Higher Education, 44*(9), 1630–1644. https://doi.org/10.1080/03075079.2018.1458222
Ruben, B. D., & Kealey, D. J. (1979). Behavioral assessment of communication competency and the prediction of cross-cultural adaptation. *International Journal of Intercultural Relations, 3*(1), 15–47.
Ryan, J. (2012). *Cross-cultural teaching and learning for home and international students: Internationalization of pedagogy and curriculum in higher education*. Routledge.
Salmi, J (2009). The Challenge of Establishing World-Class Universities, World Bank. https://lst-iiep.iiep-unesco.org/cgi-bin/wwwi32.exe/inepidoc1.in/t2000-027226/(100). https://doi.org/10.1596/978-0-8213-7865-6.

Saunders, C., Van Slyke, C., & Vogel, D. R. (2004). My time or yours? Managing time visions in global virtual teams. *Academy of Management Perspectives, 18*(1), 19–37. https://doi.org/10.5465/ame.2004.12691177
Sawir, E. (2013). Internationalization of higher education curriculum: The contribution of international students. *Globalization, Societies and Education, 11*(3), 359–378. https://doi.org/10.1080/14767724.2012.750477
Schmidt-Wilk, J. (2010). Going abroad. *Journal of Management Education, 34*, 643–644.
Schumacher, T., & Festing, M. (2020). Developing cultural intelligence in a serious-game-centered blended course. *Academy of Management Proceedings, 1*, 19018. https://doi.org/10.5465/ambpp.2020.19018abstract
Schwarzer, R., & Hallum, S. (2008). Perceived teacher self-efficacy as a predictor of job stress and burnout: Mediation analyses. *Applied Psychology, 57*(s1), 152–171. https://doi.org/10.1111/j.1464-0597.2008.00359.x
Silverman, S. K. (2008). *The teachers' sense of multicultural efficacy scale: Construction and validation.* 22nd Hayes Graduate Research Forum, 1–14. https://kb.osu.edu/handle/1811/32049.
Slavin, R. E. (1980). Cooperative learning. *Review of Educational Research, 50*(2), 315–342. https://doi.org/10.3102/00346543050002315
Smith-Maddox, R., & Solórzano, D. G. (2002). Using critical race theory, Paulo Freire's problem-posing method, and case study research to confront race and racism in education. *Qualitative Inquiry, 8*(1), 66–84. https://doi.org/10.1177/107780040200800105
Spencer-Rodgers, J., & McGovern, T. (2002). Attitudes toward the culturally different: The role of intercultural communication barriers, affective responses, consensual stereotypes, and perceived threat. *International Journal of Intercultural Relations, 26*(6), 609–631. https://doi.org/10.1016/s0147-1767(02)00038-x
Sternberg, R. J., & Detterman, D. K. (1986). *What is intelligence? Contemporary viewpoints on its nature and definition.* Ablex.
Straker, J. (2016). International student participation in higher education. *Journal of Studies in International Education, 20*(4), 299–318. https://doi.org/10.1177/1028315316628992
Strickland, D. L. (2018). Factors relating to the multicultural efficacy and attitudes of teachers. *Electronic Theses and dissertations.* 1742. https://digitalcommons.georgiasouthern.edu/etd/1742
Stromquist, N. P., & Monkman, K. (2014). *Globalization and education: Integration and contestation across cultures* (2nd ed.). R&L Education.
Su, R. (2012). Enhancing international student engagement: Interpreting business messages in visual approaches. *Student Engagement and Experience Journal, 1*(3), pp. 1–9.
Tatar, M., & Horenczyk, G. (2003). Diversity-related burnout among teachers. *Teaching and Teacher Education, 19*(4), 397–408. https://doi.org/10.1016/s0742-051x(03)00024-6
Tchaicha, J., & Davis, M. (2005). The impact of culture on technology and business: An interdisciplinary, experiential course paradigm. *Journal of Management Education, 29*(5), 738–757.
Teichler, U. (2003). The future of higher education and the future of higher education research. *Tertiary Education and Management, 9*, 171–185.
Tharapos, M. (2015). *Cultural intelligence in the transnational education classroom: The case of Australian accounting academics.* https://www.semanticscholar.org/paper/Cultural-intelligence-in-the-transnational-The-case-Tharapos/94196cf79504b32cd67dc3d8e31e29f49d32763b#references
Thomas, D. C. (2006). Domain and development of cultural intelligence. *Group & Organization Management, 31*(1), 78–99. https://doi.org/10.1177/1059601105275266
Thomas, D. C. (2015). *Cultural intelligence.* Wiley Encyclopedia of Management, 1–3. https://doi.org/10.1002/9781118785317.weom060051
Thomas, D. C., Elron, E., Stahl, G., Ekelund, B. Z., Ravlin, E. C., Cerdin, J.-L., Poelmans, S., Brislin, R., Pekerti, A., Aycan, Z., Maznevski, M., Au, K., & Lazarova, M. B. (2008). Cultural intelligence. *International Journal of Cross-Cultural Management, 8*(2), 123–143. https://doi.org/10.1177/1470595808091787

Thomas, D. C., & Inkson, K. (2003). *Cultural Intelligence: People skills for global business*. Berrett-Koehler Publishers.
Tschannen-Moran, M., Hoy, A. W., & Hoy, W. K. (1998). Teacher efficacy: Its meaning and measure. *Review of Educational Research, 68*(2), 202–248. https://doi.org/10.3102/00346543068002202
Upton, S., & Butters, L. (2019, October 19). The importance of developing cultural intelligence. *University World News*. https://www.universityworldnews.com/post.php?story=20191017135800899. Accessed 3 June 2020.
Vaira, M. (2004). Globalization and higher education organizational change: A framework for analysis. *Higher Education: The International Journal of Higher Education and Educational Planning, 48*(4), 483–510. https://eric.ed.gov/?id=EJ733389
Valentine, D., & Speece, M. (2002). Experiential learning methods in Asian cultures: A Singapore case study. *Business Communication Quarterly, 65*(3), 106–116. https://doi.org/10.1177/108056990206500314
Van Dyne, L., Ang, S., & Livermore, D. (2010). Cultural intelligence: A pathway for leading in a rapidly globalizing world. In *Leading across differences* (pp. 131–138). Pfeiffer. http://soonang.com/wp-content/uploads/2011/04/2010_VanDyne_CCL-CQ.pdf
Van Dyne, L., Ang, S., Ng, K. Y., Rockstuhl, T., Tan, M. L., & Koh, C. (2012). Sub-Dimensions of the four factor model of cultural intelligence: Expanding the conceptualization and measurement of cultural intelligence. *Social and Personality Psychology Compass, 6*(4), 295–313. https://doi.org/10.1111/j.1751-9004.2012.00429.x
Velarde, J. M., Ghani, M. F., Adams, D., & Cheah, J.-H. (2020). Towards a healthy school climate: The mediating effect of transformational leadership on cultural intelligence and organizational health. *Educational Management Administration & Leadership*. https://doi.org/10.1177/1741143220937311
Waghid, Y. (2002). Knowledge production and higher education transformation in South Africa: Towards reflexivity in university teaching, research and community service. *Higher Education, 43*, 457–488.
Wang, J., Spalding, E., Odell, S., & Klecka, C. (2011). Understanding teacher education in an Era of globalization. *Journal of Teacher Education, 62*, 115–120.
Wang, T., & Moore, L. (2007). Exploring learning style preferences of Chinese postgraduate students in Australian Transnational programs. *International Journal of Pedagogies and Learning, 3*(2), 31–41. https://doi.org/10.5172/ijpl.3.2.31
Watkins, D. (2000). Learning and teaching: A cross-cultural perspective. *School Leadership & Management, 20*(2), 161–173. https://doi.org/10.1080/13632430050011407
Watkins, D. A., & Biggs, J. B. (1996). *The Chinese learner: Cultural, psychological and contextual influences*. Hong Kong University Press.
Webster, J., & Hackley, P. (1997). Teaching effectiveness in technology-mediated distance learning. *Academy of Management Journal, 40*(6), 1282–1309. https://doi.org/10.2307/257034
Weiss, S. (2003). Teaching the cultural aspects of negotiation: A range of experiential techniques. *Journal of Management Education, 27*, 96–122.
Whetten, D. A. (2007). Principles of effective course design: What I wish I had known about learning-centered teaching 30 years ago. *Journal of Management Education, 31*(3), 339–357. https://doi.org/10.1177/1052562906298445
Wilkins, S. (2017). Ethical issues in transnational higher education: The case of international branch campuses. *Studies in Higher Education, 42*(8), 1385–1400. https://doi.org/10.1080/03075079.2015.1099624
Willcoxson, L. (1998). The impact of academics' learning and teaching preferences on their teaching practices: A pilot study. *Studies in Higher Education, 23*(1), 59–70. https://doi.org/10.1080/03075079812331380492
Williams, R., & Van Dyke, N. (2007). Measuring the international standing of universities with an application to Australian universities. *Higher Education, 53*, 819–841.
Williams, W. C. (1985). Effective teaching. *The Journal of Higher Education, 56*(3), 320–337. https://doi.org/10.1080/00221546.1985.11780693

Wong, J. (2004). Are the learning styles of Asian international students culturally or contextually based? *International Education Journal, 4*(4), 154–166.

Woods, P. R., Jordan, P. J., Loudoun, R., Troth, A. C., & Kerr, D. (2006). Effective teaching in the multicultural business classroom. *Journal of Teaching in International Business, 17*(4), 27–48. https://doi.org/10.1300/j066v17n04_03

Yang, R. (2003). Globalisation and higher education development: A critical analysis. *International Review of Education, 49*, 269–291. https://doi.org/10.1023/a:1025303303245

Zepke, N., & Leach, L. (2002). Appropriate pedagogy and technology in a cross-cultural distance education context. *Teaching in Higher Education, 7*(3), 309–321. https://doi.org/10.1080/13562510220144806

Zhao, C.-M., Kuh, G. D., & Carini, R. M. (2005). A comparison of international student and American student engagement in effective educational practices. *The Journal of Higher Education, 76*(2), 209–231. https://doi.org/10.1080/00221546.2005.11778911

Zhao, G. (2007). Culturally appropriate pedagogy: Is it always necessary? The case of East Asians learning math and science. *Intercultural Education, 18*(5), 473–486. https://doi.org/10.1080/14675980701685339

Chapter 3
Social-Psychological Intervention: Development of Cognitive Empathy

Kumaran Rajaram

Abstract This chapter presents the topic on social-psychological intervention: competency and skills development in cognitive empathy. The evidence-based approach takes an effective psychological intervention to elicit cognitive growth in a variety of contents and translates it into a university setting to develop students' cognitive empathy as part of the leadership skills. The intervention aims to prepare students for development in cognitive empathy and by extension, leadership skills in a university business course. Social-psychological interventions provoke individuals to address potential cognitive blocks that may inhibit positive learning behaviours. Prior research has found this class of interventions to be effective tools for redressing negative mindsets liked views of intelligence and learned helplessness. This research is significant for three reasons (1) It attempts to prime students for the development of a non-content-based skill with a generalizable activity sequence; (2) It compares the effects of this priming activity against students receiving more domain-specific content; (3) It introduces methods of analysing student work for holistic solutions and for indicators of graduate attributes instead of merely addressing content knowledge and domain-specific skills. This chapter presents some specific deliverables, which are easily adopted to be inculcated and for training others on the aspects of competency and skills in the area of cognitive empathy. A set of activities and learning measures for developing cognitive empathy as part of development is shared. Empathy and leadership, as competencies, fall under the university's graduate outcomes. They relate to communication, civic-mindedness, character, competency and creativity. As such, curriculum that develops empathy and leadership is valuable not only for business school courses, but across university-wide. Additionally, this study provides ways of using survey questions and coding students' work to measure the development of these constructs which could be easily applied university-wide and beyond. A template for developing social-psychological interventions is developed to facilitate the development of cognitive empathy in a measurable way. Likewise, similar interventions can be used to develop other non-content-based skills. The key to making the intervention cycle transferable is to identify the psychological

K. Rajaram (✉)
Division of Leadership, Management and Organization, Nanyang Business School, Nanyang Technological University, Singapore, Singapore
e-mail: rkumaran@ntu.edu.sg

K. Rajaram, *Learning Intelligence: Innovative and Digital Transformative Learning Strategies*, https://doi.org/10.1007/978-981-19-9201-8_3

blocks that are hindering the development and creating materials to force students to address those blocks. Different skills will have different blocks. This project will provide a tested template for the development and use of social-psychological interventions that can be modified for the development of materials for interventions that address other "tough to teach" skills and abilities. Many universities are pursuing ways of engaging instructors to look at their courses as research opportunities to further teaching and learning throughout the university. The discussion of how we built a set of processes to make such research not only viable but also valuable to all parties is discussed. The process of how the set of processes and binding infrastructure developed to facilitate such research is also discussed. This study does serve as a pioneering opportunity for the development of these resources and a concrete example to be pointed to when advocating for more scholarship of teaching and learning.

3.1 Introduction

In a management education classroom, educators often face a dilemma of whether to dedicate precious class time to teaching of course content or development of soft skills related to the content (Rubin & Dierdorff, 2009). Teaching soft skills in class may lead to an unnecessary sacrifice of content teaching (Anthony & Garner, 2016) and therefore, having to achieve both concurrently may be a challenge. Furthermore, many programmes may not have the flexibility to include relevant soft skills teaching activities into their already heavy course loads (Bedwell et al., 2014). Educators have to be referees at the interface of this educational tug-of-war—believing they must choose one side while sacrificing the other. For instance, educators must balance how much time should be spent introducing the four functions (planning, organizing, leading and controlling) of management against how much time students need to investigate, test and apply the theories. They must teach business ethics and still gather a sense of whether their students will make ethically responsible decisions (Gioia, 2002).

There has been a growing awareness among the educators to prepare students to respond to the ever-changing needs of the increasingly globalized contemporary workplace; the mere teaching of contents is not good enough. There is a demand by employers for new employees to possess soft skills which include interpersonal skills, communication skills and empathy (Andrews & Higson, 2008; Bedwell et al., 2014; Goleman, 1998). Unfortunately, it was also suggested by various reports that there is a lack of soft skills in graduates and employees (Anthony & Garner, 2016; Bedwell et al., 2014).

Soft skills differ from the "hard" and technical skills (Anthony & Garner, 2016). Apart from improving new graduate's employability (Andrews & Higson, 2008; Anthony & Garner, 2016), soft skills are also believed to be important for work performance, success as a manager and have other work-related benefits (Bedwell et al., 2014; Hayes, 2002; Morgeson et al., 2005).

Our study is particularly targeted at the development of one of the soft skills: cognitive empathy. One of the essential competencies as a leader is the ability to handle interpersonal relationships. This study partially closed this institutional gap in knowledge and provided a model for developing non-content-based learning outcomes, relevant activities and the measures that connect those activities to the outcomes. The study was executed with two primary aims, namely: (1) using a social-psychological intervention to prepare students for empathy and leadership development and (2) using students' written work and class activities as measures of cognitive empathy. We measured spontaneous displays of cognitive empathy in students' written work and analysed self-evaluations of their empathy as part of their leadership qualities. Fortunately, development in psychology has created a new way of using the same activity to achieve both greater depth of knowledge in a field and development of skills, beliefs, and identity necessary for that field (Dweck, 1986; Rogoff, 2003; Van Haneghan et al., 1992; Walton, 2014).

The ultimate question we seek to answer is whether we can get students to internalize the importance of cognitive empathy and display it in an observable way. Working within an existing curriculum, we sought to elicit and capture a measure of cognitive empathy development by introducing the Stanford d.school's version of the design thinking process (Brown, 2008). This interpretation of design thinking focuses on the process of empathize, define, ideate, prototype and test (Brown, 2008). The stages of this instantiation of the design thinking process is presented by Stanford d.school's stages of Design Thinking (Standford d.school, 2012).

The d.school's courses and projects are built on a process that leads with empathy. The designer needs to understand profoundly the needs, wants, and desires of the people he is solving the problem for (Brown, 2008; Stock et al., 2017). This must happen before the designer can formally define that problem. Successful design thinkers can understand people deeply which allows them to clarify problems before proceeding to brainstorm solutions, prototyping the promising ideas, and eventually testing whether the prototypes work.

In the management context, design thinking lends itself to transformational leadership styles where managers concern themselves with developing their workers to be better people and not just more productive employees. It can also be harnessed to inform human system design with its interconnecting layers of complexity. With empathy development as our study's destination, design thinking as the path leading towards the goal, all we needed is the transport which can bring us to our goal.

3.2 Leadership Competencies

While the terms "skills" and "competencies" are sometimes used interchangeably, they are not exactly identical. Skills is one of the three facets that comprises of a competency, the other two being knowledge and abilities. The right mix of these three facets will allow a person to perform a job successfully (Beckett, 2018) and with a higher level of efficacy that enhances productivity and quality of work. Hence, in the context of leadership, competencies are a combination of knowledge, skills and abilities that establish effective leadership within an organization (Towler, 2020).

Some significant leadership competencies have been highlighted in a study by Giles (2016). 195 global leaders were asked to rate 74 qualities. Of that, the top 10 leadership competencies include "high ethical and moral standards", "goals and objectives with non-rigid guidelines/directions" and "flexibility to change opinions", along with the other seven, that are categorized into five primary themes namely: strong ethics and safety, self-organizing, efficient learning, nurturing growth and connection and belonging. Further to these specific competencies, there are a multitude of leadership competency models advocated. Although there is no one "right" model/framework that addresses all challenges, organizations should discern the model/ framework or a mixture of some that would help them to develop their idealized version of a leader. For instance, a study by Welch and Hodge (2017) found that the development and design of a district leadership competency model increased clarity, shared understanding, and uniformity of practice, where it also supports improvements in the development of participants.

The essential competencies for leaders to have in the twenty-first century, Industry 4.0 (I4.0) and beyond need to be advocated and emphasized. The primary characteristics of leadership in the I4.0 context include agile leadership, participative leadership and collaborative leadership (Guzmán et al., 2020). Leaders today require the ability to manage digital environments, as such they need to continuously upgrade their skills to be able to sustain, work and continuously value-add in the digitalized world.

Studies have validated that the correlation between leadership competencies and leader effectiveness is largely determined by organizational or team performance (Korzynski et al., 2020). Further to this, organizational constraints could be addressed by certain competencies exemplified by the leaders. For example, professional development of students and staff would enable them to be developed and progressively become high-performing and value-adding employees and leaders of an organization. Hence, we could imply that leadership competencies led towards superior organizational performance (Rohana & Abdullah, 2017).

Leadership programmes that target individuals' skills, abilities and/or knowledge are benefiting for organizations to better the leadership competencies of their staff across all levels. The development of young adults has predominantly gained traction in recent years. Leadership programmes vary from professional practice-oriented workshops, master classes to postgraduate diplomas and executive masters programmes. While exposure and training is provided for students to develop leadership competencies before they embark in the working world, the continuity in organizations to sustain and grow individuals through leadership development programmes to upskill their managerial staff has to be a continuous process.

While these development programmes are generally useful, organizations must ensure that they are effective, and organization-focused in order to ensure that resources and costs are wisely spent in terms of optimization. For instance, one pitfall to avoid and a criticism that business schools commonly face regarding leadership development is the adoption and/or use of their "one-size fits all approach". Zaar et al. (2020) suggest that schools personalize, contextualize and customize their leadership development to explicitly suit the needs of their students. They provide three recommendations to incorporate a cognitive approach in the design and delivery of leadership development programmes. They are: (a) facilitate leadership development, not leadership; (2) ask to engage through open questions instead of providing fixed answers; and (3) engage in meaningful experiences to support students' leader identity development. Although their study centred around business schools, organizations in varying industries are able to reflect and leverage on these recommendations to train leaders more effectively. Training is imperative as it caters to every individual trainee on the basis that each individual has different starting levels of skills and competencies.

Leadership is a very complex concept. Leadership competency is defined as "the underlying characteristics of a person that lead to or cause effective and outstanding performance" (Boyatzis, 2009, p. 750). Emotional and social competencies are crucial for leaders (Boyatzis et al., 2018) in almost all industries (Bedwell et al., 2014).

As "a central characteristic of emotionally intelligent behaviour" (Salovey & Mayer, 1990, p. 194), empathy was not given much recognition on lists of management competencies by prior research (Holt & Marques, 2012) and even less recognition for its development in the context of business school courses (Brown et al., 2010). It may be due to a misperception of empathy as being opposite to the stereotype of an assertive, competitive and dominant leader. However, empathy is by no means a weakness. Research suggest that the most effective leaders are those who possess high emotional intelligence (Amdurer et al., 2014; Boyatzis, 2009; Druskat et al., 2005).

According to Goleman (1998, p. 100), "empathy is particularly important today as a component of leadership for at least three reasons: the increasing use of teams, the rapid pace of globalization, and the growing need to retain talent". Being empathetic allows the leaders to better navigate intricate work relationships. When a leader empathizes, the team members may feel more valued and understood, and therefore more trust for the leader, more motivated at work and more unity within the team. Empathy can also promote better communication and therefore improve team problem-solving and decision-making abilities.

As the world of business becomes more globalized, diversity in workplace is also becoming more common. Empathy is required from modern leaders to allow connection with team members from different cultural and racial backgrounds and understanding of diverse perspectives. Therefore, empathic leadership is expected to play an increasingly important role in leadership today. Moreover, research has shown a strong relationship between empathy and current theories of leadership (Tzouramani, 2017). For example, high levels of empathy is required for transformational leadership (Bass & Avolio, 1990) as it makes a leader effective (Ashkanasy & Tse, 2000) through the leader's ability to establish a common understanding with others (Kellett et al., 2002). This is in contrast with transactional leaders who look at their team members as means to ends or cogs in a machine. However, not everyone agrees that empathy can or should be taught in a classroom (Holt, 2012). Some feel that teaching empathy in class takes away the precious time that should be used to teach students contents of the course. The coverage demands of the undergraduate business school curriculum often preclude opportunities to develop students' propensity for cognitive empathy (Brown et al., 2010).

To resolve this dilemma, we proposed the use of design thinking in the form of a social-psychological activity embedded in the course in the form of a pre-course activity to prepare students for empathy development.

3.3 Empathy

Empathy can be viewed as one of the crucial competencies that leaders should have, and future leaders should potentially develop. Researchers often describe two types of empathy, namely cognitive empathy and affective (emotional) empathy. While both types of empathy are equally valid and vital in their own rights, cognitive empathy is substantially easier to develop as it can be taught and developed through programmes whereas affective empathy is often inherent and gained through experience, and hence harder to influence or to be taught. Further to this, cognitive empathy plays a crucial role in the absence of affective empathy as a result of sociocultural differences (Riess, 2017).

We acknowledge that the vast literature on empathy is diverse and transdisciplinary. However, there is a general agreement that empathy is multidimensional, with cognitive and affective components (Davis, 1983; Davis et al., 1994). Cognitive empathy is a conscious processing of others on the mental level and affective empathy is a physiological and unconscious processing of others (Segal et al., 2017).

Our study focused on developing the cognitive component which is also at times called perspective-taking. Cognitive empathy is a conscious and intellectual process of making one comprehend another person's emotional state or point of view (Davis, 2009; Stephan & Finlay, 1999). One can take the perspective of someone else without having to feel it oneself. It enables one to simulate another person's thoughts or physiological processes (Davis et al., 1994). It is "the tendency to spontaneously adopt the psychological point of view of others in everyday life" (Davis, 1994, p. 57). Highly cognitively empathetic individuals are aware of their own thoughts and emotions, hence could effectively use those insights when interacting with others (Carre et al., 2013). On the other hand, affective empathy, is the unconscious, affective response to another's emotional state. Highly affective empathic people are often able to "feel other people's emotions" as if they were experiencing those feelings themselves (Bryant, 1982). The affective process often involves mirroring (Lacoboni, 2008).

There are three reasons why we chose cognitive empathy as the focus of this study. First, we used design thinking as a tool for teaching empathy. The framework of design thinking that we adopted makes cognitive empathy as an important first step. Second, we have designed measurement of display of empathy in students in the form of cognitive role-taking, i.e. when students display in their writing that they had inferred the mental state of others (Davis, 1996). Also, empathy trainers distinguish teaching "basic empathy" and "trained empathy" (Alligood, 2002; Morse et al., 1992). Basic empathy is related to the affective component of empathy, and it is something that we develop through interactions with others (Howe, 2013). It is believed that trained empathy is more cognitive in nature and that is what trainers focus on when the trainees are taught how to take another person's perspective.

3.3.1 Cognitive Empathy

Cognitive empathy is "the ability to ascribe mental states to others, such as beliefs, intentions, or emotions" (Maiborn, 2017, p. 1). This can be carried out through reflecting on how events, behaviours and psychological states co-vary and by taking on a different position or perspective to comprehend how others would feel. Further to this, we could leverage on two primary theoretical frameworks on how we could possibly understand another individual's perspective, namely Theory Theory (TT) and Simulation Theory (ST) (Spaulding, 2017). Cognitive empathy can also be viewed as part of a dual route system. Affective empathy falls under the lower-level route as it is spontaneous and fast whereas cognitive empathy is the higher-level route which is slow and complex (Yu & Chou, 2018).

Most effective leaders accentuate cognitive empathy over affective empathy (Kalavana & Andreou, 2018). This could be largely related to the fact that cognitive empathy enables leaders to balance their relationships with others through a friendly and comforting environment, while reassuring their self-efficacy. On other hand, affective empathy while useful in building rapport and trust, it can be rather damaging if leaders are unable to sustain adequate emotional distance. Kalavana and Andreou (2018) reported four types of leaders categorized based on their level of cognitive and affective empathies. They used cognitive empathy and affective empathy as their two measuring variables to categorize the 4 types of leaders: (a) "low" in cognitive empathy and "low" in affective empathy—manager/leader; (b) "low" in cognitive empathy and "high" in affective empathy—friendly colleague/leader; (c) "high" in cognitive empathy and "low" in affective empathy—inspirational/effective leader; (d) "high" in cognitive empathy and "high" in affective empathy—emotional leader.

A study by Obliopas (2020) reports that cognitive empathy showed a positive relationship with leadership performance, where this reiterates that cognitive empathy is a much-required competency of an effective leader. In general, empathy is a vital competency for leaders in organizations. There could be potentially significant business costs to incur if leaders function with lack of empathy (Gourguechon, 2017). For instance, Gourguechon (2017) also pointed to how lack of empathy contributes to the many sexual harassment incidents that has caused accomplished leaders to fail in their moral principle and resign. Therefore, organizations are required to train and inculcate competency in empathy aspects to leaders who may fall low on the empathy scale.

Empathy is generally understood as a person's understanding or feeling of what another person is experiencing from that person's point of view, i.e. being in another person's shoes (Henriksen, 2018). We acknowledge that the vast literature on empathy is diverse and transdisciplinary. However, there is a general agreement that empathy is multidimensional, with cognitive and affective components (Davis et al., 1994). Affective empathy is the unconscious, affective response to another's emotional state. Our project focuses on cognitive empathy. Cognitive empathy is the non-affective component of empathy (Davis et al., 1994). Essentially, it is an understanding of what someone else is thinking or feeling without necessarily having to feel it yourself. Cognitive empathy allows a person to simulate another person's thoughts or physiological processes. It develops over time and is thought to be fully developed by the time a person is in their mid-twenties (Greimel et al., 2010). This extended time course makes cognitive empathy one of the few cognitive abilities that is still developing in most undergraduates.

From a management perspective, high level of cognitive empathy is required for transformational leadership, human systems design and transdisciplinary problem-solving where understanding how the key stakeholders think and feel is a part of understanding the problem (Kellett et al., 2002). For example, transformational leaders look at their workers and see people with wants, needs and desires (Bass, 1991). Transformational leadership is predicated on a leader's ability to establish a common understanding with others (Kellett et al., 2002). This bond, in turn, is predicated on the leader's proper application of cognitive empathy—the non-affective component of empathy.

Research in the past has found little recognition for empathy on lists of management competencies (Holt & Marques, 2012) and even less recognition for its development in the context of business school courses (Brown et al., 2010). The coverage demands of the undergraduate business school curriculum often preclude identifying student's propensity for cognitive empathy and providing opportunities to develop it (Brown et al., 2010). Fortunately, there has been a rising awareness of educators for the need of empathy in business leadership. This is because, in the increasingly globalized world, managers are required to have empathy for their employees in order to manage the culturally diverse workforce (Henson, 2016; Tzouramani, 2017; Young et al., 2017). Furthermore, empathy teaching in business schools is also recognized as crucial in students' ethical decision-making education (Baker, 2017).

3.3.2 Teaching Empathy

While some may be naturally good at expressing empathy, not everyone has the same level of competency. Therefore, to enhance a leader's performance and effectiveness, organizations must explore ways to equip their leaders how to demonstrate empathy (Gentry et al., 2016). Gentry et al. (2016) recommend organizations to: (a) talk about and emphasize the importance of displaying empathy in the workplace; (b) equip listening skills of their leaders to increase trust among their colleagues; (c) understand and resonate with others' perspectives; (d) cultivate compassion; (e) provide support for their global managers that enables them to work effectively across cultures.

Research studies highlight that the level of empathy to be ingrained to an individual could potentially change over the course of an education, though the change may either be positive or negative (Baker, 2017). Examples to increase empathy in education institutions include (a) getting learners to be involved in workshops, talks and professional development courses on topics inclined towards mindfulness, cultural, emotional and social intelligence and compassion; (b) enabling students to resonate and relate by seeing through the lens of others by using film, role-play situations and encouraging them to intermingle, interact with individuals from varying diverse cultural and social backgrounds. These approaches or methods may be adopted in the corporate world where organizations can engage experts to facilitate a workshops or customized workshops on empathy development.

The challenge in developing empathy on individuals is that it is challenging to quantify the growth in explicit sense due to its intangibility (Holt et al., 2017). Hence, any actual progress of empathy development among leaders may not be clearly obvious and difficult to measure. This further adds to the complexity and challenge of attributing improvements in the working environment directly to empathy development. Hence, this could potentially pose hindrances in gaining approval or justifying any costs spent on training and development targeted towards empathy development. There could also be other forms of challenges, for example the lack of awareness of one's own level of empathy, denial in acknowledging their lack and in a worst case, unwillingness to learn and grow. In addition, some researchers argue against the usefulness of empathy in business leadership models (Holt et al., 2017). In their advocate, they suggested that empathy can be counter-productive in decision-making as being sensitive to feedback could lead to second-guessing, decreasing management effectiveness. These contrary views and lesser perceived importance given to the trait empathy may significantly incumber the speedy acceptance of empathy as one of the essential competencies in leaders. However, we could logically agree that this may potentially be the case only if the leader is overly emotional and not able to moderate the affective nuances of the situational context. In most other contexts, an adequate level of empathy by leaders can certainly be viewed beneficial for the organization. It enables leaders to be customer-centric, resonate and relate by placing themselves in others' positions that helps to increase their awareness, extend more care and concern about the welfare of their employees, enable them to make more informed ethical decisions and many more.

Empathy is a quality trait that develops over time (Holt, 2012). Scholars found that younger-aged individuals use empathy-based emotions less than more mature-aged individuals (Greimel et al., 2010). Empathy is believed to be fully developed by early adulthood (Eisenberg et al., 2005) or mid-twenties (Greimel et al., 2010). While some studies seem to suggest that empathy appears to decline during college years (Hojat et al., 2009; Konrath et al., 2010), Eriksen (2009) found that certain aspects of empathy development can be highlighted and reinforced through the intervention of learning activities. Many scholars also found that perspective-taking can still be developed in college (e.g. Eisenberg et al., 2005; Holt & Marques, 2012), as it can be enhanced with practice and feedback (Gagne et al., 1992).

Indeed, Batt-Rawden et al. (2013) reviewed relevant articles and found that educational interventions increase empathy in students of medical field. The types of intervention used include reflective writing exercises requiring students to write about their own experience of illness (Baker, 2017; Cheung & Reeves, 2014; DasGupta & Charon, 2004; Gerdes et al., 2011; Hatcher et al., 1994). In this study, a significant increase in students' empathic content in their essay was found. Other interventions being reviewed include drama intervention where students were taught to act their role (Lim et al., 2011). This study has also found an increase in students' empathy. Also, a study done to investigate empathy for medical students, Cheung and Reeves (2014) found that students who completed an undergraduate course on Compassion in Medicine have shown greater empathy than the control group who did not complete the course. Medical students who have gone through a course on mindfulness which focuses on mind-body approaches such as meditation and guided imagery have shown greater empathic concerns in their self-reports.

Hatcher et al. (1994) found empathy developing activities, i.e. Rogerian-based curriculum in peer facilitation training to have significant effects with tertiary students. However, it was ineffective with high school students (Hatcher et al., 1994). Specifically, for managerial and leadership development, Taylor and Ladkin (2009) advocated use of art-based methods, such as theatre, music and poetry to teach empathy. Other methods of teaching suggested including using art, role-plays, interactions with people from different walks of life (Hoffman, 2000), role modelling, shadowing, mentoring (Hojat, 2009), interviews and cross-cultural exchanges (Bowen, 2014). Baker (2017) suggested that the "most authentic way of teaching students to empathize is through travel abroad programme, service-learning projects or internship in non-profit organizations" (p. 852). This is because, it could reduce in-group bias, similarity bias and here-and-now bias, which would in turn increase empathy (Baker, 2017).

3.4 Design Thinking

Design thinking is an iterative process that seeks to comprehend the user, challenge assumptions and redefine problems in an attempt to identify alternative strategies and solutions that might not be instantly apparent with our initial level of understanding (Dam & Siang, 2018). It enables a solution-based approach when tackling issues and allows organizations to develop empathy with the target audience in mind. In applying and teaching design thinking, the five-phase model proposed by the Hasso-Plattner Institute of Design at Stanford (also known as d.school) has been one of the forefront models. The five phases that comprise in the model are: empathize, define, ideate, prototype and test. For many organizations today, design thinking has become an essential tool for simplifying and humanizing matters (Kolko, 2015), where it assists in an organization's innovative capacity, specifically overcoming human tendencies that hinder innovations. Despite experienced designers often complaining that design thinking is too structured and linear, the structure of design thinking helps managers to adjust to new and reformed behaviours. This process provides managers and leaders who are not generally designers themselves, with psychological safety, enabling them to be more open and flexible to new ideas and innovations.

Further to that, a significant influence, both positively and negatively could be made on organizational cultures through the effective use of design thinking interventions (Elsbach & Stigliani, 2018). For instance, organizational cultures that were defined by collaboration and experimentation supported the use of design thinking tools in general while those that were characterized by productivity and performance hindered the use of such tools.

Empathy plays a vital role in the design process, where in accordance to Gasparini (2015), it can be addressed in varying ways. The required transformation of this emotional feeling as an attribute as well as a way to acquire insights into users' needs can be adopted and in doing so, inform the design process. In design thinking, participants need to be empathetic with users to create relevant solutions. Leveraging cognitive empathy, designers are able to apply different approaches to build competence and insights, enabling them to prioritize the need of their customers. Further to this, cognitive empathy can impact how a design team works together as there is a need to work with people from varying cultural or disciplinary backgrounds (Koppen & Meinel, 2015). The role that empathy plays in design thinking process serves as a good way to foster values on empathy within the organization. An example of an approach to gain cognitive empathic insights is the usage of "experience prototype" to examine how individuals using a product would feel (Gasparini, 2015). An organization may also wish to examine the social-psychological aspects of design thinking in order to improve their design process. The design thinker who is aware on how social-psychological aspects influence perception, engagement and behaviour can better comprehend, relate to the needs of the users and positively influence the innovation process (Thompson & Schonthal, 2020).

In general, design thinking is a highly influential process in today's dynamic and evolving business environmental context and climate. It enables the organizations to adopt a more customer-centric view that will benefit both the consumers, stakeholders and the organizations. By facilitating innovation and creating competitive advantages, organizations should adopt design thinking as a means to remain relevant in today's hyper-competitive environment.

3.5 Social-Psychological Interventions

Social-psychological interventions could be adopted by creatively designing and embedding them into individuals' activities to enhance leadership competencies. An intervention is defined as "any purposeful attempt at change" (Cohen et al., 2017, p. 658). It does not have to be a dedicated programme, set of activities or curriculum and can range from mini-, everyday interventions to large-scale ones. Regardless of the size or duration of the intervention, its impact is dependent on the meaning it brings. This explains why research has shown that even brief, single-shot social-psychological interventions have lasting impacts with diverse outcomes (Kenthirarajah & Walton, 2015). These interventions proofed to be impactful where it is found to reduce gaps in academic achievement (Spitzer & Aronson, 2015).

Many of the empathy interventions are inclined more towards developing individual's ability and capacity to empathize experience empathy (Rajaram, 2021; Weisz & Zaki, 2017). This is done largely through experience-based interventions and expression-based interventions. For experience-based interventions, learners gain an opportunity to take on a new perspective by either imagining themselves in another individual's position or by considering another individual's internal state. Such intervention enables these individuals to gain a much better understanding of others' thoughts and feelings. Expression-based interventions, on a flip side, teach learners to recognize another person's internal states and respond aptly. These comes useful and timely when one is unable to identify another's distress or is impaired in conveying empathy for another. These interventions are only likely to work where an individual person is able to empathize and is ready to empathize. Individuals often fail to empathize not because they are unable to but rather because they are unwilling to do so. Therefore, existing interventions may be largely restricted by this lack of motivation.

Hence, this is where the social-psychological interventions come into play. Most interventions introduce at least one novel element, in accordance to Cohen et al. (2017). Generally, social-psychological interventions present an element that energizes people by enabling a motivational process that subsequently is channelled into new behaviours. According to research scholars (Rajaram, 2021; Weisz & Zaki, 2017), these interventions can be used to develop empathy through (a) altering views of self; (b) transforming perceived social norms and (3) shifting people's construal of empathy-evoking circumstances. By leveraging on social-psychological interventions to comprehend the motives of people, one can preserve empathy in contexts, specifically where it is known to be unsuccessful. This can be done by using self-oriented interventions, group-based interventions and situation-based interventions. An intervention should not only guide people to empathize but also make them want to empathize. The process of shifting people's mindsets from their unwillingness to willingness to empathize is one of the goals of such interventions. Other specific social-psychological interventions revolving around empathy includes increasing perspective-taking and creating a common in-group identity (Čehajić-Clancy et al., 2016). Social-psychological interventions are highly beneficial to organizations that are keen to increase their staff's ability to empathize, especially when there is a low level of competency among managers and leaders. The absence of such interventions will only have the status quo to be repeated and have such issues regenerated (Cohen et al., 2017).

The inspiration for the development of our activity design comes from the exciting new development in psychological sciences for a class of intervention that is typically short and appears conventional and similar to everyday experience (Walton, 2014). The social-psychological interventions, under the disguise of innocuous activities, steer students to engage in effortful cognitive processing that addresses cognitive blocks and gives preference to alternative ways of thinking (Walton, 2014).

Social-psychological intervention theory can be compared to cognitive-behavioural therapy where the subject does cognitive work in preparation for future challenges and social pressures (Walton & Cohen, 2011). What makes social-psychological intervention different is that there is no requirement of licenced therapists or a long time to see progress. Also, the benefits of interventions were found to be not limited to individuals, but their social environments as well (Powers et al., 2016).

The working hypothesis for why social-psychological interventions are effective at behavioural change is because the subject must expend mental effort constructing new decision pathways to complete a task, that effort then inoculates them against challenges and helps them to maintain a stable mindset (Walton, 2014). In past research, social-psychological interventions have been developed to improve marriage quality by having subjects write undelivered letters to their spouses (Finkel et al., 2013) and change interracial perceptions (Aronson et al., 2002) by letting subjects think of positive examples that contradict racial stereotypes. Educational interventions have been used to improve student retention among freshmen at a large university (Cohen et al., 2006; Yeager & Walton, 2011), decreasing student suspension rate (Okonofua et al., 2016), and improving students' self-concept, effort and achievement in mathematics (Brisson et al., 2017).

We used the principles of social-psychological interventions to inform the design of our management competency learning activity. We extracted three design principles from the social-psychological interventions we reviewed: (1) make the students work at a novel and somewhat ambiguous task, and (2) make that task meaningful to the subject, (3) measure the psychological changes due to the activities. In classroom settings, we call psychological changes "learning outcomes".

3.6 Hypotheses

With all the pieces in place to develop a learning activity capable of developing cognitive empathy, we devised two hypotheses that addressed the efficacy of our activity design specifically.

Hypothesis 1: Students receiving resources on the design thinking process will be more likely to empathize with the problem's key stakeholders.

Hypothesis 2: Introducing students to design thinking process early in the semester would have a lasting effect on their development and displays of cognitive empathy later in their ethical assignment.

3.7 Methods

3.7.1 Settings

83 undergraduate students enrolled in a business management course voluntarily consented to making their course activity data and assignments available for analysis. The students came from two course sections of a larger cohort. The same instructor facilitated both sections. 47 of the students were female, and 36 were male. Out of the 83 students, 62 students completed an optional class activity during the first week of the semester. 33 of these students were female and 29 were male.

Students in each course section met once a week for the scheduled class session with the instructor. Each session ran for four hours. During the class time, the instructor led students through a mix of lecture slides, discussion activities and case studies. Both sections followed the same syllabus, covered the same course materials in the same sequence, experienced the same in-class activities and used the same lecture slides presented by the same lecturer. Students are first randomly selected to receive one of the two themes of the resources: principles of management or design thinking. Although the two themes of the resources and material differ, our two activity sequences proceeded through the same presentation structure: (1) an overview of the module and what students were expected to do while completing the sequence; (2) some animated videos followed by a transcript of an interview related to the sequence's theme; (3) a summary of recent psychological studies related to decision-making processes. Figures 3.1 and 3.2 show the structure of the principles of management and design thinking activity sequences, respectively.

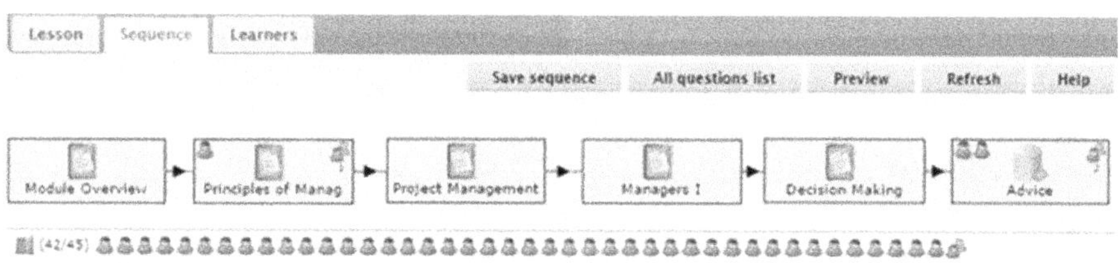

Fig. 3.1 Principles of management LAMS sequence

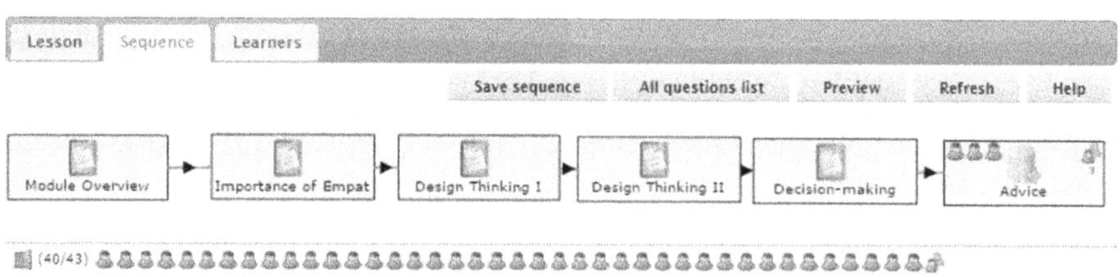

Fig. 3.2 Design thinking LAMS sequence

As for the two themes, principles of management sequence present to students with four functions of management based on Fayol's (1949) model and an abridged interview with Henry Mintzberg (1994) on the qualities of good managers. The design thinking sequence focused on the steps of Stanford d.school's design thinking process (Brown, 2008) and explicitly referenced the importance of cognitive empathy for understanding people and solving problems. While the concepts explained in the design thinking materials were new to the students, the concepts in the management material were actually a review of concepts introduced earlier in the semester.

3.7.2 Data Sources

In the current quasi-experimental study,[1] we created a research-informed activity that could be delivered to students without sacrificing time spent on teaching course content. As a team, we tested how applying social-psychological principles to the design of an optional course activity could lead to differences in the skills students utilize when completing the activity. We designed the activity combining two different movements in management education. The first movement is the incorporation of empathy into management decisions. The second movement is the emphasis on evidence-based learning designs. We will summarize each movement in turn.

For the final component of both Learning Activity Management System (LAMS) sequences, students read a short scenario embedded within a letter from a prospective university student. In the letter, a high school student explained that she had been tasked with providing input for the formation of a committee to imagine the future of learning in higher education. The scenario states that the committee must be composed of high school students from across the districts and the committee must meet up monthly for six months. At the end of the six months, the committee will present its vision and proposed plan to university and education leaders. At the end of the scenario, the prospective student asked for advice on how to approach the situation. The activity then specified to write a short letter of at least two to three paragraphs to the prospective student in response to her query. Students would then enter their responses to the scenario into a text box below the scenario description. As not to unintentionally prime students towards a particular response, none of the design thinking and the principles of management terms explained in the resources were used in the scenario description. We also intentionally left the focus of the advice and how to structure it undefined. Students completed the entire activity sequence on their own time outside of the class.

[1] Our study is considered quasi-experimental because all students within a section were assigned to the same condition rather than assigned randomly.

3.7.3 Procedures

During the fourth week of the semester, the two versions of the optional activity sequence is made available for students to complete. Each version of the sequences presented a slightly different set of resources. In one version, the principles of management condition, students received content emphasizing the functions of management, project management and decision-making. In the other version, the design thinking condition, students received content emphasizing design thinking, empathy and decision-making. Table 3.1 contrasts the differences between each condition. While all the students within each course section were assigned to the same activity condition, the instructor was blind to the activity received by each section. The same instructor taught both sections and attempted to keep the sections as identical as possible.

The optional activity was delivered online via LAMS which allows course developers to sequence online activities and resources for delivery to students (Ghiglione & Dalziel, 2007). The platform connects with the campus' Learning Management system (LMS) to record and archive students' participation in online quizzes, discussion forums, chat groups and other assignments.

Prior to the activity's release, the instructor briefed the students in each section about the activity at the end of their respective class. He emphasized that the activity was voluntary and would not be graded, but it was nonetheless important to the course's learning outcomes and objectives. The activity remained available for students' attempt for one week.

In the principle of management condition of the LAMS activity, students viewed a series of texts and videos related to the principles of management (planning, organizing, leading and controlling). These principles formed the four pillars on which the course was built upon. In the design thinking condition of the activity, students viewed a series of resources related to design thinking (empathy, defining the problem, ideating, prototyping and testing). These concepts were not officially part of the course content, but students may employ the process in problem-solving during the course. At the end of both sequences, students were to create a plan of action for a prospective student who was struggling with a management issue. They were supposed to write a letter of advice to that prospective student.

Table 3.1 LAMS sequence resource descriptions by conditions

Resource	Conditions	
	Principles of management	Design thinking
Video 1	Introduction to the principles of management	Introduction to empathy
Video 2	Introduction to project management	Introduction to design thinking
Reading 1	Interview with Henry Mintzberg on the qualities of a good manager	Interview with CEOs on design thinking's application to management
Reading 2	Summary of recent psychological findings relevant to business decision-making	

The semester comprises of a total of 13 teaching weeks. In the fifth week of the semester, students were required to submit an assignment that address the ethical behaviours of specified companies ("ethical assignment"). Students were free to analyse any ethically dubious decision of their chosen company. They were also supposed to provide a possible solution to this ethical issue. This is a compulsory assignment, and it is also graded. During the final week of the semester, a researcher unaffiliated with the course approached students in both sections to seek whether they voluntarily consent to participate in the research study. Those who consented also completed a short survey to capture their demographic information and academic motivation. The researchers did not have any prior connections to the course.

In accordance with the university's institutional review board's policies regarding voluntary consent, the instructor left the room as the researchers distributed information package to every student in attendance. The package included a description of the research study, a consent form requesting access to students' activity data and course assignments, and a learner profile questionnaire. In addition to the written descriptions, the researchers verbally informed the students about the nature of the study. The researchers explicitly mentioned that participating in the study was voluntary, and participation in the study would neither positively nor negatively affect participants' grades. The researchers also emphasized that the instructor would not be privy to the individual data and results collected by the researchers. Students then choose whether to provide or withhold consent.

Students who provided consent subsequently filled out a questionnaire focusing on their expected level of academic engagement of the remainder of the semester, the quality of their learning and their propensity for perspective-taking. The answer choices for each item were presented as a four-point, unidirectional Likert scale. Only the demographic data and expected workload measure collected by the survey will be discussed in the context of this paper.

Students who chose not to participate in the study were given the option of taking a short recess or remaining at their seats. After all the participating students had an opportunity to fill out the consent form and complete the survey, the researchers collected the package and released students for a short recess.

Throughout the study briefing and survey completion, the instructor remained outside of the room to avoid unintentional pressuring of students into participating in the research. After the end of the semester and the instructor had submitted the final course grades, we proceeded with exporting an archive of the LAMS activity sequences of the consenting students to be coded.

3.7.4 Measures and Reliability

3.7.4.1 LAMS Writing Activity

We coded the LAMS writing activity according to five variables, (1) whether a response was submitted, (2) how many of the introduced management terms from the activity was included, (3) how many of the six-introduced design thinking terms from the activity was included, (4) what the focus of the advice was and (5) whether the student empathized with the prospective student featured in the activity.

We used a binary coding scheme to indicate whether a participant completed the LAMS sequence. For the management and design thinking terms, we created categories for each of the core management functions and design thinking stages. While reading each response, a researcher assigned a binary value to each category based on the presence or absence of the given concepts. The management terms included planning, organizing, leading, controlling and goal setting. The design thinking terms included empathizing, defining, ideating, prototyping and testing, along with design thinking itself. Students received a credit for using a concept only if they mentioned the term and applied the term to their solution or explain its meaning. After the initial coding of the writings, we totalled the scores for the management terms into a single variable ranging from zero to five. We calculated the total for the design thinking terms the same way into a variable ranging from zero to six.

We also coded the LAMS writing activity for the presence or absence of cognitive empathy towards the prospective student. As an example, a student could show cognitive empathy for the prospective student in the LAMS writing activity by recognizing that the prospective student may not have had experience organizing diverse groups of individuals and therefore explained the procedure for how to set a meeting, book a room and organize people.

We also coded the focus of students' writing when responding to the prospective student. We identified four levels of focus related to process orientation: (1) the student opted out of the activity by either not submitting a response or attempting the activity, (2) the student did not provide an obvious focus, (3) the student focused on the scenario's outcome (the presentation), (4) the student focused on the process (forming a committee). For responses judged not to have a focus, students merely summarized the content of the resources and did not address the prospective student. Outcome-focused responses emphasized the presentation the committee had to give at the end of six months. When focusing on the process, students explained how or what the prospective student should consider when setting up the committee that was responsible for developing the presentation.

3.7.4.2 Ethical Assignment

After receiving consent from the students to review their coursework at the end of the semester, a researcher coded the ethical assignments for the presence of the design thinking and management terms. Additionally, the researcher coded the assignments for the display of cognitive empathy. We operationalized the display of cognitive empathy in this assignment as statements which referred to a stakeholder's perspective and explained how the conditions within the company could affect the stakeholder's reasoning.

Table 3.2 Means comparison of demographic measures between conditions

Variable	Management (SD) ($N = 41$)	Design thinking (SD) ($N = 42$)	*F* ratio	Sig
Gender	0.52 (0.51)	0.61 (0.49)	0.61	0.44
Year	2.33 (0.69)	2.27 (0.45)	0.26	0.61
Residency	1.31 (0.68)	1.27 (0.63)	0.08	0.78
Class preparation	2.26 (0.77)	2.41 (0.67)	0.93	0.34
Completed activity	0.83 (0.38)	0.68 (0.47)	2.58	0.11

3.7.4.3 Inter-Rater Reliability

For all the qualitative measures of level of focus and the presence of empathy, a second coder was used to provide a calculation of inter-rater reliability. As with the first coder, the second coder was blind to conditions. With respect to identifying the set of management and design thinking terms, a custom automated text analysis tool was used in lieu of a second coder. The average Cohen's κ for all measures was 0.81 and the kappa value for every measure exceeded 0.74 and reached significance at the 0.05 level, indicating a good level of inter-rater reliability.

3.8 Results

83 students agreed to participate in the study. Out of the 83 students, 62 of them completed the voluntary online activity. We carried out multiple analysis of variance (MANOVA) to determine whether variables such as gender, year in school or academic expectations differed by sections (Table 3.2 shows the results of the analyses). As none of the analyses were found to be significant, we proceeded with the analysis to answer the hypothesis based on the presumption that the samples from two sections were equivalent.

3.8.1 Assignment Completion by Conditions

76% of consented students completed the writing activity at the end of the LAMS sequence they have gone through. We performed a one-sample t-test which indicated that this percentage was significantly different from zero.[2] Comparing the completion percentage of students in different conditions, 68% of the students in

[2] $T\ (82) = 16.02, p < 0.001$.

Table 3.3 Mean comparison of used terms between conditions

Variables	Principles of management (SD) ($N = 35$)	Design thinking (SD) ($N = 28$)	F ratio	Sig
Management terms	3.11 (1.10)	0.71 (0.85)	83.52	0.01
Design thinking terms	0.49 (0.61)	1.86 (1.58)	19.23	0.01

design thinking condition and 83% of the students in the principles of management condition completed the writing activity. A Chi-square analysis indicated that this difference was not statistically significant.[3]

3.8.2 *Use of Management and Design Thinking Terms by Conditions*

Using the LAMS sequence conditions as the independent variables and the number of management and design thinking terms as dependent variables, we conducted a MANOVA which identified a main effect of condition for both measures. We identified a main effect of condition with respect to management terms used[4] and a main effect of condition with respect to design thinking terms used.[5] Table 3.3 shows the mean comparison of used terms between conditions and Fig. 3.3 shows a match of terms with the condition assignment. There is a greater use of management terms after the students progressed through the LAMS management sequence and there are more design thinking terms used after students progressed through the LAMS design thinking sequence.

In short, the students used the terms present in the LAMS sequence they were assigned to.

3.8.3 *Assignment Solution by Conditions*

We conducted a one-way analysis of variance (ANOVA) which indicated a significant main effect of condition at the 0.01 level.[6] As Fig. 3.4 shows, more than 75% of students under the principles of management condition completed the writing activity with a focus on the scenario's outcome (the presentation that the committee had to give at the end of the six months).

---

[3] $X^2\ (2, N = 83) = 2.57, p > 0.10$.

[4] $F\ (1, 61) = 89.24, p < 0.001$.

[5] $F\ (1, 61) = 29.26, p < 0.001$.

[6] $F\ (1, 82) = 7.41, p < 0.01$.

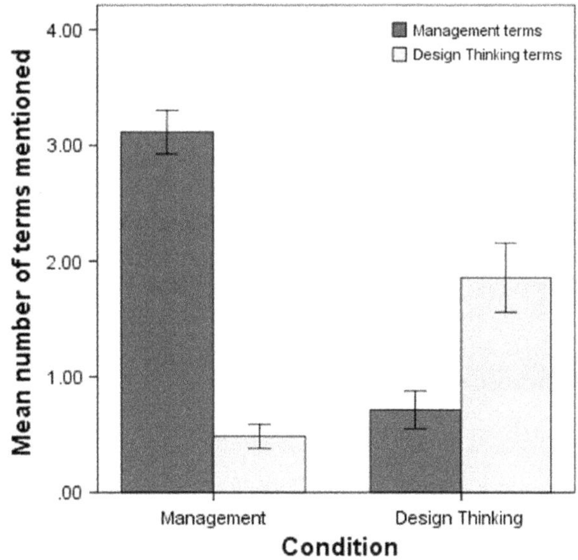

Fig. 3.3 Use of terms by conditions

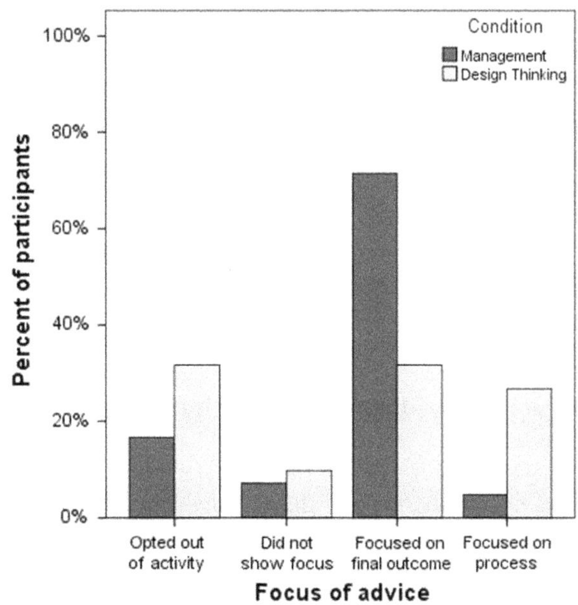

Fig. 3.4 Focus of advice by conditions

In contrast, students who completed the design thinking sequence showed a wider distribution of focuses. They also focused much more on the building up of committee than students in the principles of management condition did.

3.8.4 Presence of Empathy by Condition

18% of students who submitted a response in the design thinking condition showed indications of cognitive empathy. In contrast, only 3% (one student) showed signs of cognitive empathy in the principles of management condition. We conducted a Chi-square test to determine whether the difference in the percentage of students showing cognitive empathy in the design thinking condition was significant as compared to the percentage of students showing cognitive empathy in the principles of management condition. The results showed a significant difference in the expression of cognitive empathy between two conditions.[7] Calculating Cohen's *d* based on these percentages and associated standard deviations revealed an effect size of 0.50 in favor of the design thinking condition.

3.9 Discussion

In this section, we shall revisit each of the hypotheses and examine the outcomes that unfold from it respectively.

Hypothesis 1—Condition Effects on the Presence of Cognitive Empathy
Our analyses support the hypothesis that the Stanford d.school's design thinking process that emphasizes empathy would induce students to display cognitive empathy in their advice. The activity we have designed provided an easy-to-execute activity for students to display complex problem-solving skills and cognitive empathy in a management context.

Students in the design thinking condition were more likely to identify and consider the potential feelings of the prospective student as they offered management advice to the prospective student. The results potentially show that the effect on students was due to the learning through the activity sequence.

Hypothesis 2—Lasting Effect of Introduction to Students to Design Thinking Process
During the fifth week of the semester, students were required to submit an ethical assignment addressing ethical behaviours of a company. Students in the design thinking condition displayed signs of cognitive empathy more often ($M = 0.29$, $SD = 0.46$) than students in the principles of management condition ($M = 0.06$, $SD = 0.24$), $t\ (60) = 2.5, p < 0.05$. Students in the design thinking condition also showed a higher rate ($M = 0.68$, $SD = 0.48$) of proposing ethics-based education as a solution to unethical corporate behaviour than students in the principles of management condition ($M = 0.38$, $SD = 0.49$), $t\ (60) = 2.4, p < 0.05$. Our hypothesis is supported through the results.

---

[7] $X^2\ (2, N = 63) = 4.01, p < 0.05$.

There is no concern that students performed similarly in terms of final grades in both design thinking condition and principles of management condition. This is because the grading scheme does not favour either condition. Even though the grading rubric does not distinguish between design thinking and management functions processes, students who were exposed to the design thinking process still provided more holistic remediation plans to address the unethical corporate actions in comparison to students who received information on principles of management.

3.10 Conclusion

Our results have shown that it is possible to develop cognitive empathy as a leadership competency without sacrificing valuable course time for course content. By incorporating an optional online assignment into an existing curriculum, we managed to elicit and capture the spontaneous display of cognitive empathy from students without sacrificing class time or content coverage. Not only were students willing to complete optional assignments that were designed with the principles of academic engagement in mind, students were also willing to produce meaningful and nuanced responses to management problems that considered the needs, thoughts and feelings of stakeholders. The considered application of cognitive empathy is important for transformational leadership. The generalizable nature of the design thinking process and the structure of the activity itself makes it transferable to other courses and content domains. At its simplest level, this study tested a way of introducing and developing non-content-based skills in tertiary courses. Rather than impressing upon students the importance of psychological constructs such as empathy, leadership and academic engagement directly, the study sets the stage for students to converge on these realizations for themselves. Empathy is a fundamental concept in the design thinking framework. By tapping on the theories of social-psychological interventions, students are indirectly being introduced to the importance of this soft skill embedded in the teaching of design thinking. Our intervention results showed definite effect of the course design helping the students to internalize the importance of empathy in facilitating holistic management plans and leadership. Nevertheless, teaching and learning at the university are affected in two ways. First, it introduces a process of introducing and measuring non-content-based outcomes that can be scaled across the university. Second, the results of this study can be disseminated for use by the learning design and solution teams as evidence for transitioning more courses to use outcome-based assessments.

Out next steps will be to scale our activity beyond single instructor course sections and randomly assign all students within the course to either the principles of management or design thinking sequences. We also plan on investigating individual student learning profiles to better understand what influences some students to exhibit empathy when others do not.

In summary, there is much work to be done to transit traditional business courses towards helping their students in meeting the demands of our rapidly changing world.

Business educators may consider moving beyond traditional techniques, such as, using sanitized case studies that highlight a limited set of core business principles or small group discussions that inadvertently coax students to match course terms to decontextualized questions. Instead, we propose that adding a modicum of emphasis on humanistic design principles and processes to the curriculum may be a way forward. Our data suggests that undergraduate students are prepared to deliver on the promise of more holistic decision-making and management solutions if the situation warrants it. All we have to do is let them volunteer to do it themselves.

References

Alligood, M. R. (2002). A theory of the art of nursing discovered in Rogers' Science of Unitary Human Beings. *International Journal for Human Caring, 6*(2), 55–60.
Amdurer, E., Boyatzis, R. E., Saatcioglu, A., Smith, M. L., & Taylor, S. N. (2014). Long term impact of emotional, social and cognitive intelligence competencies and GMAT on career and life satisfaction and career success. *Frontiers in Psychology, 5*, 1447.
Andrews, J., & Higson, H. (2008). Graduate employability, 'soft skills' versus 'hard'. Business knowledge: A European study. *Higher Education in Europe, 33*(4), 411–422.
Anthony, S., & Garner, B. (2016). Teaching soft skills to business students: An analysis of multiple pedagogical methods. *Business and Professional Communication Quarterly, 79*(3), 360–370.
Aronson, J., Fried, C. B., & Good, C. (2002). Reducing stereotype threat and boosting academic achievement of African-American students: The role of conceptions of intelligence. *Journal of Experimental Social Psychology, 38*, 113–125.
Ashkanasy, N. M., & Tse, B. (2000). Transformational leadership as management of emotion: A conceptual review. In N. M. Ashkanasy, C. E. Hartel, & W. J. Zerbe (Eds.), *Emotions in the workplace: Research, theory, and practice* (pp. 221–235). Quorum Books.
Baker, D. F. (2017). Teaching empathy and ethical decision making in business schools. *Journal of Management Education, 41*(4), 575–598. https://doi.org/10.1177/1052562917699028
Bass, B. M., & Avolio, B. J. (1990). Developing transformational leadership: 1992 and beyond, *Journal of European Industrial Training, 14*(5).
Bass, B. M. (1991). From transactional to transformational leadership: Learning to share the vision. *Organizational dynamics, 18*, 19–31.
Batt-Rawden, S. A., Chisolm, M. S., Anton, B., & Flickinger, T. E. (2013). Teaching empathy to medical students: An updated, systematic review. *Academic Medicine, 88*, 1171–1177.
Beckett, S. (2018). *What's the difference between skills and competencies?* https://resources.hrsg.ca/blog/what-s-the-difference-between-skills-and-competencies
Bedwell, W. L., Fiore, S. M., & Salas, E. (2014). Developing the future workforce: An approach for integrating interpersonal skills into the MBA classroom. *Academy of Management Learning and Education, 13*, 171–186.
Bowen, J. L. (2014). Emotion in organizations: Resources for business educators. *Journal of Management Education, 38*, 114–142.
Boyatzis, R. (2009). Competencies as a behavioral approach to emotional intelligence. *Journal of Management Development, 28*(9), 749–770.
Boyatzis, R. E., Passarelli, A., & Wei, H. (2018). Assessing leader development: Lessons from a historical review of MBA outcomes. *Journal of Management Education, 41*, 55–79.
Brisson, B. M., Dicke, A. L., Gaspard, H., Häfner, I., Flunger, B., Nagengast, B., & Trautwein, U. (2017). Short intervention, sustained effects: Promoting students' math competence beliefs, effort, and achievement. *American Educational Research Journal, 54*(6), 1048–1078.
Brown, T. (2008). Design thinking. *Harvard Business Review, 86*(6), 84.

Brown, T. A., Sautter, J. A., Littvay, L., Sautter, A. C., & Bearnes, B. (2010). Ethics and personality: Empathy and narcissism as moderators of ethical decision making in business students. *Journal of Education for Business, 85*(4), 203–208.
Bryant, B. (1982). An index of empathy for children and adolescents. *Child Development, 53*, 413–425.
Carre, A., Stefaniak, N., D'Ambrosio, F., Bensalah, L., & Besche-Richard, C. (2013). The basic empathy scale in adults (BES-A): Factor structure of a revised form. *Psychological Assessment, 25*(3), 679–691.
Čehajić-Clancy, S., Goldenberg, A., Gross, J. J., & Halperin, E. (2016). Social-psychological interventions for intergroup reconciliation: An emotion regulation perspective. *Psychological Inquiry, 27*(2), 73–88. https://doi.org/10.1080/1047840x.2016.1153945
Cheung, D. H., & Reeves, A. (2014). Can we teach empathy? Evidence from the evaluation of a course title "Compassion in Medicine." *Journal of Alternative and Complementary Medicine, 20*(5), A7.
Cohen, G. L., Garcia, J., Apfel, N., & Master, A. (2006). Reducing the racial achievement gap: A social-psychological intervention. *Science, 313*(5791), 1307–1310.
Cohen, G. L., Garcia, J., & Goyer, J. P. (2017). Turning point: Targeted, tailored, and timely psychological intervention. In A. J. Elliot, C. S. Dweck, & D. S. Yeager (Eds.), *Handbook of competence and motivation: Theory and application* (2nd ed., pp. 657–686). The Guilford Press.
Dam, R. F., & Siang, T. Y. (2018). *What is design thinking and why is it so popular?* Retrieved 29 January 2022 from http://athena.ecs.csus.edu/~buckley/CSc170_F2018_files/What%20is%20Design%20Thinking%20and%20Why%20Is%20It%20So%20Popular.pdf
DasGupta, S., & Charon, R. (2004). Personal illness narratives: Using reflective writing to teach empathy. *Academic Medicine, 79*(4), 351–356.
Davis, M. H. (1983). Measuring individual differences in empathy: Evidence for a multidimensional approach. *Journal of Personality and Social Psychology, 44*, 113–126.
Davis, M. H. (1994). *Empathy: A social psychological approach.* Westview Press.
Davis, M. H. (1996). *Empathy: A social psychological approach.* Brown & Benchmark.
Davis, M. H. (2009). Empathy. In H. T. Reis & S. Sprecher (Eds.), *Encyclopedia of human relationships* (pp. 516–520). Sage Publications.
Davis, M. H., Luce, C., & Kraus, S. J. (1994). The heritability of characteristics associated with dispositional empathy. *Journal of Personality, 62*(3), 369–391.
Druskat, V., Mount, G., & Sala, F. (Eds.). (2005). *Emotional intelligence and work performance.* Erlbaum.
Dweck, C. S. (1986). Motivational processes affecting learning. *American Psychologist, 41*(10), 1040.
Eisenberg, N., Cumberland, A., Gutherie, I. K., Murphy, B. C., & Shephard, S. A. (2005). Age changes in prosocial responding and moral reasoning in adolescence and early adulthood. *Journal of Research on Adolescence, 15*, 235–260.
Elsbach, K. D., & Stigliani, I. (2018). Design thinking and organizational culture: A review and framework for future research. *Journal of Management, 44*(6), 2274–2306. https://doi.org/10.1177/0149206317744252
Eriksen, M. (2009). Authentic leadership: Practical reflexivity, self-awareness, and self-authorship. *Journal of Management Education, 33*(6), 747–771.
Fayol, H. (1949). *General and Industrial Management*. Pitman.
Finkel, E. J., Slotter, E. B., Luchies, L. B., Walton, G. M., & Gross, J. J. (2013). A brief intervention to promote conflict reappraisal preserves marital quality over time. *Psychological Science*, 1595–1601.
Gagne, R. M., Briggs, L. J., & Wager, W. W. (1992). *Principles of instructional design* (4th ed.). Harcourt Brace College.
Gasparini, A. A. (2015). *Perspective and use of empathy in design thinking.* https://www.researchgate.net/publication/273126653_Perspective_and_Use_of_Empathy_in_Design_Thinking

Gentry, W. A., Weber, T. J., & Sadri, G. (2016). *Empathy in the workplace: A tool for effective leadership*. https://cclinnovation.org/wp-content/uploads/2020/03/empathyintheworkplace.pdf
Gerdes, K. E., Segal, E. A., Jackson, K. F., & Mullins, J. L. (2011). Teaching empathy: A framework rooted in social cognitive neuroscience and social justice. *Journal of Social Work Education, 47*, 109–131.
Ghiglione, E., & Dalziel, J. (2007). Design principles for LAMS version 2 and the LAMS "Tools Contract". *Current Research on IMS Learning Design and Lifelong Competence Development Infrastructures*, 13.
Giles, S. (2016, March 15). *The most important leadership competencies, according to leaders around the world*. https://hbr.org/2016/03/the-most-important-leadership-competencies-according-to-leaders-around-the-world
Gioia, D. A. (2002). Business education's role in the crisis of corporate confidence. *The Academy of Management Executive, 16*(3), 142–144.
Goleman, D. (1998). What makes a leader? *Harvard Business Review*.
Gourguechon, P. (2017, December 26). *Empathy is an essential leadership skill—And there's nothing soft about it*. https://www.forbes.com/sites/prudygourguechon/2017/12/26/empathy-is-an-essential-leadership-skill-and-theres-nothing-soft-about-it/?sh=3192ac452b9d
Greimel, E., Schulte-Rüther, M., Fink, G. R., Piefke, M., Herpertz-Dahlmann, B., & Konrad, K. (2010). Development of neural correlates of empathy from childhood to early adulthood: An fMRI study in boys and adult men. *Journal of Neural Transmission, 117*, 781–791.
Guzmán, V. E., Muschard, B., Gerolamo, M., Kohl, H., & Rozenfeld, H. (2020). Characteristics and skills of leadership in the context of industry 4.0. *Procedia Manufacturing, 43*, 543–550. https://doi.org/10.1016/j.promfg.2020.02.167
Hatcher, S. L., Nadeau, M. S., Walsh, L. K., Reynolds, M., Galea, J., & Marz, K. (1994). The teaching of empathy for high school and college students: Testing Rogerian methods with the Interpersonal Reactivity Index. *Adolescence, 29*(116), 961–974.
Hayes, J. (2002). *Interpersonal skills at work*. Routledge.
Henriksen, D. (2018). *The 7 transdisciplinary cognitive skills for creative education*. Springer International Publishing.
Henson, R. (2016). Addressing the challenges with global mindset. In *Successful global leadership* (pp. 123–182). Palgrave Macmillan.
Hoffman, M. L. (2000). *Empathy and moral development: Implications for caring and justice*. Cambridge University Press.
Hojat, M. (2009). Ten approaches for enhancing empathy in health and human services cultures. *Journal of Health and Human Services Administration, 31*, 412–450.
Hojat, M., Vergare, M. J., Maxwell, K., Brainard, G., Herrine, S. K., Isenberg, G. A., & Gonnella, J. S. (2009). The devil is in the third year: A longitudinal study of erosion of empathy in medical school. *Academic Medicine, 84*, 1182–1191.
Holt, S. (2012). *What Do Empathy and Emotional Intelligence Have to Do with Change?* Springer.
Holt, S., & Marques, J. (2012). Empathy in leadership: Appropriate or misplaced? An empirical study on a topic that is asking for attention. *Journal of Business Ethics, 105*(1), 95–105.
Holt, S., Marques, J., Hu, J., & Wood, A. (2017). Cultivating empathy: New perspectives on educating business leaders. *Journal of Values-Based Leadership, 10*(1), 1–25. https://doi.org/10.22543/0733.101.1173
Howe, D. (2013). *Empathy—What it is and why it matters*. Palgrave Macmillan.
Kalavana, T. V., & Andreou, P. (2018, March 15). *Finding the right level of empathy*. https://www.chieflearningofficer.com/2018/03/15/finding-right-level-empathy/#:%7E:text=Look%20for%20situations%20that%20call,validate%20the%20other%20person's%20experience
Kellett, J. B., Humphrey, R. H., & Sleeth, R. G. (2002). Empathy and complex task performance: Two routes to leadership. *The Leadership Quarterly, 13*(5), 523–544.
Kenthirarajah, D. T., & Walton, G. M. (2015). How brief social-psychological interventions can cause enduring effects. *Emerging Trends in the Social and Behavioral Sciences*, 1–15. https://doi.org/10.1002/9781118900772.etrds0026

Kolko, J. (2015). *Design thinking comes of age*. https://enterprisersproject.com/sites/default/files/design_thinking_comes_of_age.pdf

Konrath, S. H., O'Brien, E. H., & Hsing, C. (2010). Changes in dispositional empathy in American college students over time: A meta-analysis. *Personality and Social Psychology Review, 15*, 180–198.

Koppen, E., & Meinel, C. (2015). Empathy via design thinking: Creation of sense and knowledge. In H. Plattner, C. Meinel, & L. Leifer (Eds.), *Design thinking research: Building innovators* (pp. 15–28). https://doi.org/10.1007/978-3-319-06823-7

Korzynski, P., Kozminski, A. K., Baczynska, A., & Haenlein, M. (2020). Bounded leadership: An empirical study of leadership competencies, constraints, and effectiveness. *European Management Journal*, 1–10. https://doi.org/10.1016/j.emj.2020.07.009

Lacoboni, M. (2008). Imitation, empathy and Mirroe Neuons. *Annual Review of Psychology, 60*, 653–670.

Lim, B. T., Moriarty, H., & Huthwaite, M. (2011). "Being-in-role": A Teaching innovation to enhance empathic communication skills in medical students. *Medical Teacher, 33*(12), 663–669.

Maiborn, H. L. (2017). *The Routledge handbook of philosophy of empathy*. Routledge/Taylor & Francis.

Mintzberg, H. (1994). Rounding out the manager's job. *Sloan Management Review, 36*, 11–26.

Morgeson, F. P., Reider, M. H., & Campion, M. A. (2005). Selecting individuals in team settings: The importance of social skills, personality characteristics, and teamwork knowledge. *Personnel Psychology, 58*, 583–611.

Morse, J. A., Anderson, G., Bottorff, J. L., Yonge, O., O'Brien, B., Solberg, S. M., & McIlveen, K. H. (1992). Exploring empathy: A conceptual fit for nursing practice? *Journal of Nursing Scholarship, 24*(4), 273–280.

Obliopas, R. (2020). Cognitive empathy and leadership performance of middle level educational managers in a State University. *Indian Journal of Science and Technology, 13*(5), 576–586. https://doi.org/10.17485/ijst/2020/v13i05/149372

Okonofua, J. A., Paunesku, D., & Walton, G. M. (2016). Brief intervention to encourage empathic discipline cuts suspension rates in half among adolescents. *Proceedings of the National Academy of Sciences, 113*(19), 5221–5226.

Powers, J. T., Cook, J. E., Purdie-Vaughns, V., Garcia, J., Apfel, N., & Cohen, G. L. (2016). Changing environments by changing individuals: The emergent effects of psychological intervention. *Psychological Science, 27*(2), 150–160.

Rajaram, K. (2021). *Evidence-based Teaching for the 21st century classroom and beyond*. Springer.

Riess, H. (2017). The science of empathy. *Journal of Patient Experience, 4*(2), 74–77. https://doi.org/10.1177/2374373517699267

Rogoff, B. (2003). *The cultural nature of human development*. Oxford University Press.

Rohana, N. S. M., & Abdullah, C. Z. (2017). Leadership competencies and organizational performance: Review and proposed framework. *International Journal of Academic Research in Business and Social Sciences, 7*(8), 824–831. https://doi.org/10.6007/ijarbss/v7-i8/3297

Rubin, R. S., & Dierdorff, E. C. (2009). How relevant is the MBA? Assessing the alignment of required curricula and required managerial competencies. *Academy of Management Learning & Education, 8*(2), 208–224.

Salovey, P., & Mayer, J. D. (1990). Emotional intelligence. *Imagination, Cognition, and Personality, 9*, 185–211.

Segal, R., Zwaal, C., Green, E., Tomasone, J. R., Loblaw, A., & Petrella, T. (2017). Exercise for people with cancer: A clinical practice guideline. *Current Oncology, 24*(1), 40–46.

Spaulding, S. (2017). Cognitive empathy. In H. L. Maibom (Ed.), *The Routledge handbook of philosophy of empathy* (pp. 13–21). Taylor & Francis.

Spitzer, B., & Aronson, J. (2015). Minding and mending the gap: Social psychological interventions to reduce educational disparities. *British Journal of Educational Psychology, 85*(1), 1–18. https://doi.org/10.1111/bjep.12067

Stanford d.school. (2012). *Design thinking steps.* http://web.stanford.edu/group/cilab/cgi-bin/redesigningtheater/the-design-thinking-process/
Stephan, W. G., & Finlay, K. (1999). The role of empathy in improving intergroup relations. *Journal of Social Issues, 55*(4), 729–743.
Stock, K. L., Bucar, B., & Vokoun, J. (2017). Walking in another's shoes: Enhancing experiential learning through design thinking. *Management Teaching Review*, 2379298117736283.
Taylor, S. S., & Ladkin, D. (2009). Understanding arts-based methods in managerial development. *Academy of Management Learning & Education, 8*, 55–69.
Thompson, L., & Schonthal, D. (2020). The social psychology of design thinking. *California Management Review, 62*(2), 84–99. https://doi.org/10.1177/0008125619897636
Towler, A. (2020, May 16). *Leadership competencies and leadership competency models: What they are and why they matter*. https://www.ckju.net/en/dossier/leadership-competencies-leaderhip-competency-models-what-they-are-why-they-matter
Tzouramani, E. (2017). Leadership and empathy. In J. Marques & S. Dhiman (Eds.), *Leadership today: Practices for personal and professional performance* (pp. 197–216). Springer International Publishing.
Van Haneghan, J. P., Barron, L., Young, M., Williams, S., Vye, N. J., & Bransford, J. (1992). The Jasper series: An experiment with new ways to enhance mathematical thinking. In D. F. Halpern (Ed.), *Enhancing thinking skills in the sciences and mathematics* (pp. 15–38). Erlbaum.
Walton, G. M. (2014). The new science of wise psychological interventions. *Current Directions in Psychological Science, 23*(1), 73–82.
Walton, G. M., & Cohen, G. L. (2011). A brief social-belonging intervention improves academic and health outcomes of minority students. *Science, 331*(6023), 1447–1451.
Weisz, E., & Zaki, J. (2017). Empathy-building interventions a review of existing work and suggestions for future directions. In M. C. Worline, S. L. Brown, E. Simon-Thomas, & E. Seppälä (Eds.), *The Oxford handbook of compassion science* (pp. 273–289). Oxford University Press.
Welch, J., & Hodge, M. (2017). Assessing impact: The role of leadership competency models in developing effective school leaders. *School Leadership & Management, 38*(4), 355–377. https://doi.org/10.1080/13632434.2017.1411900
Yeager, D. S., & Walton, G. M. (2011). Social-psychological interventions in education: They're not magic. *Review of Educational Research, 81*(2), 267–301.
Young, C. A., Haffejee, B., & Corsun, D. L. (2017). Developing cultural intelligence and empathy through diversified mentoring relationships. *Journal of Management Education, 42*(3), 105256291771068.
Yu, C.-L., & Chou, T.-L. (2018). A dual route model of empathy: A neurobiological prospective. *Frontiers in Psychology, 9*, 1–5. https://doi.org/10.3389/fpsyg.2018.02212
Zaar, S., Van Den Bossche, P., & Gijselaers, W. (2020). How business students think about leadership: A qualitative study on leader identity and meaning-making. *Academy of Management Learning & Education, 19*(2), 168–191. https://doi.org/10.5465/amle.2017.0290

Part III
Innovation and Transformation in Learning

Chapter 4
Exploiting Disruptive Innovation in Learning and Teaching

Samson Tan

Abstract With the dawn of the twenty-first century, the world has been in chaos, turmoil and a changing environment that is chaotic and difficult to predict. In the midst of rapid technological advancements, geopolitical shifts, dramatic demographic changes, ecological disasters and immigration, lives are being disrupted at a level of severity and frequency that seems to only increase. Most importantly, globalization and competitive market forces have created significant growth in the knowledge sector, a development that has a profound effect on society and higher education institutions. Together, these factors have accentuated a state of volatility, uncertainty, complexity and ambiguity that has been termed VUCA: volatility, uncertainty, complexity and ambiguity. The interaction between the four VUCA elements can lead to the breakdown of order in almost every organization, including the education and higher education sectors. Since students today have grown up with technology, they expect to have instant access all the time and anywhere to their learning materials.

As opposed to this, a black swan event is an abnormal behaviour outside the normal expected behaviour, an event that has an extreme impact and a response that is rationalized retrospectively (Taleb, 2007). Black Swan events, like the COVID-19 pandemic that has just been reported, can throw a wrench in the works in a VUCA world. The twenty-first century has experienced some Black Swan events, such as 9/11, and the 2008 financial crisis; however, the COVID-19 pandemic, a global phenomenon occurring over the next few years, will be a unique blend of VUCA and Black Swan events (Hadar et al. in Rethinking teacher education in a VUCA world: student teachers' social-emotional competencies during the Covid-19 crisis. European Journal of Teacher Education, 1–14, 2020). Therefore, in the coming years and decades, higher education has entered uncharted territory that will require a great deal of agility and profound astuteness to progress.

In reviewing the current situation and future challenges in the learning innovation space, we found that there is a need for a new set of tools and an updated framework

S. Tan (✉)
Head of Strategic Development in Libraries & Education, Civica Pte Ltd, Singapore, Singapore
e-mail: samson.tan@civica.com.sg

K. Rajaram, *Learning Intelligence: Innovative and Digital Transformative Learning Strategies*, https://doi.org/10.1007/978-981-19-9201-8_4

that will help educators support innovative learning initiatives. It is for these reasons that in the following chapter we propose a two-pronged approach: Integration of the Disruptive Innovation Framework (Bower & Christensen, 1995) and the Transformative Strategic Framework for Learning Innovation (Salmon, European Journal of Open, Distance and E-Learning 17:220–236, 2014). In order to accomplish this, the Gartner hype cycle and Roger's Diffusion of Innovation Model (Roger, 2010) are combined to create a framework for strategic planning and to provide educators with a practical framework to improve the implementation of interventions.

4.1 Introduction

In the twenty-first century, educators find themselves faced with the unenviable task of dealing with multidimensional challenges in the global environment and rapidly adopting the use of new digital technologies to improve teaching and learning (Zawacki-Richter & Latchem, 2018). The advent of the COVID-19 pandemic coincided with a time when educators were neither able to imagine the rapid rate of change in the digital world nor the tectonic shift in the demand for education services that would have caused a sea change in higher education. Before that time, higher education had to deal with economic uncertainty, accountability, globalization and emerging technologies that could be intimidating for students to learn and difficult to manage (Rabah, 2015; Tierney, 2014). As educators continue to grapple with the uncertainties, it has become clear that some of these changes are becoming irreversible. Institutional policymakers and stakeholders are increasingly compelled to develop strategies to keep up with the tide of change.

The higher education industry has evolved from being a non-competitive sector to one driven by market forces as it pursues capabilities and capacity to adapt to the new models of knowledge and information. As higher education is often portrayed as an industry today, competing in a highly competitive global marketplace, it has often been seen as an "industry" (Lane et al., 2014; Marginson, 2006). The competitive marketized higher education sector of higher education has become increasingly driven towards achieving higher standards based on students' experiences as priorities (Chow & Croxton, 2017; Mulgan, 2013). The Massive Open Online Courses (MOOCs) provide a good example of how the marketization of education is taking place. Institutions have somehow managed to make it easy for students to access high quality learning while tapping into the global market. As a result of MOOCs, students who would not have otherwise been able to afford higher education will now be able to gain access to higher education, despite the competition that leads to more market pressures on higher education. As a result, the complex, evolving, dynamic environment that global higher education is experiencing within this milieu might more properly be described as VUCA (Vague, Uncertain, Complex and Ambiguous) (Lane et al., 2014). With the transition towards a VUCA world, organizations, and higher education in particular, are challenged to create order, as VUCA conditions interact in tumultuous and sometimes conflicting ways (Yehezkel, 2020).

It is one of the challenges facing higher education institutions that traditionally have been focused on creating knowledge through research and scholarship that they have to find ways of supporting the growing demand for lifelong learning as the digital economy continues to advance (Guri-Rosenblit et al., 2007). Due to disruptive forces that are creeping into higher education and challenging conventional methods of thinking and working, the rate at which innovation is occurring to provide instruction and learning is increasing. As the demand for higher education increases, the sustainability and relevance of the various forms of postsecondary education continue to be a concern for many institutions in the postsecondary education sector. Another challenge to this issue is that corporate universities and the globalization of the educational sector have led to the growth of corporate universities (Alagaraja & Li, 2015). A great example is how the demand for IT talent has motivated big tech companies such as Google and Apple to provide training programmes to cater to their immediate needs for a growing technological workforce. Companies find that universities are taking too long to train graduates and that the skills of new graduates are not up to date as a result of the length of university degree programmes. As a result of these driving forces, higher education institutions must respond quickly to the changes. As a consequence, it is not surprising that global higher education institutions are racing to acquire broad-based capabilities and the capacity to adapt to these challenges.

In spite of educators increasingly realizing that conventional teaching methods no longer engage learners or teach them skills required to succeed in today's world, there have been many trials and errors which have resulted in uneven success rates (Westera, 2004). With emerging technologies considered to be the driving force of change, digital technologies are often perceived as an accessible solution for creating and enhancing innovative learning experiences, such as building collaborations and encouraging students to build new multimodal literacy skills to meet the needs of the future. While embracing emerging technologies and innovation in learning and teaching offers a wide range of opportunities for actively engaging students with solving problems in authentic environments, many institutions struggle to use appropriate pedagogical and systematic approaches (Hrabowski, 2011). One of the reasons that institutional transformations present such a difficulty is the fact that the complexity of institutional change is that it involves not only the use of technology but also the development of cognitive literacy, as well as an appreciation of the sociocultural forces which shape learner development and the role that communities play in supporting the acquisition of knowledge.

In 2017, the World Economic Forum's (WEF) launch of the Fourth Industrial Revolution (IR 4.0) not only heightened the sense of interest and urgency for the world leaders to acknowledge the impact of IR 4.0, but the narrative had seemingly affirmed that the confluence and convergence of emerging technologies would transform everything we know, including education (Schwab, 2017). As a result of global driving forces, a preliminary examination of WEF's advocacy appears to be impeccably in line with VUCA as the Fourth Industrial Revolution considers the rise of machine intelligence as a result of this development. As a result, WEF suggests that technological advances are having a profound impact on nearly every human along with challenges such as climate change, societal and political turmoil, as well as increasing inequality of wealth. In the wake of IR 4.0, every sector in society had to reskill and upskill in preparation for the future. At a time when many sectors of society are dealing with the ramifications of IR 4.0, the COVID-19 pandemic in 2020 will throw extra strain on the system.

In response to COVID-19, schools across the world were forced to shut down. Lockdown measures were implemented worldwide to contain the spread of COVID-19, preventing access to schools for over 1.5 billion children. Education has changed dramatically as a result, with online learning climbing to unprecedented heights, as teaching is now carried out remotely and on digital platforms. In the light of the massive rise in digital learning, many observers have wondered if the adoption of online learning will persist post-pandemic and how such a shift would impact global education (Li & Lalani, 2020, April). While the partnerships between universities and education technology providers helped ameliorate the need for online learning during the pandemic, many online teaching practices during the COVID-19 lockdown period were mere "band-aid" solutions (Kandri, 2020, July). Educators recognized that higher education institutions must develop the capability to experiment with different digital learning solutions, leverage technology to foster deeper student learning and develop into facilitators of student learning, blending their expertise as a profession (Karalis, 2020; OECD, 2020).

This approach, in tandem with the inadvertent need for a post-pandemic solution to learning, brought about the formulation of an updated strategic framework to assist institutions in making the most of available resources in order to achieve innovation in learning and teaching. This article is meant to make a contribution to the higher education sector by gleaning the strengths of the selected frameworks and recommending the one that would best suit the needs of the teachers. A review of existing innovation frameworks indicates that Christensen's Disruptive Innovation Framework (1995) and Salmon's (2014) Transformative Strategic Framework for Learning Innovation offer perceptive insights to craft a renewed strategic framework for learning innovation. There should also be two components to a realistic two-pronged strategic framework for learning innovation—one stage is for designing the plan and the second stage is for implementing it. As innovation execution in learning is as important as the design, this book adapted Roger's (2010) Diffusion of Innovation Model and Gartner hype cycle (Prinsloo & Van Deventer, 2017, September) for supporting readers to develop a pragmatic plan for undertaking innovation in learning.

4.2 Impact of Globalization on Higher Education

As defined by Gilpin (1987, p. 389), globalization consists of "increasing interdependence between national economies, particularly in trade, finance, and macroeconomic policies". It has been argued that globalization is closely related to neoliberalism and technocratic economic reforms as a predominant ideology (Apple, 2001; Zajda,

2016). In the context of globalization, the integration of markets has led to competition between countries and between institutions (Lemoine et al., 2017). On the other hand, advances in ICT (Information Communication Technologies) in the global economy have given an additional impetus to globalization and education reform (Carnoy, 1999; Castells, 1996). With respect to the rapidly globalizing world, we live in today, it is possible for different national higher education systems to be more similar in terms of their institutional forms and organizational structures as a result of the rapid development of technology. As a result of the convergence of globalization, competition in the marketplace and the reforms in education that were underpinned by the introduction of ICT, we are witnessing a massive explosion in the knowledge sector that profoundly affects societies and higher education institutions.

As governments throughout the world strive to gain excellence, quality, and accountability in education, more and more governments are turning to lifelong learning and ICT as a means to achieve these goals. The higher education institutions generally have more flexibility in determining their own academic policies and planning their own administration than do most of the national education systems. Inadvertently, this gives the higher education institutions access to a broader range of opportunities and toolsets for launching innovative programmes, setting up alliances and creating markets. At the same time, the ability to manoeuvre effectively in the global environment translates to the readiness and appetite to change (Lane et al., 2014). Nevertheless, the globalization process has seemingly led to the convergence of interests and the competition between and among nations as well as among institutions. With the development of technology in global higher education along with the mobility of people, information and ideas, the influence of technology, globalization and higher education has grown greatly.

A study by Flavin (2017) noted that globalization and a trend of increasingly diverse populations coupled with the ubiquitous use of technology have profoundly affected higher education in many ways. In the same way, Taylor and Bano (2015) corroborated those emerging digital technologies offer tremendous opportunities for revision and adaptation, which will result in greater access to education and new markets and expanded income opportunities for higher education institutions. Students, teachers and institutions as a collective must confront the opportunities and challenges presented by globalization and the rapid change in technologies.

Higher education institutions of these challenging times must contend with possibly the most significant test as they face globalization, and economic uncertainty, undergirded by emerging technologies that facilitate digitally savvy learners connecting with learning and with one. A wide range of issues at the intersection of which educators must deal has resulted in the need to rethink what they teach, how they conduct research, and how they interact with society. In the context of a continuously changing world, Mok (2015) corroborates the need for institutions to improve their ability to adapt to unexpected changes if they are to succeed. The emergence of all these dynamic developments is forcing institutions to adapt, respond and change in a fluid environment for reasons of learning and adapting. To achieve and maintain a competitive advantage to thrive in a constantly changing world, institutions need to enhance their capability to change rapidly due to the fact that adapting to unforeseen circumstances is critical to achieving and maintaining such an edge.

The increasingly expanding networks of mobile, broadband Internet and other digital technologies in the twenty-first century not only established new means for human interaction at an unprecedented scale, but the phenomenon also imbues cities and countries with diverse cultures and robust economic development (Stephens & Powers, 2020; Takaoka & Etzo, 2019). In enabling complex data transfers critical to knowledge-intensive manufacturing, globalization incorporates economic and cultural elements through the process of information and communication, resulting in the creation of new developments in the global economy (Geodecki & Głowacki, 2020). It has been demonstrated that networks and knowledge created by ICT have a significant impact on power relations and inequality.

4.2.1 Higher Education in a VUCA World

In a world where chaos, turmoil and rapid change are the norm rather than the exception, the "new normal" has arisen since the dawn of the twenty-first century (Lawrence, 2013). The accelerating globalization of these conditions is described as VUCA: Volatility (the nature, speed, volume, magnitude and dynamics of change); uncertainty (the lack of predictability of issues and events); complexity (the confounding of issues and surrounding factors); and ambiguity (the haziness of reality and the mixed meaning of conditions). In the context of higher education, a VUCA world is often used to refer to the turbulent, unpredictable and rapidly changing environment for learning and teaching. As the emergence of globalization has resulted in more people, countries and economies being hyperconnected, a series of seemingly unrelated events have contributed to the emergence of the VUCA world. The global financial crisis of 2008 was one such event that resulted in many organizations from around the world falling into chaotic economic environments due to the situation. The interconnectedness led to a domino effect on financial institutions, and by the end of 2009, not many were left unscathed. As a result, the development of new technologies, such as social media and automation, had a profound impact on the way in which people live, work and interact with their surroundings (Kaivo-oja & Lauraeus, 2018; Kaplan & Haenlein, 2016). The occurrence of global disasters has also affected lives, economies, businesses and even education as well (Dobbs et al., 2016; Susman et al., 2019). Hence, the globalization movement established a worldwide communications system, information, knowledge and culture, leaning towards a unified world community (Kaptan, 2019).

With the exponential expansion of mobile, broadband Internet and other digital technologies in the twenty-first century, we are not only introducing new interfaces for human interaction at an unprecedented scale, but the phenomenon also imbues cities and countries with diverse cultures and robust economic development (Stephens & Powers, 2020; Takaoka & Etzo, 2019). A further benefit of the networks is that since they enable complex data transfers, which is an important element of knowledge-intensive manufacturing, the blending of economic as well as cultural elements through the use of information and communication technology (ICT) and processes creates new global elements. The adoption of ICTs in teaching and learning is a natural consequence of these developments. In addition to this, the literature indicates that ICT networks and knowledge have created key dividing lines in shaping the relations of power and inequality (Ragnedda, 2017). In this case, it is evident that during the COVID-19 lockdown period, students who do not have the financial means to access their computers and the Internet have a difficult time accessing online educational material.

The higher education sector has faced an uncertain future due to globalizations, the adoption of new technologies and the coming of the VUCA era (Korsakova, 2019). In addition, Yehezkel (2020) emphasizes that the VUCA paradigm has the potential to disrupt organizations and, in particular, higher education, as the four elements interact in turbulent and sometimes conflicting ways. Taking these forces together, they drive the institutions to adapt quickly by developing and implementing operational strategies and systems that are more effective than what they currently have in place. Nevertheless, institutions must enhance their efficiency in order to remain competitive in a world of uncertainty and complexity, where globalization is playing an increasingly significant role. In an era of globalization, governments are realizing the importance of pre-employment education to sustain long-term growth and remain competitive; therefore, institutions are being compelled to shift their focus from traditional teaching and learning roles to innovative practice, entrepreneurship, creativity and marketing role development (Wihlborg & Robson, 2018).

It is imperative that leaders of higher education who flourish in a VUCA world show innovative thinking and advocate adaptability and flexibility in their work so that they can effectively address the multitude of societal, financial, management and leadership issues that the era is confronting. Providing a student's achievement is a measure of success as measured by retention or graduation, and higher education leaders must confront the demands and political dictates for increased student achievement. As a result of these seismic changes in higher education, students and faculty are now operating in a VUCA world. In short, leaders are expected to face up to the unpredictability and pressures of the changes that are of a multiplicity of facets and reconcile with the fact that change means ambiguity and challenges, as well as setbacks, stress and crises. It has been shown that globalization, when coupled with the VUCA environment, can change the world's economy, increase diversity and cause widespread usage of technology, which has major implications for higher education (Moodie, 2016). This narrative continues to challenge higher education institutions in a rapidly evolving global landscape, with a perception of innovation continuing to evolve as well (Proenza, 2010).

4.2.2 The 21st Century Learners in Higher Education

It is not surprising that students of the twenty-first century are accustomed to technology such as computers, mobile phones, online games and social media from an early age, as they have grown up with technology, so when it comes to learning and sharing, they expect instant access at any time and from any location (Galanek et al., 2018). According to Brabazon (2017), learners who have a difficult time balancing both life and school are attracted to ubiquitous anytime, anywhere learning that can be accessed via student computers. It is important to point out, however, that the literature indicates that the actual process of learning from technology is more complex than the consumption process (Lawrence & Tar, 2018). In the light of these considerations, educators might attempt to design learning in a way that is more familiar to students, while also resembling the consumption of technology. In order to develop a self-directed learning course, educators might leverage game-based learning framework design and transform it into a self-directed educational experience. Even though it is possible, it does not mean that the game has to be of the same quality as they play as casually for entertainment. A number of well-established studies have demonstrated that digitally mediated information and data are significantly changing the design and delivery of instruction, as well as the assessment of academic outcomes, and the idea of learning itself (Broadbent, Panadero et al., 2020a, 2020b; Van Nyhuis, 2018).

During a period when knowledge is fluid and distributed, it is not sufficient for faculty to act as dispensers of information, as students can access the same information easily on the Internet. The opposite is also true the faculty are expected to make a paradigm shift to helping students make sense of knowledge as opposed to simply imparting it, increasingly by utilizing technology. A significant part of this change is due to the effects of rapid technological and socio-economic development, including the development of information technology, the shift to a services-based economy and the evolution of a knowledge society (Schleicher, 2015). The thought of enhanced online learning has also emerged as the new impetus for the change in higher education learning pedagogy. It is therefore important for faculty members to be able to adapt rapidly to new technology and use it to reach and engage learners, both as facilitators of learning and as transmitters of information (Ossiannilsson, 2018). It is important to note that technology can be viewed as an inherently fundamental approach to initiating and sustaining contact with an increasing and enlarging student population that is in constant motion and striving to participate fully. Consequently, it is not surprising that students' ease in using technology for learning, which has fundamental implications on their interaction with the faculty, and the impact of institutional policies, reflects a fundamental influence on the students' sociocultural context.

The next section provides an overview of the influence of technology on teaching and learning in higher education.

4.3 The Influence of Technology on Higher Education

Since technology has advanced exponentially over the last few decades, higher education has taken on new dimensions, making technology knowledge essential for college administrators in the twenty-first century. The emergence of new technologies has facilitated higher education institutions in transforming practices and gaining greater global interconnectedness, as a consequence of which educational, cultural, social, economic and political life has been reorganized (Krause, 2020). The understanding of how information and communication technologies can be utilized for the benefit of education is imperative for the leaders of higher education in order to harness technology for the benefit of education from a local, national and global perspective. It is thus of the utmost importance than ever for higher education institutions to facilitate wide-ranging relationships and maintain an uninterrupted flow of resources so they can gain entry into global markets (Williamson, 2020). The integration of technology for the transformation of higher education provides a global focus, therefore increasing the level of interconnectedness between higher education institutions on the global scale. The following paragraphs address the potential impact that emerging technologies may have on global higher education instruction and students' learning experiences.

As the dissemination of emerging technologies is a universal phenomenon, their application usually differs in accordance with institutional management, policy and government needs (Moodie, 2016). As a result of increased technological use, knowledge and information have become more valuable and globally connected because of their increased value and globalization. In particular, the successful conduct of business in higher education is almost exclusively dependent on technology, since the unrelenting quest for information drives the need for increasing technological capabilities. While at the same time, technology has been considered one of the most important factors for achieving a higher level of efficiency within higher education institutions; however, costs, complexity and the use of technology are not without challenges.

With the rapid advancement and continuous growth of IT systems, higher education leaders have the unenviable task of balancing technology renewal in order to keep up with technological advances and manage technology obsolescence at the same time. The majority of institutions have invested significant resources into educational technology in order to be able to provide online courses to their students. While learning technologies are increasingly being adopted by institutions, this adoption has been uneven or incoherent as a result of inadequate infrastructure and deficient implementation processes (Salmon, 2014; Waller et al., 2019a, 2019b).

Towards the beginning of the twenty-first century, significant adoption of easy-to-use learning technologies by institutions began, such as Virtual Learning Environments (VLEs), which were mistaken for innovation on the part of the education system (Westera, 2004). Over the years, learning technologies have gradually been integrated into higher education, which has led to lower hardware and connectivity prices. The advent of information, communication and technology (ICT) for the purpose of learning has led to stakeholders working together from the policy level to the practice level on the transformation of education (Salmon, 2019). In spite of the potential of VLEs to transform teaching and learning since they can be used to support ubiquitous and collaborative, they are also often underused in order to achieve this goal. It is possible to transform the learning experience of students with the help of learning technologies when they trigger a significant and sustained change in the way educators respond to pedagogical innovations.

There is, however, a lack of institutional learning from the number of isolated experiments and innovations in institutions, given the fact that reward, recognition and approval systems do not promote systematic change or meaningful experimentation (Allen, 2012; Everhart & Seymour, 2017). In this respect, rather than changing pedagogical practices through VLEs, they have reaffirmed traditional, transmissive teaching modes within the educational context. A perfect analogy for this context is Salmon's (2005) description of VLE adoption as two stages of flight. Salmon indicated there are three stages in creating a VLE, beginning with "flapping", followed by transiting to "flying".' However, for the most part, he found that most institutions stayed at the "flapping" stage, seeing VLEs as an attempt at transference of existing pedagogy. During the COVID-19 pandemic lockdown, this phenomenon was most apparent and widespread. The massive online remote teaching through the use of virtual learning environments (VLEs) amplifies ineffective pedagogical practices (Kandri, 2020, May).

Using learning technologies in a way that creates effective instructional programmes that can attract students and produce graduates who are capable is the real challenge. It is essential that technology transforms the way faculty teach and enhances the students' experience of the learning process as well as the ability of online instruction to improve (Flavin, 2017). It is important to note that technology should be seen as a tool that can be utilized by educators to enhance learners' learning using technology as a learning tool. The purpose of deploying learning technologies should be to develop learners' learning capacity and capabilities and to make learners capable of making use of the technology to utilize learning and to learn instead of building up a knowledge bank.

"Education is no longer about teaching students something alone; it is more important to be teaching them to develop a reliable compass and the navigation tools to find their way in a world that is increasingly complex, volatile and uncertain. Our imagination, awareness, knowledge, skills and, most importantly, our common values, intellectual and moral maturity, and sense of responsibility is what will guide us for the world to become a better place" (Schleicher, 2019).

It is clear that technology is progressing at a rapid pace, and the world has evolved with the technology. Fast forward to the present, higher education is moving on a path towards providing information, delivering services and adjusting to the dynamic dynamics of the global economy (Esin, 2017). At a time when higher education institutions were grappling with the gradual adoption of technology, they were unprepared for the arrival of the fourth industrial revolution, which has flipped everything upside down and thrown everything back into confusion. As a result, leaders within the global higher education sector should place a higher emphasis on ensuring quality in the application and utilization of technology rather than continuing the crisis caused by the acquisition of technology. The following paragraphs discuss the implications of the fourth industrial revolution for education.

4.3.1 The Impact of the Fourth Industrial Revolution on Education

The Fourth Industrial Revolution is a complex concept which is based on the confluence of both cyber and physical systems where the machines are interconnected, and able to exchange data with one another independently throughout manufacturing and production processes. The advent of the Fourth Industrial Revolution affords humankind new capabilities; nevertheless, the disruptive digital transformation is restructuring human affairs in all aspects of work, private and social life; the advent of digitalization has changed the way that people live and work and has led to new insights into how they learn (Schröder, 2019; Tan, 2020). Specifically, the world has entered the era of Big Data, which causes individual information footprints to be generated on a daily basis, thus creating an abundance of data that enables human and societal behaviours to be objectively quantified and, as a result, easily tracked, modelled and, to a certain extent, forecast. This phenomenon surrounding the emergence of information footprints is known as datafication (Mayer-Schönberger & Cukier, 2014).

The following is the prediction about it:

> *We stand on the brink of a technological revolution that will fundamentally alter how we live, work, and relate to one another. In its scale, scope, and complexity, the transformation will be unlike anything humankind has experienced before. We do not yet know just how it will unfold, but one thing is clear: the response to it must be integrated and comprehensive, involving all stakeholders of the global polity, from the public and private sectors to academia and civil society (Schwab, 2016, p. 1).*

The digital transformation is already changing how the global workplace is organized and the division of labour is done. "Economies, businesses, societies and politics are being transformed by technological advances in such areas as artificial intelligence and machine learning, the Internet of Things, autonomous vehicles, drones, precision medicine and genomics, advanced materials, smart grids, robotics and big data" (Samans, 2019). As a result of artificial intelligence, robotics and automatization, a lot of jobs have already been lost while new and exciting ones are being created (Brougham et al., 2018; Davenport et al., 2018; OECD, 2018). The World Economic Forum estimated the impact of the robotic revolution on industries in its Future of Work 2018 report that new technologies such as mobile Internet at high speeds, artificial intelligence, big data analytics and cloud computing will fuel the Robot Revolution at unprecedented speeds across several industries between 2018 and 2022 (Tan, 2020).

According to the World Economic Forum, the number of new occupations will increase from 16 to 27% of the employee base of large firms globally by 2022, while those jobs currently affected by technological obsolescence will decline from 31 to 21%. Taking solely statistical terms, it is estimated that 75 million current positions could be replaced by machines, algorithms and humans by a shift in the division of work between them, while 133 million new positions may also emerge as a consequence of the shift. It should come as no surprise that data analysts/scientists and artificial intelligence (AI)/machine learning (ML) specialists are emerging as the top two fastest-growing jobs.

AI is an incredibly burgeoning technological field that has the potential to change every aspect of our social relationships—the advancement of cutting-edge AI algorithms that can learn from their mistakes, computing power and access to technology have proliferated rapidly across the globe (OECD, 2018). In short, artificial intelligence innovation is bringing about a rapid and imminent shift in almost every aspect of life. If one considers the impact of artificial intelligence on education, and the skills and knowledge needed to succeed in an AI-augmented future, it is critical to go beyond the current trends and identify the jobs and skills that are needed to redefine intelligence in an artificial intelligence-augmented world.

The focus of the IR 4.0 initiative is currently centred on manufacturing and the transformation of industrial processes and the significance of embracing this change for the future of business and industries. It is evident that the majority of the predictions relate to IR 4.0, regardless of the changes in demographics, life expectancy and retirement economics that have a substantial impact on personal, social and professional development (Schwab, 2017). In terms of the impact of artificial intelligence on education, there is the possibility of quite dramatic changes in the demand for knowledge and skills, as well as an expansion of the possibilities for teaching and learning (OECD, 2018). On top of all that, the millennia have never known a world without the Internet, and one in three will live to be over 100, and some to 120 (Roser, 2019). As a result, John (2019) asserts that there is also a strong case to be made that lifelong learning can be sustainable as well as personally rewarding. Nevertheless, there is an urgent need for the concerted effort and commitment of a wide range of stakeholders, including research and educational institutions, to transform and embrace the IR 4.0 for the changes to be productive and constructive.

It is essential to emphasize that the learning technology industry has begun to develop AI-powered learning and teaching solutions, which are currently being tested in a variety of contexts (Panigrahi, 2020). There are significant potential benefits associated with AI in and for education; however, there are also certain hazards and opportunities associated with this field (Tan, 2020). To these ends, educators must exercise caution when using artificial intelligence to support learners in their learning and guide learners into a future in which artificial intelligence will play an increasingly significant role.

The time is ripe to discuss what AI in education (AIEd) is, along with where institutions have already begun, or perhaps belatedly, depending on who's looking at it. It is of greater importance to educators to understand how AI can enhance teaching and learning in such a way that an improvement in learning outcomes can be observed. A deep dive into the impact of artificial intelligence on education and how it could have an impact on human cognition is provided in Chapter 9. The dawn of the COVID-19 pandemic came without warning at the beginning of 2020, hurling the whole world into a tailspin and creating chaos as higher education grappled with global IR 4.0.

4.3.2 COVID-19 Pandemic Impact on Education

In a world that has become increasingly volatile and unpredictable, the arrival of a Black Swan like the COVID-19 has extreme implications. An item that is classified as a "Black Swan" is an exceptional occurrence that lies outside the range of regular expectations, carries an extreme impact and sometimes is rationalized in retrospect (Taleb, 2007). As if the twenty-first century were not enough Black Swan events, there were also 9/11 and the 2008 financial crisis. However, the COVID-19 pandemic has proven to be an unprecedented blend of VUCA-Black Swan events (Hadar et al., 2020).

In early 2020, the outbreak of the COVID-19 pandemic crippled the global economy and shook the educational system worldwide, resulting in the closure of many schools. There are approximately 1.6 billion affected learners out of 91.3% of the total enrolled learners in 188 countries at all levels of education as of April 2020, according to UNESCO (2020). Due to this drastically changing trend, education has dramatically changed over the last few decades, with a noticeable rise in online learning, whereby classes can be taught and learned remotely through online platforms. It would have been hard for some to foresee at the end of 2019 that universities would experience such a paradigm shift, whereby predominant virtual teaching and work-from-home became the norm, because of a global pandemic that has taken hold.

Due to the unexpected closure of their physical campuses, universities have shifted their learning and teaching in the 2020 academic year to the Internet in order to maintain continuity and normality. Inevitably, the implications of this situation have not only caused disruption and anxiety within the lives of a great many, but they have also increased inequality between those students with access to resources and those without such resources (UNESCO, 2020). The first response educators took upon the discovery of an unprecedented situation was to provide a temporary "band-aid" solution in which the students were taught entirely from a virtual classroom using video-conferencing software such as Zoom and Microsoft Teams (Kandri, 2020, May). Online learning platforms have responded to an enormous surge in demand by offering free access to their services, among them BYJU'S, the world's most highly valued educational technology company that provides online tutoring and educational technology. It has also been reported that Tencent classroom has been extensively used since the Chinese government instructed a quarter of a billion full-time students to continue their studies via online platforms during the lockdown in early 2020 (Li & Lalani, 2020, April). It is therefore not surprising that the switch to remote teaching and learning has proved to be inadequate in terms of providing a successful online learning experience.

Nonetheless, a massive and sudden shift from classroom instruction occurred in many parts of the world, which caused many observers to wonder whether this trend will persist post-pandemic and how it will impact worldwide education (Kandri, 2020, July; Li & Lalani, 2020, April; OECD, 2020). It is true that the pain and anguish that have resulted from the outbreak have been significant and unsettling; however, it might just be the catalyst needed to trigger a long overdue and welcome practice of rejuvenating our educational systems. In a sense, the pandemic has been somewhat of a leveller for educators, learners, policymakers and the entire society, in general, to reevaluate our current education system's vulnerabilities and weaknesses to some extent.

To capitalize on the opportunity offered by the virus-induced virtual culture of COVID-19, higher education institutions in order to succeed need to have an innovative mindset, open leadership, and ample imagination and creativity (Kedraka & Kaltsidis, 2020). There is no doubt that the partnerships between universities and education technology providers abated the challenges for online learning during the pandemic, but it continues to be critical to optimizing the use of learning sciences to optimize the transition from face-to-face classes to blended learning and hybrid learning in the higher education sector (Kandri, 2020, July; Martin-Barbero, 2020, July). In this regard, learning design, multimedia production and data analytics may gain greater prominence. To this end, it is imperative that teaching faculty members acquire the capability in adapting and redesigning their course content according to changing pedagogical shifts. This is supported by Kedraka's and Kaltsidis' (2020) finding that students are seeking meaningful online interactions and they expect their educators to be effective with online teaching and learning methods. A further consideration is that educators must be able to transition the sociocultural interactions from a face-to-face class setting to an online classroom setting.

Given more time and space, educators must develop the capability to experiment with different digital learning solutions, leveraging technology to foster deeper student learning and developing into facilitators of student learning, blending their expertise as a profession (Karalis, 2020; OECD, 2020). Additionally, the opportunity arises for institutional leadership to explore how students can learn in different places and at different times via digital learning solutions and bring communities, homes and schools closer together, providing students with more agency by being given more autonomy. (Kedraka & Kaltsidis, 2020; OECD, 2020). COVID-19 has been a lightning bolt to our education systems and its impact has rocked our education concept to its very core; it calls for a drastic transformation for our education system to prepare our students for the future. It is in that vein that the next section is dedicated to the discussion of the need for a new framework for teaching and learning innovation.

4.4 A New Framework for Innovation in Teaching and Learning

It is crucial for educators to establish a framework that will enable them to analyse and strategize the future with a clear view of the challenges of innovating in the midst of the increasingly unstructured world. A literature review percolates two frameworks that could provide insights for innovation and teaching and learning. With the world continuing to adapt to and deal with the ravages of COVID-19, a growing number of individuals, groups and organizations within higher education are referencing Bower and Christensen's (1995) concept of disruptive innovation in an effort to explicate the current situation and subtly advise them to take action in order to navigate the turbulent times ahead. It has been widely acclaimed by both the technical and business communities that the work of this duo has been highly influential in the field of business and management, demonstrating that even successful companies can be overtaken by technologically inferior competitors because of the former's affordability, ease of use and convenience. Essentially, disruptive innovation is the process of opening up potentially large markets for innovative products and services in order to develop technically and ultimately become market leaders. As described by Christensen (1997), four criteria determine whether technology is capable of disrupting the existing market. Through being cheaper, simpler, smaller and more convenient than the rival, incumbent technologies often supplant market leaders.

In a similar vein, Salmon (2014) presented a strategic framework for supporting higher education institutions in their adoption of technologies in teaching and learning. The time has come to examine these theories and frameworks in detail and derive insights that may inform the development of a solution for current challenges.

4.4.1 Clayton Christensen and Disruptive Innovation

As Christensen's Disruption Innovation Model might not have been able to predict the COVID-19 pandemic explicitly, it lends itself to the unearthing of the disruption—proving to be more prescient than Christensen realized. It should be noted that Christensen's theory of disruptive innovation has not been designed specifically to support teaching and learning in higher education. However, it may be adapted in order to enhance the educational process.

The concept of disrupting technologies is broadly defined as technologies that disrupt conventional practices, are often implemented in small groups of users, but gain in popularity over time to the extent that they displace an already dominant technology (Christensen, 1997). Developing sustaining technologies, on the other hand, results in the further development of existing technologies. As illustrated in Christensen's Disruptive Innovation Model (1997), the difference between sustaining technologies from disruptive technologies is based on the fact that sustaining technologies improve existing products, whereas disruptive technologies create a unique value proposition that is different from the existing products. These disruptive technologies give rise to a wide variety of products that are often cheaper, simpler, smaller and, quite often, more convenient to use.

In contrast, Bower and Christensen (1995) argue that established businesses are not well positioned for going into disruptive technologies that will require a radical change in their approach, often requiring significant investment on their part. As Christensen (1997) points out, there are technologies that enable businesses to make incremental improvements as they deliver their products and services (sustaining) as well as technologies that trigger new forms of practice (disruptive). In higher education, the sustaining technology concept—in which the use of technology to enhance rather than replace existing instructional methodologies—has been utilized to enhance with the existing educational methods. According to Christensen et al. (2008), faculty greatly prefer that computer graphics be used to enhance the lecture rather than to change the pedagogical practice. Students are, on the other hand, able to use disruptive technologies to support their learning and teaching, suggesting that there is tension between students and institutions (Salmon, 2014). Taking into account the use of digital technologies in the classroom setting, it may be necessary for the lecturer to give up some of their authority in order to be able to manage the learning environment. This analysis correlates with Christensen's Disruptive Technology Theory (1997) in which new technology can disrupt established practices and that new technology can transform the way pedagogical practices are practised as well as being disruptive.

Higher education institutions have made a substantial investment in virtual learning environments (VLEs) because they are technology-based learning tools. The issue is that students and faculty have not fully embraced these technologies. Similarly, technologies can be adapted for educators and students for the purpose of facilitating teaching and learning, even though they were not designed for that purpose. The emergence of disruptive technologies usually serves as the catalyst for the emergence of new markets, and innovation originates from the ground up (Christensen, 1997; Christensen & Raynor, 2003). When translating Christensen's theory to technology-enhanced learning, innovation may come from students who combine their knowledge and experiences of technologies with their own. It is the university's leadership and faculty members who are responsible for deciding whether to embrace these disruptive technologies and fully utilize them for innovation in higher education.

In summary, the disruptive technology framework provides policymakers with a lens for making sense of their external environment; however, the disruptive technology framework does not take into consideration the strengths and weaknesses of the institutional setting in developing the innovation strategy. The next section will examine how teaching and learning innovations can be integrated into an institutional strategy to help institutions harness the disruptive technologies available within the current environment.

4.4.2 Transformative Strategic Framework for Innovation in Teaching and Learning

According to Salmon (2014), a strategic innovation framework has been conceptualized in order to improve the digital learning strategies in higher education institutions—a framework that considers the resources, structures, and innovation capabilities that universities possess, as well as the opportunities and risks created by the external environment in which the university operates. It is therefore through this framework that the university can leverage its unique assets as well as develop a multidimensional perspective with respect to digitally enhanced learning, taking into consideration the university's mission and objectives during the design of its innovation strategy for education.

The framework developed by Salmon (2014) was categorized into four quadrants. In the first quadrant, a university builds upon the existing core competencies and employs incremental innovation to solve problems and enhance the quality of learning at the institution using the technologies that are already in place. The level of risk in this quadrant is relatively low. It differs in the second quadrant from the first quadrant, where a university turns to horizontal integration or organizational development by taking its core strengths and incremental development from the first quadrant and applying them to new missions and markets, but the risk increases proportionately.

In the third quadrant, universities become more innovative in terms of deploying their core competencies to teach and learn. As a result of the imagination and prototyping involved in this quadrant, the risk is higher. In the fourth quadrant, there are crucial elements which are essential for success in developing new products, deploying emerging technologies and bringing about new markets and missions. There is an obvious risk increase with this investment, but for those who succeed, there is a potential for a higher return on investment.

It is evident that this strategic framework is valuable for institutional policymakers as it accounts for the resources, structures and innovative capabilities that universities possess as well as the cultural norms of the faculty and students, however, given the disruption of emerging technologies and Black Swan events like the COVID-19, there are some gaps in adapting to rapidly changing situations. Accordingly, the following section aims to examine the possibilities for a revised framework that could be more responsive to the institutions' needs.

4.5 A Revised Framework for Innovation in Teaching and Learning

In Salmon's (2014) strategic innovation framework for changing digitally enhanced learning strategies, a university is able to make an assessment of its internal resources and strengths and, at the same time, of the opportunities and risks created by its external environment. In contrast, Bower & Christensen's (1995) Disruptive Innovation Model provides an opportunity to examine the challenges posed to technology-enhanced learning, through disruptive innovation, and the implications of that practice with technology. In higher education, each of the frameworks offers educators a different lens through which to approach the issue of innovation in learning. In particular, the frameworks could assist educators in making effective strategic decisions regarding learning innovations.

While both frameworks are excellent in helping educators analyse the driving forces of change, they do not explicitly guide educators in implementing innovations in teaching and learning, particularly in adapting the innovations to the socio-organizational culture. The social cognition perspective provides some insights as it emphasizes the role of individuals' thought processes in the change initiative and posits that resistance to change is often attributed to a lack of understanding of change processes and the implications for one's work rather than a refusal to accept the changes (Hrebiniak, & Joyce, 1985). It is, therefore, essential that change agents be able to view the institution through a variety of different lenses in order to impact others to adopt unfamiliar worldviews. In contrast, the cultural perspective highlights the importance of context, values, beliefs, irrationality, flexibility and complexity in the change process (Collins, 2005; Corbo et al., 2016). In this view, organizational change occurs as the result of a change in culture, more specifically through the emergence of new values, beliefs, myths and rituals.

By taking into account the relevant points, particularly regarding the sociocultural aspects of organizational change, this section proposes a two-step comprehensive framework for guiding educators in designing and implementing innovations that will close the achievement gaps. The convergence of Bower & Christensen's (1995) Disruptive Innovation Theory and Salmon's (2014) Transformative Strategic Framework for Learning Innovation might allow for their strengths to be merged, possibly producing a revised disruptive innovation and Transformative Strategic Framework for Learning Innovation as highlighted in Fig. 4.1.

The first quadrant represents incremental innovation, which occurs when an institution applies the technologies already available to solve problems and enhance the quality of life of the students. Despite the fact that most institutions have invested in a VLE, Salmon (2014) points out that fewer have operated their VLEs to their full potential for fostering innovation in learning. In the wake of COVID-19, educators had been prompted to rediscover the VLEs in their institutions when they moved to remote teaching during the pandemic lockdown period during which they had moved to remote teaching. In most institutions, most of the faculty is located in this area. At a scale not seen before the pandemic, they will continue to make incremental improvements to online learning courses at a large scale. Nonetheless, the pandemic presents a rare opportunity for educators around the world to come together and form a collective resolve that will help them test out different digital pedagogies of instruction and learning.

In the second quadrant, innovation can be seen as sustainable. This signifies an institution can take its core strengths and incremental innovation in the first quadrant and apply it to new markets or fields. One possible scenario would be if the faculty was

New Market/Domain	Sustaining Innovation	Disruptive Innovation
Existing Market/Domain	Incremental Innovation	Radical Innovation
	Existing Technology	New Technology

Fig. 4.1 Revised transformative strategic framework for learning innovation

able to enhance the performance of their online courses for other courses they may offer in the future or if they are able to develop new courses from scratch. It is amply demonstrated in this example how edtech tools are embedded in a virtual learning environment to enable a seamless experience of teaching and learning for faculty and students. Educators have been hard at work experimenting with synchronous blended learning during the COVID-19 lockdown period. Through the integration of digital tools like Zoom with virtual learning environments (VLEs), students from overseas could participate in class alongside their classmates who were attending classes on campus.

In the third quadrant, there is a radical change in education, in which a university is deploying new technologies to boost its core competencies in teaching and learning. A typical example would be how educators use big data analytics to innovate in teaching and learning for existing courses. The benefits gained from new technologies might be higher, as technological affordances might be able to gain more insights; however, they may present a relatively higher risk as well. A deep dive into the use of artificial intelligence and learning analytics to enhance teaching and learning are discussed in Chapter 8 along with more examples.

In the last quadrant, the university is entrusted with disruptive innovation, in which the university utilizes emerging technologies to create new products, new markets and new missions. The remainder of this book includes examples of how universities have leveraged technologies for innovation in teaching and learning. This revised framework for innovation in teaching and learning is useful in identifying current practices in teaching and learning and enhancing institutional effectiveness in designing and implementing new teaching and learning practices; however, it does not adequately address the implementation of the new innovations that have been designed. This is why the following sections are going to explore new models that can be employed as a support for implementing innovation into the teaching and learning process.

4.6 Implementation of Innovation Through Diffusion of Innovation

The revised Transformative Strategic Framework for Learning Innovation provides educators with a useful framework for reflecting upon and designing innovations in teaching and learning, but it does not provide scaffolding to assist educators in developing the implementation strategies. In particular, the implementation process involves taking into account the institution's context, values, beliefs, irrationality, flexibility and complexity. It is therefore the intent of the next sections to examine the possibilities of adapting the Gartner hype cycle and the diffusion of innovation model for the implementation of innovations in learning.

4.6.1 The Gartner Hype Cycle

The challenge for higher education institutions today is to be competitive in leveraging technology for innovation. A model for adapting and tracking the performance of such an initiative is through the use of Gartner hype cycle for emerging technologies. The Gartner hype cycle is a graphic presentation of a pattern that emerges with each innovation in technology or otherwise, and it is published every year since 1995 (Fenn & Raskino, 2008). Taking into consideration both the horizon (y-axis) and the timeframe (x-axis), the heuristic illustrates a technology's value (Kaivo-oja et al., 2020). The hype curve shape of the value of new technologies over time can be clearly seen when viewed in a graphic (Fenn & Raskino, 2008; Steinert & Leifer, 2010). As a result of a rapid, overly optimistic response to new technology, the bell-shaped curve of expectations tends to shape up as a result. The bell-shaped curve is due to several factors including the desire for novelty in addition to social contagion and heuristic attitude when it comes to making decisions.

There are more than 90 hype cycles created every year by Gartner across various sectors to help companies and individuals monitor the maturity of technologies and their future potential. In general, the hype cycle starts with the zealous adopters and continues through five phases until the new technology is accepted and finds application on the market (Linden & Fenn, 2003). The five phases are the Technology Trigger, Peak of Inflated Expectations, Trough of Disillusionment, Slope of Enlightenment and Plateau of Productivity.

It is important to note that Gartner has used several market indicators to accurately represent the expected value and maturity phase of technology innovation. Despite all the risks and opportunities, every technological breakthrough comes with a lot of hype surrounding it. At every stage of the hype cycle, certain decisions can assist with the effective adoption of new technology when the time is right for a use case and business requirements. The hype cycle can help learning innovators assess the adoption position of a given technology; however, there are gaps in scaling and sustaining the innovation in a given population. The following section investigates the possibilities of adapting the diffusion of innovation model in order to better facilitate the implementation of teaching and learning innovations.

4.6.2 The Diffusion of Innovation Model

As far as the diffusion of innovation models are concerned, Diffusion of innovations is one of the most widely adopted models, which reflects the degree of innovation based on socio-economic characteristics (Rogers, 2010). There are four critical factors that contribute to the diffusion of innovation: Innovation, communication channels, time and social systems.

Rogers defines diffusion as "the process in which an innovation is communicated through certain channels over time among the members of a social system" (p. 5). It is evident from the above description that innovation could be defined as a new idea that spreads around the social system via specific communications channels over the course of time among its members (Rogers, 2010). According to the social system's innovativeness, the members are grouped into four categories: Innovators, early adopters, early majorities, late majorities and laggards. Each category of adopter bears some characteristics regarding their innovativeness which are common to all individuals within the group. The innovativeness of a system is the degree to which an individual or some other unit of adoption is relatively earlier in adopting new ideas than are the others within the system (Rogers, 2010, p. 22).

The term "innovators" refers to the population which represents the first 2.5 per cent of the population to adopt a new innovation. As a matter of course, the term "innovators" had also been employed in a more general sense to describe an early market that included innovators and "early adopters" which included the first 16 per cent of adopters in general (Midgley, 1977). There seems to be a continuous distribution of individuals; however, the literature indicates that there are gaps between many major adopter groups (Moore, 2002). Considering both of these gaps reflect the different perspectives on innovation, it is imperative to clearly communicate the innovation's value proposition to each adopter group (innovators, early adopters and the early majority) for achieving complete diffusion of innovation. As a result, the gap between these two markets is often described as "a chasm" which must be crossed for innovation to succeed (Moore, 2002). It is also consistent with Rogers' (2010) paradigm, according to which an innovation is considered "safely diffused" once it has achieved market penetration of at least 13–16% before gaining sufficient momentum to reach the tipping point in the Early Adopter segment (Sanderford, 2013).

The communication strategies rest on sociocultural factors and intrapreneurial orientation factors, significantly impacting perceived cross-functional strategies (Sinha & Srivastava, 2016). Glückler and Bathelt (2017) corroborate that successful innovation depends on the design of institutional contexts since inconsistent institutional contexts constrain or even impede successful innovation. Such situations require adapting innovations to the institutional context (robust design), sidestepping resistant institutional contexts (peripheral dominance) or creating new institutional contexts that support the innovation process. By applying the social cognition perspective to the change effort, change agents would be capable of viewing the institution through a variety of perspectives, considering the role that individual thought processes play within the change undertaking. To accomplish this goal, it is necessary to persuade others to adopt unfamiliar worldviews and to reduce the resistance to change, which is a result of insufficient knowledge of change processes and of the implications for one's work as opposed to refusing to accept the changed surroundings.

The diffusion of innovation model or the technology adoption life cycle provides learning innovators with a roadmap for developing appropriate strategies for implementation. However, on its own, the model does not provide sufficient insights into related technology developments and life cycles. Therein lies a gap in the model that needs to be addressed to support learning innovation. The next section will shed light on the possibility of combining the strengths of the Gartner hype cycle and the diffusion of innovation model to construct a comprehensive model that will assist companies in executing their innovation strategies more effectively.

4.6.3 The Synergy Gartner Hype Cycle and the Diffusion of Innovation Model

Reviewing the Gartner hype cycle and the diffusion of innovation model highlights their strengths and weaknesses as a guideline for potential users to use to implement their own learning innovations. This comparative approach provides users with synergistic and multidimensional insights into the status of innovation in its life cycle, in a synergistic and multifaceted manner (Vallecillo, 2014). In the case of an educator introducing an immersive technology to enhance a course, the hype cycle would indicate periodically the state of technology development, while the diffusion model is used to determine the availability of the technology to other educators. For the educator to cross the chasm between the Trough and the Chasm of Disillusionment, it is imperative to monitor and craft appropriate communication strategies. Vallecillo's (2014) integrated hype cycle and diffusion of innovation (HCDI) framework meets the implementation needs.

The HCDI (hype cycle and diffusion of innovation) model may not be validated through empirical research, but it remains an important resource for educators to use in adapting it to their respective contexts when implementing innovations for teaching and learning. Nonetheless, readers retain the prerogative and responsibility to make adjustments according to their respective institutional contexts. Due to the distinction in the life cycle of each technology, it would also be necessary for users to modify the applications in tandem with the breadth, depth and pace of development of each technology. The next step will be to apply the HCDI Model to empirical research in order to validate it.

4.7 Conclusion

Throughout higher education, the VUCA environment has been accelerated and accentuated by globalization. In the wake of this, institutions are now faced with a variety of new challenges and rapid changes, particularly when it comes to the use of digital technology to harness authentic innovation in teaching and learning. It is described in this chapter that the VUCA environment and the COVID-19 concocted the perfect storm for triggering fundamental changes and innovation in the field of education. Some of these changes such as digitalization may be more visible and immediate, but how we view education as a whole in the future may take much longer to become more apparent.

It was discovered through reviewing the immediate situation and future challenges that an updated framework is needed to support educators' learning innovations. Based on the analysis presented in this chapter, a two-pronged approach has been proposed: One approach combines out of the disruptive innovation framework (Bower & Christensen, 1995) and the transformative strategic framework for learning innovation (Salmon, 2014) to form a comprehensive approach to strategic planning, as well as the merger of the Gartner hype cycle and the diffusion of innovation model (Roger, 2010) to produce a pragmatic model that educators can use to design implementation plans for learning innovation. While this model of HCDI has not yet been validated empirically at the time of publication of this book, it does provide educators with a fairly comprehensive guide for designing and implementing innovative teaching and learning practices. Towards the end of the book, Chapters 7 and 8 provide a more detailed analysis of how the use of emerging technologies can lead to innovation in the teaching and learning process.

References

Alagaraja, M., & Li, J. (2015). Utilising institutional perspectives to investigate the emergence, rise, and (relative) decline of corporate universities. *Human Resource Development International, 18*(1), 4–23.

Allen, M. (2012). An education in Facebook. *Digital culture and education, 4*(3), 213–225.

Apple, M. (2001). Comparing neo-liberal projects and inequality in education. *Comparative Education, 37*(4), 409–423.

Bass, R., & Eynon, B. (2017). From unbundling to rebundling: Design principles for transforming institutions in the new digital ecosystem. *Change: The Magazine of Higher Learning, 49*(2), 8–17.

Borg, J., Scott-Young, C. M., & Turner, M. (2019). Smarter education: Leveraging stakeholder inputs to develop work-ready curricula. In *smart education and e-learning 2019* (pp. 51–61). Springer.
Bower, J. L., & Christensen, C. M. (1995). Disruptive technologies: Catching the wave. *Harvard Business Review, 73*, 43–53.
Broadbent, J., Panadero, E., Lodge, J.M., & Barba, P.D. (2020a). Technologies to enhance self-regulated learning in online and computer-mediated learning environments. Handbook of Research in Educational Communications and Technology.
Broadbent, J., Panadero, E., Lodge, J. M., & de Barba, P. (2020b). Technologies to enhance self-regulated learning in online and computer-mediated learning environments. In *Handbook of research in educational communications and technology* (pp. 37–52). Springer.
Brougham, D., & Haar, J. (2018). Smart technology, artificial intelligence, robotics, and algorithms (STARA): Employees' perceptions of our future workplace. *Journal of Management and Organization, 24*(2), 239–257.
Breen, J. M. (2017). Leadership resilience in a VUCA world. *Visionary leadership in a turbulent world: Thriving in the new VUCA context* (pp. 39–58). Emerald Publishing Limited.
Carnoy, M. (1999). *Globalisation and educational reform: What planners need to know?*. UNESCO, International Institute for Educational Planning.
Castells, M. (1996). *The rise of the network society*. Blackwell.
Chow, A. S., & Croxton, R. A. (2017). Designing a responsive e-learning infrastructure: Systemic change in higher education. *American Journal of Distance Education, 31*(1), 20–42.
Christensen, C. M. (1997). *The innovator's dilemma: When new technologies cause great firms to fail.*Harvard Business School Press.
Christensen, C. M. (2006). The ongoing process of building a theory of disruption. *The Journal of Product Innovation Management, 23*, 39–55.
Christensen, C. M., & Eyring, H. J. (2011). *The innovative university: Changing the DNA of higher education from the inside out*. Jossey-Bass.
Christensen, C. M. & Horn, M. B. (2013, October 4). How disruption can help colleges thrive. In The Chronicle of Higher Education (p. B30).
Christensen, C. M., & Raynor, M. E. (2003). *The innovator's solution: Creating and sustaining successful growth*. Harvard Business School Press.
Christensen, C. M., Baumann, H., Ruggles, R., & Sadtler, T. M. (2006). Disruptive innovation for social change. *Harvard Business Review, 84*(12), 94–101.
Christensen, C. M., Horn, M. B., & Johnson, C. W. (2008). *Disrupting class: How disruptive innovation will change the way the world learns*. McGraw-Hill.
Christensen, C. M., Raynor, M. E., & McDonald, R. (2015). What is disruptive innovation? *Harvard Business Review, 93*(12), 44–53.
Christensen, C. M., Bartman, Tandvan Bever, D. (2016, Fall). The hard truth about business model innovation. MIT Sloan Management Review. http://sloanreview.mit.edu/article/the-hard-truth-about-business-model-innovation/
Collins, D. (2005). *Organisational change: Sociological perspectives*. Routledge.
Corbo, J. C., Reinholz, D. L., Dancy, M. H., Deetz, S., & Finkelstein, N. (2016). Framework for transforming departmental culture to support educational innovation. *Physical Review Physics Education Research, 12*(1), 010113.
Davenport, T. H., & Ronanki, R. (2018). Artificial intelligence for the real world. *Harvard Business Review, 96*(1), 108–116.
Dobbs, R., Manyika, J., & Woetzel, J. (2016). No ordinary disruption: The four global forces breaking all the trends. PublicAffairs.
Egmond, C., Jonkers, R., & Kok, G. (2006). One size fits all? Policy instruments should fit the segments of target groups. *Energy Policy, 34*(18), 3464–3474.
Esin, J. O. (2017). *System overview of cyber-technology in a digitally connected global society*. AuthorHouse.

Everhart, D., & Seymour, D. M. (2017). Challenges and opportunities in the currency of higher education. In K. Rasmussen, P. Northrup, & R. Colson (Eds.). *Handbook of research on competency-based education in university settings*. IGI Global.

Fenn, J., & Raskino, M. (2008). *Mastering the hype cycle: How to choose the right innovation at the right time.* Harvard Business Press.

Flavin, M. (2017). *Disruptive technology enhanced learning: The use and misuse of digital technologies in higher education.* Springer.

Flavin, M., & Quintero, V. (2020). *An international study of technology enhanced learning-related strategies from the perspective of disruptive innovation.* Interactive Technology and Smart Education.

Galanek, J., Gierdowski, D., & Christopher Brooks, D. (2018). ECAR study of undergraduate students and information technology (Vol. 12, p. 12).

Geodecki, T., & Głowacki, J. (2020). Automation and robotisation in the services industry. Outsourcing in European Emerging Economies: Territorial Embeddedness and Global Business Services.

Gilpin, R. (1987). *The political economy of international relations.* Princeton University Press.

Glückler, J., & Bathelt, H. (2017). *Institutional context and innovation.* Edward Elgar Publishing.

Goldin, C., & Katz, L. (2010). *The Race between Education and Technology.* Belknap Press.

GTAI, G. (2019). Industrie 4.0.

Guri-Rosenblit, S., Sebkova, H., & Teichler, U. (2007). Massification and diversity of higher education systems: Interplay of complex dimensions. *Higher Education Policy, 20*(4), 373–389.

Hadar, L. L., Ergas, O., Alpert, B., & Ariav, T. (2020). Rethinking teacher education in a VUCA world: student teachers' social-emotional competencies during the Covid-19 crisis. *European Journal of Teacher Education*, 1–14.

Hrabowski, F. A. (2011). Institutional change in higher education: Innovation and collaboration. Policy paper: Strategies to increase STEM achievement in higher education. McGraw-Hill Research Foundation.

Hrebiniak, L. G., & Joyce, W. F. (1985). Organizational adaptation: Strategic choice and environmental determinism. *Administrative Science Quarterly*,336–349.

Iivari, N., Sharma, S., & Ventä-Olkkonen, L. (2020). Digital transformation of everyday life–How COVID-19 pandemic transformed the basic education of the young generation and why information management research should care? *International Journal of Information Management*, 102183.

John, J. (2019). *How to create: A broader, fairer and smarter education system.* https://www.jisc.ac.uk/blog/how-to-create-a-broader-fairer-and-smarter-education-system-08-mar-2019

Kaivo-oja, J. R. L., & Lauraeus, I. T. (2018). The VUCA approach as a solution concept to corporate foresight challenges and global technological disruption. Foresight.

Kaivo-oja, J., Lauraeus, T., & Knudsen, M. S. (2020). Picking the ICT technology winners-longitudinal analysis of 21st century technologies based on the Gartner hype cycle 2008–2017: Trends, tendencies, and weak signals. *International Journal of Web Engineering and Technology, 15*(3), 216–264.

Kandri, S. (2020, July). How COVID-19 is driving a long-overdue revolution in education. In The world economic forum COVID action platform. https://www.weforum.org/agenda/2020/05/how-covid-19-is-sparking-a-revolution-in-higher-education

Kaptan, Y. (2019). Global communication and culture. *Global Communication: A Multicultural Perspective*, 344.

Karalis, T. (2020). Planning and evaluation during educational disruption: Lessons learned from COVID-19 pandemic for treatment of emergencies in education. *European Journal of Education Studies, 7*(4), 125–142.

Kedraka, K., & Kaltsidis, C. (2020). Effects of the COVID-19 pandemic on university pedagogy: Students' experiences and considerations. *European Journal of Education Studies, 7*(8). https://oapub.org/edu/index.php/ejes/article/view/3176

Korsakova, T. V. (2019). Higher education in VUCA-World: New metaphor of university. *European Journal of Interdisciplinary Studies, 5*(2), 31–35.
Krause, K. L. D. (2020). Vectors of change in higher education curricula. *Journal of Curriculum Studies*, 1–15.
Lane, K. E., Lemoine, P., Tinney, T. M., & Richardson, M. D. (2014). Modify and adapt: Global higher education in a changing economy. *International Journal of Innovation in the Digital Economy (IJIDE), 5*(2), 24–36.
Lawrence, K. (2013). Developing leaders in a VUCA environment. UNC Kenan-Flagler: Business School Executive Development.
Lawrence, J. E., & Tar, U. A. (2018). Factors that influence teachers' adoption and integration of ICT in teaching/learning process. *Educational Media International, 55*(1), 79–105.
Lemoine, P. A., Hackett, P. T., & Richardson, M. D. (2017). Global higher education and VUCA–volatility, uncertainty, complexity, ambiguity. In *Handbook of research on administration, policy, and leadership in higher education* (pp. 549–568). IGI Global.
Li, C., & Lalani, F. (2020, April). The COVID-19 pandemic has changed education forever. This is how. In *World economic forum* (Vol. 29). https://www.weforum.org/agenda/2020/04/coronavirus-education-global-covid19-online-digital-learning/
Linden A., & Fenn J. (2003). Understanding Gartner's hype cycles. Strategic Analysis Report N° R-20–1971. Gartner, Inc
Marginson, S. (2006). Dynamics of national and global competition in higher education. *Higher Education, 52*(1), 1–39.
Martin-Barbero, S. (2020, Jul). COVID-19 has accelerated the digital transformation of higher education. In *World economic forum* (Vol. 29).
Mayer-Schönberger, V. and Cukier, K. (2014). *Learning with big data: The future of education.* Eamon Dolan Book.
Mense, E. G., Lemoine, P. A., Garretson, C. J., & Richardson, M. D. (2018). The development of global higher education in a world of transformation. *Journal of Education and Development, 2*(3), 47.
Midgley, D. F. (1977). *Innovation and new product marketing*. Croom Helm.
Miller, G., Benke, M., Chaloux, B., Ragan, L. C., Schroeder, R., Smutz, W., & Swan, K. (2014). *Leading the e-learning transformation of Higher Education: Meeting the challenges of technology and distance education.* Stylus Publishing.
Moodie, G. (2016). Book review of teaching machines: Learning from the intersection of education and technology. *Canadian Journal of Higher Education, 46*(2), 262–264.
Moore, G. A. (2002). *Crossing the Chasm* (revised). HarperBusiness Essentials.
Moreira, F., Ferreira, M. J., Pereira, C. S., Gomes, A. S., Collazos, C., & Escudero, D. F. (2019). ECLECTIC as a learning ecosystem for higher education disruption. *Universal Access in the Information Society, 18*(3), 615–631.
Mulgan, G. (2013). Reality checks. In M. Barber & S. Rizvi (Eds.), *Asking more: The path to efficacy* (pp. 17–22). Pearson.
OECD. (2018). Education and AI: Preparing for the future and AI, attitudes and values. Future of Education and Skills 2030: Conceptual Learning Framework.
OECD. (2019). OECD future of education and skills 2030: OECD learning compass 2030. A Series of Concept Notes.
OECD. (2020). Education responses to covid-19: Embracing digital learning and online collaboration. https://www.oecd.org/coronavirus/policy-responses/education-responses-to-covid-19-embracing-digital-learning-and-online-collaboration-d75eb0e8/
Ossiannilsson, E. (2018). Promoting active and meaningful learning for digital learners. In Handbook of research on mobile technology, constructivism, and meaningful learning (pp. 294–315). IGI Global.
Panigrahi, C. M. A. (2020). Use of artificial intelligence in education. *Management Accountant, 55*, 64–67.

Prinsloo, T., Van Deventer, J. P. (2017, September). Using the Gartner Hype Cycle to evaluate the adoption of emerging technology trends in higher education–2013 to 2016. *In international symposium on emerging technologies for education* (pp. 49–57). Springer.
Proenza, L. M. (2010). Relevance, connectivity, and productivity: Three paths to innovation in higher education. *Innovations, 5*(2), 3–11.
Rabah, J. (2015). Benefits and challenges of Information And Communication Technologies (ICT) integration in Québec English Schools. *Turkish Online Journal of Educational Technology-TOJET, 14*(2), 24–31.
Ragnedda, M. (2017). The third digital divide: A Weberian approach to digital inequalities. Taylor and Francis.
Richardson, M. D., Jenkins, W., & Lemoine, P. A. (2017). Planning for innovation and disruption in a global environment. *Educational Planning, 24*(3), 11–24.
Rogers, E. M. (2010). *Diffusion of innovations*. Simon and Schuster.
Roser, M. (2019). Hindsight, world comparisons and interactive maps about life expectancy. https://ourworldindata.org/life-expectancy
Salmon, G. (2005). Flying not flapping: a strategic framework for e-learning and pedagogical innovation in higher education institutions.
Salmon, G. (2014). Learning innovation: A framework for transformation. *European Journal of Open, Distance and E-Learning, 17*(2), 220–236.
Salmon, G. (2019). May the fourth be with you: Creating education 4.0. *Journal of Learning for Development, 6*(2). https://jl4d.org/index.php/ejl4d/article/view/352
Samans, R. (2019). Globalisation 4.0 shaping a new global architecture in the age of the Fourth Industrial Revolution: A call for engagement. World Economic Forum Report. http://www3.weforum.org/docs/WEF_Globalization_4.0_Call_for_Engagement.pdf
Sanderford, A. R. (2013). Bridging the diffusion of innovation chasm for green housing (Doctoral dissertation, Virginia Tech).
Schleicher, A. (2015). Schools for 21st-century learners: Strong leaders, confident teachers, innovative approaches. international summit on the teaching profession. OECD Publishing. 2, rue Andre Pascal, F-75775 Paris Cedex 16, France.
Schleicher, A. (2019). Presentation at the forum on transforming education, Global Peace Convention, Seoul.
Schröder, T. (2019). A regional approach for the development of TVET systems in the light of the 4th industrial revolution: The regional association of vocational and technical education in Asia. *International Journal of Training Research, 17*(suppl. 1), 83–95.
Schwab, K. (2017). The fourth industrial revolution. Currency.
Sinha, N., & Srivastava, K. B. (2016). Perceived innovation championing strategies and intrapreneurial orientation the role of social cultural context. *Journal of Management Research, 16*(2), 77–86.
Steinert, M. & Leifer, L. (2010, 18–22 July) 'Scrutinising Gartner's hype cycle approach', PICMET 2010 Proceedings, Phuket Thailand.
Stephens, K. K., & Powers, C. J. (2020). Communication technology and organizational life. *The Handbook of Applied Communication Research*, 249–265.
Susman, P., & O'KEEFE, P. H. I. L., and Wisner, B. (2019). 14 Global disasters, a radical interpretation. *Interpretations of Calamity: From the Viewpoint of Human Ecology, 4*, 263.
Takaoka, S., & Etzo, I. (2019). International human capital mobility and FDI: Evidence from G20 countries.
Taleb, N. N. (2007). *The black swan: The impact of the highly improbable, 2.* Random house.
Tan, S. (2020). Artificial Intelligence in education: Rise of the Machines. *Journal of Applied Learning and Teaching, 3*(1), 129–133.
Tierney, W. G. (2014). Higher education research, policy, and the challenges of reform. *Studies in Higher Education, 39*(8), 1417–1427.

Tokareva, E. A., Smirnova, Y. V., & Orchakova, L. G. (2019). Innovation and communication technologies: Analysis of the effectiveness of their use and implementation in higher education. *Education and Information Technologies, 24*(5), 3219–3234.

UNESCO. (2020). Global monitoring of school closures caused by COVID-19. https://en.unesco.org/covid19/educationresponse

Vallecillo, A. (2014). On the industrial adoption of model-driven engineering. Is your company ready for MDE? *International Journal of Information Systems and Software Engineering for Big Companies (IJISEBC), 1*, 52–68.

Van Nyhuis, A. (2018). Advancing globalisation by teaching with technology: Synthesising global understanding and collaborative online international learning models. *American Association of University Administrators, 33*(1), 136–143.

Wallace-Hulecki, L. (2017). Part 1: Higher education in a VUCA world the new normal in higher education.

Waller, R. E., Lemoine, P. A., Mense, E. G., Garretson, C. J., & Richardson, M. D. (2019a). Global higher education in a VUCA world: Concerns and projections. *Journal of Education and Development, 3*(2), 73.

Waller, R. E., Lemoine, P. A., Mense, E. G., & Richardson, M. D. (2019b). Higher Education In Search Of Competitive Advantage: Globalisation, Technology And E-Learning. *International Journal of Advanced Research and Publications, 3*(8), 184–190.

Wenger, A., Dunn Cavelty, M., & Jasper, U. (2020). The politics and science of the future: Assembling future knowledge and integrating it into public policy and governance. In *The politics and science of prevision: Governing and probing the future* (pp. 229–251). Routledge.

Westera, W. (2004). On strategies of educational innovation: between substitution and transformation. *Higher Education, 47*(4), 501–517.

Wihlborg, M., & Robson, S. (2018). Internationalisation of higher education: Drivers, rationales, priorities, values and impacts. *European Journal of Higher Education, 8*(1), 8–18.

Williamson, B. (2020). Making markets through digital platforms: Pearson, edu-business, and the (e) vauation of higher education. *Critical Studies in Education*, 1–17.

Zajda, J. (2016). Globalisation, ideology and politics of education reforms. *The Netherlands*. https://www.springer.com/gp/book/9783319195056

Zawacki-Richter, O., & Latchem, C. (2018). Exploring four decades of research in computers and education. *Computers and Education, 122*, 136–152.

Samson Tan is the Director of Regional Strategy and Operations at Civica (Singapore). The focus of his work is on developing education strategies with strategic customers and stakeholders for the advancement of educational innovation best practices. Samson served as the Head of the Centre for Innovation in Learning at the National Institute of Education prior to joining Civica. He is also an exco member of the Association of Problem-Based Learning and Active Learning Methodologies (PAN-PBL), and the Education Research Association of Singapore.

Chapter 5
Blended Learning

Kumaran Rajaram

Abstract This chapter focuses on engaging learners through a blended-based learning strategy, with the adoption of the contextualized framework proposed, the learning elements and resources involved in having this learning approach executed. This includes presentation, analysis and discussion of evidence-based results on various aspects, say for example, effectiveness of the learning pedagogy, self-reports of students' perspectives and experiences, the different aspects of learning outcomes it focuses on and why using such a learning approach is more inclined in preparing them for the industry or corporate world. Blended learning is defined by Maarop and Embi (2016) as a teaching and learning approach that blends online instructional methods and face-to-face interaction. Spanjers et al. (2015) conducted a meta-analysis and found blended learning on average is more effective than traditional learning. Some of the benefits of blended learning includes, increased student-to-student and student-to-instructor interaction, student engagement (Alebaikan & Troudi, 2010; Korr et al., 2012) and flexibility in class design (Alebaikan & Troudi, 2010). It has been pointed out in literature reviews that there has been many challenges implementing the blended learning environment, especially due to a high demand on the time and workload of instructors to design the right blend between the two types of learning (Maarop & Embi, 2016) as there has not been much literature revealing any detailed framework designed (Boelens et al., 2017). To address this gap, we will be presenting a tested conceptual framework of blended learning with supporting discussions and the analysis performed on it. In this chapter, the rationale and effectiveness as well as the pragmatic challenges in adopting such a learning design will be covered. Survey and interview findings will be shared to show evidence-based reflections on the claims made. Experiences and contextualized issues will be shared so to explore how these findings could be extended beyond the sample group and applicable to varying learning cultures. There will be a section that discusses how blended learning will be perceived from a social-cultural perspective and if at all educators need to be mindful in designing and implementing them from the learning effectiveness dimension.

K. Rajaram (✉)
Division of Leadership, Management and Organization, Nanyang Business School, Nanyang Technological University, Singapore, Singapore
e-mail: rkumaran@ntu.edu.sg

K. Rajaram, *Learning Intelligence: Innovative and Digital Transformative Learning Strategies*, https://doi.org/10.1007/978-981-19-9201-8_5

5.1 Introduction

Worldwide demand for higher education is increasing despite controversies relating to high costs, accessibility barriers, drop-out rates and the quality in terms of relevance and contemporariness of courses. Higher education institutes are facing challenges such as multicultural integration, students' drop-out rates, fluid transitions from educational programmes to first jobs, and implementing flexible, agile and relevant lifelong learning processes (Castro, 2019), consistently to meet the evolving needs and demands. Rajaram (2013) advocated that effective learning and optimal knowledge acquisition cannot be guaranteed by any fixed type of instructional strategy. Instructors should have a thorough comprehension of students' learning attitudes, behavioural aspects and students' profile to adopt a well-blended mixture of instructional techniques to achieve optimal learning effectiveness (Rajaram, 2013). Blended learning can potentially assist institutes in taking the first step to address and overcome these multifaceted and complex challenges. This pedagogical approach provides opportunities for institutes to respond to evolving external pressures by leveraging on the use of technological innovations in classrooms. Hence, blended learning programmes are progressively becoming more popular. Almost 50% of four-year institutes in the United States offered courses in blended learning (Castro, 2019), and this number is expected to evolve as years ahead.

This increase in blended learning programmes can be attributed to the prominence of technology and the Internet in our everyday lives. As such, higher education institutes have left with literally not much of choice but rather to align to the trend, adopt and have the technological interventions implemented in classrooms. Aside from overcoming institutional challenges, blended learning is also beneficial in many different ways. As stated by Tucker et al. (2017), blended learning enables some targeted characteristics of best teaching and learning practices such as personalization, agency notion, authentic audience, connectivity and creativity. The first section in this chapter will further elaborate and focus on the definition of blended learning as well as its benefits. In it, we shall discover that while the term blended learning may seem straightforward, there is more to it than what meets the eye. This is largely because there are many ways to categorize blended learning. Thus, we have put together a simplified and easy-to-relate framework on three separate but interlinking clusters of the types of blended learning.

Technology has certainly modernized the "in and out" of classroom learning. Classrooms are no longer just a physical place, but an experience (Hofmann, 2018). Learning today happens in the traditional classroom, on an e-learning platform, mobile devices and systems and while on the job. Since technology and digitalization plays a key role in blended learning design, we need to examine deeper into the technology-enhanced learning framework and its link to the blended learning ecosystem. With contemporary learning comes modern design where the instructional design for blended learning must be appropriately well applied. Increased complexities have resulted in many more aspects and factors to be duly considered when designing a blended learning classroom. This includes learning design, instructional techniques, assessments and the sociocultural aspects of blended learning.

As a whole, more institutions are accepting and adopting blended learning pedagogy as the new normal. The specificity of a school's programme will vary depending on their goals and capacity. However, it is vital to note that the environment is constantly changing and evolving especially due to the rapid technological developments and interventions in today's era, and so blended learning programmes must be agile to transform itself as well. A relevant example of this could be linked to Hofmann (2018) who reported that *The New York Times* declared 2012 "The Year of the MOOC", yet in 2015 this excitement dwindled down. Then, at the time of his writing, the latest revolutionary technology was the inception of the Experience API (xAPI) software which allowed content to be sent to learning management systems. However, today, the hype revolves around newer innovations such as artificial intelligence (AI) and virtual reality. Hence, while the future of blended learning looks promising, the direction it takes is uncertain which reiterates the importance of agility and to remain open to change speedily by being responsive to the evolving needs and demands.

5.2 Blended Learning

Blended learning is defined as a well-blended combination of online and conventional face-to-face classroom-based teaching and learning (Rajaram, 2021). Blended learning is a pedagogical approach that incorporates at least in part where learning occurs (a) via online, with some level of control over time, place, path and/or pace; (b) in part in a supervised physical location; (c) the modalities along each student's learning path within a course or subject are linked to provide an integrated learning experience. Rajaram (2021) defines blending as

> In blended learning, classroom time between instructors and students is not substituted by online delivery. Instead, the online component comprises of content and activities that complement in-class lessons. It usually involves online resources such as online journals, quizzes, voice-overs and/or audio podcasts, interactive games, and videos. Learners can access these online resources from anywhere and they are usually delivered through a university-wide learning management system, blogs or contextualized learning systems. The important point to understand about the blended approach is that traditional learning has not been replaced by online learning; rather, the two elements complement each other to provide learners with an inclusive and holistic learning experience. (p. 29)

Below is the conceptual framework for blended learning presented in Fig. 5.1 that was validated by Rajaram (2021), that embeds the e-learning pedagogical strategies for pre and post seminars to attain effective learning outcomes for students in higher education.

Bonk and Graham (2005) described blended learning as the combination of traditional face to face sessions supported by distributed learning systems, with the involvement of computer-based technologies. In a blended learning environment,

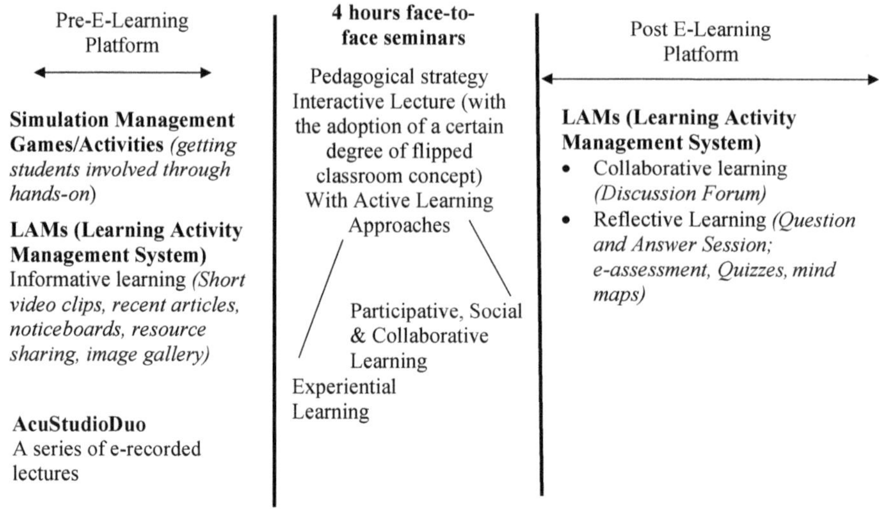

Fig. 5.1 Conceptual framework for blended learning (Extracted from Rajaram, 2021)

there is a combination of instructional delivery in a traditional face-to-face context with online learning, either synchronously or asynchronously. Blended learning is part of an ongoing amalgamation of two types of learning environments—the traditional face-to-face learning environment, and distributed learning environment—that are rapidly evolving as a result of digitalization and new technological interventions. In the past, these two learning environments remained independent and as separate entities, largely because they used different media, methodological combinations and addressed the needs of varying profile of audiences. While traditional learning occurred in a teacher-directed environment with person-to-person interaction, distance learning was more about self-paced learning. However, with the expansion of technological innovations, this has changed. This convergence of the two learning environments is illustrated by Bonk and Graham (2005) in the conceptual framework on progressive convergence of traditional face-to-face and distributed environments allowing development of blended learning systems.

On a similar context, Arbaugh (2014) described blended learning as a collation of educational experiences delivered through an avenue of thoughtful combination of face-to-face and online learning activities. Some researchers have criticized this definition as being more focused on instruction than on learning while others have acknowledged that the approach allows instructors to modify the way in which the class time is being used to provide much better opportunities for student learning. Blended learning enables students to have greater autonomy over their own learning experiences. Indeed, this blended approach strives to achieve the best of both worlds by grasping the advantages of both online and face-to-face learning design settings.

Based on the evidence-based comparative review of the academic literature on online and blended management education, it is suggested that blended learning environments have a high potential in delivering much better positive outcomes. This could be largely due to both the opportunity for and the requirement of increased learner control over the learning process, interaction and collaboration with fellow learners. This combination of self-directed and group-directed activity is enhanced by intentional and mindful instructors' consideration on the types of activities that are positioned in either aspect of the blended learning. This notion emphasizes the importance of the role the instructor plays on the blended learning courses.

Furthermore, it is interesting to see how blended learning has been adopted by higher institutions globally. In fact, evidence states that blended learning is often the preferred approach in Asia. A Japanese university found that combining face-to-face socializing events with online learning activities enhanced the level of motivation, clarity of purpose and quality of online discussion from a holistic analysis. In the next section, we shall examine the reasons that contribute to the popularity of blended learning that is all over the world by addressing some specific benefits of implementing it into higher education programmes.

5.2.1 Benefits of Blended Learning

Blended learning model is beneficial at varying levels, namely institutional, programme, course and individual levels. At the institutional level, blended learning allows for increased cost-effectiveness. Blended learning systems provide institutions the opportunity to reach out a large and global audience in a short period of time with consistent and semi-personal content delivery. Evidence also indicates that blended learning delivers large return on investments. Although the additional cost of setting up programmes and utilizing new technology may seem to be large, the subsequent cost savings is achievable once more students enroll in the programme and the costs are well spread out.

At the programme level, there is increased access and flexibility when blended learning approaches are used. Access to learning is one of the key elements that is currently influencing the growth of distributed learning environments. Many programmes may not exist today if not for the ability to provide students with distance learning. For instance, many MOOCs today allow for students to study at their own pace which is necessary as students require flexibility and convenience in learning as they may have commitments outside of school including family and work. By implementing blended learning within programmes, schools can offer this to students without compromising on the beneficial aspects of having human-related contact in face-to-face classrooms. Current teaching and learning practices are focused on transmissive rather than interactive strategy (Bonk & Graham, 2005). For instance, face-to-face learning environments tend to be lecture-dominated or instructor-centric while distance learning courses often have an overwhelming amount of information that students are expected to learn independently. Blended learning has proven to enhance levels of active learning, peer-to-peer, and learner-centred strategies used. With blended learning, instructors have more flexibility and increased autonomy to implement a wide variety of pedagogical techniques that may improve student learning experiences.

The benefits of blended learning at the student level is vast as institutes are moving towards a more student-centric approach. Nonetheless, we will examine several of these benefits though the list is not exhaustive. Blended learning is inclined towards accommodating diverse student populations. This is particularly relevant today where higher education institutions are accepting much more students globally. Blended learning approaches improve teaching and learning while accommodating the notion of student diversity and its impacts. The adoption of active blended learning to establish ethical pedagogy and shift traditional frameworks of higher education classrooms would empower international Lomer and Anthony-Okeke (2019). For instance, enabling students to blog as a means of participation in class resulted in higher level of engagement, where even if students remain silent, the active intellectual participation of students can be recognized. This chips away at the stereotype of the quiet and passive and disengaged foreign student.

The benefits of blending learning can be categorized into four main groups: ease of use, independence, advanced learning and flexibility (Sharma et al., 2019). Students are likely to interact more with the instructor and peers as there are numerous opportunities to do so in face-to-face class and the online environment. Students can participate more in class discussions through the multiple learning environment platforms in which they feel more comfortable with. Additionally, students often develop or enhance skills in time management, critical thinking and problem-solving and other employability skills, and have timely access to essential contents. Subsequently, students can acquire useful technological skills from using the Internet and digitalization as advanced learning. Finally, the students have more time flexibility, freedom and convenience working at preferred timeslots from their residences that also decreases related issues with travel that they may have.

All in all, there are plenty of advantages to using a blended or hybrid learning model. However, institutions must give due consideration on the suitability and method of implementing blended learning into their programmes. They must account for any external factors that may influence the effectiveness of blended learning within their own institution. Although the concept of blended learning may appear to be simple, the practical application is much more complex (Garrison & Vaughan, 2008). Blended learning cannot be merely viewed as an extra and costly educational layer, rather to be viewed on how the design helps to restructure the class contact hours with the goal of improving engagement and extending access to Internet-based learning opportunities. This approach is a fundamental redesign of approaches to teaching and learning. Hence, it is vital to know the varying types and models of blended learning that are available. The next section will explore the types of blended learning, its usage and related impact.

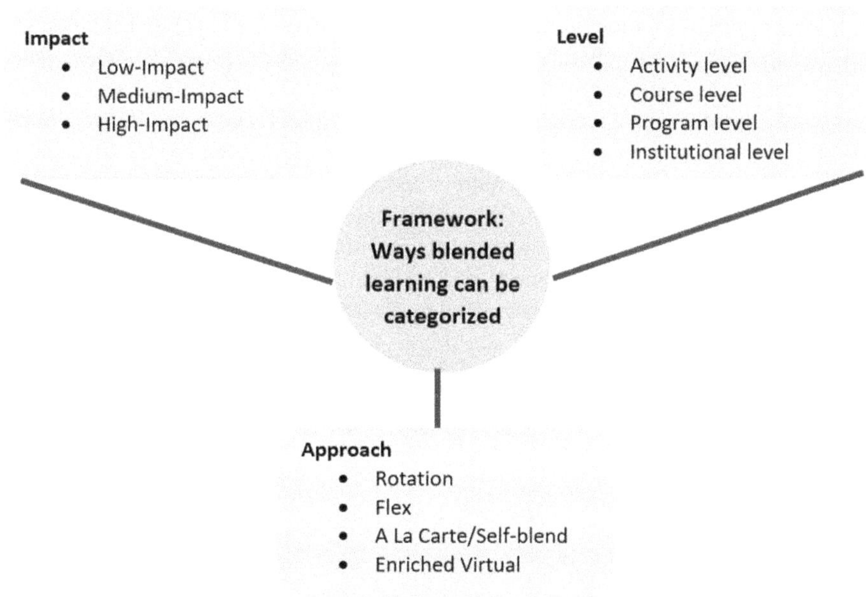

Fig. 5.2 Conceptual framework: ways blended learning can be categorized

5.2.2 Types of Blended Learning

Blended learning can be categorized and examined in multiple ways. In this section, we shall examine three ways in which blended learning is categorized. Blended learning can be clustered into three different but interlinking ways, namely by (a) approach, (b) intensity and (c) level. By comprehending the types of blended learning available, higher education institutions may gain a much better chance of implementing the most appropriate type or combination of types. Figure 5.2 presents the framework that entails the types of blended learning.

5.2.3 Approach Adopted: How Blended Learning Is Conducted?

Approach refers to how blended learning is conducted. There are various combinations of blended learning that instructors could choose to use in their classrooms. For instance, instructors need to consider where students will study, how much time they allocate to traditional classroom learning or virtual learning, and more. One such framework of blended learning that highlights different approaches comes from the Christensen Institute presented in Fig. 5.4 that categorizes four models of blended learning. In accordance to their advocate, majority of blended-learning programmes resemble one of four models, namely (a) Rotation; (b) Flex; (c) A La Carte (or Self-blend), and (d) Enriched Virtual (Staker, 2011). The rotation model includes four sub-models: (i) station rotation, (ii) lab rotation, (iii) flipped classroom and (iv) individual rotation. These models could be used individually or as in a mixed combination. Figure 5.3 presents the types of blended learning created by the Christensen Institute. These models were designed for high school (i.e. primary and secondary schools) sectors although Sharma et al. (2019) reported that the rotation and enriched virtual models are relevant to higher education institutes while the other two are educationally feasible. The varying types of blended learning was advocated by Horn et al. (2014). Hence, we examined these different models of blended learning, its applied contexts and impacts on learning in the meta-analysis Table 5.1.

5.2.4 Impact

Blended learning can be customized, aligned and re-aligned as the learning environment evolves and alters. Creating an entirely new programme to incorporate blended learning is considered high-impact, however, it is costly so institutions could instead consider implementing a low-impact intervention by adding online activities to a pre-existing course. Institutions should first determine the extent they want blended learning to be incorporated in their eco-system as well as if they have the capacity to achieve that. Three distinct design approaches in terms of the impact of blended learning was identified by Alammary et al. (2014) by examining the varying different processes of designing blended learning courses (Table 5.2).

5.2.5 Level

Level refers to the specific level of a higher education institution in which blended learning is implemented. This category is similar and correlates to the impact category, i.e. the higher the level the greater the impact, whereas the focus differs. This category looks more at which level of the institution blended learning is implemented in rather than how intense the impact is.

Blended learning approaches can occur at one of the following levels: activity level, course level, programme level or institutional level (Bonk & Graham, 2005). Across all the levels, the nature of blends is influenced by the learners, course designers and instructors. For instance, blending at the institutional and programme levels is often left to the discretion of the learner, while course designers and instructors are more likely to take a role in prescribing the blend at the course and activity levels (Table 5.3).

Table 5.1 Meta-analysis: different models of blended learning, its applied contexts and impacts on learning

Types of blended learning	Description	Applied context (states the potential situation or context, for whom and why?)	Impact on learning (states the outcomes)
Rotation	A course or subject in which students are rotated on a fixed schedule or at the instructor's discretion between learning modalities, where at least one of which is online learning. Other modalities include activities such as small-group or full-class instruction, group projects, individual tutoring and pencil-and-paper assignments. The students learn mostly on the brick-and-mortar campus, except for any homework assignments (Christensen Institute, 2018). In the rotation model, students rotate between different stations on a fixed schedule, either working online or spending face-to-face time with the teacher in a course. Activities performed through this model are small-group or full-class instruction, individual tutoring, group projects and assignments (Sharma et al., 2019)	In a seminar style class that comprises of 10 to 12 groups per class. This can also be done across seminars scheduled at a fixed timeslot. This size will enable students in the groups to perform rotation to experience varying blended activities. This design could be adopted sparingly across the course or designed to be incorporated for the entire course duration	One school involved in the study by Staker (2011) was Fairmont Preparatory Academy, applied blended programmes for students in Grade 9 to 12. Fairmont realized a 33% cost per student reduction as it was able to spread its cost per course over a larger number of participants. As for academic performance, remediation students (meaning students who were retaking a course because of a failing grade) made moderate improvements in the blended environment compared to comparable remediation students in a traditional environment in prior years. Students taking blended courses for credit advancement faired comparably, on average, to students in traditional classrooms taking the same courses in prior years
Station-Rotation	A course or subject in which students experience the rotation model within a contained classroom or group of classrooms. The station rotation model differs from the individual rotation model because students rotate through all of the stations, not only those on their custom schedules	In a seminar style class that comprises of 4 to 6 groups per class. This size will enable the students to go through all stations. This learning design model can be adopted sparingly across the course in the assigned lessons or designed to be incorporated for the entire course duration	In the study conducted in a third grade classroom, the teacher found a 21% improvement in the math performance of the students while using a blended model of the flipped classroom and the station rotation model (Truitt, 2016)

(continued)

Table 5.1 (continued)

Types of blended learning	Description	Applied context (states the potential situation or context, for whom and why?)	Impact on learning (states the outcomes)
Lab-Rotation	A course or subject in which students rotate to a computer lab for the online-learning station	In a laboratory setting that can facilitate rotating stations	Able to gain diverse collective perspectives. This enables students to appreciate the different approaches taken to resolve for example a problem-based experimental task
Flipped Classroom	Flipped classroom (FC) approaches are a special type of blended learning (BL) (Thai et al., 2017), where there is a swap of what is commonly done in the classroom with learning activities conducted outside the classroom (Lage et al., 2000; Rajaram, 2021)	"The flipped classroom serves as a platform to achieve a collaborative and organic learning environment" (Rajaram, 2021, p. 25). "The flipped classroom's primary focus is on the reversal of the traditional content delivery mode of learning. In a flipped classroom, course materials are prepared such that learners have access to the materials prior to their classes, at their own pace and time. Actual class time is then utilised to clarify concepts and run learning activities that emphasise content application, with facilitation and guidance from the instructor. The different types of online platforms adopted in-class serve to enhance and work towards higher levels of student collaboration, engagement, and a holistic learning process" (Rajaram, 2021, p. 29)	"Flipped Classroom (FC) helps students to learn at their own pace, spend more time in preparatory work, and get more involved during classroom activities (Thai et al., 2017). Rajaram (2019, 2021) advocated through the validated studies conducted that flipped learning has enabled students to think critically, apply what they learnt in a holistic context and perform quality analysis that has enabled them to achieve higher average scores
Individual-Rotation	A course or subject in which each student has an individualized playlist and does not necessarily rotate to each available station or modality. An algorithm or teacher(s) sets individual student schedules	A small-sized class that enables collaborative work at a deeper level or perhaps more individualized attention	Deeper and more intense collaborative exchanges. Learning process focuses on higher-order reflections and thinking that have an inclination towards more of tailor-made sessions

(continued)

Table 5.1 (continued)

Types of blended learning	Description	Applied context (states the potential situation or context, for whom and why?)	Impact on learning (states the outcomes)
Flex	As advocated by Sharma et al. (2019), Flex model qualifies when it is a course or subject in which online learning is the backbone of student's learning, even if it directs students to offline activities at times. Students move on an individually customized, fluid schedule among learning modalities. The teacher of record is on-site, and students learn mostly on the brick-and-mortar campus, except for any homework assignments. The teacher of record or other experts or peers provide face-to-face support on a flexible and adaptive as-needed basis through activities such as small-group instruction, group projects and individual tutoring. Some implementations have substantial face-to-face support, whereas others have minimal support. For instance, some Flex models may have face-to-face certified teachers who supplement the online learning on a daily basis, whereas others may provide little face-to-face enrichment. Even then, others may have different staffing combinations. These variations are useful modifiers to describe a particular Flex model. Within this approach, content and instructions are primarily delivered online. The teachers are present to provide face-to-face support as needed, while learning is primarily self-guided as the students independently learn and practice new concepts in a digitally enriched environment	This model is adopted when for courses which support a large number of non-traditional or at-risk students	Initial test results at the Centers of Innovation indicate that participating 9th graders on average outperformed all other students in traditional high schools in the district. Anecdotal evidence suggests that teachers have been pleased with the blended programme. Special education teachers, in particular, claim that the hybridization is much more effective for their students on a whole (Staker, 2011)

(continued)

Table 5.1 (continued)

Types of blended learning	Description	Applied context (states the potential situation or context, for whom and why?)	Impact on learning (states the outcomes)
A La Carte/Self-Blend	A course that a student takes entirely online to accompany other experiences that the student is having at a brick-and-mortar school or learning centre. The teacher of record for the A La Carte course is the online teacher. Students may take the A La Carte course either on the brick-and-mortar campus or off-site. This differs from full-time online learning because it is not a whole-school experience. Students take some courses via A La Carte mode and others via face-to-face at a brick-and-mortar campus The self-blend model gives students the opportunity to gain a different exposure and learning. While the students will attend a traditional face-to-face environment, they also opt to supplement their learning through online courses offered remotely via such learning design	In order for this pedagogical model to be successful, the students must be highly self-motivated. The self-blend model is ideal for students with interests in a subject area that is not covered in the course curriculum (Sharma et al., 2019)	The average course completion rate in 2008–2009 for all Michigan Virtual School courses (with blended learning for Grades 6 to 12) was 81%. Data for 2009–2010 suggested that the completion rate has climbed to 84% (Staker, 2011)

(continued)

Table 5.1 (continued)

Types of blended learning	Description	Applied context (states the potential situation or context, for whom and why?)	Impact on learning (states the outcomes)
Enriched Virtual	A course or subject where students require face-to-face learning sessions with their instructor and are free to complete their remaining coursework remotely. Online learning is the backbone of student's learning, particularly when the students are located remotely. Many Enriched Virtual programmes began as full-time online schools and then developed as blended programmes to provide students with brick-and-mortar school experiences. The Enriched Virtual model is used in a course where students have to attend face-to-face learning sessions with their teachers and then are free to complete their remaining coursework remotely via the online mode. In this model, the online mode is the backbone of student learning when the students are located remotely. The model differs from the flipped classroom because the students seldom meet face to face with their teachers. It also differs from fully online courses and programmes because the face-to-face learning sessions are in most cases is not part of the requirement	Recommended for subjects that students can cope up with their own and those which are more explorative in nature rather than technically inclined that requires more coaching and guidance from the experts, in this context, the instructors who are bestowed the role	The skill of multiple ways of learning and ensuring the level of efficacy in terms of knowledge acquiring and comprehension of concepts is still high. The grit and self-discipline in managing a more individualized learning

Table 5.2 Three distinct design approaches in terms of the impact of blended learning

Types of blended learning	Description	Applied context (the situation for whom and why?)	Impact on learning (outcomes)
Low-impact blend	In the low-impact approach, extra online activities are added to a traditional face-to-face course (Alammary et al., 2014)	Adding extra online activities onto an already established course normally happens when inexperienced instructors build their blended learning courses. By simply adding on to their courses, these instructors attempt to gain benefits of blended learning without investing efforts in rethinking the entire course objectives within the context of a blended learning model. In other cases, however, the added activity is a result of a pedagogical need and proves to be a valuable addition to the traditional course (Alammary et al., 2014)	In the work of McCarthy (2010), an online activity was added to a course called "Imaging Our World" to encourage students to interact more with their peers. In addition to the traditional teaching modes of lectures and tutorials, students were required to submit some work online to Facebook and to provide critiques of their peers' submissions. Resulting discussions were then transferred into the physical classroom to build meaningful relationships between students based on the embryonic online connections. The aim of adding the online activity was to strengthen the face-to-face engagements between students. The work was evaluated using weekly feedback from students, pre- and post-semester questionnaires and project-specific reflections at the end of the semester. It was discovered that the additional activity hosted by Facebook where a platform was created for students to establish preliminary academic and social interactions with their peers, while meeting the diverse learning needs (Alammary et al., 2014)

(continued)

Table 5.2 (continued)

Types of blended learning	Description	Applied context (the situation for whom and why?)	Impact on learning (outcomes)
Medium-impact blend	In the medium-impact approach, an existing course is redesigned by replacing some of the face-to-face activities by online components	The assumption behind this approach is that some parts of the course would be more effective as online activities	The redesign (of a second-year political science course) produced promising results, involving the students in more sustained and meaningful discourse (Alammary et al., 2014)
High-impact blend	In the high-impact approach, the blended learning course is built from scratch. This approach has been described in the literature in various ways such as full redesign, total redesign, radical change	Instead of looking at an entire course, the instructor needs to look at each single course learning outcome. For each outcome, the instructor needs to determine the best delivery option of that outcome	By applying this approach at the learning outcomes level, instructors can get the most effective blend of technologies and can produce a better curriculum (Alammary et al., 2014)

Table 5.3 Levels of blended learning approaches

Levels of blended learning	Description
Activity-level blending	Blending at the activity level occurs when a learning activity contains both face-to-face and computer meditated (CM) elements
Course-level blending	It entails a combination of distinct face-to-face and computer meditated (CM) activities used as part of a course. Some blended approaches engage learners in different but supportive face-to-face and computer meditated (CM) activities that overlap in time, while other approaches separate the time blocks so that they are sequenced chronologically but not overlapping
Programme-level blending	Blends in higher education are often occurring at the degree programme level. Blending at a programme level often entails one of two models: a model in which the participants choose a mix between face-to-face courses and online courses or one in which the combination between the two is prescribed by the programme
Institutional-level blending	Some institutions have made an organizational commitment to blending face-to-face and computer mediated (CM) instruction. Many corporations as well as institutions of higher education are creating models for blending at an institutional level

5.3 Technology Enhanced Learning (TEL)

Technology enhanced learning (TEL) is proving to be an attractive term as it is opens to a very broad range of interpretations. The definition does not define or restrict users to specific types of technology or pedagogical approaches. On the flip side, this term has been criticized. For instance, Bayne (2015) argues that the term "is far from being an unexceptionable and neutral term that simply in need of clearer definition, in fact carries with it a set of discursive limitations and deeply conservative assumptions which actively limit our capacity to be critical about education and its relation to technology" (p. 7). Nonetheless, some researchers have used the term loosely or simply to cover all circumstances where technology plays a significant role in making learning more effective, efficient or enjoyable. Technology can be used to support and enhance learning where it consists of both hardware and software. Hardware includes such as interactive whiteboards and handheld technologies while software includes such as learning management systems (LMS) and educational games. Both hardware and software have been constantly evolving and rapidly transforming as technology continues to change dramatically. This process enhances student learning and prepare students to work effectively with technology in their future workplaces. The affordance of technology creates many opportunities that can transform the learning process and magnify the potential of knowledge and skill acquisition (Goodyear et al., 2010).

Sociocultural perspectives are another aspect of TEL that should be duly considered. Humans are complex, hence sociocultural accounts of learning and knowing take as a premise that humans are social and cultural beings (Sutherland et al., 2009).

An instructor's understanding on the essential information and communications technology (ICT) is vital to fulfill the deliverables tied to the intended learning outcomes, students' out-of-school learning with ICT and quality of the learning resources that are developed. This also includes the quality of the interaction between the instructor and the students, and between the students. The potential and power of technology will continue shaping the educational process and the messages or information that are delivered to both teachers and students. They conclude that the quality and nature of learning are largely influenced and shaped by the varying unique individual's experiences of cultures and technologies. Such complexities must be understood well if the vision of TEL in higher education institutions is ever to be realized.

5.3.1 Impact of Technology Enhanced Learning (TEL)

The impact of TEL on learning in general could be viewed from the perspective of enhancement. Kirkwood and Price (2014) categorized how enhancement was conceived in the context and accounts of technology interventions reviewed. The notion enhancement was clustered into three core categories, namely (a) operational improvement; (b) quantitative change in learning and (c) qualitative change in learning. Operational improvement is tied closely to the enhancements of the learner's experience supported with relevant learning resources while "quantitative changes" refer to the improvements in the learner's knowledge after the TEL intervention Finally, "qualitative changes" look at the skills developed by the learner for the implementation of TEL. The benefits of TEL are placed in the three categories as highlighted (Kirkwood & Price, 2014):

- *Operational improvement*—increased flexibility, improved retention
- *Quantitative change in learning*—improved engagement or time spent on learning task; more favourable perceptions or attitudes (for example, higher ranking of satisfaction or importance), improved test or assessment scores
- *Qualitative change in learning*—deeper learning and comprehension with higher-order thinking processes and skills, more reflection and critical awareness, improved student interactions via online discussion and collaborative activities, increased sharing of experiences (related to professional practices).

Additionally, TEL plays an essential part to contribute to the process of sustainability of higher education institutes. A study by Daniela et al. (2018) examined how and the extent to which TEL can enhance teaching and learning. They found that use of technologies in the learning process promotes students' active participation. This outcome correlates primarily to assist foster students' creativity, independent thinking and problem-solving skills, with employability skills as part of the holistic learning outcomes. This further helps to promote students' awareness and willingness to examine additional information from multiple sources that is able to deliver positive effects. Overall, their study confirmed that the use of technology enhanced learning can influence a multitude of learning outcomes largely in the positive inclination.

The meaningful usage of technologies can support the notion of sustainability from a holistic perspective. We need to acknowledge that students' digital competence influences their attitude and perception towards the adoption of technology by and large. A positive attitude is required for students to be cognitively ready to correspond with their motivation. Moreover, low levels of digital competence have an influencing effect on boredom during the learning process. Therefore, although students of younger age are perceived to be digital natives, it is vital to comprehend that the development of digital knowledge, skill and competence needs support. Without it, there will be a series of challenges where the study process becomes more technologically enhanced, yet its available learning resources will not be utilized to its best potential as neither students nor instructors would be equipped with the necessary skills to use these technologies effectively.

5.3.2 The Link of TEL to Blended Learning

The term technology enhanced learning (TEL) suggests a value judgement about the use of technology. The word "enhanced" suggests that there is an improvement in the quality, intensity (volume/amount) and strength of learning. This establishes a responsibility for using this pedagogical intervention accurately that cannot be substituted or identified with other learning design interventions such as e-learning or online learning. Hence, higher education institutes find an increased obligation for ensuring that TEL embedded in the design of blended learning programmes will certainly have a positive impact on the learning experience of students (Casanova & Moreira, 2017).

TEL can be implemented in conjunction with blended or hybrid learning approaches. For instance, a study carried out by Shyr and Chen (2017) found that the technology-enhanced language learning system adopted better prepared students for flipped classrooms, a type of blended learning approach. The study also found that it improved the learning performance as compared to the traditional flipped classroom without any technological inclined interventions. The study findings proved that incorporating TEL can further boost the intended learning outcomes of blended teaching approaches in general. Aside from the integration of the appropriate TEL learning design at the operational level, the development of relevant institutional policies has to be prioritized. According to Li et al. (2015), the management of the higher education institutes have to consider whether there is a need for technological interventions, which form and type of technology they will use, and the barriers and enablers that they are likely to face when they implement the identified technology. They also have to consider whether staff, students and other stakeholders will accept the incorporation of the identified technological interventions within the learning environment.

Due to the rapid evolution and constant change in the eco-system of technologies, it complicates the matter in having the TEL seamlessly incorporated. For it to be effective and useful, the theory of blended learning is technology-neutral. This means that TEL within blended learning should not focus on specific types of technology but rather focus on successfully mixing face-to-face and online learning. Thus, technologies that are novel today become more mainstream and ubiquitous in everyday life, however theoretical development with supporting insights need to transcend specific technology offerings (Gribbins et al., 2007). In other words, in adopting blended learning, faculty should not tie themselves down or have a fixated mindset only on the technology that they are currently using.

Instructors and students must be comfortable and trained in using newer technologies to optimize the successes in blended learning classrooms. Upon receiving adequate training, blended learning has a high potential in delivering a richer learning environment compared to a traditional classroom learning (Gribbins et al., 2007). The specificity of how blended learning is implemented do matters, that has to start from policies at an institutional level to the details of the types of technology adopted. Depending on how the instructors use face-to-face and computer-mediated learning, we can expect different learning outcomes to be attained.

5.4 Blended Learning Design

Blended learning is defined as a teaching and learning pedagogical approach that combines the online instructional techniques and face-to-face learning in a brick-and-mortar location, usually referred to as traditional learning (Maarop & Embi, 2016). For a more specific design of a blended or "hybrid" learning pedagogical approach, we advocate three key components that instructors should be aware of when implementing blended learning in their classroom. We illustrated these components from the perspective of online learning and face-to-face learning separately, the two main elements that make-up blended learning. Figure 5.3 presents blended learning design framework.

The first component is the elements of the learning design, where it examines deeper at the varying specific types and the correct mixture of instructional techniques that need to be used to curate their blended learning programme. Rajaram and Collins (2013) have emphasized that a balanced approach and compatibility are required between the learning styles of students and correct mix of instructional delivery approaches for effective learning to occur. The second component looks at assessment which is crucial for both instructors and students to keep track of the progress and impact of the deployed blended learning mode. Lastly are the sociocultural aspects of blended learning which instructors should be made aware of as they can significantly influence learning outcomes. In the learning transformation framework developed by Rajaram (2021), one of the core thrusts is learning culture and culture of learning. This trust focuses on the learners' profile and culture of learning in an institution and the type of learning climate that the learners are exposed to. These insights reiterate

Blended Learning Design		
Factors for due Consideration	**Online Learning**	**Face-to-Face Learning**
Elements of Design	Animations Voice-over lectures Interactive Quizzes Online reflection journals Discussion Forums (Class, Inter & Intra Group, Peer-to-Peer)	Face-to-Face seminars Interactive lectures Active & Experiential Learning Team-Based Learning Collaborative Learning
Assessment	Online quizzes and tests Asynchronous contribution Synchronous contribution	Written and timed exams Group and individual assignments In-class MCQs Self and peer reviews
Social and Cultural Aspects	Communication styles Level of active and passive, correct mix of instructional techniques Motivation and engagement levels Open-minded versus traditional/conversative fixated mindset complexity of culture and sub-cultures Gender biases and perception Age Race, religion & ethnicity Nationality	

Fig. 5.3 Blended learning design conceptual framework

the notion of sociocultural aspects in a broader context that needs to be taken into due consideration. This point has been validated by research scholar Rajaram (2020) who advocates "learning happens in many varying forms and is shaped by personal, social, cultural, psychological and contextual influences" (p. 44).

In the next section, the core components in the blended learning design will be discussed to provide an illustrative analysis and serve as a better appreciation on the "know-hows of why and how".

5.4.1 Online Learning

Online learning is a key trust in the design composition of blended learning. More generically, and unlike pre-class online learning component, online learning does not necessarily have to occur before a physical or virtual classroom session. Online learning is an instructional technique of reaching out, engaging and supporting learners through the use of the Internet and its related technologies. Online classroom comprises of elements found in the usual classroom. Furthermore, learner-centred and resource-centred learnings are expected to evolve with the use of online learning. All in all, there are several ways teachers can engage in online learning by incorporating them in the execution of its learning design as elaborated in this section.

5.4.2 *Voice-over Lectures*

Voice-over lectures can be defined as pre-recorded audio lectures often recorded over a set of slides or contents of a subject matter that are usually uploaded online for students to view and learn the contents at their own time and space. A study by Hove and Corcoran (2008) found that psychology students who accessed online lecture resources achieved much better grades than those who did not have access to them. Such approach adopted allows students to pace their learning, and this may be especially useful for dyslexic and foreign international students to give them adequate leeway that enable them to take notes in their own time and pace (Buchanan et al., 2010).

5.4.3 *Animations*

Animations can be used as an instructional approach for several varying reasons (Berney & Bétrancourt, 2016). Firstly, they can be used to gain students' attention. Secondly, it can be used to demonstrate concrete or abstract procedures that are needed to be memorized and performed by the students. Lastly, it can assist learners to understand how complex systems function through continuous representation of the succession of steps. Evidence shows that animations overall have a positive effect when compared to static graphics. This claim is validated by a study by Liu and Elms (2019) who reported that animated instructional videos enhanced students' learning experiences. Students reported increased engagement and interest, improved understanding and greater flexibility in self-directed learning.

5.4.4 *Quizzes*

In an online environment, there is a higher ease and convenience in having different types of quizzes incorporated at a high frequency than a traditional learning environment. Technology and digitalization functionalities such as automatically grading students' answers and providing speedy formative feedback does prove rather useful for teachers. Additionally, such feedback provides students useful information on correct answers and offer themselves and teachers, with a snapshot of the concepts that have been mastered. When the feedback is given frequently to students, quizzes help them in spacing their learning activities that potentially affect their learning outcomes positively. Hence, this preparation enables students to come much more prepared for the face-to-face classroom phase. Hence, the time can be optimized in the classroom through the use of active learning activities (Spanjers et al., 2015). The before-class quiz gives additional class time to engage in application, analysis, synthesis and evaluation, and enable students to better comprehend the in-class exercises and case problems (Du, 2011). This approach improves students' performance, whereas on the flip side after-class quizzes ensure that students continue reviewing the course materials taught in class and reinforces learning.

5.4.5 Online Reflection Journal

Self-reflection is a vital skill for students to be nurtured on and developed. It requires students to think critically and analyse their own behaviours in the goal of developing a greater understanding and awareness on the impact of their actions (Gudmundsson & Laing, 2011). Reflection is an essential part of blended learning process. Hence, the instructors can promote behavioural, emotional and cognitive processes through varying active learning activities, exercises and tasks involving reflection, that includes online reflection journals. This effect was validated by Andrusyszyn and Davie's (1997) study that examined the reflections of learners who participated in interactive reflective journal writing. This task was tenaciously integrated into the design of a graduate-level technology-mediated course, where their findings suggest that the process of reflection can be actively facilitated through interactive journal writing.

5.4.6 Face-to-Face Learning

Face-to-face learning plays a vital role within the context of blended learning. In a similar context to online learning, and in a more generic sense, face-to-face learning within the blended learning context does not necessarily have to come after online learning. At the Open University Malaysia (OUM), their blended learning model consists of face-to-face learning as well as online learning, in addition to self-managed learning. The teaching strategies employed were a mix of mini lectures, discussions, exercises, hands-on activities and presentations in multiple modes. This is an example that illustrates how face-to-face and online learning can be blended. We also need to acknowledge that the design of blended learning varies across institutions. Evidence shows that students enjoy participating in a blended learning environment where face-to-face classes are supplemented with online classes. The value of face-to-face sessions is established with the presence of human connections and spontaneity. It is easier to bond and develop a social presence in a face-to-face setting or context.

5.4.7 *Face-to-Face Seminars with Technological Interventions*

Technological interventions comprise both aspects of hardware and software. When conducting seminars, lab work or tutorials, instructors can leverage on to create a blended learning environment. Blended strategies can be viewed as supplementary to the already established pedagogy rather than completely modifying it. Technology Enhanced Learning (TEL) aims to support teaching through adopting varying technological interventions to achieve increased quality, enhanced level of efficacy and better efficiency deliverables. In the face-to-face classrooms, activities that take place include class discussions, inter- and intra-group discussions, problem-based learning, team-based and collaborative learning, active and experiential learning, cooperative learning and reflective writing among other things.

Technological tools such as Google Docs, K^mAlive (pronounced as "come alive") Learning Intelligent (IQ) Application, Etherpads and Piazza are used for collaborative oriented learning. As stated by Nussbaum et al. (2010), such TEL approaches as such use computer programmes and digitalization to facilitate interactions between peers during group work. The technology meditates the interaction and collaboration among students by disseminating relevant information, regulating the required tasks to be carried out, administering rules and roles and intermediating the acquisition of new knowledge. In the past where technology was less advanced, collaborative activities suffered from limitations where the desktop computers' software is not able to support simultaneous interactions between various users. Students would often have to gather around a single personal computer and take turns using the mouse or keyboard. However, the contemporary and innovative technological interventions such as smartphones, tablets and laptops provide individualized access that help address these challenges. The applied research studies by Rajaram (2019, 2021) validate that the mobile phones are apt, easy to use and highly convenient, accessible by students for collaborative team-based work within a classroom context. Learning management systems (LMS) are also widely adopted and even customized to the institutional needs that can be accessed on devices such as smartphones and laptops. The study by Govender (2010) examined the attitudes of students on the use of LMS in a traditional face-to-face classroom setting and found a positive trend in students accepting the blended learning model. The study also reports that the efficiency and quality of education had improved due to blended learning. All in all, the face-to-face seminars can be blended with technology and digitalization be it software or hardware, in order to create much better learning environments.

5.5 Assessment of Blended Learning

Assessment is the process of measuring, documenting and interpreting behaviours that demonstrate learning (Simonson et al., 2014). Assessments can fulfill the administrative purposes of an institution through programme evaluation and improvement, facilitation of student placement in programmes, justification for funding priorities and reporting of long-term trends to state, federal or corporate entities. On top of that, the purpose assessing learning gains is to primarily provide feedback to learners and instructors as an avenue of reflection and improvement. Assessment is a vital tool used to evaluate learners' knowledge of concepts and learning progress. Assessment impacts how much a student learns, the learning strategies they adopt as well as how they manage their study time.

In the context of blended learning, assessments can be conducted either online through in web-based or cloud-based learning environments or offline in face-to-face environments. Assessments play an essential role in the instructional design process and is linked to the development of learning objectives. Hence, the type and design of assessment is significant to be duly considered when designing a blended learning programme. The following section will examine assessment methods of both online and face-to-face learning.

5.5.1 Online Learning Assessment

Online learning environments are said to comprise of unique characteristics that are not found in traditional environments. These characteristics bring both advantages and disadvantages in online learning assessment. The benefits of evaluating students online include (a) the ability to track; (b) monitor and document students' activities automatically; (c) unlimited and self-paced access to course materials and resources; and (d) an increased emphasis on students' thoughts and reflections. On the flip side, there are also disadvantages with online assessments. For instance, students may require more specific instructions on online assessments where instructors are not able to control the time and resource in terms of its accessibility when they take online exams away from a traditional monitored exam environment. Types of online assessments include online quizzes and tests, asynchronous communication, synchronous communication and online submission of papers (Simonson et al., 2014).

Online quizzes have numerous advantages over pencil-and-paper tests. Quizzes can be curated to randomize questions from a pre-made question pool, display images and videos alongside question text, provide immediate feedback, assist in spelling, allow several retakes and enable scores to be directly entered into an online gradebook. Online quizzes are effective as a formative and self-study tool that motivates students to keep up with the course materials and provide reinforcement of core concepts. Asynchronous mode of communication can be adopted to facilitate online assessments that can occur through online discussion forums. Such type of discussion or class or inter- and intra-group forums can be used as an avenue to implement the relevant assessment activities. For instance, teachers may get students to respond to questions or discuss key concepts within the secured and customized forum environment. The time taken by students to formulate their answers may result in more meaningful and well-organized contributions compared to those offered in a traditional classroom environment. Teachers can facilitate these discussions by asking thought-provoking questions that promote higher-order thinking and ad hoc critical thinking skills. Discussion forum includes student debates and student-moderated discussions. On the other hand, communication tools such as video calls and instant messaging support synchronous communication. Leveraging on such platforms allow instructors a way to conduct real-time assessments that gives them immediate sense of students' comprehension of the lessons delivered. This can be especially useful and apt in courses such as teaching foreign languages where teachers can test students on their level of fluency and provide speedy formative feedback.

Technology has also made it easier for students to submit their course work assignments and reports. Most learning management systems today have some form of drop box where students can submit assignments electronically anytime anywhere. This ensures that a student's work is directly submitted which can be only accessed by the instructor of the course, providing cyber security and confidentiality. Functions such as this one reduces the chances of human error such as misplacing papers. Factors that may hinder an instructor's ability to assess a piece of work such as poor handwriting or students forgetting to write their names on their work can be mitigated through online submissions.

Introducing computer-assisted assessments into course programmes enable practical benefits for teaching which helps to enhance student learning (Chesney & Ginty, 2007). It is especially beneficial for programmes with large cohorts of students, where teachers may be overwhelmed by the number of students' work to be assessed. Additionally, moving assessments online allows teachers to function on the go or via mobile mode, easier to access and grade anytime, anywhere and not taking up unnecessarily the physical space. The online assessment system embedded with data analytics provide instructors teachers with information on students' progress and enable them to monitor on how a cohort is performing. This data assists instructors to adjust and align their instructional techniques to improve their efficacy in executing them. Online assessments can improve student motivation as immediate feedback allows students to identify and recognize their weaknesses and act on them appropriately. The immediacy of feedback increases the value as mistakes or misconceptions can be corrected immediately rather later as it may be much more challenging to have it rectified where students have likely moved on other aspects of the lessons and/or assignments.

5.5.2 Face-to-Face Learning Assessment

The most typical face-to-face assessment methods include in-class tests such as multiple-choice questions (MCQs) and written examinations. Group as well as self and peer assessments can be well deployed within classrooms. Written and timed examinations in a moderated environment is the most salient form of face-to-face assessment. Examinations in higher education are viewed as a proven and effective way of assessing students' learning, especially to evaluate cognitive skills of subject matter knowledge. The benefits of adopting examinations as a mode of assessment includes reducing opportunities for students to cheat and providing a pathway to assess students acquired knowledge, comprehension of contents and its application. It also better prepare students by encouraging them to revise and hence develop a deeper understanding of key concepts taught. Furthermore, it offers equitable treatment to all students who are allocated the same duration of time to do a similar task or a set of tasks. This is unlike online assessments where individual circumstances such as poor Internet connection, technical challenges or a noisy home or external environment could significantly impact a student's performance. Hence, the familiarity and competence in dealing with examinations will make it easier and more convenient for teachers who are familiar with the process.

Examinations could instill anxiety in students which could affect their performance negatively (Bloxham & Boyd, 2007). Hence, this effect results in an unfair evaluation of their true ability in the subject. Additionally, examinations could encourage memorization and rote learning resulting in unauthentic and unoriginal responses as students may be pressured to replicate notes and learning resources and course materials. This implies that students may lack critical and creative thinking skills which are crucial for future workforce.

All in all, while face-to-face assessments are traditionally adopted, they seemed to be lacking the flexibility required in today's landscape. Take for example, the COVID-19 pandemic that struck seemingly out of nowhere. Examinations that were due to be held had no chance of occurring due to students being confined to their residences and institutions had to switch to online assessments immediately without any leeway given. With that, academic integrity issues arose and challenged universities. Although online proctoring or relevant software can be used to mitigate this, they were not available to most institutions because the expenses and training were too much to bear at one go or out of sudden (Nguyen et al., 2020), plus these software solutions may yet to be tailored made for large-scale purposes or for it to be exactly fitted in. We could conclude that the matter of assessment is a complex one and no one specific type of assessment can be labelled as the best. Instructors should comprehend the nature of different types of assessments and use their own discretion to implement them appropriately into their courses.

5.6 Social-Cultural Aspects of Blended Learning

In any type of pedagogical approach, it is necessary for higher education institutes to duly consider the significance of social and cultural aspects that could potentially impact the effectiveness and efficacy on specific nuances of the identified approach. One of the primary challenges in teaching across cultures is to adequately understand the application of the cultural universals, differences and sub-cultures that will potentially influence the processes and outcomes.

Higher education is often promoted as a means to achieve equality. At large, many view the purpose of education as a pathway to climb up the social ladder. Nonetheless, the graduate degree achievement is still disproportionately low for racial minorities, especially those lower on the socioeconomic scale. Evidence shows the connectivity of race and ethnicity and how that play a role in affecting one's higher education experience. This phenomenon appears to be relevant across countries, cultures globally. These considerations can become more complex and multifaceted as we examine deeper into more specific types of pedagogy. Hence, in the case of blended learning, we examine and discuss the sociocultural aspects of both of its components, namely, online and face-to-face learning.

5.6.1 Online Learning

The evolution and advancement of digitalization and technological interventions has influenced the landscape of higher education to expand their global outreach. Along with that arises concerns of the cultural adaptability, for instance, in terms of the learning resources and the process of re-engineering or transformation of courses (Liu et al., 2010). Existing research suggests that cultural differences can cause a negative effectual consequence on learners' participation in online courses. Online learners globally have reported to have felt marginalized or alienated. Different cultural communication patterns can increase the possibility of miscommunication, hence with greater awareness of cultural differences among students, this may potentially lead to even more incidents of miscommunication. However, evidence re-assures that with online learning, the cultural differences present can contribute to more culturally rich learning experiences rather than affecting students' online experiences negatively. Nevertheless, this does not mean that online learning comes without any sociocultural issues. The challenges emerge from varying contexts, for example, language, communication tool usage, plagiarism, time zone differences and a lack of diversified cases. These factors could potentially affect students' learning performance if the instructors do not take the needs of the international students into due consideration. By utilizing the theoretical models such as Hofstede's model of cultural dimensions, potential sociocultural issues can be identified. Gómez-Rey et al. (2016) used the Hofstede's model of cultural dimensions to experiment four e-learning universities in four different countries, namely Spain, the United States,

China and Mexico. The study shows that students from China and Mexico, countries with a high-power distance index, tend to be more passive that implies of lower motivation levels. Meanwhile, in countries with a low power distance index such as Spain or the United States, teachers expect students to take initiative, where students are expected to be more motivated. The study reported that individualistic societies tend to have higher motivation values compared to collectivistic societies, at least from the results of its sample size. However, we should be mindful of not simply generalizing it without large and more rigorous studies that substantiate this claim. Furthermore, students from countries with high uncertainty avoidance levels are more comfortable in a learning process that is structured by teachers, compared to countries with low uncertainty avoidance levels where students are more inclined and comfortable in an open-minded learning environment instead. Overall, the study infers that it is possible to categorize students based on their nationality and identify their proclivity towards online learning through the use of theoretical models of cultural dimensions. Despite that however, it is imperative to be mindful that cultures are evolving, dynamic and to completely generalize them may not be logical and accurate. In today's global, mobile and online inclined society, people interact with people from other cultures while assimilating and absorbing the nuances of these different cultures. The former territories of the British Empire such as India, Singapore and Hong Kong have shown that many have adopted their behavioural processes, way of doing, operating things and cognitive traits at some level. Additionally, many other Asian countries today have been absorbing Western ideas and habits often due to the media (Jung, 2014). Similarly, Western countries have also been opening up to Asian culture. Higher education Institutions have to duly consider these factors such as age, cultural experiences, multicultural experiences and sub-cultures in developing the online learning eco-system, specifically its functional processes, learning design and operational interventions. The major challenge online educators to ensure that they are well-equipped themselves to understand the complex nature of culture and how it influences teaching and learning eco-system at strategic, tactical as well as operational levels.

5.6.2 Face-to-Face Learning

In a more traditional higher education learning environments, face-to-face learning occurs within the school's campus, where it generally functions through lectures and seminars. With higher education becoming more accessible and globally interconnected through internationalization, it comes as no surprise that schools are becoming more diverse and socioculturally apt in terms of gender, age, race and nationality.

From a gender context, we can observe a growing number of women pursuing their career in Science, Technology, Engineering and Mathematics (STEM) arena which is often a male-dominated field. The stereotypes faced by women in STEM is reported in the review conducted by Blackburn (2017). Due to the long-standing sociocultural stereotypes regarding successful cisgender white males and academic

STEM disciplines, women face a phenomenon known as stereotype threat. Stereotype threat occurs when individuals fear of being a negative stereotype of a group they belong. This links to higher levels of anxiety and stress in women in general and women minority students. Another common stereotype of women in STEM can be pointed towards the perception that women have weak mathematical skills. Moreover, women in STEM face stereotypes on appearances as well as the behavioural patterns. By appearing too feminine, they are assumed to be ill-suited for the science field. As such, they may not be able to function optimally as they are not able to be themselves and adjust their gender depending on the environment they are in. Unfortunately, such stereotypes are deeply rooted in biases and sexism.

Ageism is also another growing concern as higher education institutions have seen a rise in the number of adult learners. A study by Simi and Matusitz (2016) reported that while adult learners over 24 years of age are the fastest rising population, evidence emphasizes that age as a factor alone may prevent reaping the benefits offered by higher education. Adult undergraduates have faced a lot of neglect, for instance, in terms of policy, curriculum, attitudes, teaching environment and financial aid. Although universities attempt to fulfill the needs of adult learners, they seemed to be ignored when it comes to public policies and objectives. Additionally, adult learners have their own challenges and struggles in coping with their pursuit of studies, due to their dual commitments in studies and work. Younger students may feel hostile and uncomfortable towards their older peers if they come across as too competitive or worst still intimidating, while many adult undergraduates may feel that partnering with the younger ones may not be uncomfortable, not easy or not required due to the imbalance of experience. The younger students may believe prior life experiences make adult students appear too regimented, set in their own ways and rules and lacking in openness to fresh, new ideas and perspectives.

Higher education institutions need to be aware and keep an eye out for racial discrimination. Racial discrimination can take place anywhere in the world. For example, in the United States, racism can be seen through white supremacy, white privilege and discrimination against racial minorities. White supremacy is experienced in varying ways at the student level in higher education (Cabrera, 2012). For instance, in the fraternity/sorority system, students are given a choice to select members, frequently excluding people from minority groups from participation. A study by Picca and Feagin (2007) reported the behaviour of white students that was observed to be completely different in the presence of minority students than among their white peers. Within their white peer groups, participants reported their peers consistently telling racist jokes and using the n-word, among other manifestations of racism that publicly have fallen out of favour.

Cross-border cultural challenges arise when students of different nationalities interact, explicitly for example in a collaborative group work setting or learning environment. Evidence shows that by simply placing students into groups with peers from other countries does not immediately lead to productive collaboration (Mittelmeier et al., 2017). Initially, there are often social tensions between diverse group members, which could be due to a lack of shared understanding about one another's backgrounds and experiences. Many domestic students have negative and challenging experiences working with international students. Oftentimes, many students preferred to work with those from their own backgrounds or sociocultural inclinations. In a study by Harrison and Peacock (2009), it was found that domestic students often demonstrated passive xenophobia towards international students which is described as unwillingness to interact freely and openly with international students at anything beyond the most superficial level. At its most extreme, there were some students who were worried about their academic grades and described active avoidance within the classroom setting. More usually, it was a case of viewing international students as nothing more than peers with whom they shared physical spaces, but rarely from a social or educational dimensional aspect.

All in all, there are plenty of sociocultural aspects to duly consider when examining the learning environments on campus. These social and cultural influences that emerge as both in the positive and negative aspects can greatly shape the experience of students. While there could be factors that may be beyond the institution's control, other contributing elements must be properly observed and controlled.

5.7 Application to Teaching and Learning

To have the blended learning effectively implemented in the learning eco-system, there are several considerations that go beyond just pedagogical aspects and its related nuances. This section provides an overview on other elements that must be duly considered in the implementation of the blended learning. This framework is well-illustrated that serve as a guiding framework and reference for higher education institutional leadership, administrators and faculty. Figure 5.4 presents the elements of blended learning. The elements of this blended learning framework are further elaborated thereafter in the following section.

5.7.1 Global Perspectives

Globally, there has been a rising trend towards the privatization of education in general. For example, in countries such as Australia, Canada, the United States and the United Kingdom, the privatization and internationalization of education, including higher education has become more widespread as government funding has diminished, while the demand has increased to serve the varying needs of an increasing diverse students' population (Pease, 2005; Rajaram, 2020; Rajaram & Bordia, 2011; Rajaram & Collins, 2013).

The global adoption of blended learning comes with embedded challenges, primarily due to the wide knowledge divide between developed and developing countries. Despite the growth of internet usage in developing countries, the overall gains are rather limited if productivity benefits do not come to fruition or if the adoption of technology is restricted to only an affluent minority. For instance, even

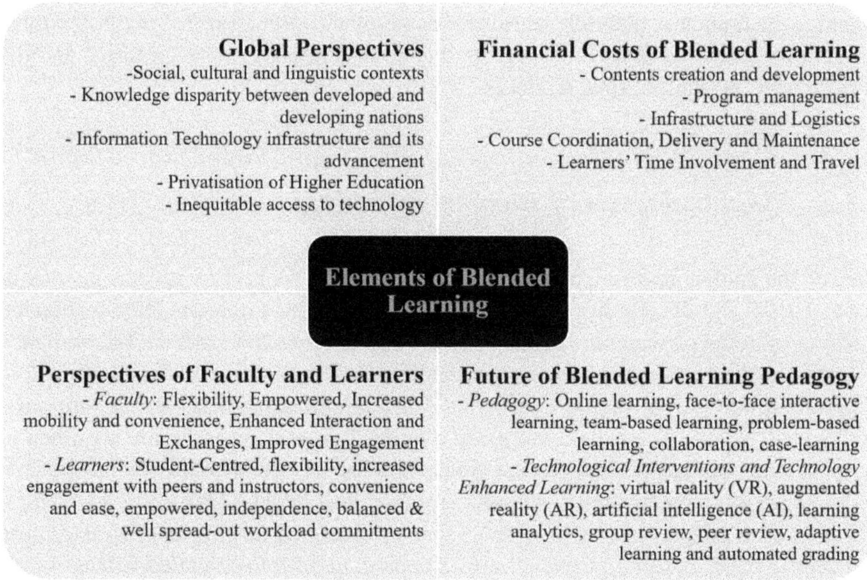

Fig. 5.4 Elements of blended learning

if all developing countries have access to the world's best knowledge resources, not much would change as the institutional capacity and individual capability to learn and apply the knowledge would still largely be lacking and remains as a pressing constraint. While technological development is certainly crucial, it cannot change educational institutions and organizations merely on its own accord. Thus, through the reduction of knowledge divide, developing countries can catch up. The knowledge divide is rather prevalent and could only possibly be overcome by effective development of country-specific learning strategies. This knowledge divide needs to be addressed through (a) improved access to Information and Communications Technology (ICT); (b) lowered costs of access and (3) relevant and contemporary contents that is of good instructional quality. Examining from a student's perspective, the main challenges include the capability and capacity to adapt and absorb locally relevant information.

All in all, cultural, social and linguistic contexts are extremely important elements to examine when considering learning strategies. The learning context becomes even more complicated due to inequitable access to technology. Computer penetration in developing countries is significantly lower than in developed countries. Incidents such as frequent power outages, atmospheric pollution and a lack of air-conditioning increase the downtime of computer equipment while worsening accessibility issues. Hence, student preparedness for the course varies between countries and even regions within the country. As a whole, it is crucial for institutes to adjust the learning environment to student-specific contexts when implementing blended learning. When planning to launch a blended learning course at the global scale, institutes must account for these various global factors that could impact their programme and the performance of international students.

5.7.2 Financial Costs of Blended Learning

One of the major goals of blended learning systems in higher education institutions (HEIs) and corporations is to save costs (Bonk & Graham, 2005). Blended learning systems provide an opportunity for HEIs to reach a large global audience in a short period of time with semi-personalized content delivery. An example that we could relate to will be the Center for Academic Transformation that supported the Pew Charitable Trust that completed a three-year grant programme designed to help universities explore methods in using technology to attain quality enhancements and cost savings concurrently. Another instance will be The University of Central Florida that attained cost savings due to cost reductions in physical infrastructure and improved scheduling efficiencies (Dziuban et al., 2005). Blended learning may not necessarily reduce costs immediately, but there is potential for a high return of investment when the students' enrollment increases.

Bersin (2004) examined the budgeting of blended learning programmes in corporations where five cost components were identified. This cost component can be similarly referenced to as they are relevant when implementing blended learning within higher education programmes as well. The five cost components are namely (a) content development costs; (b) infrastructure costs; (c) delivery costs; (d) programme management costs and (e) learner's time and travel cost. Content development costs include the initial preliminary costs of developing contents. They are usually accounted for in terms of development cost per student hour of contents, or the costs to develop per single hour of contents. Infrastructure costs refer to the amount of money spent on the technology and software used to deploy, manage and maintain the programme. The costs incurred are usually amortized over the numerous programmes which should be viewed as free, should these services already exist in the current eco-system. In the case of instructor-led programmes, delivery costs refer to the cost of instructor salaries, logistics for the course and other related variable costs that are driven by the total size of the participants. On the flip side, in the case of online learning delivery, there are also notable delivery costs that arise as well. Costs can be incurred due to the need of large servers and network bandwidth to store and deliver the required and relevant contents. The costs for programme deployment and management refer to the costs of launching the programme, marketing and advertising the programme, conducting internal and external meetings with various stakeholders and affiliated partners, and other related activities. The last component is the time involved and travel expenses for the learners themselves. In the context of higher education, this can be related to the travel costs for students travelling to campus.

5.7.3 Future of Blended Learning Pedagogy

In examining the future directions of blended learning, it clearly shows that blended learning will be dominating the higher education as it has already become a typical part of educational eco-system. In the years ahead, we could experience continued accelerating growth and new strategic directions, agendas and visions which are brought about by the blending of learning opportunities.

Evidence also validates the fact that we can potentially expect a dramatic rise in the usage of blended learning approaches in the near future and upcoming years. Additionally, online team-based (inter- and intra-group) and collaborative, inquiry-based learning activities, case learning and problem-based learning should be the preferred instructional approaches in the coming decade for online instructors in higher education. We can predict that e-books, intelligent agents, tablet PCs, virtual worlds, language support or wearable technologies would have a significant impact on the delivery of online learning in higher education settings. Today, many of these technologies are conveniently and easily used in classrooms. This reiterates that technology is unpredictable and we can never be too sure of what will potentially happen in the coming years ahead. In a more recent study by Dziuban et al. (2018), they elaborated on the next emerging blend revolving around ICTs or specialized artificial intelligence. This includes learning analytics, adaptive learning, calibrated peer review and automated essay scoring which are advanced processes that can assist teachers to focus more on the human aspects of teaching such as being compassionate, empathetic, creative and engaging in problem-solving.

5.7.4 Perspectives of Students and Instructors

It is essential to comprehend how both students and teachers largely feel about blended learning in general and the explicit aspects that surround it. If neither of these stakeholders have a positive perception of blended learning, then the intended outcomes of implementing it may not come to fruition. Waha and Davis (2014) examined Australian university students' perspective on blended learning, where of the students surveyed, only 17% of respondents indicated that they preferred the blended mode compared to fully online or face to face. These results showed that there is a still an adamant perceived view against the take-up rate of the blended mode of study. It could be logically interpreted that the low percentage indicates that students generally hold a strong preference for either online or face-to-face learning mode. However, students who did prefer blended learning found the blended mode to be beneficial to learning, where they appreciated the freedom of choice and empowerment given. Aside from the flexibility, the common reasons that emerge include, convenience, interaction with their peers and teachers, independence and balancing work commitments. It is essential to understand the type of tools used by teachers to aid students in their learning (Waha & Davis, 2014). We need to acknowledge the notion that a student may enjoy a particular instructional method or tool, but not find it particularly beneficial or in fact the learning efficacy could be low. Similarly, they may find instructional methods or tools that aid their learning or high in learning efficacy but may not enjoy using them. Teachers should not merely consider the way they deliver blended learning but also importantly look into the level of enjoyment a student feels when experiencing it.

From the perspective of instructors, faculty who have taught blended learning courses generally express their experiences as positive (Vaughan, 2007). This reiterates that generally teachers appreciated (a) blended learning structure; (b) enhanced student interactions; (c) increased student engagement; (d) flexible teaching and learning environment and (e) the eco-system that requires continuous improvement. However, a key concern among teachers on blended learning is the minimal connectivity to their students. However, studies show that much more interaction can occur in a blended learning process and certainly at a much higher quality level than a traditional face-to-face learning. This increased sense of interaction allows new ways and avenues for teachers to engage their students online. Additionally, this sense of interaction can then be transferred to face-to-face sessions in a blended course, allowing for increased class discussions and an in-depth exploration of course concepts. Evidence states that teachers adopting blended learning noticed students doing a much better in writing, learning the course materials, mastering concepts and applying their acquired knowledge much better than usual. This improvement can be largely due to students being much more engaged in the learning process. Moreover, teachers can accomplish course learning objectives more effectively within a blended course than within a traditional course due to the flexibility of the blended model. The mobility, flexibility of time and the capability to use web-based multimedia enable teachers to develop solutions to course problems and to incorporate new types of learning activities that may not be possible in traditional courses. Lastly, the blended model also allows teachers an ongoing and evolving opportunity to experiment with new approaches to learning and new types of educational technology.

5.8 Concluding Thoughts and Future Directions

In this chapter, we specifically examined the theoretical concept of blended learning in higher education. We examined plentiful academic literature addressing the various components of blended learning as well as the discussions surrounding it. Additionally, examples covered have a well-balanced mix from Western and Eastern contexts that address unique sociocultural aspects with specificity in terms of localized contexts to be applied across the higher education institutes around the world. Having a good comprehension of the influencing factors that are external to higher education institutes is vital for the successful implementation of blended learning.

All in all, blended learning is covered from two varying perspectives. We first analysed it from a pedagogical perspective and categorized the aspects in four separate yet interlinked clusters of blended learning. Institutions who are considering implementing blended learning approaches within their curriculum can consider these clusters to make them decide on how to cultivate blended learning within their context. The design of the blended learning approaches was also examined. The framework proposed informs educators of the vital elements that comprise the eco-system of blended learning. By adopting this proposed framework, teachers can customize by re-designing or modifying their pedagogy to create a more apt blended learning mode for their classrooms. We also discussed and provided insights on the aspects that go beyond the classroom context and examine various other elements of blended learning that are vital for its successful implementation. These elements of blended learning may not directly impact instructors but are crucial in the successful facilitation of blended learning. The goal of these proposed frameworks is to provide stakeholders from higher education institutes with a clear and concise overview of the core aspects of blended learning.

In today's technologically advanced and constantly evolving world, blended learning is inevitable for higher education institutes if they want to remain relevant and contemporary. Smartphones, laptops and Internet access are no longer rare commodities in today's modern societies. The use of technology in classrooms has evolved from simply using desktop computers and projectors for learning activities to implementing school-wide learning management systems, real-time streaming and recording of lectures, seminars that can be played anytime and even gamifying the learning process. Despite this evolving status, institutions should not assume that it will be all well and smooth sailing. Technology is constantly evolving and hence, higher education institutions have to continually reflect and work around the challenge to keep up to its pace and evolution. The process includes training both teachers and students to use the new technology in the most effective and optimal manner. With the school populations becoming more multicultural and diverse, faculty must ensure that they empower students with equal and fair learning opportunities. For instance, institutions have to duly consider how older and perhaps less tech-savvy students will cope with blended learning tools. Moreover, they must acknowledge the struggles of students from low-income households who may not be able to afford their own mobile devices, like smartphone or tablet or laptop that does not allow them to have Internet access at home.

The future of blended learning is promising with the emergence of technologies such as virtual reality, augmented reality, 3D printing and biometrics that help to shape the future of teaching and learning. Blended learning may potentially become the pedagogical approach of choice due to its high value to both the students and higher education institutions. However, while technology becomes smarter, automated and more capable, one might ponder and wonder how it may negatively impact the future of higher education? We may want to reflect on a few thought-provoking questions, say, will higher education institutions become too reliant on technology and diminish the role of the teacher? Or will the role of the teacher evolve into something completely different? It is hard to say for certain but for now, higher education institutes should anticipate change and future developments no matter how far or even out of reach they appear. By effectively and appropriately implementing technology into classrooms while also maintaining the social aspects of learning, institutions can create a balanced learning environment that is technologically progressive and consists of human-oriented elements concurrently. This act of intervention enables graduates to be equipped with both the hard and soft skills much expected by employers in today's rapidly evolving contemporary workforce.

References

Alammary, A., Sheard, J., & Carbone, A. (2014). Blended learning in higher education: Three different design approaches. *Australasian Journal of Educational Technology, 30*(4), 440–454. https://doi.org/10.14742/ajet.693

Alebaikan, R., & Troudi, S. (2010). Online Discussion in Blended Courses at Saudi Universities. *Procedia Social and Behavioral Sciences, 2*, 507–514.

Andrusyszyn, M. A., & Davie, L. (1997). Facilitating reflection through interactive journal writing in an online graduate course: A qualitative study. *Journal of Distance Education, 12*(1–2), 103–126. https://eric.ed.gov/?id=EJ582141

Arbaugh, J. B. (2014). What might online delivery teach us about blended management education? Prior perspectives and future directions. *Journal of Management Education, 38*(6), 784–817. https://doi.org/10.1177/1052562914534244

Bayne, S. (2015). What's the matter with 'technology-enhanced learning'? *Learning, Media and Technology, 40*(1), 5–20. https://doi.org/10.1080/17439884.2014.915851

Berney, S., & Bétrancourt, M. (2016). Does animation enhance learning? A meta-analysis. *Computers & Education, 101*, 150–167. https://doi.org/10.1016/j.compedu.2016.06.005

Bersin, J. (2004). *The blended learning book: Best practices, proven methodologies, and lessons learned* (1st ed.). Pfeiffer.

Blackburn, H. (2017). The status of women in STEM in higher education: A review of the literature 2007–2017. *Science & Technology Libraries, 36*(3), 235–273. https://doi.org/10.1080/0194262x.2017.1371658

Bloxham, S., & Boyd, P. (2007). *Developing effective assessment in higher education: A practical guide: A Practical Guide*. Open University Press.

Boelens, R., De Wever, B., & Voet, M. (2017). Four key challenges to the design of blended learning: Asystematic literature review. *Educational Research Review, 22*, 1–18.

Bonk, C. J., & Graham, C. R. (2005). *Handbook of Blended Learning: Global Perspectives, Local Designs*. (p. 2005). PfeifferPublishing.

Buchanan, B., MacFarlane, R., & Ludwiniak, R. (2010). *Student perception of online lectures within a blended learning environment for security and digital forensics*. https://www.napier.ac.uk/research-and-innovation/research-search/outputs/student-perception-of-online-lectures-with-a-blended-learning-environment

Cabrera, N. L. (2012). Exposing whiteness in higher education: White male college students minimizing racism, claiming victimization, and recreating white supremacy. *Race Ethnicity and Education, 17*(1), 30–55. https://doi.org/10.1080/13613324.2012.725040

Casanova, D., & Moreira, A. (2017). A model for discussing the quality of technology-enhanced learning in blended learning programmes. *International Journal of Mobile and Blended Learning, 9*(4), 1–20. https://doi.org/10.4018/ijmbl.2017100101

Castro, R. (2019). Blended learning in higher education: Trends and capabilities. *Education and Information Technologies, 24*(4), 2523–2546. https://doi.org/10.1007/s10639-019-09886-3

Chesney, S., & Ginty, A. (2007). Computer aided assessment. In S. Bloxham & P. Boy (Eds.), *Developing effective assessment in higher education: A practical guide* (pp. 207–220). Open University Press.

Christensen Institute. (2018, March 9). *Blended learning definitions*. https://www.christenseninstitute.org/blended-learning-definitions-and-models/

Daniela, L., Visvizi, A., Gutiérrez-Braojos, C., & Lytras, M. (2018). Sustainable higher education and Technology-Enhanced Learning (TEL). *Sustainability, 10*(11), 3883. https://doi.org/10.3390/su10113883
Du, C. (2011). A comparison of traditional and blended learning in introductory principles of accounting course. *American Journal of Business Education (AJBE), 4*(9), 1–10. https://doi.org/10.19030/ajbe.v4i9.5614
Dziuban, C., Graham, C. R., Moskal, P. D., Norberg, A., & Sicilia, N. (2018). Blended learning: The new normal and emerging technologies. *International Journal of Educational Technology in Higher Education, 15*(1), 1–16. https://doi.org/10.1186/s41239-017-0087-5
Dziuban, C., Hartman, J., Juge, F., Moskal, P., & Sorg, S. (2005). Blended learning enters the mainstream. In C. J. Bonk & C. R. Graham (Eds.), *The handbook of blended learning: Global perspectives, local designs* (pp. 220–233). Pfeiffer.
Garrison, D. R., & Vaughan, N. D. (2008). *Blended Learning in Higher Education: Framework, Principles, and Guidelines*. Jossey-Bass.
Gómez-Rey, P., Barbera, E., & Fernández-Navarro, F. (2016). The impact of cultural dimensions on online learning. *Journal of Educational Technology & Society, 19*(4), 225–238. https://doi.org/10.2307/jeductechsoci.19.4.225
Goodyear, P., & Retalis, S. (2010). *Technology-enhanced learning: Design patterns and pattern languages*. Sense Publishers.
Govender, D. W. (2010). Attitudes of students towards the use of a Learning Management System (LMS) in a face-to-face learning mode of instruction. *Africa Education Review, 7*(2), 244–262. https://doi.org/10.1080/18146627.2010.515394
Gribbins, M. L., Hadidi, R., Urbaczewski, A., & Vician, C. (2007). Technology-enhanced learning in blended learning environments: A report on standard practices. *Communications of the Association for Information Systems, 20*, 741–760. https://doi.org/10.17705/1cais.02046
Gudmundsson, A., & Laing, L. (2011). Facilitating student self-reflection in a blended learning environment. *ATN Assessment Conference 2011: Meeting the Challenges*, 107–116. https://eprints.qut.edu.au/46705/1/ATNA_-_Gudmundsson.pdf
Harrison, N., & Peacock, N. (2009). Cultural distance, mindfulness and passive xenophobia: Using Integrated Threat Theory to explore home higher education students' perspectives on 'internationalisation at home.' *British Educational Research Journal, 36*(6), 877–902. https://doi.org/10.1080/01411920903191047
Hofmann, J. (2018). *Blended learning (what works in talent development)*. Association for Talent Development.
Horn, M. B., Staker, H., & Christensen, C. M. (2014). *Blended: Using disruptive innovation to improve schools*. Wiley.
Hove, M. C., & Corcoran, K. J. (2008). Educational technologies: Impact on learning and frustration. *The Journal of Teaching of Psychology, 35*, 121–125.
Jung, I. (2014). Cultural influences on online learning. In I. Jung & C. N. Gunawardena (Eds.), *Culture and online learning* (pp. 15–24). Stylus Publishing.
Kirkwood, A., & Price, L. (2014). Technology-enhanced learning and teaching in higher education: What is 'enhanced' and how do we know? A critical literature review. *Learning, Media and Technology, 39*(1), 6–36. https://doi.org/10.1080/17439884.2013.770404
Korr, J., Derwin, E. B., Greene, K., & Sokoloff, W. (2012). Transitioning an Adult-Serving University to a Blended Learning Model. *The Journal of Continuing Higher Education, 60*, 2–11.
Lage, M. J., Platt, G. J., & Treglia, M. (2000). Inverting the Classroom: A Gateway to Creating an Inclusive Learning Environment. *The Journal of Economic Education, 31*, 30–43.
Li, K. C., Lam, H., & Lee, T. (2015). Effectiveness of technology enhancement in blended learning: An instrumental perspective. *Technology in Education. Transforming Educational Practices with Technology*, 187–198. https://doi.org/10.1007/978-3-662-46158-7_19

Liu, C., & Elms, P. (2019). Animating student engagement: The impacts of cartoon instructional videos on learning experience. *Research in Learning Technology, 27*(0), 1–31. https://doi.org/10.25304/rlt.v27.2124

Liu, X., Liu, S., Lee, S. H., & Magjuka, R. J. (2010). Cultural differences in online learning: International student perceptions. *Journal of Educational Technology & Society, 13*(3), 177–188. https://doi.org/10.2307/jeductechsoci.13.3.177

Lomer, S., & Anthony-Okeke, L. (2019). Ethically engaging international students: Student generated material in an active blended learning model. *Teaching in Higher Education, 24*(5), 613–632. https://doi.org/10.1080/13562517.2019.1617264

Maarop, A. H., & Embi, M. A. (2016). Implementation of Blended Learning in Higher Learning Institutions: A Review of the Literature. *International Education Studies, 9*(3), 2016.

McCarthy, J. (2010). Blended learning environments: Using social networking sites to enhance the first year experience. *Australasian Journal of Educational Technology, 26*, 729–740.

Mittelmeier, J., Rienties, B., Tempelaar, D., & Whitelock, D. (2017). Overcoming cross-cultural group work tensions: Mixed student perspectives on the role of social relationships. *Higher Education, 75*(1), 149–166. https://doi.org/10.1007/s10734-017-0131-3

Nguyen, J. G., Keuseman, K. J., & Humston, J. J. (2020). Minimize online cheating for online assessments during COVID-19 pandemic. *Journal of Chemical Education, 97*(9), 3429–3435. https://doi.org/10.1021/acs.jchemed.0c00790

Nussbaum, M., Gomez, F., Mena, J., Imbarack, P., Torres, A., Singer, M., & Mora, M. E. (2010). Technology-supported face-to-face small group collaborative formative assessment and its integration in the classroom. In D. D. Preiss & R. J. Sternberg (Eds.), *Innovations in educational psychology: Perspectives on learning, teaching, and human development* (pp. 295–324). Springer Publishing Company.

Pease, P. S. (2005). Blended learning goes totally virtual by design. In C. J. Bonk & C. R. Graham (Eds.), *The handbook of blended learning: Global perspectives, local designs* (pp. 266–279). Pfeiffer.

Picca, L. H., & Feagin, J. R. (2007). *Two-faced racism: Whites in the backstage and frontstage.* Routledge/Taylor & Francis Group.

Rajaram, K. (2013). Learning in foreign cultures: Self-reports Learning effectiveness across different instructional techniques. *World Journal of Education, 3*(4), 71–95.

Rajaram, K. (2019). Flipped classrooms: Scaffolding support system with real-time learning interventions. *Asian Journal of the Scholarship of Teaching and Learning, 9*(1), 30–58. http://www.nus.edu.sg/cdtl/engagement/publications/ajsotl-home/archive-of-past-issues/v9n1/flipped-classrooms-providing-a-scaffolding-support-system-with-real-time-learning-interventions

Rajaram, K. (2020). *Educating Mainland Chinese Learners in business education: Pedagogical and cultural perspectives—Singapore.* Springer.

Rajaram, K. (2021). *Evidence-based teaching for the 21st century classroom and beyond—Innovative-driven learning strategies.* Springer.

Rajaram, K., & Bordia, S. (2011). Culture Clash: Teaching western-based management education to mainland Chinese students in Singapore. *Journal of International Education in Business, 4*(1), 63–83.

Rajaram, K., & Collins, J. B. (2013). Qualitative identification of learning effectiveness indicators among mainland Chinese students in culturally dislocated study environments. *Journal of International Education in Business, 6*(2), 179–199.

Sharma, B., Nand, R., Naseem, M., & Reddy, E. V. (2019). Effectiveness of online presence in a blended higher learning environment in the Pacific. *Studies in Higher Education, 45*(8), 1547–1565. https://doi.org/10.1080/03075079.2019.1602756

Shyr, W.-J., & Chen, C.-H. (2017). Designing a technology-enhanced flipped learning system to facilitate students' self-regulation and performance. *Journal of Computer Assisted Learning, 34*(1), 53–62. https://doi.org/10.1111/jcal.12213

Simi, D., & Matusitz, J. (2016). Ageism against older U.S. college students: A view from social closure theory. *Interchange, 47*(4), 391–408. https://doi.org/10.1007/s10780-016-9286-6

Simonson, M. R., Smaldino, S. E., & Zvacek, S. (2014). *Teaching and learning at a distance*. Van Haren Publishing.

Spanjers, I. A. E., Könings, K. D., Leppink, J., Verstegen, D. M. L., de Jong, N., Czabanowska, K., & van Merriënboer, J. J. G. (2015). The promised land of blended learning: Quizzes as a moderator. *Educational Research Review, 15*, 59–74. https://doi.org/10.1016/j.edurev.2015.05.001

Staker, H. (2011). *The rise of K-12 blended learning: Profiles of emerging models*. https://www.christenseninstitute.org/wp-content/uploads/2013/04/The-rise-of-K-12-blended-learning.emerging-models.pdf

Sutherland, R., Lindstrom, B., & Lahn, L. (2009). Sociocultural perspectives on technology-enhanced learning and knowing. In N. Balacheff, S. Ludvigsen, T. de Jong, A. Lazonder, & S. Barnes (Eds.), *Technology-enhanced learning: Principles and products* (pp. 39–54). Springer Science+Business Media.

Thai, N. T. T., De Wever, B., & Valcke, M. (2017). The impact of a flipped classroom design on learning performance in higher education: Looking for the best "blend" of lectures and guiding questions with feedback. *Computers & Education, 107*, 113–126. https://doi.org/10.1016/j.compedu.2017.01.003

Truitt, A. A. (2016). *A case study of the Station Rotation blended learning model in a third grade classroom*. https://digscholarship.unco.edu/dissertations/365/?utm_source=digscholarship.unco.edu%2Fdissertations%2F365&utm_medium=PDF&utm_campaign=PDFCoverPages

Tucker, C. R., Wycoff, T., & Green, J. T. (2017). *Blended learning in action: A practical guide toward sustainable change* (1st ed.). Corwin.

Vaughan, N. (2007). *Perspectives on blended learning in higher education*. https://www.researchgate.net/publication/255567084_Perspectives_on_Blended_Learning_in_Higher_Education

Waha, B., & Davis, K. (2014). University students' perspective on blended learning. *Journal of Higher Education Policy and Management, 36*(2), 172–182. https://doi.org/10.1080/1360080x.2014.884677

Chapter 6
Authentic Learning Digital Transformation and Innovations

Kumaran Rajaram

Abstract In a rapidly evolving and changing global world, the creation, development and adoption of the transformative technological advancements by organizations and higher education institutions have become more protuberant. This chapter focuses on the key thrusts, discussion, insights and its relating nuances in authentic learning through digital transformation and innovations. The discussions address the process in achieving the intended learning outcomes with the adoption of these learning interventions. The chapter commences by addressing the aspects surrounding digitalization through transformative strategies and innovative learning interventions to be embedded within the eco-system. To keep up relevance and contemporariness, it is imperative for higher education institutions to move towards digital transformation in learning and learning innovations at strategic level through the relevant policies development. This thrust needs to be executed at the tactical and operational levels through the essential learning interventions to improve the efficacy of the entire learning process and transform the instructional strategies to attain the futurist learning outcomes. Next section discusses the social engineering strategy in context that primarily focuses on the behavioural and cognitive aspects of leaners and other relevant stakeholders. This deep and critical discussion enables us to appreciate the nuances involved in how learners' function and make decisions in general as well as situational circumstances. Hence, the process enables better learning design to be formulated with a well-grounded understanding from a socio-cultural dimension. That section also addresses the core thrust of learning culture and culture of learning. The type of learning culture across the higher education institutes globally allows the comprehension of the type of learners and their related learning characteristics, that may potentially be unique and rooted with distinctive values and beliefs. In the same vein, culture of learning enables the appreciation of how learners respond to design and relate to the specific challenges tied to the learning eco-system and tools based on their diverse social and cultural backgrounds, even prolonged exposure for international foreign students. Thereafter, the pedagogy as a key and holistic consideration explores into some of the contemporary twenty-first

K. Rajaram (✉)
Division of Leadership, Management and Organization, Nanyang Business School, Nanyang Technological University, Singapore, Singapore
e-mail: rkumaran@ntu.edu.sg

K. Rajaram, *Learning Intelligence: Innovative and Digital Transformative Learning Strategies*, https://doi.org/10.1007/978-981-19-9201-8_6

century and beyond instructional techniques and its impact. The chapter then focuses on some of the key learning notions that are critical to develop the employability (soft skills) and leadership competencies in learners to get them job-ready and nurtured for future workforce challenges. In these parts of the sections, first the functionality of the learning intervention is discussed with supporting illustrations and insights. Thereafter, the process on how the learning design could be embedded within the ecosystem structure is described with supporting explanations. Next, a meta-analysis on the aspects of the learning design, types of this intervention, approaches to enhance the functionality, its impact on learning outcomes and processes and application to employability and future work. The final part of this chapter addresses the application of the interventions to teaching and learning practice in general. It recommended learning interventions with sociocultural engineering strategies. The chapter value-adds by including the part of practical implications and recommendations that will assist readers to apply thee validated strategies immediately that enables to achieve a much higher impact in terms of efficacy. The concluding thoughts in the ending section provides a strategic overview by focusing on the key thrusts of the chapter's insights.

6.1 Introduction

In an ever-globalized world, the development and adoption of evolving technological advancements by organizations and higher education institutions have become more prominent. Research shows that approximately 13% of higher education institutes, i.e. colleges and universities are undertaking digital transformation (Grajek & the 2019–2020 EDUCAUSE IT Issues Panel, 2020).

The increasing trend of innovation and implementation of digital technology in higher education institutes can be attributed to varying factors. For instance, the recent COVID-19 pandemic has hastened the engagement of digital transformation in higher education (Iivari et al., 2020; Martin-Barbero, 2020; Rajaram, 2021). This situation has shifted and magnified the concerns and actions of higher education institutes around the globe, stimulating their interests into assuring short-term operational continuity while also committing to long-term institutional viability (Martin-Barbero, 2020). In particular, a study by Beatty et al. (2020) found that COVID-19 pandemic has allowed teachers to recognize the dramatic change in higher education that have been observed over the last 20 years, with approximately 5.5 million students taking classes online (National Center for Educational Statistics, 2017). The mode of delivery from the traditional classroom to hybrid and/or online approach is evident.

While some may question or challenge whether this trend will continue once the pandemic subsides and when campus classes resume that allow meetings in person to be facilitated in the future, what are the changes to be expected? Teachers who avoided online platforms in the past may now be required to return to physical classroom with new perspectives on the comparative teaching modalities of face-to-face, online, synchronous and asynchronous approaches (Beatty et al. 2020; Rajaram, 2021). In fact, in today's modern times, digital transformation becomes a basic essential and necessity for an institute to survive in its domain. It is critical for it to evolve integrally if it wants to persist in time and not disappear from the stage (Benavides et al., 2020). Apart from the necessity of digital transformations, the degree to which an institute's digital transformation is revolutionary may additionally serve as a competitive advantage. On top of that, digital transformation helps institutes better prepare their students for Industry 4.0 and beyond. For instance, without significant attention and the required push towards this direction, institutes may be unfamiliar and underprepared and, as a result, will not be able to adequately equip their students for the required changes. There is the urgent need and emphasis for a digital mindset and tech literacy in business management education (Allen, 2020; Rajaram, 2021).

Digital learning and its necessary interventions is one strategy in which digital transformation manifests itself. Evidence shows that OECD countries invested $16 billion into e-learning (Balasubramanian et al., 2009). At the surface level, we could we see lectures and seminar rooms being equipped with projectors and latest version of computers and laptops which are linked to the Internet and equipped with the latest applications to be utilized. As such, pedagogical practices are rarely affected at a significant level, as the control of learning is shifted from the teacher to the student (Lai, 2011). Technology in the context of higher education is largely used to complement higher education programmes than serve as a disruption (Jackson, 2019). Digital transformation today can significantly impact institutes at both the strategic and operational level. We see the increasing use of technology in pedagogical methods and instructional techniques, for instance, blended learning, e-Learning and massively online open courses (MOOCs).

Digital transformation is not only about the adoption of new digital tools and platforms, but it is also about the transformation and automation of the processes, increasing their effectiveness and efficiency through eliminating any physical barriers through increased connectivity. Hence, digital transformation of higher education is more than just mere technology or its related aspects. The goal is to adopt new ways of working to continue delivering user-focused services in the face of evolving technology, competition, changing needs and behaviours of stakeholders (Seres et al., 2018).

6.2 Digital Transformation in Learning and Learning Innovations

It is imperative to comprehend and have a clear perspective on the terms used when discussing digital transformation. Many varying terms are often used interchangeably. Digital transformation is the collation of all the necessary digitization processes geared towards the strategic change of an organization (Kopp et al., 2019). The decisive element is the "digital transformation" that encompasses more than just digitization processes. Similarly, Hinings et al. (2018) defined digital transformation as the combined effects of multiple digital innovations. Digital innovations, on the other hand, is about the creation and application of novel products and services. Wilms et al. (2017) describes digital transformation as the changes caused by digital technologies that influences multiple aspects of human life. According to EDUCAUSE, digital transformation is a series of deep and coordinated workforce, culture and technology shifts that enable new educational and operating models and transform an institution's operations, strategic directions and value proposition (Grajek & the 2019–2020 EDUCAUSE IT Issues Panel, 2020, p. 50). All in all, digital transformation includes a wide range of technologies such as cloud systems, big data, predictive analytics and integrative platform technologies, all of which have potential to generate both opportunities and challenges in contemporary organizational settings (Jackson, 2019).

It is vital to comprehend the relevance of learning innovations in the context of digital transformation in higher education. Innovations in learning assist in accomplishing better learning outcomes (Redding et al., 2013), where it happens in a specific teaching and learning context. Contemporary learning innovations, with digitalization of today's world, tend to revolve around incorporating digital technologies in classrooms. Learning innovations are the only way for improved future education and training. The underlying argument is that through learning innovations there will be numerous opportunities made available to learn, that enables one to respond to the changing times of globalization as well as to the new digital generational changes (Stracke, 2007).

Tertiary institutes that want to reinvent themselves have to take a long and hard strategic look into how their instructional methods conflict with the cognitive potentials of modern information technologies. The role of the learners changes as technological innovations and computers become smarter and more powerful. Both students and institutions should be better prepared for a different path where intelligence can be enhanced using information technologies that are deployed in strategic ways. With the coming industry revolution 4.0, industries around the globe have been disrupted in varying aspects. Although disruption in higher education may not be clearly noticeable, understanding disruption and preparing a good strategy to maintain relevancy is critical for institutes by and large. According to a study by Zulfikar et al. (2018), digital transformation will push higher Education Institutes to be more involved, engaged in using social media and other digital mediums in their customer relationships. Further to that, digital partnerships will also be key in their operations. Using both data collected from digital partners and customer relationships can assist institutes in building predictive models with the help of technology. This includes profiling student demographics using social media patterns that allow institutes to gain useful information that will play a key role in the strategic decision-making process. Furthermore, technology has enabled and increases the efficacy of global distance learning. This not only allows institutes to have a greater number of international students, but also provides them with a bigger pool of donors as a source of revenue stream. Digital transformation differs from country to country. For instance, Xiao (2019) studied the digitization of strategic development plans of 75 top universities in China, where it was found that unique to Chinese higher education institutes, were the goals of building a positive online ethos and developing political and ideological education via digital means. Hence, the strategic impacts observed will differ based on cultural contexts and circumstances. Course offerings that are influenced by digital transformation such as distance education and MOOCs programmes can also significantly alter the strategic decisions an institution may make. For instance, competitive aspects such as market size, price, the quality level of the product and institutional reputation are vital considerations when implementing distance strategies. Digital transformation will impact the main business model's dimensions. According to a study by Rof et al. (2020), the greatest emphasis brought about by digital transformation was assigned to new channels, partnerships and customer segments. This was followed by customer relationships, new technology or equipment, and new price and/or costs structures.

In fact, digital transformation may result in lower costs incurred by the institute. For instance, the use of technology in redesigning large introductory courses provides institutes an opportunity to reduce costs in the long run through reducing the amount of time instructors spend on planning and delivering their courses. However, institutes have to be mindful that redesigning courses has considerable start-up costs (Chingos et al., 2016). Nonetheless, in the long run it is possible to both improve outcomes and reduce costs as experience is accumulated using technology and integrating them into the institutes' structure. Major cost savings will likely require more strategic use of technological tools across departments and institutions along with effective leadership.

From a pedagogical perspective, digital learning environments open up new opportunities for both heteronomous and autonomous learning. These environments can be argued to make heteronomous learning even more heteronomous and, likewise, autonomous learning even more autonomous. For instance, with heteronomous learning, the pedagogically substantiated amalgamation and integration of two or more modes of presentation suggest that multimedia teaching can be offered on a multisensory basis (Peters, 2000). Hence, this process enables accurate "precise close overlapping of stimuli whereby better learning can be prepared, effected and strengthened" (Peters, 2000, p. 16). On top of that, significantly greater levels of activity and interactivity can be accomplished from digital learning environments.

Autonomous learning, on the other hand, is described as having a considerable amount of desirable preconditions. Compared to heterogeneous learning, the starting situation for autonomous learning varies as students are immediately placed into an interactive relationship with all types of information. This improves the accessibility to findings of scientific research and academic teaching programmes in the media. Hence, rather than passive learning, digital learning environments allow open learning situational contexts and learning to be based on active interactions that enable students to gain knowledge based on their own self-learning strategies. Furthermore, different methods of teleconferencing enable partnership and group work, on top of academic discourse. Teleconferencing forms a new arrangement for distance education where learners will have to get used to working with different forms of virtual partners and communities.

Learning-oriented outcomes are vital higher education even if digital technologies are not adopted or used (Lacka & Wong, 2019). These learning outcomes are enhanced when students use virtual learning environments. However, when social media is used in higher education, learning-oriented outcomes are least important and students tend to prioritize outcomes related to knowledge transfer instead. The implementation of digital tools and interventions in higher education classrooms may assist students to develop and improve their information and communications technology (ICT) outcomes, that is according to the studies is crucial when it comes to students' employability in today's context. Higher levels of ICT skills correlate to higher wages as well as the increased risk of future job losses caused by computerization and automation. Higher education institutes are obligated to implement digitization strategies that will encourage modern-day skills and enable students to use technology in flexible, adaptive and innovative ways (Bond et al., 2018).

Digital transformation also allows for developments in communication within higher education institutes. The rapidly increasing number of students accessing the Internet through mobile devices has caused more higher education institutes to accept contemporary and new communication technologies in the teaching context (Santos et al., 2019). To address the needs of this new generation of students, higher education institutes are adopting digital interventions and tools such as virtual learning environments and social media (Lacka & Wong, 2019). Results from a study by Santos et al. (2019) indicate that applications that allow for interpersonal communication, publishing and sharing technologies are preferred by students when communicating with their teachers. This is supported by a study from Ashour (2019) who found that communicating with one student at a time with an individualized context occurred more frequently online than on campus. In the study, it was found that in both small and large online classes, students would individually communicate directly with their teachers through email, messages, telephone, and in discussion forums or via video chats. In a survey, teachers responded how they perceived their relationships with online students compared to campus students. It was found that eight respondents reported that the online teacher-student relationship is closer. In contrast, some perceived their online students to be more anonymous than their campus students. We could conclude from the analysis that it depends on the learning culture and how the facilitation is conducted which eventually influence the learners' perception and experience.

There is an increasing amount of evidence suggesting that digital technology is restructuring the way students read and think in a negative manner. According to Cavanaugh et al. (2015), rigorous use of digital devices resembles a "Faustian quandary" where certain cognitive skills are gained while other deep-thinking capabilities weaken as a result of alterations in the neural circuitry of millennial brains. This could be a reason why hybrid or blended learning is often used in traditional course offerings to balance the amount of online and on-campus communication. For instance, according to a study by Ashour (2019), it was reported that blended classroom embedded with online learning that includes the formal in-person facilitation can produce significant benefits in relation to effectively improving student learning and success. To further validate this point, Chingos et al. (2016) reported that technology can be used to replace some classroom time without compromising students' learning outcomes. Hybrid courses have the potential to improve access to higher education, better learning outcomes and reduce costs to students by providing them with more flexible schedules.

6.3 Learning Interventions

Learning intervention can be defined as a strategy or methodology that is used to enhance the efficacy of the learning process and/or to perform the instructional adjustments to effectively teach that eventually improves the attainment of the intended specific learning outcomes.

In a survey of 1658 undergraduate students, Henderson et al. (2015) suggested that while data confirms that digital technology is central to the ways in which students experience their studies, they do not spontaneously transform the nature of university teaching and learning without careful learning design and its impact. As such, university educators are expected to temper enthusiasm for what might be achieved through technology-enabled learning and develop better understanding of the realities of students' encounters with digital technologies This is where learning interventions plays a vital role to enhance the learning process and eventual outcomes in the higher education classrooms.

Effective and easy collaboration has become a norm that allows students and teachers to access shared workspaces anytime (Beatty et al., 2020). Video presentations, online pitches and other similar contents can be created speedily and creatively. Micro-engagement through polls and quizzes using applications gives teachers a snapshot of students' progress in learning at any given moment and the ability to assess the shortfalls or lack of understanding immediately. Additionally, learning management systems can be used for virtual discussions to increase the chances for participation and co-creation of learning. Table 6.1 presents the digital learning interventions and tools that are available to be adopted by faculty. This section serves as a quick collated summary on various digital learning intervention tools that addresses the multifaceted learning needs that exist.

6.4 Learning Transformation

Technology is changing the nature of work within organizations and the roles within them. Organizations are aware of the importance of continuous learning for their employees in today's rapid evolving business environment. Therefore, in the higher

Table 6.1 Digital learning interventions and tools

Learning interventions—learning support systems	Primary functions
K^mAlive Learning Application	K^mAlive is designed using an evidence-based framework that focuses primarily on learning culture, social engineering and collaborative, active pedagogical learning design that can be team based or individualized. The learning App enables monitoring, assessing and storing of learners' individual, peer, intra- and inter-group contributions by engaging students in real time. The data analytics with report generation embedded within enables easy and quick extraction of learners' performance. The learning application focuses on distinctive features, namely: (1) class participation: monitor and assess learners' participation real time; (2) grouping: automate group forming with specific criteria; (3) group review: enable intra-group evaluation and inter-group peer evaluation by instructor and students; (4) critical reflection: train learners on critical thinking skills; (5) peer review: facilitate peer review and enable peer feedback; (6) polling: collate and present the statistical output of the class inputs; (7) group discussion: allow groups to discuss and collate their inputs; (8) leadership and human skills development: enable learners to enhance their leadership, communication, presentation, human skills and competencies; (9) ask questions: enable learners to pose questions, clarifications, comments or add-ons; and (10) data analytics: the learners' performance can be extracted easily, quickly and presented via the report generation functionality
Kahoot	Kahoot is a tool used to create and administer quizzes and enable discussions. Quizzes can be facilitated in real time. Questions are presented on a shared screen, and participants could answer using their own mobile devices or laptops
Quizizz	Quizizz is similar to Kahoot of being an online assessment tool. Quizzes can be facilitated real time or to be done as homework with a deadline stipulated. Once the quiz has been completed, students are able to review their answers. Teachers are also able to gather the required data from quizzes in order to analyse student performance
Slack	Slack is communication tool where users can create groups or "channels" based on different projects, teams and organizations. In the context of higher education institutes, Slack can be used in different courses, modules and project groups. Slack can also be used to facilitate project management and has functions such as app integration, video chat and screen sharing
Trello	Trello is a team collaboration platform that can be used to coordinate and communicate projects. In higher education contexts,. Trello can be used for lesson planning and teamwork projects. Boards on Trello, which are presented in a visually appealing manner, can be viewed and edited by multiple people allowing for ease of collaboration

(continued)

Table 6.1 (continued)

Learning interventions—learning support systems	Primary functions
Google Classroom	Google Classroom is a learning management system that allows teachers to create, distribute and grade assignments. At the same time, it also allows teachers to engage and communicate with their students. Google Classroom can be integrated into both students' and teachers' Google Calendar, while communication happened through Gmail, and assignment management through Google Drive
Tiki-Toki	Tiki-Toki is a software that allows users to create interactive timelines that can be shared over the Internet. In a higher education context, this allows for easier course management or for instructors to view students' group assignment progress. It can also assist in making presentations through its image and video integration function. It can help visual leaners understand events and dates easily
Hypothes.is	Hypothes.is an online social annotation tool which can be integrated with an institute's learning management system (LMS). It enables users to annotate on websites, blogs, journal articles and other pieces of information that can be accessed online. Groups can be created to share resources and annotations. Hypothes.is can be used individually or in a group where students can see annotations and comments made by their peers
Socrative	Socrative is an assessment tool where teachers can create quizzes, "space races", "exit tickets" and more. Data can be analysed in real time to improve student learning and make changes in instructional techniques. A report section is available for teachers to download data of class performance or of individual students. For higher education, Socrative recommends the Socrative PRO version of the app that includes features that cannot be found in the basic version. This includes: (a) class roster import; (b) silent hand raise; and (c) Custom folders

education context, where learning is a core function of the organization's service, learning transformation is ever crucial.

Hence, the increasing rate at which technological advancements are created and adopted has resulted in dramatic transitions in the way in which people learn. This process is what we could refer to as learning transformation. TV to classrooms led to learning transformation in the 1950s while the Internet dramatically evolved traditional classroom teaching in the 1990s. In the more recent years, Web 2.0 has been affecting the learning styles of students (Thomas, 2008). In the future, we may see how learning is transformed even further with the potential introduction of artificial intelligence (AI) and machine learning into courses. Students experience transformative learning when they meet certain specific conditions and learning climate according to Pearson's and Somekh's (2006). This includes learning creatively, learning as active citizens, engaging intellectually with powerful ideas and reflecting on their own learning. Learning transformation in higher education is vital in today's

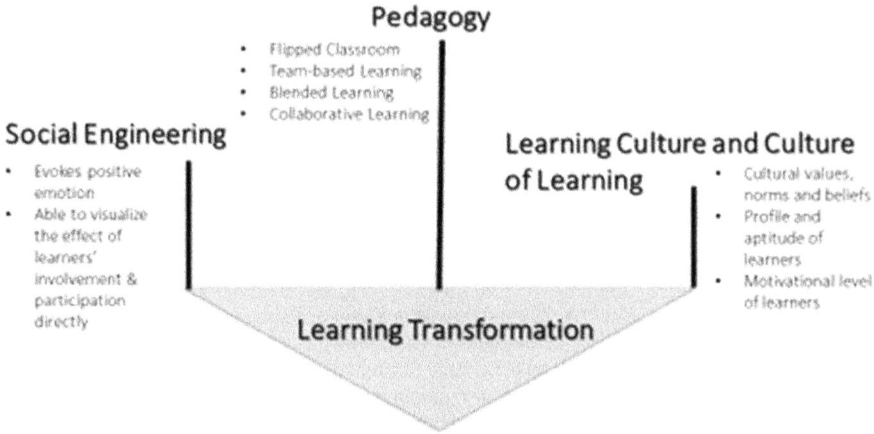

Fig. 6.1 Learning transformation framework (Adapted from @Reserach Lab for Learning Innovation and Culture of Learning, Rajaram [2020])

climate not only to meet the needs of learners, but also to adequately and appropriately train teachers to engage in relevant instructional and pedagogical techniques, methodologies that will effectively capture and engage students. Furthermore, learning transformation and development can help organizations save on costs. According to a study by Deloitte (2014), organizations can increase the value of their learning span by improving the effectiveness and efficacy of the learning programmes, efficiency of their learning operations, and alignment of their learning and business strategies.

A framework for learning transformation is presented in Fig. 6.1. It comprises of three independent but interlinking elements namely social engineering, learning culture and culture of learning, and pedagogy. In the next section, these elements will be elaborated.

6.4.1 Social Engineering

Social engineering in the context of social science is the science of masterfully directing human beings to take actions in some aspects of their lives. For instance, social engineering is used with us not even realizing it consciously, in our everyday lives where children use certain approaches to get parents to give into their demands. In a different professional context, it is also how working professionals such as doctors and lawyers retrieve information from their clients tactfully yet objectively. On a similar vein, from an educational context, it is used by educators in the way they interact with their students. All in all, we can say that social engineering approach is used in largely most of human interactions and exchange of thoughts (Hadnagy, 2010).

"Nudge theory", a concept popularized by Thaler and Sunstein (2008), can be viewed as a type of social engineering. A nudge given to an individual makes it more likely that a person will make a particular choice by involving choice architecture as a way to design the environment or context to influence people's choices. In teaching and learning, social engineering can be adopted to facilitate desired behaviours from learners including active learning through class participation, team-based learning, collaborative and cooperative learning, through engagement emotional aspects of group work and even levels of academic achievement. One such applied case study of social engineering in a higher education learning context can be one pointed at the University of Washington at Tacoma. Carmean and Frankfort (2018) discussed how the university had used predictive analytics, early alert and nudging tools that coincided with student-success strategies. The university's partnership with Persistence Plus that sent student-personalized text message nudges to them during the academic year had been providing consistently strong results, such as a 6% increase in graduation of students who had the highest risk of dropping out. The success of SMS text-based messaging nudges was also examined and validated by Castleman and Meyer (2020). Another example was illustrated by Fritz (2017) using example of the University of Maryland, Baltimore County (UMBC). Between 2007 and 2010, it was discovered that students who scored a D or F tended to use the school's learning management system (LMS) where about 40% less than students achieving a C or higher. Subsequently, a student feedback tool was developed called Check My Activity (CMA) and it allowed students to not only view a list of their own courses but also enabled them to compare their LMS activity to an anonymous summary of their course peers. Also, if instructors used the online grade book, students were able to compare their own activity with course peers earning the same, lower, or higher grade for any assignment. With a 2-year implementation phase, it was reported that students using the CMA feedback tool in spring 2012 were nearly twice as likely to earn a C or higher than students who did not (Fritz, 2017). Perhaps, feedback to students about their LMS use could redefine the LMS itself into a real-time indicator of student engagement, not just a static document repository for the syllabus, presentations and readings that it has largely become in higher education.

Social engineering links to learning transformation in the sense that the prevalence of digital devices in the minds of today's learners play a vital role in enabling higher education institutes to engage social engineering via modern technology. The success of any social engineering interventions will involve identifying channels that learners are engaging with on a regular basis and then designing ways to deliver information that will motivate engagement and informed decision-making (Castleman & Meyer, 2020).

6.4.2 Learning Culture and Culture of Learning

Culture in learning can be viewed primarily in two dimensional aspects, namely learning culture and culture of learning. Firstly, there is a type of learning culture that exists within the institute. This can vary depending on the location of the institute domestically or globally as well as the type of learners that make up its population, which subsequently form a type learning culture that comprises of certain characteristics. Secondly, culture of learning can be viewed as how learners respond to pedagogy and how well they acclimate to particular learning tools based on their diverse backgrounds. Primarily, learning culture is shaped by and can be attributed based on external factors, for example (a) cultural norms and social values; (b) the profile of the type of learners in context; and (c) national and industry related policies that could possibly affect the decision-making from an institutional strategic perspective (Rajaram, 2020, 2021). On the flip side, culture of learning refers to the internal factors, for instance (a) the learning outlook, beliefs and attitude; (b) the values that have been ingrained that enables learners to operate in a common agreed space. This requires much efforts on the institution to have built and put in place a strong eco-system in ingraining the relevant ethos and values (Rajaram, 2020; Rajaram, 2021). Learning should be viewed in terms of an environment, combined with the rich resources provided by the digital information network, where the context in which learning happens, the boundaries that define it, and the leaners, teachers and information within it all coexist and shape each other in a mutually reinforcing way (Thomas & Brown, 2011). The future culture of learning is grounded in a simple reflective question: "What happens to learning when we shift from the stable infrastructure of the twentieth century to the fluid infrastructure of the twenty-first century, where technology is consistently, constantly evolving, being created and responding to change? Culture of learning involves cultural values, beliefs and norms held by learners where it examines the profile and aptitude of learners as well as their motivational levels.

Culture is viewed as an existing, stable entity that evolves and changes over extended period of time. Individuals have a choice to join cultures, but no individual can create one totally alone. What becomes important in this traditional sense of culture is the process through which individuals join a culture and the transformation that occurs as a result. We can imagine certain people joining a culture and changing it wholesale, but, for the most part, the process works the other way. When individuals become part of a new culture, they are generally the ones who are transformed. Consider an exchange student who has just arrived in a foreign country, for example. As the student becomes immersed in the new culture, he undergoes a process of transformation in which he either adapts to the customs and conventions of the new culture and becomes integrated into it or finds he cannot adapt and decides to leave. Unlike the traditional sense of culture, which strives for stability and adapts to changes in its environment only when forced, this emerging culture responds to its surroundings organically. It does not adapt. Rather, it thrives on change, integrating it into its process as one of its environmental variables and creating further change. In other words, it forms a symbiotic relationship with the environment. This is the type of culture that exists in the new culture of learning. It makes no sense to think of people adapting to what they are already doing. But it does make sense to see them as functioning within a broader culture and creating it, rather than merely responding to it.

Many teaching practices implicitly assume that conceptual knowledge can be abstracted from the situations in which it is learned and used. This article argues that this assumption inevitably limits the effectiveness of such practices. Drawing on research evidence into cognition as it is manifest in everyday activity, it is argued that knowledge is situated, being in part a product of the activity, context and culture in which it is developed and used. The discussion focuses on how this view of knowledge affects the understanding of learning, and it was found that conventional schooling too often ignores the influence of school culture on what is learned in school (Brown et al., 1989). This correlates to learning transformation as the rise of mobile learning and technology-enabled learning results in learning transformation that gives rise to new cultures of learning that may deviate from traditional views. The use of digital technologies may support a shift of cultural practices in teaching and learning, to better meet the needs of twenty-first century higher education learners (Lai, 2011).

6.5 Pedagogy

Digital technologies have the potential to support and shape a pedagogy that is more active, participatory, personalized, flexible and inclusive (Laurilland, 2008). We shall have a succinct review and discussion on some of the emerging pedagogies that stem from learning transformation.

6.5.1 E-Learning

E-Learning comprises of the use of the Internet and other technologies to produce content for learning and teaching students and additionally regulate courses in an organization (Fry, 2001). According to Tao et al. (2006), this modern-day environment for learning has enabled higher education institutes to get individualized support. It also enables for higher levels of interaction and collaboration between educators compared to a traditional environment for learning. Although e-Learning is a workable strategy for many higher education institutes, most are resisting a full e-Learning environment (Al-Busaidi, 2013). Instead, many institutes engage in blended or hybrid forms of learning.

6.5.2 Blended Learning

Blended or hybrid learning is the integration of face-to-face and online instruction and is widely adopted by higher education institutions. Research by Dziuban et al. (2018) found that it was challenging to accurately monitor and track the growth of blended learning although studies have found that 35% of higher education institutions offered blended courses, and that 12% of the 12.2 million-documented distance education enrolments were in blended courses. Blended learning has transformative potential because there is evidence that it has the potential to be more effective and efficient when compared to a traditional classroom model. The evidence validates this as students tend to achieve as well, or better, on exams and are generally satisfied with the approach adopted (Garrison & Kanuka, 2004).

6.5.3 Flipped Classroom

The flipped classroom approach emphasizes the face-to-face interaction with educators that would enhance the efficacy of their learning process through leveraging the classroom meeting phase for active learning activities other than traditional-inclined lectures. However, lectures may not necessarily be completely removed from the course, rather the sessions could be potentially recorded in short bite-sized videos or podcasts and to be uploaded online where students can access and learn anytime, from anywhere. Class sessions will then be reserved for learners to have high intensity and deeper, meaningful interactions, reflections with their teachers and peers (Dennen, 2019; Rajaram, 2019, 2021). The flipped classroom approach is one contemporary approach to adapt to society's changes in the information and digital age era (Mortenson & Nicholson, 2015). It leverages and takes advantage of the benefits of modern and advanced technological innovations and digitalization while not ignoring the benefits of face-to-face teaching, and optimizing, enhancing the efficacy and effectiveness of learning process and improving the learning outcomes (Rajaram, 2019).

6.5.4 Virtual Reality and the Future of Pedagogy

Virtual reality has the potential to evolve learning even further in the future. The implementation of virtual reality can be revolutionary in education. Research suggests we retain more information and can better apply what we have learned after participating in virtual reality exercises (Rogers, 2019). The future of education will always be evolving so long as technology continues to find its way into our everyday lives.

6.6 Class Participation

In most higher education courses, class participation is often regarded as important, and it is not unusual to find courses in which it makes up 10–25% of the final course grade (Lyons, 1989). Of course, the importance placed through the weightage of the class participation has to be based on the overall learning outcomes and how these are tied in with the learning design. The emphasis on classroom discussions is a result of increasing interest in student-centred approaches to teaching and learning. However, the challenge is the way class participation is perceived by the faculty and students that differs. Evidence shows that the source and type of discussions, and exchanges that happens in classrooms are differed by gender, age and course levels. For instance, students in upper-level courses would participate in a different style compared to students in lower-level courses. Hence it is vital for students to be briefed and have them comprehend how the class participation is carried out and it is being assessed. The learners' behaviours can be well shaped through the class participation assessment component. This requires the specific behavioural elements to be embedded in the assessment criteria so that the expected skills and competencies can be nurtured on.

In Jones' (2008) study, the importance and intended effects of class participation were examined. To have the insights summarized, class participation (1) holds students accountable for their own learning; (2) involves more learners in the discussions and exchanges of thoughts; and (3) stimulates thinking. Firstly, when the class participation requirement is imposed, it places the responsibility upon students and have them accountable for their own learning. This involves data collection through impressionistic means or a more objective method such as using a roster or even via technological intervention to check off students who can answer questions posed by the teacher. Secondly, class participation enables more students to speak up and be involved. This can help shift conversations from being overly dominated by the teacher or by the same handful of enthusiastic students. Lastly, class participation can stimulate thinking when teachers pose a challenging question or probe or prompt and invite students to provide their answers and opinions Answering the questions requires students to relate, link ideas or scrutinize applications of that lesson's concept in new, unique and varying contexts. The primary idea is to move from consideration concepts to conceptual development or generalization.

Another possible correlation of class participation to its learning outcomes is its relation to achievement. An example can be illustrated from Reinsch and Wambsganss's (1994) study that aimed to determine whether class participation helped students improve their overall results on take-home essay examinations. Four sections were examined, namely (a) legal environment classes, which was considered and categorized to be a less technical class, and two sections of law of commercial transactions classes, which was considered and categorized to be a more technical class. Their study findings showed that participation in less technical classes benefited tests' results of sections as a whole, but not in the individual test scores. In the more technical classes, participation did not affect scores both on the section and on individual levels. All in all, they concluded that the effects of class participation primarily depend on students' preparation before class and the technical nature of the class. Evidence also pointed and highlighted that class participation has an impact on learning outcomes where specific influential factors must should be duly considered when evaluating class participation. Further to this, for student preparedness and technical nature of the class, external factors such as age, gender and culture may play a role in the level of class participation and engagement within a classroom and hence subsequently result in differing learning outcomes among students (Rajaram, 2021). For instance, while class participation does not significantly impact students' enjoyment levels (Simpson & Du, 2004), when paired together based on learning styles, that vary from culture to culture, can explain the level of enjoyment that could potentially be viewed from an engagement perspective.

In the next section, we shall discuss the correlation of class participation to the intended learning outcomes, and how educators may facilitate or execute the class participation in classrooms context.

6.6.1 Facilitation of Class Participation

Class participation is advocated by many higher education institutes as the responsibility of students to play a part in the learning environment (Czekanski & Wolf, 2013). To advocate student-centred learning, class participation can be included in the course syllabi, be it whether it is graded or ungraded. A recommended way to facilitate class participation is through the creation of rubrics that provide structure and scaffolded process for student participation and sets forth the actions they should explicitly perform. These assessment rubrics have scales to describe students' level of performance when they participate and contribute in class. In the later section below, a validated and exemplary class participation through a digitalized support platform embedded with data analytics and report generation is discussed. Other potential factors that influence students to speak up includes the size of classroom, personalities of the instructor and the perception of peers (Abdullah et al., 2012). Learning culture can be a potential contributor in influencing the levels of class participation. Research study evidence shows that generally only a minority pool of students in a class participate actively where this leaves some students who are introverts but committed, annoyed at their peers, especially those who are extremely outspoken and talkative but not necessarily contributing value to the discussions. Perhaps, primarily the existing eco-system in these higher educational institutions may not have been equipped adequately to create a student-centric learning culture, appropriate learning design and assessment structure. The inclination or unintentionally the learning design could have contributed students to be passive and view the instructor as an expert, where students are made to believe that their role was to listen quietly and take notes, but not necessarily to engage in active exchange of thoughts. It could also be the potential power distance within the classroom that causes students to take on such mindset. Here, the learning culture and culture of learning play a vital intervening and influencing role in how the class participation is facilitated.

All in all, class participation has a strong influence on many aspects of teaching and learning. The following section, Table 6.2., will present a meta-analysis on the aspects of class participation and its impact on learning outcomes and processes.

6.6.2 Meta-Analysis: Aspects of Class Participation and Its Impact on Learning Outcomes and Processes

See Table 6.2.

6.6.3 Learning Intervention: K^mAlive Learning Application—Class Participation Functionality

In this section, the validated learning intervention of class participation will be discussed, and its insights embedded with its value proposition will be presented. In Fig. 6.2, the instructor's panel view for the instructor-centred class participation functionality is presented.

For the class participation functionality, the option of instructor centred can be selected. Instructor can select the question to be posed to the students. Once the question is selected, the instructor can select the rubrics, here there is an option to decide whether the instructor would like to perform and evaluate the class participation with or without rubrics. Once the required option is selected, the session can be commenced. Once the button "start question" is selected, a raise hand icon appears via the student's panel in the mobile phone, tablet or iPad that they are using. So, students can now decide to participate. Once the student clicks on the digitally raise hand icon, those students who have selected in answering will appear under the raise hand column. For all these students who have raised their hand, their counters have now changed to R1 because they have raised their hands once. If the student selection option is set to "Auto", the student who raises the hand, digitally the fastest, will automatically appear. So, this student is now ready to answer the question posed, where the student is now given an opportunity to verbalize the answer to the open-ended question posed. Once the student has answered the question, the instructor can rate the answer provided based on the rubrics. Once this flow of sequence has been completed, the instructor can get to the next student. The next student can continue to answer the same question posed. The next student appears in the left side panel to answer, the student who has answered would automatically go back down to its original panel, and the counter increases its count to C1 because the student has contributed after raising hand digitally. This process will continue in a cyclic manner until all the students who have raised their hands digitally have completed answering the questions. The instructor can also click the button "No Answer" when a student raises hand digitally but did not answer. Once the last student is rated in the pool of digitally raised hand students, that completes everyone in having the question posed answered. Then it depends on instructor to decide if you want to pose any question and repeat the entire cycle again. Alternatively, the instructor can exit the session.

The primary difference between the student selection option "Auto" versus "Manual" is very much that the option "Auto" facilitates first come first basis where whoever raises the hand digitally first will go to the speaking panel first, but with

Table 6.2 Aspects of class participation and its impact on learning processes and outcomes

Aspects of class participation	Impact on learning outcomes/processes
Engagement	Kuh et al. (2008) examined how student engagement affected college students in 18 baccalaureate-granting colleges and universities in the United States. Their study found that student engagement in educationally purposeful activities is positively related to academic outcomes as represented by first-year student grades. Also, engagement has a compensatory effect on first-year grades and persistence to the second year of college at the same institution. The study also reported that the effects of engagement move generally in the same positive direction for students of diverse ethnic and racial backgrounds
Ad hoc articulation of thoughts	Class participation allows students to spontaneously and freely communicate, articulate and express their thoughts and ideas in both written and verbal forms. This ad hoc articulation of thoughts that generally happens in a learning climate or situation where students do not come prepared prior. This process of learning enables students to gain the confidence by allowing them to effectively communicate with their teachers as well as with fellow peers by collating, linking varying learned concepts and having that articulated in a logical manner with rigour and quality. One example that includes ad hoc articulation of thoughts and class participation is spontaneous collaborative learning (SCOLL), where a research was conducted on SCOLL, using a sample of 39 tertiary students from the Hong Kong Polytechnic. Spontaneity involved students forming study groups without any instruction or advice from teacher and having discussions with no interventions. The study found that spontaneous collaborative learning had positive effects on students' learning. The learning process facilitates discovery learning focusing on fundamental knowledge through coordinating ideas and perspectives rather than just a passive transmission of information. Essentially, when students try to express their own opinions, they are subject to higher cognitive levels. In learning contexts where students do not prepare prior, it is imperative for them to have the ability to improvise their communication. This will better prepare them for such unprepared and ambiguous situations, circumstances in their future career
Cognitive thinking process	Class participation challenges students to think at a higher cognitive level. This may place some discomfort on students as they think and reflect. It is especially vital for high-ability students or indeed students who are to be nurtured to be of high quality, who may not feel challenged to push themselves. A study by Scager et al. (2012) that examines undergraduate students found that the challenges in terms of complex tasks, high expectations and lack of teacher's direction (intentionally and unintentionally) resulted in increased efforts despite a mixture of feelings of worries and frustrations

(continued)

Table 6.2 (continued)

Aspects of class participation	Impact on learning outcomes/processes
Critical thinking	Class participation as a learning pedagogy enables students to speak up, express themselves and ask questions in class, by facilitating through an open and easy platform that lessens communication barrier (Rajaram, 2022, p. 84). Class participation can foster critical thinking among learners. "Critical Thinking can be defined as the higher order cognitively and actively conceptualizing, evaluating, applying and synthesizing information collated from or generated by experience, observation, reflection, reasoning and/or communication" (Rajaram, 2021, p. 81). Critical thinking is a higher-order cognitive skill that is essential to prepare students for evolving challenges and rapidly changing environment they potentially face in the future. In a study of four separate institutes, Tsui (2002) suggested that participation in classroom discussions encourages the exercise of critical thinking skills by allowing students to test out their ideas verbally, to reflect upon the views of one's peers and to modify critically one's own views through incorporating feedback from
Collaborative learning	Dillenbourg (1999) defined collaborative learning as "a situation in which two or more people learn or attempt to learn something together" (p.1). Class participation enables collaborative learning where students share and exchange various learning viewpoints. This enables them to learn from their peers and also gain relevant team-working skills. Rajaram (2021) advocated that one of the instructional approaches is to allow students to be engaged by participating through discussions via collaborations. He also emphasized that meaningful contributions through group and class participations can assist students to be more actively engaged in the learning process. There are many benefits of learning collaboratively including social, psychological and academic benefits as well as providing teachers and students with an alternate assessment technique (Laal & Godsi, 2012)

(continued)

Table 6.2 (continued)

Aspects of class participation	Impact on learning outcomes/processes
Individualized learning	Individualized learning enables one to learn through collating the comprises of three primary elements, namely (a) listening to others' perspectives or views in a subject matter discussion and making sense out it. This can be impactful as learners have varying values, principles and imperatively culturally diverse experiences; (b) reflection of what is being shared and how this may make some good sense for individuals analysing the information from their own perspectives; (c) sense making from collective viewpoints and thoughts. Class participation also involves aspects of individualized learning where the process involved in getting an answer differs from student to student. They core aspects of how individualized learning occurs include students listening to others' perspectives, reflecting on what is being shared and analysing it from their own "window" of lenses as well as sense making from a holistic perspective For instance, class participation and discussion can be used as a tool to facilitate critical reflection. Through these reflections and discussions, students can accomplish three crucial goals, namely (a) they begin to question traditional ideas about teaching and learning; (b)concurrently will realize that they each have a wealth of knowledge about teaching and learning through their past experiences; and (c) students can come to own the process of critical reflection, claiming it as a valuable means for learning rather than as a programme requirement (Wade, 1994)

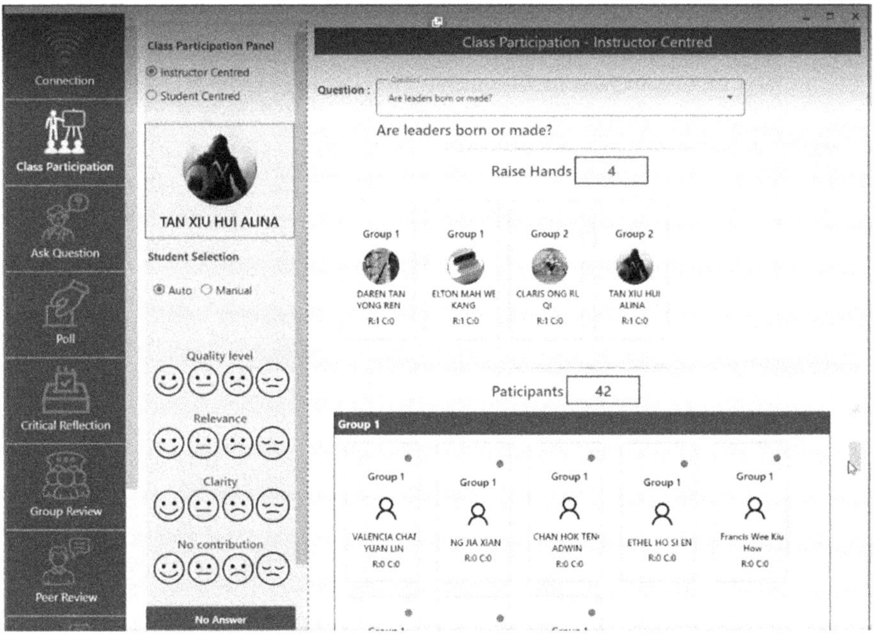

Fig. 6.2 Instructor's panel view: Instructor-centred class participation functionality

respect to the option "manual", the instructor must manually select who will be speaking from the students' pool. Next, in Fig. 6.3, the instructor's panel view for the student-centred class participation functionality is presented.

For the class participation "Student Centred" functionality, the instructor can select the "Student Centred" option and have the question selected. The instructor can see all the groups and students assigned in the respective groups. The counters are not stating zero in Fig. 6.3 because we are assuming that these contributions are from the "Instructor Centred" functionality that was executed prior. However, assuming the instructor did not start out with the "Instructor Centered" but directly with this functionality of "Student Centred", then all the counters "C" for contributions will be appearing as "0", to commence from the start. "V" is linked to the feature validation. When we select either self-validation or leader-led validation features, it enables the peers in the group to validate students' answers where the number of validations by whom would be appearing here. The members' names in the groups and the contribution the validators' names will also be appearing. If you wish to give individual students feedback, you can click the blue icon "Feedback"; alternatively if you prefer to give feedback to the entire group, you can click the orange colour icon "Feedback" so that the feedback gets to everyone in the group. You can view how the tabulated presentation looks for all groups and their respective members as well as the contributions, validation and feedback columns. Please also note that on the left-hand side, before we begin this student-centred class participation functionality, you have an option to "On" or "Off" for the validation. If you select the Yes

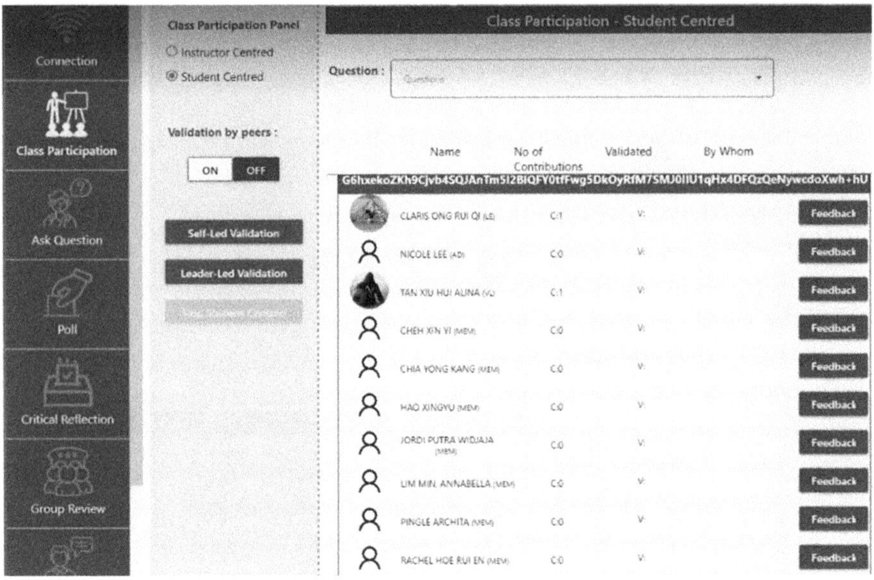

Fig. 6.3 Instructor's panel view: Student-centred class participation functionality

option for the validation, then you have two choices namely, self-led validation or instructor-led validation.

Next, we will be discussing the class participation with the option of self-led validation selected. You need to select the question to be posed, thereafter select the "Self-Led Validation" option. "Self-Led Validation" feature provides the autonomy and empowerment to students to monitor their own verbal contributions in the class, for instance, if they raise their hand physically and they contribute to the class they have to self-update their contribution via the system. You can view from the screen of how the student panel looks once the instructor has clicked the "Self-Led Validation". You can see on the students' panel screen that the question posed appears and the row that shows the student's contributions namely the number of times the student has contributed. Now the student's participation needs to be validated by another randomly assigned student within the group. Once that student has pressed the icon "validate", the counter for the validation changes to "1" as you could see from the screen. You could now see that the student So basically, for this functionality of self-lead validation, once a group member in the team contributes and acknowledge his/her contribution, a randomly assigned team member will be requested to validate the peers' participation to serve as a form of authentication. However, if the leader-led validation option is selected, then the pre-defined group member who is assigned as the leader for the group will be the sole validator. So based on whoever has been assigned previously under the leadership setting, when someone in the team contributes, the respective team members can automatically self-track their own contribution by pressing the "+" button in the students' panel screen; thereafter, based on the option of the validation selected, the validator who is assigned will validate and could see the increase in the counter. You can also provide feedback individually to the students. The instructor can also give feedback to the entire group not necessary to only one particular student.

6.7 Critical Thinking

Critical thinking is a complex and multifaceted phenomenon and thus has many varied definitions in scholarly work. On a generic basis, critical thinking can be defined as a set of abilities or cognitive skills that is linked to logical analysis and the evaluation of arguments. Through this process, an individual forms a judgement about what to do or what to believe in a particular context. Rajaram (2021) defines critical thinking as "the higher order cognitively and actively conceptualizing, evaluating, applying and synthesizing information collated from or generated by experience, observation, reflection, reasoning and/or communication" (p .81). According to Erikson and Erikson (2018), critical thinking can be positioned in two different ways: (a) as involving varying abilities in different disciplinary traditions; (b) as a general set of abilities and dispositions. In practical sense, both these two aspects can be combined as well.

The study conducted by Moore (2013) investigated the ideas of critical thinking from the perspectives of academics working in history, philosophy and cultural studies. The study discovered seven definitional groups based on their commentaries that include (a) as judgement; (b) as skepticism; (c) as a simple originality; (d) as sensitive readings; (e) as rationality; (f) as an activist engagement with knowledge; and (g) as self-reflexivity. In the context of higher education, it has been argued that there must be certain dispositions. These include of being able to distinguish contexts that require critical thinking and the motivation to in fact think critically in those situational contexts and circumstances. The notion of critical thinking includes the ability to argue and seek for clarifications (Erikson & Erikson, 2018). The role of critical thinking in higher education context can take on different meanings when examined from a strict disciplinary context compared to a generic context. We can advocate that the notion of critical thinking supports students' future roles such as an employee. For instance, critical thinking enables students to be able distinguish fake news as well as provide them with the ability to use scientific reasoning in their future careers. Higher education institutes have to acknowledge the importance of critical thinking as part of skills and competencies' framework development. The development of self-awareness is one of the most useful outcomes of critical thinking (Walker & Finney, 1999), where it allows individuals to understand where their skills lie and how they learn. With this newfound understanding in context, individuals develop a more thoughtful, inquisitive and open-minded approach in both their professional and personal lives. We could acknowledge that these are some of the many learning outcomes that can be attributed to critical thinking skills.

Research by Davies (2015) stated that various skills can be derived from critical thinking. These critical thinking skills were then categorized into four main categories: lower-level thinking skills, thinking skills, complex thinking skills, and thinking about thinking or meta-cognitive skills. Davies (2015) illustrates the various aspects of the thinking skills and the categories they fall under. Four broad categories were developed and specific skills within that were identified, namely *first category*: lower-level thinking skills ("Foundation")—(a) interpreting, (b) identifying assumptions and (c) asking questions for clarification; *second category*: higher-level thinking skills—(a) analysing claims, (b) synthesizing claims and (c) predicting; *third category*: complex thinking skills—(a) evaluating arguments, (b) reasoning verbally, (c) inference making and (d) problem-solving; and *fourth category*: thinking about thinking—(a) meta-cognition and (b) self-regulation. In the context of higher education, these skills can be seen as learning outcomes the teachers may want to achieve when trying to impart the ability to think critically onto their students.

Deep learning is another aspect of learning outcome for critical thinking. They found that the term deep learning often appears along with the term critical thinking in titles when searching online databases. Recent work by Dwyer et al. (2014) showed that students who learn the skills of analysing arguments score higher on tests of critical thinking. Hence, the line between deep learning and critical thinking blurs because the two are so highly interdependent (Franco et al., 2015). Another learning outcome is memorization abilities. Higher-order thinking skills such as critical thinking are dependent on memory since it is not possible to use higher-order thinking processes if an individual cannot remember the information that they are thinking about (Dwyer et al., 2014). In these two cases, it is hard to distinguish learning outcomes and critical thinking as completely separate entities as they are highly interlinked and co-related.

More recent research found issues of learning outcomes become even more challenging when critical thinking is brought into play (Erikson & Erikson, 2018). The first challenge involves interpretations since the use of learning outcomes is reliant on advanced but implicit interpretative frameworks. The next problem is that of educational goals which cannot be expressed easily through learning outcomes. Lastly, is the potential risk of learning outcomes establishing a potential ceiling that could be viewed as a hindrance for students' advanced, broad-level aspirations and ambitions. All in all, the relevance and importance of critical thinking in higher education is highly indisputable and comes across as a clear requirement.

6.7.1 Meta-Analysis: Instructional Approaches to Enhance Critical Thinking, Its Impact on Learning and Application to Employability

Research findings from Tsui's (1999) study suggested that writing assignments and instructor feedback on such work positively affect students' development of critical thinking skills. On the flip side, multiple choice exams seem to diminish the cultivation of critical thinking skills. The more effective instructional techniques share a similarity in that they require students to construct responses to a problem rather than ask them to memorize and select answers from a set of possible responses. Critical thinking is a higher-order ability that requires more than the ability to recall. Hence, it is vital to distinguish what useful instructional approaches can be implemented by teachers in the classroom in order to enhance critical thinking in students. In the Table 6.3, the instructional approaches to enhance critical thinking, its impact on learning and application to employability is presented.

While research scholars have provided some methods to advance critical thinking skills in students in general, the specific type of instructional techniques to be adopted and its efficacy when implemented may be influenced by other contributing factors. Hence, it becomes the responsibility of faculty to discern the most appropriate strategy for their courses. As shared by Penningroth et al. (2007), much more research on the effectiveness of various methodologies is required to appropriately comprehend the specific teaching strategies that are more inclined and validated in improving critical thinking.

6.7.2 Facilitation of Critical Thinking

The key question for us to reflect on is why facilitating and nurturing critical thinking skills in students becomes imperative in higher education classrooms? According to Davies (2015), at one level, critical thinking is about the development of skills such as argumentation and the ability to make logical judgements, that addresses the graduate employability aspects as employers look out for critical thinking skills in their employees. Critical thinking skills involve the deposition to utilize them as well. In a more recent study by Calma and Davies (2020), the study that comprises of multiple surveys reported that critical thinking is one of the most crucial skills when it comes to student employability. The specific importance of critical thinking skills may vary across disciplines. In the context of business students, for instance, to think and learn critically is often seen as an essential skill expected of every student. Further findings from Penkauskienė et al. (2019) re-iterated that critical thinking is valued not only because it contributes to professional success, but also because it assists in personal improvement and the common good. All in all, it can be concluded that critical thinking is both an individual attribute and a skill set that will benefit society and beyond. Hence, having to develop this skill becomes a vital element in the phase of higher education to have students nurtured in context before they are transited to employment.

There are numerous studies that advocate strategies for teachers to facilitate critical thinking. One of the ways is through collaborative learning. Loes and Pascarella (2017) found that exposure to collaborative-learning activities is very much linked to the improvement of critical thinking skills, where their sample size resembled White students and those who were the least well prepared academically for college.

Table 6.3 Instructional approaches to enhance critical thinking, its impact on learning and application to employability

Instructional approaches to enhance critical thinking	Description of instructional approach	Impact on Learning	Application to Employability
5-step framework (Duron, Limbach & Waugh, 2006)	The authors developed a 5-step framework which can be implemented in any classroom setting to assist the development of critical thinking skills in students. The steps are as follow: 1. Determine learning objectives 2. Teach through questioning 3. Practice before you assess 4. Review, refine, and improve 5. Provide feedback and assessment of learning	In step one, teachers should be aware of the key learning objectives that define what behaviours students should have when they leave the classroom. In the second step, teachers extend students' knowledge to develop new ideas via questions. This can stimulate interaction between the teacher and the student and challenge students to defend their opinions. The next step aims to engage students in active learning activities so that they can think about what they are doing. The fourth step requires teachers to continually refine and revise their courses to ensure that their techniques certainly develop critical thinking skills in students. Lastly, feedback enhances the quality of student learning and performance and teaches students how to assess their own performance in the future	Teachers should have this applied in context through authentic learning. For instance, if the students are trained in engineering, the instructor can simulate an engineering-based case study and see how best this framework could be implemented to optimize the development of the critical thinking skills

(continued)

Table 6.3 (continued)

Instructional approaches to enhance critical thinking	Description of instructional approach	Impact on Learning	Application to Employability
Two approaches designed for critical thinking skill development: 1. A personalized case approach 2. A group poster session approach (Powley & Taylor, 2014)	The authors developed two approaches for developing crisis leadership and consequently critical thinking skills. The first is a personalized case which is an individual writing assignment. This incorporates experiential learning and critical thinking as a way to develop significant learning. The next approach is a group poster project which takes around 2 h and involves an in-class presentation session. It occurs after the personalized case activity, and is usually the first exercise during the term. It is possible to accompany or replace the typical group project presentation with this group poster project	The first approach helps increase students' critical thinking skills as well as develops learning on how to lead in crises. The second approach provides students with the opportunity to work on a crisis leadership scenario. It helps them recognize leadership characteristics as well as build on the critical thinking aims of the course	The first approach is to be implanted in crisis-related situational training, to equip with the skills and applied knowledge "know-hows". The second approach enables students to develop leadership skills for their future work context
Operational framework for teaching critical thinking (Thomas & Lok, 2015)	Thomas and Lok developed an operational framework of critical thinking. The authors then created an illustrative checklist based on items in this framework. The checklist allows for self-assessment, and can also be made into an evaluative rubric with open columns that cater to a maximum of 5 students per rubric	Assuming an adequate learning environment, the operational framework can be used to support development of critical thinking ability and the application of this ability in disciplined performances over a specified time. It also aims to build self-awareness and self-monitoring abilities	This approach assists in developing varying aspects of critical thinking and its nuances. This is useful as the teacher relates to real-life scenarios and perhaps explicitly focusing on a few of those skills in a more targeted manner. Such skills are very useful to be exposure to for their future work operations for students

(continued)

Table 6.3 (continued)

Instructional approaches to enhance critical thinking	Description of instructional approach	Impact on Learning	Application to Employability
Web-based simulations (Lovelace et al., 2016)	The authors claimed that previous studies have found that simulations are effective tools for teaching content knowledge and achieving desired learning outcomes. In their own study, they found that participation in strategy-based simulations was an effective way to develop critical thinking skills	In simulations where student groups are required to make decisions in a complex environment, critical thinking must be used to analyse and evaluate the situation and make choices that consider the consequences and implications of the decision. The authors also found that the development of critical thinking skills was linked to simulation performance but only in simulations with shorter durations in which performance was determined only by the actions of the individual team members	Such interventions enable students to visualize and expose themselves to the actual related sort of job tasks. This prepares them to know what skills are required and get students start pondering about ow to hone on them through their own efforts

(continued)

Table 6.3 (continued)

Instructional approaches to enhance critical thinking	Description of instructional approach	Impact on Learning	Application to Employability
VaKE method (Pnevmatikos et al., 2019)	The VaKE method is an approach that fosters "scientific humanism". It enables the students to obtain and comprehend conceptual knowledge along with scientific methodologies. Moreover, it further assists students to become more aware and sensitive of the ethical aspects of science and technological activities. Through the VaKE methods, a moral dilemma is introduced to the class and students must either argue for or against a solution using moral reasoning and assessment of arguments. Dilemmas are developed in a way where new knowledge will be necessary for the moral-inclined solutions. Hence, students are motivated to find relevant information and implement their knowledge to justify their solutions	The VaKE method allows students to make use of their argumentation, reasoning, critical thinking and decision-making skills to solve problems. Thus, students learn how to separate their beliefs from factual evidence. They also learn to understand that a solution cannot be easily proposed when there is a lack of knowledge around the specific circumstances of the problem. The dilemmas introduced allow for an inquiry-based learning approach that is appropriate for developing and practicing thinking skills. Therefore, using VaKE, students can steadily engage students in the inquiry process that develops their critical thinking skills	Expose students for real-life situational skills such as argumentation, reasoning, critical thinking and decision-making skills to solve problems. These are vital skills that need to be built on which needs to be exposed to them as an awareness at this phase

(continued)

Table 6.3 (continued)

Instructional approaches to enhance critical thinking	Description of instructional approach	Impact on Learning	Application to Employability
The ACER Critical Thinking Skill Development Framework (Heard et al., 2020)	The ACER critical thinking skill development framework describes critical thinking within core elements called "strands", which are then further categorized as sub-elements or aspects. A strand refers to the overarching conceptual category for framing the skills and knowledge addressed by critical thinking assessments" while an aspect refers to "the specific content category within a strand" (p. 11). Overall, the framework consists of three strands with each containing three aspects. The strands are as follows: 1. Knowledge construction 2. Evaluating reasoning 3. Decision making	Each strand has various impacts on learning. In Strand 1, knowledge construction involves reflective and evaluative engagement with information that is needed to make accurate sense of it. Its sub-elements indicate that it requires learners to identify gaps in knowledge, discriminate information, and identify patterns and make connections. The second strand refers to the thinking that is necessary to detect the validity of whatever information that is being absorbed. It consists of applying logic, identifying assumptions and motivations as well as justifying arguments. Lastly, Strand 3 necessitates being analytical and evaluative. Its aspects include identifying criteria for decision-making, evaluating opinions, and testing and monitoring implementation. Overall, this framework can be produced into a rubric where skill development levels of students are monitored through the various strands and aspects	This process is highly relevant as it enables students to be put in the learning process of knowledge creation, reflective engagement and skills development that is much required for future workplace

Results also suggested that exposure to collaborative learning among Whites who have relatively low levels of tested pre-college academic preparation is positively associated with gains in critical thinking skills.

6.7.3 Learning Intervention: K^mAlive Learning Application—Critical Reflection Functionality

In this section, the validated learning intervention of critical reflection will be discussed, and its insights embedded with its value proposition will be presented. In Fig. 6.4, the instructor's panel view for the critical thinking functionality is presented.

For the critical reflection functionality, you must first select the question. Once the question is selected, you can click the icon "Start Critical Reasoning". In this instance, since a MCQ type question has been inputted, you can see three options. From the students' panel, they can see this selected question and choose an answer. When the students submit the answers, at the bottom of the panel, you can see the students who have submitted the answer, the group they are from and the answer they have selected. Further to this, the explanation of why they have selected that answer, in this instance one of the three options, is provided. So, primarily this functionality of critical reflection requires students to not only answer the question but more imperatively to state why they have selected that answer. From the instructor panel, you can see the responses from the students of why they have selected the answer

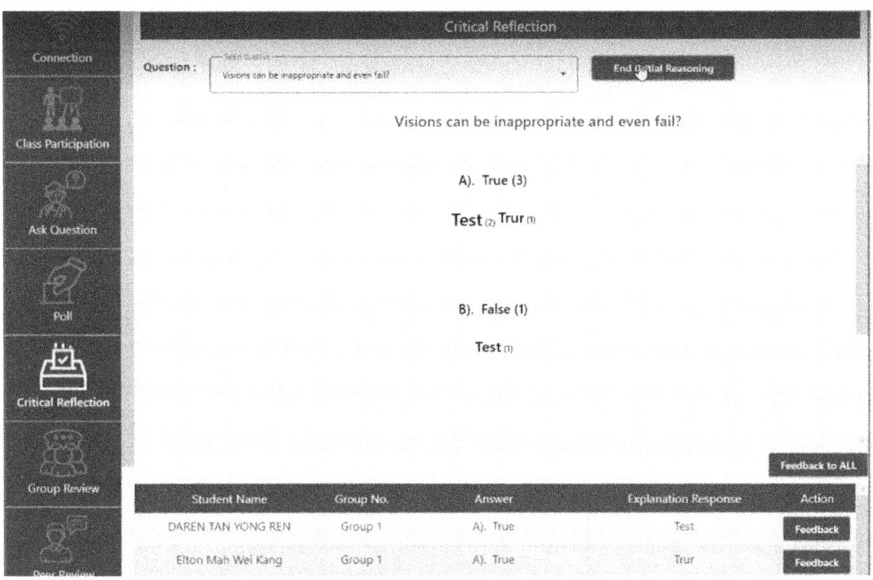

Fig. 6.4 Instructor's panel view: critical reflection functionality

and how many have selected that specific option, respectively. For this instance, you can see that two students have selected the option A and provided the explanation as "Influence" and one other student has selected option "B" and provided the explanation "More Power". You can give feedback to the students individually via pre-defined feedback that has already been pre-entered or able to send feedback to all the students by selecting the icon "Feedback to ALL". Alternatively, you can also just type in new feedback on the spot, for instance "Everyone has done well", and sent it to all where the students are able to receive it instantly. To end the session, you can click the icon "End Critical Reasoning".

6.8 Peer Evaluation

Peer evaluation, also known as peer assessment, is defined by Tillema (2010) as a process in which learners rate their peers. This is highly relevant and serves as an avenue for teachers as well as for students' development. Those in the learning process are involved in the appraisal of their own self-learning and its outcomes through joint collaboration. Students give due consideration to "the amount, level, value, worth, quality or success of learning from peers of similar status" (Topping, 1998, p. 250). Peer assessment can be viewed as a social appraisal process that includes giving and receiving feedback (Tillema, 2010), that aims to enhance the performances of learners. All things considered, interpersonal and interactional processes must be duly considered when examining peer evaluation as they play a vital role.

Along with self-assessment, peer evaluation is a crucial skill that enables students to self-monitor and self-regulate learning (Harrison, 2010). Self-assessment assists students in making judgements about the quality of their own work as well as their peers. This learning process enables students to comprehend the expectations in terms of quality for particular pieces of work and helps to understand how teachers generally assess them. Moreover, it assists teachers save time on the grading process although this will take some time as students' progress and develop their evaluation techniques. Peer evaluation may be used formatively to guide future learning, or it can be used as a summative assessment. Peer evaluation may also be used in cases where it may be challenging for teachers to determine the marks of individual group members (Cheng & Warren, 2005).

Evidence reports that the general perceptions of peer evaluation among students tend to be inclined towards positivity (Cheng & Warren, 2005; Stepanyan et al., 2009). However, it is necessary to give due consideration to the external factors that may influence this perception of peer evaluation. For example, Cheng and Warren cited Miller and Ng's work which found that Hong Kong students tended to have negative attitudes towards peer evaluation. The explanation was supported by subjectivity, unfairness, inadequate experience and being time consuming. On top of all that was the potential of loss of face which meant that students saw peer evaluation as a threat to both the evaluator and the person being evaluated. This concept is especially prevalent in Confucian Heritage Cultures. Hence, culture as an influencing element must be duly considered before implementing peer evaluation in the classroom.

Studies on peer review and evaluation have suggested that this learning intervention helps learners develop meta-cognitive skills such as communication skills, self-evaluation skills, observation skills and self-criticism (Havner & McDowell, 2007; Rajaram, 2021). Effects of peer evaluation vary with findings ranging from better attendance, learning gains, impact on the ability to self-assess and developing critical thinking, to no effects at all (Topping, 1998). This section will illustrate some examples of these findings though we need to acknowledge and note that the learning outcomes mentioned are not exhaustive.

One of the learning outcomes of peer evaluation as elaborated by Domingo et al. (2016) is improvement in students' teamwork. They found that at the individual level, the implementation of peer evaluation led to a negative relationship between students' midterm scores and the level of improvement in terms of teamwork effectiveness, meaning that the lower a student's score, the greater the improvement. This was supported by and explained with two complementary factors. Firstly, the lower the score received, the greater there is room for improvement. Therefore, with high quality feedback, low-performing students can improve much more. On the flip side, higher-performing members may be less motivated to improve since they know that they have already contributed a lot and are the backbone of the team. Therefore, high-performing members maintain their already good performance compared to lower-performing members who would potentially try and improve. Furthermore, a study from Donia et al. (2015) discovered that performance improvement also manifests when a student works with an entirely different group of peers in varying phases or circumstances.

Another learning outcome is the improvement of the quality of group presentations. A study by Babcock (1986) reported that by using rating forms to evaluate their peers, the quality and effectiveness of group presentations became much better than before they were used. According to the study, this approach became most effective when groups had multiple presentations throughout the semester and thus were able to show improvement and address the highlighted issues. Students also became more comfortable and less anxious during presentations they had later on. Despite that, this approach was still useful even when there was only one presentation to be done in the semester. Since they were informed of how they were being evaluated ahead of the presentation, students were able to well prepare for their presentations in an unique, different and more effective manner. Furthermore, evidence shows how peer evaluation enables active involvement with the rest of the class and therefore benefit the class as a whole and not just the group presenting. This learning process allows students to learn the knowledge taught better, and it also provides them with experience and exposure similar to a work town hall presentation that help them to make effective presentations in their future work.

Additionally, the practice of conducting multiple peer evaluations improves evaluation skills which may be crucial. Findings from a study by Brutus et al. (2013) of undergraduate business students found that repeated use of a standardized peer evaluation system was an effective way of increasing students' confidence in evaluating their peers while also improving the quality of evaluations provided. This process enables the manifestation of essential skills that are relevant to managerial practice since the peer evaluation system they used was similar to performance appraisal processes that are adopted in organizations. In a later study, Donia et al. (2015) found evidence that the competencies make students more effective contributors in teamwork at the university transfer to the workplace in the form of organizational citizenship behaviours. Further2011 correlations of efficacy to learning outcomes through peer assessment includes enhancing learning experience, assisting deep learning and enhancing the acquisition of critical thinking skills (Stepanyan et al., 2009). On a similar aspect, Gielen et al. (2011) advocated the goals of peer assessment where five aspects were highlighted, namely that serves as (a) social control tool; (b) assessment tool; (c) learning tool; (d) learning-how-to-assess tool; and (e) active participation tool.

6.8.1 *Meta-Analysis: Types of Peer Evaluation*

In today's teaching and learning scene, it is crucial to explicitly comprehend the learning outcomes of any approach adopted. In the context of peer review and assessment, the appropriateness and efficacy of different types of peer evaluation may differ across courses and programmes. If the peer assessment is used in a mathematics course, for instance, the appropriate criteria will illustrate an improvement in the mathematical competence of a student while in another subject domain, the criteria will be different (Gielen et al., 2011). For instance, in management courses, there may be more focus on presentation skills and group work skills while a linguistic course may focus more attention towards students' articulation and writing expressions. Based on evidence, peer evaluation can be categorized into five clusters, namely (a) behavioural; (b) content specific; (c) comparative; (d) reflective; and (e) feedback focused. These clusters describe the types of peer evaluation that may be adopted. Depending on the type of course that is being delivered, one type of peer evaluation may be more appropriate than the others. Table 6.4 presents the categorization of peer evaluation, its impact on learning and its application to future work.

6.8.1.1 Behavioural Peer Evaluation

Behavioural peer evaluation can be defined as students assessing their peers on soft skills and competencies. For example, one can evaluate their peer's ad hoc verbal articulation competencies as part of class participation, class discussion pitches and presentation skills in terms of verbal articulation and body, hand gestures, as part of nonverbal communication.

Ohland et al. (2012) developed a web-based instrument that collects and analyses self- and peer evaluation data. The instrument uses a behaviourally anchored

Table 6.4 Categorization of peer evaluation, its impact on learning and application to future work

Types of peer evaluation	Description of peer evaluation	Impact on learning	Application to future work
Behavioural	Evaluation focuses more on soft skills and competencies rather than explicit knowledge	Able to learn behavioural skills inclined and customized to the subject matter context	Awareness at the training phase enables students to navigate, respond and operate more speedily in real-life situations and circumstances in the future work settings
Content specific	Evaluation focuses on the accuracy and delivery of taught content	Detail orientation Critical thinking	Able to be equipped with the essential knowledge to get started while building on that foundation to grow progressively in work setting
Comparative	Evaluation aims to allow students to compare their work with that of their peers	Agile; growth and learning mindset; humility; builds confidence; receptive to changes	Mindset shift to be receptive to feedback; trained not to be too over-confident, but receptive to inputs for improvements
Reflective	Evaluation aims to get students to reflect on their own work and what they themselves can do to improve	Self-awareness and mindfulness	Builds the ability to be more socially and culturally mindful;
Feedback-focused	Evaluation aims to target students' ability to provide appropriate feedback to their fellow peers	Evaluation skills	Have confidence to be able to evaluate and provide concrete feedback, supported with rationale and why so in terms of the thought process adopted

rating scale to measure team member contributions in five core areas. The tool is useful for instructors who use team-learning methods where they require a relatively easy to use, simple instrument that is closely aligned with team member effectiveness. Generally, teams often have problems, such as, team members who prefer to work independently rather than collaboratively, poor communication, conflict, differences in team members' skills, motivation and goal levels, and free riding or social loafing. For instance, we recommend that for courses such as leadership, management, marketing and especially those that are more qualitative inclined, peer evaluations are already widely used, where teachers may want to place more emphasis on behavioural traits that will improve students' employability in the field.

6.8.1.2 Content-Specific Peer Evaluation

Content-specific peer evaluation is adopted when there is a heavy focus and importance placed on the contents of students' works. Hence, feedback provided by fellow peers will mainly be focused on contents and how the contents are delivered. Usually, grading occurs via strict guidelines provided by the instructor. This type of peer evaluation is generally inclined towards teachers instilling and advocating the importance of contents knowledge to be acquired by the students to eventually attain desirable grades. Hence, relevant evidence was further examined on peer grading to gain a better sense and comprehension of why content-specific peer evaluation is preferred or rather occurs.

In a study, Kerr et al. (1995) evaluated a 2-year programme involving peer grading of essays in a principles of microeconomics course. Results showed that students with less developed writing ability apparently benefited the most from the peer grading experience. From the study, we can deduce that peer grading was focused primarily on the content produced by the students. We can therefore include content-specific peer evaluation as a type of assessment teachers can use when they prefer to know if the students have understood what was taught or for them to improve the way students communicated their knowledge.

6.8.1.3 Comparative Peer Evaluation

The primary goal of comparative peer evaluation is to get students compare their work with that of their peers. This will allow them to learn from comparative evaluation and sensible judgement of their peers rather than just merely following random or ambiguous feedback or simply fixating to the scope of the rubrics.

Comparative judgement happens when evaluators are given a set of students' work and asking them to judge which one is better in their perspective (Jones & Alcock, 2014). As a result, the work can be ranked from best to worst. In this context, comparative judgement is advocated to be better than criterion-based approaches when it is used to examine elusive constructs that are central to a discipline and well understood by experts, but that are challenging to define accurately and comprehensively. The study provided the example of undergraduate mathematics as one type of course that could benefit from comparative judgement. To conclude, the study found that students performed well and were able to assess their peers' work reliably despite the lack of assessment criteria.

We can deduce that this nature of peer evaluation aims to empower or facilitate students to compare their work with their peers. It draws on principle that people are better at comparing one object against another more than they are at comparing an object against specified criteria. In a later study by Jones and Wheadon (2015), it was concluded that comparative judgement offers an approach for teachers and researchers who wish to implement peer evaluation in contexts in which inter-rater reliability and validity are necessary, such as in summative assessments.

6.8.1.4 Reflective Peer Evaluation

Unlike self-evaluation, peer evaluation allows students to potentially receive a less biased review of their work. Reflective peer evaluation is defined as a method of assessment that aims to get students to reflect on their own work and what they could do to improve. In the learning process, reflection plays a vital role and is beneficial in improving learning performance. Many higher education institutes are actively trying to enhance students' reflection skills so that they are able to deal with the fast-changing world they will enter when they graduate (Chen et al., 2009).

Studying in an online learning environment enables high-level prompts with high-quality observation, that could be classified as an element of peer evaluation, which had a moderating effect on students' reflection levels. No studies have found significant influence of peer feedback from the various levels of reflections. Thus, we can deduce that it is possible to have a type of peer evaluation that focuses on students' reflective abilities. Hence, if teachers want students to be better at reflecting and gain from this learning intervention's learning outcomes, using strategies and methods to engage in reflective peer evaluation may be most apt.

6.8.1.5 Feedback-Focused Peer Evaluation

While peer feedback does almost come with peer evaluation, feedback-focused peer evaluation places much greater emphasis on the delivery and type of feedback that each student gives rather than peer grading. Teachers could encourage elaborated feedback and even provide a structured and detailed manner in which feedback is presented.

Nelson and Schunn (2009) differentiate feedback into cognitive and affective categories. Cognitive feedback involves the content of the work and requires summarizing, specifying and explaining elements of the work under scrutiny. Affective feedback looks at the quality of work and uses affective language or nonverbal expressions to give praise and criticism. This can also be done in online learning environments through the use of emoticons. Aside this, in a study by Lu and Law (2011), they found that peer grading was not a significant predictor of project performance, and that positive affective feedback was related to the performance of those being evaluated. This study explains the benefits of online peer assessment in general and highlights the importance of specific types of feedback. All in all, these studies imply that there may be occasions where peer feedback is more effective than peer grading. Hence, a cluster explicitly focused on feedback-focused peer evaluation becomes a necessity.

6.8.2 Facilitation of Peer Evaluation

Studies have examined on how instructors may facilitate peer evaluation. Some findings include that of Stepanyan, Mather, Jones and Lusuardi's (2009), who strongly suggest that design, delivery techniques, facilitation methods and specific features of technology (such as those that allow anonymity) are necessary in order to create learning environments that will promote greater participation in peer evaluation. This section will examine some of these strategies and methods advocated.

Tillema's (2010) work relates to design and delivery techniques that enable the facilitation of peer evaluation. Tillema explains how framing features in the arrangement of peer evaluation may influence on how students first approach the process of appraising others' learning results. In the study, Tillema describes that a first set of framing features requires that the contextual arrangement of the assessment is specified. This includes:

> the why, that is, reasons for utilizing peer assessment; the what, that is, objectives, teaching areas and products/outcomes; when, that is, time; where, that is, place; and how, that is, is it supplementary to grading or required; compulsory or voluntary? (Tillema, 2010, p. 566)

Following that, a second set of framing features must be mindful of the interaction between peers during the appraisal. This involves the directionality in peer evaluation—meaning that peer evaluation could occur as a one-way interaction (from evaluator to the person being evaluated), reciprocal (peers assessing one another, potentially in pairs) and mutual (peers assessing every other peer). Furthermore, there may also be variation in the level of privacy (anonymous, confidential or public) and the nature of contact (distanced of face-to-face). Lastly, the third set of framing features refers to the composition of the peer group that provides feedback.

The use of technology is another way teachers may facilitate peer evaluation. Technology-facilitated peer evaluation aims to conduct peer assessment through the use of technologies. A meta-analysis done by Zheng et al. (2019) revealed that the use of technology-facilitated peer assessment along with the use of supporting strategies had positive and medium effects on students' learning achievements. Peer evaluation through the use of technology also allows for anonymity. Studies on anonymous peer evaluation provide advantages in terms of students' perceptions about the learning value of peer assessment, delivering more critical peer feedback, increased self-perceived social effects and a slight tendency for more performance, especially in higher education and with less peer assessment aids. This could be especially useful for classrooms where the majority of the students come from cultures that are sensitive to maintaining "face", as illustrated in an earlier section. However, anonymous assessment had a medium effect on learning achievements (Zheng et al., 2019), while results from another study are not consistent. In Panadero's and Alqassabb's (2019) study, they found that general anonymity seems to have mixed results when supporting peer assessment interventions' outcomes. Their results as well as previous discussions on this topic suggest that non-anonymous versions of peer assessment might be needed for deeper formative interventions. All in all, while the efficacy of anonymity is not clear, privacy is certainly a factor that teachers have to consider when facilitating peer evaluation.

Additionally, the practice of conducting multiple peer evaluations improves evaluation skills which may be crucial. Findings from a study by Brutus et al. (2013) of undergraduate business students found that repeated use of a standardized peer evaluation system was an effective way of increasing students' confidence in evaluating their peers while also improving the quality of evaluations provided. This process enables the manifestation of essential skills that are relevant to managerial practice since the peer evaluation system they used was similar to performance appraisal processes that are adopted in organizations. In a later study, Donia et al. (2015) found evidence that the competencies make students more effective contributors in teamwork at the university transfer to the workplace in the form of organizational citizenship behaviours. Further correlations of efficacy to learning outcomes through peer assessment include enhancing learning experience, assisting deep learning and enhancing the acquisition of critical thinking skills (Stepanyan, Mather, Jones & Lusuardi, 2009). On a similar aspect, Gielen et al. (2011) advocated the goals of peer assessment where five aspects were highlighted, namely that serves as (a) social control tool; (b) assessment tool; (c) learning tool; (d) learning-how-to-assess tool; and (e) active participation tool.

6.8.3 Learning Intervention: K^mAlive Learning Application—Peer Review Functionality

In this section, the validated learning intervention of peer review will be discussed, and its insights embedded with its value proposition will be presented. In Fig. 6.5, the instructor's panel view for the peer review functionality is presented.

For the functionality of peer review, you will be able to select the question for peer review under the drop-down menu. You can turn the timer on or off. If you decide to turn on, you can indicate the time that you wish to allocate. There are a couple of options here, you click the "student response" option so that students are allowed to respond from their mobile phones, tablets or iPads. You could tick off the "Cloud Display" to ensure the students' inputs are appearing in the screen for class discussion and you are able to select "Tabulated Statistics" if you would like to have the specific details presented in a tabulated manner. Next you can launch the question by clicking the icon "Activate Question" and the students will answer the question and submit their answers. You can then see the pie chart that indicates the outcome of students' responses. For instance, one of the students has indicated option A and similarly for option B that has been selected. The number of students and its corresponding percentage who have selected the option will be presented here. In the table, the students' name and their responses will be all listed here so that we could view all the answers that they have given. The next phase is to get to the peer review, for that, the first step is to click the icon "Stop Question", thereafter

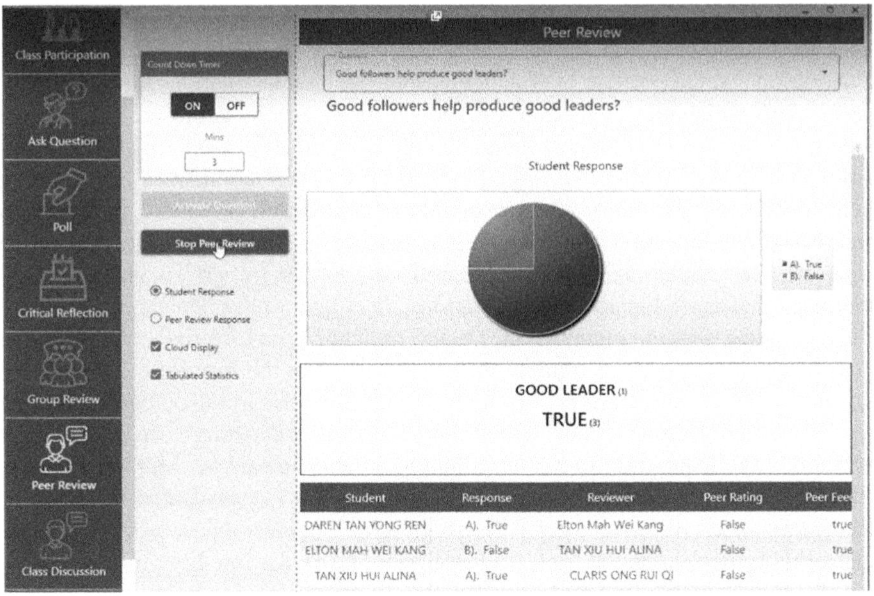

Fig. 6.5 Instructor's panel view: Peer review functionality

click the icon "Start Peer Review". At this juncture, each of the students' answers will be randomly exchanged with another student to be reviewed and for them to select their own answer as well as to provide feedback of their peers' answers. Once you click the "Start Peer Review" icon, you can see what happens in the students' panel, the students are asked to select the answer and based on their peers' answer provided they provide peer feedback. In the tabulated summary, you could see that there will be a reviewer. So in this table of tabulated statistics, you could view the inputs by the students and the peer reviewers under the varying columns. You can also view the cloud display here, where the common feedback responses by their peers are collated, captured and presented. If you have many students participating, you will potentially see that the common responses will be much larger in size. To end the session, you have to click the icon "Stop Peer Review".

6.9 Group Discussions and Group Review

Over the last two decades, the importance of group-related and collaborative learning has significantly increased in higher education. This trend is a result of the following reasons: (a) the rising demand for faculty members to be both productive researchers and quality teachers; (b) larger class sizes generally with classes often having 40 or more students; (c) the growing importance of technology and digitalization and the urgent need for cultural diversity training; and (d) finally, budget restrictions that has limited the funding of new programmes at many universities. Group learning can be described as individuals coming together as a group to verbally communicate or share their knowledge, where group discussion can be categorized as one of its elements (by Stenlund et al., 2017). In a teaching and learning context, the instructor will often introduce concepts or questions to be discussed or will ask student groups to analyse problems or carry out specific tasks. Group discussion is an effective active learning technique as alluded by Clinton and Kelly (2017) that enhances student engagement and learning.

Group assessments are largely connected with group work and discussions. Group assessment in higher education is often commonly implemented by dividing students into teams with each one working on an elaborate group project (Sadler, 2010). Upon completion of the assigned task, the work is assessed by the teacher, or by members of other groups, or by everyone involved. Grades awarded vary from awarding the same marks to all group members or apportioned marks based on each member's contribution to the work. If handled appropriately, quality, productivity and student satisfaction with group assessment can be high. On the other hand, if poorly handled, disputes may arise. This section focuses on group assessments in terms of group work evaluated by other groups. This method of group assessment can be labelled as group peer review (Odom et al., 2009), inter-group peer review (Kritikos et al., 2011), collaborative peer review (Rajaram, 2021) or group review (Rajaram, 2021). For the purpose of cohesion, we will be using the term group review throughout this section. Baruah, Ward and Jackson (2018, p. 4) analysed the effects of group review at the MSc Engineering Management programme at York in the UK. The benefits highlighted includes, (a) reduction of bias in grade allocations and peer assessments; (b) justified and fair grades for peer interactions; (c) multiple perspectives among team members; (d) team interaction and exchanges encouraged; (e) enhancement of group dynamics; (f) initiates a sense of responsibility among team members based on their roles, for instance team leader, devil advocate, scribe and so on; (g) motivates team for future group activities; and (h) deeper comprehension of academic grades and feedback.

Evidence states that both group discussion and peer review are intertwined and correlated to learning outcomes. Group discussion that comprises of collaboration among students promotes retention of course contents in a much better manner than via the mode of lectures alone (Clinton & Kelly, 2017). Evidence shows that even when all students struggle with deriving at answers or do not know the answer to a question posed by an instructor, the engagement within the group discussion eventually enhances the learning process as well as accuracy of reaching a common consensus to possible remedies. The opportunity for students to explain the required information to each other among them enables a much better understanding of learning resources. Moreover, interacting in groups enables the development of critical thinking, independent learning and collaborative skills. Research conducted by Pollock et al. (2011) reported positive learning outcomes of group discussions, where not only it helps to improve students' oral communication skills but also better learning outcomes. Group discussions are also viewed as an active learning technique that promotes critical thinking and deep learning. Research shows that students benefit from the effects of group discussions, especially in larger classes. But in the flip side, smaller groups tend to stimulate more equal discussion participation from students from diverse ethnic backgrounds and equipped with a wider range of previous academic achievements.

In terms of group review, Miller and Emery's (2018) study on collaborative peer review has shown benefits when implemented in the classroom. This includes students embracing the peer response process, improving the level of quality of their projects as well as report writing, and gaining practice at receiving and responding to peer feedback in a way that is disjointed from their grades. Imperatively, these skills are viewed as critical to the future workplace. Students' reactions to feedback go from defensiveness to having then being welcomed and viewing feedback affirmatively as they gain more experience and exposure. Other benefits include greater speed of students in completing their initial drafts of projects and more engagement in revisions with better changes that improves the overall project's quality. Group reviews may also be more useful in collectivist cultures where peer reviews threaten students' losing face or being embarrassed by being challenged. In a study by Thanh and Gillies (2010) that comprises of Vietnamese undergraduate students, the study's results showed that the students resisted and refused to participate in intra-group peer assessment as they were not confident in exchanging feedback directly and on a face-to-face context. However, inter-group peer assessment or group review was more interesting for the students because they were able to avoid direct conflict with their peers and had group members who were able to make them save their face with multiple varying views. Thus, the students in this situation had more opportunities to give and receive formative feedback. This study also illustrated the relevant correlations to learning outcomes and the degree to which they are influenced and affected by other influencing factors.

6.9.1 Meta-Analysis: Approaches to Group Discussion and Its Impact to Learning

Tables 6.5 and 6.6 present the categorization of group discussion and group review, its impact on learning and its application to future work.

6.9.2 Facilitation of Group Discussion and Group Review

We should emphasis and acknowledge the fact on how teachers facilitate group discussions and group reviews which is vital to fully and effectively reap the benefits of both. In this section, we will discuss some of these strategies and their resultant outcomes.

Table 6.5 Categorization of group discussion, its impact on learning and its application to future work

Approaches to group discussion	Description	Impact on learning	Application to future work
Face-to-face (Behrens & Kret, 2019; Meyer, 2019)	Traditionally, face-to-face discussions require students to be physically present in a designated learning environment. Behrens and Kret (2019) suggest that face-to face contact is an important predictor of cooperation. They highlight how face-to-face contact makes nonverbal communication more conspicuous	In terms of learning, Meyer (2019) found that face-to-face discussions allow students to seize emotions, feelings and tones of specific exchanges which allow them to better remember and form memories that may help them with their learning. Additionally, their study agrees with most other literature that a clear majority of students tend to favour face-to-face discussions compared to online discussion which have been gaining traction in recent times	The skills of relating to emotions, sense behaviours and verbal tonations are useful for students to deal with their future colleagues and clients. The exposure at this phase enables them to learn, unlearn and relearn from their mistakes that make them more confident to apply these acquired practice-oriented skills in the actual circumstances in their future employment
Computer-mediated / Online (Olaniran et al., 1996)	Computer-mediated communication (CMC) is any human communication that occurs through two or more electronic devices. Similarly online communication facilitates human connection through the Internet. Olaniran et al. (1996) suggest that CMC can be used for collaborative and decision-making activities in the learning environment. Thus, this includes the facilitation of group discussions through such means	Olaniran et al. (1996) found that CMC enabled students to develop more students to ideas when compared to groups of students who only worked face to face. Other benefits they report include greater and more equalized participation among group members as well as reduced impact of evaluation apprehension due to the fact that participants were less likely to feel personally offended by comments and criticism. The latter point may be especially significant in today's globalized world, where students come from different cultural backgrounds and thus have different perceptions of communication	The ability to work in inter- and intra-teams virtually and via varying online/e-platforms is a skill that is very essential with the highly globalized and mobile work environment in today's context and the future

(continued)

Table 6.5 (continued)

Approaches to group discussion	Description	Impact on learning	Application to future work
Gamified (Ding et al., 2017, 2018)	Ding et al. (2018) refer to gamification as the incorporation of game elements into a non-game activity to make the activity more motivating and engaging. This includes group discussions which was the target of Ding, Kim and Orey (2017) who developed a gamified online discussion tool called "gEchoLu". Game elements such as a badge system and experience points were included in this tool	In both studies, it was found that this gamification approach had a positive effect on student engagement. More specifically, the gEchoLu tool had positive effects on student behavioural engagement, emotional engagement, and cognitive engagement (Ding et al., 2017). It was also found that gamification impacted medium achievers the most (Ding et al., 2018)	The skill of cognitive, emotional and behavioural engagement is vital as students take on leadership positions in their employment. Such exposure only makes them reflect and pick up skills which they could leverage on and hone further in their work context in the future
Reflective (Tsang, 2011)	According to Tsang (2011), group reflective discussion is a pedagogy that is embedded in a multitude of teaching and learning approaches such as peer learning and collaborative learning. This refers to when group members reflect together. Tsang's study involved two steps. First the students were told to share a critical incident that had occurred with a small group, and the group chose one to reflect on. Subsequently, there would be another reflective discussion where the instructor would choose a critical incident to discuss	The key benefits of reflective group discussions as highlighted by Tsang (2011) included peer learning, peer and/or tutor support and multi-perspective critical thinking. Reflective discussions were appealing to students as they were interactive, supportive and multi-perspective	The mindset shift and skill of embracing diverse perspectives embedded with critical thinking allow students to be equipped with the capability that is vital for their future work. The training through such methodology allows them to identify their areas of weakness and provide them opportunity to have them addressed before the actual work setting in the near future

(continued)

Table 6.5 (continued)

Approaches to group discussion	Description	Impact on learning	Application to future work
Small group (Al Jawad & Abosnan, 2020)	Small group discussion refers to dividing the classroom into small groups in order to achieve specific learning objectives	Results from Al Jawad and Abosnan's study at the English language department at Faculty of Arts and Science Kufrah—Benghazi University proved that the mean performance-speaking skills of the students who experienced small group discussion had a better technique than those exposed to large group discussion	The exposure and training provided to enhance on the students' speaking skills is crucial in negotiating, engaging others with tact and improving the working relationships in their future workplace
Cross-cultural (Jones, 1999; Young & Schartner, 2014)	Jones' (1999) work tackled the differences in levels of academic group discussion tied to cultural factors. Cross-cultural discussions occur when group members come from various cultural backgrounds. For example, Jones highlighted non-native English-speaking students and their struggles with oral communication when it comes to group discussion. He suggests several approaches teachers can adopt in order to facilitate cross-cultural group discussions—"One is to acquaint them, before or at an early stage of their studies, with the ethos of the tutorial or seminar in a Western English-speaking country. The other is to build up their interactional skills and command of the discourse norms that they will need inorder to become equal partners with NS students" (p. 249)	By adopting these approaches, teachers can enable equal and active participation among students of diverse backgrounds. Additionally, Young and Schartner (2014) found that students who engage in cross-cultural communication had a significantly greater performance in various measures of academic achievement compared to students in a similar programme but lacked a specific focus on cross-cultural communication. They also found that students experienced increased self-confidence and a greater sense of understanding and open-mindedness	The skills and knowledge to communicate and deal in a cross-cultural and diverse climate and environment is vital. This skill of cultural intelligence plays a pivot role in their future work setting with an increased probability of a diverse workforce

Table 6.6 Categorization of Group Review, its impact on learning and its application to future work

Approaches to Group Review	Description	Impact on Learning	Application to Future Work
Online	Rajaram's (2019) research and practice-oriented innovative applied work on the 5 activity sequences created by "doKumaran" tool or "dKT" tool serves as powerful validated group review and collaborative learning support system. The "dKT" tool is a functionality feature integrated within the LAMS system that enables teachers to create powerful and collaborative learning designs on real-time document. It allows students to collaborate on a single or multiple documents in "real time" attaining a learning outcome while influencing each other's thoughts. Five activity sequences have been created in the environment of LAMS together with the use of newly created "doKumaran" or "dKT" tool. These five sequences allow for: (a) intra-group collaborative activities; (b) peer review activities; (c) inter-group collaborative activities; (d) jigsaw activities; and (e) unstructured and other collaborative activities	The activity support system allows an instructor to maximize effective use of class time in a flipped classroom design, through assisting the instructor in coordinating learning activities, organizing student responses and scaffolding more effective class discussions. Through the use of the activity support system, students are expected to: (a) be more engaged in their learning process; (b) have more opportunities to learn collaboratively; (c) facilitate more opportunities for engaged students to interact with peers and instructors; (d) provide marginally engaged students with more meaningful activities to maintain their engagement; (e) improve their critical thinking and higher-order cognitive thinking skills; (f) minimize disruptions between learning activities to maintain student engagement; and (g) scaffold activity models for instructors who are especially new and inexperience to flipped classrooms	The ability and skill to collaborate with high efficacy via online becomes an essential skill at workplace today. Such "know-hows" i.e. digitalization literacy in an online collaborative setting serve as useful and required skill to be acquired

(continued)

Table 6.6 (continued)

Approaches to Group Review	Description	Impact on Learning	Application to Future Work
Technology enabled	Rajaram (2021)'s research and practice-oriented applied work on the learning intelligence (LQ) application comprises two of the functionalities, namely group review and group discussion K^mAlive (pronounced as "come alive") is designed using an evidence-based framework that focuses primarily on learning culture, social engineering and collaborative, active pedagogical learning design that can be team based or individualized. The learning App enables monitoring, assessing and storing of learners' individual, peer intra- and inter-group contributions by engaging students in real time. The data analytics with report generation embedded within enables	The K^mAlive Learning Intelligence (LQ) Application enables (a) evaluation of individualized and team-based collaborative contributions real time, with certain functionalities via assessment rubrics; (b) interpretation of meaningful and useful analysis through data analytics which enables extraction of useful students' performance information The primary functionalities and its core role are as follows: (1) group review—enable intra-group evaluation and inter-group peer evaluation by instructor and students; (2) group discussion—allow groups to discuss and collate their inputs; (3) class participation—monitor and assess learners' participation real time; (4) peer	The multi-levelled and higher-order learning intelligence (LQ) skills that are being exposed via this learning application prepares students for the future workforce. This combination of these skills and "know-hows" becomes the forefront skills and applied knowledge that is expected of future employers

(continued)

Table 6.6 (continued)

Approaches to Group Review	Description	Impact on Learning	Application to Future Work
	easy and quick extraction of learners' performance	review—facilitate peer review and enable peer feedback; (5) ask questions: enable learners to pose questions, clarifications, comments or add-ons; (6) critical reflection—Train learners on critical thinking skills; (7) polling—collate and present the statistical output of the class inputs; (8) leadership and human skills development—enable learners to enhance their leadership, communication, presentation, human skills and competencies; (9) data analytics—the learners' performance can be extracted easily, quickly and presented via the report generation functionality; and (10) grouping—automate group forming with specific criteria	
Face to face (Kritikos et al., 2011)	The traditional approach of working in groups with individuals directly in person	Students became more engaged, confident, and motivated, and developed a range of self-directed, life-long learning skills	This is always an essential skill that requires consistent and continuous exposure so as to gather more diverse experiences. Such exposure only allows students to hone their skills through developing their self-confidence to deal with individuals of varying personalities and how to enhance the efficacy in such circumstances or situational contexts

Teachers can facilitate group discussions or group work by assigning students into teams that comprise of an assigned group size. Instructors should form small groups of three to five students that give due considerations to students' characteristics such as gender and race when planning formal group work (Wilson et al., 2018). Rightfully, the group comprises of members who use different problem-solving approaches. This diversity has proven to result in rather a balanced collaboration. An alternative method to facilitate group discussion is to allow students to choose their own teams in more informal settings. When facilitating group discussions, teachers should be aware of varying factors that may potentially impact the effectiveness and efficacy of group discussions in different environments. For instance, it could be simply the number of team members in a group.

For facilitating group reviews, the most typical approach instructors adopt is to get students in a group to exchange their work with another group for a stipulated period to review. Subsequently, each group will make suggestions, comments and critique the other group's work. After stipulated time is up, the work is returned to the original group and students will have time to read, reflect on the comments from the other team and modify their work accordingly. This can be done physically where students move from their station to another group's station to view their work. It can also be done online through learning platforms, for instance the "dKT" collaborative tool with 5 authentically created activity sequences by Prof Kumaran RAJARAM, from Nanyang Business School, Nanyang Technological University, Singapore (Rajaram, 2019).

Another approach that teachers may adopt is by using a framework designed by Miller and Emery (2018) where project teams and review teams are considered as separate entities. They experimented this framework on engineering students who are assessed in part by team projects. Each student has been assigned a project team that they work with over a full semester. Concurrently, each member of the team is also assigned to a different review team for peer response activities. There must be careful preparation before the first review session. There are strict criteria to adhere to in the formation of review teams where there are several benefits in adhering to these guidelines advised. Firstly, since no two students in a review team would be in the same project team, it becomes less likely that students misuse their time with their review team to discuss their own group projects. Additionally, while each member of the review team individually reviews one project, the team members will collectively review the breadth of other students' work to evaluate and identify strong suits and downfalls of other projects. These will enable the students to involve to bring back new ideas, thoughts and apply it to their own projects. All in all, we believe that this approach although requires more time and preparation, it will especially be beneficial in summative group work where issues revolving around bias may be prevalent. Hence, this could be potentially innovative alternative to traditional methods of group review.

6.9.3 Learning Intervention: K^mAlive Learning Application—Group Discussion and Group Review Functionality

In this section, the validated learning intervention of group discussion and group review will be discussed, and its insights embedded with its value proposition will be presented. In Fig. 6.6, the instructor's panel view for the group review functionality is presented, and in Figs. 6.7a and b, the instructor's panel view for the group discussion functionality is presented.

For the "Group Review" functionality, its primary function is enabling group or groups to evaluate another presenting group. For instance, if there are total of seven groups, assumed if one group assigned to perform a pitch or do a presentation, the other six groups including the instructor will be able to evaluate the presenting group. First, you need to select the group to be reviewed, for instance, in this case, let identify Group One to be reviewed. The description can be spelled out as, for example, "Review for Group 1″. You can turn "ON" the timer as follows and input, for example, 3 min for the group to have the pitch or presentation to be done. You can tick the box that states"Show Teacher Score In Attendee Window" so that the score can be seen in the instructor's participation panel. Firstly, you need to download the sample file, once you click the icon "Download Sample File", you can see the first file name as "Assessment Rubrics" and save type as the CSV file. Decide the location that you wish to save in your PC or laptop and click the "Save" button.

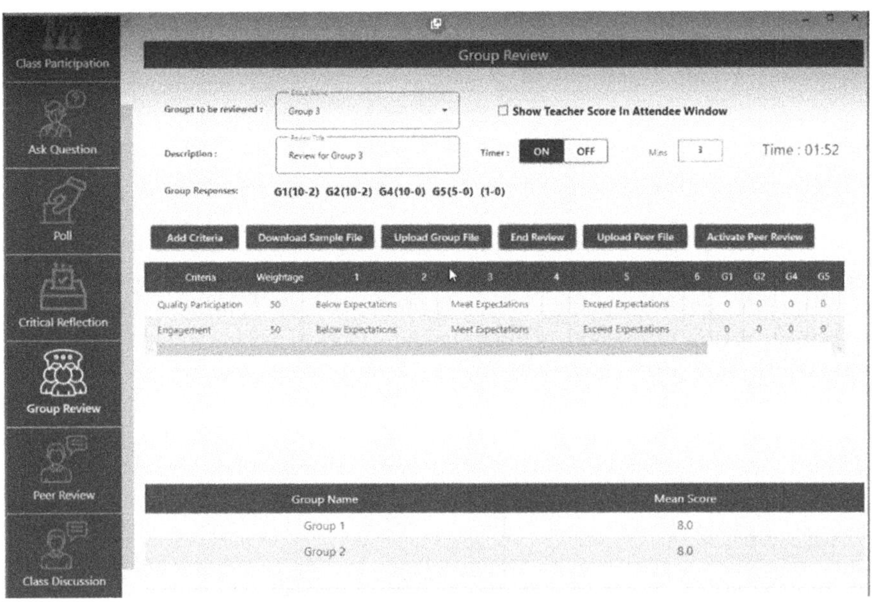

Fig. 6.6 Instructor's panel view: Group Review functionality

Fig. 6.7 Instructor's panel view: Group Discussion functionality

You will see the pop-up small screen with the text that states, "file downloaded successfully", click "O.K." You now see another pop-up window where you see the file name as "Assessment Rubrics—Peer Review" and save type as CSV file. Click the "Save" button. You will see the pop-up small screen with the text that states, "file downloaded successfully', click "O.K." Basically two files have been downloaded in your PC or Laptop. Next you click the icon "Upload Group File", and then you select the "Assessment Rubrics" which has been downloaded earlier, when you click open, you could see the. This rubric can be adjusted or the inputs changed and inputted by the instructor. In this instance, there are two rubrics, one that evaluates" Quality Participation" and other on "Engagement", so there's an equal weightage of 50 50 percent and the scale ranges from 1 to 6 but the instructors can input more columns if they will like to extend the scale rating to 10. For instance, in this case, we have "Below Expectations", "Meet Expectations" and "Exceed Expectations" over a rating scale of 1 to 6. The groups are presented here and instructor's scoring is indicated here. To get started on the group review, you have to click the icon "Activate Group Review". Now the students will be able to evaluate. In this instance, Group 1 is to be reviewed by the rest of the groups. What you see here is Group 2 has evaluated Group 1, this indicates that there are 5 group members but only one has evaluated similarly for Group 3, so on and so forth. This is an indication of how many group members have evaluated. This also shows all of the participating group responses. You can have a sense of the number of groups and its respective group members who have been evaluated. To end the session, you can click the icon "End Review". You can see the Mean Score appears, in this instance, Group 2 has evaluated Group 1 and the mean score is 5/6 for each of these rubrics. You as the instructor can also evaluate the group which provides your expert assessment that could be compared to the students' peer's assessment. Assuming we have Group 2 to be reviewed, we can replicate the same procedure, where we activate the group review, so once it's activated, you can see of what the students will be seeing and how they will do their evaluation accordingly. They are to select the rubrics in accordance and evaluate their group members in Group One. You can see the indication comes up for Group 1, where there are a total of five members, two of them have been reviewed. To end the session, you can click the icon "End Review". Immediately, you could see that the scores for the evaluation would appear in the table. Let us now move on to the next aspect which is the peer review. First, the instructor must upload the peer review file so click the icon "Upload peer review file", a pop-up window appears, select the "peer assessment rubrics" that you have uploaded in your system earlier and click "open". The assessment rubrics is now made available. You can now launch the peer review by clicking the icon "activate peer review". You can now see that each of the team members are able to evaluate their peers based on the rubrics. If you look at the bottom of the table, you can view the details. Once the students have completed the review, you as the instructor can click the "End Review" icon to complete the session.

Next, let us examine the group discussion functionality.

For the class discussion functionality, you can select the question. Upon the selection of the question, you have a choice to choose from the two options of the answer type, namely "Individual" or "Group". If the option "Individual" is selected, every individual team member in the group will be able to answer; if the option "Group" is selected, then only the leader of the group will be able to answer on behalf of the group. So, let us select the "answer type" option to be individual. You can then turn "ON" the timer and for this instance lets input 3 min for the discussion. You can commence the session by clicking the icon “Start Class Discussion”. Upon the commencement of the session, the timer starts to count down. You can see from the student’s panel the question appears with possible options of answers. All students in the group are allowed to participate since option for the answer type selected was “Individual”. The students can answer the question as well as provide the comments or feedback under the feedback column that is available. Once the student has made the necessary inputs, it appears in instructor panel. All these answers that have been inputted by the students are collated. If the answers are longer, you can adjust the columns from the top row, so that the contents presented will be visible. To end the session, you can click the icon “End Group Discussion” so that it stops the group discussion inputs from all of the team members from the groups. The next sub-functionality will be class discussion review. This functionality allows intra-group review, for example, group 1’s answers will be reviewed by group 3, so on and so forth. For this feature, only an assigned representative from the group or the leader has to input the necessary on behalf after the group discussion. To commence this, you can click the icon “Start Class Discussion review”. You can see from the students’ panel that they are to view their peers’ response, select their choice of answer and then provide the required feedback. With a random swap via an intra-group approach, for example, “Group 1” answer could go to “Group 3” or rather “Group 2” and “Group 2” answer can come to “Group 1” and so on. They able to see each other’s answer and start reviewing the answers accordingly. We could see students are reviewing the answers of their peers and giving their feedback. Hence, you can see which group is reviewing, so for “Group 1’s” answer, “Group 2” is reviewing, and they have given their answer and also the feedback based on the evaluation of “Group 1’s” answer. All these are collated to provide the instructors a clearer view to facilitate a class discussion based on the groups answer as well as the groups who have reviewed them. To end the discussion, you can click the icon “Stop Group Discussion Review”. Till now we have been going through the individual contributions from all group members in a group where it is reviewed by another intra-group at a group level. If we select the “Answer Type” as “Group”, then only the group leaders of the groups are able to answer the question. This assists in terms of collaboration among the team members to discuss together as a group and decide on a particular answer unanimously and then provide feedback based on that answer they have selected and submitted. Thereafter, you can then end the session by clicking the “End Group Discussion” and click the icon “Start Group Discussion Review”, where the above explained for the “individual” answer type applies here as well.

6.10 Leadership, Human and Soft (Employability) Skills and Competencies

Leadership and soft skills competencies within the higher education context can manifest itself in both faculty and students. In this section, we will focus on its impact on students, how instructors can facilitate its development as well as why these skills are vital for students' development.

According to Davies et al. (2001), on the study performed on UK Higher Education Institutes, there has been a shift in focus from developing administration to management to leadership skills in students. Management is inclined towards coping with complexity while leadership, by contrast, is about dealing and coping with change (Davies et al., 2001). Therefore, there is no surprise that higher education institutes have emphasized and re-iterated that leadership development is a vital part of their curriculum, especially with the rapid and evolving developments in globalization, technology, sustainability, climate change and societal aspects. These interventions have caused much higher demand and the need for leadership in the workforce to deal with complex and challenging problems that require innovative solutions (Campbell et al., 2012) and perhaps a vision with a transformative approach.

Dempster and Lizzio (2007) reported on young people's perceptions of leadership as an appropriate response to a social context that is characterized by high levels of cultural change and social pluralism. This is largely due to the inclusion and social cooperation which have become even more challenging and complex than ever before. In this new context, leadership skills can now be defined as the ability to self-regulate in facing changes and challenges, and to be able to successfully navigate diversity and differences. Diversity, where factors such as gender, race and sociocultural aspects are to be duly considered when we examine the efficacy of leadership in context. A study of students enrolled in American colleges found that women's leadership competence was higher than men's although men are reported to have more self-confidence in their leadership abilities when compared to women (Dugan & Komives, 2007). Evidence also shows that African American students often secured top scores across the values of the social change model of leadership while Asian American often had the lowest scores. Hence, it is important for instructors to be mindful and adequately aware of the influences that may impact the development of student leadership.

Alongside with leadership skills, there has been a great emphasis on the need to foster soft skills in students. Politicians, educational researchers and corporate practitioners have all stressed the importance of non-academic attributes such as the ability to cooperate, communicate and solve problems (Chamorro-Premuzic et al., 2010). Soft skills are also labelled or referred to as employability skills. Unlike academic knowledge which is subject based, content specific and often formally assessed, soft skills are made up of a wide set of competencies that are separate from yet developed by formal curricula and is seldom assessed explicitly. Soft skills can be described as abilities and personal attributes that can be used within the wide range of working environments that graduates operate in throughout their lives. Although the specific set of attributes reported by institutions and governments may differ, there is growing acceptance that soft skills enable students to achieve both academic and occupational goals.

Higher education institutes need to understand the impact of both leadership and employability/soft skills on learning outcomes that will make them understand the evolving need for increased facilitation in the development of both. While the outcomes may vary from institute to institute, some illustrations are provided in this section.

One example is from Deng et al. (2019) who explored the influence of leadership experience in multiple periods, including primary school, junior high school, senior high school and college. They collected data from Chinese undergraduate students and discovered several pieces of information. Firstly, they found that being a student leader can enhance academic performance in both the short and long term. They also found that previous leadership experience, in particular from primary school, most effectively improves contemporary academic achievement. Additionally, they found that specific leadership positions such as being a class monitor were generally more effective in promoting academic performance when compared to other positions. Lastly, despite reducing study time, being a student leader improves learning consciousness which ultimately improves overall academic performance. Chamorro-Premuzic et al. (2010) conducted three studies to examine the importance and development of 15 different soft skills that focuses on the correlation of soft skills to learning outcomes. One study found that IQ was negatively associated with soft skills ratings. This meant that individuals with higher cognitive ability were less likely to believe that soft skills played a significant role in attaining academic excellence or an attractive job upon graduating. They rationalize that lower cognitive ability students would compensate for their poorer reasoning skills using soft skills. The other two studies found the importance placed and improving soft skills predicted academic performance and accounted for the effects of personality on academic performance. It also revealed higher soft skills ratings in "softer" or less technical courses such as humanities. A more recent study by Obilor (2019) examined the influence of soft skills on students' academic achievement. He found that skills such as time management, problem-solving, communication, self-motivation, conscientiousness and willingness to learn influenced the academic achievement of students to a large extent. This is further supported by the results of a study by Mohamed, Abozeid, Mohammed and Ahmed (2019) which found a positive correlation between soft skills in 4th year nursing students and their academic achievements.

6.10.1 Meta-Analysis: Leadership, Human and Soft (Employability) Skills Development, Impact on Learning and Application to Future Work

Tables 6.7 and 6.8 present the leadership, human and soft (employability) skills development, its impact on learning and application to future work.

Table 6.7 Presents the leadership skills development, its impact on learning and application to future work

Leadership		
Impact on Learning	Description	Application to Future Work
Confidence and motivation (Gannouni & Ramboarison-Lalao, 2016)	The authors found that leadership experience elevates students' confidence and motivation which results in an inner drive to have high aims and to persevere and achieve their goals	The elements of confidence and motivation is vital for students to identify the specificities and build up the explicit aspects of these skills. It makes them know how to deal and navigate with the evolving challenges
Compassion and Empathy (Gialamas, Grigoropoulos, Pelonis & Cherif, 2020)	The authors found that students have a higher likelihood to be prepared to assume desirable leadership roles in their own learning and in their current and future lives should leadership skills be infused with ethics, empathy and compassion. Developing resilience, kindness and empathy leads to mental strength as well	Skills such as compassion, empathy and grit are vital as it assists students to deal with unprecedented circumstances and challenging, complex and demanding work situations. To ride through such phases, these skills are even more imperative than the technical competency to stay afloat and navigate through such phases
Cooperation (Thomson, 2012)	When asked what they learnt from leadership activities, primary and secondary school students in an English school responded that they learnt to play a part in a team and to work cooperatively. They also gained confidence. The authors suggest that this could benefit student-led monitoring and formative assessments	The concept of teamwork and cooperation is vital as students have to know how to win over and buy in individuals with different mindsets, values and beliefs. More importantly, the ability to get consensus from all members to work on a common ground or goal. That requires support with cooperation, although members in the team can agree to disagree, but willing to work towards the common good for the organization in their future work

(continued)

Table 6.7 (continued)

Leadership		
Impact on Learning	Description	Application to Future Work
Communication (Bialek & Lloyd, 1998)	The authors examined the impact of student leadership experiences on the personal and professional lives of graduates several years after leaving the institute. Among many other themes, it was found through interviews with the alumni that personal and professional interpersonal communication skills improved due to previous student leadership experience. This manifested as a heightened sense of appreciation for and the ability to work with a diverse group of people	The ability to negotiate, pitch it with quality yet fitting in the context, buy-in, engage and win over conversation in unprecedented and new circumstances cannot be under-estimated
Creative problem-solving (van der Meer et al., 2019)	The authors found that peer leadership experiences positively impacted creative problem-solving the most. This component includes items that relate to problem-solving skills such as critical thinking skills, decision-making skills, creativity and adaptability. It also includes items that involve innovative or creative problem-solving processes such as analysing a problem from a new perspective, bringing together information learned from different places, creating innovative approaches to complete a task	The ability to resolve issues in a creative manner is a skill well received by employers. Hence, the development of such skills serve as a competitive edge for their future work standing

(continued)

Table 6.7 (continued)

Leadership		
Impact on Learning	Description	Application to Future Work
Reflective Peer-Leadership Feedback: Leadership Development (Rajaram, 2021)	This research by Rajaram (2021) takes an effective intervention known to elicit leadership competencies growth through a reflective peer review analysis after every activity-based learning. The intervention aims to prepare students for the development of leadership competencies and, by extension, leadership in a university business course. Rather than impress upon students the importance of psychological construct such as leadership directly, the project sets the stage for students to converge on the realization of leadership competencies for themselves. Social psychological interventions provoke individuals to address potential cognitive blocks that may inhibit positive learning behaviours	This intervention helps students develop non-content-based skills with various types of activity-based learning. This will be useful in ingraining and cultivating such variety of skills in a more impactful manner that becomes part of their "DNA" while they pursue their education. As such, when they transit to their future workplace, these skills have become part of their habitual cognitive and behavioural traits

Table 6.8 Presents the human, soft (employability) skills development, its impact on learning and application to future work

Soft Skills Competencies		
Types of Soft Skills	Impact on Learning	Application to Future Work
Critical thinking (Walker & Finney, 1999)	Students suggest that one of the most useful outcomes of critical thinking is the development of self-awareness through reflection. Self-awareness relates to their perception of where their skills lie and becoming more cognizant of how they learn. As a result, this manifests as a more thoughtful, enquiring and open-minded approach, in both professional and personal life	The trait of self-reflection helps students to easily understand where they could improve on their weakness and address those aspects speedily. This is a much-required skill that future employers will value as they want their knowledge workers to be continually putting their best to optimize their deliverables
Creativity (de Alencar & de Oliveira, 2016)	Participants in the study agree that creativity is relevant in higher education especially in graduate programmes. Reasons for the importance placed on creativity include the fact that it helps one organize and classify thoughts, facilitates innovation and necessarily is meeting societal demands	Creativity is a vital behavioural trait that needs to be ingrained as an ethos. The element should be intervened as part of an assessment process in context to varying specialization. This skill serves as a competitive edge and value-adding for students to function in their future workplace
Goal setting (Friedman & Mandel, 2009)	In accordance with the goal setting theory, individuals who set goals are more likely to perform better than those who do not. By simply setting challenging goals and partaking in the goal setting process, one can positively influence performance. Other factors such as goal specificity, relevancy, challenge, commitment, participation, goal feedback, and peer competition also improve performance	The varying exposure given in the goal setting is essential. This serves a training ground to build students' confidence and grit in comprehending the practice challenges in having them executed while working around potential challenges. The exposure and experience serve to level them up quicker when the students are operating in the actual work environment to produce deliverables

(continued)

Table 6.8 (continued)

Soft Skills Competencies		
Types of Soft Skills	Impact on Learning	Application to Future Work
Adaptability (Collie et al., 2016)	Adaptability refers to the degree to which students are able to effectively cope and deal with changes. The study revealed that adaptability was linked with higher positive behavioural engagement that includes factors such as persistence, planning and task management. It is also linked with lower negative behavioural engagement such as disengagement and self-handicapping	A critical skill that is highly sought after by employers. In today's rapid evolving climate and work environment, the one aspect which is expected from future workforce is agility and adaptability
Compassion and empathy (Bove, 2019, p. 31)	The study found that empathy can reduce anti-social, revenge, discrimination and unethical behaviours in service settings. The author also discovered that empathy can also improve value-in-context experiences for users of service innovations	These people-related skills are vital to build good work relationships and develop deeper authentic ties with clients and corporate partners

6.10.2 Training of Leadership, Human and Soft (Employability) Skills

There has been increasing emphasis and focus placed on developing leadership in higher education students (Dugan & Komives, 2007; Rajaram, 2021). Many trends have amalgamated in the recent few years that have resulted in support for a new focus in developing critical leadership outcomes in students. This movement has gained a much-increased momentum in recent years as the prominence of accountability for learning has increased and the employability demands have been rapidly evolving. Some of these trends include the development of new leadership frameworks or models for higher education, the empowerment of social identity groups and their distinct leadership needs. As a result, the techniques for leadership training and development have evolved and transformed over the years. This section will discuss some of these strategies as well as explicit methodologies on how to develop leadership, human and soft (employability) skills in students. Educators in general need to comprehend such techniques well enough so as to be better able to effectively and appropriately facilitate the development of these skills in their students.

Training leadership can be performed through leveraging the appropriate grounded theoretical frameworks which can be applied to curricula. One such framework developed by Skalicky et al. (2018) provides guidelines to support quality assurance across the wide range of leadership development strategies in higher education. It was labelled as the developing and supporting student leadership (DaSSL) framework, which was part of a multi-institutional research project led by the University of Tasmania. The goal of the framework is to assist programme developers and coordinators to plan for and support student leadership development in a more scaffolded, organized and well-intentional manner. Student leadership includes experiences that provide students with the opportunity to learn about, experience and/or display leadership qualities. The four key components of the framework are: (a) a reflection tool and action plan; (b) a set of good practice principles and guidelines; (c) a series of case studies; and (d) supporting tools.

All in all, higher education institutes should be advocated to leverage, adopt the existing frameworks and customize or perhaps which may implement or develop their own frameworks such as this one in order to systematically facilitate leadership development in their course programmes. There are many varying methods in developing leadership that may require much less intense preparatory work. One example is by leveraging the use of entertainment media. McMahon and Bramhall (2004) use entertainment media to teach leadership concepts to students, where it includes movies, television, literature and music. Entertainment media has the ability and power to make complex concepts more salient which is much needed for successful leadership development.

For the development of soft skills, a large part of it lies within one's personal traits and habitual behaviours. Hence, it is recommended for institutions to facilitate such training and development through methodically planned approaches. One key aspect that is necessary for this to successfully occur is awareness and acknowledgement of specific behavioural inadequacies or bad habits that are aspects that are necessary for such training and development to successfully happen (Schulz, 2008). Without such recognition, any trainings undertaken will most likely be unsuccessful especially if the person is not completely convinced that it will lead to any improvement or if they do not believe that such efforts will be beneficial. Students' awareness about the importance of soft skills and the consequences of having shortcomings need to be emphasized. Students should be encouraged to improve their soft skills by, for instance, reading interdisciplinary books, attending professional, self-improvement and skills-based courses, and join associations, clubs and societies. A more formal method will be to incorporate soft skills courses into formal course curriculums. For example, offering a management skills course that tackles the hands-on practice skills expected of a project manager or supervisor in an organization, say focusing on skills tied to problem-solving, negotiation, conflict management, project management, ad hoc communications skills, time management and other relevant soft skills. Often, however, courses are overloaded with teaching technical skills and hence incorporating deep development of soft skills may be too overwhelming for both teachers and students. To cope with his, institutions may offer soft skills training by embedding them within the teaching of technical knowledge and hard skills. This will not require any changes to programme offerings, but changes are instead reflected on instructors' teaching learning design, methodology and instructional techniques. For instance, an instructor could increase the occurrences of group discussions or ad hoc presentation pitches that emphasizes on the go thinking. This enables the development of self-confidence, teamwork, collaborative abilities communication and presentation skills among the other vital human and soft skills. To make this possible, careful re-thinking, re-planning and re-organizing on the training and development of hard skills is required.

6.10.3 Learning Intervention: K^mAlive Learning Application—Leadership, Human and Soft (Employability) Skills Functionality

In this section, the validated learning intervention of leadership, human and soft (employability) skills will be discussed, and its insights embedded with its value proposition will be presented. The following are presented, namely, in Fig. 6.8, the instructor's panel view for the pre-evaluation functionality; in Fig. 6.9 the instructor's panel view for the in-class evaluation functionality; in Fig. 6.10, the instructor's panel view for post evaluation functionality; in Fig. 6.11, the instructor's panel view of peer evaluation; in Fig. 6.12, the instructor's panel view of role-based evaluation: leader evaluation; in Fig. 6.13, the instructor's panel view of role-based evaluation: scribe evaluation; in Fig. 6.14, the instructor's panel view of role-based evaluation: devil's advocate evaluation; and in Fig. 6.15, the instructor's panel view of within-group evaluation;

Pre-Evaluation

In this section, we will be examining the Leadership and Human Skills functionality with the option "pre-evaluation" selected. You can choose any of the options, namely "Pre-Evaluation", "Post Evaluation", "In-Class Evaluation" or "Peer Review Evaluation". Let us choose the option "Pre-Evaluation", you can then select the question in this instance it reads as "How would you rate your leadership skills?". Students could be asked to reflect on this question before the class commences. To start the session, click the icon "Launch Question" from the instructor panel, students will be able to see the question immediately as they are able to evaluate themselves. As this's a pre class evaluation, students perform a pre-evaluation on themselves and give a rating together with qualitative feedback. For instance, at the table presented on the bottom, the student Zhi Wei has scored "9" upon "10" on his leadership skills and has given self-qualitative feedback indicating that he has good quality leadership skills. There is also a pie chart that helps you to have a holistic perspective of the proficiency of the skill set evaluated. For instance, when you the instructor mouse over the pie chart, 25% of students are in the weak category, whereas in the "Good" category, it stands at 50%. This provides an overview of the proficiencies of the students' leadership

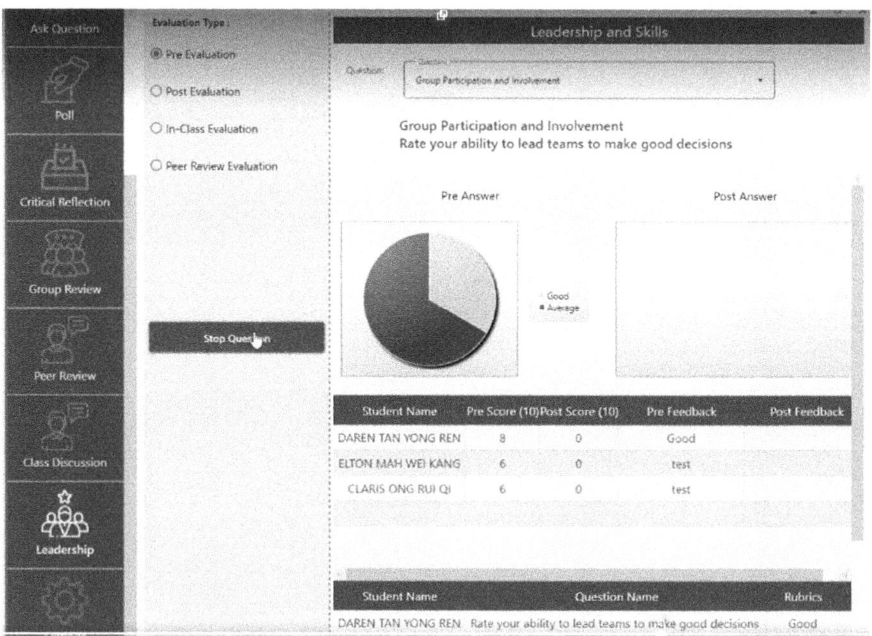

Fig. 6.8 Instructor's panel view for the pre-evaluation functionality

qualities that were reflected on. You can end this session by clicking the icon "Stop Question".

In-Class Evaluation

This section will be focused on examining the "Leadership and Human Skills" functionality with the "In Class Evaluation" as the selected feature. In this functionality, you are able to evaluate the group's performance in terms of skills and competency. For instance, you select "Group 1". Upon selection of group 1, you will be able to view the team members in that group and the evaluation question that you will be evaluating them on and the "Score" rating. For instance, for the student Elton, you will be able to give a "Score" from 1 to 10 based on his performance. For example, the student Elton is given rating score of 8 and you can give qualitative feedback immediately, say "Good Job, very active in participation within the group". For another student, perhaps who is weaker, you can give a rating score of "5" in terms of 10 and qualitative feedback say "To be a better listener and understand the perspectives from the group members". So once done, you can click on the icon "Save Evaluation", the pop-box "Instructor evaluation saved successfully" appears and you can click "Ok". You can then release evaluation to the students by clicking on the "Release Instructor Evaluation" icon where students will get feedback immediately, as you could see appearing in their device.

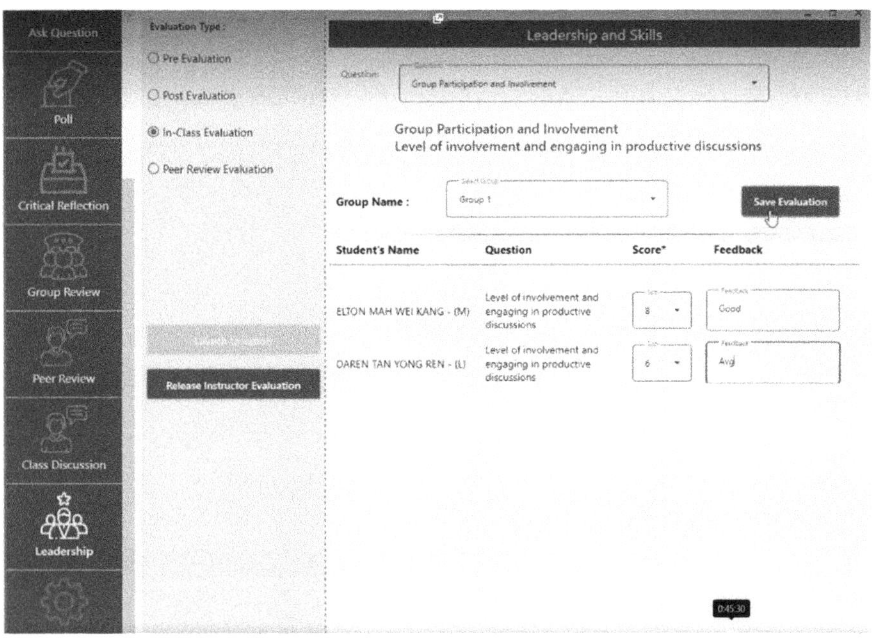

Fig. 6.9 Instructor's panel view for the in-class evaluation functionality

Post Evaluation

In this section, we will be discussing leadership and human skills functionality with option post evaluation selected. First, you should select the "Post Evaluation" option and then select the question, in this instance, is "How would you rate your ad hoc communication skills?". You can then click the icon "launch question" to have the question launched. You could view from the students' panel that they are able to rate their communication skills, for instance for that lesson or activity. They are able to evaluate themselves and give a rating. For instance, the student Zhi Wei has self-evaluated with a high score which could be an indication an improvement as a "Post Feedback". To end the session, you can click the icon "Stop Question".

Peer Review Evaluation

For the functionality of "Peer Review Evaluation", there are four sub-aspects, namely "Leader Evaluation", "Scribe Evaluation", "Devil's Advocate Evaluation" and "Within Group Evaluation". The first three evaluation is primarily a role-based evaluation, that is "Leader Evaluation" is about evaluating the assigned leader, the "Scribe Evaluation" is about evaluating the assigned scribe and "Devil's Advocate Evaluation" is about evaluating the assigned devil's advocate.

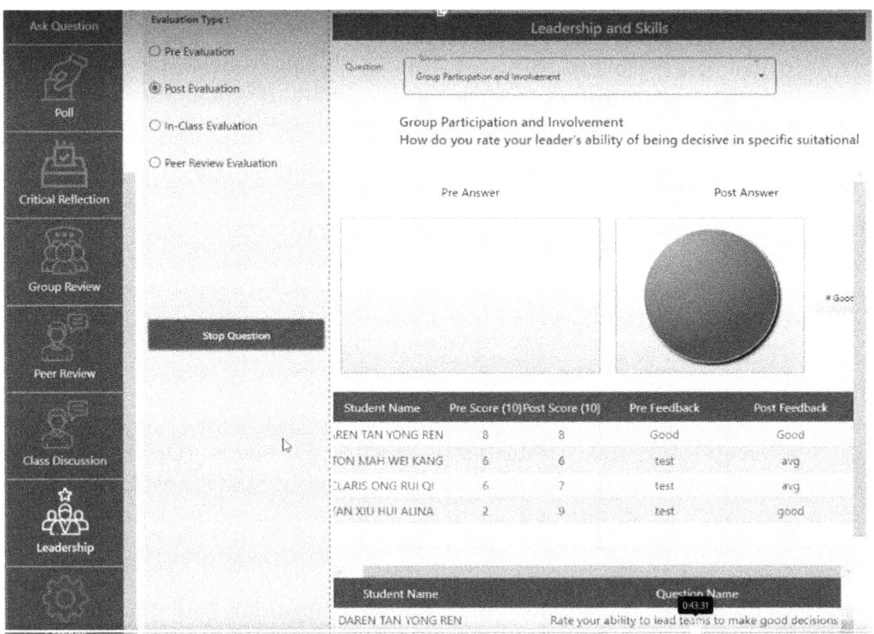

Fig. 6.10 Instructor's panel view for post evaluation functionality

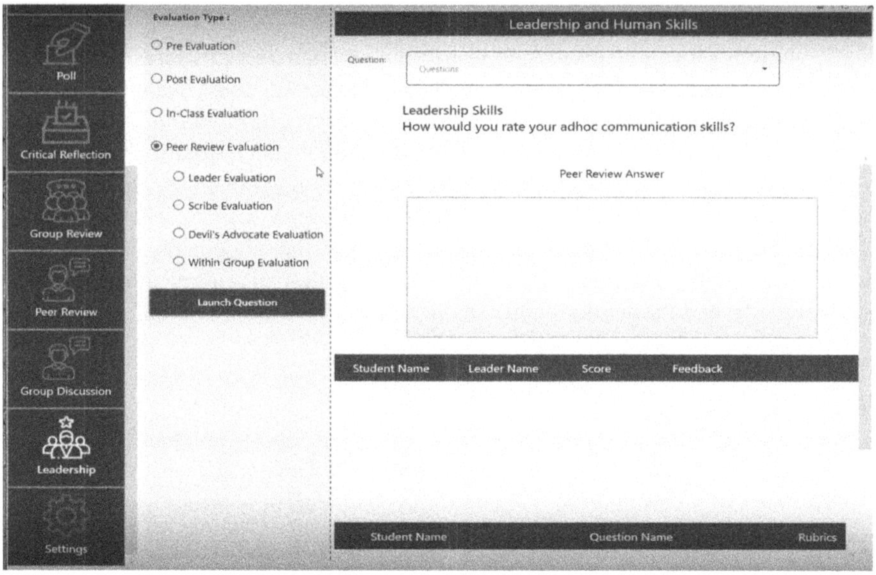

Fig. 6.11 Instructor's panel view: Peer evaluation functionality

Role-Based Evaluation: ***Leader Evaluation***

First, let us examine the feature of "leader evaluation". Here, only the leaders assigned will be evaluated, and, in this instance, the skills and active participation of the leader will be evaluated. Once the question is launched the leader assigned will be evaluated by the group members. You can then click the icon "Stop Question" to end the session.

Role-Based Evaluation: ***Scribe Evaluation***

Next for the "Scribe Evaluation", click the option that states "Scrive Evaluation" and you can click the icon "launch question" to have the evaluation started. Group members can now evaluate the Scribe. Once done, you can end the session by clicking the "Stop Question" icon.

Role-Based Evaluation: ***Devil's Advocate Evaluation***

Next for "Devil's Advocate Evaluation", we click the option "Devil's Advocate Evaluation" option. You can click the "launch question" to start the evaluation. Once done you can stop the session by clicking the icon "stop Question" icon.

Within Group Evaluation

Let us now move on to the feature "Within Group Evaluation", first select the option "Within Group Evaluation". This feature allows the students to evaluate the group members within the group. To start the evaluation, click the icon "Launch Question". This enables team members to evaluate their peers within the group. For instance, the student Zhi Wei has evaluated the student Elton on a score of 10 and provided the feedback as "Good skill". Similarly, the student Adwin has evaluated the student Hui

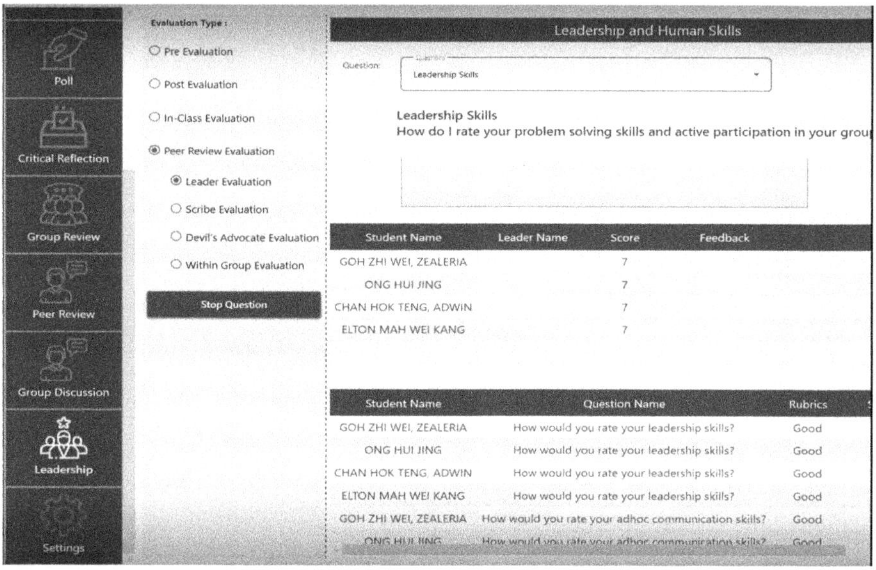

Fig. 6.12 Instructor's panel view of role-based evaluation: leader evaluation

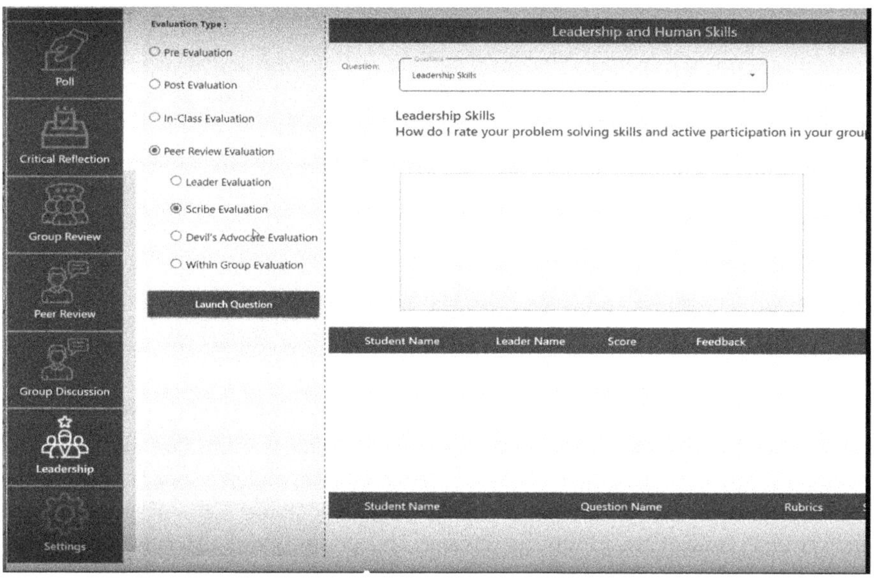

Fig. 6.13 The instructor's panel view of role-based evaluation

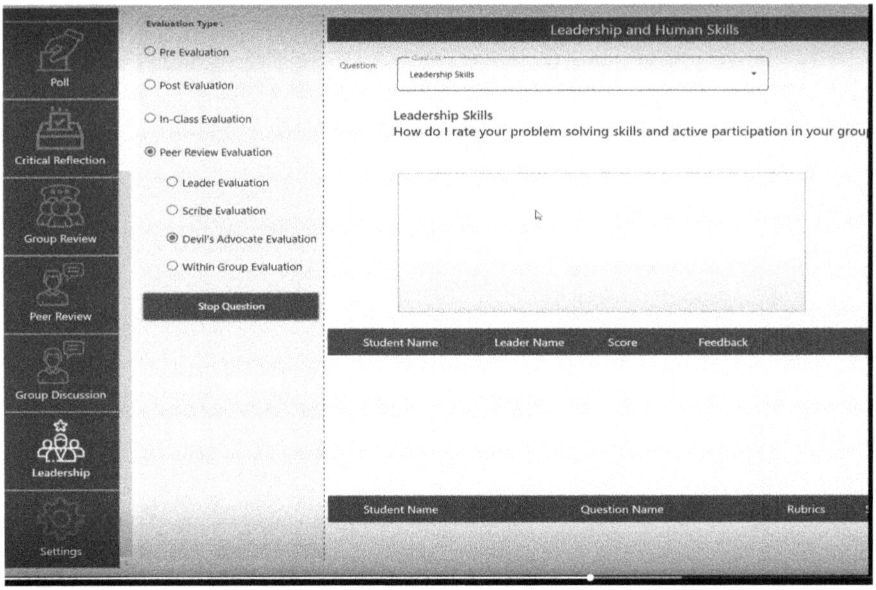

Fig. 6.14 Instructor's panel view of role-based evaluation: devil's advocate evaluation

Jing with a score of 6 and provided the feedback as "Average skill. This process allows each of the group members to evaluate their peers within their group that enables you as the instructor to comprehend their proficiency on the evaluated criteria. To end the session, you can click the icon "Stop Question" and then click on "Release Peer Evaluation" so that the feedback will be provided to all the group members, respectively.

6.11 Application to Teaching and Learning Practice

In this chapter, we discussed on three themes that comprises learning transformation, namely social engineering, pedagogical interventions and learning culture and culture of learning. Subsequently, we examined on learning interventions such as class participation, methods of developing critical thinking, leadership and soft skills competencies, peer evaluation, group discussions and group review. Hence, the primary question is: "How do these learning interventions play a key role in learning transformation and how are they co-related and connected to the sociocultural aspects of teaching and learning? It is especially vital to comprehend these nuances in today's evolving globalized and multicultural learning environments.

At the operational level (classroom), effective and appropriate communication among teachers and students is required. Thus, instructors need to be mindful on how they conduct the classroom discussions. When examined from a cultural dimension,

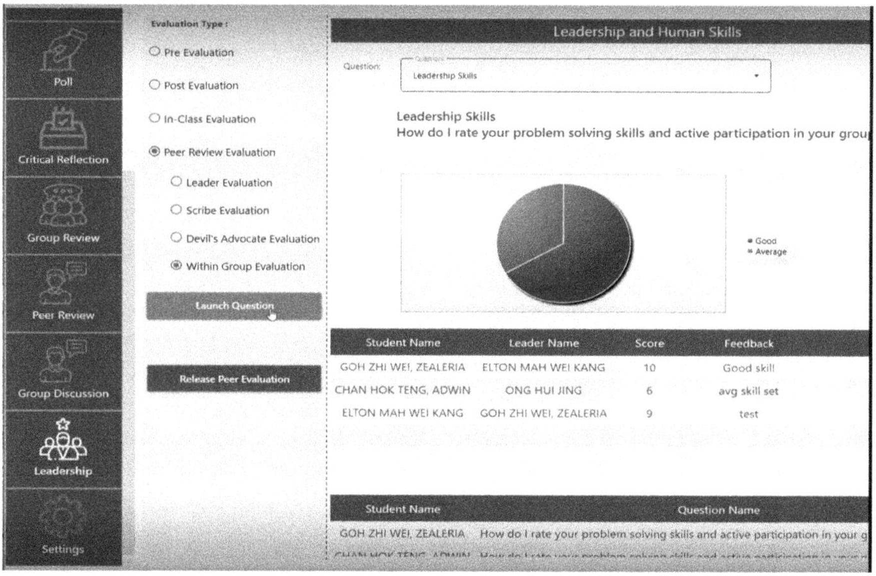

Fig. 6.15 Instructor's panel view of within group evaluation

there are preferences in choices and certain behavioural inclination ingrained in varying cultures and social norms. For example, students from collectivist cultures tend to be more quiet and less outspoken in class versus those from an individualist culture. This is so that they could avoid feeling embarrassed in front of their peers in case they were challenged, or their responses are criticized. In contrast, those from individualistic cultures may appear more dominating in terms of being sharing their thoughts openly. Social aspects such as perceptions of race and religion. Teachers must acknowledge how varying social aspects (for example, perceptions of race and religion) may impact the levels of participation. A study by Howard, Zoeller and Pratt (2006) found that White students are likely to participate at a significantly higher rate than non-White students. Instructors must be mindful of the profile and the diversity pool of students present in the classroom to ensure equality is upheld. On the flip side, teachers should acknowledge and embrace the differences openly and authentically as ignoring race completely could result in colour-blind racism (Bonilla-Silva, 2006).

At the group or group work level, student discussions and review require students to assimilate and work together at both the social and cultural levels. One such consideration is the perception of time. Western cultures tend to view time as linear while other cultures may perceive time as cyclical and endless (Pant, 2016). This could potentially cause issues when leaving students to do work on their own and at their own space independently. From a social context, teachers should be aware and mindful of any inherent biases and beliefs held by students of peers from particular races. For instance, students may perceive non-native English-speaking students to be of weaker links due to their language abilities and put them down or rather to have them grade lower even if they perform just as well as their peers.

When conducting work at the peer level, similar issues as mentioned above should be taken into consideration. There could be possible misunderstandings or conflicts among students due to differences in sociocultural aspects. For instance, students may find it challenging to understand one another's accents. Additionally, students from some cultures may feel uncomfortable in giving candid feedback to their peers as it may cause both parties to lose face. With regard to any pedagogical interventions that target specific traits such as critical thinking and leadership, it is imperative for students to understand the necessity to develop such traits as its importance may not have been emphasized to them in their home country. For example, critical thinking may not be viewed highly by students from certain cultures who are often assumed to understand concepts through memorization, rote learning and knowledge regurgitating. All in all, in order for learning transformation to happen, simply looking and modifying pedagogical methods will not be adequate. Social engineering and learning culture notions are intertwined with pedagogy. Higher education institutions must duly consider social and cultural contexts which enables the creation of a safe and comfortable learning environment for students of different backgrounds. Schools must engineer an institutional culture that allow students globally to thrive in learning, and teachers must enforce and advocate equal treatment of students.

6.12 Recommended Learning Interventions with Sociocultural Engineering Strategies

To summarize the above detailed discussions and its supported illustrations, the key learning interventions are collated and have provided supporting elaboration on their purposes, learning outcomes and sociocultural aspects that are required to be considered. Figure 6.16 presents the summary of the learning interventions and its relevant aspects on sociocultural considerations.

6.12.1 Class Participation

The objective of class participation is to enable active involvement and engagement of as many students as possible. Such a learning intervention allows students to take control of their own learning and teaches them how to speak up and get involved. Evidence shows that class participation improves academic performance. The willingness of a student to participate in class may be influenced by their cultural and social background. Students who are afraid of losing face may appear to be disengaged in class but would potentially approach teachers after class with their questions and clarifications. Social norms play a vital role in student's class participation level. For instance, students from India who are from a lower caste may potentially feel as if their voices would not be heard or taken seriously should they speak up.

Class Participation

- Promotes student-centered learning by holding students responsible for their own learning, involving more students in active learning and by stimulating thinking

- Improves academic achievement

- Students from certain cultures and/or social groups may prefer to be passive

Critical Thinking

- A higher order set of cognitive abilities linked to the logical evaluation of arguments. It is A vital part of skills development

- Develops self-awareness and other cognitive skills such as deep learning, interpreting, analysing and reasoning

- Students from different cultures may not place the same value on critical thinking

Peer Evaluation

- Allows learners to rate their peers and hence students can self-monitor their own learning

- Helps develop metacognitive skills such as communication and self-evaluation

- Students may feel uncomfortable to provide feedback on their peer's work. They may feel worried that they and the individual that they are evaluating will "lose face"

Group Discussion and Group Review

- Both can occur when students engage in group work. Discussion is an effective active learning technique that engages students

- Promotes better retention of course resources, improves communication skills and quality of group projects in general

- Those from collectivist cultures may prefer group review to peer review. Issues such as passiveness and racial bias may still occur when students from different backgrounds come together

Leadership and Soft Skills Competencies

- Leadership experiences teach students on how to cope with change while soft skills may help students achieve both academic and occupational goals

- These skills have been labelled as important for students to attain in order to succeed in the working world. The skills influence academic achievement.

- The importance placed on different types of soft skills may vary from culture to culture. Social norms may also impact result in male-dominated leadership

Fig. 6.16 Framework of learning interventions and socio-cultural considerations

6.12.2 Critical Thinking

Critical thinking enables students to be engaged in high-level cognitive thinking and problem-solving. Students should have the ability and the motivation to think critically. There is a wide range of learning outcomes associated with critical thinking, including deep learning. Although there are various frameworks available for teachers to adopt and facilitate this higher-order cognitive skills development, the effectiveness of these frameworks largely lies in external factors such as social and cultural beliefs and behaviours. For instance, cultures that place an emphasis on rote learning may not value critical thinking as much and as a result, students may not feel the need to engage in or develop critical thinking skills.

6.12.3 Peer Evaluation

Peer evaluation enables students to monitor and to take charge of their own learning process. Students can receive feedback from their peers who, in terms of the academic knowledge acquired, could be seen as equals. This provides students involved in this peer review process with fresh perspectives on their work. Teachers also benefit from peer evaluation not just through managing valuable time from grading work but the ability of highlighting the gaps in their students' understanding. This allows them to re-align and adjust the facilitation, learning design on the curriculum to better engage and teach. From a sociocultural dimensional perspective, some students may feel uncomfortable in providing feedback as students who are sensitive to the concept of face would want to avoid situations in which they may experience embarrassment themselves or cause someone to feel embarrassed. Students from various sociocultural backgrounds may have varying unique ways in delivering feedback. Some may be more straightforward than others and cause peers to feel offended while others may give more vague feedback that causes peers to be dissatisfied due to ambiguity.

6.12.4 Group Discussions and Group Review

Group discussions are beneficial active learning techniques that enable students to be more involved and engaged in their own learning. It also promotes the retention and re-adopting of learning materials and relevant resources in a much-organized manner plus other positive impacts such as improving inter- and intra-group verbal as well as written communication skills. Group reviews serve as a useful assessment method that potentially reduces the bias in instructor's grading and peer reviews while concurrently supports the development of teamwork and collaborative skills. These can be useful when done repeatedly as students not only become more open to candid and critical feedback but also in having their evaluation skills improved. Group reviews may also be more suitable and appropriate for students who come from collectivist cultures as they feel less fearful of losing face. Socially, students should be made aware of and taught how to release any negative biases they may have on people of different ethnicities, gender and economic backgrounds. These biases may affect how students interact with others during group discussions. It could also lead to unfair and unjustified group reviews.

6.12.5 Leadership and Soft Skills Competencies

Being equipped with leadership competencies and relevant soft skills will not only improve students' academic life, help attain the graduate attributes but also well prepare them for their professional career upon their graduation. The effectiveness of developing leadership and soft skills may be influenced by social and cultural factors. For example, it could be due to the unequal treatment of men and women in leadership positions. As such, female student leaders may face more issues than their male counterparts due to the underlying sexist beliefs some may hold. For instance, a male leader may be perceived to be "decisive" whereas a female leader exemplifying the same trait may be labelled "bossy" instead. In terms of soft skills and cultural influences, different cultures may place different levels of importance and emphasis on different skills set. For instance, cultures that value cooperation and respecting authority may not place high value on individuality. As a result, students may not recognize the need to develop certain specific soft skills and its related nuances.

6.13 Practical Implications and Recommendations

All in all, learning transformation is not just merely about pedagogical learning design. The change in pedagogy requires a certain adequate level of sociocultural considerations. Instructors must be able to handle the increasingly diverse classrooms of today to provide and facilitate students with equal learning and assessment outcomes. To comprehend the sociocultural topics, it may not be so straightforward or easy, there are many explicit nuances as each culture is unique and the social norms within that cultural context may also distinctively differ in context. While institutes should ideally provide and equip instructors with continuous and consistent professional training and development, we have to be reminded that it might be costly. Hence, we recommend explicit and targeted steps that instructors can take to create an inclusive and diverse classroom environment that will allow them to better facilitate learning transformation in multicultural classrooms.

- Leverage on evidence and scholarly work
  Teachers should be equipped with some level basic understanding of classroom diversity. There are numerous studies that teachers can look up pertaining to multicultural classrooms that can provide them with a better understanding than they previously had. Scholarly frameworks, for example such as Hofstede's cultural dimensions, can provide teachers with a steppingstone in comprehending the aspects that make cultures different from each other and how those differences that intertwines with social values, norms and beliefs could be better understood and applied. It is also imperative for teachers to keep up to date with social justice issues, relate and empathize with students' concerns.
- Get to know your students (their background, context and profile)

While facts and evidence can be useful and helpful to help lay a concrete and fundamental grounding, teachers should not assume that their students will think or act a certain way as a form of prescription. Teachers should avoid compartmentalizing students. For instance, generalizing and treating all Asian students similarly or uniformly may be detrimental as it would potentially come across as being "taking away" their unique cultural nuances and experiences, and stereotyping them without respecting their sociocultural norms and values. Likewise, completely ignoring racial differences would be perceived as being taking away from students the struggles, embedded, unspoken challenges and hardships they face as individuals from a marginalized community or as a minority population. Hence, it is essential for instructors to acknowledge and understand what makes everyone different and unique in their own rights.

- Be a role model ("Actions speaks louder than words")
  As a role model, teachers should encourage and inspire students, especially local students in that context, to get to know their peers. Teachers must ensure that students themselves are to let go of any inherent biases and assumptions they may hold about people from varying backgrounds that are dissimilar to their own. This help create an inclusive learning environment for everyone involved. Teachers must also deal with any obvious signs of exclusion and advocate to students the value, strength and benefits of being in a diverse learning environment and climate. For instance, teachers should ensure, when students are involved in group work or tasks assigned, that groups formed are diverse. This expectation re-iterates and send a strong, clear message to all students the importance put in place to be working in teams of diversity. Teachers must also deal with any micro-aggressions that may occur in the classroom, for example, a male student talking over his female peer or students mocking a non-native English speaker's accent and so on. Such possible occurrences should be intervened by addressing the incorrect and discriminatory behaviours, imperatively ensuring the students do not repeat such behaviours rather learn from their mistakes by having them monitored till they show improvements and eventually making the required behavioural corrections addressed.
- Encourage students to step out of their comfort zone ("breaking point versus comfort zone"—the discomfort notion, advocated by Rajaram (2021); (Video podcast interview of Dr. Rajaram, hosted by National University of Singapore, NUS-CELC https://www.youtube.com/watch?v=sgEac7Xwe60
  While the learning environment must remain safe and secured for all students to participate and be themselves, teachers should ensure that students learn and are facilitated with the eco-system to push their boundaries. For instance, teachers can encourage, but not force or put pressure, especially on the passive students to speak up and improve their ad hoc verbal communication skills. This is especially important to prepare them for their future work/employment upon their graduation as they will most likely be put in a similar situational contexts in their future careers. With globalization, more and more companies will have a multicultural and diverse workforce and thus, gaining cultural intelligence skills at the tertiary level will be of a great help.

- Adopt a life-long learning and growth mindset with an agility outlook (open mind, humility and being vulnerable of what you don't know)

  With the complex and multifaceted sociocultural contexts and rapidly evolving external circumstances, it will be merely impossible for teachers to easily comprehend every sociocultural context and its overarching implications. Nonetheless, teachers must always keep an open mind when it comes to individuals from diverse sociocultural backgrounds. With adequate time and practice, teachers can continue improving their ability to work with students from such varied backgrounds.

6.14 Concluding Thoughts

This chapter discusses the broad thrust of learning transformation through varying design of learning interventions, more specifically on how it is not as simple as it seems to be. Learning design and pedagogical approaches certainly play a vital role in the process of the strategic learning transformation. As we progress, we have more choices of innovative approaches to adopt as compared to the past. However, the question that we all should ponder on is "what is the point of having the latest technology and the newest ideas when instructors cannot effectively implement them in our classrooms?" Hence, we examined how social and cultural norms, beliefs and nuances impact learning transformation by discussing its effects on varying types of learning interventions.

As school communities become more diverse, teachers must be mindful of the particular behaviours and mindsets of learners with diverse backgrounds. These cultural differences can have ramifications and spill-over effects that could potentially influence teaching strategies adopted for the diverse groups of students at large. Hence, it is the responsibility of the leaders in higher education institutes to perform social engineering to an institutional culture that enables students globally to have equal learning opportunities. The importance of social and cultural norms within learning transformation is not widely discussed in the literature even though the two aspects are highly intertwined. By providing a safe and secured learning environment for students, not only do they get to learn with high level of efficacy, but they can also learn to comfortably navigate cross-cultural situations embedded with multifaceted social complexities and challenges. This is an important skill to learn and be equipped with, especially working in organizations that are embedded with a global presence or simply any organizations where the external environment of globalization overarches or somewhat intervenes in the business strategies execution and operational processes.

Finally, institutes should ingrain the culture of humanizing that has to be part of the ethos and values to be advocated among the faculty and all employees within the institution and its affiliated partners related with it. So, when we say to humanize a situation or condition, we are striving to improve it by changing it in a way that makes it more appropriate and relevant, suitable and pleasant for people within that community, working and living space. It is the ability to embed adequate social-cultural intelligence to be able to resonate with the varying diverse cultures, sub-cultures and social norms. This is essential to have strong values advocated to build a rooted culture with respect, tolerance and understanding that allows diverse students to benefit from the rich varying beliefs, values, norms, learning culture and culture of learning.

References

Abdullah, M. Y., Bakar, N. R. A., & Mahbob, M. H. (2012). Student's participation in classroom: What motivates them to speak up? *Procedia—Social and Behavioral Sciences, 51*, 516–522. https://doi.org/10.1016/j.sbspro.2012.08.199

Al Jawad, A. S. H., & Abosnan, S. H. (2020). The impact of using small group discussion technique on enhancing students' performance in speaking skill: A case study of Benghazi University. *International Journal of Linguistics, Literature and Translation, 3*(7), 189–198. Retrieved from http://www.ijllt.org/the-impact-of-using-small-group-discussion-technique-on-enhancing-students-performance-in-speaking-skill-a-case-study-of-benghazi-university/.

Al-Busaidi, K. A. (2013). An empirical investigation linking learners' adoption of blended learning to their intention of full e-learning. *Behaviour & Information Technology, 32*(11), 1168–1176. https://doi.org/10.1080/0144929x.2013.774047

Allen, S. J. (2020). On the cutting edge or the chopping block? Fostering a digital mindset and tech literacy in business management education. *Journal of Management Education, 44*(3), 362–393. https://doi.org/10.1177/1052562920903077

Ashenafi, M. M. (2015). Peer-assessment in higher education—Twenty-first century practices, challenges and the way forward. *Assessment & Evaluation in Higher Education, 42*(2), 226–251. https://doi.org/10.1080/02602938.2015.1100711

Ashour, S. (2019). How technology has shaped university students' perceptions and expectations around higher education: An exploratory study of the United Arab Emirates. *Studies in Higher Education, 45*(12), 2513–2525. https://doi.org/10.1080/03075079.2019.1617683

Babcock, J. A. (1986). Encouraging better group presentations through peer evaluation. *Journal of Management Education, 10*(4), 101–104. https://doi.org/10.1177/105256298601000413

Baker, D. F. (2007). Peer Assessment in small groups: A comparison of methods. *Journal of Management Education, 32*(2), 183–209. https://doi.org/10.1177/1052562907310489

Balasubramanian, K., Clarke-Okah, W., Daniel, J., Ferreira, F., Kanwar, A., Kwan, A., … West, P. (2009). *ICTs for higher education*. Retrieved from https://unesdoc.unesco.org/ark:/48223/pf0000183207.

Baruah, B., Ward, T., & Jackson, N. (2018). Should higher education encourage the use of intergroup peer assessment among students? *2018 17th International Conference on Information Technology Based Higher Education and Training (ITHET)* (pp. 1–7). https://doi.org/10.1109/ithet.2018.8424618.

Beatty, J. E., Leigh, J., & Lund Dean, K. (2020). The more things change, the more they stay the same: Teaching philosophy statements and the state of student Learning. *Journal of Management Education, 44*(5), 533–542. https://doi.org/10.1177/1052562920932612

Behrens, F., & Kret, M. E. (2019). The interplay between face-to-face contact and feedback on cooperation during real-life interactions. *Journal of Nonverbal Behavior, 43*(4), 513–528. https://doi.org/10.1007/s10919-019-00314-1

Benavides, L. M. C., Tamayo Arias, J. A., Arango Serna, M. D., Branch Bedoya, J. W., & Burgos, D. (2020). Digital transformation in higher education institutions: A systematic literature review. *Sensors, 20*(11), 3291. https://doi.org/10.3390/s20113291

Bialek, S. C., & Lloyd, A. G. (1998). *Post-graduation impact of student leadership*. Retrieved from https://eric.ed.gov/?id=ED417669.

Bond, M., Marín, V. I., Dolch, C., Bedenlier, S., & Zawacki-Richter, O. (2018). Digital transformation in German higher education: Student and teacher perceptions and usage of digital media. *International Journal of Educational Technology in Higher Education, 15*(1), 1–20. https://doi.org/10.1186/s41239-018-0130-1

Bohnsack, R. (2004). Group discussions and focus groups. In U. Flick, E. von Kardorff, & I. Steinke (Eds.), *A companion to qualitative research*. Sage.

Bonilla-Silva, E. (2006). *Racism without racists: Color-blind racism and the persistence of racial inequality in the United States* (2nd ed.). Rowman & Littlefield Publishers.

Bove, L. L. (2019). Empathy for service: Benefits, unintended consequences, and future research agenda. *Journal of Services Marketing, 33*(1), 31–43. https://doi.org/10.1108/jsm-10-2018-0289

Breen, R., Lindsay, R., Jenkins, A., & Smith, P. (2001). The role of information and communication technologies in a university learning environment. *Studies in Higher Education, 26*(1), 95–114. https://doi.org/10.1080/03075070123233

Brown, J. S., Collins, A., & Duguid, P. (1989). Situated cognition and the culture of learning. *Educational Researcher, 18*(1), 32–42. https://doi.org/10.3102/0013189x018001032

Brutus, S., & Donia, M. B. L. (2010). Improving the effectiveness of students in groups with a centralized peer evaluation system. *Academy of Management Learning & Education, 9*(4), 652–662. https://doi.org/10.5465/amle.9.4.zqr652

Brutus, S., Donia, M. B. L., & Ronen, S. (2013). Can business students learn to evaluate better? Evidence from repeated exposure to a peer-evaluation system. *Academy of Management Learning & Education, 12*(1), 18–31. https://doi.org/10.5465/amle.2010.0204

Calma, A., & Davies, M. (2020). Critical thinking in business education: Current outlook and future prospects. *Studies in Higher Education, 1–17*,. https://doi.org/10.1080/03075079.2020.1716324

Campbell, C. M., Smith, M., Dugan, J. P., & Komives, S. R. (2012). Mentors and college student leadership outcomes: The importance of position and process. *The Review of Higher Education, 35*(4), 595–625. https://doi.org/10.1353/rhe.2012.0037

Carmean, C. M., & Frankfort, J. (2018). *The right way to nudge students*. Retrieved from https://www.chronicle.com/article/the-right-way-to-nudge-students/.

Castleman, B. L., & Meyer, K. E. (2020). Can text message nudges improve academic outcomes in college? Evidence from a West Virginia initiative. *The Review of Higher Education, 43*(4), 1125–1165. https://doi.org/10.1353/rhe.2020.0015

Cavanaugh, J. M., Giapponi, C. C., & Golden, T. D. (2015). Digital technology and student cognitive development. *Journal of Management Education, 40*(4), 374–397. https://doi.org/10.1177/1052562915614051

Chamorro-Premuzic, T., Arteche, A., Bremner, A. J., Greven, C., & Furnham, A. (2010). Soft skills in higher education: Importance and improvement ratings as a function of individual differences and academic performance. *Educational Psychology, 30*(2), 221–241. https://doi.org/10.1080/01443410903560278

Chang, J., & Chen, W. (2020). Research on the application of group discussion approaches in graduate courses. *DEStech Transactions on Social Science, Education and Human Science*, 224–229. https://doi.org/10.12783/dtssehs/mess2019/33757.

Chen, N.-S., Wei, C.-W., Wu, K.-T., & Uden, L. (2009). Effects of high level prompts and peer assessment on online learners' reflection levels. *Computers & Education, 52*(2), 283–291. https://doi.org/10.1016/j.compedu.2008.08.007

Cheng, W., & Warren, M. (1997). Having second thoughts: Student perceptions before and after a peer assessment exercise. *Studies in Higher Education, 22*(2), 233–239. https://doi.org/10.1080/03075079712331381064

Cheng, W., & Warren, M. (2005). Peer Assessment of Language Proficiency. *Language Testing, 22*, 93–121.

Chingos, M. M., Griffiths, R. J., Mulhern, C., & Spies, R. R. (2016). Interactive online learning on campus: Comparing students' outcomes in hybrid and traditional courses in the University

System of Maryland. *The Journal of Higher Education, 88*(2), 210–233. https://doi.org/10.1080/00221546.2016.1244409

Cleveland, S., Jackson, B. C., & Dawson, M. (2016). Microblogging in higher education: Digital Natives, knowledge creation, social engineering, and intelligence analysis of educational tweets. *E-Learning and Digital Media, 13*(1–2), 62–80. https://doi.org/10.1177/2042753016672130

Clinton, V., & Kelly, A. E. (2017). Student attitudes toward group discussions. *Active Learning in Higher Education, 21*(2), 154–164. https://doi.org/10.1177/1469787417740277

Collie, R. J., Holliman, A. J., & Martin, A. J. (2016). Adaptability, engagement and academic achievement at university. *Educational Psychology, 37*(5), 632–647. https://doi.org/10.1080/01443410.2016.1231296

Czekanski, K. E., & Wolf, Z. R. (2013). Encouraging and evaluating class participation. *Journal of University Teaching & Learning Practice, 10*(1), 1–12. Retrieved from http://ro.uow.edu.au/jutlp/vol10/iss1/7.

Davies, M. (2015). A Model of Critical Thinking in Higher Education. *Higher Education: Handbook of Theory and Research, 30*, Springer.

Davies, J., Hides, M. T., & Casey, S. (2001). Leadership in higher education. *Total Quality Management, 12*(7–8), 1025–1030. https://doi.org/10.1080/09544120120096197

Davies, M., & Barnett, R. (2015). *The Palgrave handbook of critical thinking in higher education* (1st ed. 2015 ed.). Palgrave Macmillan.

de Alencar, E. M. L. S., & de Oliveira, Z. M. F. (2016). Creativity in higher education according to graduate programs' professors. *Universal Journal of Educational Research, 4*(3), 555–560. https://doi.org/10.13189/ujer.2016.040312.

Deloitte. (2014). *Deloittee Insights - Trends - Business Trends.* Retrieved from https://www2.deloitte.com/us/en/insights/focus/businesstrends/2014.html.

Dempster, N., & Lizzio, A. (2007). Student leadership: Necessary research. *Australian Journal of Education, 51*(3), 276–285. https://doi.org/10.1177/000494410705100305

Deng, W., Li, X., Wu, H., & Xu, G. (2019). Student leadership and academic performance. *China Economic Review, 60*, 101389. https://doi.org/10.1016/j.chieco.2019.101389

Dennen, V. P. (2019). Digital pedagogies and theories of learning and instruction. *Technology, Instruction, Cognition & Learning, 11*(2/3), 115–119.

Developing Leadership Capacity in College Students: Findings from a National Study. (2007). Retrieved from https://www.researchgate.net/publication/237536892_Developing_Leadership_Capacity_In_College_Students_Findings_From_a_National_Study.

Dillenbourg P. (1999). What do yuo mean by collaborative leraning? In P. Dillenbourg (Ed.), *Collaborative-learning: Cognitive and Computational Approaches*, (pp. 1–19). Oxford: Elsevier.

Ding, L. (2018). Applying gamifications to asynchronous online discussions: A mixed methods study. *Computers in Human Behavior, 91*, 1–11. https://doi.org/10.1016/j.chb.2018.09.022

Ding, L., Er, E., & Orey, M. (2018). An exploratory study of student engagement in gamified online discussions. *Computers & Education, 120*, 213–226. https://doi.org/10.1016/j.compedu.2018.02.007

Ding, L., Kim, C. M., & Orey, M. (2017). Studies of student engagement in gamified online discussions. *Computers & Education, 115*, 126–142. https://doi.org/10.1016/j.compedu.2017.06.016

Dochy, F., Segers, M., & Sluijsmans, D. (1999). The use of self, peer and co-assessment in higher education: A review. *Studies in Higher Education, 24*(3), 331–350. https://doi.org/10.1080/03075079912331379935

Dolence, M. G., & Norris, D. M. (1995). *Transforming higher education : a vision for learning in the 21st century.* Retrieved from https://www.researchgate.net/publication/31655851_Transforming_higher_education_a_vision_for_learning_in_the_21st_century_MG_Dolence_Donald_M_Norris.

Domingo, M., Petkova, A., & Lamm, E. (2016). Let's be frank: The real improvement in student teamwork effectiveness following peer feedback. *Academy of Management Proceedings, 2016*(1), 12754. https://doi.org/10.5465/ambpp.2016.90

Donia, M., O'Neill, T. A., & Brutus, S. (2015). Peer feedback increases team member performance, confidence and work outcomes: A longitudinal study. *Academy of Management Proceedings, 2015*(1), 12560. https://doi.org/10.5465/ambpp.2015.21
Duron, R., Limbach, B., & Waugh, W. (2006). Critical thinking framework for any discipline. *International Journal of Teaching and Learning in Higher Education, 17*(2), 160–166. Retrieved from https://www.isetl.org/ijtlhe/pdf/IJTLHE55.pdf.
Dugan, J. P., & Komives, S. R. (2007). Developing Leadership Capacity in College Students: Findings from a National Study. A Report from the Multi-Institutional Study of Leadership. *National Clearinghouse for Leadership Programs.*
Dwyer, C. P., Hogan, M. J., & Stewart, I. (2014). An integrated critical thinking framework for the 21st century. *Thinking Skills and Creativity, 12*, 43–52. https://doi.org/10.1016/j.tsc.2013.12.004
Dziuban, C., Graham, C. R., Moskal, P. D., Norberg, A., & Sicilia, N. (2018). Blended learning: The new normal and emerging technologies. *International Journal of Educational Technology in Higher Education, 15*(1), 1–16. https://doi.org/10.1186/s41239-017-0087-5
Eggenberger, A. L. B. (2019). Active listening skills as predictors of success in community college students. *Community College Journal of Research and Practice,* 1–10. https://doi.org/10.1080/10668926.2019.1706667
Eich, D. (2008). A grounded theory of high-quality leadership programs. *Journal of Leadership & Organizational Studies, 15*(2), 176–187. https://doi.org/10.1177/1548051808324099
Erikson, M. G., & Erikson, M. (2018). Learning outcomes and critical thinking—Good intentions in conflict. *Studies in Higher Education, 44*(12), 2293–2303. https://doi.org/10.1080/03075079.2018.1486813
Fahim, M., & Masouleh, N. S. (2012). Critical thinking in higher education: A pedagogical look. *Theory and Practice in Language Studies, 2*(7), 1370–1375. https://doi.org/10.4304/tpls.2.7.1370-1375
Fornaciari, C. J., Forte, M., & Mathews, C. S. (1999). Distance education as strategy: How can your school compete? *Journal of Management Education, 23*(6), 703–718. https://doi.org/10.1177/105256299902300608
Franco, A. H. R., Butler, H. A., & Halpern, D. F. (2015). Teaching critical thinking to promote learning. *The Oxford Handbook of Undergraduate Psychology Education,* 1–20. https://doi.org/10.1093/oxfordhb/9780199933815.013.007
Freeman, M. (1995). Peer assessment by groups of group work. *Assessment & Evaluation in Higher Education, 20*(3), 289–300. https://doi.org/10.1080/0260293950200305
Freeman, S., & Parks, J. W. (2010). How accurate is peer grading? *CBE—Life Sciences Education, 9*(4), 482–488. https://doi.org/10.1187/cbe.10-03-0017.
Friedman, B. A., & Mandel, R. G. (2009). The prediction of college student academic performance and retention: Application of expectancy and goal setting theories. *Journal of College Student Retention: Research, Theory & Practice, 11*(2), 227–246. https://doi.org/10.2190/cs.11.2.d
Fritschner, L. M. (2000). Inside the undergraduate college classroom. *The Journal of Higher Education, 71*(3), 342–362. https://doi.org/10.1080/00221546.2000.11780826
Fritz, J. (2017). Using analytics to nudge student responsibility for learning. *New Directions for Higher Education, 2017*(179), 65–75. https://doi.org/10.1002/he.20244
Fry, K. (2001). E-learning markets and providers: some issues and prospects. *Education + Training, 43*(4/5), 233–239. https://doi.org/10.1108/eum0000000005484.
Gannouni, K., & Ramboarison-Lalao, L. (2016). Leadership and students' academic success: Mediating effects of self-efficacy and self-determination. *International Journal of Leadership in Education, 21*(1), 66–79. https://doi.org/10.1080/13603124.2015.1123300
Garrison, D. R., & Kanuka, H. (2004). Blended learning: Uncovering its transformative potential in higher education. *The Internet and Higher Education, 7*(2), 95–105. https://doi.org/10.1016/j.iheduc.2004.02.001
Gellin, A. (2003). The effect of undergraduate student involvement on critical thinking: A meta-analysis of the literature 1991–2000. *Journal of College Student Development, 44*(6), 746–762. https://doi.org/10.1353/csd.2003.0066

Gialamas, S., Grigoropoulos, J. E., Pelonis, P., & Cherif, A. H. (2020). How can manifesting leadership skills infused with ethos, empathy, and compassion better prepare students to assume leadership roles? *International Journal of Progressive Education, 16*(1), 54–66. Retrieved from https://eric.ed.gov/?id=EJ1245093.

Gielen, S., Dochy, F., Onghena, P., Struyven, K., & Smeets, S. (2011). Goals of peer assessment and their associated quality concepts. *Studies in Higher Education, 36*(6), 719–735. https://doi.org/10.1080/03075071003759037

Grajek, S. & 2019–2020 EDUCAUSE IT Issues Panel. (2020, January). *How colleges and universities are driving to digital transformation today.* Retrieved from https://er.educause.edu/articles/2020/1/how-colleges-and-universities-are-driving-to-digital-transformation-today.

Hadnagy, C. (2010). *Social engineering* (1st ed.). John Wiley & Sons.

Harrison, C. (2010). Peer and self-assessment. In P. Peterson, E. Baker, & B. McGaw (Eds.), *International encyclopaedia of education.* Elsevier.

Havnes, A., & McDowell, L. (2007). *Balancing dilemmas in assessment and learning in contemporary education (Routledge Research in Education)* (1st ed.). Routledge.

Heard J., Scoular, C., Duckworth, D., Ramalingam, D., & Teo, I. (2020). Critical thinking: Skill development framework. Australian Council for Educational Research. https://research.acer.edu.au/ar_misc/41.

Henderson, M., Selwyn, N., & Aston, R. (2015). What works and why? Student perceptions of 'useful' digital technology in university teaching and learning. *Studies in Higher Education, 42*(8), 1567–1579. https://doi.org/10.1080/03075079.2015.1007946

Hinings, B., Gegenhuber, T., & Greenwood, R. (2018). Digital innovation and transformation: An institutional perspective. *Information and Organization, 28*(1), 52–61. https://doi.org/10.1016/j.infoandorg.2018.02.004

Hinrichs, R., & Wankel, C. (2011). *Transforming virtual world learning (Cutting-edge technologies in higher education).* Emerald Publishing Limited.

Howard, J., Zoeller, A., & Pratt, Y. (2006). Students' race and participation in sociology classroom discussion: A preliminary investigation. *Journal of Scholarship of Teaching and Learning, 6*(1), 14–38. Retrieved from https://eric.ed.gov/?id=EJ854909.

Iglesias Pérez, M. C., Vidal-Puga, J., & Pino Juste, M. R. (2020). The role of self and peer assessment in Higher Education. *Studies in Higher Education,* 1–10. https://doi.org/10.1080/03075079.2020.1783526

Iivari, N., Sharma, S., & Ventä-Olkkonen, L. (2020). Digital transformation of everyday life—How COVID-19 pandemic transformed the basic education of the young generation and why information management research should care? *International Journal of Information Management, 55*, 102183. https://doi.org/10.1016/j.ijinfomgt.2020.102183

Jackson, N. C. (2019). Managing for competency with innovation change in higher education: Examining the pitfalls and pivots of digital transformation. *Business Horizons, 62*(6), 761–772. https://doi.org/10.1016/j.bushor.2019.08.002

Jones, I., & Alcock, L. (2014). Peer assessment without assessment criteria. *Studies in Higher Education, 39*(10), 1774–1787. https://doi.org/10.1080/03075079.2013.821974

Jones, I., & Wheadon, C. (2015). Peer assessment using comparative and absolute judgement. *Studies in Educational Evaluation, 47*, 93–101. https://doi.org/10.1016/j.stueduc.2015.09.004

Jones, J. F. (1999). From silence to talk: Cross-cultural ideas on students participation in academic group discussion. *English for Specific Purposes, 18*(3), 243–259. https://doi.org/10.1016/s0889-4906(97)00059-8

Jones, R. C. (2008). The "why" of class participation: A question worth asking. *College Teaching, 56*(1), 59–63. https://doi.org/10.3200/ctch.56.1.59-64

Kaharuddin, K., & Rahmadana, A. (2020). Problem-based group discussion: An effective ELT technique to improve vocational high school students' transactional speaking skills. Jurnal Ilmu Budaya, *8*(2), 247–258. https://doi.org/10.34050/jib.v8i2.11032

Kerr, P. M., Park, K. H., & Domazlicky, B. R. (1995). Peer grading of essays in a principles of microeconomics course. *Journal of Education for Business, 70*(6), 357–361. https://doi.org/10.1080/08832323.1995.10117778

Kopp, M., Gröblinger, O., & Adams, S. (2019). Five common assumptions that prevent digital transformation at higher education institutions. Inted2019 Proceedings, 1448–1457. Retrieved from https://library.iated.org/publication_series/INTED

Kritikos, V. S., Woulfe, J., Sukkar, M. B., & Saini, B. (2011). Intergroup peer assessment in problem-based learning tutorials for undergraduate pharmacy students. *American Journal of Pharmaceutical Education, 75*(4), 1–12. https://doi.org/10.5688/ajpe75473

Kuh, G. D., Cruce, T. M., Shoup, R., Kinzie, J., & Gonyea, R. M. (2008). Unmasking the effects of student engagement on first-year college grades and persistence. *The Journal of Higher Education, 79*(5), 540–563. https://doi.org/10.1080/00221546.2008.11772116

Laal, M., & Ghodsi, S. M. (2012). Benefits of collaborative learning. *Procedia—Social and Behavioral Sciences, 31*, 486–490. https://doi.org/10.1016/j.sbspro.2011.12.091

Lacka, E., & Wong, T. C. (2019). Examining the impact of digital technologies on students' higher education outcomes: The case of the virtual learning environment and social media. *Studies in Higher Education, 1–14*,. https://doi.org/10.1080/03075079.2019.1698533

Lai, K.-W. (2011). Digital technology and the culture of teaching and learning in higher education. *Australasian Journal of Educational Technology, 27*(8), 1263–1275. https://doi.org/10.14742/ajet.892.

Laurilland, D. (2008). The teacher as action researcher: Using technology to capture pedagogic form. *Studies in Higher Education, 33*(2), 139–154.

Ledwith, A., & Rísquez, A. (2008). Using anti-plagiarism software to promote academic honesty in the context of peer reviewed assignments. *Studies in Higher Education, 33*(4), 371–384. https://doi.org/10.1080/03075070802211562

Lin, M.-H., Chen, H., & Liu, S. (2017). A study of the effects of digital learning on learning motivation and learning outcome. *EURASIA Journal of Mathematics, Science and Technology Education, 13*(7), 3553–3564. https://doi.org/10.12973/eurasia.2017.00744a.

Liu, M., Zha, S., & He, W. (2019). Digital transformation challenges: A case study regarding the MOOC development and operations at higher education institutions in China. *TechTrends, 63*(5), 621–630. https://doi.org/10.1007/s11528-019-00409-y

Liu, O. L., Mao, L., Frankel, L., & Xu, J. (2016). Assessing critical thinking in higher education: The HEIghten^{TM} approach and preliminary validity evidence. *Assessment & Evaluation in Higher Education, 41*(5), 677–694. https://doi.org/10.1080/02602938.2016.1168358

Liu, X., Li, L., & Zhang, Z. (2017). Small group discussion as a key component in online assessment training for enhanced student learning in web-based peer assessment. *Assessment & Evaluation in Higher Education, 43*(2), 207–222. https://doi.org/10.1080/02602938.2017.1324018

Loes, C. N., & Pascarella, E. T. (2017). Collaborative learning and critical thinking: Testing the link. *The Journal of Higher Education, 88*(5), 726–753. https://doi.org/10.1080/00221546.2017.1291257

Loignon, A. C., Woehr, D. J., Thomas, J. S., Loughry, M. L., Ohland, M. W., & Ferguson, D. M. (2017). Facilitating peer evaluation in team contexts: The impact of frame-of-reference rater training. *Academy of Management Learning & Education, 16*(4), 562–578. https://doi.org/10.5465/amle.2016.0163

Lomonosova, N. V., & Zolkina, A. V. (2018). Digital learning resources: Enhancing efficiency within blended higher education. *Novosibirsk State Pedagogical University Bulletin, 8*(6), 121–137. https://doi.org/10.15293/2226-3365.1806.08.

Lovelace, K. J., Eggers, F., & Dyck, L. R. (2016). I do and I understand: Assessing the utility of web-based management simulations to develop critical thinking skills. *Academy of Management Learning & Education, 15*(1), 100–121. https://doi.org/10.5465/amle.2013.0203

Lu, J., & Law, N. (2011). Online peer assessment: Effects of cognitive and affective feedback. *Instructional Science, 40*(2), 257–275. https://doi.org/10.1007/s11251-011-9177-2

Luo, H., Robinson, A. C., & Park, J.-Y. (2014). Peer grading in a MOOC: Reliability, validity, and perceived effects. *Online Learning, 18*(2), 1–14. https://doi.org/10.24059/olj.v18i2.429.

Lyons, P. R. (1989). Assessing classroom participation. *College Teaching, 37*(1), 36–38. https://doi.org/10.1080/87567555.1989.10532154

Martin-Barbero, S. (2020). *COVID-19 has accelerated the digital transformation of higher education.* Retrieved from https://www.weforum.org/agenda/2020/07/covid-19-digital-transformation-higher-education/.

McDowell, L. (1995). The impact of innovative assessment on student learning. *Innovations in Education and Training International, 32*(4), 302–313. https://doi.org/10.1080/1355800950320402

McMahon, T. R., & Bramhall, R. (2004). Using entertainment media to inform student affairs teaching and practice related to leadership. *New Directions for Student Services, 2004*(108), 61–70. https://doi.org/10.1002/ss.142

Merry, S., & Orsmond, P. (2018). Peer assessment: The role of relational learning through communities of practice. *Studies in Higher Education, 45*(7), 1312–1322. https://doi.org/10.1080/03075079.2018.1544236

Meyer, K. A. (2019). Student Perceptions of face-to-face and online discussions: The advantage goes to . . . *Online Learning, 11*(4), 53–69. https://doi.org/10.24059/olj.v11i4.1715.

Miller, L., & Emery, D. (2018). A Framework for Collaborative Peer Review for Group-written Documents. *2018 ASEE Annual Conference & Exposition*, 1–15. Retrieved from https://www.asee.org/public/conferences/106/papers/23504/view.

Mohamed, A. S., Abozeid, H. A. A., Mohammed, F. M., & Ahmed, Z. A. (2019). Relationship between soft skills and academic achievement among 4th year nursing students. *IOSR Journal of Nursing and Health Science, 8*(4), 15–23. Retrieved from https://www.researchgate.net/publication/340487606_Relationship_between_Soft_Skills_and_Academic_Achievement_among_4_th_Year_Nursing_Students.

Moody, D. L., & Sindre, G. (2003). Evaluating the effectiveness of learning interventions: An information systems case study. *ECIS 2003 Proceedings, 80*, 1–18. Retrieved from https://aisel.aisnet.org/ecis2003/80.

Moore, M. G., & Diehl, W. C. (2019). *Handbook of distance education* (4th ed.). Routledge.

Moore, T. (2013). Critical thinking: Seven definitions in search of a concept. *Studies in Higher Education, 38*(4), 506–522. https://doi.org/10.1080/03075079.2011.586995

Mortensen, C. J., & Nicholson, A. M. (2015). The flipped classroom stimulates greater learning and is a modern 21st century approach to teaching today's undergraduates. *Journal of Animal Science, 93*(7), 3722–3731. https://doi.org/10.2527/jas.2015-9087

National Center for Education Statistics. (2017). *Distance learning.* Retrieved from https://nces.ed.gov/fastfacts/display.asp?id=80.

Nelson, M. M., & Schunn, C. D. (2009). The nature of feedback: How different types of peer feedback affect writing performance. *Instructional Science, 37*(4), 375–401. https://doi.org/10.1007/s11251-008-9053-x

Nielsen, N. C., Dotiwala, F., & Murray, M. (2020). A transformation of the learning function: Why it should learn new ways. Retrieved from https://www.mckinsey.com/business-functions/mckinsey-accelerate/our-insights/a-transformation-of-the-learning-function-why-it-should-learn-new-ways.

Obilor, E. I. (2019). Soft skills and students' academic achievement. *The International Journal of Community and Social Development*, 7(2), 27–37. Retrieved from https://www.researchgate.net/publication/343609946_Soft_Skills_and_Students'_Academic_Achievement.

Odom, S., Glenn, B., Sanner, S., & Cannella, K. A. S. (2009). Group peer review as an active learning strategy in a research course. *International Journal of Teaching and Learning in Higher Education, 21*(1), 108–117. Retrieved from https://files.eric.ed.gov/fulltext/EJ896250.pdf.

Ohland, M. W., Layton, R. A., Loughry, M. L., & Yuhasz, A. G. (2005). Effects of behavioral anchors on peer evaluation reliability. *Journal of Engineering Education, 94*(3), 319–326. https://doi.org/10.1002/j.2168-9830.2005.tb00856.x

Ohland, M. W., Loughry, M. L., Woehr, D. J., Bullard, L. G., Felder, R. M., Finelli, C. J., & Schmucker, D. G. (2012). The comprehensive assessment of team member effectiveness: Development of a behaviorally anchored rating scale for self- and peer evaluation. *Academy of Management Learning & Education, 11*(4), 609–630. https://doi.org/10.5465/amle.2010.0177

Olaniran, B. A., Savage, G. T., & Sorenson, R. L. (1996). Experimental and experiential approaches to teaching face-to-face and computer-mediated group discussion. *Communication Education, 45*(3), 244–259. https://doi.org/10.1080/03634529609379053

Panadero, E., & Alqassab, M. (2019). An empirical review of anonymity effects in peer assessment, peer feedback, peer review, peer evaluation and peer grading. *Assessment & Evaluation in Higher Education, 44*(8), 1253–1278. https://doi.org/10.1080/02602938.2019.1600186

Pant, B. (2016). *Different cultures see deadlines differently*. Retrieved from https://hbr.org/2016/05/different-cultures-see-deadlines-differently.

Patchan, M. M., Schunn, C. D., & Clark, R. J. (2017). Accountability in peer assessment: Examining the effects of reviewing grades on peer ratings and peer feedback. *Studies in Higher Education, 43*(12), 2263–2278. https://doi.org/10.1080/03075079.2017.1320374

Paulsen, M. B. (Ed.). (2015). Higher education: Handbook of theory and research. *Higher Education: Handbook of Theory and Research*, 1–605. https://doi.org/10.1007/978-3-319-12835-1

Pearson, M., & Somekh, B. (2006). Learning transformation with technology: A question of sociocultural contexts?1. *International Journal of Qualitative Studies in Education, 19*(4), 519–539. https://doi.org/10.1080/09518390600773353

Penkauskienė, D., Railienė, A., & Cruz, G. (2019). How is critical thinking valued by the labour market? Employer perspectives from different European countries. *Studies in Higher Education, 44*(5), 804–815. https://doi.org/10.1080/03075079.2019.1586323

Penningroth, S. L., Despain, L. H., & Gray, M. J. (2007). A course designed to improve psychological critical thinking. *Teaching of Psychology, 34*(3), 153–157. https://doi.org/10.1080/00986280701498509

Peters, O. (2000). Digital learning environments: New possibilities and opportunities. *The International Review of Research in Open and Distributed Learning, 1*(1), 1–19. https://doi.org/10.19173/irrodl.v1i1.3.

Phye, G. D. (1996). *Handbook of classroom assessment: Learning, achievement, and adjustment (educational psychology)*. Academic Press.

Pnevmatikos, D., Christodoulou, P., & Georgiadou, T. (2019). Promoting critical thinking in higher education through the values and knowledge education (VaKE) method. *Studies in Higher Education, 44*(5), 892–901. https://doi.org/10.1080/03075079.2019.1586340

Pollock, P. H., Hamann, K., & Wilson, B. M. (2011). Learning through discussions: Comparing the benefits of small-group and large-class settings. *Journal of Political Science Education, 7*(1), 48–64. https://doi.org/10.1080/15512169.2011.539913

Powley, E. H., & Taylor, S. N. (2014). Pedagogical approaches to develop critical thinking and crisis leadership. *Journal of Management Education, 38*(4), 560–585. https://doi.org/10.1177/1052562913519081

Privateer, P. M. (1999). Academic technology and the future of hjigher education. *The Journal of Higher Education, 70*(1), 60–79. https://doi.org/10.1080/00221546.1999.11780754

Rajaram, K. (2019). Flipped Classroom: Scaffolding support system with real time learning interventions. *Asian Journal of the Scholarship of Teaching and Learning, 9*(1), 30–58.

Rajaram, K. (2020). *Research lab for learning innovation and culture of learning*. https://learningintervention.wixsite.com/researchlab

Rajaram, K. (2021). *Evidence-based teaching for the 21st century classroom and beyond—Innovative-driven learning strategies*. Springer

Rasoal, C., Danielsson, H., & Jungert, T. (2012). Empathy among students in engineering programmes. *European Journal of Engineering Education, 37*(5), 427–435. https://doi.org/10.1080/03043797.2012.708720

Redding, S. (2013). What is an innovation in learning? In J. S. Twyman & M. Murphy (Eds.), *Handbook on innovations in learning* (pp. 3–14). Philadelphia, PA: Center on Innovations in Learning, Temple University and Information Age Publishing.

Reinsch, R., & Wambsganss, J. R. (1994). Class participation: How it affects results on examinations. *Journal of Education for Business, 70*(1), 33–37. https://doi.org/10.1080/08832323.1994.10117721

Roberts, T. S. (2006). *Self, peer and group assessment in e-learning*. Information Science Publishing.

Rof, A., Bikfalvi, A., & Marquès, P. (2020). Digital transformation for business model innovation in higher education: Overcoming the tensions. *Sustainability, 12*(12), 4980. https://doi.org/10.3390/su12124980

Rogers, S. (2019). *Virtual reality: The learning aid of the 21st century*. Retrieved from https://www.forbes.com/sites/solrogers/2019/03/15/virtual-reality-the-learning-aid-of-the-21st-century/?sh=16b636f0139b.

Roscoe, R. D., Walker, E. A., & Patchan, M. M. (2018). Facilitating peer tutoring and assessment in intelligent learning systems. In S. D. Craig (Ed.), *Tutoring and intelligent tutoring systems* (pp. 41–68). Nova Science Publishers.

Sadler, D.R. (2010). Assessment in higher education assessment in higher education. In P. Peterson, E. Baker, & B. McGaw (Eds.), *International encyclopaedia of education*. Elsevier.

Santos, H., Batista, J., & Marques, R. P. (2019). Digital transformation in higher education: The use of communication technologies by students. *Procedia Computer Science, 164*, 123–130. https://doi.org/10.1016/j.procs.2019.12.163

Scager, K., Akkerman, S. F., Pilot, A., & Wubbels, T. (2012). Challenging high-ability students. *Studies in Higher Education, 39*(4), 659–679. https://doi.org/10.1080/03075079.2012.743117

Schulz, B. (2008). The importance of soft skills: Education beyond academic knowledge. *Journal of Language and Communication*, 146–154. Retrieved from https://www.researchgate.net/publication/41936500_The_importance_of_soft_skills_Education_beyond_academic_knowledge.

Seres, L., Pavlicevic, V., & Tumbas, P. (2018). Digital transformation of higher education: Competing on analytics. In *Proceedings of INTED2018 conference 5th-7th March, Subotica: Serbia*, (pp. 9491–9497). https://doi.org/10.21125/inted.2018.2348.

Simpson, C., & Du, Y. (2004). Effects of learning styles and class participation on students' enjoyment level in distributed learning environments. *Journal of Education for Library and Information Science, 45*(2), 123–136. https://doi.org/10.2307/40323899

Skalicky, J., Warr Pedersen, K., van der Meer, J., Fuglsang, S., Dawson, P., & Stewart, S. (2018). A framework for developing and supporting student leadership in higher education. *Studies in Higher Education, 45*(1), 100–116. https://doi.org/10.1080/03075079.2018.1522624

Sluijsmans, D. M. A., Brand-Gruwel, S., van Merriënboer, J. J. G., & Bastiaens, T. J. (2002). The training of peer assessment skills to promote the development of reflection skills in teacher education. *Studies in Educational Evaluation, 29*(1), 23–42. https://doi.org/10.1016/s0191-491x(03)90003-4

Smith, G. F. (2003). Beyond critical thinking and decision making: Teaching business students how to think. *Journal of Management Education, 27*(1), 24–51. https://doi.org/10.1177/1052562902239247

Stenlund, T., Jönsson, F. U., & Jonsson, B. (2017). Group discussions and test-enhanced learning: Individual learning outcomes and personality characteristics. *Educational Psychology, 37*(2), 145–156. https://doi.org/10.1080/01443410.2016.1143087

Stepanyan, K., Mather, R., Jones, H., Lusuardi, C. (2009). Student engagement with peer assessment: A review of pedagogical design and technologies. In M. Spaniol, Q. Li, R. Klamma, & R. W.H . Lau (Eds.), *Advances in web based learning*. ICWL 2009. Elsevier.

Stracke, C.M. (2007). Learning innovations and learning quality: Relations, interdependences, and future. In M. Stracke (Eds.), *The future of learning innovations and learning quality*. Berlin: GITO 2012.

Tan, D. A. L., Ganapathy, M., & Kaur, M. (2018). Kahoot! It: Gamification in higher education. *Pertanika Journal of Social Science and Humanities, 26*(1), 565–582. Retrieved from https://www.researchgate.net/publication/320182671_Kahoot_It_Gamification_in_Higher_Education.

Tang, K. C. C. (1993). Spontaneous Collaborative learning: A new dimension in student learning experience? *Higher Education Research & Development, 12*(2), 115–130. https://doi.org/10.1080/0729436930120201

Tao, Y., & -. H., Yeh, C. R., & Sun, S. -. I. (2006). Improving training needs assessment processes via the Internet: System design and qualitative study. *Internet Research, 16*(4), 427–449. https://doi.org/10.1108/10662240610690043

Tatum, H. E., Schwartz, B. M., Schimmoeller, P. A., & Perry, N. (2013). Classroom participation and student-faculty interactions: Does gender matter? *The Journal of Higher Education, 84*(6), 745–768. https://doi.org/10.1080/00221546.2013.11777309

Terenzini, P. T., Springer, L., Pascarella, E. T., & Nora, A. (1995). Influences affecting the development of students' critical thinking skills. *Research in Higher Education, 36*(1), 23–39. Retrieved from https://doi.org/10.1007/BF02207765. *The benefits of student involvement in leadership: An annotated bibliography of underpinning research.* (2015). Retrieved from https://www.researchgate.net/publication/299428458_Student_involvement_in_leadership

Thaler, R., & Sunstein, C. (2008). *Nudge : Improving decisions about health, wealth, and happiness.* Yale University Press.

Thanh, P. T. H., & Gillies, R. (2010). Designing a culturally appropriate format of formative peer assessment for Asian students: The case of Vietnamese students. *International Journal of Educational Reform, 19*(2), 72.

Thomas, M. (2008). *Handbook of rsearch on web 2.0 and second language learning.* Information Science Reference.

Thomas, D., & Brown, J. S. (2011). *A new culture of learning: Cultivating the imagination for a world of constant change* (1st ed.). CreateSpace Independent Publishing Platform.

Thomas, K., & Lok, B. (2015). Teaching Critical Thinking: An Operational Framework. In: Davies, M., Barnett, R. (eds) *The Palgrave Handbook of Critical Thinking in Higher Education.* Palgrave Macmillan.

Thomson, P. (2012). Understanding, evaluating and assessing what students learn from leadership activities: Student research in Woodlea Primary. *Management in Education, 26*(3), 96–103. https://doi.org/10.1177/0892020612445677

Tillema, H. (2010). Formative assessment in teacher education and teacher professional development. In P. Peterson, E. Baker, & B. McGaw (Eds.), *International encyclopaedia of education.* Elsevier.

Topping, K. (1998). Peer assessment between students in colleges and universities. *Review of Educational Research, 68*(3), 249–276. https://doi.org/10.3102/00346543068003249

Topping, K. J. (2010). Methodological quandaries in studying process and outcomes in peer assessment. *Learning and Instruction, 20*(4), 339–343. https://doi.org/10.1016/j.learninstruc.2009.08.003

Tsang, A. (2011). In-class reflective group discussion as a strategy for the development of students as evolving professionals. *International Journal for the Scholarship of Teaching and Learning, 5*(1), 1–20. https://doi.org/10.20429/ijsotl.2011.050107.

Tsui, L. (1999). Coures and instruction affecting critical thinking. *Research in Higher Education, 40*, 185–200. Retrieved from https://link.springer.com/article/https://doi.org/10.1023/A:1018734630124.

Tsui, L. (2002). Fostering critical thinking through effective pedagogy. *The Journal of Higher Education, 73*(6), 740–763. https://doi.org/10.1080/00221546.2002.11777179

Van den Berg, I., Admiraal, W., & Pilot, A. (2006). Design principles and outcomes of peer assessment in higher education. *Studies in Higher Education, 31*(3), 341–356. https://doi.org/10.1080/03075070600680836

Van der Meer, J., Skalicky, J., & Speed, H. (2019). "I didn't just want a degree": Students' perceptions about benefits from participation in student leadership programmes. *Journal of Leadership Education, 18*(1), 25–44. https://doi.org/10.12806/v18/i1/r3.

Vasagar, J. (2014). *Countries that excel at problem-solving encourage critical thinking*. Retrieved from https://www.ft.com/content/e512db9c-c643-11e3-ba0e-00144feabdc0.

Wade, R. C. (1994). Teacher education students' views on class discussion: Implications for fostering critical reflection. *Teaching and Teacher Education, 10*(2), 231–243. https://doi.org/10.1016/0742-051x(94)90015-9

Wagner, R. J., Scharinger, D., & Sisak, J. (1992). Enhancing teaching effectiveness using experiential techniques: Model development and empirical evaluation. *Paper Presented at the Annual Meeting of the Midwest Region of the Academy of Management* (pp. 1–9). Retrieved from https://eric.ed.gov/?id=ED345908.

Walker, P., & Finney, N. (1999). Skill development and critical thinking in higher education. *Teaching in Higher Education, 4*(4), 531–547. https://doi.org/10.1080/1356251990040409

Warschauer, M. (2007). The paradoxical future of digital learning. *Learning Inquiry, 1*(1), 41–49. https://doi.org/10.1007/s11519-007-0001-5

Wei, L., Murphy, P. K., & Firetto, C. M. (2018). How can teachers facilitate productive small-group talk? An integrated taxonomy of teacher discourse moves. *The Elementary School Journal, 118*(4), 578–609. https://doi.org/10.1086/697531

Wildman, S. M. (1988). The question of silence: Techniques to ensure full class participation. *Journal of Legal Education, 38*(1/2), 147–154. Retrieved from https://www.jstor.org/stable/42893014

Wilms, K. L., Stieglitz, S., Fröhlich, L., Schaulies, S., Meske, C., Meske, H., … Rudolph, D. (2017). Digital transformation in higher education—New Cohorts, New requirements? *Twenty-Third Americas Conference on Information Systems* (pp. 1–10). Retrieved from https://www.researchgate.net/publication/317717549_Digital_Transformation_in_Higher_Education_-_New_Cohorts_New_Requirements

Wilson, K. J., Brickman, P., & Brame, C. J. (2018). Group work. *CBE—Life Sciences Education, 17*(1), fe1. https://doi.org/10.1187/cbe.17-12-0258.

Woodhouse, J., & Wood, P. (2020). Creating dialogic spaces: Developing doctoral students' critical writing skills through peer assessment and review. *Studies in Higher Education, 1–13*,. https://doi.org/10.1080/03075079.2020.1779686

Xiao, J. (2019). Digital transformation in higher education: Critiquing the five-year development plans (2016–2020) of 75 Chinese universities. *Distance Education, 40*(4), 515–533. https://doi.org/10.1080/01587919.2019.1680272

Xiao, Y., & Lucking, R. (2008). The impact of two types of peer assessment on students' performance and satisfaction within a Wiki environment. *The Internet and Higher Education, 11*(3–4), 186–193. https://doi.org/10.1016/j.iheduc.2008.06.005

Yoo, Y., Kanawattanachai, P., & Citurs, A. (2002). Forging into the wired wilderness: A case study of a technology-mediated distributed discussion-based class. *Journal of Management Education, 26*(2), 139–163. https://doi.org/10.1177/105256290202600203

Young, T. J., & Schartner, A. (2014). The effects of cross-cultural communication education on international students' adjustment and adaptation. *Journal of Multilingual and Multicultural Development, 35*(6), 547–562. https://doi.org/10.1080/01434632.2014.884099

Zheng, L., Zhang, X., & Cui, P. (2019). The role of technology-facilitated peer assessment and supporting strategies: A meta-analysis. *Assessment & Evaluation in Higher Education, 45*(3), 372–386. https://doi.org/10.1080/02602938.2019.1644603

Zulfikar, M. W., Hashim, A. I., Ahmad Umri, H. U., & Dahlan, A. R. A. (2018). A business case for digital transformation of a Malaysian-Based University. *2018 International Conference on Information and Communication Technology for the Muslim World (ICT4M)*, 106–109. https://doi.org/10.1109/ict4m.2018.00028

Part IV
Digital Transformation and Data Analytics in Learning

Chapter 7
Harnessing Immersive Technologies for Innovation in Teaching and Learnings

Samson Tan

Abstract Immersive technologies, due to their transformative potential, do indeed attract the attention of educational researchers. Educators in various fields are beginning to take advantage of VR technologies, and as a result, a growing number of them seek to integrate the technology into their specific areas of expertise. It has been widely documented and addressed extensively that immersive technologies will contribute to learning and teaching, particularly with the rapid rise of augmented reality, virtual reality, and mixed Reality hardware and applications over recent years. As part of the World Economic Forum's latest survey on the Future of Jobs, which was conducted in December 2019, 58% of the businesses surveyed indicated that they are close to adopting immersive technologies by 2022. It was predicted in a report by Goldman Sachs (2018) that 15 million people could benefit from virtual reality and related technologies by the year 2025. In the future, conversational platforms, which range from virtual personal assistants to chatbots, may incorporate expanded sensory channels through which the platform may be able to detect emotions based on facial expressions. As a result, they will become more conversational in interactions. It is the anticipated growth and possibilities of immersive technologies and media in teaching and learning that generate great optimism and excitement for technologists and educational researchers, but it is clear that their attention is insufficiently directed to the instructional design and learning outcomes that result from integrating immersive technologies in such teaching and learning. The educators and learning scientists concerned about the use of these new technologies within educational systems are more concerned with the driving factors that are not pedagogical in nature, but rather technological in origin. It is for this reason that this chapter focuses on a limited but growing body of literature which explores the science of immersive learning beyond simply improving student engagement in the classroom. According to the literature, there are a number of learning affordances that can be identified, including immersion, interactivity, presence and student agency. As important as this chapter's pedagogical framework, instructional design and learning outcomes are, it is intended to facilitate educators' consideration and adoption of immersive technologies in their content and context. In the context of prevailing instructional design models which

S. Tan (✉)
Head of Strategic Development in Libraries & Education, Civica Pte Ltd, Singapore, Singapore
e-mail: samson.tan@civica.com.sg

K. Rajaram, *Learning Intelligence: Innovative and Digital Transformative Learning Strategies*, https://doi.org/10.1007/978-981-19-9201-8_7

are complex and more appropriate for research, this chapter proposes a revised model that puts a greater emphasis on learning than on technologies.

7.1 Introduction

Educators have been progressively adapting digital technologies over the twenty-first century as a means of enhancing teaching and enhancing learning (Zawacki-Richter & Latchem, 2018). The transformational potential of immersive technologies captures the imagination of educational researchers and continues to capture their attention. Immersive technology has become popular as a means to support the teaching and learning processes, and this is increasingly cited and documented, particularly of late with the growing popularity of virtual, augmented and mixed reality hardware and applications. According to the latest World Economic Forum Future of Jobs report conducted in December 2019 by the IDG World Economic Forum, 58% of the businesses in the survey indicated that they would like to implement immersive technologies by 2022. In a similar vein, Goldman Sachs (2018) estimated that by 2025, virtual reality (VR) and other related technologies would reach 15 million learners. It is probably best to mention that the most exciting immersive technology news in 2020 is the name change of Facebook to Meta, referring to metaverse as the company's ambitious plan to work and play in a virtual world (Rodriguez, October 2021). As a concept, metaverse is a persistent, online, massive, dynamic and interoperable virtual environment for sharing and exchanging information on many levels, spanning both digital and tangible realms, which has been around for more than a decade (Nevelsteen, 2018; Ondrejka, 2004). It is therefore not surprising that a growing number of educators across the board are seeking to harness the immersive nature of VR and, increasingly, other immersive technology types into their respective subject matter. Between 2011 and 2020, there has been an increase in the use of virtual reality (VR) in education and training to provide a more authentic learning environment for students (Checa & Bustillo, 2019; Snelson & Hsu, 2020).

It is generally accepted that immersive technologies allow students to immerse themselves in different simulated contexts, providing them with personal experiences and enabling them to engage with different learning processes and tasks. It is evident that VR has been around for a while, but with the rapid advances in immersive technologies, VR has become increasingly appealing to educators. With the latest high-end VR head-mounted displays (HMDs), users are able to experience a high degree of immersion in a virtual environment, which they will feel disconnected from the real world, creating a sense of presence in the virtual environment.

The most advanced headsets are equipped with controllers that allow the user to play games, providing high-fidelity user experiences. On the other hand, low-budget HMDs, such as Google Cardboard, have the technical features that enable them to support gaze control or allow users to interact with the virtual environment. It is actually this propensity of VR to embody not only tangible but also intangible phenomena with high fidelity of visual perception that makes it so attractive (Tacgin, 2018). It is also important to consider that the high level of realism with which the environment is presented helps to create a sense of immersion and presence in the user. The enjoyment of the immersive VR environment is therefore foreshadowed to enhance users' perceptions in various contexts like that of a chrysalis, in a wide range of different scenarios.

While there is growing interest in immersive learning, as well as studies indicating that users perceive HMDs in a positive manner, there is insufficient empirical evidence demonstrating the effectiveness of the technology in terms of learning (Han, 2020; Makransky et al., 2019). As a result of several comprehensive studies, systematic mappings of VR-based educational applications were conducted (Jensen & Konradsen, 2018; Radianti et al., 2020; Wu et al., 2020). While Jensen and Konradsen (2018) emphasize the benefits of HMD technologies to learning that involve the learning experience and the learning outcomes, Radianti et al. (2020) are more specific about the target audience they are addressing. Neither of these studies examine the underlying learning theories that guide the development of VR applications and the design elements that are used in their creation. It is clear that the adoption of immersive media has grown exponentially in the last few decades; however, recent studies (Radianti et al., 2020; Wu et al., 2020) point to a lack of an overarching framework grounded in sound educational principles to guide the development of applications as a significant challenge facing the field. It is in this context that this article focuses on learning outcomes in conjunction with user experience, with a particular emphasis on the design elements of existing research for implementing immersive technologies in higher education, based on the methods of meta-analyses derived from systematic mapping reviews. It is based on the selection of essential information from documents indexed in scientific digital libraries, which have been in turn systematically sieved by using methods of exclusion and inclusion.

It is readily apparent that the majority of the research in immersive learning is being conducted across a wide spectrum of disciplines. However, this chapter is intended to drive the attention to the quality of teaching and learning by placing a strong emphasis on learning outcomes and the design of instructional materials based upon theories of learning. As such, it is imperative to define the parameters in the following section by reviewing the literature on immersive learning.

7.2 Literature Review Immersive Learning

The review of several recent studies has revealed gaps in immersive learning research and significant insights that can be applied to the present book. Radianti et al. (2020) examined VR characteristics in an educational context on a more abstract level, but the other three studies did not pay much attention to the design elements that underpin what is taught and learned through HMD-based teaching and learning. It should also be noted that a mapping of VR design elements that fit the needs of specific forms of learning content has not been produced yet. It is the purpose of this book to underscore the importance of immersive learning in higher education by focusing on how to improve the quality of both teachings and learning across subject matters in higher education institutions.

The disciplines in universities are largely industry oriented; thus, it applies to workplace training as well. In the case of systematic reviews, some of them focused on a specific application area such as science and engineering, while others took treated education as just one application among many (Suh & Prophet, 2018). While the four reviews focused on the application of immersive technologies, only Radianti et al. (2020) provided a more in-depth review of VR applications in education, which is closer to the purpose of this chapter. The following are the details of each review.

7.2.1 Jensen and Konradsen (2018)

In Jensen and Konradsen (2018), a systematic review was conducted in order to update the body of knowledge about the use of head-mounted displays (HMDs) in education and training. They identified and assessed the quality of 21 studies that reported experimental studies, and then assessed the quality of those studies through a comprehensive search. According to the review, there are several situations where HMDs can be useful for the acquisition of various skills including (1) cognitive skills related to remembering and understanding spatial and visual information and knowledge; (2) psychomotor skills related to head movement, such as visual scanning or observational skills; and (3) affective skills related to controlling ones emotional response to stressful or difficult situations. Aside from these situations, they found that the HMDs do not appear to have a distinct advantage over less immersive technologies or traditional instruction. Moreover, in some cases, their examination indicates that HMDs even proved counterproductive due to widespread cybersickness, technological challenges or the immersive experience that distracted learners from the task at hand.

It is also important to note that, even though the focus of Jensen and Konradsen's (2018) study has been on immersive VR technologies, there are still several critical points that have been left out. The study does not analyse immersive VR applications according to learning content, design elements, underpinning learning theories and domains in which they may be used. Additionally, the findings are restricted to the domains of conceptual knowledge, gesture skills and emotional control. Even though Jensen and Konradsen's (2018) study focuses on education, it is unable to address the fundamental objective of learning, which pertains to the instructional content, design elements, underlying learning theories and the domains in which VR applications are used.

7.2.2 Merchant et al. (2014)

A meta-analysis conducted by Merchant et al. (2014) examined the effects of instructional design principles on immersive learning. In comparison with simulations and virtual worlds, the study demonstrates that learners exhibited better learning outcomes through the use of games. Interestingly, they discovered that the number of treatment sessions is inversely proportional to the increase in learning outcomes. As a consequence of the study findings, too much exposure to virtual worlds can be detrimental to learning outcomes. In simulation studies, elaborated explanation feedback is more useful for conceptual tasks, whereas correct responses are more suitable for procedural tasks. The study covers both K-12 and higher education settings equally and examines desktop VR technologies that are not included in this study. Also, the authors examined the appropriateness of a particular VR instructional design when applied to specific learning outcomes. Therefore, this chapter might fill in gaps in Merchant et al.'s (2014) work and provide an inclusive platform for other immersive environments.

In their systematic study examining immersive VR technology research at the present time, Suh and Prophet (2018) employed a different approach by studying the current state of immersive technology research—a classification framework that considered the stimuli (sensory, perceptual, and content), the organism (cognitive and affective reactions), the response (positive and negative outcomes) and the individual differences in the use of VR (gender, age, sensation-seeking tendency, and personal innovativeness). Using immersive technologies, they discovered four prevalent research fields: education, entertainment, health care and marketing. Furthermore, there are two major streams of research that have been developed: firstly, the research focuses on the effects of unique system features of immersive technology on the user experience. Secondly, studies that examine how immersive technologies improve users' performance are focused on learning and teaching effectiveness, task performance and pain management. According to their findings, it is imperative that immersive technology's technological affordances be explored further in order to improve our understanding of how users perform in immersive environments. Due to the lack of evidence, it can be concluded that there are still many unknowns regarding how immersive technologies affect user performance, and in particular the pedagogical effectiveness of immersive learning. A thorough discussion of this issue is given in Sect. 7.5 of this chapter. It is a critical gap that this chapter attempts to address.

A literature review conducted by the authors was also focused on integrating IVR with augmented reality (AR) and mixed reality (MR) and covered studies that were not in the field of education specifically. As a result, we considered that many theoretical frameworks were used in the existing immersive technology studies including flow theory, conceptual blending theory, cognitive load theory, the constructive learning theory, experiential theory, motivation theory, presence theory, situated cognitive theory, media richness theory, stimulus–organization–response model and technology acceptance theory. Despite the fact that Suh and Prophet (2018) conducted a systematic review of immersive VR for education, they also included several other applications besides education, such as health care and marketing. It should be noted, therefore, that immersive VR applications in the education field were not discussed in depth in their study, another gap that is hoped to be filled in this chapter.

7.2.3 Wu et al. (2020)

It was in this context that Wu et al. (2020) conducted a systematic review of literature on immersive learning published between 2013 and 2019. The purpose of the study was to sum up the findings of the overall effects of immersive learning using HMDs, in comparison to less immersive desktop virtual reality (DVR) or other traditional means of instruction. For the purpose of calculating the pooled effect size, they identified 35 randomized controlled trials (RCTs) or quasi-experimental studies and used the random-effects model (REM). Several characteristics of these studies were examined to determine which factor of their characteristics had a moderating effect on the outcome measure, such as learner stage, learning domain, type of learning application, testing format, control group treatment and learning duration. The results showed that IVR using HMDs is more effective than non-immersive learning approaches with a small effect size. This study has revealed the following key findings: HMDs have a more significant impact than typical glasses (a) on students in K-12; (b) in the fields of science education and specific abilities development; (c) when offering simulation or virtual world representations, and (d) when compared with lectures or real-world practices. The authors' meta-analysis also suggested that HMDs can improve knowledge and skill development and maintain learning effectiveness. However, this study does not explain the impact of learning theories and design on the effective application of immersive learning technologies. On top of that, contrary to other research, their results indicate that immersive learning is less effective for higher education in comparison to other studies (Jensen & Konradsen, 2018; Radianti et al., 2020). Lastly, the authors conceded that most of the previous studies that they reviewed did not address theory-driven instructional design with regard to HMD-based immersive learning, thus restricting the analysis of technological-pedagogical symbiotic relations. This is an essential measurement of the effective integration of technology to enhance modern teaching and learning, and this topic is explained in more depth in Sect. 7.5 of this chapter.

7.2.4 Radianti et al. (2020)

The study conducted by Radianti et al. (2020) was a systematic mapping of research design elements already available for implementing VR in higher education. The reviewers extracted crucial information from documents indexed in four digital scientific libraries and used exclusion, inclusion, semi-automatic and manual methods of filtering to identify relevant studies. In comparison to other studies, this review is unique in that it investigates the domain structure in relation to the learning contents, the immersive design elements and the learning theories as a basis for successful VR-enhanced learning. There was a mapping procedure performed between application domains, learning contents, design elements and learning contents. During the review of the VR applications that could be applied in higher education, several gaps were discovered. This study addresses a common issue of learning theories considered in VR application development to guide learning outcomes.

Except for this study, reviews tended to focus only on broad immersive media application domains in education without examining in more detail particular types of learning content that were best suited to immersive technology applications. Furthermore, another gap is that the evaluation of immersive educational applications is mainly based on how well they perform instead of how well they assist students in learning. Immersive virtual reality has tended to be part of research and development activities rather than being used frequently for actual instruction. On the other hand, this study identified 18 application domains, indicating better acceptance of this technology in many spheres. The identified gaps suggest VR design for education has yet to be explored, inspiring future research in this area. In this regard, Radianti et al.'s (2020) study provide clarity, insights and a reference for analysing the innovation in immersive learning and appears to be the most aligned with the purpose of this chapter.

7.3 Meta-Analysis of Immersive Learning

It is Radianti et al.'s (2020) systematic review of selected studies published between 2013 and 2020 which blended existing data collection methodologies in qualitative and quantitative studies that provided the essential findings for the meta-analysis, which includes descriptive statistics. As a result, the following section describes the implications, suggests research agendas, deduces recommendations, highlights limitations and suggests further research.

In the review, the term "immersion" and the application of immersive technology are interpreted differently. During the evaluation process, many papers were excluded because they used an incompatible definition of immersion, which is often applied to non-immersive technologies. In this review, we included a variety of terms related to the immersive technology industry, such as Oculus, Samsung Gear, Samsung Odyssey, Vive and Google Cardboard, among others. On the other hand, many non-immersive technologies could not be included in the list, such as Desktop VR and 360° videos, CAVEs and panoramic videos. There still exists ambiguity and a non-homogeneous identification of the equipment that can be considered "immersive technology" despite the best efforts made in screening the studies. Sixteen application domains were identified, indicating a strong interest in using immersive VR technologies across a range of areas. These include engineering and computer science, to name a few. It should be noted that most studies did not report lessons learned from implementing VR in actual university courses. The majority of reports focused either on the development process or on the potential applications of VR-based learning.

Immersive technology seems to have progressed enough in some fields to teach procedural, practical and conceptual knowledge, as evidenced in fields such as fire safety, surgery, nursing and astronomy. In these cases, professional VR applications were utilized and proven to be appropriate for higher education-related learning. It should be noted, however, that most studies showed that VR development is still in its infancy. New prototypes are being created and pilot tests are being carried out with students. Likewise, there have been few papers which discuss learning outcomes from VR implementation. Rather, the vast majority of the evaluations were usability tests, indicating that immersive technology is still in its infancy when it comes to innovation for teaching and learning. Therefore, it remains a barrier to its widespread adoption in regular courses.

There has been a considerable amount of research done regarding the potential of VR for developing a realistic environment for almost all learning contents, with specific outcomes in mind. There is an observation to be made that there are two distinct levels of interaction between the user and the hardware: (1) interactivity within the immersive environment and (2) interaction with the hardware itself. Nevertheless, the vocabulary of realism does not seem to be uniform in the field of virtual reality. In some studies, for instance, a realistic environment is defined as a high-fidelity virtual environment that includes complex and high-quality graphics. Other researchers, however, advocate that moderation in making the environment of objects "realistic enough" for the users to identify the objects is sufficient. Further details and parameters applicable to this chapter are provided in the following subsections.

7.3.1 *Immersive Technology*

A total of 72% of the studies that were comprised of high-end HMDs, such as the Oculus Rift or HTC Vive, were used. Many of these high-end VR systems used a variety of accessories, including touchpads, controllers and haptic feedback suits. In contrast, out of 38 VR technology counts, nine of them used low-budget mobile VR, as demonstrated by Masuoka et al. (2019). A virtual reality environment that included smartphones and Google Cardboard was used to complete this activity. Taking advantage of low-budget devices and platforms is an approach that this chapter advocates. As a result, not only does this lower the barrier of entry for educators, it shifts the emphasis from relying on the technological affordances to that of focusing on maximising the pedagogical affordances of immersive learning. An in-depth discussion of this topic can be found in Sect. 7.5.

The majority of the hardware did not use enhanced virtual reality technology. Accordingly, Wade et al. (2016) used a gaze-contingent adaptive virtual reality environment, and Shattuck (2018) adopted the use of a multi-user virtual reality environment to visualize neural imaging data. In 3% of the studies, the VR technology used in the study did not make a specific mention, which does not necessarily cause concern. There has also been a point to note that, in some experiments, two technologies have been tried, like in Bujdosó et al. (2017), Song and Li (2018) and Markowitz et al. (2018). As a whole, high-end HMDs were the most commonly used immersive VR technology overall. While this is not surprising, it is at the same time disturbing, as most researchers tend to overwhelmingly focus on the latest technological capabilities when undertaking educational research.

7.3.2 Learning Outcome Evaluation

In most of the reviewed studies, the learning outcome evaluation was not specified. In a few studies (12%), questionnaires or user activities were used while logged on to the VR application. It is worth noting that summative assessments, expert judgments and focus group discussions accounted for a combined total of less than 10% of the studies, with the remaining studies using observation data. Many studies does not include usability or user experience evaluations of developed VR applications. Nonetheless, Farra et al. (2018) and Zhang et al. (2017) measured or evaluated how much students' knowledge or skills had progressed after immersion in VR.

One of the most important aspects of teaching and learning innovation is the learning outcome. Together with the subject content, it represents one of the key pillars of the learning design model developed in this chapter.

7.3.3 Application in Domain Knowledge

Not surprisingly, engineering was identified as the most popular domain of application by 24% of the articles. In terms of application domains, the most popular ones were computer science (12%) and astronomy (8%). Taking the total number of articles together, there are more than 30 articles because some articles cross multiple categories. It should also be noted that several articles were generic and did not state a specific domain. Specifically, this applied to the works of Misbhauddin (2018), Webster and Dues (2017), Yang et al. (2016) and Zizza et al. (2019).

It is interesting that medical education was not mentioned in the review, despite the fact that immersive technology is thought to potentially enhance learning in physiology and anatomy, which require a three-dimensional understanding of human organ systems and structures (Hanna et al., 2018; Moro et al., 2021). Nevertheless, the contribution of this chapter to the education community lies in addressing the broad spectrum of domains that could be enhanced by harnessing immersive learning. The following section provides an overview of innovative learning content through leveraging immersive technology.

7.3.4 Defining the Types of Knowledge or Learning Content

The review indicates that virtual reality applications for higher education were most frequently used to teach: (1) **procedural-practical knowledge** (33%), such as filing a report (Shamsudin et al., 2018) or extinguishing fires (Zhang et al., 2017); (2) **conceptual knowledge** (25%), such as learning about corrosion prevention (Webster, 2016) or theoretical concepts in organic chemistry Edwards et al. (2019); and (3) **analytical and problem-solving skills** (12%), such as diagnosing patients (Cecil et al., 2018) or learning how to code (Dass et al., 2018, April). The rest of the learning content categories found in the literature were communication, collaboration and soft skills (10%), behavioural impact (6%) and learning a language (2%). The categories others and not specified accounted for 6% and 4%.

It is by far the most important act in analysing and evaluating the impact of immersive learning on learning outcomes to organize the immersive learning research by the types of knowledge or content that will be studied. The categorization of knowledge based on the revised Bloom's taxonomy allows educators to design and revise their learning design based on the data obtained (Krathwohl, 2002). Following is a comprehensive discussion of key aspects of innovation in teaching and learning, divided into subsections.

7.3.5 Contextualising Immersive Technologies for Innovation in Teaching and Learning

In the systematic reviews, it was found that the "realistic surroundings" and "basic interaction" design elements were seen in all types of virtual reality applications. As a result, these elements can be considered basic design requirements for educational immersive applications. In immersive technology research, the majority of the literature focuses on the content and technological affordances of immersive media, with little or very little attention being paid to the learning outcomes or the learning theories. During the writing of this chapter, it was noted that learning outcomes such as factual, conceptual and procedural knowledge as well as the transfer of knowledge were closely related to the use of immersive learning environments in education. As a result, these outcomes have been derived from Anderson et al.'s (2001) taxonomy for learning, teaching and assessing, as well as the addition of transfer of knowledge, which is widely accepted to be a benchmark for the most important outcome of education (Dede, 2009; Eraut, 2012; Mayer, 2014).

Conceptual knowledge is primarily taught in lectures, and students are expected to memorize what they have learned for exams in the courses. In this sense, immersive applications can be used for teaching conceptual knowledge as well as ensuring that learning keeps students engaged. The design elements of most conceptual knowledge applications are based on only two elements. In other words, these design elements can be a soft start for immersive learning development, making them easy for students and lecturers to use. In addition, there might not be any curriculum changes required. The implementation of immersive applications that improve conceptual understanding can be recommended as an introduction to immersive learning in the classroom.

Anderson et al. (2001) classify procedural knowledge as a type of knowledge about how to perform a particular task in a particular way and demonstrates itself as a behaviour rather than conscious memory, which fits perfectly with the previous section's findings showing that immersive learning environments lend themselves readily to the teaching of procedural and practical knowledge. Immersion learning environments have been found to provide the optimal conditions for learning by practising procedures with appropriate sensors such as hand-control devices, gloves or camera-based hand-tracking devices. The immersive learning environment, therefore, allows learners to rehearse the performance of a procedure as many times as necessary in a safe-to-fail environment where they can slow down the process as needed. The application of an immersive learning environment can be found in acquiring procedural knowledge that is difficult to acquire or dangerous to acquire in real life, such as fire safety practices (Sankaranarayanan et al. 2018) and complex surgical procedures (Xin et al., 2019), or aviation (Oberhauser & Dreyer, 2017).

In the case where teaching faculty has already had successful immersive learning experiences in their lessons, they can adapt more sophisticated applications to make more practice-oriented interventions. The majority of the reviews reviewed describe immersive learning applications for teaching procedural knowledge. Moreover, the reviews of these applications indicate that they have the greatest number of design elements, an indication that the development of such applications could be complex and demanding. As a result, teaching faculty, as well as students, may need more exposure to immersive learning in order to use them effectively. In addition, the curriculum may need to undergo complex transformations in order to shift from the teaching of conceptual knowledge to a more practice-oriented focus. It is therefore imperative that faculty members acquire a more advanced level of expertise in learning design in order to maximize the pedagogical benefits of immersive learning innovation.

There is no doubt that immersive technology has the potential to improve communication, collaboration and other soft skills that are crucial to twenty-first-century learning; however, the review provided limited insight into the most suitable design elements for meeting specific learning objectives. It has been shown that it is beneficial to provide the teaching faculty with preliminary ideas about the use of immersive learning as a scaffold to get a better understanding of how it works, what it can be used for and what kind of technology to use.

It is common for emerging technologies to progress through different stages of hype with heightened expectations that surround a technology over time from its initial launch (Bosch-Sijtsema et al., 2021). Undoubtedly, immersive technology is an exciting topic in the technology world, and educators can take advantage of this momentum by becoming early adopters and contributing to the development of immersive learning experiences. It is therefore imperative that educators who are interested in immersive learning become equipped with the appropriate capabilities as well as work in collaboration with the industry to develop immersive learning environments specifically tailored to their curriculums.

The natural development of immersive learning applications builds on the existing use cases of immersive learning applications in a multitude of domains. It was found that robust use cases can be used as a suitable indicator in the absence of best practices in a particular field. Ideally, a robust case should contain clear learning outcomes, practical design elements and an immersive application in higher education, based on reliable technology in order to make the case. It is, therefore, necessary to nurture, sustain and scale up the pioneering works beyond the institutions and in the domain of the original work. As discussed in Sect. 7.5, educators need to go beyond just the wow factor of rich visualizations and focus on instructional support and learning processes (Chandler, 2009; Makransky & Petersen, 2021).

Lastly, transfer of learning is described as the act of transferring skills and knowledge learned in one context to another context or when the effects of past learning affect or impact the performance or performance of a subsequent activity (Mestre, 2002). In terms of immersive learning technology, it can be used to create learning experiences that incorporate learners' digital fluency in a way that fosters engagement, learning and transferability between the classroom and real-life situations (Dede, 2009). In particular, the ability of learners to sequester problem-solving and prepare for future learning can be considered evidence of the transfer of learning (Schwartz et al., 2005). Sequestered problem-solving focuses on near transfer, allowing learners to apply the knowledge acquired in one context to another context with somewhat different surface characteristics. In contrast, future-oriented learning preparation emphasizes learners acquiring skills in "learning how to learn" and using their learning to solve authentic, real-world problems, which requires applying the knowledge learned in a different context. In this regard, it is reassuring to note that immersive learning for situated learning has the potential to offer learners simulated simulations of real-world issues and contexts that learners must grasp as part of the near transfer to prepare them for future education. The following section of the chapter is devoted to investigating the learning design of immersive learning after redefining the technological and pedagogical affordances of immersive learning.

At the time of writing, the cost of HMDs has continued to decline, as the metaverse gains traction, causing immersive technology vendors to transition from custom development for customers to Software as a Service (SaaS) subscriptions. There is still a barrier to entry for educators since the subscription price (based on the number of users inclusive of instructors and students) is so high that it may not be convincing for educators to pay the subscription until there is evidence of a positive impact on learning. Towards that end, what is recommended is that pilot lessons should be conducted, starting small and adjusting the application to the dimensions and time frame of the application that seem to be realistic and achievable. There is a significant risk of a costly failure if the whole course is adopted, regardless of the fact that there is an abundance of funds and other resources available to give the course a successful outcome. However, integrating low-cost mobile headsets or adapting immersive applications to a few selected lessons over the course of the semester can lay the groundwork for wider adoption of immersive learning in the institution by virtue of serving as scaffolding. After adopting measurable dimensions and embedding them in educational contexts, the following section reviews some of the technological affordances of immersive technologies for teaching and learning innovation.

7.4 Reframing Immersive Technology for Innovation in Teaching and Learning

With a wide variety of technologies available for integrating with immersive learning, the task of understanding immersive learning becomes an untenable one, as the literature on immersive learning abounds with its long list of possibilities. As a result, it is necessary to discover the theoretical underpinnings for immersive learning and learning efficacy. It is possible to analyse the application of immersive learning in the context of educational institutions by combining these topics. Learning enhancement through the application of immersive technology is so widely accepted as being beneficial to learning that educators and learning specialists have been analysing this technology extensively. With modern technology such as virtual and augmented reality, as well as the rise in free development platforms, it has become easier to create engaging online experiences that are a welcome addition to people's lives. As a matter of fact, its single greatest strength lies in the ability to render both tangible and intangible phenomena in an incredibly realistic way. The highly realistic depiction of the learning environment directly relates to the sense of presence and immersion experienced by the user.

Research indicates that the use of immersive technologies helps students retain knowledge, particularly in the context of learning (Araiza-Alba et al., 2020; Krokos et al., 2019; Parong & Mayer, 2020; Tacgin & Dalgarno, 2021). As global revenues from HMDs are expected to reach USD 25 billion by 2022, growing at a Compound Annual Growth Rate (CAGR) of 39.52% between 2019 and 2025 (Global Augmented Reality, 2019), the industry believed the market has reached the point of mass adoption. The new developments also warrant further research to establish the immersive efficacy of immersive learning, mainly due to the enhanced capabilities of the technology and reduced costs that are associated with the new developments. The new cordless Oculus Quest HMD is an example of the latest innovation since it allows the user to move more freely while keeping the same price as the previous generation Rift with cables.

There were two systematic reviews on immersive learning that is undertaken in recent years by Radianti et al. (2020) and Wu et al. (2020), and these reviews provided a solid foundation upon which this article is based to glean the best practices in the applications of immersive technologies in higher education. Due to the features of the technologies for creating virtual learning environments, they can be categorized as either immersive or non-immersive, based on their characteristics. In this context, mobile immersive learning devices, high-end head-mounted displays and enhanced immersive technologies are considered to be immersive technologies that enable users to immerse themselves completely in a virtual environment (Khalifa & Shen, 2004; Martín-Gutiérrez et al., 2017). As opposed to Cave Automatic Virtual Environment (CAVE) or desktop virtual reality systems, which still allow users to see the screen or the desktop workstation, CAVE or desktop virtual reality is considered non-immersive (Biocca & Delaney, 1995; Robertson et al., 1997).

It is important to note, however, that there are many different immersive technologies revolving around virtual reality (VR), augmented reality (AR), mixed reality (MR) and extended reality (XR); most of the reported research focuses on VR (Milgram & Kishino, 1994; Radianti et al., 2020). Cross reality, or XR, is actually a term applied to a group of technologies and applications which include mixed reality (MR), augmented reality (AR), virtual reality (VR) and virtual worlds (VW) (Ziker et al., 2021). It is evident that, even though these emerging immersive technologies are gaining traction with educators and the technology industry, there is a lack of research to guide educators in implementing these new technologies to innovate in the teaching and learning environment.

While immersive learning environments are typically perceived by users as fully immersive environments where they can interact with an artificial world in a unique way (Pan & Hamilton, 2018; Roo & Hachet, 2017, October), Biocca and Delaney (1995) take a broader position when defining immersive learning technologies as a combination of hardware and software systems that are intended to result in an all-encompassing sensory impression of being in a synthetic environment. In spite of the ability of the virtual world to simulate some properties of the real world, it can go beyond physical reality's limitations by creating a world where physical laws no longer apply. In the world of immersive technologies, there is such a variety of ways to describe immersive environments generated by them that stakeholders find it challenging to make sense of the myriad terms used. It is helpful, therefore, that Milgram and Kishino (1994) were able to point out that the term 'virtual reality' that is frequently used in conjunction with a number of other environments that might not necessarily correspond to total immersion or complete synthesis, but which might fall somewhere along the *virtuality continuum*. The continuum provides a virtual and reality gradation corresponding to the transition from virtual to physical reality, which encompasses immersive technologies from the perspective of the continuum or spectrum of immersive experiences.

Since research in immersive learning often classifies immersion, presence and interactivity as the three most fundamental elements of immersive learning, (Kim & Ko, 2019; Mütterlein, 2018) the following section attempts to clarify these definitions and provide a better understanding of these pillars.

7.4.1 Immersion

It is still unclear how exactly the concept of immersion should be defined, while researchers generally agree on the definitions of interactivity and presence. There is one school of thought that advocates immersion as a technological attribute that users can objectively assess (Slater, 2009; Slater & Wilbur, 1997), as opposed to others who viewed immersion as a synthesis of virtual reality that creates the illusion of a real world that is supported by cognitive processes. It is Jensen and Konradsen's (2018) work which offers a different perspective on the positive effects of immersion and presence on learning outcomes. In their study, the researchers found that learners who used an immersive head-mounted display (HMD) were more engaged, spent more time on learning tasks and developed better cognitive, psychomotor and affective skills. Nevertheless, individual personality characteristics may also affect one's ability to acquire skills associated with the use of immersive technologies.

Given the wide range of vague descriptions of immersion, it is gratifying that Slater and Sanchez-Vives (2016) provided greater clarity asserting that immersion is determined by how effectively an immersive platform replaces the real world's perception with that of the virtual one, thereby allowing the user to perceive through natural sensorial exigencies. Immersion is a measure that focuses specifically on how the system in question is able to exclude the outside world from a user's experience as well as the intensity of the experience offered. Adding to this consideration, Ryan (2015) provided further clarity in that cognitive immersion can be divided into three kinds, including **spatial immersion**, **temporal immersion** and **emotional immersion**.

With a better understanding of the concept of immersion, it is important to examine the degree of immersion, since it is the fundamental aspect that distinguishes an immersive learning lesson via head-mounted display from a virtual reality session via a desktop computer. Simulators or 3D worlds that can be accessed from a desktop computer or a mobile device are classified as low immersion. Depending on the technology and type of the hardware, the degree of immersion can vary considerably. However, immersive learning experiences that can be accessed via an HMD are generally regarded as having a high degree of immersion (Bailey & Bailenson, 2017). It is also possible to access XR via HMD, blending reality with virtual content based on a virtual environment (Ziker et al., 2021).

As immersion is interconnected with the sense of presence that the user feels when they are in the space, the following section clarifies the sense of presence that occurs from immersion.

7.4.2 Presence

Presence is defined as "a psychological state in which users experienced virtual objects as actual objects in either sensory or nonsensory ways" (Lee, 2004). As an alternative, Witmer and Singer (1998) define presence as "the subjective experience of being in a place or environment even in cases where you are physically situated in another place". As the term presence implies, it includes the subjective elements of physical, social and self-presence, referring to all the different aspects of the human experience.

According to the psychological perspective of a user's sense of presence, immersion is a psychological state in which the user perceives isolation of the senses of the real world while using the augmented reality system. It is important to note that the degree of immersion perceived by individuals varies according to their level of technological sophistication, with technological attributes barely making a difference (Mütterlein, 2018). On the other hand, Slater (2018) has argued that immersion should be viewed from an objective perspective independent of the perspective of the user as an objective description of technological immersion. Specifically, the degree to which physical reality is excluded in the simulation, the range of sensory modalities, the spatial scope of the external environment, the resolution and the accuracy of the simulation are all taken into account. The findings from Ijsselsteijn and Riva's study (2003) provided more specific details and proposed three types of factors that determine presence: (1) the extent of sensory information presented, (2) the amount of control one has over the sensors in the environment and (3) the degree to which one can modify the environment and its objects. The first element of the system to be taken into account is the degree of immersion it offers. Contrary to the first element, the second and third elements are explained by the kind of control provided by the environment, where the proximity of activation is also an important consideration.

The fidelity of the immersive environment is another important aspect of presence that is dependent on the realism of the environment as well as the consistency of views that are changing (Dalgarno & Lee, 2010). Similarly, Witmer and Singer (1998) indicate that the control factors include variables such as the degree of control, the proximity to control and the control mode. There are several variables that are considered to be part of representational fidelity, including realism of display, smoothness of display and consistency of object behaviour (Dalgarno & Lee, 2010). Nevertheless, it is Makransky et al. (2018) study that has provided clarity by demonstrating three dimensions of presence: **physical, social and self-presence**. As a result, physical presence in the actual state of psychological awareness requires a user to feel physically present in a virtual environment as if they were physically present in that environment, either in a sensory or a non-sensory manner. As social presence has been defined as users' psychological state in experiencing virtual social actors as real social actors in any sensory or non-sensory medium, the state of self-presence can be described as the state of a user in experiencing their virtual selves as their actual self in either sensory or non-sensory platforms. When starting a project in the field of immersive learning, this is an important point for learning innovators to keep in mind. The technological capability and therefore the cost of integrating the social presence can be rather high. As such, it is advisable for learning innovators new to immersive technologies to start with small steps before scaling up.

Since this chapter includes all types of immersive technology that can be applied for developing an immersive learning environment, the affordances of cross reality or extended reality are discussed in more detail. Beyond academic institutions, there has been an increasing interest in employing cross reality and extended reality for workplace learning and development. Microsoft's HoloLens 2 is a prime example of innovation in the workplace through the introduction of "instinctual interaction" in the application of XR. In a similar vein, Ziker et al. (2021) assert that collaborative virtual environments within the workplace can facilitate co-designing and co-development when scenarios or problem-solving questions are incorporated into immersive environments. In the immersive learning environment, presence is interwoven with the need for interaction; therefore, the following section examines how interaction is related to the sense of presence and the degree of immersion found therein.

7.4.3 Interactivity

Over the past few decades, researchers have tended to consider interaction as a parameter that allows the user to adapt to the virtual environment in real time, which has prompted them to focus their efforts on how the interaction element in the learning experience can affect the level of engagement in learning, attention to learning resources and reliance on them (Jensen & Konradsen, 2018; Song et al., 2012; Steuer, 1995; Zhang et al., 2019). As a result, the focus has largely been on technology, such as the use of immersive head-mounted displays (HMDs) in order to stimulate students' interest and help them acquire comprehensive cognitive, psychomotor and affective skills.

In this regard, Dalgarno and Lee (2010) make a refreshing point stating that immersion is determined by both the interactivity of the simulation environment as well as its fidelity. As a result, immersion and interaction are critical aspects of an immersive learning environment that must be considered together. In the same way, Bowman and McMahan (2007) find that immersion surprisingly does not result in more realistic and detailed methods of interaction with the environment, but the research lacks a comprehensive understanding of the effects immersion and interactivity have on each other. To be more specific, interaction can be considered as a technical characteristic of a virtual environment that is associated with the degree of freedom that the learner can experience and the level of fidelity with which the exercise is implemented (Kilteni et al., 2012). Immersive learning environments focus on interactivity within the learning environment, which is another distinguishing characteristic of immersive learning as opposed to traditional multimedia lessons. However, it is crucial that these concepts work together in order to support future research on the way users engage with technology-mediated experiential interfaces, which is why it is important to understand how immersion and interactivity are interrelated.

On the basis of these concepts, Lyons and Mallavarapu's (2021) study provided critical insights on the collective usability as an expression of the ability of a group of concurrent users to interact effectively with a computerized system where a combination of inter-human and inter-computer interactions operates to provide a holistically integrated system. The deployment of an agent-based model simulation provided a basis for exploring how changes in the number of simultaneous users as well as the duration, size and the number of extended interactives may have an impact on the overall usability of immersive learning environments. The most important point is that these developments enable educators to shift their attention from the technological affordances to balance with the pedagogical affordances in learning design. More specifically, the aim of this chapter is primarily on harnessing immersive technologies for imbuing, among other educational imperatives, critical twenty-first-century skills in the classroom. As such, this chapter referred liberally to Radianti et al.'s (2020) findings on the current domain structure regarding the learning contents, the immersive learning design elements and the learning theories' foundation for successful immersive technology-based learning. However, there was no mention of student agency in the review, despite the fact that it is a crucial component of education in the twenty-first century. In the following section, agency is discussed in more detail in relation to other educational research.

7.4.4 Agency

It is important that immersive learning environments foster a sense of student agency rooted in the belief or perception that students are able to make a positive impact on their own lives and the world, or a sense of generating and controlling actions on behalf of themselves (OECD, 2018). Essentially, the feeling of agency or character of agency has been defined as a sense of generating and controlling actions (Moore & Fletcher, 2012). As a result, agency provides learners with an opportunity to contribute to their learning experience rather than just consume it.

According to research studies, agency is conceptualized as an interactive process between students and the learning environment which allows students to execute the actions that they wish to perform (Wardrip-Fruin et al., 2009, September). By giving learners the ability to exercise agency, they are able to make informed decisions to support their engagement, motivation and learning (Rowe et al., 2011; Snow et al., 2015). The agency is shown to be effective when a learner deems a learning activity too easy and chooses to skip it, moves on to a more challenging exercise, realizes that they are not familiar with some pre-requisite knowledge and reviews some prior instructions before beginning the challenge. Specifically, Metcalfe et al. (2013) argue that a learner's decision to take action to achieve a learning goal stems from the learner having a learning goal, taking the appropriate steps to accomplish the goal and reflecting on the outcome of these steps.

The fact remains, however, that most advances in technology-enhanced learning (TEL) have focused on the use of technology as a platform for delivering educational content, as well as facilitating interaction between students (Buchem et al., 2014; Lindgren & McDaniel, 2012). As a result, in an immersive learning environment, student agency is mostly determined by the ability of learners to control their own actions (Johnson-Glenberg, 2019). A virtual environment where interaction is impossible, where a narrative is fixed and where interaction is impossible results in low agency. To develop a sense of agency, learners must first recognize that they can exercise agency in how they perceive the learning environment. In planning their immersive learning programmes, learning innovators should endeavour to include technological affordances that enable agency as a crucial pedagogical affordance. In the light of the essential role of agency in developing immersive learning designs, the following section discusses agency in relation to sociocultural dynamics in the immersive learning environments.

7.4.5 Sociocultural Dynamics

The immersive learning environments are part of the expectation that they are capable of providing immersive and interdisciplinary experiences that support students' motivation and learning while also being tailored to meet student needs and allowing for student agency (Oyserman & Dawson, 2021). It is important to highlight that this point is applicable broadly, but it may be particularly pertinent when considering ways of creating immersive learning environments that ensure that underrepresented minority groups or students with special needs are both meaningfully represented and actively engaged in the learning process (Foster & Shah, 2021). Hence, immersive learning environments can be used as a theoretical framework to explain sociocultural practices and situated reality, with a view to shaping students' identities. Immersive learning could be adapted as an alternative for students' field trip if the students are not able to do field work due to mobility issues. During the COVID-19 pandemic lockdown period, teachers had curated or created immersive 360 videos for students so that they could do their "fieldtrip" using inexpensive headsets at the comfort of their homes. Also, these students may still view the place-based learning using the computer even though that compromises the fidelity of the learning experience.

In dealing with the need to transit to meaningful blended learning in the post-COVID-19 world, Colreavy-Donnelly et al. (2022) argued that well-designed immersive learning environments maybe that is able to enhance students' social learning experiences. Sociocultural perspectives are based on the notions of social constructivism. As a result, they emphasize the social and cultural contexts in which cognition takes place, the origins of cognition, and the ways in which a person's appropriation of language allows them to construct their own meaning from it. Taking a sociocultural approach to designing an immersive learning environment is crucial for creating an immersive learning environment that is fitting for the twenty-first century. Having established the role of social and cultural elements in the design of immersive learning, the stage has been set for the analysis of the instructional design models.

7.5 Immersive Learning Design Model

There have been numerous studies that have explored immersive learning, but few of them have introduced a systematic process that can be used for the development of these courses. Most of those who reported on systematic design processes have tended to focus on instructional design models which work well in non-immersive learning environments. As a result, these instructional design models do not take into account the unique affordances of immersive learning environments. Aside from the above, those designing processes generally tend to be theoretical, and they often have not been validated against the real-life practice. In this regard, this chapter is arguing that in order to design immersive learning environments that incorporate the distinctive characteristics of immersive environments, a fresh approach must be taken.

In the review of Sect. 7.3, it is found that several elements are crucial considerations for harnessing the pedagogical affordances of immersive learning. Firstly, the types of learning content as long coupled with the subject domains is observed that most types of immersive applications have at least one factor in common: "realistic surroundings" and "basic interaction" designs. In this regard, immersive applications can be used to teach conceptual knowledge to create a more engaging learning experience. In this way, these design elements may function as a soft start for immersive learning development, as they are easy to use for lecturers and students, and may not require any curriculum alterations. It is possible for the faculty to adopt more sophisticated applications to more procedural knowledge teaching if they already have successful immersive learning experiences in their lessons. However, most reviews portray immersive applications for teaching procedural knowledge. Hence, it is imperative to adopt the appropriate design for the type of learning content according to the domains when deploying immersive learning innovation.

Secondly, the review in Sect. 7.3 also revealed that there is a dearth of studies that emphasize learning theories in the design of immersive learning. Compounding the problem, it is found that the majority of the immersive learning studies do not include learning outcomes in the evaluation of the findings. The lack of focus in these two critical areas not only exposes the glaring gaps in designing immersive learning innovation but also brings to question the educational benefit of such learning innovation.

A vast majority of immersive learning studies tend to focus on the technological affordances of immersive learning; however, there is a broader spectrum of hardware and applications that are used when using different types of platforms. The review carried out in Sect. 7.4 concluded that the combination of immersion, presence, interactivity and agency are the technological affordances that are most suited for the design of immersive learning.

It is intended that this section would integrate the reframed technological and pedagogical affordances to contribute to developing an appropriate instructional design model which supports immersive learning environments. In the following section, several instructional models are reviewed and evaluated for their potential use in designing immersive learning.

7.5.1 *Tacgin's Instructional Design Model for Immersive Virtual Reality Learning Environments*

Conventional instructional design models rely on learning space to present learners with information. Hence, the use of computers to represent knowledge on screens as a direct result of linking learning components for interaction is essential for traditional teaching models. On the other hand, the dynamics of immersive learning environments are different, and knowledge representation in immersive learning environments should be more flexible than in non-immersive learning environments. The application allows users to interact with each virtual object in a realistic way; for example, they can use the door instead of an exit button to quit the application. As these navigation panels or texts are not part of our physical reality, providing them using transparent interfaces is an important component of enhancing immersion within an immersive learning environment.

In consideration of these issues, Tacgin (2018) developed an instructional design model consisting of three main components: (1) a virtual environment, (2) a learner interface and (3) content knowledge. During the development process, the following model is used sequentially and iteratively, as shown in the following figure. There are distinct characteristics associated with each step that can assist in the teaching of concepts.

Based on these findings, it became apparent that Tacgin's (2018) instructional design model is strengthened by its emphasis on learning theories, learning contents and clear learning outcomes. They represent the pillars of pedagogical affordances that are absent from other pedagogical design models for immersive learning. Nonetheless, it is important to note that the absence of student motivation and agency in this model has to be taken into account as an area for improvement.

7.5.2 *Dalgarno and Lee's (2010) Affordance Model for 3D Virtual Learning Environments*

Dalgarno and Lee (2010) developed an instructional model that illustrates the unique characteristics and learning benefits that are associated with an immersive learning environment with the objective of revealing the essential features associated with each category of outcomes and connecting these features to those particular categories. For example, presence, interaction and fidelity constitute the critical components of

3D VRLEs. Moreover, this model emphasizes the necessity of spatial knowledge representation.

This model is purportedly suitable for collaborative, experimental and context-based learning. However, it fails to take into consideration the most critical components of learning and, in particular, the students' motivation and their autonomy. For inclusive learning experiences to be designed, agency needs to be included in the design of the learning experience, so that social interaction and the team culture of learners are taken into consideration. This is an area that needs to be strengthened for further improvement.

7.5.3 Makransky and Petersen's (2021) Cognitive Affective Model of Immersive Learning (CAMIL)

Using the cognitive learning theories, Makransky and Petersen (2021) developed a model for instructional design that integrates cognitive neuroscience methods with human perception, in order to facilitate knowledge acquisition—the Cognitive Affective Model of Immersive Learning (CAMIL). A theoretical framework for exploring immersive media lessons is based on a theory stating that the instructional method of such a lesson is effective if it facilitates the distinctive affordances of the medium of change rather than the immersive medium media that arouses learning. As a result, psychological constructs that arise from immersion and interaction, such as the learners' presence and agency, would be higher in immersive technology, indicating that approaches that increase learning through increased presence or agency would also increase learning through immersive technologies. The embodiment principle from the social agency theory as discussed by Makransky and Petersen (2021) also leads to their claim that (Mayer, 2014) using the embodiment principle could prime a learner's social presence and increase their motivation to do more work in order to grasp the concepts being presented.

The purpose of CAMIL is to foster the emergence of two pedagogical affordances that are most necessary for learning to take place in an immersive media environment—presence and agency (Makransky & Petersen, 2021). The model provides an explanation for how these two pedagogical affordances are derived from technological functionality while facilitating learning through cognitive and affective processes. Out of all the models reviewed, this is the only one that includes agency as part of its immersive learning design. In particular, this is of utmost importance for learning innovators to consider when they are in the process of embarking on immersive learning, as agency is one of the essential elements for the future of learning.

The CAMIL model relates six affective and cognitive factors, including interest, intrinsic motivation, self-efficacy, embodiment, cognitive load and self-regulation, which allow individuals to acquire factual, conceptual and procedural knowledge as well transfer their knowledge into different contexts (Lee et al., 2010; Makransky & Lilleholt, 2018; Makransky & Petersen, 2019). Connecting cognitive and affective factors with the types of knowledge is another valuable contribution made by CAMIL that would be useful to learning innovators.

Lastly, a key element of CAMIL is the integration of perspectives from previous research in virtual reality, multimedia, educational psychology and educational technology. It is also important to note that the framework focuses on learning outcomes as well as the socio-emotional aspects of learning. CAMIL has many attributes that are conducive to educational research; however, it is a sophisticated model that may prove to be challenging for educators to adopt in a classroom setting, particularly for those who are venturing into immersive learning for the first time. There is therefore an urgent need to develop a flexible and updated instructional model that can easily be adapted in order to embrace immersive learning both in teaching and in learning. Hence, CAMIL is recommended for educators who are experienced in immersive learning or intended for robust educational research. With three good instructional models for consideration, the following section examines the feasibility of developing an updated instructional design model based on an analysis of the strengths of the instructional design models reviewed in this section.

7.5.4 Revised Instructional Model for Immersive Learning

A review of current models for instructional design models of immersive learning provided insights into the elements that are crucial to facilitate the rethinking and the redesigning of an immersive learning environment for learning innovation. Each model offers a unique set of benefits and in some instances shares several common characteristics. Thus, even though these instructional models are useful in designing immersive learning environments and exploring immersive learning environments, there are still some gaps when it comes to maximizing the effectiveness of harnessing immersive technology for teaching and learning. In addition, these instructional models are rather complex, making it difficult for teachers, especially those who are not familiar with immersive technology, to readily adapt to their curriculum through the use of these tools.

It is for this reason that this article attempts to glean the strengths of the instructional models reviewed in this section, streamline the processes and propose a revised model that is more practical for teachers. The following Fig. 7.1 illustrates the revised model.

It is proposed that this new instructional model should focus on three main areas for adapting immersive technologies and incorporating them into a curriculum. These areas include functional affordances, afforded learning theories and afforded learning practices. There are three elements in the diagram that can be recognized as elements of functional abilities: interaction, immersion and presence, and they can also be identified in other instructional models. The notion of agency is nevertheless included

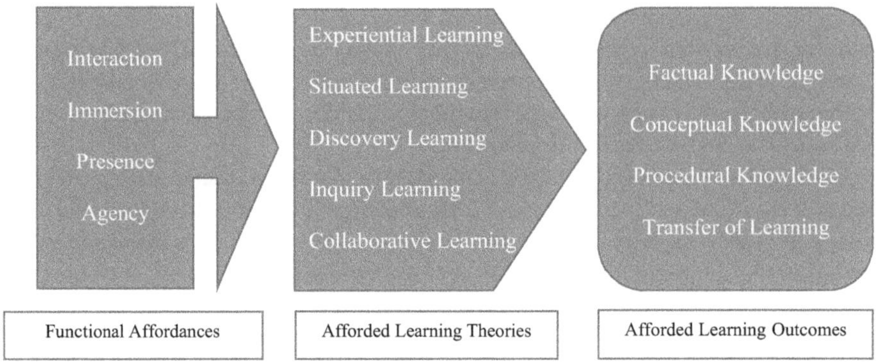

Fig. 7.1 Proposed instructional design model

in the course because it is considered a foundation component of providing students with autonomy in their learning, and it is also regarded as the most essential part of the future of learning.

Among the significant differences between this model and its predecessors that the reader might notice is the absence of any prescriptive causal links from one affordance to another. This is done with the intent of allowing the educators to exercise their freedom in deciding which functional affordances will be mapped onto learning affordances. With the rapid maturation of cloud computing and big data, the barrier for entry is increasingly lowered as more immersive technology providers adopt a cloud service business model just like music and movies are consumed (Marr, December 2020). In the light of this, educators have increasingly overcome initial challenges of technical expertise in order to create an immersive learning environment to facilitate teaching and learning in the classroom. Also, educators are able to access a multitude of low-coding or no-coding immersive learning technologies, such as virtual reality 360 videos and 360 images. When paired with authoring tools and VR headsets, these VR 360 resources can be transformed into immersive lessons with a moderate level of fidelity that is good enough to yield optimal learning outcomes. The massive shift in online learning during the COVID-19 lockdown periods provided the opportunity for educators to experiment with these immersive learning innovations. With the concerns about technological huddles addressed, this model provides educators with the opportunity to focus on the essentials of learning rather than the peripherals of learning.

This revised instructional model may be considered by some readers to be neither sufficiently sophisticated to support research nor valid for assessing its efficacy, but it is intended to serve as a pragmatic scaffold for educators focusing on the essential aspects of teaching and learning. It is the readers' prerogative to apply the model in their particular contexts so as to best suit their needs for innovation in teaching and learning. It is also the author's intention to refine this design model in the future by conducting further empirical research.

7.6 Conclusion

One of the aims of this article is to provide a broader perspective on immersive learning and support educators in harnessing immersive technologies in the classroom and at home. The advent of immersive technologies has led to the emergence of virtual reality (VR), augmented reality (AR), mixed reality (MR) and cross reality (XR), but among educational researchers, virtual reality emerged as the most researched and established (Milgram & Kishino, 1994). The rapid emergence of other forms of immersive technologies has resulted in a gap in this area due to the lack of research done to date. It is important to include all known forms of immersive technologies and to ensure that the knowledge delivered is future-ready and that it meets educators' evolving needs.

As with many aspects of educational research in the field of immersive learning, a lack of emphasis placed on learning theories and learning outcomes has led to an overemphasis placed on functional and technological affordances as the primary focus. It is for this reason that the proposed instructional model is proposed to aid educators in incorporating learning outcomes and theories when adapting an immersive learning environment to ensure that learners are engaged in learning. The next step which follows the successful completion of this project is the implementation of a robust empirical study to validate the proposed model.

References

Anderson, L. W., Krathwohl, D. R., Airasian, P., Cruikshank, K., Mayer, R., Pintrich, P., & Wittrock, M. (2001). *A taxonomy for learning, teaching and assessing: A revision of Bloom's taxonomy.* Longman Publishing.

Araiza-Alba, P., Keane, T., Matthews, B., Simpson, K., Strugnell, G., Chen, W. S., & Kaufman, J. (2020). The potential of 360-degree virtual reality videos to teach water-safety skills to children. *Computers and Education, 163*, 104096.

Bailey, J. O., & Bailenson, J. N. (2017). Immersive virtual reality and the developing child. In *Cognitive development in digital contexts* (pp. 181–200). Academic Press.

Biocca, F. (1999). The cyborg's dilemma: Progressive embodiment in virtual environments. *Human Factors in Information Technology, 13*, 113–144.

Biocca, F., & Delaney, B. (1995). Immersive virtual reality technology. In *Communication in the age of virtual reality* (pp. 57–124). Lawrence Erlbaum Associates, Inc.

Bosch-Sijtsema, P., Claeson-Jonsson, C., Johansson, M., & Roupe, M. (2021). The hype factor of digital technologies in AEC. *Construction Innovation.*

Bowman, D. A., & McMahan, R. P. (2007). Virtual reality: How much immersion is enough? *Computer, 40*(7), 36–43.

Buchem, I., Tur, G., Hoelterhof, T., Rahimi, E., van den Berg, J., Veen, W., & Rivera-Pelayo, V. (2014). Learner control in personal learning environments: A cross-cultural study. *Learning and Diversity in the Cities of the Future, 15*(2), 14–53.

Bujdosó, G., Novac, O. C., & Szimkovics, T. (2017, September). Developing cognitive processes for improving inventive thinking in system development using a collaborative virtual reality system. In *2017 8th IEEE International Conference on Cognitive Infocommunications (Coginfocom)* (pp. 000079–000084). IEEE.

Cecil, J., Gupta, A., & Pirela-Cruz, M. (2018). An advanced simulator for orthopedic surgical training. *International Journal of Computer Assisted Radiology and Surgery, 13*(2), 305–319.
Chandler, P. (2009). Dynamic visualisations and hypermedia: Beyond the "Wow" factor. *Computers in Human Behavior, 25*(2), 389–392. https://doi.org/10.1016/j.chb.2008.12.018
Checa, D., & Bustillo, A. (2019). A review of immersive virtual reality serious games to enhance learning and training. *Multimedia Tools and Applications, 79*, 1–27.
Colreavy-Donnelly, S., Ryan, A., O'Connor, S., Caraffini, F., Kuhn, S., & Hasshu, S. (2022). Leveraging immersive technologies to support blended learning post Covid-19.
Concannon, B. J., Esmail, S., & Roduta Roberts, M. (2019, August). Head-mounted display virtual reality in post-secondary education and skill training. In *Frontiers in education* (Vol. 4, p. 80). Frontiers.
Dalgarno, B., & Lee, M. J. (2010). What are the learning affordances of 3-D virtual environments? *British Journal of Educational Technology, 41*(1), 10–32. https://doi.org/10.1111/j.1467-8535.2009.01038.x
Dass, N., Kim, J., Ford, S., Agarwal, S., & Chau, D. H. (2018, April). Augmenting coding: Augmented reality for learning programming. In *Proceedings of the Sixth International Symposium of Chinese CHI* (pp. 156–159).
Dede, C. (2009). Immersive interfaces for engagement and learning. *Science, 323*(5910), 66–69.
Dede, C. J., Jacobson, J., & Richards, J. (2017). Introduction: Virtual, augmented, and mixed realities in education. In *Virtual, augmented, and mixed realities in education* (pp. 1–16). Springer.
Edwards, B. I., Bielawski, K. S., Prada, R., & Cheok, A. D. (2019). Haptic virtual reality and immersive learning for enhanced organic chemistry instruction. *Virtual Reality, 23*(4), 363–373.
Eraut, M. (2012). 1 Transfer of knowledge between education and workplace settings. In *Knowledge, values and educational policy* (pp. 75–94). Routledge.
Farra, S. L., Smith, S. J., & Ulrich, D. L. (2018). The student experience with varying immersion levels of virtual reality simulation. *Nursing Education Perspectives, 39*(2), 99–101.
Foster, A., & Shah, M. (2021). Framing and studying learning and identity in virtual learning environments: Introduction to the special issue. *The Journal of Experimental Education, 89*(3), 445–449.
Global Augmented Reality. (2019). https://www.prnewswire.com/news-releases/global-augmented-reality-ar-and-virtual-reality-vr-market-in-healthcare-marketto-reach-11-14-billion-by-2025--300831306.html
Goldman Sachs. (2018). Profiles in innovation report. http://www.goldmansachs.com/ourthinking/pages/technology-driving-innovation-folder/virtual-and-augmented-reality/report.pdf
Goodwin, M. S., Wiltshire, T., & Fiore, S. M. (2015). Applying research in the cognitive sciences to the design and delivery of instruction in virtual reality learning environments. Paper presented at the International Conference on Virtual, Augmented and Mixed Reality. https://doi.org/10.1007/978-3-319-21067-4_29
Han, I. (2020). Immersive virtual field trips in education: A mixed-methods study on elementary students' presence and perceived learning. *British Journal of Educational Technology, 51*(2), 420–435.
Hanna, M. G., Ahmed, I., Nine, J., Prajapati, S., & Pantanowitz, L. (2018). Augmented reality technology using Microsoft HoloLens in anatomic pathology. *Archives of Pathology & Laboratory Medicine, 142*(5), 638–644.
Jensen, L., & Konradsen, F. (2018). A review of the use of virtual reality head-mounted displays in education and training. *Education and Information Technologies, 23*(4), 1515–1529.
Johnson-Glenberg, M. C. (2019). The necessary nine: Design principles for embodied VR and active stem education. In *Learning in a digital world*, (pp. 83–112). Springer.
Khalifa, M., & Shen, N. (2004). System design effects on social presence and telepresence in virtual communities. In *ICIS 2004 Proceedings* (p. 43).
Kilteni, K., Groten, R., & Slater, M. (2012). The sense of embodiment in virtual reality. *Presence: Teleoperators and Virtual Environments, 21*(4), 373–387.

Kim, D., & Ko, Y. J. (2019). The impact of virtual reality (VR) technology on sport spectators' flow experience and satisfaction. *Computers in Human Behavior, 93*, 346–356.
Krathwohl, D. R. (2002). A revision of Bloom's taxonomy: An overview. *Theory into Practice, 41*(4), 212–218.
Krokos, E., Plaisant, C., & Varshney, A. (2019). Virtual memory palaces: Immersion aids recall. *Virtual Reality, 23*(1), 1–15.
Lee, K. M. (2004). Presence, explicated. *Communication Theory, 14*(1), 27–50.
Lee, E. A.-L., Wong, K. W., & Fung, C. C. (2010). How does desktop virtual reality enhance learning outcomes? A structural equation modeling approach. *Computers and Education, 55*(4), 1424–1442. https://doi.org/10.1016/j.compedu.2010.06.006
Lindgren, R., & McDaniel, R. (2012). Transforming online learning through narrative and student agency. *Educational Technology and Society, 15*(4), 344.
Liu, Y., Liu, Z., & Jin, Y. (2019, July). Virtual dome system using HMDs: An alternative to the expensive and less accessible physical domes. In *International Conference on Human-Computer Interaction* (pp. 312–328). Springer.
Lyons, L., & Mallavarapu, A. (2021). *Collective usability. Educational Technology & Society, 24*(2), 120–135.
Makransky, G., & Lilleholt, L. (2018). A structural equation modeling investigation of the emotional value of immersive virtual reality in education. *Educational Technology Research and Development, 66*(5), 1141–1164. https://doi.org/10.1007/s11423-018-9581-2
Makransky, G., & Petersen, G. B. (2019). Investigating the process of learning with desktop virtual reality: A structural equation modeling approach. *Computers & Education, 134*, 15–30.
Makransky, G., & Petersen, G. B. (2021). The Cognitive Affective Model of Immersive Learning (CAMIL): A theoretical research-based model of learning in immersive virtual reality. *Educational Psychology Review*, 1–22.
Makransky, G., Terkildsen, T. S., & Mayer, R. E. (2019). Adding immersive virtual reality to a science lab simulation causes more presence but less learning. *Learning and Instruction, 60*, 225–236.
Markowitz, D. M., Laha, R., Perone, B. P., Pea, R. D., & Bailenson, J. N. (2018). Immersive virtual reality field trips facilitate learning about climate change. *Frontiers in psychology, 9*, 2364
Marr, B. (2020). The future of virtual reality. *Forbes.*
Martín-Gutiérrez, J., Mora, C. E., Añorbe Díaz, B., & González-Marrero, A. (2017). Virtual technologies trends in education. *EURASIA Journal of Mathematics Science and Technology Education, 13*(2), 469–486.
Masuoka, Y., Morikawa, H., Kawai, T., & Nakagohri, T. (2019). Use of smartphone-based head-mounted display devices to view a three-dimensional dissection model in a virtual reality environment: Pilot questionnaire study. *JMIR Medical Education, 5*(1), e11921.
Mayer, R. E. (2014). The Cambridge handbook of multimedia learning, second edition. In *The Cambridge handbook of multimedia learning* (2nd ed., Vol. 1, Issue 3). https://doi.org/10.1017/CBO9781139547369.
Merchant, Z., Goetz, E. T., Cifuentes, L., Keeney-Kennicutt, W., & Davis, T. J. (2014). Effectiveness of virtual reality-based instruction on students' learning outcomes in K-12 and higher education: A meta-analysis. *Computers & Education, 70*, 29–40.
Metcalfe, J., Eich, T. S., & Miele, D. B. (2013). Metacognition of agency: Proximal action and distal outcome. *Experimental Brain Research, 229*(3), 485–496.
Mestre, J. (2002). *Transfer of learning: Issues and research agenda.* National Science Foundation.
Milgram, P., & Kishino, F. (1994). A taxonomy of mixed reality visual displays. *IEICE TRANSACTIONS on Information and Systems, 77*(12), 1321–1329.
Misbhauddin, M. (2018). VREdu: A framework for interactive immersive lectures using virtual reality. In *2018 21st Saudi Computer Society National Computer Conference* (pp. 1–6). IEEE.
Moore, J. W., & Fletcher, P. C. (2012). Sense of agency in health and disease: A review of cue integration approaches. *Consciousness and Cognition, 21*(1), 59–68. https://doi.org/10.1016/j.concog.2011.08.010

Moro, C., Phelps, C., Redmond, P., & Stromberga, Z. (2021). HoloLens and mobile augmented reality in medical and health science education: A randomised controlled trial. *British Journal of Educational Technology, 52*(2), 680–694.
Mütterlein, J. (2018, January). The three pillars of virtual reality? Investigating the roles of immersion, presence, and interactivity. In *Proceedings of the 51st Hawaii International Conference on System Sciences*.
Nevelsteen, K. J. (2018). Virtual world, defined from a technological perspective and applied to video games, mixed reality, and the Metaverse. *Computer Animation and Virtual Worlds, 29*(1), e1752.
Oberhauser, M., & Dreyer, D. (2017). A virtual reality flight simulator for human factors engineering. *Cognition, Technology & Work, 19*(2), 263–277.
Ondrejka, C. (2004). Escaping the gilded cage: User created content and building the metaverse. *NYLS Law Review, 49*, 81.
Organisation for Economic Cooperation and Development (OECD). (2018). *The future of education and skills: Education 2030* (OECD Education Working Papers).
Oyserman, D., & Dawson, A. (2021). Successful learning environments support and harness students' identity-based motivation: A primer. *The Journal of Experimental Education, 89*(3), 508–522.
Pan, X., & Hamilton, A. F. D. C. (2018). Why and how to use virtual reality to study human social interaction: The challenges of exploring a new research landscape. *British Journal of Psychology, 109*(3), 395–417.
Parong, J., & Mayer, R. E. (2020). Cognitive and affective processes for learning science in immersive virtual reality. *Journal of Computer Assisted Learning*.
Radianti, J., Majchrzak, T. A., Fromm, J., & Wohlgenannt, I. (2020). A systematic review of immersive virtual reality applications for higher education: Design elements, lessons learned, and research agenda. *Computers and Education, 147*, 103778
Robertson, G., Czerwinski, M., & Van Dantzich, M. (1997). Immersion in desktop virtual reality. In *Proceedings of the 10th Annual ACM Symposium on User Interface Software and Technology* (pp. 11–19). Citeseer.
Rodriguez, S. (2021, October 29). *Facebook changes company name to Meta*. CNBC. https://www.cnbc.com/2021/10/28/facebook-changes-company-name-to-meta.html
Roo, J. S., & Hachet, M. (2017, October). One reality: Augmenting how the physical world is experienced by combining multiple mixed reality modalities. In *Proceedings of the 30th Annual ACM Symposium on User Interface Software and Technology* (pp. 787–795).
Rowe, J. P., Shores, L. R., Mott, B. W., & Lester, J. C. (2011). Integrating learning, problem solving, and engagement in narrative-centered learning environments. *International Journal of Artificial Intelligence in Education, 21*(1–2), 115–133.
Ryan, M. L. (2015). *Narrative as virtual reality 2: Revisiting immersion and interactivity in literature and electronic media* (Vol. 2). JHU Press.
Sankaranarayanan, G., Wooley, L., Hogg, D., Dorozhkin, D., Olasky, J., Chauhan, S., Fleshman, J. W., De, S., Scott, D., & Jones, D. B. (2018). Immersive virtual reality-based training improves response in a simulated operating room fire scenario. *Surgical Endoscopy, 32*(8), 3439–3449.
Schwartz, D. L., Bransford, J. D., & Sears, D. (2005). *Transfer of learning from a modern multidisciplinary perspective*. IAP.
Shamsudin, N. M., Mahmood, N. H. N., Rahim, A. R. A., Mohamad, S. F., & Masrom, M. (2018). Virtual reality training approach for occupational safety and health: A pilot study. *Advanced Science Letters, 24*(4), 2447–2450.
Shattuck, D. W. (2018). Multiuser virtual reality environment for visualising neuroimaging data. *Healthcare Technology Letters, 5*(5), 183–188.
Slater, M. (2009). Place Illusion and plausibility can lead to realistic behaviour in immersive virtual environments. *Philosophical Transactions of the Royal Society of London, 364*, 3549–3557. https://doi.org/10.3389/frobt.2016.00074

Slater, M. (2018). Immersion and the illusion of presence in virtual reality. *British Journal of Psychology, 109*(3), 431–433.
Slater, M., & Wilbur, S. (1997). A framework for immersive virtual environments (FIVE): Speculations on the role of presence in virtual environments. *Presence: Teleoperators and Virtual Environments, 6*(6), 603–616.
Snelson, C., & Hsu, Y. C. (2020). Educational 360-degree videos in virtual reality: A scoping review of the emerging research. *TechTrends, 64*, 404–412.
Snow, E. L., Allen, L. K., Jacovina, M. E., & McNamara, D. S. (2015). Does agency matter?: Exploring the impact of controlled behaviors within a game-based environment. *Computers and Education, 82*, 378–392.
Song, Q., He, L., & Hu, X. (2012). To improve the interactivity of the history educational games with digital interactive storytelling. *Physics Procedia, 33*, 1798–1802.
Song, Y., & Li, L. (2018, August). Research on application of VR technology in art design teaching. *In 2018 International Conference on Engineering Simulation and Intelligent Control (ESAIC)* (pp. 343–345). IEEE.
Steuer, J. (1995). Defining virtual reality: Dimensions determining presence. In *Communication in the age of virtual reality* (pp. 33–56). Lawrence Erlbaum Associates.
Suh, A., & Prophet, J. (2018). The state of immersive technology research: A literature analysis. *Computers in Human Behavior, 86*, 77–90.
Tacgin, Z. (2018). Proposing an instructional design model with designing and developing sensory immersive VRLE to teach concepts and procedures. In *Academic studies in educational science.* IVPE.
Tacgin, Z., & Dalgarno, B. (2021). Building an instructional design model for immersive virtual reality learning environments. In *Designing, deploying, and evaluating virtual and augmented reality in education* (pp. 20–47). IGI Global.
Wade, J., Zhang, L., Bian, D., Fan, J., Swanson, A., Weitlauf, A., Sarkar, M., Warren, Z., & Sarkar, N. (2016). A gaze-contingent adaptive virtual reality driving environment for intervention in individuals with autism spectrum disorders. *ACM Transactions on Interactive Intelligent Systems (TiiS), 6*(1), 1–23.
Wardrip-Fruin, N., Mateas, M., Dow, S., & Sali, S. (2009, September). Agency reconsidered. In *DiGRA Conference.*
Webster, R. (2016). Conceptual knowledge acquisition in immersive virtual learning environments. *Interactive Learning Environments, 24*(6), 1319–1333.
Webster, R., & Dues, J. F. (2017, June). System usability scale (SUS): Oculus Rift® DK2 and Samsung Gear VR®. In *ASEE Annual Conference and Exposition, Conference Proceedings* (Vol. 2017).
Witmer, B. G., & Singer, M. J. (1998). Measuring presence in virtual environments: A presence questionnaire. *Presence, 7*(3), 225–240.
Wu, B., Yu, X., & Gu, X. (2020). Effectiveness of immersive virtual reality using head-mounted displays on learning performance: A meta-analysis. *British Journal of Educational Technology, 51*(6), 1991–2005.
Xie, B., Nelson, G. L., Akkaraju, H., Kwok, W., & Ko, A. J. (2020, August). The effect of informing agency in self-directed online learning environments. In *Proceedings of the Seventh ACM Conference on Learning@ Scale* (pp. 77–89).
Xin, B., Chen, G., Wang, Y., Bai, G., Gao, X., Chu, J., … & Liu, T. (2019). The efficacy of immersive virtual reality surgical simulator training for pedicle screw placement: A randomized double-blind controlled trial. *World neurosurgery*, 124, e324–e330.
Yang, X., Cheng, P.-Y., & Yang, X. (2016). The impact of three types of virtual reality scene on learning. In *2017 International Conference of Educational Innovation Through Technology* (pp. 322–324). IEEE.
Zawacki-Richter, O., & Latchem, C. (2018). Exploring four decades of research in computers and education. *Computers and Education, 122*, 136–152.

Zhang, K., Suo, J., Chen, J., Liu, X., & Gao, L. (2017). Design and implementation of fire safety education system on campus based on virtual reality technology. In *2017 Federated Conference on Computer Science and Information Systems* (pp. 1297–1300). IEEE.
Zhang, L., Bowman, D. A., & Jones, C. N. (2019, September). Exploring effects of interactivity on learning with interactive storytelling in immersive virtual reality. In *2019 11th International Conference on Virtual Worlds and Games for Serious Applications (VS-Games)* (pp. 1–8). IEEE.
Ziker, C., Truman, B., & Dodds, H. (2021). Cross reality (XR): Challenges and opportunities across the spectrum. *Innovative Learning Environments in STEM Higher Education*, 55.
Zizza, C., Starr, A., Hudson, D., Nuguri, S. S., Calyam, P., & He, Z. (2019). Towards a social virtual reality learning environment in high fidelity. In *2018 15th IEEE Annual Consumer Communications and Networking Conference* (pp. 1–4). IEEE.

Samson Tan is the Director of Regional Strategy and Operations at Civica (Singapore). The focus of his work is on developing education strategies with strategic customers and stakeholders for the advancement of educational innovation best practices. Samson served as the Head of the Centre for Innovation in Learning at the National Institute of Education prior to joining Civica. He is also an exco member of the Association of Problem-Based Learning and Active Learning Methodologies (PAN-PBL), and the Education Research Association of Singapore.

Chapter 8
Harnessing Artificial Intelligence for Innovation in Education

Samson Tan

Abstract In the field of educational technology, Artificial Intelligence in Education (AIEd) is an emerging field that is projected to have a profound impact on the teaching and learning process. The AIEd has already been around for more than 30 years, but educators may still have concerns about scaling the pedagogical benefits of the AIEd and how it could positively impact the teaching and learning process. The purpose of this chapter is to demystify artificial intelligence (AI), its impact on society and how to harness the power of AI for transformational change in education. Taking the first step is clarifying the definition of artificial intelligence (AI) to differentiate it from human intelligence (HI). With this understanding in place, an open learner model by design can be applied as a framework which explains how AI can be used to enhance teaching and learning in general (Luckin et al., 2016). It is the purpose of this chapter to advocate for teachers' roles to be augmented and evolved to be AIEd-enabled, and to consider AIEd applications from three different perspectives: (i) learner-facing, (ii) teacher-facing and (iii) system-facing AIEd (Baker and Smith, 2019). There has been significant progress in the area of student-facing AIEd, especially when it comes to the development of personalized adaptive learning systems based on big learning data. The open model adaptive system as presented by Luckin et al. (2016) provided insights into the design of a learner-facing, personalized learning system. It was discussed that a personalized adaptive learning system (PALS) framework was proposed as an example of how artificial intelligence can be applied to a situation for student-facing purposes (Palanisamy et al., 2021). There are two aspects of teacher-facing AIEd that have garnered a lot of interest: automatic grading and prompt feedback on the learners' progress. As a system-facing solution, AIEd offers academic administrators insights into learners' profiles and predictions, admission decisions and course scheduling, attrition and retention and student models and academic achievement. An evaluation of the literature on AIEd suggests that the future of AIEd is intertwined with the ability of AI to be integrated with other emerging technologies, like immersive technology and the Internet of Things, to create new innovations in teaching and learning.

S. Tan (✉)
Head of Strategic Development in Libraries & Education, Civica Pte Ltd, Singapore, Singapore
e-mail: samson.tan@civica.com.sg

K. Rajaram, *Learning Intelligence: Innovative and Digital Transformative Learning Strategies*, https://doi.org/10.1007/978-981-19-9201-8_8

8.1 Introduction

Educators working in the field of Artificial Intelligence in Education (AIEd) have been investigating the uses of AI for creating learning technologies for improving education since the early 1970s (du Boulay, 2016). It is an emerging technology capable of radically transforming all aspects of our social interactions. AI has already begun to produce new ways of learning and teaching and is currently being tested in different educational scenarios. Over the last thirty years, the academic community associated with AIEd has examined, deliberated and discussed the potential benefits of the discipline. Over the last few years, the convergence of emerging technologies such as the surge in computing power and big data analytics have contributed to the rise of sophisticated AI algorithms that can learn and improve on their own (Tan, 2020).

The digital footprint leaves behind by each individual is the result of the generation of copious amounts of data in the age of big data, allowing societal and individual behaviour to be empirically quantified, thereby being much easier to trace, model and in some cases even predict. It has been noted that this phenomenon, known as datafication, has now begun to affect every segment of society, and it is no different with education (Mayer-Schonberger & Cukier, 2013). As a result of the development and application of artificial intelligence, a significant and rapid change is taking place in almost every aspect of our lives, which is consistent with the assertions of Agrawal et al. (2018) that leveraging data to make predictions has enabled the recent series of AI systems to improve organizations' capability and has lowered the cost of making predictions significantly.

The application of AI to an educational context offers an opportunity to shed light on the "black box of learning", and offer a deeper, more comprehensive and fine-grained understanding of student learning (Luckin et al., 2016). It is generally acknowledged by most people that computers of today are intelligent in the sense that they are able to learn and make decisions based on data that has been gathered. This is, however, a distinctly different kind of intelligence from what is currently available. In more precise terms, the combination of big data analytics and artificial intelligence has inherent risks, such as ethical concerns, the need for a concerted policy response and the arising of new possibilities associated with personalized learning and assessment.

Gartner's survey of 2018 technological trends ranked artificial intelligence as the top strategic technology, providing insight into how leaders in the industry are looking for ways to harness artificial intelligence (AI) to improve decisions, reimagine business models and environments and create a more immersive customer experience that will drive digital initiatives through 2025. While the Gartner survey indicates that 59% of organizations are still at the initial data gathering phase to develop their AI strategies, the rest have made some progress in piloting or adopting AI-powered solutions (Panetta, 2018). IBM's Leaderboard predicts that by the early 2020s, artificial intelligence will enter deeper domains of self-learning as well as become capable of being able to assist, collaborate, coach and mediate by the early 2030s.

As a result, it is imperative to examine how artificial intelligence impacts education and future citizens in terms of their knowledge and abilities. There is a need for educators to look beyond the current trends and determine the kinds of jobs and skills that the world will need going forward, with a focus on the core issue of being intelligent in an AI-enhanced world in the twenty-first century. It is nonetheless worthwhile to synthesize the work of experts on the topic of how susceptible jobs are to being automated. The most important feature of this phenomenon is that it provides an impetus for reconceptualizing human intelligence.

The purpose of this chapter is to support education policymakers and practitioners in understanding and anticipating the extent to which artificial intelligence will influence the education sector to enable them to formulate effective policy responses. Thus, it is critically important to proceed cautiously and conscientiously into a new educational environment in which artificial intelligence (AI) is used to support students and teachers and prepare them for a future in which AI will be an increasingly integral part of learning (Taguma et al., 2018). Despite the fact that there are many frameworks for studying the application of AI in education, this chapter refers to the three dimensions of Baker and Smith (2019), namely student-facing, teacher-facing and system-facing. Before examining the application of AI in education, it is important to clarify what AI is from the myriad definitions in the literature.

8.2 What Is Artificial Intelligence (AI)?

According to John McCarthy in 1955, artificial intelligence refers to the process of making machines behave in ways that would be considered intelligent by humans if a human performed those actions (McCarthy et al., 1955). Despite the fact that there has been artificial intelligence technology for nearly six decades, there have not been any significant breakthroughs until recently, as the advent of big data, affordable access to computing power and machine learning have dramatically changed the technological landscape (Luckin et al., 2016; Tan, 2020).

It is infamous that artificial intelligence (AI) is difficult to define, and this has both proved to be a boon and a bane (Tan, 2020). As a result of the inherent broadness of the term, an extremely diverse range of techniques are able to inhabit the space defined by the term, ranging from data-intensive machine learning techniques like neural networks to model-based deduction logics and the use of techniques from statistics to derive psychological models for decision-making. As all these efforts have been made to emulate existing forms of intelligence or create new ones, they have sparked debates about the future of intelligence.

The fact remains that although there is no standard and straightforward definition of artificial intelligence, there are a number of widely recognized and generally accepted classifications of AI, including McCarthy, J. et al. (2006), Nilsson (2014) and ITU (2018). Defining artificial intelligence (AI) can be a difficult task, even for the experts in the field. As we discussed earlier, one of the challenges in defining AI is being able to identify how computers differ from human intelligence. When

AI research becomes sufficiently common and widely accepted, advanced AI applications become general applications without the AI label. (Bostrom, 2017; Luckin et al., 2016).

Baker and Smith (2019) defined artificial intelligence as "Computers which perform cognitive tasks, usually associated with human minds, particularly learning and problem-solving" (p. 10). The term AI is considered an umbrella term covering a wide range of technologies and methods, including machine learning, natural language processing, data mining, neural networks and algorithms. Pedro et al. (2019) advocated another approach to the understanding of artificial intelligence by categorizing it into four dimensions.

Artificial Intelligence and Big Data are two of the most significant technologies expected to have the greatest impact on human life in the future (World Economic Forum, 2020). It is also important to note that there are a number of other emerging concepts within AI such as machine learning and learning analytics (Luckin et al., 2016). Currently, artificial intelligence research is mostly focused on learning, reasoning, problem-solving, perception and language, resulting in two types of artificial intelligence (AI): knowledge-based AI through Machine Learning and data-driven AI through data mining (Pedro et al., 2019). The success of AI today is primarily due to advances in data-driven artificial intelligence (AI), which is commonly called machine learning. In a more precise sense, machine learning is a method for making predictions that are based on observed patterns (Cope et al., 2020).

In machine learning, deep learning is a particular subfield focused on the development of representations from data that is based on the notion of learning successive layers of representations that are increasingly meaningful over time (Perrotta & Selwyn, 2020). There are layered representations that create new models that are referred to as neural networks: multilayered statistical sequences that identify patterns within patterns (Krizhevsky et al., 2012). With neural networks requiring vast amounts of data and computational power in order to function, the computer utilizes big data to build its own intelligence, including the ability to learn by recalculating its calculations on an ongoing basis. In this context, it is reasonable to posit that there can be no data-driven artificial intelligence without big data. It is generally regarded that big data is a system of collecting vast amounts of data but growing in volumes exponentially along the way. As a result of the large size and complexity of the data, there are no traditional data management tools which will be able to store or process it efficiently (Najafabadi et al., 2015). There are two types of data sets in these data sets, namely structured and unstructured data.

Learning analytics (LA) is an emerging knowledge area that is related to the use of big data in education. By evaluating massive amounts of data, critical analytics (i.e. learning analytics), and generating patterns to illustrate learner learning behaviours, predict learner responses and provide timely feedback (Siemens, 2013). Specifically, LA enhances the ability to make decisions, enhances the ability to customize the content, simplifies authentic assessments and provides enhanced supervision of the learning process (Verbert et al., 2013). As a result of that, the end goal is to enhance learners' achievement by scaling the instantaneous capitalization of LA by learners, instructors and learning management systems through the use of knowledge management.

It was due to the rise and convergence of cloud computing power and big data analytics that accelerated the development of sophisticated AI algorithms, which led to the consideration of the possibility of AI taking over the world. The following section explores the dystopian scenario of humans being subsumed by artificial intelligence in the future.

8.3 Will AI Take Over from Humans?

There is a segment of the scientific community that is concerned that artificial intelligence may one day take over the world, which will eventually lead to humanity's demise (Tan, 2020). A school of thought originating from Vernon Vinge's notion of singularity is defined as the point at which an artificially intelligent computer or robot is able to redesign itself or create artificial intelligence more advanced than the one it is currently using (Vinge, 1993). According to Vinge, allowing artificial intelligence to develop at the current pace would lead to AI reaching intelligence levels far exceeding human intelligence, a situation in which the human era would end. While it's easy to dismiss such a concept as "science fiction" rather than real science, some more recent scientific thinkers like Stephen Hawking, Stuart Russell, Max Tegmark and Frank Wilczek have warned that artificial intelligence may become more and more intelligent and thus less beneficial to humans in the long run (Hawking et al., 2014). In an interview with BBC, Stephen Hawking even cautioned: "The development of full artificial intelligence could spell the end of the human race" (Cellan-Jones, 2014). In light of Hawking's reputation and authority, it has been a sufficient reason for attention and a cause for concern.

Due to the nature and potential of artificial intelligence, scientists have good reasons to be wary of the possibility of humans inadvertently creating a general AI—a machine that could perform any intellectual task that a human could perform. It is important to note that even under the current state of AI research and development, there is no general AI at this time (Luckin et al., 2016). Sadly, Hollywood sci-fi movies such as The Matrix and Terminator have conspired to exaggerate the fear of artificial intelligence in the public. In this regard, it is not helpful that many people have insufficient understanding of machine learning, neural networks and artificial intelligence (Gurkaynak et al., 2016). Instead of worrying about whether we might accidentally develop a general artificial intelligence that would lead to unintended consequences of the greatest magnitude, it would probably be more productive for us to determine whether AI is capable of the same level of intelligence as humans. The following section provides a realistic assessment of AI's development and the potential impact it may have on society in the future.

8.3.1 *Human Intelligence (HI) and Artificial Intelligence (AI)*

AI currently has the capability of learning from its experience through its Machine Learning component (ML) along with its Deep Learning component (DL). This enables AI to adjust to new inputs and achieve human-like performance. Despite the fact that artificial intelligence is still developing and advancing, the time needed to train AI systems is substantially prolonged, which is not possible without human intervention. A wide range of sophisticated technologies, such as autonomous cars and robots, as well as natural language processing and image processing, rely on human intelligence on a daily basis. As per Luckin et al. (2016), humans need to redraw the concept of HI in light of the sophisticated AI that is permeating the vast majority of society today. AI implementations today offer a broad spectrum of capabilities.

Though AI systems have been able to develop intelligent machines that are able to outperform humans in some areas, they have a long way to go before they can match the capabilities of the human mind. Human beings have the unique capability at their disposal of learning and applying acquired knowledge while employing logic, reasoning and understanding to do so. In the real world, there is a need for an integrated, logical, rational and emotional approach to decisions that is specific to humans. AI, however, cannot understand the meaning of "cause" and "effect" in different contexts, nor can it apply its capabilities in multiple contexts at the same time. In reality, while there has been a strong correlation between the capabilities of AI systems with regard to decision-making in relation to the data used to train them, and the events the systems are able to resolve, these systems are unable to make meaningful decisions in the context of human societies. Specifically, human intelligence encompassed the ability of an individual to generalize the knowledge gained to accomplish significant tasks and activities such as creating and sustaining culture, collaborating with others on art projects, and forming social relationships with other individuals.

As opposed to assuming that artificial intelligence and human intelligence are mutually exclusive, artificial intelligence could work together to enhance human intelligence by handling tasks they are better at than humans. In the same way that human knowledge is embedded in culture, AI cannot comprehend culturally embedded aspects of human knowledge (Siemens, 2019). In the future, humans will need to learn, think and work with machines, rather than working with one another, since the new world order is characterized by the idea that "what we know is not as important as how we know", and this is reflected in the notion of "ongoing knowing", which points to a context in which sense-making, meaning-making, as well as wayfinding become the primary knowledge activities (Siemens, 2017; Siemens et al., 2020).

A different definition of intelligence is the ability to coordinate complex cognitive processes, while also having a holistic understanding of others and our abilities, knowledge and skills (Luckin, 2018). In other words, human intelligence refers to the ability to learn, apply the knowledge acquired, synthesize what has been learned, communicate with others, understand, formulate decisions, think, to be able to express one's learning and learn from one's experiences. Coincidentally, Luckin et al. (2016) state that machines are not capable of contextualizing and making sense of subjective knowledge at this point in time, which corresponds with Siemen's (2019) postulation that the future of AI will be dominated by HI, with AI complementing HI and cognizance, which is embodied in our meta-subjective and meta-contextual intelligence.

In summary, rather than worrying about whether AI is going to take over the world one day, it would be far more valuable to spend the time and effort on figuring out how AI can complement the developments in Health Information Technology. The following section gives a brief overview of the profound effects of AI on society.

8.3.2 *Impact of AI on Society*

According to the discussion in the previous section, there is a scenario where an intelligent machine surpasses human intelligence in a wide array of skills only if an AI becomes a general agent (AI) capable of acting in a wide range of different contexts. A review of the literature on artificial intelligence shows, however, that we are still far away from achieving general AI for a number of reasons. As Jebari and Lundborg (2020) suggest, for machines to be able to acquire human intelligence, they need a productive drive to direct behavior in a variety of contexts. To acquire human intelligence, it is not possible for an AI to produce such desires spontaneously, that is, through an endogenous procedure, at the present time. As such, the authors of the study contend that it is not plausible for general agency to suddenly appear in a non-general AI. Moreover, AI is still incapable of surpassing human intelligence due to the current limitations of deep learning—AI must shift from a limited 2D space to a tera-dimensional space representing the million billion synapses connecting neurons within the cortex of the human brain seamlessly as one dimension in order to achieve general artificial intelligence (Bartholomew, 2020).

Despite the fact that we have not yet reached the level of general AI, AI is rapidly becoming more advanced and is having a profound impact on our economy. The study by Frey and Osborne (2013), using machine learning to study 702 detailed occupations, concludes that 47% of the total US employment could be at risk. However, there is a more concerning finding: they found that wages and educational attainment show significant negative associations with an occupation's odds of being computerized (Ford, 2015). The inaugural report of the World Economic Forum (WEF), titled "The Future of Jobs", published in 2016, cautions that humankind must take immediate steps to ensure that all workers are prepared for the changes facing our workplaces in the near future. Further, the WEF posits that AI's potential cannot be realized without a substantial amount of public and government buy-in, based on trust that applications and technologies using AI are developed and deployed ethically.

> During previous industrial revolutions, it often took decades to build the training systems and labour market institutions needed to develop major new skill sets on a large scale. Given the upcoming pace and scale of disruption brought about by the Fourth Industrial Revolution, however, this is simply not an option.

In the latest "The Future of Jobs" 2020, WEF expects that the pace of technology adoption is expected to remain unabated and may accelerate in specific fields and automation, in tandem with the COVID-19 recession creating a "double-disruption" scenario for workers. Among the companies we surveyed, 43% indicate that they are willing to reduce their workforce due to the integration of technology, 41% plan to increase the outsourcing of tasks that require specialized skills and 34% plan to expand their workforce due to the integration of technology. The shift in the division of labour between humans and machines can also result in the displacement of 85 million jobs. In the same period, 97 million new roles may be created in the future that is more suited to the new division of labour between humans and algorithms. The WEF predicts, by 2025, that humans and machines will spend the same amount of time working on current tasks at work. There are four industries that are seeing the most adaptation of artificial intelligence (AI) among the many others: Digital Information and Communications, Financial Services, Healthcare and Transportation.

The experience of previous industrial revolutions has shown that societies were adaptive to economic changes by changing the scope and the quality of education and learning as much as possible. The WEF argues, however, that IR 4.0 is nothing like what has been experienced in the past, and that therefore, humanity is responsible for a collective response. In order to best meet the needs of the twenty-first century, the guiding principle is that the workforce can be retrained and upskilled as needed, so as to remain competitive (Goldin & Katz, 2010; World Economic Forum, 2020).

As a result of AI, humanity is affected by every dimension and everything that we know. This includes our knowledge about education. According to a market survey, there is no shortage of companies offering artificial intelligence-powered tools that can significantly improve educational outcomes (Baker & Smith, 2019). It is noteworthy that there is still a substantial gap between the "hype" of the future potential and the reality of current practice. In order to determine if these AI-powered applications have pedagogical value before implementing them, educators must evaluate them for pedagogical effectiveness before moving forward with implementing them. The following subsection provides an overview of a pedagogical framework for adopting AI in education as it appears in the current context.

8.4 A Framework for Artificial Intelligence in Education

According to a review of the pedagogical literature, there are several frameworks for integrating technology into the classroom in order to facilitate learning and teaching (Xie et al., 2019). It is important to note that many of these studies are adapted generic learning design frameworks for putting AI to use in educational settings. This is a suboptimal outcome because these frameworks are not designed to take advantage of the unique technological and pedagogical affordances of artificial intelligence in education. Hence, a pedagogical framework that is dedicated to studies of AI in education and to the design of innovative learning tools is essential to gaining insights and determining their effectiveness.

According to Luckin et al. (2016), AI is the combination of software designed to interact with the world in ways that require human intelligence. In other words, artificial intelligence requires access to the world's information and algorithms to do an intelligent analysis of the information. Three central models of AIEd have been proposed so far: the pedagogical model, the domain model and the learner model.

The learner models represent the interfaces between the computer and the individual. An AIEd programme can employ the interactions that are represented by the model, such as the students' previous achievements, current activities, emotional qualities and propensity to learn from feedback, which can be employed by the domain and pedagogy components of an AIEd programme to infer or predict the learner's success rate (Sergis & Sampson, 2019). The data would also be fed into the domain model and the pedagogy model so that the best learning activities could be decided upon. In particular, the learner's activities are continually fed back into the learner model, resulting in a rich and comprehensive model, thus resulting in a more intelligent system.

Luckin et al. (2016)'s model-based adaptive tutor combines predictions from three central models. By using AIEd algorithms, which are embedded in the system's computer code, the system selects the most relevant content to be delivered to the learner, according to their situation and capabilities. It is important for the continuous analysis of learners' interactions with this digital content to inform the delivery of feedback and the use of this feedback to help learners learn the content.

As a result of the learning analytics gathered from students' interactions, the learner model can be modified to elicit more precise assessments of whether each student is on track to reaching the goal. With this feedback loop, it is ensured that each student's learning experience is personalized to their capabilities and requirements in a way that supports their learning. The Open Learner Models can be used to present learning analytics data back to learners and teachers in an interactive and practical way (Bull, 2020; Luckin et al., 2016). Having access to these outcomes can provide valuable information about the learner's achievements and any misconceptions or emotional states the person may have. It is useful for teachers to recognize their students' learning styles and shape learning opportunities accordingly. The Open Learner Model can also motivate the learners by tracking their progress and encouraging them to reflect on their learning as they progress through their learning.

An important benefit that is offered by AI-driven adaptive systems is the ease with which they collect a large corpus of data, which can then be computed and applied to dynamically improve pedagogy and domain models. It is through this work that one can create more effective, individualized and contextualized support while testing and refining one's understanding of the teaching and learning process. The AIEd researchers have explored and developed models that take into account social, emotional and metacognitive aspects of learning so that their systems can encompass the full range of influences that affect and influence education. After having established a firm grounding of the pedagogical frameworks for the effective integration of artificial intelligence into education in the context of teaching and learning, the following section will focus on the specific areas in which artificial intelligence can be effectively deployed in educational settings.

8.5 Applying Artificial Intelligence in Education (AIEd)

The rapidly expanding field of education is being transformed to an entirely new level with the advent of the AIEd, which presents a great deal of excitement and a number of breakthroughs in demonstrating a wide spectrum of tools and applications. According to a literature review in AIEd, the vast array of potential AI applications in higher education to support students, faculty members and administrators is summarized in this chapter. It also illustrates steps that people can take in order to help fulfil that potential while minimizing the risks they may face. In this regard, Baker and Smith's (2019) paper provided much-needed clarifications for classifying and applying artificial intelligence in education. There are three broad categories of educational contexts categorized by the authors: learner-facing, teacher-facing and system-facing, all of which have the potential to profoundly transform education.

The use of AI-powered applications in student-facing applications provides an exceptional opportunity for better designing intelligent student support systems and scaffolding student learning in adaptive and personalized learning environments (Zawacki-Richter et al., 2019). Intelligent tutoring systems (ITSs) can be used to personalize education, and are one of the most promising aspects of artificial intelligence for transforming education. Currently, the growth of this potential is unfolding as the present technologies begin experimenting with new models of learning, thereby generating new opportunities in education. With the application of Artificial Intelligence-powered algorithms, ITSs are able to replicate the assistance provided by a tutor, such as providing personalized assistance in solving problems. Carnegie Learning's adaptive learning programmes such as MATHiaU and Zulama are recognized models of this class of ITS (Ritter et al., 2015).

According to Peng et al. (2019), ITS differs from personalized adaptive learning, in that personalized adaptive learning is a blend of personalized learning and adaptive teaching. As a result of the scientific advancement of big data technology, they posit that the new learning paradigm of adaptive personalized learning will emerge that will be able to record and interpret the characteristics of students and their real-time state in every aspect of their learning. Before reviewing the AI-powered ALSs, it is crucial to introduce Learning Analytics (LA), the critical technology that powers ALSs. The Learning Analytics field is still in its infancy but it is already proving to be a powerful tool that enables educators to make informed decisions and be able to reach better learning results. As a result of the digital revolution, LA can now collect (big) data that can be analysed to extract insights or even to develop useful, intelligent applications for educational or administrative purposes.

The use of personal adaptive learning systems (PALS) has immense potential in online and blended learning where one-to-one human tutoring is not possible. Research suggests that learning is a social activity where interaction and collaboration play an important role in the process (Bonk & King, 2012; Desjardins & Bullock, 2019). Since collaborative learning using online means must be facilitated and moderated in order to be effective (Salmon, 2000), PALS can help to establish an effective collaborative learning environment by supporting the formation of adaptive groups based on the learner characteristics. The AI-powered PALS can also facilitate online group interaction or review discussions where a human instructor can guide students in their learning process by facilitating online discussion sessions. Due to the importance of the pedagogy of personalized learning being learner-centred as well as inclusive, it is a process designed to meet the needs of all learners, regardless of whether they are vulnerable or difficult to reach (BECTA, 2007). It is known that for analysing and extracting the most value from data, advanced data analysis techniques are used, which rely on other disciplines, such as statistics-based big data technologies, for processing large volumes of data efficiently. With the help of data and visualization, machine learning algorithms can learn and communicate with humans who, in the end, will be making decisions. As more software layers are implemented for intelligent data processing, data insight can be gained, learning patterns can be examined, future scenarios can be predicted or resources can be optimized.

The concept of personalized learning functionalities can therefore be described as encompassing a wide variety of approaches, such as mastery-based learning, differentiated instruction, learning by doing, and adaptive learning, among other approaches (Palanisamy et al., 2021, December). Additionally, the analysis is imperative in developing future AI-powered applications that rely on resource-rich libraries, natural language understanding, translation and perhaps even game theory to create avatars that are robots that can be manipulated to portray a virtual teacher for students or a teaching assistant for teachers (Pedro et al., 2019). Considering the future development of artificial intelligence in a more optimistic view, an AI eco-system could be developed that is capable of helping humanity overcome the various challenges involved in the learning analytics field.

With the firm foundation established in LA, the AI-powered ALSs benefited greatly over the last decade and became a significant part of the AIEd research. The consideration of research in these fields lends itself well to the development of these conclusions. Given the immense benefits of personalized adaptive learning, there has been no lack of research and development of such systems with and without AI. As such, the following section of this chapter provides a systematic review of the trends and development of personalized adaptive learning.

8.6 Trends and Developments of Personalized Adaptive Learning Systems (PALS)

A review of literature on the trends and developments of Adaptive Learning Systems in the last ten years has provided excellent insights into specific areas in the education landscape. In particular, many key findings from Xie et al.'s (2019) systematic review became evident, such as PALS, learning support, learning outcomes, subjects, participants and hardware, which are important aspects of configuring and developing PALS.

8.6.1 Distribution of Learning Content

Not surprisingly, the most popular subject matter in learning content for PALs has been engineering and computer science. In contrast, learning content such as health care, medical/nursing, social sciences, art/design, business and management was seldom selected in the PALs studies.

It may be the case that science, language and mathematics are core subjects in school, and researchers are typically well trained in their fields and possess knowledge of the context in which their research takes place. Conversely, researchers with degrees in fields other than health care, medical/nursing, social science/studies, art/design or business and management are unlikely to be familiar with relevant domains (Alexander et al., 1992; Lee et al., 1997). By using deep-neural networks to build knowledge graphs, Shi and Weringer (2017) suggest that insufficient domain knowledge can be addressed by automatically extracting knowledge structures in these disciplines. In this way, researchers can identify the domain knowledge structure in these disciplines and then organize the teaching and learning content of the PALS in accordance with it.

For a university which is considering the design of a new PALS, the suggestion of constructing knowledge graphs can be insightful and instructive as PALS can include as much learning content as there are willing faculty to participate in the learning innovation programme. This could be a crucial pre-implementation step as it could potentially diminish resistance, lower the risks in crossing the "chasm" and reach the early majority faster as described in Hype Cycle and Diffusion of Innovation in Chap. 4.

8.6.2 Distribution of System Support/Hardware

One of the key aspects of PALS is the essential systems that support PALS, including personalized interfaces, personalized learning content, personalized learning paths, personalized diagnosis and suggestions, personalized recommendations and personalized prompts/feedback, personalized professional learning guidance, lower-order personalized interfaces and other personalized functions. As indicated in the review, the most frequently adopted learning support in these PALs is personalized learning content, as featured in 29 of the 70 theoretic studies, with personalized learning paths following in the second place with 17 out of 70 studies. The frequency of personalized interfaces, personalized diagnostics and suggestions, personalized recommendations and personalized feedback is similar to that of personalized prompts/feedback and is about 10 out of 70. Lastly, the review categorized 14 studies as other personalized functions, which used different order thinking skills.

The findings from the review indicate that learning content and learning paths were the top dimensions identified as crucial in supporting PALS, which suggest that the majority of researchers may want to empower students with some degree of freedom in deciding their learning paths as they engage with the learning content. As discussed in Chap. 7, student agency is crucial in 21st-century learning, which is why this finding is particularly important to learning innovators considering integrating PALS into their practice.

As for the type of hardware used in research, the most frequently used hardware studies used "traditional computers" as a means of administering their PALs, including personal computers, notebooks and PDAs, 46 out of 70. Smartphones (Android, iOS, or Windows mobile) and tablet computers (Android and iPads) come in a distant second at 7 out of 70. As 6 of the 70 studies were categorized as "not specified", their PALs did not focus on any specific category of devices. One important thing to note is that none of these studies included wearable devices or intelligent electronic devices in any of their research, which suggests that smart devices might be peripheral in the implementation of PALS.

It is evident that most PALS are built based upon the development packages and existing systems for computers, thus reducing the number of human resources and time needed for development, resulting in "traditional computers" emerging as the most frequent hardware deployed. While the new computational devices such as the exciting new developments of wearables are gaining traction, the challenge of developing the PALS for wearable devices requires specialized IT skillsets. As a result, the technological challenge was probably too overwhelming, which is why no study was found during the review period. However, wearables represent an integral part of current information technologies, and as the development of wearables rapidly advances, it will likely be possible to see a rise in wearable learning as a trend in personalized adaptive learning. In terms of big data analytics, these results represent a very important outcome since wearable devices might be considered a subset of the Internet of Things (IoT) in some respects. It may be possible for educators to harness the power of more than one emerging technology for learning innovation, depending on both the learning content and the learning outcomes, which is particularly relevant to the following section on learning outcomes.

8.6.3 Distribution of Learning Outcomes

According to Xie et al. (2019), there are seven categories of learning outcomes: affect, cognition, skills, behaviour, correlations, others and no experimental results for coding the learning outcomes. There is no surprise that affection and cognition emerged as the most common learning outcomes at the end of their review. Of the 70 studies, 54.2% reported that affection was measured during learning, while 61.4% reported that cognition was measured. It is noteworthy that the results show that the studies looking at skills, behaviours, correlations and others are in the range of 8.6–28.6%. Additionally, around 11.4% of the studies had no precise experimental results, primarily reviews or conceptual modelling studies.

As affection and cognition were deemed to be the primary measured learning outcomes across all categories, the authors examined the subcategories associated with these two dimensions. The authors classified affection into eight subcategories: technology acceptance/learning intention, learning attitudes/expectation of learning engagement, learning motivation, self-efficacy/confidence, interest/satisfaction, cognitive load, learning anxiety and opinions/learning experiences of students. Technology acceptance/learning intention, interest/satisfaction and opinions/learning experiences of students account for about 20 of the 40 studies that involve affection. In contrast, only one measured learning anxiety and four on cognitive loads. It is interesting to note that most of the participants in this review showed positive responses to the PALS, suggesting that it is helpful for them. The findings of this study are encouraging for learning innovators as the majority of respondents believe that PALS have a positive impact on learning despite their limitations.

Cognition can be classified into three subcategories: learning achievements, higher-order thinking/competence and collaboration/communication. Among these three subcategories of cognition, learning achievements appear to be the most commonly measured learning outcome, with 37 of the 43 studies involving cognition measuring learning achievements. In addition, two subcategories, higher-order thinking/competence and collaboration/communication, are included in seven and four studies, respectively. There is something intriguing, but it is not surprising, that most of the research is focused on learning achievement, as PALS is designed to support learners in achieving their learning goals. It is for this reason that learning innovators who are embarking on PALS may be able to integrate the classification of outcomes into their learning design.

It should be noted that higher-order thinking skills and communication receive less attention than learning achievements, as they are harder to measure than learning achievements in the classroom (Brookhart, 2010). Also, higher-order thinking skills and communication skills also require that learning outcomes are supported in a way that is unlikely to be facilitated by existing PALS. On the other hand, with the growing popularity of collaborative and immersive learning environments that are supported by virtual reality techniques, interest in studying higher-order thinking skills and communication in PALS is expected to increase (Greenwald et al., 2017). It is imperative that learning innovators comprehend the implications when seeking to adapt or develop a PALS that integrates higher-order thinking skills and communication to ensure that these new PALS are future-ready.

As a result, these developments would likely lead to an increasing need for a new generation of AI-powered PALS which could inform the development of intelligent virtual agents in the near future. Since the topic of integrated intelligent virtual agents to support students in their online learning courses has been gaining a tremendous amount of attention during the COVID-19 lockdown period, it is reasonable to expect that there will be more research and applications of artificial intelligence in this area in the post-COVID-19 education landscape. In Sect. 8.7, more in-depth discussion on designing a new generation of PALS will be covered.

8.6.4 Distribution of Parameters of Personalized Adaptive Learning

Adaptive learning systems (PALS) were evaluated in two dimensions: parameters of the systems to support personalized adaptive learning, and also the hardware used in these studies. In PALS, the parameters consist of the difficulty level of the learning materials, the sequence in which they are presented, the students' learning achievements, preferences, learning styles, learning perceptions, cognitive styles, profiles, portfolio or logs and platform/technical support. The parameters that are used most frequently to facilitate PALS are students' learning achievement and platform/technical support. They are used 28 times each on average. Contrary to that, the cognitive styles of students are the least frequent factor, yielding a fivefold increase. Besides the second least adopted parameter, the sequence of learning materials, which is adopted at a frequency of 9 times, the six remaining parameters—the difficulty level of the learning materials, students' preferences, students' learning styles, students' learning perceptions, students' profiles and portfolio or logs are about the average frequency of 17.2 for all parameters.

Students' perceptions of their learning were classified into three subcategories based on the review: (i) learning attitudes, learning motivation or hard work and high expectations; (ii) self-efficacy or self-confidence; and (iii) satisfaction or interest. There are seven, three and four studies in these three facets, respectively. Lastly, the subcategory of learning attitudes captures 50% of all studies using learning perceptions as PALS parameters.

According to these findings, it seems that most scholars are interested in how the PALS can help students to achieve better academically. Considering the fact that many institutions are competing with one another by leveraging technology to improve their students' performance, it is natural that this would occur. Intriguingly, platform/technical support was also listed as the top concern for faculty and students, suggesting that they might encounter challenges utilizing the existing PALS without technical support. It is a valuable insight for learning innovators when evaluating and implementing PALS for their respective contexts. In conclusion, we also found that 50% of all studies included students' learning attitudes when evaluating PALS, suggesting the purpose of such research was to examine motivation among students. Taking into account, this dimension is particularly important when measuring the success of learning innovation, as discussed in Chap. 4.

In summary, Xie et al.'s (2019) study provided insights into the trends and issues in deploying personalized adaptive learning, providing rich insights for potential learning innovators and researchers. The findings suggest that existing technologies such as personalized adaptive learning systems (PALS) may not be able to keep up with the new educational demands, being particularly incompatible with a broad spectrum of potential applications such as wearable personal learning technologies and collaborative, immersive personalized learning. As a result, the following section explores the characteristics of such a new generation of PALS that may meet such demands in the future.

8.7 Designing an AI-Powered New Personalized Adaptive Learning

There is little information available in the educational research literature regarding how to design PALS. The literature review uncovered several different conceptual frameworks that might be applicable for educational research, but it is challenging to find a framework that is easily adaptable to educators' academic courses. It was serendipitous that Palanisamy, Thilarajah and Chen (2021, December) shared their findings in their attempt to acquire an appropriate PALS for their institution. They conducted a study on the market for learning technologies and evaluated several commercial PAL platforms. As a result, the authors found the following gaps in the PALS that fell short of their expectations about an intelligent PALS:

1. Ineffective content—authoring tools.
2. Limited learner-centred learning tools.
3. Lack of functionality for repurposing reusable content in adaptive environments such as adding, modifying and re-creating content.
4. Dearth of broad-based adaptive engines to self-trained to teach other subjects across various disciplines.
5. Limited capability in providing multilayered adaptivity in content and practice difficulty adjustment, learning loops and customized feedback style.

In the absence of any suitable commercial PALS available for purchase, the authors designed and developed a PAL system that met their requirements for the PAL integration with their institution's learning management system.

The Diagnostic Check model is used to compare the entry-level competency of a learner with the entry-level competency of the lesson. With a diagnostic check report with the learner's proficiency level, the Learner Model is updated in real time and tracks the learner's performance, proficiency and behaviour as they progress. The Curriculum Model provides detailed information regarding the content, prerequisite content, practice items, assessment and the relationships between the content and prerequisite content. Content authoring techniques include, but are not limited to, creating, uploading and customizing test elements, instructional content and assessment. The Predictive Mode connects data in real time from the learner and curriculum models to develop algorithms that would create the individualized learning pathways, which would include learning activities such as instructional content, practice items, personalized feedback and assessment in the adaptive learning module. In the event that the learner is not considered competent, the system automatically scaffolds content in real time by providing instruction and practice in prerequisite concepts. It is also significant to note that although Palanisamy, Thilarajah and Chen's design model of a PALS (2021, December) is not backed up by empirical research, it serves as a guide for educators to consider what kinds of PALS they may be able to adapt or develop to match their respective learning environments, and possibly integrate with other emerging technologies.

In general, PALS are classified as a student-facing AIEd, and it is easily the most researched topic with many AI-powered applications already on the market. However, readers should note that the development in AIEd in the three areas as depicted by Baker and Smith (2019) are interrelated. While assessment is classified as teacher-facing AIEd, the data generated from assessment provides valuable insights for PALS to develop personalized learning pathways for learners. The following section offers a discourse on teacher-facing AIEd.

8.8 Teacher-Facing AIEd

As Baker and Smith (2019) suggest, teacher-facing AIEd can be used by teachers as a method of reducing their workload, gaining students' insights and facilitating classroom innovation. These AIEd systems are designed to assist teachers and reduce their workload by automating assessment, plagiarism detection, administration, as well as feedback mechanisms. It is also possible for these AI-powered applications to provide teachers with insights into their students' learning progress, so they can provide additional guidance and support as necessary. Among the potential transformational change that can be made in education with the use of AI-powered assessment, Cope et al. (2020) assert it has the highest potential. In contrast to conventional assessments, in which distinctive and atypical artefacts have been employed to select and provide response tests for retrospective, summative sampling, these two authors argue that AI-enabled assessment systems could support recursive feedback systems integral to learning processes.

In light of the advancement of AIEd and the accessibility of (big) data and learning analytics, Luckin et al. (2016) assert a "Renaissance in assessment" (p. 35). In contrast to conventional assessments that are different artefacts that appear at the end of a period of instruction, a stop-and-test assessment, powered by artificial intelligence, can be embedded in learning activities for continuous assessment of the student's progress. As algorithms are already used for predicting the probability of a student failing an assignment or dropping out of a course with a high accuracy rate, these developments can radically transform education institutions (Cope & Kalantzis, 2017; Kalantzis & Cope, 2015). To learning innovators, these findings are of great value because, in lieu of tests that provide a standardized comparison of learners, learners and teachers are able to access incremental progress panels that can help to facilitate customized and adaptive learning pathways. The subsequent subsection provides further granular details on AI-powered assessment support for teachers.

8.8.1 Automated Grading or Marking

Among the AI-enabled assessments, one of the most popular is automatic grading which uses Automated Essay Scoring (AES) systems (Zawacki-Richter et al., 2019). It was found that this AI-powered tool could be used in a wide variety of disciplines, but there was a focus on experimenting with its use in undergraduate courses. There are various ways to evaluate writing using AES systems, including statistical modelling, natural language processing (NLP), Latent Semantic Analysis (LSA) and other methods from AI (Dikli, 2006). The review highlighted Gierl et al. (2014) findings of using an open-source Java software, LightSIDE, to grade postgraduate medical student essays indicates an agreement between the computer classification and human raters between 94.6 and 98.2%. This process reportedly has the potential benefit of reducing costs and reducing the time associated with employing multiple human assessors for large-scale assessments (Barker, 2011; McNamara et al., 2015). It is still important to note that the authors pointed out that AES might not be suitable for every writing genre as it would be unfeasible to apply it in small classrooms as the system needs to be calibrated using many pre-scored assessments.

In another study, Ma and Slater (2015) discussed the benefits of using algorithms that identify patterns in text responses and prompt students to revise their responses. In this sense, AES could potentially allow educators to consider a broader range of assessment approaches than just testing students' knowledge and abilities using multiple-choice tests only. There is some evidence, however, that an increase in the likelihood of students questioning their grades is a result of the increasing detail in the feedback provided (Barker, 2011). This result has thus led to a rethinking of feedback in the classroom for students who are beginning to study a language (Aluthman, 2016).

There is considerable evidence that AI-powered essay ratings are comparable to human ratings in general, even if there are some areas of concern, indicating good efficacy in general. AES, on the other hand, has been associated with a high degree of efficacy when students are provided with quality feedback. It appears that, despite the growing body of knowledge about how to harness AES for automated grading, little attention has been paid to the feedback delivered to students. It is therefore vital that learning innovators pay attention to this area while adapting or developing AI-based assessment tools. A continuing discussion about providing feedback to students can be found in the subsection that follows.

8.8.2 *Feedback*

The review found that an AES software for pilot training was capable of alerting trainee pilots when they lose situation awareness during flight (Thatcher, 2014). The use of machine learning systems with lexical to provide automatic feedback to the students and improve their writing skills is another popular application (Chodorow et al., 2010; Garcia-Gorrostieta et al., 2018; Quixal & Meurers, 2016). The automated feedback system is another example of this technique, as it operates on adaptive testing to establish the appropriate answers based on Bloom's cognitive levels and recommend additional learning resources and challenges (Barker, 2010).

On the whole, the automated scores generated by these systems are generally reliable in terms of accuracy. Nonetheless, the efficacy of these systems is likely to be very strongly correlated to the nature and quality of the feedback they receive. It is within this context that machine learning has a particular advantage. Multilayered statistical sequences can identify patterns within patterns, and the resulting predictions can be based on the identified patterns. While these teacher-facing AI systems can potentially support and enhance teachers in developing an effective learning environment and in helping them to develop innovative learning experiences, it is crucial for teachers to ensure that they do not abdicate their professional judgement and let the AI systems take charge of their engagement with the students. Having established the benefits of AI systems in supporting teachers in their direct classroom intervention activities, the next section examines how AI applications within academic administration can be useful to students and teachers.

8.9 System-Facing AIEd Applications

The system-facing AI-powered applications provide academic administrators and managers with information on a macro level, such as monitoring attrition patterns across schools or institutions, but this area received the least attention and, thus, the fewest number of existing AI-powered applications in the market (Baker & Smith, 2019). It is not surprising that there is a scarcity of research and a knowledge gap in this area. Fortuitously, Zawacki-Richter et al. (2019) review offers an overview of modest research in these areas: profiling and prediction, admission decisions and course scheduling, drop-out and retention, and student models and academic achievement.

8.9.1 *Profiling and Prediction*

In many AI-powered applications, predictability is enabled by learner models or profiles that are the basis for the algorithm. It is, for instance, important not only to consider the odds that a student will drop out of a course or be accepted into a programme but also to offer timely support and give feedback and guidance on all relevant content-related topics throughout the learning process. In educational data mining, categorization, modelling and prediction are all essential components (Phani Krishna et al., 2018). Among the studies involving students' profiling and prediction, there were three subcategories: seven dealt with admissions decisions and course scheduling, 23 focused on drop-out and retention and 27 examined student models and academic achievement.

It is evident that these findings indicate similar data that are required for the development of student-facing AI systems such as PALS. As a result, it is crucial for learning innovators to design learning analytics purposefully, so that data can be utilized for developing various AI applications.

8.9.2 Admission Decisions and Course Scheduling

The importance of being able to predict students' academic performance is paramount for making informed admission decisions and providing better educational services to students (Chen & Do, 2014). The review found four studies that attempted to predict the probability of a prospective student being admitted to a university-based on the characteristics of the prospective student. Acikkar and Akay (2009) used the support vector machine (SVM) technique to predict applicants' admission to a School of Physical Education and Sports in Turkey based on a physical ability test, their scores in the National Selection and Placement Examination, and their graduation grade point average (GPA). They could predict admission decisions with an accuracy rate of 97.17% in 2006 and 90.51% in 2007. Similarly, Andris et al. (2013) applied SVM to uncover spatial patterns that might favour prospective college students from specific geographic regions in the United States. Feng et al. (2011) used an artificial neural network (ANN) model to analyse enrolment data from 25 Chinese provinces to predict registration rates in other provinces.

Additionally, machine learning techniques and ANN are utilized to predict student course selection behaviour to support course planning. Kardan et al. (2013) developed a model to predict course selection with an ANN in two Computer Engineering and Information Technology Masters programmes based on factors influencing student course selection, including course and instructor characteristics, workload, the approach of delivery and examination time.

In general, findings from these studies suggest that AI-powered applications can predict admission decisions at a high accuracy rate, which means that administrators are able to free up time to focus their efforts on more complicated cases. It is likely that these low hanging fruits would be attractive to university administrators in such a way that would help them to overcome any inhibitions they might have regarding investing in AI for student-facing and teacher-facing AIEd. Taking note of the convergence of the three types of AIEd systems when constructing an AIEd Strategic Framework for Learning Innovation plan, as discussed in Chap. 4, is critical to the success.

8.9.3 Drop-Out and Retention

In general, the purpose of research on drop-out and retention is early warning systems to identify students at risk of dropping out during the first year (Alkhasawneh & Hargraves, 2014; Aluko et al., 2016; Hoffait & Schyns, 2017; Howard et al., 2018), and to predict the attrition of undergraduate students (Oztekin, 2016; Raju & Schumacker, 2015).

To predict drop-outs, Delen (2011) used three classification methods: artificial neural networks (ANNs), decision trees (DTs) and logistic regression with data from 25,224 students enrolled as Freshmen in an American university over a period of eight years. The data included a number of variables that were related to the students' demographic, academic and financial characteristics. The ANN model performed best, with an accuracy rate of 81.19%, and determined the most significant predictors of student drop-out were related to the student's past and present academic achievement, in addition to whether they receive financial aid. A similar study was conducted in which both cognitive and non-cognitive characteristics of undergraduate engineering students were used to predict academic performance (Sultana et al., 2017). In contrast to other studies, their study focused on non-cognitive variables such as self-concept, self-appraisal, time management, leadership and community support to improve the precision of prediction.

These findings indicate that system-facing AIEd applications are capable of predicting students' drop-out and retention rates at fairly high accuracy. Not only this is important to administrators for planning purposes, but this prediction also offers the academic leaders and faculty valuable insights to provide targeted intervention programmes to support students who are at risk of dropping out. It is likely that the institutional leadership would take an interest in the AIEd Strategic Framework for Learning Innovation plan since the student retention rate is another important determinant of the success of an institution. The following subsection delves more into the issue of academic achievement, which is closely related to retention.

8.9.4 Student Models and Academic Achievement

There is a growing trend towards profiling students and modelling their learning behaviours to better predict their academic achievements as the graduation rate has become a critical performance indicator for institutions. Using several machine learning algorithms, Hussain et al. (2018) investigated the behaviour of students at the Open University in the UK to predict their engagement, in order to develop an intelligent predictive system that allows the instructors to identify low-engaged students and automatically provide early intervention. In a similar vein, Blikstein et al. (2014) explored how undergraduate students learned computer programming by analysing over 150,000 code transcripts generated in software development projects. Using the programming process, they found that the model they derived from this yielded a better predictive ability than the model derived from mid-term grades. In a related study, Spikol et al. (2018) applied face-tracking and hand-tracking to assess the effectiveness of project-based learning in classes with engineering students. It has been demonstrated that the findings of the research could be utilized to inform teachers about critical aspects of project-based learning activities.

In various studies, the results suggest that research on student models would be the essential building block for designing intelligent tutoring systems and personalizing adaptive learning environments. In short, while the system-facing AIEd applications are not well-researched as the student-facing and teacher-facing dimensions, it is evident from the literature reviewed that the data required for training the AI algorithm and learning models for all three AIEd dimensions has a great deal in common. In other words, educational institutions should take a holistic approach when making a strategy for AI innovation, as is recommended in Chap. 4. The following section describes possible AIEd trajectory scenarios that reflect possible futures for AIEd's development.

8.10 Future of Artificial Intelligence in Education (AIEd)

Advances in AIEd in the foreseeable future are unfolding fast, and some of these will happen sooner than others bringing both opportunities and challenges. More importantly, these developments usher in the exciting potential that AIEd has to improve education for all. The future of AIEd is intricately coupled with the development of AI. As the economy and job markets evolve, new roles would emerge in AI technology, among other emerging technologies (World Economic Forum, 2020). The emerging professions reflect the greater demand for roles at the forefront of the data and AI economy. However, as the pace of innovation and development is at an unprecedented rate, the current attractiveness of AI should suggest that AIEd is a focus of attention for an increasing number of businesses. Simply put, the imperative is that as humans live and work alongside progressively intelligent machines, our education systems would need to rediscover new frontiers like never before. The following examines the affordances of AI-powered applications due to the convergence of AI with other emerging technologies.

8.10.1 AIEd Augment Our Physical Landscape

In examining the developments of PALS, Greenwald, Corning and Mae, (2017) posit the potential of PALS to be enhanced by the increasing appeal of collaborative and immersive learning environments. Luckin et al. (2016) corroborated, asserting that augmented reality systems (AR), and the full spectrum of extended reality (XR), could potentially transcend intelligent virtual reality systems by facilitating learners and teachers to experience and interact differently with the physical world. In short, immersive technology (such as AR and XR) can present an overlay of information about a learner's physical environment, enabling formal classroom content in virtual reality to overlay the learner's physical reality. A case in point could be that the age, species or vegetation habitat surrounding a learner could be visualized as they undertake a learning journey in the physical world.

There are already existing AIEd systems embedded with socially and culturally intelligent avatars that guide and support virtual learning environments (Bos et al., 2019). Inherently, the extension of such AIEd systems to include AR or XR systems could enable personalized, adaptive learning experiences with virtual mentors guiding students through field trips or learning journeys, allowing teachers to focus on those learners whose needs are most significant (Luckin et al., 2016). Also, teachers will be freed up from the most rote tasks and afforded the time and space, flexibility and creativity to pursue professional development or other educational goals (Schiff, 2021). Readers can refer to Chap. 5 of this book to adapt immersive technologies for teaching and learning.

8.10.2 AIEd Connect to the Internet of Things

The Internet of Things (IoT) refers to a system of interrelated, Internet-connected objects or "things" with embedded computing systems and sensors that can collect and transfer data over a wireless network without human intervention. IoT enables the interconnection of any networked object with any other networked objects or machines. Coupled with big data analytics, the convergence of these emerging technologies opens up new dimensions of possibilities for AIEd systems.

The increasing range of data capture devices such as biological data, voice recognition and eye-tracking enable AIEd systems to provide other forms of data and evidence for currently challenging to assess skills (Luckin et al., 2016). IoT is evident in the form of "wearable personal learning technology" that collects data from the person wearing the device or the surrounding environment to enhance differentiation of instruction and student engagement (Borthwick et al., 2015). For illustration, a skills-based learning experience that integrates fundamentals of problem-solving or collaboration might employ a mix of data sources to assess learners' progress, including the voice recognition device for identifying which learner is doing and saying what in a team activity, and an eye-tracking device for detecting which learner is focusing on which learning resources (Luckin et al., 2016).

Finally, AIEd has created tools and techniques to conduct the fine-grained analysis that enables tracking of each learner's skills and capabilities as they interact and learn. The data yielded of individual learners can be interpreted as required to provide insights into the learner's progress at various levels, laying the foundation for the future of learning, such as 21st-century skills.

While the possibilities that AIEd holds for the future of education are exciting, it drives further research to unlock the potential. Luckin et al. (2016) recommended three following steps to help assure AIEd's developments. UNESCO's report revealed the challenges and opportunities of AIEd for a sustainable development dealing with various areas which are critical to pedagogical, social and ethical dimensions: ensuring inclusion and equity in AIEd, preparing teachers for AI-powered education, developing quality and inclusive data systems, or ethics and transparency in data collection, use and dissemination (Pedro et al., 2019).

8.11 Conclusion

This article begins by examining the developments of AI and its impact on society and the world, mainly focusing on the future of work (World Economic Forum, 2020). Given AI's aptitude to accelerate, exaggerate and amplify, care must be taken to ensure that AIEd is not employed to reiterate the current priorities of schools. More importantly, AIEd can serve as a vehicle or platform for reimagining the design of our education system so that it is fit for the future. The rapid developments AIEd promises many exciting transformative changes to education, making a solid case for the potential of a wide range of tools and applications—learner-facing, teacher-facing and system-facing—to change education in profound ways (Baker & Smith, 2019). A literature review in AIEd provided an overview of the vast array of potential AI applications in higher education to support students, faculty members and administrators. More importantly, it illustrates actions we can take to help fulfil that potential while minimizing risk.

In the student-facing systems, the AI-powered applications provide enormous pedagogical opportunities for designing intelligent student support systems and scaffolding student learning in adaptive and personalized learning environments (Zawacki-Richter et al., 2019). The meta-analysis provided insights into the design and development of a new generation of Personalized Adaptative Learning Systems (PALS) that could be potentially more effective in supporting teaching and learning.

The teacher-facing AIEd systems can help teachers to reduce their workload, gain insights about students and innovate in their classroom. These AIEd systems support the teachers and reduce their workload by automating assessment, plagiarism detection, administration and feedback. These AI-powered applications also provide insight into students' learning progress so that the teacher can provide guidance and support when needed.

While the system-facing AIEd systems received the least attention in educational research, they provide critical insights for academic administrators and managers on the institutional level, such as monitoring attrition patterns across schools or institutions. These AI-powered systems focus on profiling and prediction, admission decisions and course scheduling, drop-out and retention, student models and academic achievement. However, as the data required for training the AI algorithms and learning models for all three dimensions of AIEd are interrelated, institutions should take a holistic approach when mapping out an AI strategic innovation plan.

As the future of AIEd is coupled with the future of AI, new affordances of AI-powered applications may arise due to the convergence with other emerging technologies. The coupling of AIEd with wearable personal learning technologies, a type of IoT device that collects data from the person wearing the device or the surrounding environment could give rise to a spectrum of new applications to enhance differentiation of instruction and student engagement (Borthwick et al., 2015). Also, AI-powered PALS could potentially enhance collaborative and immersive learning environments (Greenwald et al., 2017). Lastly, this article highlights that the next steps for the development depend on various factors such as ensuring inclusion and equity in AIEd, preparing teachers for AI-powered education, developing quality and inclusive data systems or ethics and transparency in data collection.

References

Acikkar, M., & Akay, M. F. (2009). Support vector machines for predicting the admission decision of a candidate to the School of Physical Education and Sports at Cukurova University. *Expert Systems with Applications, 36*(3 PART 2), 7228–7233. https://doi.org/10.1016/j.eswa.2008.09.007.

Agrawal, A., Gans, J., & Goldfarb, A. (2018). *Prediction machines: The simple economics of artificial intelligence*. Harvard Business Press.

Alexander, R., Rose, J., & Woodhead, C. (1992). Curriculum organisation and classroom practice in primary schools: A discussion paper. The Department of Education and Science of United Kingdom.

Alkhasawneh, R., & Hargraves, R. H. (2014). Developing a hybrid model to predict student first year retention in STEM disciplines using machine learning techniques. *Journal of STEM Education: Innovations & Research, 15*(3), 35–42. https://core.ac.uk/download/pdf/51289621.pdf.

Aluko, R. O., Adenuga, O. A., Kukoyi, P. O., Soyingbe, A. A., & Oyedeji, J. O. (2016). Predicting the academic success of architecture students by pre-enrolment requirement: Using machine-learning techniques. *Construction Economics and Building, 16*(4), 86–98. https://doi.org/10.5130/AJCEB.v16i4.5184

Aluthman, E. S. (2016). The effect of using automated essay evaluation on ESL undergraduate students' writing skill. *International Journal of English Linguistics, 6*(5), 54–67. https://doi.org/10.5539/ijel.v6n5p54

Andris, C., Cowen, D., & Wittenbach, J. (2013). Support vector machine for spatial variation. *Transactions in GIS, 17*(1), 41–61. https://doi.org/10.1111/j.1467-9671.2012.01354.x

Barker, T. (2010). An automated feedback system based on adaptive testing: Extending the model. *International Journal of Emerging Technologies in Learning, 5*(2), 11–14. https://doi.org/10.3991/ijet.v5i2.1235

Barker, T. (2011). An automated individual feedback and marking system: An empirical study. *Electronic Journal of E-Learning, 9*(1), 1–14. https://www.learntechlib.org/p/52053/.

Baker, T., & Smith, L. (2019). Educ-AI-tion rebooted? Exploring the future of artificial intelligence in schools and colleges. Retrieved from Nesta Foundation website: https://media.nesta.org.uk/documents/Future_of_AI_and_education_v5_WEB.pdf

Bartholomew, B. Y. (2020). Why AI will never surpass human intelligence. *Journal of Consciousness Exploration & Research, 11*(3).

BECTA (2007). The impact of ICT in schools: A landscape review. Coventry: BECTA. http://www.pedagogy.ir/images/pdf/impact_ict_schools.pdf

Blikstein, P., Worsley, M., Piech, C., Sahami, M., Cooper, S., & Koller, D. (2014). Programming pluralism: Using learning analytics to detect patterns in the learning of computer programming. *Journal of the Learning Sciences, 23*(4), 561–599. https://doi.org/10.1080/10508406.2014.954750

Bonk, C. J., & King, K. S. (2012). Searching for learner-centered, constructivist, and sociocultural components of collaborative educational learning tools. In *Electronic collaborators* (pp. 61–86). Routledge.

Borthwick, A. C., Anderson, C. L., Finsness, E. S., & Foulger, T. S. (2015). Special article personal wearable technologies in education: Value or villain? *Journal of Digital Learning in Teacher Education, 31*(3), 85–92.

Bos, A. S., Pizzato, M., Ferreira, V. A., Schein, M., Zaro, M. A., & Tarouco, L. (2019). The impact of effective communication between users in 3d collaborative virtual environments: The conversational agent use case. *International Journal of Advanced Engineering Research and Science, 6*(8).

Bostrom, N. (2017). Strategic implications of openness in AI development. *Global Policy, 8*(2), 135–148.

Brookhart, S. M. (2010). *How to assess higher-order thinking skills in your classroom*. ASCD.

Bull, S. (2020). There are open learner models about! *IEEE Transactions on Learning Technologies, 13*(2), 425–448.

Cellan-Jones, R. (2014). Stephen Hawking warns artificial intelligence could end mankind. *BBC News, 2*(10), 2014.

Chen, J.-F., & Do, Q. H. (2014). Training neural networks to predict student academic performance: A comparison of cuckoo search and gravitational search algorithms. *International Journal of Computational Intelligence and Applications, 13*(1). https://doi.org/10.1142/S1469026814500059.

Chodorow, M., Gamon, M., & Tetreault, J. (2010). The utility of article and preposition error correction systems for English language learners: Feedback and assessment. *Language Testing, 27*(3), 419–436. https://doi.org/10.1177/0265532210364391

Cope, B., Kalantzis, M., & Searsmith, D. (2020). Artificial intelligence for education: Knowledge and its assessment in AI-enabled learning ecologies. *Educational Philosophy and Theory*, 1–17.

Cope, B., & Kalantzis, M. (2017). Conceptualising e-learning. In B. Cope & M. Kalantzis (Eds.), *E-learning ecologies* (pp. 1–45). Routledge.

Delen, D. (2011). Predicting student attrition with data mining methods. *Journal of College Student Retention: Research, Theory and Practice, 13*(1), 17–35. https://doi.org/10.2190/CS.13.1.b

Desjardins, F., & Bullock, S. (2019). Professional Development Learning Environments (PDLEs) embedded in a Collaborative Online Learning Environment (COLE): Moving towards a new conception of online professional learning. *Education and Information Technologies, 24*(2), 1863–1900.

Dikli, S. (2006). An overview of automated scoring of essays. *The Journal of Technology, Learning and Assessment, 5*(1).

du Boulay, B. (2016). Artificial intelligence as an effective classroom assistant. *IEEE Intelligent Systems, 31*(6), 76–81.

Feng, S., Zhou, S., & Liu, Y. (2011). Research on data mining in university admissions decision-making. *International Journal of Advancements in Computing Technology, 3*(6), 176–186. https://doi.org/10.4156/ijact.vol3.issue6.21

Ford, M. (2015). *Rise of the robots: Technology and the threat of a jobless future*. Basic Books.

Frey, C. B., & Osborne, M. (2013). The future of employment.

Garcia-Gorrostieta, J. M., Lopez-Lopez, A., & Gonzalez-Lopez, S. (2018). Automatic argument assessment of final project reports of computer engineering students. *Computer Applications in Engineering Education, 26*(5), 1217–1226. https://doi.org/10.1002/cae.21996

Gierl, M., Latifi, S., Lai, H., Boulais, A., & Champlain, A. (2014). Automated essay scoring and the future of educational assessment in medical education. *Medical Education, 48*(10), 950–962. https://doi.org/10.1111/medu.12517

Goldin, C., & Katz, L. F. (2010). *The race between education and technology*. Harvard University Press.

Greenwald, S. W., Corning, W., & Maes, P. (2017). Multi-user framework for collaboration and co-creation in virtual reality. In *Proceedings of 12th International Conference on Computer Supported Collaborative Learning* (pp. 1–2). ISLS.

Gurkaynak, G., Yilmaz, I., & Haksever, G. (2016). Stifling artificial intelligence: Human perils. *Computer Law & Security Review, 32*(5), 749–758.

Hawking, S., Russell, S., Tegmark, M., & Wilczek, F. (2014). *Transcendence looks at the implications of artificial intelligence—But are we taking AI seriously enough?* Independent.

Hoffait, A.-S., & Schyns, M. (2017). Early detection of university students with potential difficulties. *Decision Support Systems, 101*, 1–11. https://doi.org/10.1016/j.dss.2017.05.003

Howard, E., Meehan, M., & Parnell, A. (2018). Contrasting prediction methods for early warning systems at undergraduate level. *Internet and Higher Education, 37*, 66–75. https://doi.org/10.1016/j.iheduc.2018.02.001

Hussain, M., Zhu, W., Zhang, W., & Abidi, S. M. R. (2018). Student engagement predictions in an e-learning system and their impact on student course assessment scores. *Computational intelligence and neuroscience.*

ITU. (2018). Artificial Intelligence (AI) for development series module on AI. Ethics and Society.

Jebari, K., & Lundborg, J. (2020). Artificial superintelligence and its limits: Why AlphaZero cannot become a general agent. *AI & SOCIETY*, 1–9.

Kalantzis, M., & Cope, B. (2015). Learning and new media. The Sage handbook of learning, 373–387.

Kardan, A. A., Sadeghi, H., Ghidary, S. S., & Sani, M. R. F. (2013). Prediction of student course selection in online higher education institutes using neural network. *Computers and Education, 65*, 1–11. https://doi.org/10.1016/j.compedu.2013.01.015

Krizhevsky, A., Sutskever, I., & Hinton, G. E. (2012). ImageNet classification with deep convolutional neural networks. In F. Pereira, C. J. C. Burges, L. Bottou & K. Q. Weinberger (Eds.), *Neural information processing systems 2012* (pp. 1097–1105).

Lee, V. E., Croninger, R. G., & Smith, J. B. (1997). Course-taking, equity, and mathematics learning: Testing the constrained curriculum hypothesis in US secondary schools. *Educational Evaluation and Policy Analysis, 19*(2), 99–121.

Luckin, R. (2018). *Machine learning and human intelligence: The future of education for the 21st century*. UCL IOE Press. UCL Institute of Education, University of London, 20 Bedford Way, London WC1H 0AL.

Luckin, R., Holmes, W., Griffiths, M., & Forcier, L. B. (2016). *Intelligence unleashed. An argument for AI in education*. Pearson.

Ma, H., & Slater, T. (2015). Using the developmental path of cause to bridge the gap between AWE scores and writing teachers' evaluations. *Writing & Pedagogy, 7*(2), 395–422. https://doi.org/10.1558/wap.v7i2-3.26376

Mayer-Schonberger, V., & Cukier, K. (2013). Big data: the essential guide to work, life and learning in the age of insight.

McCarthy, J., Minsky, M. L., Rochester, N., & Shannon, C. E. (1955). A proposal for the Dartmouth summer research project on artificial intelligence. *AI Magazine, 27*(4), 12–14.

McCarthy, J., Minsky, M. L., Rochester, N., & Shannon, C. E. (2006). A proposal for the dartmouth summer research project on artificial intelligence, August 31, 1955. *AI Magazine, 27*(4), 12–12.

McNamara, D. S., Crossley, S. A., Roscoe, R. D., Allen, L. K., & Dai, J. (2015). A hierarchical classification approach to automated essay scoring. *Assessing Writing, 23*, 35–59. https://doi.org/10.1016/j.asw.2014.09.002

Najafabadi, M. M., Villanustre, F., Khoshgoftaar, T. M., Seliya, N., Wald, R., & Muharemagic, E. (2015). Deep learning applications and challenges in big data analytics. *Journal of Big Data, 2*(1), 1–21.

Nilsson, N. J. (2014). *Principles of artificial intelligence*. Morgan Kaufmann.

Oztekin, A. (2016). A hybrid data analytic approach to predict college graduation status and its determinative factors. *Industrial Management and Data Systems, 116*(8), 1678–1699. https://doi.org/10.1108/IMDS-09-2015-0363

Palanisamy, P., Thilarajah, S., & Chen, Z. H. (2021, December). Providing equitable education through personalised adaptive learning. *ASCILITE.*

Panetta, K. (2018). *Gartner top 10 strategic technology trends for 2019*. Gartner.

Pedro, F., Subosa, M., Rivas, A., & Valverde, P. (2019). Artificial intelligence in education: Challenges and opportunities for sustainable development.

Peng, H., Ma, S., & Spector, J. M. (2019). Personalised adaptive learning: an emerging pedagogical approach enabled by a smart learning environment. *Smart Learning Environment 6*(9). https://doi.org/10.1186/s40561-019-0089-y

Perrotta, C., & Selwyn, N. (2020). Deep learning goes to school: Toward a relational understanding of AI in education. *Learning, Media and Technology, 45*(3), 251–269.

Phani Krishna, K. V., Mani Kumar, M., & Aruna Sri, P. S. G. (2018). Student information system and performance retrieval through dashboard. *International Journal of Engineering and Technology (UAE), 7*, 682–685. https://doi.org/10.14419/ijet.v7i2.7.10922.

Quixal, M., & Meurers, D. (2016). How can writing tasks be characterised in a way serving pedagogical goals and automatic analysis needs? *Calico Journal, 33*(1), 19–48. https://doi.org/10.1558/cj.v33i1.26543

Raju, D., & Schumacker, R. (2015). Exploring student characteristics of retention that lead to graduation in higher education using data mining models. *Journal of College Student Retention: Research, Theory and Practice, 16*(4), 563–591. https://doi.org/10.2190/CS.16.4.e

Ritter, S., Carlson, R., Sandbothe, M., & Fancsali, S. E. (2015). Carnegie Learning's adaptive learning products. Educational Data Mining, 2015, 8th.

Schiff, D. (2021). Out of the laboratory and into the classroom: The future of artificial intelligence in education. *AI & Society, 36*(1), 331–348.

Sergis, S., & Sampson, D. (2019). An analysis of open learner models for supporting learning analytics. In *Learning technologies for transforming large-scale teaching, learning, and assessment* (pp. 155–190). Springer.

Siemens, G. (2013). Learning analytics: The emergence of a discipline. *American Behavioral Scientist, 57*(10), 1380–1400.

Siemens, G. (2017). Connectivism. Foundations of learning and instructional design technology.

Siemens, G. (2019). Learning analytics and open, flexible, and distance learning. *Distance Education, 40*(3), 414–418.

Siemens, G., Rudolph, J., & Tan, S. (2020). 'As human beings, we cannot not learn'. An interview with Professor George Siemens on connectivism, MOOCs and learning analytics. *Journal of Applied Learning and Teaching, 3*(1), 108–119.

Spikol, D., Ruffaldi, E., Dabisias, G., & Cukurova, M. (2018). Supervised machine learning in multimodal learning analytics for estimating success in project-based learning. *Journal of Computer Assisted Learning, 34*(4), 366–377. https://doi.org/10.1111/jcal.12263

Sultana, S., Khan, S., & Abbas, M. (2017). Predicting performance of electrical engineering students using cognitive and non-cognitive features for identification of potential dropouts. *International Journal of Electrical Engineering Education, 54*(2), 105–118. https://doi.org/10.1177/0020720916688484

Taguma, M., Feron, E., & Lim, M. H. (2018). Future of education and skills 2030: Conceptual learning framework.

Tan, S. (2020). Artificial intelligence in education: Rise of the machines. *Journal of Applied Learning and Teaching, 3*(1), 129–133.

Thatcher, S. J. (2014). The use of artificial intelligence in the learning of flight crew situation awareness in an undergraduate aviation programme. *World Transactions on Engineering and Technology Education, 12*(4), 764–768. https://www.semanticscholar.org/paper/The-use-of-artificial-intelligence-in-the-learning-Thatcher/758d30530515l1cde2f28fc6b2181b8e227f8ea2.

UNESCO. (2018). *Artificial intelligence in education: Challenges and opportunities for sustainable development* (UNESCO Working Papers on Education Policy, [7], pp. 1–48).
Verbert, K., Duval, E., Klerkx, J., Govaerts, S., & Santos, J. L. (2013). Learning analytics dashboard applications. *American Behavioral Scientist, 57*(10), 1500–1509.
Vinge, V. (1993). Vernor Vinge on the singularity. Presented at the VISION-21 Symposium sponsored by NASA Lewis Research Center and the Ohio Aerospace Institute.
World Economic Forum. (2020). *The future of jobs report 2020.* World Economic Forum.
Xie, H., Chu, H. C., Hwang, G. J., & Wang, C. C. (2019). Trends and development in technology-enhanced adaptive/personalised learning: A systematic review of journal publications from 2007 to 2017. *Computers & Education, 140*, 103599.
Zawacki-Richter, O., Marín, V. I., Bond, M., & Gouverneur, F. (2019). Systematic review of research on artificial intelligence applications in higher education–where are the educators? *International Journal of Educational Technology in Higher Education, 16*(1), 1–27.

Samson Tan is the Director of Regional Strategy and Operations at Civica (Singapore). The focus of his work is on developing education strategies with strategic customers and stakeholders for the advancement of educational innovation best practices. Samson served as the Head of the Centre for Innovation in Learning at the National Institute of Education prior to joining Civica. He is also an exco member of the Association of Problem-Based Learning and Active Learning Methodologies (PAN-PBL), and the Education Research Association of Singapore.

Part V
Assessment and Feedback for Learning

Chapter 9
Assessment, Assessment Rubrics and Feedback

Kumaran Rajaram

Abstract This chapter presents the topic on qualitative indicators on the perceived learning effectiveness of the assessment rubrics adopted. Students' performance in higher education is closely intertwined with the effectiveness of feedback because it influences learning quality. Giving timely, effective feedback to students is a complex task and not all feedback may be equally effective. The use of assessment rubrics assists in making assessment more uniform, better in communicating expectations and performance standards to students, measuring students' progress over time and helping to lay the foundation for rigorous long-term assessment. A section will discuss on how assessment rubrics are perceived from a social-cultural perspective and at the aspects that all educators need to be mindful in designing and implementing them from the learning effectiveness dimension. This exploratory study investigates the usage of assessment rubrics by business management students, instructors teaching management courses and course designers who are involved in the learning design of these courses. With evolving technology, e-assessment rubrics have become an increasingly useful and productive evaluation tool. Twenty consenting students from 200+ diverse business management students, three instructors and two course designers teaching and/or managing a management course participating in a larger study were selected for face-to-face interviews on the effectiveness of e-assessment rubrics adopted and their impact on students' learning outcomes. This study summarizes the qualitative "consultations" with learners, instructors and course designers and argues for holistic yet standardized and detailed assessment rubrics to serve as a platform for formative and normative feedback.

K. Rajaram (✉)
Division of Leadership, Management and Organization, Nanyang Business School, Nanyang Technological University, Singapore, Singapore
e-mail: rkumaran@ntu.edu.sg

K. Rajaram, *Learning Intelligence: Innovative and Digital Transformative Learning Strategies*, https://doi.org/10.1007/978-981-19-9201-8_9

9.1 Introduction

Assessment serves as one of vital element in the learning process as it drives effective learning processes. We do not know exactly if students learn, or much they learn when we teach. Anyone who has been in a class for a few hours will know that it's simply not practical to organize and catalogue all the learning experiences from the start to the end, which may be a potential substitute for assessments. Hence, it is only feasible through assessment where we find out whether the instructional activities in which we engaged our students resulted in the intended learning. The assessment component serves as a vital and central process in teaching and learning which enables instructors to assess what the students have been taught. The design of assessments determines how students learn and acquire knowledge. Hence, assessment serves as the connecting link between teaching and learning.

Assessment plays a vital role facilitating high efficacy in learning, to attain the intended learning outcomes and as a control mechanism in improving the learning process. As reported by Wyatt-Smith and Cumming (2009), research points us to the fact that teachers characteristically spend around one-third to one-half of the class time engaged in a particular type of assessment or learning evaluation activity (Wyatt-Smith & Cumming, 2009). Evidence shows that the knowledge pertaining to assessment-related matters that teachers hold is rather limited. In a holistic general sense, there needs to be much more attention and conscious efforts required to be placed on the teacher preparation programmes and related matters, taking in due consideration the relevance of assessment and accountability has increased in muti-folds over the past decade. Assessments are rather embedded in a social-cultural settings which are stated transparently in some cases and implicit in others (Mislevy et al., 2003).

Conventionally, assessment is used by higher education institutes as a means to measure students' learning outcomes that are tied to learners' performance on participating, for instance, in an academic degree programme. This allows institutions to clearly have a mechanism to authenticate the expected requirements to be met and imperatively serve as validated evidence of knowledge gained and essential competencies acquired. The direct measuring of students' learning could be attributed to three primary reasons, namely (a) to provide students accurate feedback on their learning progress and provide advice, feedback on their improvements, for example, to fulfil the course requirements; (b) to reflect and improve on the collated outcomes obtained from measuring students' learning outcomes that pin-points both the strengths and weaknesses of the course contents, deliver and so on, that assist institutions in their pursuit of continuous improvement; and (c) to provide both internal and external stakeholders with relevant information relating to the course, programme and the contributing success factors in having the educational goals to be met.

Feedback and assessment rubrics are among the significant components of assessment as these elements facilitate the process of continuous improvement in students' learning and promote essential shifts, transformations to take place in the classroom and beyond. The impact of assessment on learning is influenced by how students perceive feedback and the learning environment in which it occurs (Pereira et al., 2016). Feedback could also be obtained by students upon the completion of an assessment task where it could potentially present assessment rubrics typically feature evaluation criteria, descriptions of the criteria, quality definitions and a scoring strategy, where while they are generally used to grade students' work, they indeed serve a much bigger role in providing concrete directions tied to the learning outcomes. Assessment rubrics assist students in comprehending the targets for their learning as well as the expected standards of the tasks to be fulfilled. The rubrics enable them to make reliable judgements about the learners' own work and highlight areas for improvement or development.

In today's dynamic and complex global learning environment, higher education institutions must duly consider the impacts of social and cultural diversity issues intertwined with evolving contemporary aspects. For instance, student populations are more racially diverse than ever before. The Association of American Colleges & Universities (2019) revealed that students of colour made up 45.2% of the undergraduate student population in the United States in 2016. This number had increased from 29.6% in 1996. Other differences could include gender, disability, religious beliefs, nationality and so on. Institutions must acknowledge and recognize that these social-culturally diverse students function optimally in different learning environment. This point is emphasized by research scholar Rajaram (2021) who advocates that a high efficacy of outcomes in terms of teaching deliverables (from educators), process of learning (by learners) and assessment rigour (its design by educators and learning performance by learners) requires a good comprehension of the learning culture and culture of learning by the Higher Education Institutions Technology is increasingly prevalent in modernized classrooms, where a study by McGraw-Hill (2016) reported that 81% of college students in the United States found that digital learning technology was helpful in improving their grades while more than 69% felt it helped them to be more focused. Hence, this makes us ponder on how assessments will be potentially influenced both positively and negatively through technology disruptions.

In general, the assessment and its associated components are more complex with varying categories of interventions beyond the surface level. Hence, the goal of this chapter is to provide readers with a deeper appreciation and comprehension of assessments at higher education context, while proposing conceptual and practical frameworks as broader guidelines that are to be used to increase the efficacy and implement effective assessments in today's classrooms.

9.2 Assessment

Assessment is defined as a process for documenting in measurable terms the knowledge, skills, attitudes and beliefs of the learner (Capraro et al., 2011). The term assessment is often used interchangeably with the terms "examination", "test" and "measurement". Is that explicitly accurate? From a broad perspective, assessment enables gathering of information, for educational purposes in terms of what students know and what they are capable of (Mislevy, 2017). The process of executing assessments with rigour and high level of effectiveness in classrooms has its own set of demands and complexities embedded with varying challenges. At the classroom level, teachers must decide on matching the level of knowledge, competencies, attitudes and beliefs require with the correct types of assessments. It must also be figured out when and why that type of assessments should be adopted to optimize the intended learning outcomes and interconnectivity to the expected deliverables (Capraro et al., 2011).

The significance of how assessments are executed is also closely observed from an institutional level. There is a rise in numbers on the implementation of methodical strategies for the assessment of students' learning to meet the increased demands for educational accountability. Higher Education Institutions are becoming more conscientious to their accountability to the varying stakeholders they are expected to account for. Firstly, legislators and taxpayers who subsidize higher education institutions have strict expectations on what constitutes students' learning. Secondly, employers want some way to affirm that the graduates they hire are knowledgeable and equipped with the essential competencies. Thirdly, parents who pay for their child's tuition fees want to see that they receive quality education from the institutions. Finally, students want to be re-assured and self-validated that they have the required skills and knowledge to start employment upon graduating.

Assessment is of primary importance to education and students' learning (Koshy, 2008; Taylor, 2006). Measurements of learning effectiveness and outcomes are essential for institutions to attain quality educational deliverables (Rajaram & Collins, 2013). In any assessment, learning should be positioned at the core for its design and execution. Assessment has the capacity to contribute to learning because students will work diligently to meet the requirements to perform well to achieve their intended learning outcomes (Carless et al., 2017). Entwistle and Ramsden (1983) emphasized that students are mindful of their overall aims and interests, hence careful in aligning to the assessment requirements to achieve them. For students, the assessment serves as a primary driver and agenda that drives their behavioural action that leads to the expected deliverable that is measured. Hence, the design of the assessment is vital and should be mindfully designed to enhance and advance students' learning process that leads to achieving the intended learning outcomes. Instructors should be clear of their learning outcomes of the course that they are designing. Secondly, the assessment must be designed where the key touch points of how the learning happens, and their potential outcomes should be defined and described explicitly. Third, instructors must think through carefully on the type of learning design and the supporting pedagogy to be adopted to ensure the learning happens through the type of assessment embedded within it. If these three basics are well put in placed, the intended quality and rigour of the assessment process will be well achieved.

While largely scholar's perspectives on assessments tend to be similar, there are some alternative perspectives of assessments that comes from scholars Rajaram (2021) and Boud et al. (2016) who advocates that criteria for the assessments needs to be broaden to incorporate a multifaceted and much more rigorous development of the learners. They highlighted that research has focused on ways that emphasize measurement on students' learning or institutional policies, while they advocate viewing assessment from a practice-oriented perspective, developing more on the competencies related to the respective subject specializations. They believe this approach or direction will help position assessment in general to re-look and re-create learning design and curriculum practices that helps shape future ready workforce focusing on the competences to be developed on. In doing so, they propose that research on assessment, specially in developing the criteria for the assessment rubrics, its phenomena and aspects that constitute it. For instance, the process should involve a larger range of experts, for example, subject matter practice experts, employers that offer strategic perspective, besides the faculty designing it.

All in all, we can agree that assessment plays an integral role in higher education curricula. The next section will elaborate on why this is the case.

9.2.1 Importance of Assessments

Assessment is a crucial driver of student learning, and its effective and efficient implementation facilitates positive impact and meaningful learning. On the flip side, unorganized, feebly executed assessments could potentially lead student learning in unproductive directions (Carless, 2017). The assessment strategies undertaken by courses will have a major impact on students' learning process and how the learning activities will be executed, the depth of knowledge and its application aspects focused on (Bloxham & Boyd, 2007; Rajaram, 2021). Apparently, evidence reiterates that poorly executed assessment strategies will negatively impact students' learning. The emphasis to pay attention on the assessment strategy is vital, where these studies suggest that while assessments by itself are important, so is its design.

Authentic assessments differ from traditional types of assessment such as essays and examinations which have no specific application in most real-world contexts. For instance, authentic assessments, where the focus is in applying knowledge and skills in real-life settings, where it is found to provide the foundation in attaining much higher academic standards and working towards adopting best practices globally. Evidence points us to enhance student learning through teaching them competencies, skills beyond technical and applied knowledge that vastly improve their employability potentials (Rajaram, 2021; Sotiriadou et al., 2019). Likewise, authentic assessments are positively related to students' satisfaction and promoting good behaviour (James & Casidy, 2016). Students who view their subjects to be authentic are more inclined to be involved, affirmative when exchanging ideas, having dialogue about the subject. Ultimately, such collective positive responses could only potentially better the university's reputation which potentially help in attracting more prospective students.

A study by Lam (2015) reinforces that assessment as a part of the learning process promotes teacher competence in teaching writing, student motivation for learning and text improvement. In a similar vein, Carless (2017) mentioned that assessment for learning (AfL) is defined as any form of assessment designed to promote students' learning. Some of the key impacts of AfL are: (a) a clear focus on the intended outcomes is designed and work towards to; (b) there is a validation and authentication of the specific skills, applied knowledge or competencies attained; (c) controls that serve as feedback for improvements from the current to the desired state, in terms of cognitive or behavioural skills. The next section discusses the common categories of assessment that provide us with a better comprehension of how assessments are administered in schools in today's contemporary context.

9.2.2 Categories of Assessments

Simonson et al. (2014) highlights that assessment can be categorized into two schemas. The first schema can be classified as being objective or subjective that revolves around the attributes of the assessment itself while the second schema is categorized as being formative or summative that is based on how the results are used.

Subjective assessments are designed in a manner such that learners are expected to produce similar results, but the submissions still require individual scrutiny to determine each student's progress and score. On the other hand, objective assessments do not typically require human intervention and learners are expected to have identical results as all the correct answers should match. The key aspect is not about comparing which of these two types of assessments are more superior, rather one must be mindful and clear to understand why that type of assessment is used based on the expected outcomes in terms of developing the correct mixture of technical knowledge and conceptual skills required.

Another way of categorizing the assessment measures is by sorting them out by their intended purpose. Formative assessments are intended to lead for betterment of the instruction itself. An example will be reviewing and reformulating the instructions for an assignment after realizing that a number of students have not understood task, perhaps in terms of clarity and simplicity at least from their lenses of view. Many instructional designers hold a more inclusive view of formative assessments where it is defined as assessment that provides the relevant information about a learner's progress towards the identified mastery of objectives. Some teachers use formative tests as a means to prepare their students for summative tests; however, this is not ideal. A study by Grosas et al. (2014) shows that the final exam performances of students they had examined were disappointing despite their positive attitudes towards the formative tests. It was concluded that it would be more sensible to use formative tests as a means to address weakness or areas of improvements rather than as a way to provide exam practice.

On the flip side, summative assessments are more outcome-focused and place emphasis on the overall final results. Standardized exams such as the ACT, GRE or GMAT fall into this category. These types of tests provide a snapshot of knowledge and skills that are used for administrative purposes such qualifying assessment standards, awarding validations or certifications, whereas summative assessments are typically comprehensive and measure the mastery or a specific body of knowledge.

9.2.3 Assessments for Developing Varying Learning Outcomes

While the categories of assessments discussed above are useful in making us comprehend the different types of assessment, the goal is to recommend a more holistic, broader and practice-oriented framework that allows educators and researchers to much better appreciate the range of assessment methods and potentially to be adopted for their research or course execution. We decided to leverage and expand on Jimaa's (2011) work that categorizes assessment in four ways, namely:

- **Knowledge and understanding**: assessed through a combination of unseen examinations and in-course assignments, for example quizzes, essays, presentations, reports and problem-solving-based assessments.
- **Intellectual skills**: assessed through a combination of unseen written examinations, coursework related to engineering that requires analysis and problem-solving.
- **Practical skills**: assessed through a combination of continuous formative assessment, summative assessments and objective structured and/or practical examinations.
- **Transferable skills**: assessed through a range of assignments built into the curriculum, including coursework reports, oral presentations and research exercises.

In our recommend framework, we categorized the assessment approaches into three clusters, namely: (a) cognitive development; and (b) behavioural development and hybrid, comprising both of these aspects. These categories are further broken down into subcategories to provide a deeper context to be appropriately adopted. This provides educators, researchers and practitioners with a conceptual framework that assists them in choosing the most appropriate assessment methods based on their individual needs and learning goals for their courses.

The cognitive interventions include all the psychological processes and activities revolving thinking and knowing. This includes how information is acquired, processed and organized. Cognitive development is the study of how these processes develop in individuals and how they become more efficient and effective in their understanding of the world and mental processes. We identified three primary ways in which cognitive development can manifest itself in the higher education context, namely (a) knowledge in terms of theoretical and conceptual understanding, where it refers to the technical knowledge that learners learn from textbooks or lectures or through facilitations.; (b) applied knowledge and interpreted contents, where this revolves around the comprehending of how to apply the knowledge in specific contexts; and (c) cognitive relational skills where it refers to higher-order thinking skills that are vital aspects in teaching and learning. This includes the ability and capacity to analyse, evaluate and create which differs from lower order thinking skills such as remembering, understanding and applying (Tanujaya et al., 2017).

On the other hand, behavioural development relates to the acquisition and growth of certain skill sets and behaviours. In its subcategories, we have incorporated competencies and skills that are primarily imperative for graduate employability in today's contexts. These include presentation skills, communication skills and teamworking skills. Character education embedding values refer to teaching students to understand and act on ethical values such respect, compassion and justice among other things.

Lastly, for the hybrid development, we have catered this category for assessment approaches that falls into the mix in combination of both cognitive and behavioural development. Some assessments may have an impact in both aspects on a similar or varying levels. This purpose of this is intentional where we want the learners to acquire both cognitive and behavioural development, especially in circumstances that enable them to do so. Table 9.1 presents the three-tier conceptual framework for categorization of assessment methods.

9.3 Feedback

Students' performance in higher education is closely intertwined with the effectiveness of feedback because it influences learning quality.

Feedback can be described as brief information provided to learners in written or oral forms on their progress of learning and performance, for example, could be deliverables or in the form of the expected behavioural actions. From a scientific perspective, feedback is defined as a mutual exchange (Carless, 2006; Getzlaf et al., 2009; Hattie, 2012; Hattie & Timperley, 2007; Nicol & Macfarlane-Dick, 2006; Sadler, 1983; Stiggins & Chappuis, 2006; Wolsey, 2008) of information that is imperative and critical (Ackerman & Gross, 2010; Ferguson, 2011; Hattie & Jaeger, 1998; Higgins et al., 2002; Wolsey, 2008) provided in timely and efficient manner (Hattie & Timperley, 2007; Higgins et al., 2002; McCabe et al., 2011; Nicol & Macfarlane-Dick, 2006; Stiggins & Chappuis, 2006) to promote learning (Black & Wiliam, 1998; Case, 2007; Crisp, 2007; Duncan, 2007; Hattie & Jaeger, 1998; Hattie & Timperley, 2007; Higgins et al., 2002; Lipnevich & Smith, 2009; Nicol & Macfarlane-Dick, 2006; Sadler, 1983; Stiggins, 2007; Stiggins & Chappuis, 2006, 2008; Taras, 2003; Wolsey, 2008) and self-correction (Case, 2007; Ferguson, 2011; Getzlaf et al., 2009; Hattie, 2012; Hattie & Timperley, 2007; Lipnevich & Smith, 2009; Nicol & Macfarlane-Dick, 2006; Sadler, 1983). Feedback is defined as the information provided regarding aspects of an individual's performance or understanding of a certain matter (Hattie & Timperley, 2007). This process is facilitated

Table 9.1 Three-tier conceptual framework for categorization of assessment methods

Target to be assessed	Assessment methods	Scholarly evidence
Cognitive development		
Knowledge (theoretical and conceptual understanding)	Written examinations Closed-book exams Quizzes/MCQs Online quiz/test/exam Group work	Downing (2002) Aziz (2002) and Gokcora and DePaulo (2018) Chiriac (2014)
Applied knowledge and contents	Coursework Case-study analysis Presentations Open-book exams Portfolios	Slapcoff, Dobler and Tovar (2011) Escartin et al. (2015)
Cognitive relational skills (cognitive empathy, intellectual skills, higher-order skills)	Reflective essays	Lew and Schmidt (2011); Rajaram (2021)
Behavioural development		
Competencies and skills	Group work Oral exams Book/article review Exchange programme/study abroad	Hassanien (2006) Ahmed et al. (1999)
Character education embedding values	Reflection journals Exchange programme/study abroad	Rajaram (2021)
Hybrid *(Behavioural, affective and cognitive with application)*		
Practical hands-on skills	Internships/Industrial Experience Practical examinations	Crowell (2016) Gwynne and Morgan (2014) and Rajaram (2021)
Transferable skills	Internships/Industrial Experience	Crowell (2016) and Rajaram (2021)

through an agent such as through a teacher, peers, book, parent, self and/or experience. A teacher can provide corrective inputs or required information for corrections, while a peer can provide alternative perspectives or strategies to make enhancements or amendments. A book can help clarify ideas that leads to potential betterment and a parent can provide encouragement with possible areas of improvement. A learner can possibly engage in self-correction by looking up the answer to evaluate the response provided. We need to acknowledge that feedback is a consequence of performance. Hence, in contemporary higher education systems, the process of assessment and feedback is viewed as coexisting activities (Rajaram, 2021; Winstone & Boud, 2020).

Winstone and Boud (2020) argue that there is a need to disentangle assessment and feedback as its rudimentary purpose is to serve as an evaluation and to act as a certification function. On the flip side, we could debate that the goal and use of feedback goes beyond which is to also influence learners' future work and learning strategies.

A teacher who is grading students' work is enacting two distinct purpose: (a) to be provide a grade award and supporting justifications, after giving due consideration to the past achievement and the provision of feedback to influence or positively impact future progress and achievement. While both of these aspects are vital, the assessment processes could potentially lead to conflict between the two functions where the dominance of assessment hinders the purpose of feedback (Winstone & Boud, 2020). Therefore, we need to be mindful of how one function could possibly obstruct the other, so the aspects of feedback should not be diminished.

As such, one way for teachers to relate fully appreciate and understand the implication of feedback is to view it as a process that makes a difference to students' performance. Feedback is not a one-way, as rightfully intervention Henderson, Ajjawi et al. (2019) emphasizes that the feedback process does not merely stop at the juncture when students' work is returned to them. Learners' follow-up action is necessary for feedback to be meaningful. This aspect emphasizes on the shift from a teaching-centred process to a learning centred one. The quality of comments matter in terms of the efficacy of feedback where there is a necessity to observe if these comments serve as a positive influence on students' learning.

The goal of feedback could be viewed as the bridge that assists students to lessen the gap between their current understanding of learning and the intended learning goals/outcomes (Hattie & Timperley, 2007; Mory, 2004; Poulos & Mahony, 2008; Sadler, 1989). Feedback has an extensive impact on students' learning (Ackerman & Gross, 2010; Black & William, 1998; Fraser et al., 1987; Hattie, 2012; McCabe et al., 2011; Metcalfe & Kornell, 2007), plays a pivotal role in enhancing their performance (Carless et al., 2011; Evans, 2013; Ferguson, 2011; Hattie & Timperley, 2007). Feedback can be categorized as formative (information that is meant for progressive students' improvement on their learning) or summative (to provide a holistic analysis of a standard attained, characteristically through marks and grades) (Sinclair & Cleland, 2007). Feedback enables learners to reflect on their performance against the criteria that they were measured on, hence focusing on the specific "gaps." The instructor's comments, suggestions in the form of feedback enable students to reflect and understand where they could improve taking reference to the expected outcomes described explicitly in the assessment criteria. The feedback is valued by students as they are aware of where they could improve on explicitly. Through the meta-analyses, it shows that there is a beneficial and positive consequence of feedback on learning with unfavourable effects in a subset of learners (Hattie & Timperley, 2007). Feedback increases students' confidence and motivation to learn (Yuan & Kim, 2014). Not all feedback provided qualifies spontaneously to be effective. Scholars (Duncan, 2007; Gibbs & Simpson, 2004; Gielen et al., 2010) reports that even if the feedback is to be well crafted, its effectiveness could only be realized if the students act on it. For students to make a more informed decisions and act on it, the feedback needs to come from multiple sources (Van den Berg et al., 2006). The effectiveness of feedback could be viewed to exist in a range of scale, where consideration is to be given to the individuality of each of the student, plus the ability to balance with the correct amount of feedback supported with appropriate and relevant elements such as clarity, delivery, depth, focus and type. Students' confidence and motivation to learn is enhanced through instructors' positive feedback (Ferguson, 2011; Narciss, 2008). Evidence also shows that the contrary of not acknowledging effort will have a negative effect of making the students want to give up (Ferguson, 2011). Scholars (Hattie & Timperley, 2007; Narciss, 2008) advocates that by incorporating metacognitive strategies in feedback they can be instrumental in nurturing students to transform to self-regulated learners. The metacognitive strategies involve (a) setting clear goals to monitor the learning process; and (b) evaluate outcomes and so forth (Narciss, 2008).

Giving effective feedback to students is a complex task and not all feedback may be equally effective. The effectiveness of feedback is a key factor that needs to be reflected upon mindfully. Weaver (2006) highlights that students are aware of the viral role of feedback and how it has a consequential effect on their learning. The question is are the feedback provided to students effective? In the literature, there are several attributes that are discussed on effective feedback. Shute (2008) studied the "specificity" (p. 157), "complexity and length" (p. 159) and "timing" (p. 163) of feedback. Evans (2013) provides some guidelines for effective feedback design focusing on timely feedback, post-feedback, feed-forward, sources of feedback as well as interactions about feedback.

9.3.1 Importance of Feedback

While most would agree that feedback is important, Henderson, Phillips et al. (2019) claim that students expressed much dissatisfaction largely because they are not given timely feedback and when they receive them, it is not adequately comprehensive and value-adding in their perspective. This could be due to common challenges of teachers giving concise comments instead of elaborative and detailed comments with adequate coverage on their explicit weakness and how they could improve on these areas. Teachers, on the other hand, find the process of giving feedback burdensome and are cynical that their efforts will go to waste should students are not willing to be engaged with the given feedback. Hence, the significance role of feedback as part of the continuous learning process with a growth mindset, its implications and why it is required as post-assessment inputs in higher education contexts must be consistently reflected upon.

Feedback is critical for effectively promoting continuous learning emphasizing on the ethos of growth mindset and self-development. Without it, learners are limited in how they can make self-evaluations or judgements on their own progress and change, make positive impact in their future performance. Feedback is vital to learners' (a) as a self-reflection and development; (b) as an opportunity to appreciate the diverse perspectives and to appreciate them for betterment; and (c) for effective decision-making which is the foundation for improved learning outcomes. In fact, feedback could be viewed as one of the most powerful influences on learning and achievement (Hattie & Timperley, 2007). The significance is also validated by Bellon et al. (1991) who reports that academic feedback is strongly and consistently related to achievement of learners than any other teaching behaviours, where this relationship remains consistent regardless of grades, socioeconomic status, race or school setting.

There are varying factors that could possibly influence the outcomes of feedback, for instance, in terms of its correlation intertwined link to assessments. Feedback is perceived as more relevant, effective and is perceived more positively by learners who are assessed through learner-centred methods compared to those assessed by traditional approaches (Pereira et al., 2016). From this study, the emphasis on perception is reiterated on how both learners and instructors perceive feedback from their own dimensions and how that becomes relevant to how it is provided, received and used. Hence, one must mindful and empathetic when the feedback is articulated keeping in mind a few vital aspects such as (a) what are the key aspects that makes the feedback given is of high in efficacy?; and (b) what are the factors to keep in mind to ensure the feedback is easily comprehensive and relatable to the learners or the individuals receiving it. Experience influences the way examiners evaluate and provide feedback on students' work (Jansson et al., 2017). Evidence shows that with more experience, examiners tend to utilize less menu-marking and articulate more openly with very much of flexibility. They provide instructions for students rather than limiting themselves to only evaluative text. Experienced examiners were identified to use more explanatory text and less descriptive text in their evaluations. Hence, the impact on the effectiveness of feedback is influenced and determined by how exactly feedback should be facilitated. The next section discusses on the guidelines in providing effective feedback.

9.3.2 Guidelines to Provide Effective Feedback

The ability to provide quality feedback requires us to comprehend and apply the art and science of delivering feedback. The science encompasses the "know-hows" of what to include, how to articulate that focuses on the technical aspects of providing feedback, whereas the art involves the way it is delivered, be in written or verbal, in terms of the choice of words, articulation and tonation. Feedback is viewed as of quality if it has the potential to effectively impact students' learning and it leads to improved learning outcomes, where it relates to the efficacy rather than perceived value.

The factors that influence perceptions of feedback can be categorized in three domains: (a) the feedback itself; (b) the context of the feedback; and (c) the assessment literacy and expectations of students (O'Donovan et al., 2019). The domains of influence are very much varied, difficult to prioritize, and are not mutually exclusive. Strong interdependencies exist between them. Effective feedback practices are influenced by its design, the competency of the individuals involved in facilitating the process and the institutional culture (Henderson, Phillips et al., 2019). By simply replicating, an effective feedback practice from one context does not guarantee success in the next. Hence, to sustain and continuously deliver effective and quality feedback, much efforts and resources are to be invested must be inputted in addressing the contributing elements, respectively. When we focus on the efficacy of feedback, instead of only focusing on the quality of the teacher's input, the quality of the whole process, including the active role of students need to be duly considered (Henderson, Phillips et al., 2019). Majority of students do optimize the feedback they receive, hence fail to realize and maximize the potential it would potentially offer. Despite the complex nature of providing quality feedback that is viewed as such by all stakeholders involved, we have collated and advocated guidelines on how potentially quality, relatable and effective feedback can be accomplished.

9.3.2.1 Instructor to Students

Traditionally, feedback is provided by instructors to students after they have reviewed their submitted work or verbal presentations, by providing feedback, comments for improvements. Effective feedback is influenced by learning design, the learners and the educator's capacities and dispositions (Henderson, Phillips et al., 2019). The effect of feedback is also influenced by the competing and layered demands of classroom, faculty, specializations, disciplines and university contexts.

After thoroughly analysing the evolving scholarly works and conceptual frameworks in academic literature as well as taking into due consideration of the contemporary practices adopted, a new framework is created with five core thrusts, namely Capability and Competency of Stakeholders, Learning Designs and Cultural and Social Contexts, Timing and Efficacy. Table 9.2 presents the conceptual framework of guidelines in providing effective feedback.

Efficacy for feedback refers to optimizing the quality of the deliverable and its positive impact. Hence, for instance, how much of the feedback provided is useful and meaningful for the learners. Capacity and competency of stakeholders for feedback refers to the ability, competency and capacity of the people involved in the feedback process, for instance, both learners and instructors, their motivations, actions, and dispositions towards the feedback process. Timing for feedback refers to the appropriate and right phase of intervention in providing the inputs. Learning Designs primarily refers to how the feedback process is implemented and its efficacy of being received by the learners. Cultural and social contexts revolve around how the feedback provided is perceived by different culturally and socially varying learners as well as stakeholders at all levels of the institution. The success of feedback is attained when the institutions are committed, value through its appropriate implementation in its systems, policies and activities. Effective feedback on assessment much be a valued and vital part of the university's eco-system and culture. Feedback is not simply just providing some inputs or comments to students, instead it is a process that requires students to make sense on the quality of their performance on the assigned tasks so as to improve their future learning performance. Teachers must ensure and emphasize that students reflect, relate and comprehend what the feedback is for in order to achieve the efficacy of the feedback provided. However, Universities need to recognize that providing effective feedback is complex, comprises of a well-fitted eco-system put in place where its effectiveness is unlikely to be achieved unless the conditions of efficacy, capacity and competency, timing, learning designs and cultural and social contexts are met. Aside this, teachers must duly consider students' perceptions of feedback as negative perceptions may deter students from acting on the feedback and take it seriously. Interestingly, according to the study by Ackerman

Table 9.2 Conceptual framework: guiding principles—conditions for high efficacy and effective feedback

Key thrusts	Conditions that enable effective feedback
Efficacy	1. The focus and emphasis on the aspects of feedback provided must align to the learning needs, intended learning outcomes and growth of the learners 2. To understand the learners' ability by relating to the context so that the feedback could be customized, applied and provided to their future tasks' undertakings 3. The type, approach of feedback to be adopted and how it is delivered to the learners' must be duly considered and executed
Capability and competency of stakeholders	1. Educators must be trained appropriately and equipped with relevant, contemporary skills and applied knowledge to be able to facilitate quality and effective feedback. This enables them to be well aware of identifying the correct channels to enhance its efficacy as well as mindful and sensitive in the way the feedback is delivered 2. Educators should be highly encouraged to adopt evidence-based approach in their planning and evaluation phases on the effectiveness of feedback given 3. Educators and learners must be given the appropriate space and autonomy 4. Learners must be proactive and forthcoming by being engaged, involved that enables them to optimize from the feedback process 5. The values of growth mindset and ability to embrace diverse perspectives must be embedded in the process of learning. These interventions are to be consistently advocated to learners to have them take the feedback provided in the right spirit with humility to attain greater heights 6. Instructors must believe and acknowledge the value in taking time, efforts to provide quality feedback as a continuous growth for betterment of students 7. The positive mindset and correct outlook is imperative to anchor its essence which is primarily depended on the instructor who is giving the feedback and the learner who is in the receiving end
Timing	1. Understand the motivation of learners receiving feedback and when will be the right juncture that assists them to reflect and apply the learnings 2. The intervention has to be targeted when there is adequate space provided for some deep reflection and seek clarification, if required
Learning designs	1. The feedback must be contextualized and customized to its best means to address the varying and unique needs of the different profile of learners. This personalized approach addresses specific aspects in a more targeted manner 2. Learning outcomes of multiple tasks must be carefully and thoroughly thought through and aligned to attain consistency 3. A variety of sources and modes must be evaluated to examine its effectiveness. Among it, identify and adopt one that is of the most relevance to improve the efficacy of implementation 4. Ensure the information shared or made available is relevant, usable and the learners are aware on how to use it

(continued)

Table 9.2 (continued)

Key thrusts	Conditions that enable effective feedback
Cultural and social contexts	1. There must be adequate awareness and the ability to relate well mindfully with sensitivity to the varying complex, mutilayered social-cultural values, norms and practices 2. There must be well-validated processes and controls in place to ensure consistency, rigour and quality 3. Leaders of institutions and educators must emphasis on continuity of vision and commitment to high quality and rigour, despite the differences and challenges that potentially arise 4. Educators must be empowered and have the flexibility to deploy resources to its best effect to deal with potential hindrances and roadblocks 5. The diversity of composition involved in any circumstances must be respected, valued, perceived positively and unanimously accepted by all stakeholders

and Gross (2010), it was found that students generally prefer to receive adequately sufficient rather than overwhelmingly more feedback comments on assignments. The evidence reiterates the point that offering too much of comments causes negative effect on their perceptions that could potentially be equated to not providing any feedback at all.

9.3.2.2 Students to Students

Feedback between students or peer feedback is a form of activity or feedback process that is a common occurrence in classrooms. This aspect occurs when students are required to evaluate the quality of work or performance of their fellow peers. Peer feedback can be confirmatory, suggestive or corrective and have positive effects on learning when it is well-received and is vital for the development of self-regulatory skills (Topping, 2009).

Peer feedback is a valuable learning and reflection activity for students, while learning how to give and take feedback should be viewed as a vital lifelong skill (Nilson, 2003; Rajaram, 2021). However, for the feedback to be valuable and to be of high efficacy, the core challenges and pitfalls must be avoided. The benefits of peer feedback can be enhanced by the following two guidelines, namely (a) to have the students identify and/or to respond to specific parts of the paper or project; and (b) to encourage candid and useful feedback, the audience needs to be authentic/real, at least in the revision stages. These guidelines put the students in a position of writing to communication, empowered with a high responsibility. Under such circumstance, these students are less likely to face challenges such as blandness, superficiality, inaccuracies, inconsistencies and other related issues present in judgement-based feedback.

9.3.2.3 Students to Instructors

Applying a flipped approach, students should be made to provide feedback on instructors' teaching, the execution of the course learning design lead by the instructor, engagement and the ability to resonate to the students involved as a key stakeholder and the professional relationship, i.e. in terms of approachability, service leadership facilitated and cultural and social connectivity with the students. In higher education institutions (HEIs), student feedback is taken as a primary source of information to evaluate and enhance the level of teaching efficacy and its effectiveness (Seldin, 1997).

The importance and usefulness of feedback are validated and supported by Universities along with teachers (Flodén, 2016). Evidence also states that attitude and outlook of how feedback is perceived by the teachers has an impact on the efficacy of feedback usage, i.e. teachers with a positive attitude towards feedback find it more useful and use it more compared to teachers inclined towards an undesirable attitude and perception. Teachers should be advocated and facilitated via formal process to better comprehend and value feedback for them to be more receptive towards it, thus more likely to continuously improve their learning design, curriculum and delivery methods in accordance with the changing learners' needs.

Evidence emphasizes that learning to provide quality and comprehensive feedback requires a certain motivation level by an individual, unswerving teaching and having optimal conditions for practice. Learners' motivation levels are vital in determining the quality and quantity of feedback they would want to give spontaneously and willingly. It is also imperative for teachers to have the self-belief and positive outlook re-iterating their belief that the feedback given to students will potentially make a difference in their future performance. One possible strategy is to provide students with the opportunity to give feedback very early on in their weekly class sessions and observe how the feedback is acted upon in a positive and appropriate manner. This approach sends a clear signal to reiterate to the students that the instructor is serious about feedback and in fact have it put to use. Evaluations have shown that collating and reflecting on feedback early in the semester enables instructors to turn around even the most challenging classes (Svinicki, 2001). Creating an eco-system to training students can certainly be viewed as a strategy in enhancing the efficacy of providing feedback. This could be started by illustrating exemplary models of quality feedback. Once students have acquired the skill of giving useful and quality feedback, the instructor can establish the conditions for students to practice and perform that skill. By enabling multiple opportunities to practice, students' progress and opinions can be tracked, where subsequently, and arguably as a vital follow-up action, teachers must be prepared to receive feedback with an open and growth mindset. No matter how high-quality student feedback is, all we result in naught if teachers choose to ignore them.

9.4 Types of Feedback

Formative feedback is what most people have in mind when they first think of feedback giving feedback (Naylor et al., 2014). Formative feedback often occurs while students are learning and is used to improve learning and the effectiveness of teaching delivery. With formative feedback, students gain a better understanding of the subject contents and learn to address or avoid the mistakes they make. Contrastingly, summative feedback is viewed as the final verdict on student performance and achievement. It is used to check on students' learning after the teaching event is complete. It is also an avenue used to grade, accredit or rank students and is typically presented as marks or grade that may or may not be accompanied with formative feedback. While these two types of feedback are distinct, most assessments at higher education institutes comprise of both formative and summative elements. For instance, students may find their final grade is accompanied by qualitative feedback from the assessor. Teachers are to design their assessments with a clear goal to decide whether its primary goal is to develop the abilities of students or to assess what they have learnt.

Further to these two primary types of feedback, we could add two more to the list, namely formal feedback and informal feedback (Hardavella et al., 2017). Formal feedback comes as part of a structured assessment and is generally planned and scheduled to be part of the assessment process. Informal feedback, on the flip side, occurs more frequently than formal feedback. It usually happens on a day-to-day basis, with the inputs provided by anyone in the students' learning journey, including instructors and peers. Table 9.3 presents examples of the various types of feedback that are categorized based on its nature and context. The contents presented are further improvised and add-on from the initial work from "Types of feedback" (University of Florida, n.d.).

9.4.1 *Formative Feedback*

The primary goal of formative feedback is for students are to increase their knowledge, skills and understanding of the contents taught (Shute, 2008). Students who utilized the formative feedback provided subsequently improved in the areas in which they had been previously criticized and did not receive the same criticisms again. They also established a strong linkage between the use of formative feedback and improvements in writing. It is worth noting that repeated feedback assisted many students improve their academic writing at a much quicker pace than usual.

Formative feedback can be used to evaluate the activities of staff and serves as an input to their professional development. According to Irons (2007), by examining the manner in which students respond to formative feedback enables teachers to review the efficacy of teaching and learning techniques adopted in classrooms. Through such avenues of generating feedback, teachers are able to identify specific gaps in students' learning process and their performance in terms of intended learning outcomes. For instance, if a teacher is required to provide analogous feedback to many students on a particular topic or aspect of it, then it is a clear indicator that their students have not fully understood what has been taught or that the question in the assessment was not easily understandable.

Table 9.3 Categorization on the types of feedback

Description of feedback	Formative feedback	Summative feedback	Formal feedback	Informal feedback
Peer review and/or evaluation by learners of their submissions as part of the class participation assessment		✓	✓	
Demonstrating tutorial questions for students to view or having them work out the questions on the i-pad or laptops and have them shared with others during class discussion	✓			✓
Asynchronous e-learning with self-assessment activity and e-reflection journal as part of the pre-class online learning assessment component		✓	✓	
Reviewing and going through solutions to practice problems or question sets	✓	✓	✓	
Comments via markup of student report or tutorial question submissions and other assignment drafts	✓		✓	
Sharing exemplar report or presentation slides submission together with relevant assessment rubrics		✓	✓	

(continued)

Table 9.3 (continued)

Description of feedback	Formative feedback	Summative feedback	Formal feedback	Informal feedback
Providing explicit feedback on students' performance, highlighting what they are doing well and skilled at and areas of improvement, say at the end of the lesson or course		✓		✓
Extending help by focusing on their behavioural skills performance tied to their future job related aspects		✓		✓
Adhoc verbal feedback on impromptu questions during group, class discussions as well as the presentation pitch	✓			✓
Reflecting on the performance on questions attempted, reviewing the correct answers and providing justifications for each of the answer		✓	✓	

All in all, when viewed from the benefits and efficacy aspect of students' learning perspective, formative feedback is ranked the most important (Naylor et al., 2014). Further to this, they also emphasized that summative assessment delivered without any constructive formative feedback can be detrimental to students' learning, as it may potentially demoralize, confuse them without much concrete, clear directions ahead and hence, causing them to feel anxious.

9.4.2 Summative Feedback

It is a common practice by teachers to grade students' class work, informal assessments, tests and provide feedback through the award of grades. Sometimes the grading systems are simple and clear, highlighting what is correct and other times complex grading criteria is used (Harlen, 2002).

The goal of summative feedback is to assist students understand how well they have performed by adequately meeting the learning goals of the course. This intervention is essential for students to know how much they have learnt, acquired in the course and what they need to work on and focus on next. Summative feedback can have major implications for life choices that students make such as the field of study they wish to pursue. It can also influence students' self-perception and their academic disciplines upon graduation (Stanford Teaching Commons, n.d.).

Even though formative feedback is often given more emphasis and viewed as more imperative than summative feedback, that said, it cannot be categorized as not important and valuable. In a higher education context, summative feedback is essential for professional accreditation and the awarding of honours placements and scholarships. Nonetheless, it must always be preceded by adequate formative feedback to enable students to be prepared for their final assessments (Naylor et al., 2014).

9.4.3 Formal Feedback

Effective feedback is generally described to be targeted, specific and timely (Goodwin & Miller, 2012). Hence, it is easier for teachers to meet those conditions through formal feedback since it is often planned and systematically timed in the assessment process. Perhaps, this formal feedback situation could also possibly be a face-to-face dialogue between the tutor and student, or between peers, or be provided in written form (Värlander, 2008).

Peer feedback can also be used as part of the formal feedback process. This may be useful in situations where power asymmetries between teachers and students may have the possibility to negatively impact feedback. If an instructor lacks power or recognition in instructor-student relationships, they may experience feelings of fear, anxiety and low self-esteem (Värlander, 2008). Obviously, this will subsequently impact students' motivation and likeliness to learn. Hence, by conducting formal peer feedback instead, teachers can negate any perceived power asymmetry felt by students as it shifts power from the instructor to students.

Formal feedback is also applicable to students' feedback. For example, in almost all British institutions, some type of formal collection and reporting of course-level feedback is required and is usually included in programme annual reports. The method of collating feedback in this case is often unspecified and left to the instructors to decide (Harvey, 2003).

9.4.4 Informal Feedback

Informal feedback can arise from a variety of sources and methods. For instance, it thrives in seminars, lecture halls and classrooms where teachers engage students in meaningful and interactive discussions, with the relevant tasks and activities.

Students can learn from informal feedback as they participate and be involved in everyday learning activities (Centre for the Enhancement of Teaching and Learning, The University of Hong Kong, n.d.).

For teachers, feedback on courses is a vital aspect for continuous improvement (Harvey, 2003). Both informal and formal feedback allow teachers validate the effectiveness of their teaching. But informal feedback allows teachers to reflect on instantaneous perceptions shared, say for a particular lesson. This allows for immediate corrective action to be taken should it be necessary.

9.5 Assessment Rubrics

The term "rubrics" is often defined in different ways. The most common definition taking reference to Reddy and Andrade (2010) is it is referred to a source that articulates the expected deliverables and expectations of an assignment by listing and illustrating the criteria and levels of quality. Assessment rubrics can be defined as a specific set of criteria adopted for evaluating a task or work performed and offers more details than just the grade or marks. Brookhart (2013) defines a rubric as "a coherent set of criteria for students' work that includes descriptions of levels of performance quality on the criteria" (p. 4). Assessment Rubrics are regarded as: a descriptive scoring instructional tool (Egodawatte, 2010; Moskal, 2000; Oakleaf, 2009). An effective and versatile assessment tool for knowledge acquisition and the development of professional skills (Mertler, 2001), they form the basis on which instructors make academic judgement about students' performance and measure their achievement and progress (Egodawatte, 2010; Reynolds-Keefer, 2010). From these definitions, we could derive that there are two primary aspects, namely (i) a definite set of criteria; and (ii) the brief explanation of the levels of performance of these criteria (Brookhart, 2013). Eshun (2011) and Gasaymeh (2011) consider that a well-constructed, criterion-based assessment approach: (a) Facilitates the purpose of instruction, inspiration and evaluation in constructivist learning environment; and (b) Allows assessment to take a lead role in the learning process. The use of rubrics is becoming an emergent trend in education due to their positive impact on teaching and learning (Andrade, 2000; Dornisch & McLoughlin, 2006). The usage of rubrics could be seen across various disciplinary context in higher education. Rubrics is a scoring tool that highlights the expectations of an assignment (Stevens & Levi, 2005). Rubrics categorizes an assignment into varying components and provide a succinct description of what is considered the acceptable or unacceptable levels of performance for each individual component. All in all, rubrics can be used for assignments such as research papers (individual and group), group work reports, individual portfolios, presentations (individual and group) and other various forms of assessments.

Rubrics must be designed for assisting assessors in evaluating the quality of students' performance. To accomplish this, rubrics comprises of three fundamental features, namely (a) information on specific aspects or criteria that examines students' deliverables or performance output that helps instructors to identify the specific aspects of elements that are being assessed; (b) the descriptions of students' performance that assists instructors in judging the quality; (c) a scoring strategy. The combination of these three features put together enables the formation of an assessment rubric (Jönsson & Panadero, 2017).

It is vital to clarify any misconceptions held in the aspects of teaching and learning. Most of the misconceptions stem from instructors using rubrics as a tool while integrating it with their understanding of assessment that relates to grading (Brookhart, 2013) One of the common mistake or incorrect perception by instructors is when they use rubrics with performance assessment that focuses on the task, product and not the learning outcomes or proficiency the task the students are expected to demonstrate. Another misconception is to confuse the criteria embedded in the rubrics with the specific task requirements to be done. By using rubrics as the guide and direction for doing up the assignment, it becomes more like a checklist to be fulfilled by students. Such use of rubrics can be viewed as being tied to a more grade-focused approach, hence the focus is shifted away from the learning which is what it is supposed to represent.

The primary purpose of rubrics is to assess performances (Brookhart, 2013). To assess learning, one must observe learners' action, behaviours and outcome in the form of relevant deliverables over time. Hence, the assessment rubrics serve as a form of scaffolded document of explicit skills demonstrated, behaviours exemplified and actions performed. Research evidence reiterates that teacher spend 20–30% of their time allocated for various forms of assessment (Stiggins, 1998). Assessment Rubrics enables grading to be performed more objectively upholding impartiality as there are organized and scaffolded criteria to adhere to. Aside this, it enables to describe the specific requirements to be met in the form of evaluating criteria of the assignment; it serves as a quick formative feedback that helps students to reflect on their work and improve. Rubrics provide a scaffolded and organized structure to evaluate the actions and deliverables expected. The scaffolded observations and evaluations performed of a student's work to the explicit descriptions articulated enables one to make informed choices in the grading process. The much thought through judgement for the grading made through the rigorous and quality-based assessment rubrics with explicit descriptions enables the instructors to provide accurate and objective feedback where students can appreciate, reflect and learn.

Rubrics guides and provides students explicit expectations that needs to be fulfilled. The goal is to make it clear, easy to understand from the students' perspective. The criteria to be included in the rubrics should be focused on what the students are expected to learn. Brookhart (2013) re-iterated the point that the lack of clarity on the learning outcomes will cause ambiguity in knowing what exactly to be taught; hence, rubrics assist with lucidity of both content and learning outcomes. The rubrics serve as coordinating tool for providing instructions to students on their assessment (Brookhart, 2013). The entire process of pre-during-post phases of using the rubrics enhances the process of learning and its intended outcomes. This is validated as Brookhart (2013) advocates:

> The criteria and performance-level descriptions in rubrics help students understand what the desired performance is and what it looks like. Effective rubrics show students how they will know to what extent their performance passes muster on each criterion of importance, and if used formatively can also show students what their next steps should be to enhance the quality of their performance. This claim is backed by research at all grade levels and in different disciplines

Assessment rubrics are categorized into two types, namely analytic and holistic rubrics (Brookhart, 2013). Each of the criterion is explicitly spelled out and described in the analytic rubrics, whereas for the holistic rubrics, the criteria are applied concurrently to facilitate an overall judgement on the quality of work. Analytic rubrics are recommended when the students are to use the graded assessment rubrics as formative feedback. The holistic rubrics are adopted when all the criteria are used together concurrently. This type of rubric is recommended especially the graded rubrics are not supposedly to be used as a formative or summative feedback for students, where the evaluated information is usually only to award a grade. In such circumstances and as the need arises, using such rubric is productive and more efficient as only an overall decision must be made instead of separate decisions for each criterion.

The effectiveness of the assessment rubrics is very much linked to its design. It is vital for instructors to avoid the common pitfalls in designing and developing the assessment rubrics. The lack of a good understanding and having misconceptions on grading has a drastic effect on students' learning. We must acknowledge that instructors may already have misconceptions about grading (Brookhart, 2001). Brookhart (2013) highlights primary misconceptions about rubrics (a) confusing learning outcomes with tasks. Instructors tend to focus on the task and not the learning outcome or competency and/or skills the task is supposed to have the students demonstrate. This is validated by scholars (Chappuis et al., 2012, Goldberg & Roswell, 1999–2000) who reiterates that the problem is on instructors focusing on task or instructional activity and not the learning outcomes; (b) confusing rubrics with requirements or quantities. Instructions must not design the rubric where the criteria involve requirements for the assignment not about descriptive aspects in terms of counting things. This incorrect approach inclines towards more to the grade-focused instead of learning focused; (c) confusing rubrics with evaluative rating scales. Instructors identify the criteria to be assessed and tag each of it to a rating scale and call it a "rubric". In other words, rubrics that contains evaluative scales instead of descriptive scales to assess the quality of the output by "grading" it which defeats the primary goal of rubrics. The primary function of rubrics is to align the performance of the task to a description instead of judging it instantly. The description serves as the bridge between the student's deliverable and the observation on the learning process.

We need to acknowledge that without a reliable and effective assessment rubric, two major concerns may arise: (a) Over-subjective and/or inconsistent evaluation, leading unfairness to students; (b) The unreasonable time involved in giving feedback to or grading students (Dornisch & McLoughlin, 2006). Sivan (2002) argue that: (a) Simply following the assessment rubric during assessment does not enhance students' learning experience; (b) A more innovative approach is required which guarantees that students experience ownership of learning. Egodawatte (2010) debates that it may be challenging to reduce discrepancies and intrinsically motivate students to learn if there is lack of training and guide on the use of rubrics.

With the availability of technological platforms, the rubrics could be embedded on the e-platform such as, in our case, eUreka platform, hence, to make it simpler and easier to relate, we will be using the term e-assessment rubrics which represents the rubrics embedded in the e-platform, eUreka which could be used virtually. This makes it easier for instructors to facilitate group discussions via online forums, discussion boards and real-time virtual platforms for students to have their thoughts/views on the e-assessment rubrics and criteria shared through collaborative session(s). In addition, this approach enables personalized access of e-assessment rubrics via online anytime, anywhere. The e-collaborative session(s) are usually followed by a physical class discussion to share thoughts, debate and to interpret the assessment criteria by engaging students. The embedment of the assessment rubrics in the e-platform allows better standardization and consistency in terms of the implementation process across many seminar groups. The e-assessment rubrics serves as an enhanced approach in disseminating clear definitions of explicit expectations within the respective assessment criteria quickly to a large no. of students, respectively.

With evolving technology, *e-assessment rubrics* have become an increasingly useful and productive learning tool. The use of e-assessment rubrics assists in making assessment: (a) More uniform; (b) More effectual in communicating expectations and performance standards to students; (c) By measuring student progress over time and helping to lay the foundation for rigorous long-term assessment; and (d) By enabling comprehensive and quick feedback for students' reflection and improvement.

If the rubrics are appropriately used it can be very beneficial in numerous ways. Rubrics can be used to pursue a student-centred approach to assessments that assist in teaching and evaluation. Students can use rubrics to enhance their comprehension of goals set for their learning as well as the level of expectation in terms of quality standard and outcomes. Further to that, rubrics can help students perform self-reflection of their own work which assist them to improve. The other reasons for rubrics adoption in higher education will be elaborated in the next section.

9.5.1 Use of Assessment Rubrics

Research on the use of rubrics has revealed that it helps assessors attain acceptable levels of consistency when grading assignments. Other documented positive impacts in using rubrics include assisting students to become independent leaners and improving their performance in school. Rubrics make expectations and criteria of assignments clear which enables students to interpret the different quality deliverable standards and to have it served as a feedback avenue. Aside these benefits, there are several other reasons as to why instructors implement the use of rubrics in their classes. This is elaborated by Stevens and Levi (2005) who identify six reasons as to why rubrics are used. The reasons are as follow (1) enable timely feedback, (2) prepare students to use detailed feedback, (3) encourage critical thinking, (4) facilitate communication with others, (5) help instructors refine their teaching and (6) assist in overcoming inequities in classrooms.

Firstly, rubrics allow teachers to provide timely feedback. Time has been found to be a significant factor in making feedback meaningful and useful to students. Rubrics can save an assessor's time and allow them to provide students feedback while they still have their mind on the assignment. With rubrics, this can also be done without compromising the relevant details and specificity of feedback for students. Secondly, rubrics prepare students to use detailed feedback. Students tend to say that they want detailed feedback yet hardly seem to read or understand it. Rubrics can provide students with a detailed description of the highest level of achievement possible while at the same time provide detailed feedback through explanations of why a student did not achieve the highest level. This allows students to easily comprehend what they are doing right and/or wrong. Rubrics also allow students to keep track of their progress and improvement. Thirdly, rubrics encourage critical thinking. By encouraging students to think critically about their own learning, rubrics can inspire the pattern of self-assessment and serve as a self-improvement intrinsic intervention, creating motivated and creative students. Fourthly, rubrics facilitate communication with others. Rubrics allow teachers to communicate their goals and intentions to all participants involved such as teaching assistants, students and fellow academic staff, where at times without not being aware that such communication is taking place. Sharing rubrics can help in ensuring the grading is performed consistent. Fifthly, rubrics help teachers refine their learning. Rubrics show students' development over time and can provide teachers with a better understanding of teaching gaps as well as strengths. Finally, rubrics can be a means or avenue where students of diverse backgrounds gain equal footing. There are many social and cultural inequities that could disadvantage certain groups of students in learning environments. Rubrics can help instructors pinpoint problems in communication and deal with them explicitly. While they are not the only way to address inequities, they could play a vital role in creating more equitable classrooms.

While the practicality of rubrics is certainly a reason to use them, as illustrated above, it is imperative to duly consider the perceptions of both instructors and students towards the rubrics. Its benefits will not be reaped unless both parties are agreeable, understand its use and put them into practice. Mostly, the perceptions towards rubrics tend to lean positively. In a review by Reddy and Andrade (2010), they indicate that postgraduate and undergraduate students' value rubrics as they help to clarify the goals of their assignments, allow them to monitor their progress, and make grades transparent and fair. The study also reported positive perceptions of instructors, where they felt rubrics provided an (1) objective basis for evaluation; (2) helped them grade work more consistently, reliably and efficiently; and (3) enabled the change in evaluation procedures from subjective observations to specific performances. Although both students and instructors view rubrics in a positive light, but the variation lies in their perceptions towards the purpose of rubrics. Students viewed rubrics as serving learning and achievement, whereas instructors viewed them as a way to quickly, objectively and accurately assign grades. This limited view on rubrics may potentially cause instructors to become more unwilling to use them. Therefore, it is important that higher education management ensure that instructors understand the adoption of rubrics and use it beyond evaluation, where it can be a useful tool to enhance teaching.

9.5.2 *Types of Assessment Rubrics*

Scholarly literature describes four types of assessment rubrics that lie on two separate schemas—holistic versus analytic and general versus task specific. Whether a rubric is analytic or holistic is independent of whether it is general or task specific, and that rubrics can be described on both factors (Nitko & Brookhart, 2013). Analytic rubric requires the instructor to score individual components of the task or assignment and thereafter sum up the scores for the final marks. On the other hand, a holistic rubric necessitates that the score relates to the overall process or product without judging components of the task separately. The general rubrics apply across a family of similar tasks while task specific rubrics specify the facts, concepts and procedures that a students' response should contain (Brookhart, 2018). Brookhart (2018)'s research work discussed on the specific definition of the four types of rubrics, namely (a) Analytic, (b) Holistic, (c) General, and (d) Task Specific as well as its advantages and disadvantages.

9.5.2.1 Analytic Rubrics

Analytic rubrics allow assessors to evaluate each component or criterion of a task separately with each criterion being scored on a different descriptive scale. The criteria should be decided in the initial stages of developing the rubrics (Moskal, 2000). For instance, in a writing task, one criterion could be the appropriate use of grammar and punctuation among the other aspects.

Analytic rubrics are the best for most classroom purposes as it focuses on one criterion at a time (Brookhart, 2013). This approach is more appropriate for instruction and formative assessment since students are able to view and acknowledge what aspects of their work requires attention. It is also useful for summative assignments as it allows instructors to comprehend how to modify their teaching in specific circumstances. The design of analytic rubrics allows a clear view of the strengths and weaknesses of students. This rubric does not only provide students the guidance on how they can improve but also facilitate instructors in the enhancement of their teaching. For instance, a rubric could point out a specific element on students' answers that is of the weakest, and as such the instructor can redirect more energy into covering that particular topic again. With the analytic rubrics, instructors are able to give specific feedback on the elements that students excelled in. Although the use of analytic rubrics is more time-consuming due to its composition of high-level details involved, it is especially useful to help students understand expectations and their performance in contrast to that (Nitko & Brookhart, 2013). However, by choosing the analytic rubrics, it does not completely rule out the possibility of a holistic factor (Moskal, 2000), where a holistic judgement could be built as one of the components. However, the challenge is to avoid an overlap between criteria for the holistic judgement and the other evaluated factors. In this instance, the assessor needs to consider whether the overlap results in certain criteria being weighted more than it was originally intended for. Hence, it must be ensured that students are not intentionally penalized for a given mistake.

9.5.2.2 Holistic Rubrics

There are instances where it is not possible to divide an evaluation into independent components. In that case, a holistic rubric may be more appropriate. In a holistic rubric, criteria are combined into one single descriptive scale, where it allows for broader judgements of the quality of the process or product (Moskal, 2000). Holistic rubrics is preferred at instances when the result of an assessment is not provided to the students and information is not used for anything other than a grade (Brookhart, 2013). The access to overall evaluation allows teachers to save time since it is faster to make a single decision as compared to many separate decisions, say in the case of the analytic rubrics. This implies that holistic rubrics are easier to use, and less time is spent per student (Nitko & Brookhart, 2013), where it is especially useful for teachers who have large class sizes.

9.5.2.3 General Rubrics

General rubrics use descriptions of work that apply to a whole set of assignments. When the same general evaluation framework is applied to all assignments in a particular subject, students can continuously apply and improve their learning. This can be tied to the fact that these assignments or tasks have the same learning outcomes. Research has shown that students' achievement improves when general analytic types of rubrics are used in classroom (Nitko & Brookhart, 2013).

General rubrics have advantages over task specific rubrics. General rubrics (1) assist planning and monitoring of students' work; (2) improve flexibility when using with many varying tasks; (3) allows description of students' performance by allowing multiple paths to success; (4) help in developing students' learning of skills instead of task completion; and (5) do not need to be rewritten for every assignment. General rubrics target the knowledge and skills that students are expected to be acquiring. If the rubrics remain the same each time a student does a similar kind of assignment or task, they can learn the general qualities of good performance of different skills such as essay writing or problem-solving. On the other hand, if a rubric is always changing for similar kinds of tasks, students will not be provided an opportunity to look past a particular problem or task. This implies that a student may not potentially learn to develop a specific skill, rather they will only learn how to overcome a specific mistake. All in all, general rubrics encourage students to focus on building up general knowledge and skills instead of simply thinking about completing an assignment.

9.5.2.4 Task Specific Rubrics

A task specific rubric is designed and used for an explicit task or assignment. Task specific rubrics cannot be shared with students ahead of time unlike general rubrics. Task specific rubrics contain information on specific answers to a challenge or provide explanation and reasoning for the usage by a student. It lists facts or concepts that are crucial for a student to mention in their work (Brookhart, 2013; Nitko & Brookhart, 2013).

Grading students' responses with task specific rubrics is lower inference work as compared to using a general rubric. We can relate this to the task specific rubrics which is more detailed and clearer to assessors on what to look out for in a student's work. Hence, it is faster to train teachers to become reliable assessors in large-scale assessments using task specific rubrics. It is also easier for instructors to apply task specific rubrics consistently with minimal practice as compared to general rubrics which takes much longer to apply (Brookhart, 2013). All in all, task specific rubrics allow for both reliability and efficiency throughout the grading process of assessments (Nitko & Brookhart, 2013).

9.6 Social-Cultural Aspects of Assessment

The learning process and assessment is influenced by the social and cultural contexts, for example in the type of learning design adopted, the relationship between learners and instructors, classroom assessments and the level of learner's autonomy. We must acknowledge that without an adequate understanding on the social-cultural impact, assessment for learning may well be "part of the futile search for a universal, culture-free, 'teacher-proof' approach to education" (Wells & Claxton, 2002, p. 6). Therefore, it is advisable for instructors to adopt the sociocultural outlook that enables instructors to be empowered to deal with the challenges and complexities to optimize the students' learning process and achieve the intended learning outcomes.

Sociocultural theory advocates that activities operate within the eco-system of broader systems of relations and social structures and do not exist in isolation (Murphy et al., 2006). In the sociocultural framework, learning is seen as a process of engagement, exchange of perspectives and participation, logically within a community of practice. The expert knowledge is collective built up through the social and cognitive means using appropriate supporting sociocultural mechanisms in partnership with the members within that community of learning. Lave (1993) emphasized correlational elements of culture such as assessment activities, language of the classroom, the relationships among the people, the social structure and power relations that define the possibilities for learning. Rajaram (2010) advocates that sociocultural elements are a vital aspect in having the appropriate learning design developed and correct mix of instructional approaches adopted for its execution. The nuances present in the social, cultural values and norms of learners are an essential part that needs to be adequately understood that affects the effectiveness of the learning process and the appropriate learning assessments to be accurately adopted and optimized. Learning is a socially embedded process where it "cannot be pinned down to the head of the individual or to assigned tasks or to external tools or to the environment but lie[s] instead in the relations among them" (p. 9). Cowie (2005) mentioned learning assessment are practices that enables instructors to develop patterns of participation and eventually lead to students' identities as learners and knowers. Sociocultural aspect is a complex perspective of significance that closely aligns with the development of learner autonomy through assessment for learning practices (Willis, 2009).

The interrelationship, emerging social and cultural contexts of teacher and student beliefs about learning and assessment, learner identity and issues of power and control (Black et al., 2006; Keppell & Carless, 2006; Marshall & Drummond, 2006; Munns & Woodward, 2006), has been well advocated in the simplified representation of sociocultural contents influencing Assessment for Learning practices (Willis, J., 2009). In this framework, the interconnectivity of six elements, namely (1) learner autonomy (2) beliefs about learning and assessment (3) aligning teacher beliefs and practices (4) learner identity (5) teacher and student relationship and (6) culture and policy contexts were presented.

The interrelationships are more complex than what Fig. 4.2 suggests. Assessment can be viewed as a complex cultural activity positioned within "the relationship between the learner, the teacher and the assessment task in the social, historical and cultural context in which it is carried out" (Elwood, 2006, p. 22). Every classroom context comprises of its distinctive patterns in what Gipps (1999, p. 378) refers to as "assessment relationship". Figure 4.2 provides instructors a basic framework which allows to comprehend and examine the sociocultural contexts of the classroom.

With greater access and opportunities created for higher education, university populations are becoming increasingly diverse today. Dissimilarities in gender, age, sexuality, disability, nationality and ethnicity are some of more obvious differences that make up diversity today. As a result, it is inevitable that social and cultural differences will influence on how higher education functions. Hence, it is imperative for teachers to adopt a sociocultural perspective and open mindset to be empowered to work around these complexities and achieve higher learner autonomy (Willis, 2009). By viewing through this dimensional lenses, learning can be viewed as a process of engaging in a community of practice, where expertise is developed in social and as cognitive aspects through the adoption of cultural interventions by partnering with expert members (Willis, 2009). The varying aspects of learning and assessment strategies influence and impact the culture of learning and learning culture, thus, define the learning potential and efficacy of classroom learning.

According to Gipps and Stobart (2009), Fair assessments in the twenty-first century and beyond must not be viewed as a technical concern due to the influences of social and cultural contexts. Equity and fairness in assessment involves primarily what precedes an assessment such as access to resources as well as its consequences, for instance interpretations of results and impacts, besides the design of the assessment itself. Hence, performances on an assessment may be due to unequal access to learning or the assessment is biased in favour of one group. Evidence shows that assessment has to be carefully examined from a sociocultural dimension so that higher education institutes provide an equal opportunity for all students to do well. The importance of assessments can be well acknowledged as it determines the final outcome of a student's degree classification that could in turn influence the type of career or job they bestowed themselves upon graduation.

Gender is one sociocultural aspect to be duly considered. According to the UNESCO Institute for Statistics (2020), tertiary school enrolment of females across the globe has been steadily increasing. The number has increased from around 8% in 1970 to about 41% in 2019, extracted from the statistical analysis retrieved from "School enrollment, tertiary, female (% gross)" (UNESCO Institute for Statistics, 2020).

Research shows that there is a gender gap in language and art observed in most countries (Brookhart, 2009). This gender gap favours girls, and its effect sizes tend to be in the small to medium range. In other subjects, observed differences vary among countries. For example, some countries have gender gaps which favour boys in mathematics while others do not. Countries have responded to this gender gap issue with varying degrees of alarm and through diverse range of educational policies.

Another dimension to examine and explore would be social and cultural interventions. There are many studies that have examined on the impact of culture on student's academic achievement. This includes that of Kao and Thompson (2003) who elaborates on the achievement gaps between different ethnic groups, where they identify the reasons for these differences can be categorized into two general categories. Firstly, they claimed that certain ethnic groups may promote or discourage academic achievement. Secondly, they suggested that the different structural positions of ethnic groups affect students' environments. Hence, consequently, these two factors influence the levels of achievement. Other studies like Smith-Maddox's (1998) emphasized the achievement gap, where their study found that cultural contexts such as parents' socioeconomic status and percentage of minorities in school have an impact on eighth grade students' academic achievements.

From a strategic perspective, when students come from all over the world to study in a common institute, culture does bound to impact students' learning experience. Cultural contexts of education play a critical role in comprehending how and why students respond in a particular manner in a learning environment. By well understanding the cultural differences, teachers are better able to handle students from diverse backgrounds. They are able to design, deliver courses and implement assessment with increased sensitivity to the varying needs (Manikutty et al., 2007). On the flip side, addressing cultural differences in teaching and learning is controversial as well Mora-Bourgeois (2000). The diverse backgrounds that students come from along with the wide achievement gap between minority and non-minority students are aspects that make culture a vital factor to be duly considered and addressed. However, controversies could potentially emerge where stereotyping and indulging in ignorant explanations as to defend the differences in achievement can happen.

Instructors must review and consider of how sociocultural dimensions influence the perception and acceptance of feedback. For instance, a study by Eriksson et al. (2020) using data from an international assessment of mathematics and science achievement found that the link between teachers' use of mistake-based feedback and their students' achievement varied between countries. For example, the United Arab Emirates reported a positive association while the United States reported a negative one. They suggest that it is culture that moderates the effectiveness of mistake-based feedback and found that it is more effective in cultures where teachers have more authority. Hence, this study highlighted how cultural differences could potentially influence and impact the reception of feedback. This matter of discussion becomes even more complicated, complex and multifaceted when students move to a different country for their pursuit of studies.

Culture plays a key role in feedback seeking behaviour. The concept of "face", which is prevalent in Chinese societies, affects students' feedback seeking behaviour. The value of face stems from shame and embarrassment, and in the socialization process there becomes a necessity for one to be respected by others and not be embarrassed in social interactions or public domain. This is as highlighted by Hwang et al. (2002) who emphasized that when face is of concern for students, they may become unwilling to participate or communicate due to fear of their views being perceived as unacceptable by their instructor or peers. In this study, it was concluded that while face-gain desires do not facilitate feedback seeking, fear of face-loss was what led students to seek out their instructor privately to ask questions rather than asking them during class.

There are varying sociocultural elements that influence the design of assessments in higher education. Figure 9.1 presents the major social-cultural aspects of assessments and feedback in a summarized version.

Despite the benefits to diverse student populations, institutes must give due considerations by scrutinizing the potential implications, especially some of which that are discussed in this section. In the next section, we will examine and discuss strategies underpinning the scholarly work on how to effectively adopt and execute assessment and feedback.

9.7 Background of Study

This exploratory and qualitative research study investigates the perceived effectiveness of usage of the e-assessment rubrics from the perspectives of: (a) Students (users); Instructors teaching the courses (users); and Course curriculum designers (course chairs). The goal of this study is to engage through qualitative "consultations"

Sociocultural Aspects of Assessment

Culture

- Address the achievement gap between ethnicities
- Avoid cultural stereotyping
- Teachers should be sensitive to cultural contexts
- Rubrics may help with impartiality

Gender

- Increasing number of female students in tertiary education
- Potential gender gaps in academic achievement
- Policies should account for disparities in performance

Sociocultural Aspects of Feedback

Culture

- Reception of mistake-based feedback varies between countries
- Culture moderates the effectiveness of mistake-based feedback
- Mistake-based feedback is more effective in cultures where teachers have more authority

'Face' value

- Prominent concern in Chinese societies
- Face-gain desires do not facilitate feedback seeking
- Fear of face-loss facilitates feedback seeking behaviour

Fig. 9.1 Social-cultural aspects of assessments and feedback

with *learners*, *instructors* and *course designers* on the effectiveness of usage of the e-assessment rubrics. The study aims to collate and analysis the perspectives. Through the study, the eventual goal is to create a holistic, standardized and detailed assessment rubric that aligns in providing quality, effective and timely feedback inline to the course's learning outcomes. The aims of the study are: (a) Enable students to have a clear understanding on the learning outcomes, learning assessment criteria, objectives and expectations; (b) Comprehend and investigate the feedback channels and approaches to enhance the speed, quality, effectiveness of the feedback provided to students for their reflection and improvement; and (c) Acknowledge and reflect on the challenges and limitations from students', instructors' and course designers' perspectives so as to formulate a well-integrated e-assessment and feedback system.

This study is timely and vital to address two primary issues: (1) To provide an effective, user-friendly and comprehensive assessment system accepted by all stakeholders involved; (2) To enable timely, quality and effective formative feedback to students for their reflection and improvement. Hence, to achieve these two aspects, a study was initiated, designed to understand the perspectives from all stakeholders that could be carefully and mindfully examined to be interpreted as useful feedback to calibrate the assessment rubrics operated in a virtual platform.

9.8 Method

Interviews were conducted with students, instructors and course designers who have accessed, adopted, used these assessment rubrics embedded via virtual platforms in their respective courses. This serves as a preliminary source for us to investigate the participants' perspectives of effectiveness on the assessment rubrics operated in a virtual platform.

9.8.1 Participants

Sample size
A total of 21 students from year 2 and 3 course programmes were randomly identified. The selection criteria include the following: (a) Students should have used the assessment rubrics embedded in the e-platform eUreka in their course modules at least over 2–3 semesters; and (b) Students should have used the assessment rubrics in at least one qualitative and one quantitative subject.

A total of 5 instructors and 5 course designers were identified to be consulted on perspectives of the perceived effectiveness of assessment rubrics. The selection criteria include: (a) The instructors and course designers should have been using the assessment rubrics for at least over 2–3 semesters; and (b) A mix of instructors and course designers who had experienced teaching and designing qualitative and quantitative subjects were identified.

9.8.2 Procedure

The 31 participants which includes the students, instructors and course designers were each interviewed for approximately 2 h. Interviews were conducted in a semi-structured manner by an external consultant from higher education has vast experience and knowledge in using the assessment rubrics. All interviews were recorded and then individually transcribed over a period of approximately three months. All interview transcriptions were re-vetted by the principal researcher and a research assistant to ensure its consistency and accuracy.

The primary research question is:

RQ1: What is *the effectiveness* of assessment rubrics and their *impacts* on students?

The following *sub-questions* also helped in forming exploratory interviews:

<u>Usage, Usefulness and Benefits</u>

RQ1a: How is assessment rubrics used in your course(s)?
RQ1b: What are the benefits of using assessment rubrics for you and your students?

RQ1c: How is assessment rubrics system useful to you as a learner?
RQ1d: Which features do you like most in the online platform, eUreka?
RQ1e: How does the feedback provided by your instructor through the assessment rubrics help you in the learning?
RQ1f: How do you think peer evaluation assessment rubrics is useful to you and your peers in performing the group work?

Operationalizing the Assessment Rubrics

RQ1g: Did you let the students view and reflect on the peer evaluation assessment rubrics first so that they know the grading criteria?
RQ1h: Did you allow the students to discuss and debate on the assessment criteria so that they are fully aware of how one will be graded?
RQ1i: Did you share exemplars or case-studies with the students on how they could potentially achieve higher scores based on the criteria presented in the assessment rubrics?

Challenges and Encouragement

RQ1j: What are the challenges you faced in using the online assessment rubrics as a faculty?
RQ1k: Do you allow the students to discuss and debate on the assessment criteria so that they could clarify their queries?

9.9 Analysis

The interviews were first analysed using consensual qualitative research (CQR) (Hill et al., 2005). Main themes were classified into broad clusters. The frequencies of similar responses were tallied within each broad cluster. Responses to every interview question were examined to determine: (a) What participants reported? and (b) How they justified their thinking? (c)What key themes emerged from the specific question asked?

9.10 Findings

Table 9.4 presents the key emerging themes from the interview conducted to collate the students' perspectives on the effectiveness of the online assessment rubrics and its impacts on students' learning.

When the students are asked on the usage of the assessment rubrics, four clusters of emerging themes were identified, namely (a) preparation for course assignment; (b) serve as a progressive guidance; (c) Understand and clarify the assessment during class discussion; and (d) Source of feedback. Students mentioned that the assessment rubrics were useful as it helps in guiding them to understand what is required in

Table 9.4 Students' perspectives—key emerging themes

Interview findings	
Qualitative "consultations" with students: Perspectives on effectiveness of e-assessment rubrics and its impact on them	
Scope of question	**Key emerging themes**
Usage of assessment rubrics	Preparation for Course Assignment
	Serve as progressive guidance
	Understand and clarify the assessment during class discussion
	Source of feedback
Usefulness of assessment rubrics	Learners' perspectives
	Likeable Features
Feedback via assessment rubrics	Likability of feedback
	Impact of feedback on students' learning
	Usefulness of peer evaluation
Impact of assessment rubrics on students' learning	Students' perceived reasons on why the online assessment rubrics should be used
Qualitative "consultations" with instructors and course designers: Perspectives on effectiveness of e-assessment rubrics and its impact on students' learning	
Usefulness, context of usage and benefits of the online assessment rubrics for students	Benefits of using the online assessment rubrics for instructors
	Benefits of using the online assessment rubrics for students
	Most likeable features in the online assessment rubrics system (eUreka)
Approach taken in using the online assessment rubrics	Nil
Challenges and Encouragement	Challenges
	Advantages outweigh challenges
Benefits of peer evaluation	Benefits to students
	Benefits to instructors

preparing for their course assignments. In addition, it enables them to calibrate their quality of deliverable based on the specific expectations stated in the assessment criteria. With the assessment criteria requirements stated upfront transparently, it facilitates students to clarify their doubts inline to what they have interpreted and have been working on. Importantly, after the assessment rubrics has been graded, it allows students to review how well they have performed on their assignment based on the assessment criteria. This serves as a platform for formative feedback for their self-reflection and improvement.

Next, for the usefulness of assessment rubrics, two primary aspects emerged namely (a) the learners' perspectives on why it is useful from their opinions were shared and (b) the explicit likeable features in the assessment rubrics that operated through an online mode. Next, for the feedback obtained via the assessment rubrics, three aspects were identified, namely (a) likeability of feedback; (b) impact of feedback on students' learning and (c) usefulness of peer evaluation.

On the question that addresses the impact of assessment rubrics on students' learning, we were able to collate students' perceived reasons on why e-assessment rubrics should be used. In the Table 4.2, the compiled findings are presented. The top reason for the usage of the e-assessment rubrics is claimed to be convenience for students to access it anytime, anywhere. Students reported that the ease and autonomy in providing them the space in accessing the e-assessment rubrics for their understanding and learning purposes enhances efficiency and ease. They also mentioned on the aspect of the clarity and comprehensiveness of the guidelines, imperatively assisting to reflect and learn on how the assessments are graded. Instead of focusing on their marks obtained, the assessment rubrics allow students to see where they stand in the grandeur context of performance. This enables students to be more objective on their reflections to improve rather than diverting the energy on comparing specific marks with their peers that affects their moral and esteem. Students also expressed their happiness as they indicated that feedback is easily accessible and instantly wherever and whenever they want to. Another accolade refers to the ability to provide individualized and concise qualitative feedback to students for improvement and reflection. Students view this feature a true value-add as it helps them to perform a quick reflection of their work and improve. Finally, students reported that the design of the e-assessment enables facilitate easy communication between the instructors and students (Table 9.5).

Next on the scope of perspectives on effectiveness of e-assessment rubrics on students' learning, we have 4 broad scope of questions. The first focuses on the usefulness, context of usage and benefits of e-assessment rubrics for students. Three primary themes emerged from this first question, namely (a) Benefits of using e-assessment rubrics for instructors; (b) Benefits of using e-assessment rubrics for students; and (c) Most likeable features in e-assessment rubrics system (eUreka).

Table 9.5 Themes and responses of students' perceived reasons for e-assessment rubrics to be adopted

Students' perceived reasons why e-assessment rubrics should be used	
Themes	Responses
Provides convenience for students to access anywhere, anytime	21 agreed
Provides clear and comprehensive instructions and guidelines with clear expectations and how the assessments are graded	19 agreed
Enables east access of feedback immediately once the results are released and able to review it whenever required	18 agreed
Able to provide individualized and concise qualitative feedback to students for improvement and reflection	15 agreed
Good communication between instructors and students	07 agreed

Table 9.6 presents the benefits of using e-assessment rubrics for instructors where the collective perspectives were collated from instructors and course designers who also double up on the role as instructors. The responses are presented in three clusters as (i) pre-phase usage of e-assessment rubrics; (ii) in-progress usage of e-assessment rubrics and (iii) post-stage usage of e-assessment rubrics.

Pre-phase is defined as the phase where students use the rubrics to reflect and understand the requirements of the assessment. In-phase refers to the period, where students use the assessment rubrics while they are preparing their course work assignments and reports. Post-stage refers the time when students view the graded assessment rubrics and qualitative comments as a form of formative feedback.

During the pre-phase, instructors and course designers reported that the e-assessment rubrics serve as a one-stop avenue to communicate to the students in a clear written form of what is expected of them. This enables students to pull out anytime, anywhere this rubric to view and take time to reflect that enables them to ask questions or seek clarifications during assignment briefs or class discussions or even from an individualized context. Whereas during the in-phase usage of the e-assessment rubrics phase, the mobility, ease in accessing and evaluating the rubrics anywhere/anytime was reiterated as the primary benefit. Quite a few aspects were highlighted under the post-phase usage of the e-assessment rubrics. Instructors and course designers reported that the e-assessment rubrics facilitates as a structured guide to marking and providing feedback to the students on their performance. It assists in maintaining standardization and equity in grading, especially in large cohorts where different instructors conduct classes for the same course over a semester. It also serves as platform to have speedy and easy access to students' assignments' feedback and grades. This is vital as it enables instructors to have a one-stop reference point in terms of extracting the information and engaging the learning needs of the students respectively. Moreover, this certainly eases the administrative aspect to be handled by the instructors. The e-assessment platform enables automated computation and provides some basic data analysis that is required for the post-course report. This helps the instructors to be able to focus more on the interpretative analysis, for example, a meaningful pattern of grade distribution, the mean across the classes on the respective assessment criteria for the post-course report rather than the administrative aspects. Instructors also reported that the e-assessment rubrics helps in maintaining consistency in marking and grading within stipulated tolerance levels across classes taught by different instructors for the same course. It was mentioned that the e-assessment rubrics serve as a constructive and comprehensive post-assignments feedback mechanism. Instructors also reported that the e-assessment rubrics can provide a well-rounded and holistic evaluation inline to both quantitative, in terms of the rating scale as well as qualitative feedback where the specific areas for improvements and areas done well are emphasized.

Next in Table 9.7, the perspectives by the instructors and course designers on benefits for students are tabulated and presented. The insights are clustered into three sections, namely pre-phase, in-phase and post-phase usage of the e-assessment rubrics. For the pre-phase usage of e-assessment rubrics, instructors reported that the approach of adopting the e-assessment rubrics provides transparency where it

Table 9.6 Themes and responses for benefits of using e-assessment rubrics for instructors

Benefits to instructors of using e-assessment rubrics (Perspectives from 05 instructors and 05 course designers)		
Themes	Responses: instructors	Responses: course designers (also as instructors)
Pre-phase usage of e-assessment rubrics		
Allows to communicate to the students in a clear written form of what is expected of them	03 agreed	03 agreed
In-phase usage of e-assessment rubrics		
Able to access and evaluate the rubrics anywhere/anytime that makes the mobility much easier	04 agreed	05 agreed
Post-phase usage of e-assessment rubrics		
Facilitates as a structured guide to marking and providing feedback to the students on their performance	05 agreed	05 agreed
Effective platform (quick and easy for usage) to access students' assignments feedback and grades	05 agreed	05 agreed
Ease of administration—it has a record of all students' results in one database	05 agreed	05 agreed
Ease of automated computation of data analysis which is required for the post-course report	05 agreed	05 agreed
e-rubrics instantly computes the grades, hence provides the instructor a meaningful picture of the pattern of grade distribution	05 agreed	05 agreed
Consistency of marking and grading for all students across various seminar groups	03 agreed	04 agreed
Serve as a constructive and comprehensive post-assignments feedback mechanism	02 agreed	03 agreed
Able to provide a more holistic evaluation inline to both quantitative, (i.e. in terms of the rating scale) as well as qualitative feedback where the specific areas for improvements and areas done well are emphasized	01 agreed	02 agreed

enables students to comprehend on how the assignments are evaluated based on predefined criteria prescribed in the assessment rubrics. As for the in-phase usage of e-assessment rubrics, instructors emphasized the ease on mobility as students can access and review the rubrics anywhere and anytime. This convenience makes it a value-add for students' learning process as it enables them to access it on their convenience that fits to their own study pace and schedule. For the post-phase usage of e-assessment rubrics, instructors reported that it serves as a constructive and comprehensive formative feedback platform for students to reflect on how they could improve. The clear categorization on their level of performance enables students to understand the areas they have done well and those that needs improvement. It was also reported that students can receive feedback online with much ease and quicker even if they are unable to be present in class.

We could acknowledge that it, with the current students' contemporary trend of learning and style of communication, it is imperative and timely to leverage on the online assessment mode. As advocated by scholars Rajaram (2010), Rajaram (2011), and Rajaram and Bordia (2013), the comfort and familiarity level of approaches adopted affects the students' learning process.

9.11 Discussion

To enable us to have a clear overview of the emerging themes, Table 9.8 presents the qualitative indicators of effectiveness in three clusters, namely "highest", "high" and "moderate", where a total of twelve themes, six from students and another six from instructors and course designers *emerged* as distinctively most effective as perceived by these two groups respectively. In this category of "highest", the students' perceived effectiveness on the e-assessment rubrics are attributed to (a) it's ability to serve as a source of feedback; (b) easier retrieval of information; (c) clarity in providing understandable instructions and guidelines on how assessments are graded; (d) enhancement on team dynamics and synergy; (e) easier access of feedback; and (f) facilitates individualized and concise qualitative feedback. Whereas the instructors' perceived effectiveness on the e-assessment rubrics are attributed to (a) ability to access and evaluate anywhere and anytime that makes the mobility much easier; (b) facilitates as a structured guide to marking and providing feedback; (c) ease of administration; (d) ease of automated computation of data analysis; (e) user-friendly; and (f) transparency on the evaluation process.

In the next category of "high", the students' perceived effectiveness on the e-assessment rubrics are attributed to (a) enables brainstorming; and (b) enables more holistic student evaluation. Whereas the instructors and course designers' perceived effectiveness of instructors and course designers are summarized as follows: (a) enables to communicate to students in a clear written form of what is expected of them; (b) ease of administration and (c) consistency of marking and grading.

Table 9.7 Themes and responses for benefits of using e-assessment rubrics for students

Benefits to students of using e-assessment rubrics (Perspectives from 05 instructors and 05 course designers)		
Themes	Responses: instructors	Responses: course designers (also as instructors)
Pre-phase usage of e-assessment rubrics		
Transparency: Enable students to understand how the assignments are evaluated based on pre-defined criteria stated in the assessment rubrics	04 agreed	05 agreed
In-phase usage of e-assessment rubrics		
Able students to access and review the rubrics anywhere/anytime that makes the mobility much easier	05 agreed	05 agreed
Post-phase usage of e-assessment rubrics		
Serve as a constructive and comprehensive feedback mechanism for the students	04 agreed	04 agreed
Easier and faster for students to receive feedback online, i.e. even if they are unable to be present in class	03 agreed	05 agreed
Usage of e-assessment rubrics across all stages		
In line with the students' trend of learning and style of communication, it comes timely to leverage on the online assessment platform. This is vital as the comfort and familiarity level of approaches adopted affects students' learning process (refer to Rajaram (2010), Rajaram (2011), and Rajaram and Bordia (2013)	05 agreed	05 agreed

In the next category of "moderate", the students' perceived effectiveness on the e-assessment rubrics are rubrics are attributed to (a) good communication between instructors and students; (b) fair grading, peer evaluation component where the students have a voice in their peers' contribution; (c) creates a fear or consequential factor of peer evaluation incorporated to prevent free-riding; (d) facilitates self-reflection; and (e) act as a driving and motivating force. Whereas for the instructors and course designers' perceived effectiveness of instructors and course designers are summarized as follows: (a) Able to provide holistic evaluation; and (b) More efficient than working on hardcopy document.

The e-assessment rubrics must be viewed and used as a learning and reflective means instead of solely as an assessment device. This is a vital point as by leveraging

Table 9.8 Emerging key indicators for effectiveness of e-Assessment Rubrics: Perspectives from students and instructors and course designers

Qualitative indicators for perceived effectiveness of e-assessment rubrics and their impacts on students' learning		
Priority scale	Students' perspectives	Instructors and course designers' perspectives
Highest	(a) Source of feedback (b) E-access: Easier retrieval of information (c) Provides comprehensive instructions and guidelines with clear expectations on how assessments are graded (d) Improves team dynamics and synergy (peer evaluation) (e) Easy access of feedback (f) Provides individualized and concise qualitative feedback	(a) Able to access and evaluate the rubrics anywhere/anytime which makes the mobility much easier (b) Facilitates as a structured guide to marking and providing feedback (c) Ease of administration (d) Ease of automated computation of data analysis (e) User-friendly (f) Transparency: Enable students to know how assignments are evaluated
High	(a) Facilitates brainstorming (b) Facilitates more holistic student evaluation (peer evaluation)	(a) Allows to communicate to students in a clear written form of what is expected of them (b) Ease of administration (c) Consistency of marking and grading
Moderate	(a) Good communication between instructors and students (b) Fair grading (peer evaluation) (c) Prevent free-riding (peer evaluation) (d) Facilitates self-reflection (e) Act as a driving and motivating force	(a) Able to provide holistic evaluation (b) More efficient than working on paper

on the learning aspects, students can benefit multi-fold in process of learning endeavours. Instructors should not make assumptions that by merely providing the students the access and briefing them on the e-assessment rubrics, they will completely comprehend the performance standards that have been articulated and described. We must acknowledge that the fact just because the assessment rubrics make sense to the instructors, that will also automatically make sense to their students.

The general presumption that the usage of hardcopy assessment rubrics is preferred due to its the ability to mark in between the rating scale and is more user-friendly is not so unilaterally confirmed. Instructors may not necessarily be performing the entire marking process efficiently and effectively but rather maybe accustomed to the style of doing it in the traditional paper method. Instructors' preference in marking via hardcopies should not be equated to them perceiving that it is a more effective way of doing so, perhaps it could be due to more of the habitual convenience.

This study serves as a bridging platform to address the rudiments of perceived effectiveness of e-assessment rubrics and its impacts of students' learning. To facilitate the quality and effective learning process for business students, it requires a good understanding of the issues intertwined in usage of the e-assessment rubrics.

Students' ability to learn optimally and deliver tangible results inline to the learning outcomes depends on: (a) how well and clearly the course assessment criteria are disseminated to students; and (b) the comprehensive and timely feedback provided for their reflection and improvement.

We could draw the following recommendations from this study: (a) able to validate with evidence insights that the usage of e-assessment rubrics and the formative feedback provided are perceived as worthwhile and useful from the students' perspective; (b) the e-assessment rubrics must provide comprehensive and explicit details on the performance and deliverable standards of students; (c) the e-assessment rubrics must be the common point of reference for all students to maintain consistency; (d) detailed, constructive and explicit qualitative feedback are crucial, for example, specific areas of weakness/opportunities for improvements should be addressed, in addition to the scale ratings; (e) to have the e-assessment rubrics discussed in class with prior preparation with the assigned group on the assessment criteria—this enables students to reflect, think through and have a deeper understanding; (f) to show and discuss exemplars or case-studies for student reflection on the e-assessment rubrics; (g) peer evaluation could be done during the semester and at the end of the semester for students' reflection and self-monitoring; (h) instructors' encouragement and advocacy of e-learning is most likely to motivate students to use the e-assessment rubrics more frequently; and (i) e-assessment rubrics can be reviewed via a focus group consisting of students and instructors to assist in calibrating and interpreting from the context of clarity and multiple perspectives.

9.12 Strategies for the Effective Adoption of Assessments and Feedback

In this section, we will be examining the validated framework that is put together from collated years of experience having this eco-system, interventions and strategies executed, observed and fine-tuned. This framework advocates guided direction for teachers to effectively implement assessment and feedback, taking into due consideration and acknowledging the varying contexts. We will discuss general strategies, interventions from varying dimensional contexts that should be addressed, the contemporary concerns, that includes sociocultural diversity and technology-enhanced learning. Figure 9.2 presents the framework on recommended strategies for effective adoption of assessments and feedback.

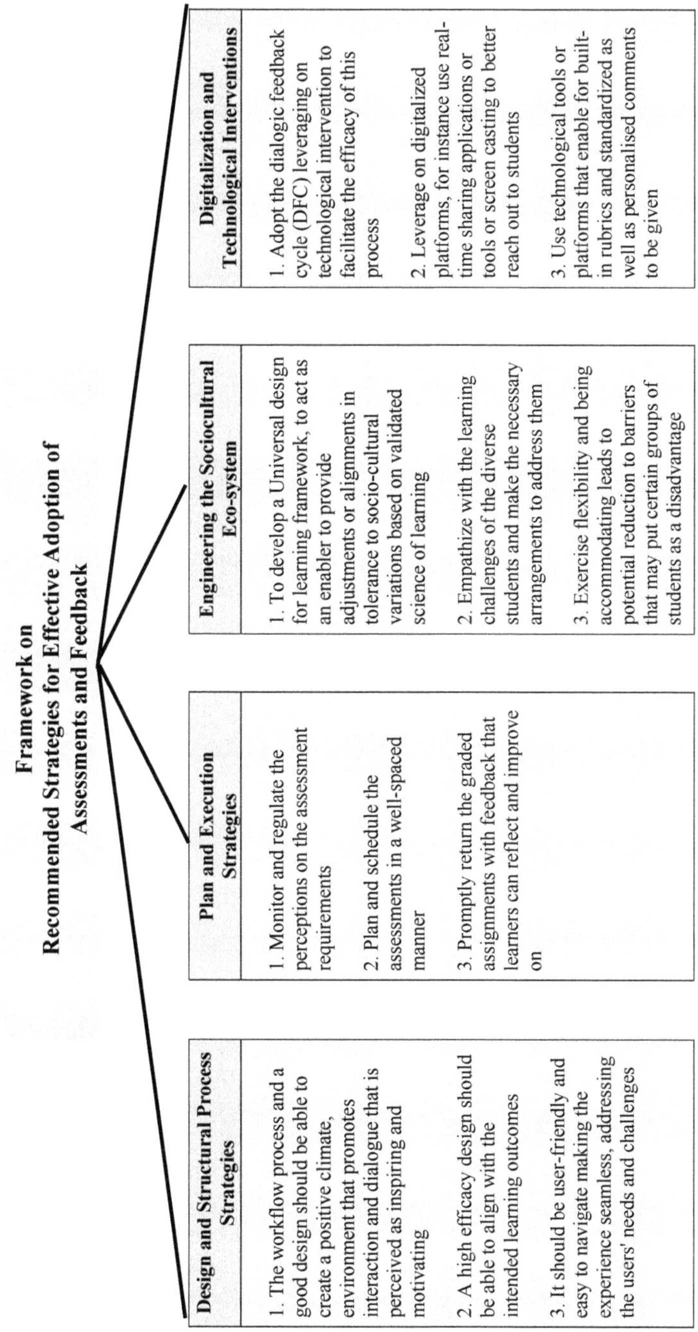

Fig. 9.2 Recommended strategies for effective adoption of assessments and feedback

9.12.1 Effective Design and Structural Process of Assessments

The design of an assessment is crucial in determining the learning progress of students towards the intended learning goals and its outcomes. A poorly and not well thought through designed assessment can obstruct students' thinking and learning (Ragupathi, 2016). Aside students, other stakeholders, for instance, quality assurance regulators, employers and staff are also impacted by the design of assessments (University of Reading, n.d.). Similar sentiments on the efficacy of good design of assessment is echoed by Jisc (2015), who reiterates that it can make students' and teachers experience with assessments more positive, inspiring and motivating while also helping students achieve much better learning outcomes. Primarily, well-designed assessments will be (a) relevant and authentic that encompasses effective mechanisms to enable high-quality feedback; (b) create a positive environment that promotes interaction and dialogue; (c) set clear expectations and establish a reasonable workload; (d) provide students with opportunities to self-learn, rehearse, practice, and receive feedback; (e) provide students with feedback on their progress; and (f) should be aligned with intended learning outcomes.

Online assessments are becoming increasingly popular and well received due to its ease, convenience, and efficacy in having it executed. Effective online assessment design should: (a) be accessible to all students including those with special needs (Walker, 2007); (b) not test a student's information technology skills or their ability to use an online assessment tool unless that is the purpose of the assessment; (c) the assessment should be easy to navigate; and (d) the time phase or timing of the assessment should be given due consideration, especially when students profile comprises of individuals from various parts of the world.

9.12.2 Well-Devised Plan and Effective Execution of Strategies

While effective design is vital, so is effective execution of the said design. Without it, the effort put into designing the assessment strategy may well go simply to waste. In addition, the intended outcomes of the assessment may not come to fruition. Instructors themselves have a significant influence on the assessment strategy of the course as it links to how students perceive and engage on the assessed tasks even if they had nothing to do with the design of the assessment. Through effective execution, instructors can ensure that the assessment process facilitates students' learning without compromising on the demands of institutional quality assurance. The three primary crucial elements of assessments include (a) assessment information; (b) scheduling of assignments and (c) returning work to students.

Firstly, teachers must regulate students' perceptions of what assessment tasks require. There are many varying processes that are required to be communicated regarding the assessment expectations to students. Among that, one of the most primary features is the written information about each course that provides the fundamental guide on what to expect. The information has to be written in an accurate and clear manner as possible to avoid the uncertainty that may potentially cause anxiousness in students. Adopting this approach will be particularly beneficial for students with disabilities, personal responsibilities, or those with high workloads as it enables them to plan and organize their time effectively. By doing so, instructors are creating an inclusive assessment practice that is certainly an exemplary assessment practice.

Secondly, teachers must also manage the scheduling of the assessments mindfully taking into due consideration of students' workload and conflicts that could possibly arise with other courses' assessments. The distribution of assessment deadlines should be discussed and decided at a programme level, so instructors should engage, discuss and clarify with the programme director on the specificity of assessments such as fixated deadlines and overview course assessment timetables for the semester. The assessment deadlines must be scheduled after the essential and relevant topics are covered, where the scheduling should be planned to work around the lessons. Additionally, teachers must spread of assessments across the course duration to ensure that students do not have multiple deadlines bunched together. As a general guide, we should have at least four to five weeks' notice for summative and higher weightage assignments or assessments, with a slightly shorter notice of one to two weeks for small-scale and lesser weightage ones. It is crucial to ensure teachers are allocated adequate time to grade and provide feedback. For instance, it would be more helpful for students' learning if they are able to work on a second assignment after they have received feedback for the first.

Thirdly, it is imperative for teachers to be aware of the benefits and positive effects arising from a prompt return of marked assignments with adequate feedback. In cases where returning of the assignments are not possible, teachers can deploy strategies to work around it. For instance, one approach is to relay holistic, collated feedback comments on the key strengths and weaknesses observed and the actions that may be taken for improvement. Basically, teachers partake a significant role in the assessment process to have it effectively executed.

9.12.3 Engineering the Sociocultural Eco-System: Strategies to Handle Diverse Student Population

Green and Johnson (2010) emphasized that that universal design for learning is a vital framework in comprehending the needs and necessary arrangements and accommodations for diverse learners. Accommodations should enable instruction and assessments to be designed in a way that reduces the barriers which may put these students at a disadvantage. The insights offered by Green and Johnson (2010) were taken as an inspiration to create new, contemporary and re-modified guiding principles that offer recommendations on how teachers can manage, accommodate and deal with diversity for the varying types of analytical assessments.

Ignorance and Lack of Familiarity with Social Norms and Values
In such circumstances, educators have to empathize, be more tolerant and exercise extended patience in performing their grading. Next, learners are to be educated through pre-assessment awareness programmes, talks and/or workshops. Further to this, pre-assessment workshops are to be conducted to ingrain learning values that respect diversity, embrace discomfort and ambiguity. Such approach adopted becomes useful in group project assessments, for example.

Ambiguity and Lack of Understanding of the Institution's Learning Culture
Educators are to establish the level of depth and extent of information and knowledge of the unknown facts or "unspoken rules" of the institution's culture. They are to be equipped with relevant pre-skills on questioning techniques that come in handy, for instance, during class participation facilitation and discussion that may be required to be evaluated. Educators are to be well informed on the student-instructor roles and responsibilities that intertwine in-course work assessments, for instance, how much guidance and formative feedback can be provided.

Mastery and Application of Learning Goals Across Social and Cultural Contexts
Educators are to address the pre-unit assessment aspects in a scaffolded approach that is primarily complex and abstract. Moreover, they are to mindfully engage on matters that intertwine with social and cultural aspects of learning.

Challenges with fine Motor Skills
In such circumstances, learners would have difficulties in their body's ability to manage the process of movements. Hence, educators must think thorough and explore alternative ways to facilitate, for example, facilitating verbal answers to questions instead of written for assessments. Aside that, they should leverage on technology and embrace digitalization to facilitate and enhance its efficacy.

Attention Deficit and Restlessness
In such situational contexts, instructors must be mindful and resonate by designing and creating the assessment contents and the way they are presented, for example, in terms of figures, tables, graphics and checklists. A scaffolded approach is to be designed to enable the task required to be completed one step at a time. The time allocated for questions and assigned tasks is to be carefully managed and highly limited. Another creative way to increase the level of engagement is to enhance the novelty of the assessment tasks. This excites and draws attention by creating a new distraction to be involved.

Proficiency in English language and the ability in having it learned
Instructors are to use the English language in the simplest and easiest form without complex syntax and cultural references. This enables easier and faster understanding of issues at hand for learners. Learners must be checked on for their comprehension of explicit vocabulary and provided with adequate opportunities for repeated access. Instructors must facilitate engaging questions and prompters that enable succinct

answers. They should also use visual cues to be able to better relate, engage students by using more verbal than written questions and articulate the relevant messages across with clarity. Further to this, opportunities must be provided to exhibit understanding through creative drawings, mind-maps, conceptual maps, tables, figures and diagrams. Students should be allowed to use translation dictionaries to ease their articulation.

Literacy skills for individuals who have learning disabilities (behavioural and cognitive)
Instructors are to check for students understanding on the use of vocabulary required for the course. To facilitate adequate practice opportunities, repeated access is to be provided. The language used should be without complex syntax to ease understanding. Students are to be encouraged to ask questions and use visual cues where answers are to be provided within their comfort zone. Instructors must be open and be prepared to provide flexibility in using oral or written mode based on the conditional circumstance. Further to that, instructors should be advocated to adopt creative and contemporary ways to demonstrate understanding through visuals/pictures, mind-maps, drawings, figures and concept maps.

Although the items presented may not necessarily be exhaustive, but the goal is to provide an adequate guiding framework for teachers to perform the required adjustments to their assessment practices. These modifications are to be made taking the learning environment, climate and learning of the institution individual schools.

9.12.4 Utilizing Digitalization and Technological Interventions to Enhance Feedback

With the evolving and rapid technological developments, higher education institutes need to re-think in incorporating and integrating technology, embracing digitalization in their assessment process. Primarily, the goal is to enable the assessment processes to be more effective and efficient. Technological interventions can influence assessment through the feedback process. Moscrop and Beaumont (2017) examined technology-enhanced feedback using the Dialogic Feedback Cycle (DFC) that is viewed a good practice in assessment feedback.

Beaumont et al. (2011) has advocated a 3-stage framework on dialogic feedback cycle that focuses on (1) preparatory guidance; (2) in-task guidance and (3) performance feedback. This served as a foundational guidance to facilitate feedback in a scaffolded manner. However, there were rapid changes over the decade, on the past and evolving literature analysis as well as the contemporary practices adopted. To address the evolving demands and multi-layered complexities, a new and detailed "Conceptual Framework: Feedback Process Cycle" is created, which is presented in Fig. 9.3. This proposed new conceptual framework comprises of 5 key thrusts, namely (1) Co-Creation of Assignment and Assessment Criteria; (2) Introductory Direction; (3) In-Progress Mentoring; (4) Feedback on Deliverable and (5) Post Feedback. This

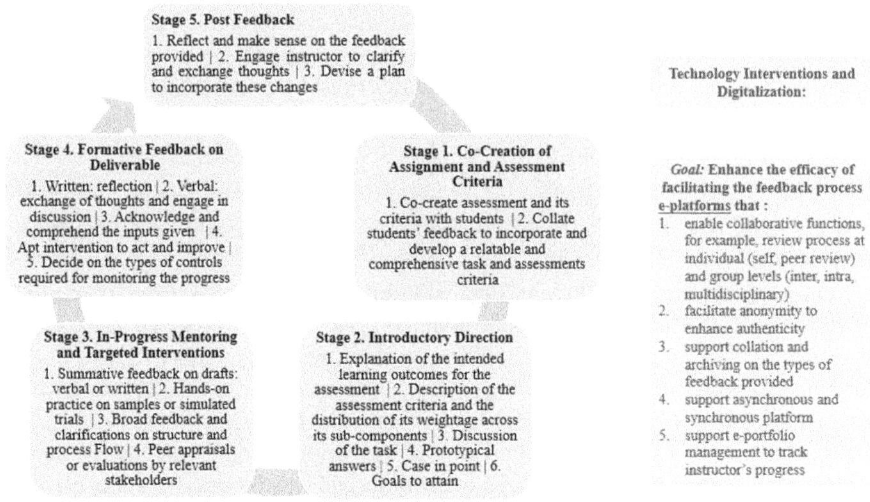

Fig. 9.3 Conceptual framework—scaffolded guiding principles on feedback process cycle

enhanced and new dialogic feedback cycle framework can be used to incorporate with the technology-enhanced learning intervention. In this section, we will discuss on how technological interventions and digitalization can be incorporated within each of these stages to enhance providing of feedback.

In the first stage, the key thrust is to co-create the assignment and assessment criteria with students in partnership. Collaborative e-platforms could be used to engage students to seek their perspectives and understand the efficacy that is perceived from their lenses. This could be performed in both asynchronous and synchronous mode. For asynchronous mode, the single document could be placed in a collaborative e-platform, for example, google document and have both the identified students and faculty to input their comments. It could also be carried out in the synchronous mode by engaging them verbally via a virtual setting. This process will eventually enable to incorporate and develop a relatable and comprehensive task and assessments criteria.

In the second stage, varying approaches are adopted to engage students to explain the intended learning outcomes for the assessment and describe the assessment criteria with the distribution of its weightage across its sub-components. One way is to present students with exemplars which enables them to relate and resonate to the given assessment criteria. While this can be potentially viewed as an effective approach, instructors may struggle as it can be time-consuming for large class sizes due to the amount of dialogue and exchanges that needs to occur between students and their peers as well as students and the instructor. Technology interventions can be adopted to address this issue, for example, teachers may consider leveraging on screen casting that allows students to be empowered as they are able to share their perspectives on the exemplar against the assessment criteria. This enables a shared understanding among students. Alternatively, teachers could use of real-time sharing and analysis of assessment descriptors, for example using collaborative software such as Google Documents, where these are ways in which technological interventions could assist. In this stage, instructors are to engage the students to discuss the task by addressing the challenges faced by working around it somewhat. They could use past case scenarios to draw relevant experiences and learning pointers to relate and provide necessary feedback that helps students. The emphasis in this stage is also to have students reflect and self-identify learning goals to be attained.

The third stage of the cycle focuses on in-progress mentoring and targeted interventions. It revolves around supporting students to develop their ideas, clarify misconceptions and analyse the task at hand. Summative feedback on drafts is provided both verbally and/or in a written manner. For physical circumstances or situational settings, hands-on practice on samples or simulated trials is facilitated. This stage allows students to identify an appropriate approach to tackle the assignment. Activities at this stage generally consist of formative assessments through draft submissions, reflecting on generic feedback, clarifications on structure and process flow and peer assessments. For peer assessments or evaluations by relevant stakeholders, technological tools can be used to facilitate peer feedback is a more efficient, easy to use and effective manner. For example, this can be done through the use of Wikis, K^mAlive Learning Application or other e-platforms.

In the fourth stage, feedback is usually delivered in both written to serve as a reflection and verbal forms where it provides an opportunity for dialogue and discussion to occur on explanations regarding assessment criteria and strategies for future improvement. Students should acknowledge and comprehend the inputs given. They could also follow-up to take the necessary actions to improve. Instructors should ponder on the types of controls required for monitoring the progress. At this stage, efficiency in terms of speed is a major concern especially when managing a large size of students. The use of assessment rubrics and standardized comments within tools such as Turnitin may be useful in assisting instructors to create a bank of commonly written comments while still being able to provide personalized feedback, if necessary. Technology can be leveraged in providing feedback through podcasts (audio) and video recorded platforms. Adopting such approach can be speedy while at the same time improves students' engagement and heighten their satisfaction since it is more personal and adds a human element although it is delivered in an asynchronous form, for example. By adopting technological tools, teachers can increase the speed and efficiency of the assessment process, while maintaining or even improving the overall effectiveness.

In the final stage of the post feedback, students are to reflect and make sense on the feedback provided. This is a vital phase as it makes students think through on how the feedback provided benefits them to reflect and improve. They are to engage instructors to clarify their queries and exchange of thoughts. Through this process, the clarity and comprehension of the feedback provided is well received by the learners. Lastly, a plan is to be devised to have these changes incorporated. This serves as a monitoring mechanism to see through the required improvements to be made that enhances the efficacy of the intended purpose.

9.13 Concluding Thoughts

Assessment has conventionally been treated as a means to evaluate students' learning that enables them to progress and improve. However, for one to perceive or view assessment to be only from that dimension diminishes or seems to be brushing off the other benefits of assessments by and large. Assessments do not only help students improve their understanding of a subject, but also assist teachers identify gaps in their teaching and enable to rectify them accordingly. Teachers can consciously integrate the intended learning outcomes into their assessment design. However, effective assessments do not manifest from simply the design alone as other aspects of assessment are also to be considered to facilitate the entire process to be beneficial. For instance, a well-designed assessment will bring no benefits or positive impact, if its execution is feeble.

In this chapter, we examined and discussed on elements of assessments, for instance, feedback and assessment rubrics. Feedback is vital and necessary for promoting learning and to assist learners, teachers to comprehend what and how they can do much better. Assessment rubrics help clarify the assignment requirements and intended learning outcomes which facilitate the assessors to grade their work in a speedy and effective manner. By examining the assessments at a more micro level, it enables teachers to modify the assessment process via a more specific approach.

We also examined the social-cultural aspects of assessments that are of an increasing relevance today as higher education population profile become more diverse. For higher education institutes to provide a fair and equitable learning climate and environment for their students, they must first understand how the differences in social and cultural norms have potential ramifications and spill overs. The teachers' actions, outlook and attitudes adopted will subsequently affect how students learn and perform during their assessments. Hence, when designing assessments, there should be due consideration on social and cultural intertwined influences. If the design of an assessment is not able to be modified, then teachers should make the necessary arrangements to help even out the playing field for disadvantaged groups of students.

Assessment is a crucial aspect of the higher education curriculum, and it is unlikely to have that removed from the eco-system of university learning due to its strong anchoring in terms of its validated measure. The extension of technological and digitalization tools has certainly reached classrooms that has enabled for more innovative ways to approach assessments. For instance, online assessment tools have allowed students located anywhere in the world to take the same real-time assessments without travelling out of the comforts of their home. Higher education institutes should pay closer attention to assessments and how they are conducted. Management must provide more support to teachers in the aspects of assessment through teacher preparation programmes and foster a culture where assessments are viewed as more than a measurement tool.

Appendix A: Interview Questions for Instructors and Course Designers

Perceived effectiveness of e-assessment rubrics and their impacts on students' learning

Usefulness, context of usage and benefits of e-assessment rubrics

1. How is e-assessment rubrics used in your course? Why do you use it for your class?
2. What are the benefits of using e-assessment rubrics to you as an instructor?
3. What do you think are the benefits of e-assessment rubrics to your students?
4. Which features do you like most in e-assessment rubrics platform, eUreka?
5. How often do you visit the e-assessment rubrics, eUreka site?

The Approach taken—in using the e-assessment rubrics

6. Do you let the students view the e-assessment rubrics prior to their assignments so that they could reflect on them and understand the grading criteria?
7. Do you allow the students to discuss and debate on the assessment criteria so that they are fully aware on how they will be graded?
8. Do you show exemplars or case studies to the students on how they can achieve higher ratings based on the evaluation rubrics?

Challenges and Encouragement

9. What are the challenges that you faced in using the e-assessment rubrics as an instructor?
10. Do the advantages outweigh the challenges? Would you use the e-assessment rubrics again for other semesters?
11. Any advice for other instructors who have not started using the e-assessment rubrics?

Benefits of Peer Evaluation

12. Do you let the students do self and peer evaluation so that they can reflect on their own performance while evaluating their peers?
13. What are the benefits to students?
14. What are the benefits to instructors?

Appendix B: Interview Questions for Students

Perceived effectiveness of e-assessment rubrics and their impacts on students' learning

Usage of e-assessment rubrics by students

1. How is e-assessment rubrics used in your course?
2. How often do you visit the e-assessment rubrics site, eUreka?

Usefulness of e-assessment Rubrics by students

3. How is e-assessment rubrics system useful to you as a learner?
4. Which features do you like most in e-assessment rubrics platform, eUreka? Assessment or the peer evaluation feature?

Feedback through e-assessment rubrics by students

5. Did you see value and benefits on the feedback provided by your instructor through the e-assessment rubrics and how does this feedback help you in the learning?
6. Did the e-assessment or e-peer evaluation rubrics give you a much better idea of the evaluation criteria and how you will be graded? How does it improve your learning process?
7. Did the feedback given by your instructor through e-assessment rubrics help you to think and reflect on your own learning? Did it motivate you to ask more questions and learn even more?
8. How do you think e-peer evaluation rubrics is useful to you and your peers in group work?

Impact of e-assessment Rubrics on students

9. Do you think other courses should use e-assessment rubrics as well and if so why?

References

Andrade, H. G. (2000). Using rubrics to promote thinking and learning. *Educational Leadership, 57*(5), 13–18.

Ackerman, D. S., & Gross, B. L. (2010). Instructor feedback: How much do students really want? *Education, Psychology Journal of Marketing Education, 32*(2), 172–181. https://doi.org/10.1177/0273475309360159

Ahmed, A., Pollitt, A., & Rose, L. (1999). *Assessing thinking and understanding: Can oral assessment provide a clearer perspective?* Paper presented at 8th International Conference on Thinking, Edmonton Canada. https://www.researchgate.net/publication/237117218_Assessing_Thinking_and_Understanding_Can_Oral_Assessment_Provide_a_Clearer_Perspective.

Aziz, S. M. (2002). *Online quizzes for enhancing student learning in a first year engineering course.* https://www.researchgate.net/publication/228400601_Online_Quizzes_for_Enhancing_Student_Learning_in_a_First_Year_Engineering_Course

Bellon, J. J., Bellon, E. C., & Blank, M. A. (1991). *Teaching from a Research Knowledge Base: A Development and Renewal Process* (Facsimile). Prentice Hall.
Black, P., & Wiliam, D. (1998). Assessment and classroom learning. *Assessment in Education, 5*(1), 7–74.
Black, P., McCormick, R., James, M., & Pedder, D. (2006). Assessment for learning and learning how to learn: A theoretical inquiry. *Research Papers in Education, 21*(2), 119–132.
Beaumont, C., O'Doherty, M., & Shannon, L. (2011). Reconceptualising assessment feedback: A key to improving student learning? *Studies in Higher Education, 36*(6), 671–687. https://doi.org/10.1080/03075071003731135
Bloxham, S., & Boyd, P. (2007). *Developing effective assessment in higher education: A practical guide: A Practical Guide* (1st ed.). Open University Press.
Boud, D., Dawson, P., Bearman, M., Bennett, S., Joughin, G., & Molloy, E. (2016). Reframing assessment research: Through a practice perspective. *Studies in Higher Education, 43*(7), 1107–1118. https://doi.org/10.1080/03075079.2016.1202913
Brookhart, S. M. (2001). Successful Students' Formative and Summative Uses of Assessment Information. *Assessment in Education Principles Policy and Practice, 8*(2), 153–169.
Brookhart, S. M. (2009). Assessment, gender and in/equity. In J. Cumming & C. Wyatt-Smith (Eds.), *Educational assessment in the 21st century: Connecting theory and practice* (2009th ed., pp. 119–136). https://doi.org/10.1007/978-1-4020-9964-9
Brookhart, S. M. (2013). *How to create and use Rubrics for Formative Assessment and Grading.* ASCD.
Brookhart, S. M. (2018). Appropriate criteria: Key to effective rubrics. *Frontiers in Education, 3*, 22. https://doi.org/10.3389/feduc.2018.00022
Carless, D., Bridges, S.M., Chan, C.K.Y., & Glofcheski, K. (2017). *Scaling up assessment for learning in higher education.* Springer.
Chappuis, J., Stiggins, R., Chappuis, S., & Arter, J. (2012). *Classroom assessment for student learning: Doing it right—using it well* (2nd ed.). Pearson.
Case, S. (2007). Reconfiguring and realigning the assessment feedback processes for an undergraduate criminology degree. *Assessment & Evaluation in Higher Education, 32*(3), 285–299.
Carless, D., Salter, D., Yang, M., & Lam, J. (2011). Developing sustainable feedback practices. *Studies in Higher Education, 36*(4), 395–407. https://doi.org/10.1080/03075071003642449
Carless, D. (2006). Differing perceptions in the feedback process. *Studies in Higher Education, 31*(2), 219–233. https://doi.org/10.1080/02075070600572132
Cowie, B. (2005). Pupil commentary on assessment for learning. *The Curriculum Journal, 16*(2), 137–151.
Crisp, B. R. (2007). Is it worth the effort? How feedback influences students' subsequent submission of assessable work. *Assessment & Evaluation in Higher Education, 32*(5), 571–581. https://doi.org/10.1080/02602930601116912
Capraro, R. M., Roe, M. F., Caskey, M. M., Strahan, D., & Bishop, P. A. (2011). *Research summary: Assessment* (pp. 1–6). Association for Middle Level Education. https://pdxscholar.library.pdx.edu/cgi/viewcontent.cgi?article=1006&context=ci_fac
Care, E., Griffin, P., & Wilson, M. (2018). *Assessment and teaching of 21st century skills (Educational assessment in an information age)* (1st ed.). https://doi.org/10.1007/978-3-319-65368-6
Carless, D. (2007). Conceptualizing pre-emptive formative assessment. *Assessment in Education: Principles, Policy & Practice, 14*(2), 171–184. https://doi.org/10.1080/09695940701478412
Carless, D. (2017). Scaling up assessment for learning in higher education. In D. Carless, S. M. Bridges, C. K. Y. Chan, & R. Glofcheski (Eds.), *Scaling up assessment for learning in higher education* (pp. 3–18). https://doi.org/10.1007/978-981-10-3045-1.
Centre for the Enhancement of Teaching and Learning, The University of Hong Kong. (n.d.). *Join-the-conversation: Enhancing feedback.* https://www.cetl.hku.hk/teaching-learning-cop/high-impact-feedback/.

Chappuis, S., Stiggins, R. J., Chappuis, S., & Arter, J. A. (2013). *Classroom assessment for student learning: Pearson new* (International). Pearson Education.
Chiriac, E. H. (2014). Group work as an incentive for learning—Students' experiences of group work. *Frontiers in Psychology, 5*, 1–18. https://doi.org/10.3389/fpsyg.2014.00558
Cortes, A. (2006). Using informal student feedback to enhance learning. *Journal of Aviation/Aerospace Education & Research, 15*(2), 9–12. https://commons.erau.edu/jaaer/vol15/iss2/3
Crowell, T. L. (2016). Academic internships: To take or not to take? Students' assessments of public health fieldwork. *Pedagogy in Health Promotion, 4*(1), 19–34. https://doi.org/10.1177/2373379916684850
Dornisch, M. M., & McLoughlin, A. S. (2006). Limitations of web-based rubric resources: addressing the challenges. *Practical Assessment, Research & Evaluation, 11*(3). Accessed 14 October 2013. http://pareonline.net/pdf/v11n3.pdf
Duncan, N. (2007). 'Feed-forward': Improving students' use of tutors' comments. *Assessment & Evaluation in Higher Education, 32*(3), 271–283. https://doi.org/10.1080/02602930600896498
Demmert, W. G. (2005). The influences of culture on learning and assessment among native american students. *Learning Disabilities Research and Practice, 20*(1), 16–23. https://doi.org/10.1111/j.1540-5826.2005.00116.x
Downing, S. M. (2002). Assessment of knowledge with written test forms. In C. P. M. van der Vleuten, D. I. Newble, & G. R. Norman (Eds.), *International handbook of research in medical education (Springer international handbooks of education (7)* (pp. 647–672). https://doi.org/10.1007/978-94-010-0462-6.
Eshun, E. F. (2011, September 26–27). Report on the action research project on adopting innovative assessment for learning in communication design in higher education. Paper presented at the *Conference on Design, Development & Research* (pp. 382–395).
Egodawatte, G. (2010). A rubric to self-assess and peer-assess mathematical problem-solving tasks of college students. *Acta Didactica Napocensia, 3*(1), 78.
Entwistle, N., & Ramsden, P. (1983). *Understanding student learning*. Croom Helm.
Elwood, J. (2006). Formative assessment: Possibilities, boundaries and limitations. *Assessment in Education, 2*, 215–232.
Evans, C. (2013). Making sense of assessment feedback in higher education. *Review of Educational Research, 83*(1), 70–120.
Eriksson, K., Lindvall, J., Helenius, O., & Ryve, A. (2020). Cultural variation in the effectiveness of feedback on students' mistakes. *Frontiers in Psychology, 10*, 1–13. https://doi.org/10.3389/fpsyg.2019.03053
Escartín, J., Saldaña, O., Martín-Peña, J., Varela-Rey, A., Jiménez, Y., Vidal, T., & Rodríguez-Carballeira, Á. (2015). The impact of writing case studies: Benefits for students' success and well-being. *Procedia—Social and Behavioral Sciences, 196*, 47–51. https://doi.org/10.1016/j.sbspro.2015.07.009
Flodén, J. (2016). The impact of student feedback on teaching in higher education. *Assessment & Evaluation in Higher Education, 42*(7), 1054–1068. https://doi.org/10.1080/02602938.2016.1224997
Flowers, M. A., & Drake, D. D. (1994). Making effective student assignments: Practices for improving student learning. *American Secondary Education, 22*(4), 2–5. https://www.jstor.org/stable/41064078
Ferguson, P. (2011). Student perceptions of quality feedback in teacher education. *Assessment & Evaluation in Higher Education, 36*(1), 51–62.
Fraser, B. J., Walberg, H. J., Welch, W. W., & Hattie, J. A. (1987). Syntheses of educational productivity research. *International Journal of Educational Research, 11*(2), 147–252. https://doi.org/10.1016/0883-0355(87)90035-8
Gielen, S., Peeters, E., Dochy, F., Onghena, P., & Struyven, K. (2010). Improving the effectiveness of peer feedback for learning. *Learning and Instruction, 20*(4), 304–315. https://doi.org/10.1016/j.learninstruc.2009.08.007

Gipps, C., & Stobart, G. (2009). Fairness in assessment. In J. Cumming & C. Wyatt-Smith (Eds.), *Educational assessment in the 21st century: Connecting theory and practice* (2009th ed., pp. 105–118). https://doi.org/10.1007/978-1-4020-9964-9

Gokcora, D., & DePaulo, D. (2018). Frequent quizzes and student improvement of reading: A pilot study in a community college setting. *SAGE Open, 8*(2), 215824401878258. https://doi.org/10.1177/2158244018782580

Goodwin, B., & Miller, K. (2012). Research says/good feedback is targeted, specific, timely. *Feedback for Learning, 70*(1), 82–83. http://www.ascd.org/publications/educational-leadership/sept12/vol70/num01/Good-Feedback-Is-Targeted,-Specific,-Timely.aspx

Green, S., & Johnson, R. (2010). *Assessment is essential* (1st ed.). McGraw-Hill Education.

Griffin, P., & Care, E. (2015). *Assessment and teaching of 21st century skills: Methods and approach (Educational assessment in an information age)* (2015th ed.). https://doi.org/10.1007/978-94-017-9395-7

Grosas, A. B., Raju, S. R., Schuett, B. S., Chuck, J.-A., & Millar, T. J. (2014). Determining if active learning through a formative assessment process translates to better performance in summative assessment. *Studies in Higher Education, 41*(9), 1595–1611. https://doi.org/10.1080/03075079.2014.988704

Gwynne, K., & Morgan, S. (2014). An introduction to practical examinations. *Veterinary Nursing Journal, 29*(6), 207–209. https://doi.org/10.1111/vnj.12149

Gasaymeh, A-H. (2011). The implications of constructivism for rubric design and use. Higher Education International Conference (HEIC 2011). Accessed 21 October 2013. http://heic.info/assets/templates/heic2011/papers/05-Al-Mothana_Gasaymeh.pdf

Goldberg, G. L., & Roswell, B. S. (1999–2000). From perception to practice: The impact of teachers' scoring experience on performance-based instruction and classroom assessment. *Educational Assessment, 6*(4), 257–290.

Gibbs, G., & Simpson, C. (2004). Conditions under which assessment supports students' learning. *Learning and Teaching in Higher Education, 1*, 3–31.

Gipps, C. (1999). Socio-cultural aspects of assessment. *Review of Research in Education, 24*, 355–392.

Getzlaf, B., Perry, B., Toffner, G., Lamarche, K., & Edwards, M. (2009). Effective instructor feedback: Perceptions of online graduate students. *Journal of Educators Online, 6*(2), 1–22.

Hardavella, G., Aamli-Gaagnat, A., Saad, N., Rousalova, I., & Sreter, K. B. (2017). How to give and receive feedback effectively. *Breathe, 13*(4), 327–333. https://doi.org/10.1183/20734735.009917

Harlen, W. (2002). *A systematic review of the impact of summative assessment and tests on students' motivation for learning.* https://dspace.stir.ac.uk/bitstream/1893/19607/1/SysRevImpSummativeAssessment2002.pdf

Harvey, L. (2003). Student feedback [1]. *Quality in Higher Education, 9*(1), 3–20. https://doi.org/10.1080/13538320308164

Hassanien, A. (2006). Student experience of group work and group assessment in higher education. *Journal of Teaching in Travel & Tourism, 6*(1), 17–39. https://doi.org/10.1300/j172v06n01_02

Hattie, J., & Timperley, H. (2007). The power of feedback. *Review of Educational Research, 77*(1), 81–112. https://doi.org/10.3102/003465430298487

Hatziapostolou, T., & Paraskakis, I. (2010). Enhancing the impact of formative feedback on student learning through an online feedback system. *Electronic Journal of E-Learning, 8*(2), 111–122. https://files.eric.ed.gov/fulltext/EJ895699.pdf

Henderson, M., Ajjawi, R., Boud, D., & Molloy, E. (2019a). *The impact of feedback in higher education: Improving assessment outcomes for learners* (1st ed.). https://doi.org/10.1007/978-3-030-25112-3

Henderson, M., Phillips, M., Ryan, T., Boud, D., Dawson, P., Molloy, E., & Mahoney, P. (2019b). Conditions that enable effective feedback. *Higher Education Research & Development, 38*(7), 1401–1416. https://doi.org/10.1080/07294360.2019.1657807

Hwang, A., Ang, S., & Francesco, A. M. (2002). The silent Chinese: The influence of face and Kiasuism on student feedback-seeking behaviors. *Journal of Management Education, 26*(1), 70–98. https://doi.org/10.1177/105256290202600106
Hattie, J. (2012). Know thy impact. *Educational Leadership, 70*(1), 18–22.
Hattie, J., & Jaeger, R. (1998). Assessment and classroom learning: A deductive approach. *Assessment in Education, 5*(1), 111–122.
Higgins, R., Hartley, P., & Skelton, A. (2002). The conscientious consumer: Reconsidering the role of assessment feedback in student learning. *Studies in Higher Education, 27*(1), 53. https://doi.org/10.1080/03075070120099368
Hill, C. E., Knox, S., Thompson, B. J., Williams, E. N., Hess, S. A., & Ladany, N. (2005). Consensual qualitative research: An update. *Journal of Counseling Psychology, 52*, 196–205.
Irons, A. (2007). *Enhancing learning through formative assessment and feedback*. Taylor & Francis.
James, L. T., & Casidy, R. (2016). Authentic assessment in business education: Its effects on student satisfaction and promoting behaviour. *Studies in Higher Education, 43*(3), 401–415. https://doi.org/10.1080/03075079.2016.1165659
Jansson, M., Carle, J., Gunnarsson, A., & Ekbrand, H. (2017). How experience affects assessment—A longitudinal study of assessment of university students' essays. *Studies in Higher Education, 44*(4), 719–732. https://doi.org/10.1080/03075079.2017.1398227
Jimaa, S. (2011). The impact of assessment on students learning. *Procedia—Social and Behavioral Sciences, 28*, 718–721. https://doi.org/10.1016/j.sbspro.2011.11.133
Jisc. (2015, n.d.). *Assessment design*. https://www.jisc.ac.uk/guides/transforming-assessment-and-feedback/assessment-design
Johnson, G., & Connelly, S. (2014). Negative emotions in informal feedback: The benefits of disappointment and drawbacks of anger. *Human Relations, 67*(10), 1265–1290. https://doi.org/10.1177/0018726714532856
Jonsson, A. (2012). Facilitating productive use of feedback in higher education. *Active Learning in Higher Education, 14*(1), 63–76. https://doi.org/10.1177/1469787412467125
Jönsson, A., & Panadero, E. (2017). The use and design of rubrics to support assessment for learning. In R. Glofcheski, C. K. Y. Chan, S. M. Bridges, & D. Carless (Eds.), *Scaling up assessment for learning in higher education* (pp. 99–112). https://doi.org/10.1007/978-981-10-3045-1
Kao, G., & Thompson, J. S. (2003). Racial and ethnic stratification in educational achievement and attainment. *Annual Review of Sociology, 29*(1), 417–442. https://doi.org/10.1146/annurev.soc.29.010202.100019
Korn, C. W., Fan, Y., Zhang, K., Wang, C., Han, S., & Heekeren, H. R. (2014). Cultural influences on social feedback processing of character traits. *Frontiers in Human Neuroscience, 8*, 1–18. https://doi.org/10.3389/fnhum.2014.00192
Keppell, M., & Carless, D. (2006). Learning-oriented assessment: A technology-based case study. *Assessment in Education, 13*(2), 179–191.
Koshy, S. (2008, June 12). *Using making criteria to improve learning: An evaluation of student perceptions*. University of Wollongong of Dubai, UWOD-ESC-WP-77.
Lam, R. (2015). Assessment as learning: Examining a cycle of teaching, learning, and assessment of writing in the portfolio-based classroom. *Studies in Higher Education, 41*(11), 1900–1917. https://doi.org/10.1080/03075079.2014.999317
Lew, D. N. M., & Schmidt, H. G. (2011). Writing to learn: Can reflection journals be used to promote self-reflection and learning? *Higher Education Research & Development, 30*(4), 519–532. https://doi.org/10.1080/07294360.2010.512627
Linn, R. L. (2000). Assessments and accountability. *Educational Researcher, 29*(2), 4–16. https://doi.org/10.3102/0013189x029002004
Lave, J. (1993). The practice of learning. In S. Chaiklin & J. Lave (Eds.), *Understanding practice. Perspectives on activity and context*. Cambridge University Press.
Lipnevich, A. A., & Smith, J. K. (2009). "I really need feedback to learn:" students' perspectives on the effectiveness of the differential feedback messages. *Educational Assessment Evaluation and Accountability, 21*(4), 347–367. https://doi.org/10.1007/s11092-009-9082-2

Maestri, V. (2017). Can ethnic diversity have a positive effect on school achievement? *Education Economics, 25*(3), 290–303. https://doi.org/10.1080/09645292.2016.1238879

Manikutty, S., Anuradha, N. S., & Hansen, K. (2007). Does culture influence learning styles in higher education? *International Journal of Learning and Change, 2*(1), 70–87. https://doi.org/10.1504/ijlc.2007.014896

McGraw-Hill. (2016). *New survey data: Four out of five college students say digital learning technology helps improve their grades.* https://www.mheducation.com/news-media/press-releases/2016-digital-study-trends-survey.html#:%7E:text=The%20report%20shows%20that%20four,technology%20helps%20them%20to%20focus

McLoughlin, C. (2001). Inclusivity and alignment: Principles of pedagogy, task and assessment design for effective cross-cultural online learning. *Distance Education, 22*(1), 7–29. https://doi.org/10.1080/0158791010220102

Meikleham, A., & Hugo, R. (2018). Understanding informal feedback to improve online course design. *European Journal of Engineering Education, 45*(1), 4–21. https://doi.org/10.1080/03043797.2018.1563051

Mislevy, R. J. (2017). On measurement in educational assessment. In B. D. Denison & C. Secolsky (Eds.), *Handbook on measurement, assessment, and evaluation in higher education* (2nd ed., pp. 37–64). Routledge.

Mislevy, R. J., Steinberg, L. S., & Almond, R. G. (2003). Focus Article: On the Structure of Educational Assessments. *Measurement: Interdisciplinary Research & Perspective, 1*(1), 3–62. https://doi.org/10.1207/s15366359mea0101_02

Moore, S., & Kuol, N. (2005). Students evaluating teachers: Exploring the importance of faculty reaction to feedback on teaching. *Teaching in Higher Education, 10*(1), 57–73. https://doi.org/10.1080/1356251052000305534

Mora-Bourgeois, G. (2000). *Reflections on the impact of culture in the classroom.* http://education.gmu.edu/assets/docs/lmtip/vol3/G.Mora-Bourgeois.pdf

Moscrop, C., & Beaumont, C. (2017). Technology-enhanced assessment feedback. In D. Carless, S. M. Bridges, C. K. Y. Chan, & R. Glofcheski (Eds.), *Scaling up assessment for learning in higher education* (pp. 193–208). https://doi.org/10.1007/978-981-10-3045-1

Moskal, P., Ellis, T., & Keon, T. (2008). Summary of assessment in higher education and the management of student-learning data. *Academy of Management Learning & Education, 7*(2), 269–278. https://doi.org/10.5465/amle.2008.32712624

McCabe, J., Doerflinger, A., & Fox, R. (2011). Student and faculty perceptions of e-feedback. *Teaching of Psychology, 38*(3), 173–179.

Metcalfe, J., & Kornell, N. (2007). Principles of cognitive science in education: The effects of generation, errors, and feedback. *Psychonomic Bulletin & Review, 14*(2), 225–229.

Mory, E. H. (2004). Feedback research revisited. In D. H. Jonassen (Ed.), *Handbook of research on educational communications and technology* (2nd ed., pp. 745–783). Lawrence Erlbaum Associates.

Mertler, C. A. (2001). Designing scoring rubrics for your classroom. *Practical Assessment, Research & Evaluation, 7*(25). Accessed 18 October 2013. http://pareonline.net/getvn.asp?v=7&n=25

Moskal, B. M. (2000). Scoring rubrics: What, when and how? *Practical Assessment, Research & Evaluation, 7*(3). Accessed 17 October 2013. http://PAREonline.net/getvn.asp?v=7&n=3

Marshall, B., & Drummond, M. (2006). How teachers engage with Assessment for Learning: Lessons from the classroom. *Research Papers in Education, 21*(2), 133–149.

Murphy, P., Sharp, G., & Whitelegg, E. (2006). Girls' experience of physics: A problem of identification and marginalization? Open University Press. *(17) (PDF) Assessment for Learning—Why the Theory Needs the Practice.*

Munns, G., & Woodward, H. (2006). Student engagement and student self-assessment: The REAL framework. *Assessment in Education, 13*(2), 193–213.

Naylor, R., Baik, C., Asmar, C., & Watty, K. (2014). *Good feedback practices: Prompts and guidelines for reviewing and enhancing feedback for students*. https://www.researchgate.net/publication/266797954_Good_Feedback_Practices_Prompts_and_guidelines_for_reviewing_and_enhancing_feedback_for_students
Nilson, L. B. (2003). Improving student peer feedback. *College Teaching, 51*(1), 34–38. https://doi.org/10.1080/87567550309596408
Nortvedt, G. A., Wiese, E., Brown, M., Burns, D., McNamara, G., O'Hara, J., Altrichter, H., Fellner, M., Herzog-Punzenberger, B., Nayir, F., & Oya Taneri, P. (2020). Aiding culturally responsive assessment in schools in a globalising world. *Educational Assessment, Evaluation and Accountability, 32*(1), 5–27. https://doi.org/10.1007/s11092-020-09316-w
Narciss, S. (2008). Feedback strategies for interactive learning tasks. In J. M. Spector, M. D. Merrill, J. van Merrienboer, & M. P. Driscoll (Eds.), *Handbook of research on educational communications and technology* (pp. 125–143). Lawrence Erlbaum Associates.
Nicol, D. J., & Macfarlane-Dick, D. (2006). Formative assessment and self-regulated learning: A model and seven principles of good feedback practice. *Studies in Higher Education, 31*(2), 199–218. https://doi.org/10.1080/03075070600572090
Oakleaf, M. (2009). Using rubrics to assess information literacy: An examination of methodology and interrater reliability. *Journal of the American Society for Information Science and Technology, 60*(5), 969–983.
Oakley, L. (2004). *Cognitive development*. Taylor & Francis.
O'Donovan, B. M., den Outer, B., Price, M., & Lloyd, A. (2019). What makes good feedback good? *Studies in Higher Education, 46*(2), 318–329. https://doi.org/10.1080/03075079.2019.1630812
Pereira, D., Flores, M. A., Simão, A. M. V., & Barros, A. (2016). Effectiveness and relevance of feedback in higher education: A study of undergraduate students. *Studies in Educational Evaluation, 49*, 7–14. https://doi.org/10.1016/j.stueduc.2016.03.004
Poulos, A., & Mahony, M. J. (2008). Effectiveness of feedback: The students' perspective. *Assessment & Evaluation in Higher Education, 33*(2), 143–154.
Ragupathi, K. (2016). *Designing effective online assessments*. https://www.nus.edu.sg/cdtl/docs/default-source/professional-development-docs/resources/designing-online-assessments.pdf
Rajaram, K. (2010). Culture clash: Teaching western-based business education to mainland Chinese students in Singapore. *Doctoral dissertation. University of South Australia, Adelaide, Australia.*
Rajaram, K. (2011). Culture clash: Teaching Western-based management education to mainland Chinese students in Singapore. *Journal of International Education in Business, 4*(1), 63–83.
Rajaram, K., & Bordia, S. (2013). East Versus West: Effectiveness of Knowledge Acquisition and Impact of Cultural Dislocation Issues for mainland Chinese Students across ten commonly used Instructional Technqiues. *International Journal for the Scholarship of Teaching & Learning, 7*(1), 1–24.
Rajaram, K., & Collins, J. (2013). Qualitative identification of learning effectiveness measures among mainland Chinese students in culturally dislocated study environments. *Journal of International Education in Business, 6*(2), 179–199.
Rajaram, K. (2021). *Evidence-Based Teaching for the 21st Century Classroom and Beyond,* Springer.
Reddy, Y. M., & Andrade, H. (2010). A review of rubric use in higher education. *Assessment & Evaluation in Higher Education, 35*(4), 435–448. https://doi.org/10.1080/02602930902862859
Reynolds-Keefer, L. (2010). Rubric-referenced assessment in teacher preparation: An opportunity to learn by using. *Practical Assessment, Research & Evaluation, 15*(8). Accessed 25 May 2020. https://scholarworks.umass.edu/pare/vol15/iss1/8/
Sadler, D. R. (1983). Evaluation and the improvement of academic learning. *Journal of Higher Education, 54*(1), 60–79.
Sadler, D. R. (1989). Formative assessment and the design of instructional systems. *Instructional Science, 18*, 119–144.
Sackstein, S. (2017). *Peer feedback in the classroom: Empowering students to be the experts* (1st ed.). ASCD.

Sambell, K. (2011). *Rethinking feedback in higher education: An assessment for learning perspective.* https://www.plymouth.ac.uk/uploads/production/document/path/2/2729/RethinkingFeedbackInHigherEducation.pdf

Seldin, P. (1997). Using student feedback to improve teaching. *To Improve the Academy, 16*, 335–346. https://doi.org/10.3998/tia.17063888.0016.021

Shute, V. J. (2008). Focus on formative feedback. *Review of Educational Research, 78*(1), 153–189. https://doi.org/10.3102/0034654307313795

Simonson, M. R., Smaldino, S. E., & Zvacek, S. (2014). *Teaching and learning at a distance.* Van Haren Publishing.

Sinclair, H. K., & Cleland, J. A. (2007). Undergraduate medical students: Who seeks formative feedback? *Medical Education, 41*, 580–582. https://doi.org/10.1111/j.1365.2923.2007.02768.x

Sivan, A. (2002). Implementing Peer Assessment to Enhance Teaching and Learning. *New Horisons, 1*, 10–11.

Slapcoff, M., Dobler, E., & Tovar, M. (2011). *Using coursework to enhance students' understanding of research/scholarship: A report from the Inquiry Network.* Montreal: Teaching and Learning Services, McGill University. https://www.mcgill.ca/tls/files/tls/slapcoff_et_al_using_coursework_to_enhance_students_understanding_0.pdf

Smith-Maddox, R. (1998). Defining culture as a dimension of academic achievement: Implications for culturally responsive curriculum, instruction, and assessment. *The Journal of Negro Education, 67*(3), 302. https://doi.org/10.2307/2668198

Sotiriadou, P., Logan, D., Daly, A., & Guest, R. (2019). The role of authentic assessment to preserve academic integrity and promote skill development and employability. *Studies in Higher Education, 45*(11), 2132–2148. https://doi.org/10.1080/03075079.2019.1582015

Stanford Teaching Commons. (n.d.). *Summative assessment and feedback.* https://teachingcommons.stanford.edu/explore-teaching-guides/feedback-assessment/summative-assessment-and-feedback#:%7E:text=Summative%20assessments%20are%20given%20to,learning%20goals%20of%20the%20course

Stevens, D. D. & Levi, A. J. (2005). Leveling the field: Using rubrics to achieve greater equity in teaching and assessment. *Essays on Teaching Excellence, Professional and Organizational Development Network in Higher Education, 17*(1).

Stiggins, R. (2007). Assessment through the student's eyes. *Educational Leadership, 64*(8), 22–26.

Stiggins, R., & Chappuis, J. (2006). What a difference a word makes. *Journal of Staff Development, 27*(1), 10–14.

Stiggins, R., & Chappuis, J. (2008). Enhancing student learning. *District Administration, 44*(1), 42–44.

Stiggins, R. (1988). Revitalizing classroom assessment: The highest instructional priority. *PHI DELTA KAPPAN, 69*(5), 363–368.

Svinicki, M. D. (2001). Encouraging your students to give feedback. *New Directions for Teaching and Learning, 2001*(87), 17. https://doi.org/10.1002/tl.24

Tanujaya, B., Mumu, J., & Margono, G. (2017). The Relationship between higher order thinking skills and academic performance of student in mathematics instruction. *International Education Studies, 10*(11), 78. https://doi.org/10.5539/ies.v10n11p78

Topping, K. J. (2009). Peer assessment. *Theory into Practice, 48*(1), 20–27. https://doi.org/10.1080/00405840802577569

Taras, M. (2003). To feedback or not to feedback in student self-assessment. *Assessment & Evaluation in Higher Education, 28*(5), 549–565. https://doi.org/10.1080/0260293032000120415

Taylor, J. A. (2006, July 12–14). Assessment: A tool for development and engagement in the first year of University study, proceedings of engaging students. *9th Pacific Rim in Higher Education Conference*, Griffith University, Gold Coast. Accessed 20 May 2020. www.fyhe.qut.edu.au/past-paper/2008/program.html

UNESCO Institute for Statistics. (2020). *School enrollment, tertiary, female (% gross).* https://data.worldbank.org/indicator/SE.TER.ENRR.FE

University of Florida. (n.d.). *Types of feedback*. https://citt.ufl.edu/resources/assessing-student-learning/providing-effective-feedback/types-of-feedback/
University of Reading. (n.d.-a). *Getting started with assessment design*. https://www.reading.ac.uk/engageinassessment/assessment-design/eia-getting-started-with-assessment-design.aspx
University of Reading. (n.d.-b). *Why is feedback important?* https://www.reading.ac.uk/internal/engageinfeedback/Whyisfeedbackimportant/#:%7E:text=studied%20and%20gives%20them%20clear%20guidance%20on%20how%20to%20improve%20their%20learning.&text=Providing%20students%20engage%20with%20feedback,learning%20and%20improve%20assessment%20performance
Värlander, S. (2008). The role of students' emotions in formal feedback situations. *Teaching in Higher Education, 13*(2), 145–156. https://doi.org/10.1080/13562510801923195
Van den Berg, I., Admiraal, W., & Pilot, A. (2006). Design principles and outcomes of peer assessment in higher education. *Studies in Higher Education, 31*(3), 341–356.
Walker, D. J. (2007). *Principles of good online assessment design*. https://ewds.strath.ac.uk/reap/reap07/Portals/2/CSL/feast%20of%20case%20studies/Principles_of_good_online_assessment_design.pdf
Wiliam, D. (2013). *Assessment: The bridge between teaching and learning*. https://www.researchgate.net/publication/258423377
Willis, J. (2009). *Assessment for learning: A sociocultural approach*. In Proceedings of: Changing climates: Education for sustainable futures, 30 November–4 December 2008. http://eprints.qut.edu.au/29323
Wingate, U. (2010). The impact of formative feedback on the development of academic writing. *Assessment & Evaluation in Higher Education, 35*(5), 519–533. https://doi.org/10.1080/02602930903512909
Winstone, N. E., & Boud, D. (2020). The need to disentangle assessment and feedback in higher education. *Studies in Higher Education, 1–12*,. https://doi.org/10.1080/03075079.2020.1779687
Wyatt-Smith, C., & Cumming, J. (2009). *Educational assessment in the 21st century: Connecting theory and practice* (2009th ed.). Springer.
Weaver, M. R. (2006). Do students value feedback? Student perceptions of tutors' written responses. *Assessment & Evaluation in Higher Education, 31*(3), 379–394.
William, D. (2013). Assessment: The bridge between teaching and learning. *National Council of Teachers of English, 21*(2), 15–20.
Wells, G., & Claxton, G. (Eds.). (2002). *Learning for life in the 21st century: Sociocultural perspectives on the future of education*. Blackwell Publishing.
Wolsey, T. D. (2008). Efficacy of instructor feedback on written work in an online program. *International Journal on E-Learning, 7*(2), 311–329.
Yorke, M. (2003). Formative assessment in higher education: Its significance for employability, and steps towards its enhancement. *Higher Education, 45*, 477–501. https://doi.org/10.1023/A:1023967026413
Yuan, J., & Kim, C. (2014). Guidelines for facilitating the development of learning communities in online courses. *Journal of Computer Assisted Learning, 30*, 220–232. https://doi.org/10.1111/jcal.12042
Yuan, J., & Kim, C. M. (2015). Effective feedback design using free technologies. *Journal of Educational Computing Research, 52*(3), 408–434. https://doi.org/10.1177/0735633115571929

Part VI
Conclusion

Chapter 10
Concluding Thoughts

Kumaran Rajaram

Abstract This chapter covers the holistic insights and future directions of teaching and learning towards twenty-first century and beyond. In this chapter, the "gaps" in terms of where universities and higher education institutions should emphasize would be discussed and suggestions advocated. The implications and ripple effects are highlighted, and possible recommendations proposed with supporting discussions.

The evolving, unpredictable and continual changes have affected the world, causing ambiguity and uncertainty that has meaningfully influenced internal and external stakeholders of higher education institutions and universities. Technological transformations and evolution serve as a fundamental impetus for change management. The latter has a large impact in making nations globally much closer, where boundaries have blurred. A borderless world has been shaped through the progressive vagueness emerged in the boundary. This contemporary global physiognomy calls for substantial transformations and change management in the way organizations are managed and organize their cross-border relationships. On a similar context, with no lesser importance, business schools are rethinking, hence organizing themselves to successfully nurture today's students as future globally competent and effective business leaders. Managers are expected to re-think, re-design and strategize with higher level of social, cultural intelligence and the companies to be more adaptable and flexible. Managers must realize that the totality of success is much dependent on humans in this ever-challenging environment, more so in terms of the creation and dissemination of knowledge. Moreover, managers' motivation to adopt a humanistic perspective largely roots from the basis that organizations fundamentally comprise of a "community of individuals" and "individuals have different opinions and perceptions on similar matters". Contemporaneously, we need to consider the phenomenon of growing digitalization while, on the one hand, it is vital to acknowledge the

K. Rajaram (✉)
Division of Leadership, Management and Organization, Nanyang Business School, Nanyang Technological University, Singapore, Singapore
e-mail: rkumaran@ntu.edu.sg

K. Rajaram, *Learning Intelligence: Innovative and Digital Transformative Learning Strategies*, https://doi.org/10.1007/978-981-19-9201-8_10

increasing borderlessness of the world, where it constitutes the current generation of students; scholars use the term "digital native" to describe this group.

In this concluding chapter, the necessity to acquire relevant skills and competencies to be "well-equipped and competent teachers" will be addressed. This is essential in creating a sustainable and rigorous economic eco-system to instil students' essential values to work productively in a borderless world. This chapter serves as a collective wisdom for scholars and teachers to reflect and re-think to identify activities, approaches and strategies they could adopt as teaching philosophies and guiding principles to develop a more collaborative and cohesive learning environment. There will also be discussion on the manner educators in universities could integrate the evolving digitalized and borderless dimension of the 21st-century business operations that permeates its activities and the need to teach students the humanistic, conceptual and technical skills to be "job-ready", competent in the dynamic, demanding and competitive workforce.

10.1 Cultural Intelligence in Teaching and Learning

The world today is evolving rapidly with varying interventions and is like never before. We no longer have to travel to a foreign land to experience diverse cultures as it could now be experienced in our own countries domestically. We could link this to globalization which is very well the primary suspect for this current climate. Organizations are becoming increasingly global and universities, Higher Education Institutions (HEIs) are enrolling progressively more and more international students each year. It almost now seems like the world has become one and that the concept of borders no longer exists. Nevertheless, as much as we try to overlook or ignore our differences, it is apparent that there are some aspects that would distinctively separate people, the habits, values and perceptions that individuals develop are all varying aspects of culture that have been imposed on us depending on the environment we grew up in. These differences impact on how we work with others; hence, it comes as no surprise that there is an increasing emphasis for the workforce and students alike to be competent in working across cultures. One's capability to do so is referred to as cultural intelligence (CQ), and it has been proven to enhance one's effectiveness in working in culturally diverse situations (Livermore, 2011).

In higher education, CQ has become a key skill that students are to develop for them to prepare to be competent as part of the future workforce. CQ is a vital skill not only for students, but also for educators as well. After all, the question is how do we expect our students to be culturally competent if the teacher is not and does not set a good example? Teachers must be able to adapt to culturally diverse classrooms by being able to engage these students who may have varying learning needs and distinctive differences in the efficacy of their learning processes.. As the foremost step, teachers must identify their own level of cultural knowledge, competency and evaluate their feelings, behaviours and attitudes during cross-cultural encounters (Lopes-Murphy, 2014). This enables the teachers to know if they are ready to deal, manage and navigate cross-cultural learning challenges and complexities. Administrators must examine how CQ-related operational matters are relevant and how these social-cultural issues can potentially impact various levels of the institution. For instance, at the strategic (institutional) level, higher education senior leaders must consider re-evaluating their recruitment and training & development policies to ensure that teachers are adequately competent in their social and cultural inclinations. Institutions must consider analysing the admission rates and the quality level of international students while giving due considerations on its potential implications. Giving due consideration to have CQ included in the curriculum means, the learning design and pedagogical approaches to be deployed in classrooms have to embed these social-cultural nuances. Teachers must review, reevaluate and adjust their deliverables from an instructional perspective to facilitate the development of cross-cultural skills and competencies. CQ also inevitably shifts the importance and emphasis towards a more student-centric learning design as well as inclined to student-to-student (peer-to-peer) interactions.

No matter how the diverse what one thinks of internationalization of higher education, it is rather clear that it will continue to grow, despite the contrary views of shifting inwards and overly protective through domestically focused. It is evident in today's workforce on how the diverse composition of workforce is, which reiterates the importance of working with culturally diverse individuals. Hence, Higher Education Institutions should prepare students as "job-ready" graduates to deal with such real-life situational contexts Unlike Intelligence (IQ) which is very much tied to an individual's birth cognitive ability which can be stretched but unlikely to significantly change no matter how much it put that in training where in comparison, whereas anyone and everyone can potentially improve their CQ abilities. For instance, institutes can collaborate with other foreign institutes across the world to provide their students with the opportunity to study abroad for a period of time for them to gain exposure to different cultural settings. Such international exposures, experiences as studying abroad have been found to positively affect CQ (Eisenberg et al., 2013; Holtbrügge & Engelhard, 2016). If such international experiences are not always possible for varying constraints, for instance, such as COVID-19 pandemic, or a crisis, institutions can incorporate cross-cultural management courses (CCM) in their programmes, which is reported according to Eisenberg et al. (2013)'s study to be effective in developing the cognitive and metacognitive aspects of CQ. Moreover, to improve their CQ abilities, students must be encouraged to work cross-culturally through experiential learning activities (Kurpis & Hunter, 2016).

The concept of CQ and its related cross-cultural learning, management aspects are expected to grow even more in prominence as the world becomes increasingly globalized. High schools, including universities, higher education institutes, need to recognize this and ensure that they are consistently and adequately doing enough at the strategic, tactical and operational levels to enable the development of CQ abilities in their students. This strategic intervention and emphasis are essential as it impacts the graduate employability and thus the reputation and the credibility of the higher education institution. Hence, institutes should put in the required processes and ecosystem to have both the teachers and students to be competent and equipped with the essential "know-hows" to have them competent in working cross-culturally.

10.2 Blended Learning Strategy

There are a significant number of core factors that influences the direction in which higher education is headed towards. For instance, globalization has influenced major shifts in students' demographics while technology has changed how learning is being delivered in today's contemporary and rapid evolving learning climate and context. As a result, higher education institutes have been looking for ways to review, modify the curricula in order to better cope with these disruptions and changes. These effects will potentially result in an increased adoption of the blended learning model in higher education institutes. The blended learning model is not only useful in dealing with evolving environmental changes and shifts but it also brings about varying plentiful of benefits to both the higher education institutions and its stakeholders.

At the institutional level, blended learning makes economic sense and is well positioned in terms of strategic direction towards futurist learning. This blended learning (BL) learning design allows institutes to open up to more students in a relatively short period of time without much need to be concerned about resources utilization, for instance, the lack of classrooms to accommodate all learners. This approach becomes a strategic method to reach out to students who otherwise will not have access to face-to-face educational opportunities in a mode or location that is convenient for them and to be accommodative to the increasing enrolment without making major facilities investments. Institutional infrastructure can be built virtually rather than physically, often at lower cost (Ross & Gage, 2005). For students as a key stakeholder, such blended learning design embedded in programmes provide them with higher flexibility in their learning that can be beneficial for students in terms of flexibility and self-directed learning that emphasizes on values such as autonomy and empowerment to shape an effective learning culture. The blended learning design and instructional approach in general increases the adoption of active and authentic learning, peer-to-peer review and learner-centred strategies adopted in real-time classroom sessions (Bonk & Graham, 2005; Rajaram, 2021). All of these individual pedagogical interventions bring about its own set of benefits that enhance the holistic students' learning experience. For instance, active learning enables far more opportunities to be able to provide instant feedback to students, deepening their comprehension of the subject contents. Further to that, peer-to-peer review strategies enable learners to experience different or contrary perspectives, self-directed learning allows students to take control of their own learning progress, while the more space made available for interactions and dialogues enhances students' collaboration skills while learner-centred strategies can promote active participation with consistent reflections.

Blended learning can be rather powerful when it is well-designed and effectively executed (Hofmann, 2018). The design facilitates creation of individualized resources that helps support both formal and informal learning. Additionally, aside from allowing increased flexibility in learning, its learning design can easily accommodate students with physical impairments, where a hybrid approach facilitates and provides a wider choice on how it could be adjusted to fit such circumstances or needs by students as such. The learning design put a large emphasis authentic learning as students are made to learn, recall and apply what they have learnt and acquired. Furthermore, it enables teachers to create personalized learning paths for their students that allows them to assess their own capabilities and make much better-informed decisions on how and what they need to learn.

Implementing blended learning is certainly much more complex than it seems at the surface level. Hence, it is recommended that institutions give due consideration to the various contributing factors before committing to its considerably high start-up costs. A good start could be potentially having to break down the blended learning into two core clusters, namely online asynchronous learning and face-to-face (physical or synchronous-virtual) learning. Learning designers can then optimize the resources involved in each of these clusters and thereafter merge them together to obtain an overall total costing. We should adopt guided frameworks that offers implementation recommendations in a structured manner, where one such framework that addressed and provided some foundational guidelines was by Porter et al. (2014). The scope of insights covered is on purpose, advocacy, definition, infrastructure, scheduling, governance, evaluation, professional development, support and incentives.

However, with the rapid evolving changes and contemporary, multilayered issues emerging, a new and contemporary scope that comprises of recommendations for blended learning was created. The newly developed framework is presented in Table 10.1 as illustrated below.

As we propel ahead embracing the numerous evolving changes and disruptions, higher education institutions (HEIs) have to shift their focus and emphasis to explore how exactly they can incorporate the varying aspects of blended learning to deliver quality, relevant and contemporary learning. Moreover, with the new technological innovations and digital transformation embedment emerging at a rapid pace, HEIs will have to be more open to enable varying type of technologies to be incorporated within the learning design curricula. Hence, HEIs will have to act swiftly and cautiously in discerning that type of technologies that will be most beneficial and value-adding to their students. In addition, the face-to-face aspect of blended learning is expected to change as disruptions and new pedagogical learning designs are uncovered and its intended learning outcomes evolve.

10.3 Future of Learning: Teaching and Learning Strategies

Responding to changes in the external and internal environment alone is not adequately sufficient to meet the rapid, evolving disruptions and changes. Higher Education Institutions (HEIs) must radically shift their outlook and transform their strategic approach from one that is reactive to a proactive one, if they have already not

Table 10.1 Institutional implementation strategies for blended learning

Interventions	Scope	Recommendations
Broad strategic emphasis and leadership direction	Goal	Universities and Higher Education Institutions (HEIs) should (a) comprehend the efficacy, its impact on learning outcomes and effectiveness in the students' learning process through adopting blended learning (BL); (b) see the common purpose and align with their institutional, stakeholders, faculty goals and values; and (c) align their emphasis on the specific aspects of students' learning development by BL, primarily by resonating on what is required of the external stakeholders, for example: The applied "know-hows"; employability skills of ad hoc verbal articulation skills, problem-solving with analytical evidence-based approaches, compassion & empathy and so on
	Creating and Establishing an Eco-system: Change Catalyst	Universities and HEIs should (a) develop an eco-system where champions or change catalysts should be implanted at multiple institutional levels, including school, division and centre/department administrations, faculty resource centres, faculty members and students; (b) get the senior leadership and management to show their commitment by emphasizing the adoption and its expected positive impact on its students
	Instituting a collectively consented description of Blended Learning (BL)	Universities and HEIs should consult the pedagogical experts to establish a standardized definition of BL that details out BL's structural dimensions such as the integration of face-to-face and online instruction. Imperatively, faculty should be fully empowered and given the autonomy to exercise the flexibility to make pedagogical learning designs regarding their BL course re-design
	Anchored and Supported through Evidence-Based and Contemporary Approaches	Universities and HEIs should advocate its stakeholders through well-researched evidence of BL that shows clear indication and positive impact on the increased efficacy of the learning quality, effectiveness and its applied contents knowledge

(continued)

Table 10.1 (continued)

Interventions	Scope	Recommendations
Structural Processes, Governance and Professional Development	Institution's Infrastructure	Universities and HEIs should plan and devise initiatives to scale initial BL adoption efforts by upgrading their information technology servers, bandwidth and other structural infrastructure processes. This means to be forward looking in allocating and sourcing for additional funding towards these initiatives
	Marketing outreach and value proposition	Universities and HEIs should include BL as a value-add proposition and as an appropriate pedagogical learning design. There should be an emphasis on how the BL could make the students achieve their learning goals as well as prepare them for the workforce
	Scheduling	Universities and HEIs should clearly and explicitly designate their BL offerings in their programme and course catalogues in a manner that accurately reflects any consistent reductions in seat time
	Authority	BL governance should involve institutional, school and divisional/department administrators as well as the faculty inputs. There should be adequate transparency in sharing the performance statistics and the impact of BL adopted and implemented across all levels
	Assessment	Universities and HEIs should establish managerial controls through assessments and reflections based on programme, course assessments and outcomes in classes where BL is incorporated. The efficacy of its implementation should be measured and reviewed for improvements. The continuous feedback should be used to correct, fine-tune and align the required aspects. These continuous changes being incorporated through such feedback mechanisms enable the rigour and quality of the system
	Training and Development, Professional Growth and Life-Long Learning	Universities and HEIs should give due consideration on varying multilayered, embedded factors when deciding on their professional, training development strategies & methodologies, including setting up internal training centres or leveraging on potential expert & specialized training providers. This also largely depends on the sustainable and prolonged number of adopters that require training and participants' needs
Management of rewards, recognition and extension of support and resources	Support & Resources	Universities and HEIs should make conscious efforts to determine both faculty and student BL adopters' resources needs, support required and have them addressed
	Rewards Management	Universities and HEIs should give incentives and rewards to blended learning (BL) adopters such as recognition to be champions/advocates. Such BL adoption should be tied to their appraisal performance, duly considered during tenure & promotion and even in terms of financial compensation. Moreover, more time for design, adoption and implementation should be allowed which shows the importance given for the change to be undertaken

done so. While a reactive approach may possibly allow HEIs to get by for that phase, it will not be adequate if their aspiration is to remain relevant and progress in the long term. Many may say that future cannot be predicted with a hundred percent certainty or concrete plan, so why bother putting in efforts in planning ahead or attempt to speculate even? While we can acknowledge we predict exactly or guarantee what's the exact future, we could have the plan devised based on certain consistent trends that point in a specific or common direction convergently. These trends are indicators or touchpoints of what is likely to be expected or emerge, perhaps not in the immediate future, but at least within the next few years. By anticipating the future, institutions can put in place required measures that will not only help them stay afloat and abreast in a highly competitive environment, but certainly equip them with a competitive edge that distinguishes and differentiates themselves from others.

Evidence shows that technology and digital transformation are clearly the core focus that requires HEIs to re-think and transform their learning design to be aligned for the future of learning. We have well entered the digital age and phase where students entering the higher education institutions are labelled as "digital natives". That means the profile of students is consistently different and changing while concurrently the external environments are rapidly transforming. The question that we need to ask will be (a) how this change affects students' learning efficacy; (b) learning process; (c) acquisition of knowledge; and (d) their preference in how they want to learn. Students today learn differently, where vast amount of information on a myriad of topics are readily available to them 24/7 for free that enables them to connect to their peers and teachers or anyone conveniently through mobile devices, tablets and in varying different platforms. Technology and digital transformation interventions are enabling multimodal teaching, changing curricula and creating rich forms of online research and collaboration (The Economist Intelligence Unit, 2008). Besides this, other significant trends and drivers of the future of learning include globalization, changes in students' demographics and in employers', external stakeholders' demands.

Aside from digitalization literacy and skills, students of the future are expected to have competencies that enable them to be adaptable, agile and relevant to the future workforce. Sixteen of these skills were identified by Ehlers and Kellermann (2019) that includes autonomy, creativity, cooperation skills and more. But the question is not simply about the general skills to be laid out rather the ability to deeply understand the key thrusts, have them ingrained in one's behaviours and outlook. Teachers of the future are expected to be equipped with specific learning design, facilitation, teaching and people management skills effectively teach and fulfil the changing learning demands. For instance, it is crucial for teachers to be open-minded, practice self-awareness and are willing to unlearn and relearn with a growth mindset. Particularly, for older teachers, the interventions of technology into classroom facilitations may be daunting. Nonetheless, with the correct mindset and sufficient support from the Higher Education Institutes (HEIs), teachers will be able to cope, deal with the evolving classroom environments.

In the future, institutions can expect to have major shifts in the manner in which course programmes are generally delivered. With the rapid evolution of technological disruptions and digital transformation, teachers are no longer bound by the traditional face-to-face model of instruction. Online asynchronous and synchronous platforms, together with the support of Artificial intelligence, virtual and augmented reality interventions, with varying application tools mean that teachers are now exposed to a varied diverse option to leverage their deliveries where students are no longer required to be at campus to learn. Teachers can design the delivery of learning where students could potentially learn the course materials at their residence at their own pace, while use the physical classroom time for students to apply their learnings through a blended learning model. All in all, technological interventions will continue to impact the creation of new innovative modes of facilitation and teaching deliveries.

Higher education institutions (HEIs) are recommended to review their curriculum by sensing the "pulse" of the industry, their continuously changing needs and act as a bridge to be relevant, updated, be consistently agile to look out for the external interventions to readily prepare for future ready graduates. This includes training teachers in the areas such as information technology, data analytics, reassessing intended learning outcomes, re-designing course programmes and re-evaluating policies of HEIs. HEIs must give due considerations to the potential implications of any major changes that are being introduced. Some vital and reflective questions to consider include: "Will shifting to a blended learning model put students of lower socio-economic status at a disadvantage?"; "Are there adequate resources, facilitates and accommodations made for students with disabilities?" and "Do students from the minority groups feel secure of the learning environment?" among other things. While the future of learning preparations may generally look promising, exciting and forthcoming, it is imperative to have it approached with careful deliberation to maximize its outcomes and output results.

10.4 Innovation and Transformation in Learning

With constant and rapid developments in society, higher education institutes (HEIs) must follow suit and must keep up with the trend to remain relevant in today's rapid evolving world. For instance, developments in information and communication technology have changed how people communicate. Hence, that has implications and spillover effects when these aspects are implemented into course programmes, as it changes how students learn and acquire knowledge. Factors influencing innovation and transformation of learning are many and rather complex. However, what comes across clearly as the key driver is that it is necessary for institutes to pursue adaptability and creativity with today's climate.

Serdyukov (2017) advocates that to innovate is to look beyond the current ways of doing things and to develop a novel idea that enables one to do a job in a creative and different manner. In education, innovation is intended to enhance productivity and efficiency of learning, hence resulting in better learning quality. It can be directed towards varying aspects of the educational eco-system, such as "theory & practice, curriculum, teaching and learning, policy, technology, institutions and administration, institutional culture, and teacher education" (Serdyukov, 2017, pp. 8). Innovation can be potentially integrated and applied in any aspects of education where it can positively impact learning and its learners, respectively. Further to this, there are varying levels of degrees in which innovation can impact education where it could range from minor adjustments to moderate modifications and to even massive alterations, where the final phase of which is to be considered to be transformative. Primarily, for innovations to be transformative and its effects to make an adequate impact on the relevant stakeholders, it must be executed and promptly diffused within the higher education institutes (HEIs) at a large scale.

Besides just allowing HEIs to maintain their relevance, contemporaneous and futurist inclinations in learning, it also serves to benefit the institute from a holistic perspective. At the institutional level, strategic innovative transformations help to create competitive advantages that enable them to outperform their rivals, hence help to generate more cashflow and profits. Taking a more granular look, innovative strategies and interventions in varying forms can positively impact the pedagogical techniques deployed in specific programmes or at specific schools in the HEIs. For students, innovations may encourage and facilitate deeper development of specific skills and competencies, which is becoming a core central focus of graduate attributes. Further to this, the effects of innovative practices and interventions can help re-design learning experiences to be more personalized inline to students' abilities while being more sensitive to the learning cultures and rooted identities (Northwest Missouri State University, 2018). Aside that, teachers also become beneficiaries of these innovations as it facilitates their job to be much easier allowing them to focus less on arduous and tiresome administrative work such as grading and more on teaching workload of students.

The higher education industry is expected to deal with further evolving disruptions in the future, hence enabling even more innovations and transformations in learning becomes rudimentary and not a preferred option. Globalization, technological developments and other such related factors will continue to influence the level of competition within the higher education industry. Higher education institutes should ensure continuous, consistent innovations and transformative interventions to not only keep up with dynamic environmental changes, but to also set them apart from competitors. While competitive advantages are crucial in saturated markets, they do not often last due to the volatile nature of industries today (McGrath, 2013), including that of higher education. Perhaps, HEIs could adopt the "blue ocean strategy" that involves the pursuit of both differentiation and low cost to create a new market space and new demand (Kim & Mauborgne, 2005). By doing so, HEIs will attain new profit and growth opportunities. For instance, Vanderbilt University worked on innovating and changing their career centre services as a way to assist the university stand out (Blue Ocean Team, n.d.). It is vital to acknowledge that while technology seems to be the most palpable way to transform learning, innovation goes beyond technology and can be done in many other ways. Leaders in higher education should keep an open mind and be proactive in thinking of the newest and most effective ways to make their HEIs stand out from the crowd.

10.5 Social-Psychological Intervention

Evidence points us to two primary types of empathy, namely cognitive empathy and affective (emotional) empathy. Empathy consists of a dual route system that comprises a lower-level route that is automatic and fast, and a higher-level route that is slow and complex. While affective empathy falls under the lower route, cognitive empathy falls under the higher route. Cognitive empathy is effortful and requires attention and time. Cognitive empathy refers to the ability to comprehend or reason the subjective mental states, perspectives and intentions of others. On the other hand, affective empathy is defined as a person's emotional response to the affective state of another. While both types of empathy are vital for a person to have, we chose to focus on cognitive empathy development in our study because it is more straightforward to train as compared to affective empathy, where it is inherent and much harder to influence. Further to that, with increasingly diverse work and school environments, cognitive empathy must play a primary role when there is a lack of affective empathy due to racial, ethnic, religious or physical differences (Riess, 2017).

In general, empathy is imperative for students because it (a) encourages prosocial behaviour; (b) creates a safer and much secured learning culture, (c) fosters positive student relationships; and (d) leads to an institution's success (Greater Good in Education, n.d.). These aspects could be also applied to students in higher education institutions. For instance, with technology and the Internet, students would potentially engage in cyberbullying as they can remain anonymous. A study by Ang and Goh (2010) examined empathy in adolescents in Singapore aged 12 to 18, where it was found that students who had both low cognitive and affective empathy were found to have higher scores on cyberbullying compared to those who had high cognitive empathy. This reiterates and emphasizes the implication of empathy in creating safe and secured school environments for all students.

Further to this, empathy is crucial for students in higher education to enhance their competencies, equip them with the skills to develop their future job performance. For instance, empathy plays a vital role in certain jobs that require a high emphasis in the social interaction aspects. For example, the skill of empathy is imperative in the medical profession, say for doctors to ensure there is a well-established doctor-patient rapport. This skill enables them to be good listeners, hence facilitates a smooth delivery of bad news, and helps them assist their patients in coping with their illness more effectively (Dehning et al., 2013). Unfortunately, evidence suggests that medical students experience a decline of empathy during their time in medical school instead of retaining or enhancing it. Hence, it is essential for higher education institutes (and schools in general) to facilitate the development of empathy in the learning eco-system, learning processes to their students through relevant interventions and controls. Empathy can also enable students to better work in groups and across cultures, which are key thrust and one of the traits that many employers are looking out for in graduate hires in today's fast-evolving industry.

Higher education institutes can advocate, promote the development of cognitive empathy through social-psychological interventions as brief activities that do not teach academic content but instead target students' thoughts, feelings and beliefs in and about school (Yeager & Walton, 2011, pp.268). These interventions are proven to be powerful when adopted in classroom settings as supported by various studies. Several experiments have found that even seemingly small-scale, social-psychological interventions had significant effects on educational achievements. For example, Wilson (2006) describes how a 15-min intervention can reduce the racial achievement gap by 40%. Hence, with a similar conceptual design, it is plausible that interventions will enhance the development of the cognitive empathy.

With the current complex, multifaceted human relational challenges there will be an increased importance and emphasis placed on empathy and its unique value to be equipped among the workforces. As technology evolves and becomes more advanced, jobs traditionally held by humans will potentially be replaced, however, social skills which are unlikely to be replicated will become vital for workers to be equipped with specific skills such as empathy that is viewed as a value proposition in the new world.

Studies by Rajaram (2021), Hartman et al. (2017) and Numanee et al. (2020) suggest that cognitive empathy skills can be learned through reasoning, relating and interconnecting with others through meaningful and thoughtful reflections. These studies found that incorporating empathy training in the classroom is essential for the successful orientation of students to empathy and its application. Hence, higher education institutes should encourage their faculty to integrate learning activities creatively revolving around empathy in their classroom facilitation beyond just mere contents facilitation and delivery. Faculty should also demonstrate empathy in their teaching to lead by example for their students. From a strategic intervention aspect, it is vital that social-psychological interventions are enacted in higher education to advocate the development of soft skill of empathy.

10.6 Digital Transformation: Data-Driven Learning

Digital technology is prevalent in our everyday lives, and this intervention has made an impact on many industries including higher education. This has influenced the landscape of higher education through digital transformation as institutes use a wide variety of digital tools to transform or change how things have been traditionally performed.

Digital transformation can be viewed as a vital thrust and could be one of higher education institutes' priorities. Digital transformation is defined as the profound transformation of business and organizational activities, processes, competencies and models to fully leverage the opportunities of a mix of digital technologies and their accelerating impact across society in a strategic and prioritized way, with present and future shifts in mind (i-SCOOP, 2018). It enables educational processes to become more effective and hence influence students' learning through digital technologies that include big data, predictive analytics and many more. For instance, using data-driven learning (DDL) as a methodology for foreign language learning can contribute to the digital transformation. DDL attempts to eliminate the middleman and provide direct access to the data so that the learners can participate in developing his or her own profiles of meaning and uses, respectively (Johns, 1994). DDL emphasizes the way in which digital tools can transform the eco-system and the sequential flow in which students learn.

Data analytics, on the other hand, can assist higher education institutes to respond effectively from a strategic aspect, especially to be able to respond promptly and speedily to any changes in their internal and external environment. With big data, institutes are better able to advocate and make more effective decisions for their organization. Further to that, data analytics can be implemented at the micro-level where it has the potential to assist learners and teachers identify, recognize warning signs of threats to learning success before they occur (Daniel, 2014). Altogether, technological tools are becoming increasingly interconnected due to the proliferation of the Internet. The Internet of Things (IoT) refers to the network of devices connected via the Internet. With many students now owning their own mobile and digital devices with Internet capabilities, teachers are seamlessly able to interact with and teach them through these technologies. Institutions should create a digital campus that will reduce costs, improve security and enable staff and students by equipping them with useful tools (Aldowah et al., 2017).

Digital transformation has an impact on both strategic and operational aspects of higher education. It affects on how key decisions are made and can potentially enable the development of novel pedagogical techniques. Institutes should also duly consider the impact technology has on students' learning process and outcomes. These digital natives may find the increased use of technology to be useful and relevant to their lives. On the flip side, students may find themselves rather distracted if there are not appropriately advised on the correct use of technology. Further to this, the steps to be digitally equipped and operational may negatively impact students, especially from lower-income families who may not be able to afford high-speed Internet or a decent mobile device.

As the world continues making progress in technological developments in a fast pace, institutes can expect increasingly more options becoming available to them. For instance, virtual reality and the gamification of programmes could be a fundamental desired choice. Despite the emergence of new technologies, it is vital that the eco-system of digital transformation for a higher education institute needs to be comprehensive and contemporary (Benavides et al., 2020). An institute should carefully distinguish the technological tools that are deployed in their programmes and monitor the efficacy of its usage. While new technologies may seem to be appealing and interesting, the bottom line should still be its relevance, efficacy of usage and impact on learning. Further to this, teachers themselves should be trained adequately to smoothly facilitate lessons and resolve technical issues. Institutes should also duly consider the varying sociocultural implications of its digital transformation strategy.

10.7 Assessment and Feedback for Learning: Now and the Future

Assessment has always been and will continue to be a crucial aspect of higher education eco-system. This could be primarily due to, especially accreditation mandatory requirements that require assessments as a methodological intervention of evaluating and discerning students based on their abilities. While assessments remain as a fundamental requirement within the eco-system, higher education institutes are discovering a broader purpose of assessments, beyond just merely validating and endorsing students' learning. Assessment can be used to measure student learning outcomes, evaluate teaching efficacy and an avenue for a particular course or programme's areas of improvement. How the higher education institutes assess students is also changing. The traditional pen-and-paper type of exam is one of the numerous ways that students could be assessed today. Some examples of assessment approaches include group work reports, fieldwork essays, reflection journals, portfolio creation with reflective analysis interventions, multiple choice tests and many more. Each of these types of assessments has their pros and cons, where it has to be carefully selected based on learning deliverables and outcomes to be measured. Many studies suggest an inclination of other assessment methods over the traditional ones primarily because the former stimulate learning and understanding rather than merely focused on memorization (Pereira et al., 2016).

Feedback is a vital aspect of the assessment process as it enhances the quality of students' learning. Feedback should be provided by teachers to help students to be aware of their level of understanding of the contents taught, their performance level on a task assigned for example and identify the specific areas for them to improve on. Feedback can be both given in a detailed manner and other times in a more generic fashion. Either way, feedback serves a useful and reflective avenue for both teachers and students. Like assessment, how feedback is perceived and delivered is evolving and transforming. For instance, peer feedback is increasingly used in classrooms today as form of intervention to have a different dimension in providing feedback. It is imperative for teachers ensure they are providing students with feedback that have high efficacy in terms of quality, usefulness and avenue for self-improvement. Teachers should ensure the feedback are of (a) quality, (b) relevance and whether it would resonate positively to influence students' learning (Henderson et al., 2019).

Assessments and feedback provide varying benefits for both at the institutional (strategic), divisional (tactical) and programme and/or course (operational) levels. At the institutional (strategic) and divisional (tactical) levels, assessments and feedback results are essential to be aligned with the accreditation purposes which are primarily used to report the findings/results to the relevant stakeholders. At the programme and/or course levels, we would focus on two major stakeholders, namely teachers and students. For teachers, assessment and feedback serve as avenues where the "gaps" in students' learning and/or in their own teaching allow them to make the necessary adjustments or alignments to increase the efficacy of the lessons in terms of quality, engagement and relevance. For students, assessments provide them with concrete evidence on their learning progress and learning outcomes, while feedback serves a reflection, aspects that they need to work to improve on. In the future, technology and digitalization have a much higher stake in terms of its role and impact it has on the design of assessment and feedback. Technology embedment in its design has already shown positive signs where it is able to produce efficient and consistent assessment outcomes (Ibarra-Sáiz et al., 2020). Automation embedded in the grading and feedback systems can lessen the load on teachers, enabling them to focus more on teaching while eliminating any potential biases that may occur during human grading and reduce the labour-intensive approach adopted. Further to this, technology allows for speedier grading and feedback, enabling students with more time to reflect, be engaged and learn from their feedback or assessment outcomes, respectively.

Higher education institutes should consider allowing students to be assessed via a wide varying approach. Not only will this open and flexible approach allow schools to evaluate students' learning performance, but more imperatively, it will provide students with the opportunity and appropriate avenue to reflect, learn varying and competencies. For instance, timed and/or real-time assessments allow students to learn beyond contents, that is how to seamlessly address the questions calmly with anxiety, primarily the ability to learn the soft skill of stress management, while take-home assessments teach these students on effective utilization of time-management skills. However, it is imperative for institutes to understand the risks and the possible ramifications that is involved in changing assessment design and methodologies without having a deep comprehension of its potential consequences. Ultimately, assessments do have an impact on students' performance that somewhat/way affect students' lives, in particular, their future job prospects and career progression, at least in the initial phases after their graduation, if organizations are rather particular and would like to place weightage on fresh graduates' academic performance to have it as a reflection of their cognitive capacity (Boud & Falchikov, 2007). However, employers today are also increasingly looking out and putting the weightage on soft skills and competencies in their graduate hires, although grades do still play a vital role in their decisions for the most part as that is generally seen as a validated performance measure that they could trust and take reference from.

10.8 Artificial Intelligence and Immersive Learning for the Future

Artificial Intelligence (AI) is one of the key driving technological forces of today's rapid evolving world (Holmes et al., 2019). AI is defined as an automatic simulation system of collating knowledge and information to process the intelligence of universe. Primarily, it involves collating and disseminating it to targeted group in the form of actionable intelligence (Grewal, 2014). Fundamentally, artificial intelligence is the ability for computers and machines to replicate human cognition and actions.

AI has the potential to impact many industries significantly, including higher education. In accordance with Holmes et al. (2019), the application of AI in education is predicted to become a market worth almost $6 billion by 2024. Despite this huge potential, the application in AI in education does seem to be lagging compared to other industries (Bates et al., 2020; Bughin et al., 2017). Nonetheless, AI has been embedded and applied to a certain degree in higher education, such as in administration, instruction or teaching and learning (Chen et al., 2020). The use of artificial intelligence in education (AIED) in classrooms can be acknowledged through the use of adaptive or personalized learning systems which collate and analyse large amounts of data (Holmes et al., 2019). The rapid evolving changes that occur in higher education certainly impact the manner in which AIED is adopted and executed. Shifts in educational goals, practices, both external & internal environments and the role adopted by the teacher are some of the vital influential factors (Roll & Wylie, 2016). The use of intelligent tutoring systems (ITS) and interactive learning environments (ILEs) are examples of how AI manifests itself speedily in the future of learning, broadly education.

AI influences on the way educators teach and how students learn. AI can potentially provide students with more personalized learning through individualizing the pace of learners, customizing to their specific needs and assisting to better facilitate their students' learning through automation of administrative processes and data analytics on learners' performance. For instance, intelligent tutoring systems (ITS), one of the most common applications of AI, provides individualized learning by evaluating a student's understanding of the subject and spontaneously automatically adjusting, aligning to the level of difficulty of activities and learning resources, materials based on learners' determined skills and competencies level (Holmes et al., 2019). This enables teachers to overcome the differences in abilities among their students and ensures that all students are learning at a pace that is most suitable for themselves. AI assist institutions to overcome the ineffectiveness of the "one-size fits all" approach. Further to this, AI is expected to empower teachers and reduce the time that they spend on menial and monotonous tasks. These AI interventions allow teachers to allocate their focus and energy towards more productive, impactful aspects such as transforming of learning design, incorporating new teaching methodologies and research that keeps them well informed through evidence-based knowledge. Hence, the implementation of AI is highly beneficial to make positive impact to both the educators and learners. At the institutional level, AI can assist in streamlining the arduous labour-intensive administrative processes, for instance, institutions make use of automated algorithms that leverages on AI to target marketing advertisements to prospective students, estimate class sizes, plan curricula and allocate resources, such as financial aid and facilities (Zeide, 2019).

In the future, AI is expected to play an even much bigger role in higher education. While it is highly unlikely that automated learning systems, robots in learning ecosystems and AI learning interventions will replace teachers, we can certainly expect an increasing range of AI applications to be adopted widely in higher education. The emergent trend on the flexible mixed-initiative systems incorporate a variety of teaching and learning methodologies (McArthur et al., 2005). Therefore, higher education institutes are recommended to embrace and integrate AI into their ecosystems to leverage on its potential benefits to meet the rapid changing needs of learners and the demands to get them job-ready to the future workforce. However, it is crucial that institutes do not ignorantly fall into the trap of letting AI interventions, automated learning robotic systems and high-end algorithms auto-run their institutional processes, without major interventions from a human decision-making control aspect. For example, ITS should not completely replace human and face-to-face teaching due to the compelling need and benefits of human interactivity and the social connection that value-adds to the entire learning process. Ultimately, while AI is useful in guiding decisions, it should be used in conjunction or in partnership with human knowledge and abilities where it should be viewed as a complementary and not as a mere substitute. The ideal outcome and impact could happen only when we are able to incorporate the correct mix of strengths of AI as well as human skills (Rouhiainen, 2019), as neither one should be viewed as superior or substitute to the other, rather complementary elements that work well together in partnership hand in hand.

Virtual reality (VR) and augmented reality (AR) are trending topics in the education industry as they both have great potential to make positive impact in the manner in which teaching and learning could be conducted. VR can be defined as computer-generated simulation of a three-dimensional image or environment that can be interacted in a seemingly real or physical way by a person using special electronic equipment, such as a helmet with a screen inside or gloves fitted with sensors (Freina & Ott, 2015). There is substantial amount of research done on VR in education, specifically on university or pre-university learning, with an inclination on scientific subjects. AR is defined as technologies that augment the sense of reality, allowing the coexistence of digital information and real environments (Shiue et al., 2019). Many industries use simulations to train and provide their trainees with realistic learning experiences, including the airline industry, the military and medical schools (Herrington et al., 2007).

VR and AR are not just merely interactive, rather when we discuss and reflect on the two concepts, the term "immersion" often emerges. The concept of immersion causes an absence of awareness of time and of the real world, as well as giving a sense of being in the task environment (Freina & Ott, 2015). As for the VR, immersion refers more to spatial involvement where there is a perception of being physically present in a nonphysical world. These immersive simulations that are now made possible through technological advancement, which was not available 2 to 3 decades ago are a way to capture the attention and engage a particular group of targeted audience.

In the case of higher education, simulations can be considered as a powerful and highly beneficial approach to incorporate in teaching students. Some positive benefits of VR and AR include improved learning outcomes, increased level of interest in learning, improvement or acquisition of skills and increased knowledge retention among the many other things (Chavez & Bayona, 2018; Shiue et al., 2019). Simulations are highly productive and beneficial in certain subjects, for instance, it assists nursing students to apply what they have learnt without the fear of harming real patients out of inexperience (Damewood, 2016).

The adoption of VR and AR systems in classrooms assists to revolutionize the instructional techniques used by educators in general (Adnan, 2020). Its adoption rate in higher education space will certainly gain much greater traction in the coming years ahead as the web-based technologies and applications, broadband and computer graphics improve in folds. Virtual learning and gamification of learning are highly relevant to today's context of rapid transformation arena and climate where the new generation who have grown or are growing up in with increased exposure to virtual worlds, such as that of Club Penguin, Roblox and so on. As these technologies become the norm in our everyday lives, institutes should explore and re-think on how to best integrate them into their course learning design and curriculum. When implementing immersive learning, institutes should carefully consider primary factors such as the learning curves in embracing new technology for both students and teachers as well as the potential disruptions and technical issues that are bound to arise. Accessibility is another critical aspect, for instance, the lack of access to relevant resources, equipment or having adequate IT infrastructure support, i.e. broadband, Internet speeds that may hinder a students' overall learning experience. There are varying new possibilities that immersive learning and virtual reality can bring into higher education. Despite these pros, institutes should cautiously plan the integration of such technologies into classrooms due to its high costs incurrence and potentially require large-scale investments to sustain it and make it work effectively.

10.9 Cultural and Social Perspectives

While innovation and digital transformation brings benefits to higher education institutes (HEIs), one must examine and look beyond its core implications. With globalization playing a significant role in changing students' demographics, HEIs must be increasingly aware of the potential consequences rising from this increased diversity. The notion of embracing ethos of diversity brings many positive growth and learning benefits to students and their peers. Interacting with others different from oneself creates awareness embedded with varying unique experiences and enables students to be nurtured with a global mindset. However, for HEIs to authentically transform themselves, especially with technological interventions, they must relate, comprehend how these unique diverse social-cultural experiences and backgrounds will affect the entire integration of technology onto campus.

Although there is certainly an increase in the adoption of personal technological devices and tools, such as laptops, tablets and smartphones, there is still an adequate digital divide that needs to be acknowledged. Students, especially from lower-income families, may not be able to afford their own device that allows online learning. Further to that, students who live abroad may also lack the required Internet speeds to access course resources, materials or classes online. Students not having equal access to technology and Internet may potentially cause this group of students to be left behind in terms of their learning progress and overall school experience. Therefore, it is crucial that HEIs provide adequate support and assistance to their disadvantaged students. This can be in the form of financial aid, learning spaces and quiet environments for virtual assessments or self-directed learning, or simply ensuring that there are enough desktops available in the common shared areas and good, consistent Internet connectivity on campus grounds.

Additionally, social-cultural differences can potentially impact the level of acceptance when it comes to technology in classrooms. Some students who are labelled "digital natives" may find the use of technology in classrooms to be more relevant, apt and essential while other students who are less competent with less information computer technology (ICT) and computer skills may be apprehensive instead. The profile of students could be from different social, cultural and technology-exposed backgrounds. They will also some with varying degrees of ICT skills and abilities. This obviously means that students who have had less exposure to technology prior and naturally less tech-savvy will struggle to keep up the pace. On the flip side, students with superior ICT skills can feel bored or disdain towards their peers as they perceive that their peers who are slower are hindering their learning process or becoming a barrier in their development.

All in all, it is crucial that HEIs are to be aware of the varying sociocultural factors that play a key role in influencing their school environment. It is vital to put in place the necessary interventions to either amplify the benefits or to reduce or eliminate the shortcomings of sociocultural differences.

References

Adnan, A. H. M. (2020). From interactive teaching to immersive learning: Higher Education 4.0 via 360-degree videos and virtual reality in Malaysia. *IOP Conference Series: Materials Science and Engineering*, *917*, 012023. https://doi.org/10.1088/1757-899x/917/1/012023

Aldowah, H., Ul Rehman, S., Ghazal, S., & Naufal Umar, I. (2017). Internet of things in higher education: A study on future learning. *Journal of Physics: Conference Series, 892*, 012017. https://doi.org/10.1088/1742-6596/892/1/012017

Ang, R. P., & Goh, D. H. (2010). Cyberbullying among adolescents: The role of affective and cognitive empathy, and gender. *Child Psychiatry and Human Development, 41*(4), 387–397. https://doi.org/10.1007/s10578-010-0176-3

Bates, T., Cobo, C., Mariño, O., & Wheeler, S. (2020). Can artificial intelligence transform higher education? *International Journal of Educational Technology in Higher Education, 17*(1), 1–12. https://doi.org/10.1186/s41239-020-00218-x

Benavides, L., Tamayo Arias, J., Arango Serna, M., Branch Bedoya, J., & Burgos, D. (2020). Digital transformation in higher education institutions: A systematic literature review. *Sensors, 20*(3291), 1–22. https://doi.org/10.3390/s20113291

Blue Ocean Team. (n.d.). How one university is trying to break out of the read ocean. https://www.blueoceanstrategy.com/blog/how-one-university-is-trying-to-break-out-of-the-red-ocean/

Bonk, C. J., & Graham, C. R. (2005). *The handbook of blended learning: Global perspectives, local designs* (1st ed.). Pfeiffer.

Boud, D., & Falchikov, N. (2007). *Rethinking assessment in higher education: Learning for the longer term* (1st ed.). Routledge.

Bughin, J., Hazan, E., Ramaswamy, S., Chui, M., Allas, T., Dahlström, P., … Trench, M. (2017). *Artificial intelligence, the next digital frontier?* https://www.mckinsey.com/~/media/mckinsey/industries/advanced%20electronics/our%20insights/how%20artificial%20intelligence%20can%20deliver%20real%20value%20to%20companies/mgi-artificial-intelligence-discussion-paper.ashx

Chavez, B., & Bayona, S. (2018). Virtual reality in the learning process. *Advances in Intelligent Systems and Computing*, 1345–1356. https://doi.org/10.1007/978-3-319-77712-2_129

Chen, L., Chen, P., & Lin, Z. (2020). Artificial intelligence in education: A review. *IEEE Access, 8*, 75264–75278. https://doi.org/10.1109/access.2020.2988510

Damewood, A. M. (2016). Current trends in higher education technology: Simulation. *TechTrends, 60*(3), 268–271. https://doi.org/10.1007/s11528-016-0048-1

Daniel, B. (2014). Big Data and analytics in higher education: Opportunities and challenges. *British Journal of Educational Technology, 46*(5), 904–920. https://doi.org/10.1111/bjet.12230

Dehning, S., Gasperi, S., Krause, D., Meyer, S., Reiß, E., Burger, M., … Siebeck, M. (2013). Emotional and cognitive empathy in first-year medical students. *ISRN Psychiatry, 2013*, 1–6. https://doi.org/10.1155/2013/801530

Ehlers, U. D., & Kellermann, S. A. (2019). *Future skills—The future of learning and higher education. Results of the international future skills delphi survey*. https://www.researchgate.net/publication/332028491_Future_Skills_-_The_Future_of_Learning_and_Higher_education_Results_of_the_International_Future_Skills_Delphi_Survey

Eisenberg, J., Lee, H.-J., Brück, F., Brenner, B., Claes, M.-T., Mironski, J., & Bell, R. (2013). Can business schools make students culturally competent? Effects of cross-cultural management courses on cultural intelligence. *Academy of Management Learning & Education, 12*(4), 603–621. https://doi.org/10.5465/amle.2012.0022

Freina, L., & Ott, M. (2015). *A literature review on immersive virtual reality in education: State of the art and perspectives*. https://www.itd.cnr.it/download/eLSE%202015%20Freina%20Ott%20Paper.pdf

Greater Good in Education. (n.d.). Empathy for Students. https://ggie.berkeley.edu/student-well-being/empathy-for-students/#tab__2

Grewal, D. S. (2014). A critical conceptual analysis of definitions of artificial intelligence as applicable to computer engineering. *IOSR Journal of Computer Engineering, 16*(2), 09–13. https://doi.org/10.9790/0661-16210913

Hartman, K., Rajaram, K., & Koh, J. (2017, August 4–8). When practitioners and scientists collide: An evidence-based activity for management education. *Academy of Management Meeting 2017*, Atlanta, Georgia, United States.

Henderson, M., Ajjawi, R., Boud, D., & Molloy, E. (2019). *The Impact of Feedback in Higher Education: Improving Assessment Outcomes for Learners* (1st ed. 2019 ed.). Cham, Switzerland: Palgrave Macmillan.

Herrington, J., Reeves, T. C., & Oliver, R. (2007). Immersive learning technologies: Realism and online authentic learning. *Journal of Computing in Higher Education, 19*(1), 80–99. https://doi.org/10.1007/bf03033421

Hofmann, J. (2018). *Blended learning (what works in talent development)*. Association for Talent Development.

Holmes, W., Bialik, M., & Fadel, C. (2019). *Artificial intelligence in education*. The Center for Curriculum Redesign.

Holtbrügge, D., & Engelhard, F. (2016). Study Abroad Programs: Individual Motivations. *Cultural Intelligence and the Mediating Role of Cultural Boundary Spanning, Academy of Management Learning and Education, 15*(3), 435–455.

Ibarra-Sáiz, M. S., Rodríguez-Gómez, G., Boud, D., Rotsaert, T., Brown, S., Salinas Salazar, M. L., & Rodríguez Gómez, H. M. (2020). The future of assessment in Higher Education. *RELIEVE—Revista Electrónica De Investigación y Evaluación Educativa, 26*(1), 1–6. https://doi.org/10.7203/relieve.26.1.17323

i-SCOOP. (2018). Digital transformation: Online guide to digital transformation. https://www.i-scoop.eu/digital-transformation/

Johns, T. (1994). From printout to handout: Grammar and vocabulary teaching in the context of Data-driven Learning. *Perspectives on Pedagogical Grammar*, 293–313. https://doi.org/10.1017/cbo9781139524605.014

Kim, C. W., & Mauborgne, R. (2005). *Blue ocean strategy: How to create uncontested market space and make competition irrelevant* (1st ed.). Harvard Business Review Press.

Kurpis, L. H., & Hunter, J. (2016). Developing students' cultural intelligence through an experiential learning activity. *Journal of Marketing Education, 39*(1), 30–46. https://doi.org/10.1177/0273475316653337

Livermore, D. (2011). *The cultural intelligence difference: Master the one skill you can't do without in today's global economy* (1st ed.). AMACOM.

Lopes-Murphy, S. A. (2014). Experiences in postsecondary education that may lead to cultural intelligence: Exploring and proposing practices. *International Journal of Teaching and Learning in Higher Education, 26*(2), 287–296. https://files.eric.ed.gov/fulltext/EJ1060833.pdf

McArthur, D., Lewis, M., & Bishary, M. (2005). The roles of artificial intelligence in education: Current progress and future prospects. *I-Manager's Journal of Educational Technology, 1*(4), 42–80. https://doi.org/10.26634/jet.1.4.972

McGrath, R. G. (2013). Transient advantage. https://hbr.org/2013/06/transient-advantage.

Northwest Missouri State University. (2018, January 8). Why innovation absolutely matters in education. https://online.nwmissouri.edu/articles/education/innovation-matters-in-education.aspx.

Numanee, I. Z., Zafar, N., Karim, A., & Ismail, S. A. M. M. (2020). Developing empathy among first-year university undergraduates through English language course: A phenomenological study. *Heliyon, 6*, 1–12. https://doi.org/10.1016/j.heliyon.2020.e04021

Pereira, D., Flores, M. A., Simão, A. M. V., & Barros, A. (2016). Effectiveness and relevance of feedback in Higher Education: A study of undergraduate students. *Studies in Educational Evaluation, 49*, 7–14. https://doi.org/10.1016/j.stueduc.2016.03.004

Porter, W. W., Graham, C. R., Spring, K. A., & Welch, K. R. (2014). Blended learning in higher education: Institutional adoption and implementation. *Computers and Education, 75*, 185–195. https://doi.org/10.1016/j.compedu.2014.02.011

Rajaram, K. (2021). Social-psychological intervention: Cognitive empathy development, Chapter 4, pp. 121 – 167, Evidence-Based Teaching for the 21st Century Classroom and Beyond—Innovative-Driven Learning Strategies, Springer.

Riess, H. (2017). The science of empathy. *Journal of Patient Experience, 4*(2), 74–77. https://doi.org/10.1177/2374373517699267

Roll, I., & Wylie, R. (2016). Evolution and revolution in artificial intelligence in education. *International Journal of Artificial Intelligence in Education, 26*(2), 582–599. https://doi.org/10.1007/s40593-016-0110-3

Ross, B., & Gage, K. (2005). Global perspectives on blending learning. In C. R. Graham & C. J. Bonk (Eds.), *The handbook of blended learning: Global perspectives, local designs* (1st ed., pp. 182–194). Pfeiffer.

Rouhiainen, L. (2019, October 14). How AI and data could personalize higher education. https://hbr.org/2019/10/how-ai-and-data-could-personalize-higher-education

Serdyukov, P. (2017). Innovation in education: What works, what doesn't, and what to do about it? *Journal of Research in Innovative Teaching and Learning, 10*(1), 4–33. https://doi.org/10.1108/jrit-10-2016-0007

Shiue, Y.-M., Hsu, Y.-C., Sheng, M.-H., & Lan, C.-H. (2019). Impact of an augmented reality system on students' learning performance for a health education course. *International Journal of Management, Economics and Social Sciences, 8*(3), 195–204. https://doi.org/10.32327/ijmess/8.3.2019.12

The Economist Intelligence Unit. (2008). *The future of higher education: How technology will shape learning.* https://files.eric.ed.gov/fulltext/ED505103.pdf

Wilson, T. D. (2006). The power of social psychological interventions. *Science, 313*(5791), 1251–1252. https://doi.org/10.1126/science.1133017
Yeager, D. S., & Walton, G. M. (2011). Social-psychological interventions in education. *Review of Educational Research, 81*(2), 267–301. https://doi.org/10.3102/0034654311405999
Zeide, E. (2019). *Artificial intelligence in higher education: Applications, promise and perils, and ethical questions.* https://er.educause.edu/articles/2019/8/artificial-intelligence-in-higher-education-applications-promise-and-perils-and-ethical-questions

Index

A
Activity level, 184
Adaptability, 97, 100, 273, 276
Admission decisions and course scheduling, 353, 354, 358
Agency, 322–327
Agility mindset, 18
AI-augmented IR 4.0 initiative, 160
A La Carte/Self-blend, 184, 188
Analytical and problem-solving skills, 314
Analytic rubrics, 389, 392–393
Animations, 197
Application to teaching and learning, 206
Appropriateness, 100
Articulation of thoughts, 234
Artificial Intelligence (AI), 159, 160, 167, 336, 337, 339–345, 349, 351, 356
Assessment of blended learning, 200
Assessment rubrics, 368, 369, 371, 384, 387–390, 392, 398–402, 407, 415, 416
Assessment(s), 5, 17, 20, 27, 28, 31, 33–35, 72, 77, 82, 88, 98, 179, 193, 195, 200–202, 418, 435, 442, 443, 447
Augmented Reality (AR), 309, 317, 318, 320, 329
Authentic assessments, 371
Authentic learning, 242
Authority, 435
Automated grading, 352
Autonomous learning, 221
Autonomy and empowerment, 432

B
Behavioral development, 374
Behavioural, 58, 63, 75, 79, 84, 87, 91, 95, 97, 99, 100
Behavioural peer evaluation, 250–251
Big data, 336–339, 344, 345, 347, 357
Biometrics, 211
Blended learning, 21–22, 30, 31, 38, 47, 79–80, 177–212, 432–433, 437
Bodily-kinesthetic, 13, 14
Broadband connectivity, 33, 34

C
Capabilities, 8, 10, 12, 14, 19, 20, 30, 34
Capability and Competency of Stakeholders, 379, 380
21st century classroom, 4, 19, 25, 34
21st century learners, 156
Change catalyst, 434
Class participation, 80, 83, 88, 224, 227, 230–239, 250, 263, 284, 286
Classroom teaching, 4, 9
Co-creation, 28, 29
Cognitive, 58–60, 63, 77, 81, 87, 90, 93, 94, 97, 99, 100
Cognitive development, 373, 375
Cognitive empathy, 121, 124, 125–126, 129, 131, 133, 136, 140, 141
Cognitive thinking process, 234
Collaborative dialogues, 4
Collaborative learning, 4, 8, 16, 24, 28, 30, 35, 234, 235, 241, 247, 256, 260, 262
Communication, 65, 67, 74, 79, 82, 87, 96, 97, 222, 224, 235, 239, 249, 250, 257, 271, 273, 278, 284, 288, 290
Comparative peer evaluation, 251, 252

K. Rajaram, *Learning Intelligence: Innovative and Digital Transformative Learning Strategies*,
https://doi.org/10.1007/978-981-19-9201-8

Compassion, 272, 276
Competency and skills development, 121
Computer-mediated, 259
Conceptual knowledge, 308, 312, 314, 315, 324
Confidence, 234, 249, 251, 255, 261, 270, 272, 278
Connectedness, 28, 29–30
Content-specific peer evaluation, 250–252
Cooperative learning, 79
Course level, 184
COVID-19 pandemic, 152, 158, 161, 163
CQ abilities, 431
Creative problem-solving, 273
Creativity, 5, 8, 12, 273, 275
Critical thinking, 224, 235, 239–248, 249–251, 255, 257, 260, 275, 284, 286, 287
Cross-cultural, 85, 105, 261, 291
Cross-cultural competence, 25
Cultural and social contexts, 379, 381
Cultural and social perspectives, 446–447
Cultural differences, 7
Cultural intelligence, 9, 58–66, 71, 72, 80, 86, 90, 96, 97, 99, 100
Culture of learning, 226–228, 232, 284, 292

D

Data-driven learning, 440–441
Data systems, 33, 34
Design thinking, 121, 124, 128–129, 132–134, 136–141
Diffusion of innovation, 152, 168, 169
Diffusion of Innovation Model, 168–171
Digital citizenship, 33, 34
Digitalization and Technological Interventions, 413
Digital transformation, 21, 218–222, 433, 436, 437, 440–441, 446
Disruptive innovation, 152, 163, 166, 167, 171
Diversity, 6, 7, 17, 18, 25, 26, 33, 36, 43–45
3D printing, 211
Drop-out and retention, 355

E

Eco-system, 380, 382, 408, 411, 416
Educational climate, 6
Educators, 4, 10, 13, 17, 23–27, 29, 34, 37, 39, 45
EDUCAUSE, 218, 220
Efficacy, 369, 376, 378–383, 385, 395, 410, 412, 414, 415
Efficacy in learning assessment, 368
Efficacy of learning, 7, 10
E-learning, 219, 229, 241
Elements of design, 195
Emotional intelligence, 58, 59
Empathy, 5, 25–26, 120, 121, 123, 124–125, 128–130, 133, 134, 137, 140, 141, 272, 276
Employer demands, 4, 8, 39
Engagement, 218, 227, 232, 234, 239, 246, 257, 258, 260, 268, 276, 286
Engagement of stakeholders, 34
Engineering, 373, 411
Enriched virtual, 184, 189
Evidence-Based and Contemporary Approaches, 434
Evidence-based approach, 3, 26
Evolving, 430, 432, 433, 436–438, 440, 442–444
Existential, 14
Experiential learning, 80, 88, 94, 97
Experiential learning activities, 431
Extended Reality (XR), 318–321, 329

F

Face-to-face, 230, 254, 258, 259, 264
Face-to-face learning, 180, 181, 189, 195, 198, 210
Face to face learning assessment, 202
Face-to-face seminars, 195, 199
Facilitation, 222, 223, 232, 241, 254, 258, 259, 270, 288
Feedback, 338, 343, 347, 350–352, 353, 354, 358, 367–418
Feedback-focused peer evaluation, 253
Financial costs of blended learning, 208
Flex, 184, 187
Flipped classroom, 78, 230, 262
Formal feedback, 383, 386, 387
Formative feedback, 383–385, 386, 388, 389, 398, 401, 403, 405, 408, 412
Fourth Industrial Revolution (IR 4.0), 151, 152, 158–161
Future of blended learning pedagogy, 179
Future of learning, 4, 5, 38, 46, 48
Future of pedagogy, 230
Futuristic learning, 19

G

Gamifications, 10, 23

Gamified, 260
Gartner Hype Cycle, 168, 170, 171
General rubrics, 392–394
Globalization, 58, 66–73, 76, 100, 105
Globalization on higher education, 152
Global perspectives, 206–208
Goal, 434, 444
Goal setting, 275
Google Classroom, 225
Group discussion, 224, 256–261, 263, 265–269, 278, 284, 288
Group review, 224, 256–258, 262–266, 268, 269, 288
Growth mindset, 9, 18, 26, 30, 44

H
Harnessing, 313, 322, 324, 327, 329
Head-Mounted Displays (HMDs), 306–308, 310, 312, 313, 316, 317, 319, 321
High-impact, 184, 191
Holistic rubrics, 389, 393
Human Intelligence (HI), 337, 339–341, 343
Hypothes.is, 225

I
Immersive learning, 307–329
Immersive technology, 306–309, 311–318, 320, 322, 326–329, 312–313
In-class evaluation, 278–280
Incremental innovation, 165, 166
Individualized learning, 7, 34, 236
Informal feedback, 383, 386–387
Informalization, 5
Information Communication Technology (ICT), 153–155, 157
Innovation and transformation in learning, 437–439
Innovation in teaching and learning, 314, 317, 328
Innovation(s), 8–10, 12, 28, 30, 38, 46, 218–220, 230
Institutional level, 181, 184, 192, 195
Institution's infrastructure, 435
Instructional techniques, 178, 179, 195, 196, 201
Intellectual skills, 373, 375
Interactivity, 312, 318, 321–322, 324
Inter-intra feedback, 4, 22
Internationalization, 431
International students, 6, 7, 36, 39
Interpersonal, 8, 13
Intrapersonal, 13

J
'job-ready', 431, 445

K
K^mAlive Learning Intelligence (LQ) Application, 224, 233, 247, 255, 263, 266, 278
Kahoot, 224
Knowledge and understanding, 100, 373

L
Labour market, 5, 8, 9
Leadership development, 270, 274, 277
Leadership, Human & Soft (Employability) Skills & Competencies, 269–284
Leadership skills development, 25
Learning Activity Management System (LAMS), 132–138
Learning analytics, 338, 343–345, 351, 354
Learning and development, 10, 12, 13
Learning culture, 7, 17–19, 222, 224, 226–228, 232, 263, 284, 286, 292
Learning design(s), 4, 17, 21, 22, 27, 32, 42, 47, 178–180, 194–197, 204
Learning intelligence, 10, 12
Learning Management System (LMS), 5, 10, 23
Learning orientation, 84, 89
Learning process, 10, 13–16, 30, 31, 44, 47
Learning strategies, 20, 24
Learning styles, 73, 77, 82, 84, 89, 94, 95, 105
Learning transformation, 223–226, 227, 229, 284, 286, 289, 291
Lifelong learning, 5, 8, 26, 27, 35, 38
Life-Long Learning Support & Resources, 435
Logical-mathematical, 13
Low-impact, 184, 190

M
Machine Learning (ML), 159, 160
Medium-impact, 191
Metacognition, 59, 62, 77
Meta-cognitive skills, 5
Mindfulness, 97, 100
Mixed Reality (MR), 306, 309, 318, 329
Mobile learning, 22–23, 30, 35

MOOCs, 181
Motivation(al), 59, 60, 65, 228, 239, 251, 272, 287
Multicultural teaching efficacy, 86–91, 92, 105
Multiple intelligence, 13–18
Musical-rhythmic, 14

N
Naturalist, 14
Networked learning, 27

O
Online, 218, 219, 221, 222, 227, 229, 240, 253, 259, 262, 265
Online learning, 18, 21, 22, 32, 34, 36, 38, 47, 48, 180, 181, 194–196, 198, 200, 203, 204, 208, 209
Online learning assessment, 200–201
Online reflection journal, 195, 198

P
Pedagogy, 4, 21, 30, 33, 34, 36, 47, 226, 228, 229, 260, 286, 289
Peer evaluation, 224, 248–250, 251, 254, 284, 288
Peer feedback, 4
Peer learning, 5
Perceived learning effectiveness, 397, 405
Personalised Adaptative Learning Systems (PALS), 345–351, 354, 356, 358, 359
Personalization, 5, 35
Personalized learning, 5, 15, 17, 35, 36, 43, 47
Perspectives of faculty and learners, 210
Post evaluation, 278, 279–281
Practical hands-on skills, 375
Practical skills, 373
Pre-evaluation, 278, 279–280
Procedural-practical knowledge, 314, 315
Professional growth, 435
Professional learning, 27, 33, 34
Proficiency, 88, 95, 96
Profiling and prediction, 353–354, 358
Program level, 184

Q
Qualitative indicators, 405, 407
Quizizz, 224
Quizzes, 195, 197–198, 200

R
Radical innovation, 164, 167
Reflective, 228, 246, 250, 251, 260
Reflective peer evaluation, 253
Reflective Peer-Leadership Feedback, 274
Reskilling, 8, 18
Rewards management, 435
Role-based evaluation, 278, 281–284
Rotation, 184, 185

S
Scheduling, 433, 435
Simulations, 23
Slack, 224
Small group, 260, 261, 265
Social and cultural aspects, 195, 203
Social engineering, 224, 226–227, 263, 284, 286, 291
Social learning, 5, 9
Social-psychological intervention, 129–131, 141
Socio-constructivist process, 14
Sociocultural, 18, 33, 36, 37, 394–397, 408
Socio-cultural aspects, 179, 195, 196, 203, 206, 210
Sociocultural dynamics, 323
Sociocultural engineering strategies, 286
Socio-organizational culture, 166
Socrative, 225
Strategic decision-making, 220
Strategic level planning, 12
Strategic road map, 12
Student-centric, 182
Student-centric/oriented learning environment, 4
Student engagement, 85, 92–95, 105
Student models and academic achievement, 335, 353, 354, 355–356
Student-teacher relationships, 85–86, 89
Summative feedback, 383, 385–386, 389, 415
Support systems, 68, 344, 358
Sustaining innovation, 169
System-facing AIEd applications, 353, 355, 356

T
Tactical level planning, 12
Task specific rubrics, 392–394

Teacher-facing AIEd, 351–352, 354
Teacher thinking, 26
Teaching empathy, 123, 124, 126–128
Teaching methodologies, 20, 30
Teaching strategies, 4, 6
Technological disruptions, 9, 18, 28, 30, 31, 39, 42
Technological innovations, 9, 30
Technological interventions, 178, 180, 194, 199, 203
Technology, 78, 85, 89, 95, 96, 105
Technology-enabled, 223, 229, 263
Technology-enhanced learning, 164, 166
Teleconferencing, 221, 222
Tiki-Toki, 225
Timing learning designs, 380
Training & development, 431, 435
Transferable skills, 373, 375
Transformation, 4, 6, 10, 12, 18, 21, 33, 39, 46
Transformational leadership styles, 121
Transnational education, 69, 74
Trello, 224

U
Unfamiliarity, 96, 100
Unpredictable and continual changes, 430
Upskilling, 8, 18

V
Verbal-linguistic, 13
Virtual learning, 78
Virtual Learning Environments (VLEs), 157, 158, 164, 166, 167
Virtual Reality (VR), 230, 306, 311, 312, 314, 318, 319, 325, 327–329
Visual-spatial, 13
Voice-over lectures, 195, 197
VUCA world, 150, 154, 155

W
Web-based simulations, 244
Workforce fragility, 8

GPSR Compliance
The European Union's (EU) General Product Safety Regulation (GPSR) is a set of rules that requires consumer products to be safe and our obligations to ensure this.

If you have any concerns about our products, you can contact us on

ProductSafety@springernature.com

In case Publisher is established outside the EU, the EU authorized representative is:

Springer Nature Customer Service Center GmbH
Europaplatz 3
69115 Heidelberg, Germany

www.ingramcontent.com/pod-product-compliance
Ingram Content Group UK Ltd.
Pitfield, Milton Keynes, MK11 3LW, UK
UKHW021257031026
15588UKWH00001B/493

9789811992025